MOVING MOUNTAINS

Roland Miller

MOVING MOUNTAINS

CREATING THE NURSE PRACTITIONER AND RURAL EMS

A memoir by

MARIE OSBORN ARNP
& JOHN OSBORN MD

CAXTON PRESS
Caldwell, Idaho
2025

ISBN 978-087004-656-8
Library of Congress Control Number: 2024950996
Printed and bound in USA

First Printing December 2024

Published by Caxton Press
312 Main Street
Caldwell, Idaho 83605
Visit caxtonpress.com

In Dedication to:

My five children — Calvin, Jerry, John, Melinda, Debbie — and their families;
The many volunteer EMTs, ambulance drivers, and people of Stanley, Idaho;
My physician preceptor and enduring friend, Bryan Stone MD;
College of Idaho premeds and WWAMI medical students; and
Nurses and Nurse Practitioners everywhere

Roland Miller

The Stanley ambulance and crew

Roland Miller

The Osborn family on Shaw Mesa, August 12, 2000
FRONT, LEFT TO RIGHT: *Debbie, Melinda, Marie;* BACK: *Cal, Jerry, John, Cal Jr.*

CONTENTS

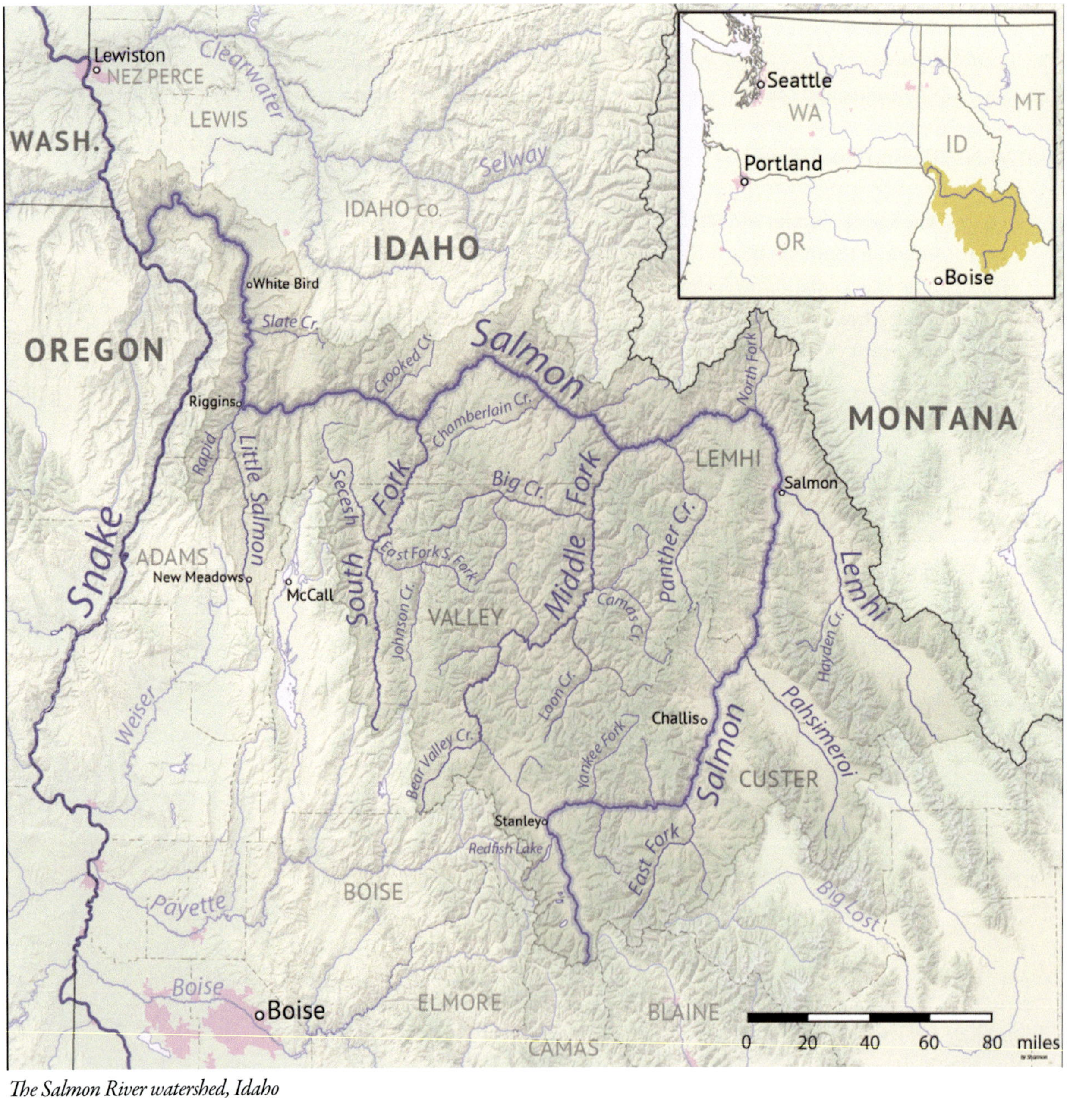

USGS National Map and NASA SRTM data, created by Shannon1 (Wikipedia)

The Salmon River watershed, Idaho

FOREWORD

Do not go where the path may lead,
go instead where there is no path
and leave a trail.

Ralph Waldo Emerson

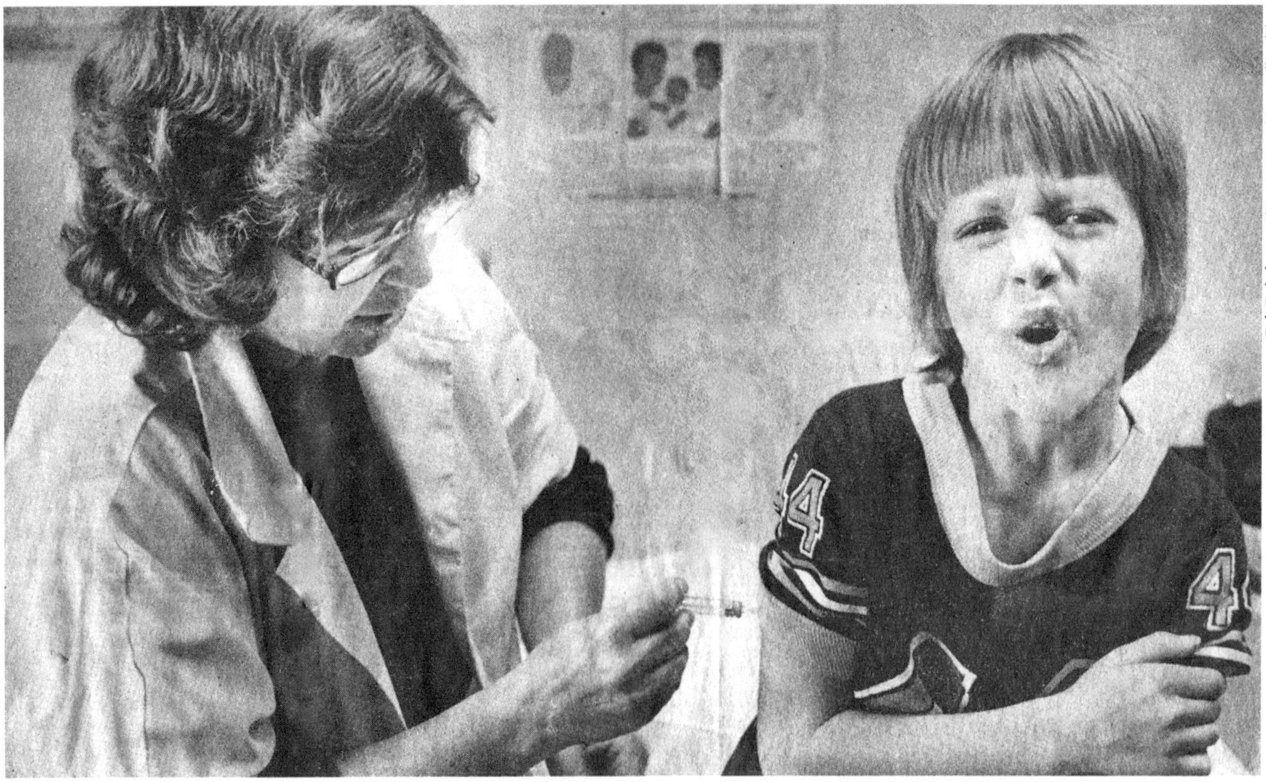

Future NFL quarterback and Stanley elementary pupil Jake Plummer receiving an injection from nurse practitioner Marie Osborn. He passed out.

Physicians as a profession began several thousand years ago. The nurse practitioner profession (NP) started in the 1960s. By 2020, the number of licensed NPs in the United States was over 300,000, and the profession is expanding internationally. This is the story of the first licensed NP, Marie Osborn.

Although Marie Osborn was the first licensed, she was not the first NP. That distinction belongs to Loretta Ford. Advanced practice nursing started in Colorado in 1965 with Loretta Ford RN, who, along with Henry Silver MD, focused on underserved pediatric populations. Six years later, Idaho became the first state to license NPs. Marie, an RN committed to providing emergency services in Idaho's Sawtooth country, was the first licensed by Idaho.

Marie, my mother, stood 4 feet 11 — five feet in her cowboy boots. Her personal story as an RN, wife, and mother crochet into the creation stories of the NP profession and rural EMS. "Someone needs to do something," Marie said. She knew the lack of rural healthcare in Idaho. That someone ended up being her. Once Marie started, she wouldn't stop. She was on a mission to prove that an advanced practice RN — a woman — could do it. For nearly 30 years, Marie was the sole healthcare provider, covering 6,000 square miles of Idaho's Sawtooth and Salmon River country.

"What's a nurse practitioner?" people asked in those first years. Marie replied, "Think of me as a 'super nurse,' not a 'mini-doctor.'"

Marie's life divides at age 40. Before, she was an IBM wife and mother of five who trained as an RN. After 40, she was a nurse practitioner. The dividing line occurred poolside at the resort in Sun Valley, Idaho. Marie and her husband, Cal, an IBM executive, were in Sun Valley to help Idaho co-host the National Lieutenant Governors Association's annual meeting in July 1971.

Marie, wearing her one-piece white bathing suit, sunbathed by the Sun Valley pool. Her trusted babysitter, Mrs. Beasley, kept an eye on her five kids in Boise. Also at the poolside was the head of the Idaho Hospital Association, John Hutchinson. John and Marie's chit-chat turned to rural healthcare.

In that unguarded moment, with freshly painted toenails and covered with suntan lotion, Marie unleashed about the sheer lack of rural healthcare. She worried about her five children spending time in Idaho's Sawtooth country, a wilderness landscape without healthcare or emergency services. The response from the Idaho Hospital Association's director? "We can help get you started."

Marie did not set out to change the world or be a revolutionary healthcare figure. And yet, in the early 1970s, for a 40-year-old woman to provide emergency services and primary care in isolated, rural Idaho also meant changing the world.

After their chance encounter, John Hutchinson assigned his college intern, Gary Steinbach, to help Marie find funding and training. In her nursing journals, Marie had read about a new concept in patient care called a "nurse practitioner." Marie had her BSN and had worked briefly as an RN at Seattle's Harborview in 1953 during the third trimester of her first pregnancy. Five children and 18 years later, Marie faced a steep learning curve to open an emergency clinic in Stanley.

Few, if anyone, with whom Marie trained at Harborview in Seattle and, later, Cook County in Chicago had heard of an NP. Forty years later, in 2011, when Marie hung up her white coat and stethoscope for the last time at age 80, NPs were fully integrated into healthcare as a new profession. Marie's work as an NP in Stanley, Idaho, prompted fundamental questions about what a nurse practitioner is, including training, scope of practice, physician oversight, prescriptive authority, and service reimbursement. In those early years, institutions struggled to adapt to Marie and other rural NPs beginning to provide rural healthcare. When the pushback came, and it did, many physicians — including Wood River Valley physicians who served as her preceptors — defended Marie's work in Stanley.

If you wonder how Marie could be central to so many NP controversies and outcomes that defined the profession, remember there was no other healthcare in that part of central Idaho. Marie was the sole provider, 24/7, for nearly 30 years. If she was in the Valley, she was on call for emergencies. For Marie to do her work, fundamental change had to come: for women, NPs, and rural EMS.

In the words of Mother Teresa, "We can do no great things, only small things with great love." There is a direct line in history between the NPs you see today in clinics, emergency departments, or hospital wards and the work of these pioneering women in rural healthcare during the 1960s and 1970s.

"Where the hell is Stanley, Idaho?" is displayed on T-shirts of Salmon River rafters, wilderness hikers, and anglers wading the Salmon River headwaters on dreamy summertime Sawtooth afternoons.

Where is this place foundational to the NP as a profession and rural EMS? If you don't know, pull out a map of Idaho and look for Stanley within the Sawtooth National Recreation Area (Sawtooth NRA) in the heart of Idaho. Or, find Sun Valley and follow Highway 75 north over Galena Summit into the Sawtooth Valley and then to Stanley. Further north is the Frank Church River of No Return Wilderness; to Stanley's east, the White Cloud Mountains.

During the winter in Stanley — which competes with International Falls, Minnesota, as the coldest place in the United States' lower 48 — the population runs to 99 or fewer. Sawtooth winters bring blizzards and temperatures dropping to minus 20 below zero or colder. Avalanches close Highway 21 to Boise, notably in the canyon below Banner Summit. At times, deep snows and avalanches in mountain passes and downriver cut off residents from the outside world.

Longer days and melting snows in the high country and mountain valleys bring an explosion of mountain flowers and tourists. For local businesses — whitewater rafting, outfitting, and guiding, hotels and restaurants, grocery stores, and gas stations—summer's tourist season is make-or-break. Stanley's short, frenetic tourist season contrasts with Stanley's long, sleepy winter.

People come to the Sawtooths and Salmon River country from all over America and the world. Each of the three approaches to the Valley is jaw-droppingly beautiful.

The high country provides an escape from southern Idaho's summer heat. On Friday nights, long lines of car lights pour over Galena and Banner Summits into the Sawtooth Valley and Stanley Basin ("the Valley").

People come for camping, wilderness hiking, fishing and hunting, bicycling and motorcycle riding, and river rafting. They also come to drink and party, attend music and craft fairs, marry, give birth, and die, be close to God, and experience spiritual renewal. Over a million people visit the Sawtooths during the summertime tourist season for these reasons and more.

The closest ER is 60 miles south over the 8,700-foot Galena Summit in Ketchum. Before Marie arrived, when good times turned bad with trauma or illness, the U.S. Forest Service responded to emergency calls.

IBM's annual company campout at Redfish Lake first brought the Osborn family to the Sawtooth Mountains. IBM is the erstwhile acronym for "I've Been Moved." Having transferred from Bellingham, Washington to Boise in 1963, and with the family settled in Idaho, Marie insisted, and her husband Cal agreed, that their five children would not continue moving to enable Cal to climb IBM's corporate ladder. IBM accommodated, and the Osborn family remained in Idaho.

After years of annual IBM campouts at Redfish Lake and family camping at Stanley and Alturas Lakes in the Sawtooths, Cal and Marie bought retirement property on Shaw Mesa overlooking the Sawtooth Valley and Salmon River. They knew there was no healthcare in this rural, isolated, and beautiful place. Still, Marie was an RN.

Just before Marie and the Idaho Hospital Association director, John Hutchinson, met poolside at Sun Valley in 1971, a terrible auto accident occurred near Galena Summit. Four teenagers were severely injured. The ambulance making its way from Hailey took nearly three hours to arrive. For Marie, those injured teenagers easily could have been her own.

Marie graduated with a BSN from Ball State in Indiana in 1953. She spent her childhood in Kentucky and Indiana during the Great Depression and World War II. While finishing her BSN, Marie met Cal Osborn, recently discharged from the US Air Force. They fell in love, married, and moved west to Seattle. As the wife of an IBM employee living in Seattle, Bellingham, and then Boise, Marie focused on raising her five children.

In transitioning to a health care provider at age 40, Marie went from homemaker and IBM wife wearing high heels and dresses to a white coat, stethoscope, jeans, and boots. With the Salmon River Emergency Clinic ("Stanley Clinic") opening in 1972, Marie began providing emergency care services as Idaho's first NP.

A devoted husband who was proud of his wife, Cal helped Marie open the Stanley Clinic. On Fridays, Cal would pick up supplies in Boise for the clinic, drive 129 miles on winding mountain roads to Stanley, and then return to Boise on Sunday night to work at IBM through the week.

Marie needed more training. Demands on her time increased, juggling her roles as wife, mother, and healthcare provider. Her training in trauma took her to Seattle's Harborview and Chicago's Cook County, where she trained in emergency rooms (ERs), with paramedics and firefighters, and in the Cook County morgue. She entered the first family NP class at the University of Utah, and invested hundreds of hours of additional training at Boise hospitals, St. Luke's and St. Alphonsus, and the Wood River Valley.

At the Osborn family cabin in the Sawtooths, a place intended to be without TV and telephone, the CB radio with emergency calls increasingly interrupted family mealtimes. When Cal and Marie went out for dinner in Stanley, people saw Marie and pulled up a chair seeking free medical advice. After that first summer of trauma in 1972, community leaders asked Marie to keep the clinic open year-round.

Demands on Marie increased as the sole provider in a rural community. The impact on the Osborn family was profound, with a wife and mother on 24/7 emergency calls without assistance, backup, or relief. In 1977, after 24 years of marriage and five children, Cal and Marie divorced.

With the passage of time and the influence of the connection they shared with their children, the rupture of divorce faded to friendship. Over the years Cal often sought out Marie's medical advice, and in time, Marie assisted with Cal's hospice. Cal died in 2014 surrounded by his family.

Marie trained hundreds of EMTs who volunteered in Stanley and other rural communities for emergency calls. Moving Mountains is their story, too.

Marie's work would never have been possible without physicians who served as her teachers, consultants, and preceptors. Dr. Michael Copass, a legendary figure in EMS who helped launch Airlift Northwest, agreed to teach Marie when she arrived for trauma training at Harborview in February 1972. Another physician, Dr. Bryan Stone of the Ketchum Medical Clinic and medical missionary in Africa, stands out for his unwavering support of Marie, commitment to teaching, and devotion to his patients. Both Dr. Copass and Dr. Stone agreed to interviews for this history.

Dr. Stone's wife, Ann, died before we completed the chapter about her husband. Still, we remember her through this book, including hosting WWAMI medical students in her home. We also honor her patience with her husband, who was called out day and night for deliveries and often returned home late from Stanley, seeing patients with Marie.

Marie's women-care clinics in Stanley and downriver in Challis and Salmon were robust. She knew many rural women had little or no access to GYN care. Yet, when it came to OB, Marie insisted that all deliveries be done "over the hill," where obstetrical hospital backup was close if things went wrong.

Marie loved to sew clothes for her family, so transitioning from cloth to human skin was nearly seamless. From suturing the first spiculated facial laceration for an intoxicated patient at the Harborview ER, Marie did excellent work. She also mastered the art of extracting fishhooks stuck in human skin.

Today, we take for granted the paramedics, EMTs, emergency medicine specialists in hospital ERs, urgent care centers, and ambulance and helicopter transport of patients — a system of EMS that networks together resources to save lives. Yet, in 1971, almost none of these resources existed, and certainly not in central Idaho. This book is about the creation of rural EMS in addition to the NP profession. I want to especially thank Paul Anderson for his help recounting his personal history with EMS. Paul was the first director of Idaho EMS, appointed by Gov. Cecil Andrus, and a friend of the Stanley Ambulance and Stanley Clinic.

Marie may also be remembered by the premeds, medical students, and nurse practitioner students she trained, introducing them to rural medicine. The College of Idaho still sponsors the Stanley Clinic pre-med internship program we started in 1975. Two of Marie's students, Dr. Ken Harris and Dr. KT Fisher, graciously agreed to sit for interviews for this book.

Starting in 1982, medical students also rotated through the Stanley Clinic as part of WWAMI. Pronounced "whammy," the cooperative medical program is based at the University of Washington and serves Washington, Wyoming, Alaska, Montana, and Idaho. For pre-meds and medical students, nighttime knocks on the Stanley Clinic door by patients complaining of crushing chest pain or needing suturing after a bar fight are memories that endure a lifetime.

While veterinary medicine was forbidden, dogs with faces filled with porcupine quills, prized horses with nasty lacerations, or a pregnant goat in a difficult delivery found their way to Marie. If she didn't provide the care, animals suffered or died. Veterinarians Tom and Marie Bulgin lifted that burden briefly when they lived in the Valley. The Idaho Board of Veterinary Medicine warned Marie, and she was careful to avoid stepping over lines.

Marie lived alone in her log cabin home at 7,100 feet elevation for nearly thirty years. She insisted she was never lonely — her dog Mousse and her beloved Sawtooth Mountains were her constant companions. In the winter, "Grandma Snowmobile" would drive her snow machine at temperatures down to 40 degrees below zero nearly two miles to the highway, where she'd crank up her car and drive another twelve miles to the clinic.

Marie survived colon cancer, but the years took their toll. The 24/7 emergency call became increasingly difficult, especially during all-night ambulance runs and busy clinic days in the summertime. In 1999, the community gathered at Redfish Lake Lodge to thank and honor Marie — and say goodbye. As fate would have it, a car accident and ambulance run nearly upended the occasion. Marie arrived late to her honoring event, splattered with blood and mud. People brought gifts, cards, and flowers, many speaking through tears of gratitude about how Marie had touched their lives and others. Marie loved the community she served, and they loved her. She was 68 years old.

For the next twelve years, Marie continued caring for patients in the rural towns of Idaho City, Emmett, and Horseshoe Bend, and then primarily low-income patients in Boise. Her vision worsened due to macular degeneration. When she turned 80, Marie took off her white coat and stethoscope for the last time. Still, her heart and home remained in the Sawtooth Mountains.

Where once Marie examined bulging ear drums and sore throats and reviewed Gram stains, macular degeneration eventually left her blind. Where once Marie joined teams of EMTs in moving patients out of the backcountry or wrecked cars in the Salmon River, asthma and deteriorating lung function increasingly required an oxygen concentrator nearby. Aging may be cruel, but it is inevitable.

What is not lost is Marie's legacy. As a new healthcare profession, the nurse practitioner endures and thrives far beyond Idaho's Sawtooth Range and Salmon River country. Gone are the days when people stared blankly and asked, "What is a nurse practitioner?"

In every step of her journey, Marie was not alone. Her family, the people of Stanley, EMTs and ambulance drivers, Idaho Emergency Medical Services (EMS), medical professionals and hospitals, editorial boards and reporters, academic institutions and training programs for medical students, premeds, and nurse practitioners, elected officials, and — if reluctantly at times — the Idaho Boards of Medicine, Nursing, and Pharmacy all supported Marie. Especially in those early years, no one else would provide healthcare in the Sawtooth country.

The NPs with whom I've worked knew little about the origins of their profession; all wanted to know more. My urban physician colleagues, who work alongside NPs in ERs, clinics, and hospital wards, may be intrigued by the realities of rural healthcare. Physicians are essential in supporting advanced practice providers (NPs and PAs) as colleagues within our healthcare teams, just as physicians made my mother's journey possible as the first licensed NP.

"Marie, you're too feminine to be a doctor," Dr. Tucker told a young girl who revealed she wanted to be a doctor. "You should go into nursing." This book is also about women in healthcare. For those working in healthcare today, it's hard to fathom a time when doctors were men and nurses were women. For Marie, the doors to medical school were closed. But, other doors opened through nursing.

Born in Kentucky during the Great Depression, Marie also dreamed of becoming one of the "Kentucky Nurses on Horseback." Instead, she became an "Idaho Nurse Practitioner on Snowmobile." As singer-songwriter Carole King states in her chapter on rural EMS, "I don't think it ever occurred to Marie, who was small of stature and big of heart, that she couldn't do something because she wasn't a man. Marie just did it."

Marie (our mother) always planned to write her memoir. Her income was almost nothing in those first years; a book might bring in some retirement income. Marie knew her life had become part of something bigger. Over the decades, I began searching for a writer and publisher. The recurring answer was: you, her son, should work with your mother and write her story. In telling this story, I've tried to let the story tell itself.

At age 84, four years after she stopped seeing patients, Marie sat for her first interview. Over the next three years, the interviews took place at her Sawtooth cabin, while driving Highway 21 from Stanley to Boise, in her townhouse in Boise, and finally, in 2019, in her independent living apartment in Boise using a smartphone recorder.

The older of Marie's daughters, Melinda ("Lindy"), who lives in Stanley with her daughter Ashley, transcribed her mother's interviews during long, snowy Sawtooth winters. Many quotes in this book are Marie's favorites, once framed and located on the walls of the Salmon River Emergency Clinic in Stanley. Today, these quotes, photos, awards, and other memorabilia crowd her apartment walls, reminders of her role in medical history and her contributions to nursing and patient care.

Interviews of EMTs, physicians, and others varied. Some were done in person at Marie's cabin or care facility, taking notes on a laptop computer. Dr. Copass was interviewed in person at a nursing home in Gig Harbor; Carole King, by telephone. Eventually, many of the interviews were conducted by video conferencing with Marie present, recorded, and transcribed. Some stories were unsolicited, including Craig Pierce's recounting of the emergency childbirth: he had read about Marie in a newspaper story. He wanted to share his experience as a College of Idaho pre-med.

Many people made this book possible, including the book reviewing team: Amy Klingler, Dr. Bryan Stone, Bev Angel, Bunny Siemers, Dave Kimpton, Gary and Laurii Gadwa, Julie Meissner, Ken and Sarah Harris, Ken and Bernie Hartz, Dr. KT Fisher, Sparky and Maryellen Easom, Noah Carter, Paul Anderson, Phil Coonts, Randall Hudspeth PhD APRN, Steve and Teresa Lipus, Roland Miller, Jack Cafferty, and Tom Kovalicky.

I want to thank Lucy Copass for assisting with the interview with her husband, Dr. Michael Copass. The Seattle VA Emergency Department team I work with provided inspiration, suggestions, and insight. My friends, Dr. Dave Burica and Dr. Kelly Mutch, are also part of this story and helped in ways they may never fully appreciate.

I want to thank the Idaho Statesman, Twin Falls Times-News, Idaho Falls Post Register, Challis Messenger, Spokesman-Review, Seattle Times, and Salt Lake City Tribune for permission to use newspaper stories and photos.

So many people and institutions made their photographs available: Craig Henty at the London Ambulance Service/National Health Service, Paul Anderson/Idaho EMS, Cook

County Health in Chicago, College of Idaho, University of Louisville in Kentucky, Indian University Health-Ball Memorial Hospital in Muncie, University of Washington, Idaho Power Company, Steve Lipus, Sawtooth Avalanche Center, Medic One Foundation, Airlift Northwest and UW Medicine, Wake Forest University School of Medicine, Sanford Health, Miles Canfield with the Ketchum Fire Departement, Life Flight, Kurt Conger (son of Dean Conger for the Stanley Stomp 1973 photo), Gary Gadwa, Ron Dunagan, and Jim Stark. I especially want to thank Roland Miller, whose many photographs are in this book.

As a pre-med at the College of Idaho, I was a Lawrence Henry Gipson Scholar and am honored to have Scott Gipson as the publisher of a book so closely connected to the college. Letitia Thornton, as editor, made this book a better read. Layout is an art form, and we thank Lori Kurts for her artistry in the look and feel of *Moving Mountains*.

The Osborn and Clark families provided helpful guidance, especially Melinda "Susie" Rider, Marie's youngest sister. My friend and author Derrick Jensen, who is starting a book on his mother, provided unwavering encouragement and guidance. In so many ways, this book would not have been possible without the support of my wife, Rachael.

Finally, I want to thank my mother. As her health has declined, we talk every day. "John, remember the best cases when you're seeing patients in the ER. I want to hear about them."

For many of us in the healthcare professions, who we are is what we do. When the day finally came that Marie stopped seeing patients, a part of her died. In a heartbeat, she would gladly have returned to caring for her patients at the Stanley Clinic, taking the emergency call from EMS dispatch, coordinating EMTs while grabbing her bag, and running out the door to the motor vehicle accident on Highway 21. People needed her. In that moment, nothing else mattered.

—John Osborn, MD

A DEDICATION TO DEDICATION

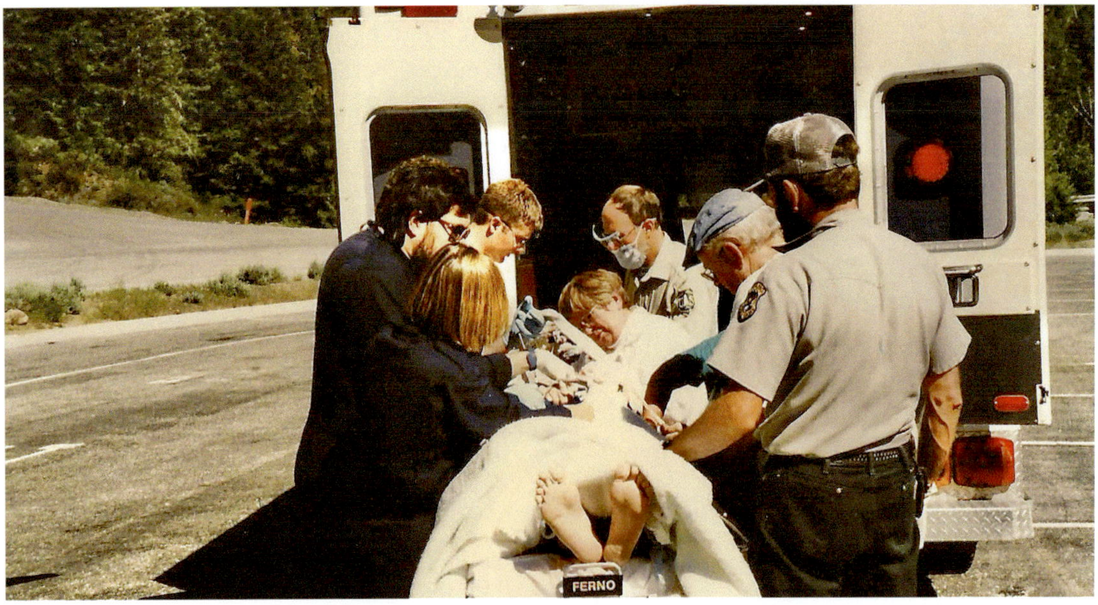

THE DEDICATION OF THAT MARIE!

By Sparky Easom

(With apologies to Sam McGee and Robert W. Service)

Read on May 30, 1999 at the Stanley community's going-away bash for Marie at Redfish Lake Lodge

There are strange things done in the mountain sun by folks in the Stanley Basin.
The Sawtooth trails have traumatic tales that would set your pulse a-racin'.
The clinic lights have seen queer sights, but one thing is for certain:
That Marie will heed a person's need whenever they are hurtin'.

Whether fever checks or auto wrecks in the hours long before dawn,
No matter the season, if there's a reason, you can count on her to respond.
But it never fails, the pager wails when she's home on the hill snug and warm.
So I guess it was fate on a luckless date in a late December storm:

That winter's day, making crochet and enjoying Monday night football,
No sooner spoken, her rev'rie was broken by the tones of a 9-1-1- call.
Adrenaline pumping, Marie started jumping and monitored dispatch in Challis,
"What could be worse?" She thought with a curse: Denver had just tied with Dallas!

To no-one's relief the report was quite brief: no milepost, no vitals, no detail.
Just a couple of fellows from Pocatello prob'ly drank just a bit too much ale.
Ten miles from the bar they'd capsized their car on a treacherous patch of black ice.
The snow had ceased squalling but with temperatures falling, those boys would need help in a trice!

She threw on warm clothes and trundled outdoors, then mounted her snow machine.
Once at the car, it wouldn't be far to drive to the accident scene.
But poor snow and bad luck, her machine got quite stuck, so she commenced to walk.
Her feet were slipping, her nose was dripping and she new she was racing the clock.

"Dispatch!...Unit One. This isn't much fun. I am having a slight delay.
Get LifeFlight on standby, let's hope they can fly. Send extrication right away."
"But, communication! We need information! Give us pulse rates, breath sounds, their condition!
What about their B.P.'s? What about I.V.'s? Or complications that warrant suspicion?"

Alas! What a pain! Her call was in vain, the repeater'd malfunctioned again.
She howled out her woes to the homeless snows. God, how she loathed that thing!
When at last down the hill she managed to spill and shoveled her car from the berm,
She clambered inside and started to ride, determined, unshaken, and firm.

'Til she came to the scene near a steep ravine, where the fire trucks all had gathered.
The ambulance crew was parked there too; patient care was now all that mattered.
Spotlights flashed while rescuers dashed across and down the slick slope,
She whispered a prayer to counter despair, 'At least where there is help, there is hope.'

She grabbed her kit, and shouldered it, then edged for the slippery abyss,
But something among the searchers was wrong. Something was surely amiss.
They'd looked through the wreck, rounded and under it checked: where did the victims go?
Had the poor souls been thrown into darkness unknown, lying battered, exposed in the snow?

They had searched all around, yet no patients were found, 'til they reached a telling moment:
Snowy footprints revealed what the dark had concealed, those rascals had hitchhiked to Lowman.
From out of the blue, then the dispatch came through: "Cancel ambulance...stand down Stanley Fire!"
Some dark oaths were hurled as the story unfurled that this wreck had occurred the day prior.

After all gear was stowed, rescue crews hit the road, nothing left, then, but for documentation.
You must not shirk that darn paperwork, one must have all the right information.
And Marie is particular, she is quite a stickler, for someone who is so short.
Woe to you if you're one of the few that fails to complete a report!

So home she went, her anger spent, as she breathed a silent prayer,
Thankful for all who had answered the call to render emergency care.
As she trudged up the hill through the dark and the chill, she dreamed of a time with no strife.
That struck snowmobile was not a big deal compared to her future life.

Stomping into her kitchen she conjured a vision as she warmed herself next to the fire,
Of a more tranquil state on some distant date: that time when she'd finally retire.
As she sipped her tea, her reverie abruptly began a tailspin.
What could disengage her? Why...that pesky ol' pager had started to wail again.

There are strange things done in the mountain sun by folks in the Stanley Basin.
The Sawtooth trails have traumatic tales that would set your pulse a-racin'.
Though the clinic lights have seen queer sights, one thing is a certainty:
For pure dedication, no one in creation compares to that Marie!

Roland Miller

Vehicle wreckage on Redfish Lake Road's Outlet Curve. Mostly men drinking and driving too fast added to the workload of the Stanley Ambulance, volunteer EMTs and drivers, and the region's sole healthcare provider.

PART ONE

HEALTHCARE COMES TO THE SAWTOOTH COUNTRY

Galena Summit, driving into the Sawtooth Valley and headwaters of the Salmon River

1

CHAMPAGNE AND HORSESHIT

Will Success Spoil Stanley, Idaho?

Residents used to say that you had a better chance of surviving an injury in Vietnam than one right here; today if someone guns you down in the woods or whacks you with a motorcycle — a very real hazard — your chances are somewhat better. Thanks to local perseverance and considerable generosity, Stanley now has a sparkling 1958 ambulance and a capable nurse-practitioner, one of the first in the nation.

The clinic is a red log building donated by a Valley resident. Mrs. Marie Osborn, a registered nurse with advanced training, is patching up one of the weekend victims of motorcycle accidents, a young man who swears he was going five miles an hour when he hit unexpected gravel and tumbled. (There are several other weekend cycle wrecks on the books, including a head-on crash, in itself quite a feat of precision.) In this case, more bloody than damaging, Mrs. Osborn just sews the guy up and lets him go. The only unusual thing about the procedure is that a young man in a yellow undershirt keeps thundering in, offering his injured buddy the "Klutz-of-the-Year Award" and thundering out again, like a non sequitur character in an absurdist play.

"We get just about everything here," says Mrs. Osborn, who has been trained to give emergency care with the telephone aid of two doctors 60 miles away. "I do a pretty good business in fishhooks."

Michael Parfitt, *The New York Times*. January 7, 1973

Call me Marie.

If you wrecked your vehicle while driving in Idaho's Sawtooth country, survived the crash, and were still conscious, you'd be looking up at a four-foot, eleven-inch, middle-aged woman wearing a white coat, stethoscope, and cowboy boots. That woman? Since 1972, and for nearly thirty years, that was me.

I am a nurse practitioner. The NP idea started in Colorado in 1965, led by Loretta Ford, RN, and Henry Silver, MD, focusing on underserved pediatric populations. Six years later, Idaho became the first state to license NPs. To respond to emergencies in Sawtooth country, I became Idaho's first nurse practitioner — and the first licensed NP.

Becoming an NP was not the profession I chose as much as it chose me. I trained as an RN, married, became an IBM executive's wife, and the mother of five great kids. But there was this desperate need and, in the end, there was no one else. So, I did what had to be done. I certainly didn't do it alone. This book is a testament to the many people who helped and, in doing so, saved lives and unexpectedly wrote a chapter in medical history.

As the sole healthcare provider covering 6,000 square miles of backcountry, I was on emergency call 24/7. I lived through tragedy in rivers and lakes, on mountains, and along highways. Yes, tragedy, but joy and laughter, too: champagne and horseshit.

You might have seen that T-shirt, "Where the Hell is Stanley, Idaho?" Stanley sits at the confluence of Valley Creek and the main Salmon River. If you're coming from Boise, you'll likely drive Highway 21, which ends in Stanley at a T-intersection with Highway 75 (formerly Highway 93).

Stanley was famous for its "stomp." Three bars, live music, drinking and dancing, cowboys, river rafters, sheepherders, hippies, and highway crews made the Stanley Stomp well known, once even making the cover of National Geographic magazine.

Stanley was a wild, rootin'-tootin' town on the weekends when the Osborn family first arrived in the early 1960s. There was so much fun, and, on the surface, you'd think, "This is the greatest place ever." People didn't know. Maybe not knowing is better. You never forget the deaths, especially the kids.

If you are coming into the valley on Highway 21, once you cross Banner Creek Summit, you can drive sixty-five mph most of the way. Driving fast, you can easily miss the turnoff to Boundary Creek, where thousands of rafters start their float down the Salmon River's Middle Fork.

On one particularly memorable summertime Sunday afternoon, we already had several ambulance runs, mostly trauma from car wrecks. From Stanley, transporting a patient by ambulance to the closest ER meant going south on Highway 75 over Galena Summit to Sun Valley and the ER at Moritz Hospital.[1]

On a summer afternoon in 1972, our volunteer ambulance crew was still "over the hill" in Sun Valley with another patient when I got an emergency call at the clinic: a toddler at the Boundary Creek turnoff. Two families had pulled off Highway 21 at the turnoff. The mother left her child with friends and was on the other side of the highway. The child was a beautiful girl, too young to know to look both ways. The toddler saw her mother — "Mommy!" — and ran onto the highway. Just then, a car passed another vehicle. The driver never saw the little girl until he hit her.

When accidents stack up in the backcountry, you can wait hours for the coroner before moving a body. Not wanting to leave the dead child, I placed her in my car, returning to Stanley with grieving parents. I carried her body into the clinic, the small log cabin across from the Kasino Club, a local bar and restaurant. As I walked into our reception room, a man suddenly stopped me. He was impeccably outfitted in cowboy clothes with beautiful Tony Lama cowboy boots — and he was upset. The "cowboy" demanded, "Where have you been? I've been waiting for almost an hour!" The man stood in front of me, blocking my way. "I have a tick. It's on my butt," he added. He wanted that tick out — now.

Wasn't it obvious? I'm cradling a little girl's limp, lifeless body. Meanwhile, the man perseverated about the tick on his butt. Couldn't he wait until I got her into the treatment room to lay her down? What a horseshit memory.

My children are a big part of my becoming an NP. I have two daughters and three sons. As a mother, my children are never far from my thoughts and life decisions. I have so many beautiful memories of my children growing up. Our family first came to the Sawtooth country in the early 1960s, when Highway 21 from Lowman to Stanley was still a dirt road.

Our favorite place to camp was Stanley Lake, quintessential Idaho: tranquil, a mirror reflecting the rugged Sawtooth peaks. The lake water is crystal clear and deadly cold. When my five kids were little, our family of seven often camped at Stanley Lake's Inlet Campground. Unfortunately, the 2020 earthquake collapsed that popular beach into the lake.

The kids would get on air mattresses, floating on the stream to the lake and sandy beach, nearly oblivious to the frigid water. Just a few feet from shore, the clear water turned deep blue. That abrupt change from turquoise to deep blue is a telltale marker for deep water just offshore.

Ours was a great Sawtooth family vacation: fishing, hiking, cooking outside, fresh-caught trout for breakfast, scary stories and marshmallows around the campfire, and sleeping bags in a tent. We rented a sixteen-foot trailer for several summers, the most luxurious camping of my life. So many treasured Osborn champagne memories live at Stanley Lake.

There are horseshit memories, too. When you see Stanley Lake, isn't it lovely? When I see Stanley Lake, all the memories return.

We started the Stanley Ambulance before the state created Idaho EMS. During those first years, the local emergency dispatch directed me to car wrecks by the highway mile marker.

After a morning of seeing patients, I broke for lunch at Stanley's Armada Cafe. June was "the quiet before the storm," with tourist season beginning the July Fourth holiday. Cafe

1 Moritz Hospital is now gone, demolished in 2019, and replaced by St. Luke's Wood River Medical Center south of Ketchum.

owner Maxine Baptiste greeted me with her big smile and laughter. The cafe's cook was a premed student and my third son, John. Unfortunately, my lunch and the emergency call came at the same time. There'd been a car wreck at Redfish Lake. I dashed for the door.

Redfish Lake, an Idaho classic, is seven miles south of Stanley, off Highway 75. Redfish Lake is named for Sockeye salmon, which swim 900 miles from the Pacific to spawn. Today, if you drive the road into Redfish Lake, you will slow for a traffic circle. But not back then: almost every curve on that road was the scene of a bad accident.

Testosterone, teenagers, and driving can be deadly. Teenagers got in a car at Redfish Lake and headed for Stanley. For those curves, the driver drove too fast. Lodgepole pine forests line the road. Law enforcement noted that the wrecked car's odometer stuck at ninety mph. Going that fast, the teenage male driver lost control, missed the curve, and hit a tree.

The front-seat passenger was critically injured. When I arrived, he was still breathing. We strapped the patient into the back of a Forest Service Bell 206 helicopter. In those early years of revolutionary EMS change, we used Forest Service and military helicopters for air ambulance transport.

The Stanley EMT who volunteered to go in the helicopter was Fred Judd. Fred headed the local fire crew for the Forest Service and had just finished his EMT training. Once airborne and headed for the ER in Sun Valley, the patient started having airway problems. Fred was up front with the pilot and couldn't suction and clear the airway.

So much of what we did in trying to save lives during those early years of EMS was by the seat of our pants. We had to make do with what we could put together. We had a helicopter. We had a critical patient. We put them together. If we had tried to transport the critically injured boy over Galena Summit by ground ambulance, he never would have made it alive to the ER. Luckily, he survived the air transport.

For Fred, this was the final straw. He'd already lost an infant patient to SIDS, despite us performing CPR all the way over the mountain pass to the ER in Sun Valley. Being in a helicopter with a young trauma patient losing his airway was too much. With that car accident, we lost an excellent volunteer EMT.

Another emergency call came while I was at a Snowmobile Club meeting, helping to plan Stanley's 100 Mile Race. A car wreck on Highway 21, near the Boundary Creek turnoff, involved a young man, a freshman at Boise

Operator error can get snowmobilers into trouble

State University. We found him lying in the middle of the road with a massive head injury. Our radio couldn't reach Boise because of the mountains. We loaded him into the ambulance, headed for Stanley, and finally got through to dispatch for helicopter transport. We met up with Life Flight on the way to Sun Valley. Like so many bad traumatic brain injuries, we did everything we could, but he didn't survive.

Snowmobiling was part of my commute to the clinic during the winter. In Idaho's high country, winters come early and stay late. Stanley often competes with International Falls, Minnesota, as the coldest place in the nation. With my home two miles off the highway, I depended on my snowmobile to get to the clinic and respond to emergencies. Unfortunately, operator error can get riders into trouble.

A group of snowmobilers from Twin Falls was traveling from Stanley to Smiley Creek, a small settlement at the southern end of the Sawtooth Valley not far from where the highway leaves the valley floor and climbs to Galena Summit. The snowmobilers were zooming across snowfields. One snowmobiler, around sixty years old and experienced, was flying. He didn't see the small creek, hit the bank, and dropped in. When he landed, his body lunged forward. His abdomen struck the handlebars of the snowmobile, ripping and perforating his intestines.

Patients with an acute abdomen need a surgeon—now. We were a long way from an operating room in that snowfield. Indeed, our first challenge was to transport the patient out of the snowbank to the ambulance waiting on the highway before we could transport him over the hill to Sun Valley.

The patient was in agony. In those years, NPs were limited on what drugs we could use for pain management. We could use Demerol, but not morphine, hydromorphone, or fentanyl—analgesics ER clinicians might use today. So, I gave him what I had: Demerol. We got him alive to the ER in Sun Valley, and he survived, barely.

When you are the only clinician caring for a patient with major trauma or life-threatening illness, you hope your training will be enough. To prepare, I trained in ERs, including Harborview in Seattle, Cook County in Chicago, and Boise. In addition, so that I could provide primary care, I completed the first nurse practitioner class at the University of Utah in family medicine.

Ask yourself: what other clinician is going to help these people? In rural Idaho, there was no one else. When I started as a nurse practitioner, not everyone approved. In the early 1970s, when women stepped out of traditional homemaker roles, men dominated the healthcare field. Today, we take for granted the collegial relationships and team approach between physicians and NPs, women and men.

Among physicians at the Sun Valley hospital, all men, there were many heated discussions about "that woman over there in Stanley practicing medicine." You can imagine the conversation: "She's some sort of — what's the name? Nurse practitioner!" After one physician ranted, another responded, "Well, why don't you go over there and do what she's doing?" None would. As a middle-aged woman, I took the 24/7 call because no man would.

Physicians did step up to help me, including Ketchum physician Bryan Stone. In time Dr. Stone would become my preceptor, colleague, and lifelong friend.

Physician support was essential for me and for establishing the NP profession. Let me be clear: physicians were there when I needed them.

Stanley is a whitewater mecca, a jumping-off place for river adventures on the Middle Fork and main Salmon River, and consequently, home to several professional river-rafting companies. Their guides are well-trained. Before passengers get in the rafts, guides go through extensive training. Drownings are bad for business. Companies are good at following the rules. Unfortunately, the same does not always apply to private parties.

Combining novice boaters with a late, rapid snowmelt and high water levels can be deadly. Immersed in cold water, humans lose their ability to swim.

A group of fathers and sons from Chicago came to Stanley to float the fabled Salmon River, "River of No Return." Unfortunately, the river was in flood. Group leaders talked to the Forest Service about floating the river and were advised not to launch.

The day was gray — the river was gray and angry. The boaters reasoned they had come from Chicago, had their sons with them, and were in Stanley to float the Salmon River. So, they launched their rafts upriver from Stanley.

Roland Miller

EMTs training for water rescue in Idaho's Salmon River country

Their rafts flipped when they hit rough water, throwing them into the roiling river.

At that moment, National Guard troops were returning to Montana from training in Boise. In an amazing coincidence, the soldiers prevented an even worse tragedy. They formed a human chain and saved quite a few of the rafters. But not everyone. The coroner was in Challis and had to drive sixty miles upriver. Until the coroner and sheriff arrived, we had nowhere to put the bodies except on folding tables at the laundromat.

People should not place themselves in harm's way. But then again, I always figured God doesn't play favorites. What you may have done wouldn't make any difference if it was your turn. As the sole healthcare provider in an isolated community, I lucked out sometimes. Other times, I did everything I could think of, and nothing worked.

When people say, "Marie, you saved their life," that doesn't sit well with me. A higher power than me has control. I never felt that I was the ultimate person in charge. I always hoped that God was on my side and the patient's side, but it didn't always work that way.

Some memories never leave you. A fellow I knew was driving a dirt road near the Salmon River, lost control, and went into the river.

Flows were high with spring runoff. We got the call. The volunteer EMTs and I arrived to find him on his truck in the river. Some EMTs wanted to tie a rope around their waists, wade into the floodwaters, and try to save him. No, I couldn't let them. The risk was too great. We watched in horror as the pickup started to move, floated away, then disappeared into the floodwaters. He was gone.

You have someone who desperately needs your help and pleads for you to do something, and you have no way of helping. And they die. Those are horseshit memories.

I would insist the EMTs practice river rescues and get people out of the water. We'd go out on the bridge to Jay Neider's ranch near Stanley and practice. And practice again until we were solid in our water extrication skills, our ability to pull people out of the river. But still, no matter how often you practice, you will lose people.

Behind these beautiful Sawtooth Mountains is a shadow. You never know when and whether the shadow will fall across you or whether you'll pass through without harm. I've seen so much; the shadow is always there. I don't know of any deserved accident: people were innocent bystanders caught up in life. When it's your time, it's your time.

On the other hand, Sawtooth champagne memories? There are many.

When I first came into the Valley, it was beautiful and peaceful — I fell in love with the Sawtooth Mountains. We camped at Redfish, Stanley, and Alturas Lakes. Cal and I built our cabin to make the Sawtooths part of our kids' lives and, eventually, our retirement home.

As I got more involved, life's realities tempered the beauty of the mountains. That's not to say the mountains haven't sustained me through the years. But sometimes, you start on a journey in life that takes you on a completely unexpected path. Otherwise, how do you explain being born in Kentucky during the Great Depression, training as an RN in Muncie, Indiana, being an IBM executive's wife and mother of five in Boise, and then becoming Idaho's first nurse practitioner covering 6,000 square miles of the Salmon River backcountry for nearly thirty years?

When I turned forty, doors opened for me in a way I could never have imagined, allowing me to do what I love.

At the beginning, no one, including me, knew what a nurse practitioner was. By necessity, we made some of it up as we went along.

The NP you know today was created, at least partly, to meet the very real needs of providing emergency services and primary care in places like Stanley, Idaho.

The only reason I left the clinic in Stanley is that, at age sixty-eight, I physically could not continue providing 24/7 care. My home is two miles off the highway and twelve highway miles from the clinic in Stanley. Getting on the snowmobile at ten below zero or colder to go to the clinic to see patients gets harder with age. In the summer, being up much of the night with emergency calls and seeing patients the next day, week after week through the busy tourist season, takes a toll.

Was it hard to say goodbye to the clinic in Stanley, the EMTs, and the beauty of the Sawtooths and White Cloud Mountains? Once I came into the Valley, I never really left. I became part of these mountains. My ashes will be here. These mountains will always be my home.

After the Stanley years, I continued to care for patients in Idaho City, Horseshoe Bend, Emmett, and Boise. Forced at age eighty to hang up my white coat and stethoscope for the last time, I would see patients in a heartbeat — if only I could see. I am blind.

My hope in telling this story is for you to understand better the challenge of providing EMS care in rural areas, how it is that we came to have nurse practitioners as a profession, and how the people with whom you may not always agree may also be the ones who will someday save your life.

2

"CAN ANYBODY HELP ME?"

"Until the 1970's there was no local fire department, ambulance crew, search and rescue, or law enforcement in the Stanley area, so those duties usually fell on the ranger.

If someone got shot, *call the ranger*.
Sombebody was having a baby, *call the ranger*.
Somebody turned their truckoad of cows over, *call the ranger*.

I was plum wore out by the end of my first summer here."

Tom Kovalicky, Stanley District Ranger, 1970 – 1973
Stanley Museum, Sawtooth Interpretive and Historical Association

Tom Kovalicky has a twinkle in his eye and an easy smile. He served as the Stanley District Ranger from 1970 to 1973 and then as the Sawtooth National Recreation Area's (NRA) Assistant Superintendent from 1973 to 1976.

The Tom Kovalicky mannikin stands in a 1932 log house, once the Stanley Ranger's home, now Stanley Museum. Tom, a walking, talking part of Sawtooth lore, was the last Ranger to live in this historic building. He was also the Ranger when I opened the Stanley Clinic. Before the Stanley Clinic and Stanley Ambulance, emergency calls usually went to Tom.

Our Stanley Clinic started when it was unclear whether the Forest Service or the Park Service would manage the Sawtooths and the White Cloud Mountains. Both federal agencies compete for public land management in the United States, and the Sawtooth country is no exception. In the late 1960s and early '70s, with open-pit mining and real estate development posing threats, Congress deliberated the fate of the Sawtooths and White Clouds.

The Park Service moved staff to Stanley. Not to be outdone, the Forest Service built a new Stanley Ranger Station upriver from town in 1971. In this contest, the Forest Service prevailed when Congress passed, and President Nixon signed enabling legislation, creating the Sawtooth National Recreation Area (Sawtooth NRA).

A young, handsome, and talented Forest Service Ranger, Tom became the Sawtooth NRA's first "Area Ranger."

Tom spent fourteen years growing up on a ranch in Wisdom, Montana, served in the Army's 9th infantry division, was a smokejumper based in Missoula, and in 1962 graduated in forestry from the University of Montana — all before joining the Forest Service as a professional forester. His first posting was as an assistant ranger in Pinedale, Wyoming, in a big timber district. Next, Tom was in Rocks Springs, Wyoming, where the Park Service and Forest Service competed: Congress poised to establish the Flaming Gorge National Recreation Area. Rock Creek was a tough town. Easygoing, Tom built relationships with the locals. There, as in the Sawtooths, Congress selected the Forest Service for the leadership team for that NRA.

Tom led the Sawtooth NRA from 1972 until 1976. To start, he moved from Stanley to rented offices in Ketchum, awaiting the completion of the new Sawtooth

NRA headquarters. Tom had three assistant rangers: Dave Kimpton, the Stanley Ranger who figures prominently in the history of the Stanley Clinic, Dave Lee, the Wilderness Ranger, and Jerry Green, Tom's assistant for the Hailey Zone.

While a smokejumper in 1961, Tom's twenty-man team nearly burned to death in the Nez Perce National Forest. The Higgins Ridge Fire exploded from twelve to several thousand acres in forty minutes, leaving the team stranded. The helicopter pilot who saved them, Rod Snider of Boise, had been told to return to Boise; his wife was about to deliver their baby. The pilot stayed, lucky and lifesaving for the smokejumpers who otherwise had no way out.

The Bell G-3 included baskets on the skids for moving wounded GIs. Smokejumpers climbed inside and onto the baskets, hanging on without straps. In 1976, the American Forestry Association awarded Rod Snider the North American Forest Fire Medal for his heroism. Experiences like these helped Tom prepare for emergency calls in the Sawtooths: keep your head and control your panic.

At the Stanley Museum, a few steps from Mannikin Ranger Tom is a display about the Stanley Clinic. Medical instruments and furniture donated by doctors to help us start the clinic are now museum pieces. Stepping from one display to the next is stepping from one chapter to the next in medical history.

Fritz Wolfram

Tom Kovalicky, who served as Stanley Ranger and the Sawtooth NRA's first Administrator, was a smokejumper first

TOM KOVALICKY, IN HIS OWN WORDS

In May 1970, I came to Stanley as the new Ranger for the Stanley District of the Challis National Forest. My first house is now the museum's main building, and my office was a converted garage. I stored ice in the ice house, which once used ice cut and hauled from Redfish Lake. Seasonal employees set up their tents for the summer over by the barn. The CCC built a tile-line pool, which we used.

I got acquainted with US Forest Service employees running emergency care services in Stanley. I quickly learned that the Stanley assignment was unique.

I want to thank those who responded to emergency calls before Marie opened the clinic. Compared with any place else I have ever worked, local volunteers in Stanley responded to emergency calls. The Ranger before Lee Presley was Harold Wadley. Harold was a combat marine who served in Korea and Vietnam. He and Bill James were the two key Forest Service people leading the effort to respond to trauma. Other Forest Service staff were Julene Steele (my secretary), Mel Sanderson, Dave Mathias, and – later – Bruce Kauffman and Dave Kimpton.

Betty Rember (1917 – 2008) was a trained nurse in the community and pitched in. Betty grew up on a farm in southern Idaho, trained as an RN, and worked as a nurse in Sun Valley under Dr. John Moritz, marrying Craig Rember in 1941. Lucille Denny, Stanley's Postmistress, helped us communicate with Sun Valley and Hailey ambulance dispatchers. In addition, Bud and Stella Critchfield had access to the state radio network. That was a critical link because the state could radio troopers and Highway Department staff when Forest Service radio bands could not.

I drove into Stanley in my station wagon, which became a convenient substitute for an ambulance until the 1958 Pontiac ambulance arrived in Stanley in 1972. My three-year-old station wagon soon looked more like 50. If emergency calls came during the workday, we used Forest Service rigs. At night, we drove our personal vehicles to the scene.

I didn't anticipate that my Forest Service staff would become first responders in the field for medical emergencies. Calls for help were coming in 24/7. Most emergencies happened from snowmelt to first snow. Snowmobiling added to the demand for emergency services, with temperatures at 30-40 below zero.

When I started, I was concerned agency staff were being taken off their jobs to do search and rescue and emergency runs – and falling short in completing agency work plans. But what are you going to do? Emergency calls come in. Lives are on the line. People could – and did – die. You can't just look the other way, "Sorry, not in my job description, work plan, or budget." Here is the reality: before the Stanley Clinic, the U.S. Forest Service, as the land management agency and authority, bore a substantial part of the burden for emergency services.

As the new Stanley Ranger, I wasn't completely unprepared. My Army training helped. In Basic Training, you learn some essential life skills, including self-care and self-control. As a smokejumper, I had a 40-hour trauma training. The Forest Service also provided a 30-40 hour advanced first aid training. Training helps but never really prepares you for what you may face. You find yourself turning corners you've never turned before. What the Hell? I never got this in my EMT training!

Demerol was available for major trauma cases, provided by the Regional Office in Ogden, and kept in my desk drawer under lock and key. We always tried to dispatch someone trained in administering pain medications. In the Stanley District, some staff had training to use Demerol, including Dave Lee, who became an early leader in establishing Search and Rescue.

We never kept statistics. Before Marie, we were busy all weekend with emergency calls. That became routine, especially on a Saturday night with the Stanley Stomp. We responded to people who were shot, knifed, pummeled with bare knuckles, and slashed with beer bottles.

At about 1 am, someone showed up at one of the bars. The man was frantic. A car had wrecked west of Stanley on Highway 21. The car was upside down. Four people were trapped inside and injured. The bars had telephones back then. "We need to call the Ranger!"

Most emergency calls came to my home at the Ranger Station. Next, I started making phone calls to see who was available and who wasn't already committed in the morning. Bill James was one of my go-to staff. Once we were on the scene and started to help, we called Sun Valley's ER and described the injuries. We'd call for one if we needed an ambulance – although it could be a long wait. If not available, then we used my station wagon. Forest Service staff volunteered. I never had an employee ask me for time off as compensation for an emergency call.

Stanley's "new" 1958 Pontiac ambulance and the community's first graduating class of EMTs opened a new era in emergency services. You could feel the body shift the other way when you drove that recycled 14-year-old ambulance and turned the wheels.

At midnight, I was enjoying a beer at the Kasino Club when a young man burst through the door. "I need help! Can anybody help me?" "The Ranger is right over there," the bartender replied, pointing at me. Then, the young man recounted how a group of college-age kids camped at Bull Trout Lake had imbibed alcohol and eaten mushrooms: Death Angels (Amanita).

We jumped into the Stanley Ambulance and headed for the scene. Two people were okay. Two others were unresponsive, and we loaded them into the ambulance and headed for the Sun Valley ER. When we left the valley floor straight-aways entering the curves leading up to Galena Summit, the '58 Pontiac was fishtailing pretty badly. Combining queasy movements with fumes coming up through the Pontiac's floorboards made people feel car sick. Our two comatose patients certainly did.

We grabbed plastic bags as our patients started throwing up. By the time we pulled up at the ambulance bay in Sun Valley, our patients were beginning to respond. ER staff asked us to wait. About 30 minutes later, the ER doc came out and thanked us, "Great job! They might not have survived if you hadn't made them vomit." Our reward for the night: saving two young people from mushroom poisoning and wiping vomit inside our ambulance.

In those years, sometimes you just had to do your best with limited or no equipment. One emergency call came at 10 pm from a Boy Scout leader. A Boy Scout troop had been hiking to Dagger Falls on the Marsh Creek trail. One of the Scouts fell, fracturing a leg. Boy Scouts used their first aid training to splint the fracture. However, the Scouts needed help to move him. We sent two teams of four men each – volunteers right out of the bar and from the Forest Service. We didn't have a stretcher, so we used sapling poles and coats to carry the boy. We moved the boy to the trailhead, loaded him in a Forest Service truck, and transported him to the ER in Sun Valley.

Some emergency calls I wish I could forget. A young man in college worked one summer helping Joe Leonard. Joe managed Robinson Bar Ranch and was a renowned climber, kayaker, and backcountry skier who later would write his memoir, "The Son of the Madam of Mustang Ranch." On a lovely Sawtooth summer day, the young man rode his 10-speed bicycle from Redfish Lake into town. A car hit him. It was 1972, and we were in our new Ranger District office when the emergency call came in. When we got to the scene, the people who stopped to give first aid had to leave. The young man died in my arms.

Before the Stanley Clinic, most of what we saw were nonlife-threatening injuries: broken wrists and legs and sprained ankles. We weren't called for many heart attacks, strokes, or other internal organ failures. Before Marie was coroner, when we had a death, sometimes the wait was long. We kept one body on ice in the laundromat for 2-3 days, waiting for the coroner.

In an emergency, you have to keep track of personal belongings — generally wallets, purses, and valuables. For example, a sheepherder at Cape Horn wrecked a sheep-hauling truck, flipping it. He had a head injury and was comatose. We transported him by station wagon to the Sun Valley ER. When the sheepherder woke up, he called his employer, who called me. The sheepherder had a pouch in the truck containing $24,000. I returned to the truck, found the purse, and handed the cash to law enforcement.

Some people run toward emergencies. Others run in the other direction. Despite my Army, smokejumper, and Ranger training, I was never at ease responding to emergencies. But it had to be done. So, as the Ranger for the Stanley District, I did it.

The U.S. Forest Service, not the Park Service, is the authority responsible for the Sawtooth NRA. With that authority come unexpected and unaccounted-for responsibilities. A deep tradition of helping exists within the Forest Service. Agency staff respond to emergency calls, and they volunteer at their own expense.

When I arrived in Stanley, the tradition was that the Forest Service served as first responders. Within a few years, Marie opened the Salmon River Emergency Clinic. Forest Service staff continued to respond to emergency calls as EMTs and ambulance drivers, volunteering with the Stanley Clinic and Stanley Ambulance.

The Forest Service has skin in the game. If the Stanley Clinic and Stanley Ambulance weren't here, emergency calls would again be coming to the Forest Service. As with the rest of the Stanley community and visitors to the Sawtooth NRA, Forest Service staff and their families need healthcare. The Forest Service has to find a way to ensure the clinic and ambulance are supported and endure.

3

IDAHO HOSPITAL ASSOC.: OPENING DOORS

Do you receive any of your healthcare from an NP? Today, the profession has expanded, providing patient care in urban and rural settings. NPs are now essential to delivering healthcare in America, and the profession has expanded internationally. Yet, the NP profession began as a solution to a problem: RNs would provide healthcare where doctors couldn't, such as in isolated towns like Stanley, Idaho. Otherwise, rural people had no medical care.

I want to take you back to a time not so long ago when no one had heard of NPs, let alone knew what an NP does.

IBM's annual campout at Redfish Lake in 1963 was how our family first came to the Sawtooths. The more time we spent in the Valley, the more I felt uneasiness about the lack of emergency care services.

"Help, I need help!" yelled a man running through the Inlet Campground at Stanley Lake, where the Osborn family camped.

He and his wife had been hiking. They left the trail to take a shortcut. She lost her footing and fell. She was hurt and needed emergency care.

We pulled together a rescue party and brought her out to the campground. The young woman was hurting and scared. Her left forearm was angulated and swollen. At a minimum, she needed x-rays to confirm the fracture. We didn't even have a blood pressure cuff. We had nothing much to offer her except for our family's meager first aid supplies. I splinted the fracture and used one of my pillowcases to fashion a sling.We helped load her into their car. The husband was upset, and I warned him not to speed or risk a car wreck.The couple headed out into the night for the ER in Sun Valley, more than 70 miles over Galena Summit.

Cal, who managed IBM's office products division in southern Idaho, was active in the Boise community. Cal and I helped to host the National Lieutenant Governors Association at the Sun Valley Resort on July 14-17, 1971. We stayed at the Sun Valley Lodge, danced, spent time at the poolside, walked to Ketchum, and even took a bus trip to Redfish Lake for a wildlife dinner hosted by the Idaho Department of Fish and Game.

With five kids, getting away for a weekend was a vacation. Little did I know that this weekend would forever change the trajectory of my life.

While lying beside the pool in my one-piece white swimsuit, next to me was John Hutchinson, who headed the Idaho Hospital Association. Soaking in the sun, John and I struck up a conversation. Pleasantries gave way to deeper discussions about rural healthcare, including emergency services.

I was going through that incident at the Stanley Lake campground and a recent car accident near Galena Summit. Teenagers about the age of my sons were injured, some badly. Getting an ambulance from Hailey to the wreck site took nearly three hours. The kids were lucky: all survived. An older person with those injuries and delays in emergency care probably would not have made it.

My anxieties bubbled to the surface as I talked about inequities in rural healthcare. Despite all of our modern medical technology and advancements, we did almost nothing for rural America. Rural communities struggled, often with no medical care and no ambulances. Nothing. Just look at Stanley, Idaho.

As we talked, John Hutchinson mentioned that he had a college intern named Gary Steinbach. Gary had excellent communication skills. For Gary to focus on creating emergency medical services in Stanley might be a good project for an energetic college intern. And with that offer to help from the head of the Idaho Hospital Association, I returned to the pleasure of the pool, Sun Valley Lodge, and the National Lieutenant Governors Association meeting.

Gary latched onto this new rural healthcare project. First, we looked at a new "MEDEX" program arising from the Vietnam War. In the late 1960s, the program trained Vietnam War and Korean Conflict veterans with military medical experience to become physician assistants serving rural communities.

I knew the ideal person for Stanley: Stan Irikari. Stan was married, had kids, and had set down roots in the community. He was a mechanic and owned the Rock Garage in town, living on the second floor with his family and pet crow. Stan had been a military medic — and a good one. Yes, Stan was ideal for the MEDEX program. There was just one problem. Stan said, "No."

I wasn't a veteran and ineligible for the MEDEX program. I was an RN but hadn't worked in nursing since my first child was born in Seattle 18 years earlier. What kept going through my mind was that Galena Summit car accident with those injured kids and the ambulance from Hailey taking almost three hours.

Those kids could have been my kids. Who else could start up a clinic in the Sawtooths? There was no one. Well, there was someone. Me.

In my nursing journals starting in the mid-1960s were articles about nurse practitioners — advanced practice nurses — filling gaps in pediatric care caused by a national shortage of physicians. I had never met an NP. I didn't really know what an NP was, but I was about to find out.

As CEO of the Idaho Hospital Association, John Hutchinson opened doors for me. John and I already knew each other; we'd met on a plane from Boise to Moscow to inaugurate the University of Idaho's new president. Academic tradition called for universities nationwide to send an alumnus dressed in regalia to walk in the "parade of universities" during the inauguration. John represented the University of Mississippi while I, in turn, represented Ball State University.

Representing Idaho's community hospitals, John lobbied the Legislature for solutions for severe healthcare shortages in rural Idaho.

JOHN HUTCHINSON, IN HIS OWN WORDS

Marie and I crossed paths in Sun Valley in July 1971. She and Cal were co-hosting the National Lieutenant Governors Association meeting, and I was there on an unrelated education project. I knew Cal through IBM and had talked with Cal and Marie on the football field: my son and the three Osborn boys played on little league football teams in Boise. On that July day in Sun Valley, Marie was upset about the lack of rural healthcare, notably for the Sawtooth country.

"John, thousands of tourists come to the Sawtooths every summer," Marie said. "We have this huge influx of people. Yet, there's nothing if they get hurt."

Could the Idaho Hospital Association help establish a new Stanley Clinic? The W.K. Kellogg Foundation had awarded us a grant to improve rural healthcare in Idaho. We used those funds to expand medical library support services to small hospitals to help with medical records. After talking with Marie in Sun Valley, I returned to my office in Boise and checked on the wording of the grant. And yes, we could use some of those funds for Marie's project.

Our intern, Gary Steinbach, was excited about the idea. With a Master's in Hospital Administration from the University of Minnesota, Gary handled the Idaho Hospital Association's grant programs, including our Kellogg Foundation grants.

Gary was a big help to Marie. He was personable with strong organizational skills. Gary helped with one crucial element: for Marie to staff a new Stanley Clinic, she would do it as an NP. Recently written regulations required Marie to have a physician preceptor. Gary wrote letters and set up a meeting for Marie with physicians in Sun Valley about serving as her preceptors, and they said, "No." Next, Gary turned to the two physicians in Hailey, Dr. Packer and Dr. Gwinner, and they said, "Yes."

Marie needed training, especially in trauma care. Gary found a local women's group in Boise to provide funding for Marie's training at Harborview Medical Center, a teaching hospital associated with the University of Washington in Seattle. At about the same time, the Legislature amended the Nurse Practices Act to include licensing for NPs.

What the Idaho Hospital Association did for Marie in opening the Stanley Clinic fit our commitment to rural healthcare.

Along with the Idaho Medical Association, we were the two leading organizations in the Legislature on healthcare. People I worked for — and with — responded to rural Idaho's needs. Doctors weren't going to small towns to practice medicine. That reality prompted legislative action to license NPs and, later, to support a physician assistant (PA) training program at Idaho State University. Then as now, our Legislature, Governor, and members of Congress are essential decision-makers for rural healthcare.

The 1960s and '70s were pivotal years for healthcare, and we spent much time in the Legislature. Idaho was not alone in seeking solutions. Improving rural healthcare captured people's time, attention, and commitment nationwide.

Idaho has a citizen Legislature, a chamber of people with full-time occupations besides being a legislator. There are so many types of issues that come before a Legislature. Legislators look to their elected colleagues or lobbyists for help understanding specific legislation and taking positions. I was one of those lobbyists representing the Idaho Hospital Association. People say bad things about lobbyists. Integrity is essential when working with a Legislature. You have to give straight answers even if it hurts your position.

Credit for legislation to improve rural healthcare belongs to many, including Dr. John Edwards. Dr. Edwards was a native of Washington, D.C., who graduated from medical school at George Washington University before becoming a physician in Council, Idaho, in 1947. So much of Idaho healthcare, especially rural healthcare, is a tribute to the contributions of this physician.

Dr. Edwards was the go-to person in the Idaho Legislature on healthcare at a critical time. As a physician from a small town, his Legislative colleagues trusted John. He knew first-hand the challenges and potential solutions. Whether adding Idaho to WWAMI or Idaho being the first to license NPs, John was a legislative visionary and leader in rural healthcare.

In the summer of 1972, at age 54, while running as a Republican for a fourth term in the Legislature, Dr. Edwards had a heart attack and died at the Council hospital. Gov. Cecil D. Andrus eulogized Dr. Edwards, emphasizing his death was "a tremendous loss to the people and the Legislature of the state of Idaho." Dr. Edwards' untimely death was a significant loss for everyone — his wife and six kids, his patients, his colleagues in the Legislature, and the people of Idaho. However, his legislative legacy lives on, training Idaho physicians and licensing NPs who provide medical care for thousands of patients.

After I retired from the Idaho Hospital Association in 1992, Pat and I had a home up Thompson Creek downriver from Stanley — before the big molybdenum mine. My wife is a nurse. One day, a car drove up. In the back was another man curled on the seat. "He's bad off," said the driver. After her initial assessment, Pat said, "Better if you take him to Marie." Off they went.

As it turned out, the fellow's condition was due to severe alcohol intoxication. But in these isolated places, you never make assumptions — people can die from failure to diagnose correctly and treat appropriately, including cases of acute alcohol poisoning.

Roland Miller

Stanley Ambulance. EMTs with Marie, who is in the ambulance doorway, standing on steps

Nearly 50 years later, after that fateful meeting with Marie at the Sun Valley poolside, I remember walking out the door of my independent living apartment, looking across the hallway, and seeing a new name on the apartment door: "Marie Osborn."

I spoke with one of the administrators at our independent living facility, "Yes, she was the nurse practitioner in Stanley," she said. Later, I saw Marie, went over to her table, "Marie!" and hugged her.

Marie's story — endless hours day and night providing healthcare for that isolated Valley, enduring the harsh winters for nearly 30 years — is a dramatic saga.

But beyond the Valley's healthcare needs, Marie set the rural healthcare movement on fire. After the Stanley Clinic opened in 1972, we started seeing more and more nurse practitioners, and many of them began practicing in Idaho's larger towns and cities, joining physicians' offices.

The nurse practitioner movement was right for Idaho and took off. It is a movement that spread across the nation and across the world.

What came out of that conversation by the Sun Valley pool is astounding. You should never underestimate what people can accomplish if they set their minds to it.

Marie set out to prove that the nurse practitioner idea could work — and she succeeded.

Reflecting on our chance meeting in Sun Valley and all that has happened since for the nurse practitioner profession and EMS, I am utterly amazed.

I am proud that the Idaho Hospital Association was part of it and helped to open those doors.

4

EMERGENCY CALL: DAVE KIMPTON

No chewing tobacco when you're driving the Stanley Ambulance. Thank Dave Kimpton, the Stanley ranger, for that rule. Dave, a Vietnam veteran and ever the gentleman, offered to share his chew with a patient's wife during his first-ever ambulance run.

We all have our first days of something. Dave's first day as an EMT was unforgettable.

That summer morning in 1972, Dave Kimpton, Bill James, and other Forest Service staff got the emergency call at the Stanley Ranger Station. Two vehicles had collided head-on a few miles up Highway 75 (then Highway 93) at the Steel Bridge over the Salmon River. (Later in the 1980s, after more car wrecks, the Idaho Department of Transportation replaced that death trap of a bridge.)

As Dave later recalled for the federal judge in the Boise courtroom, based on information provided by the widow, "Mr. Harris was driving the van onto the bridge. His grandkids were fighting, distracting him. Mr. Harris nearly ran into the abutment. That bridge was narrow for two vehicles. He overcorrected. On the bridge, in the opposite lane, was a pickup truck. The van collided with the pickup."

In a van, there's no engine to buffer the impact of a head-on collision. Upon impact, the pickup collapsed the van's front onto Mr. Harris. The dash collapsed while the area under the dash penetrated Mr. Harris's thigh. When we got to him, blood was puddling on the bottom of the van and the pavement. We had to extricate Mr. Harris from the wrecked van and clear the bridge before transporting him and Mrs. Harris over Galena Summit to the Sun Valley ER.

The two wrecked vehicles blocked the Steel Bridge. The Forest Service rigs and the Stanley ambulance parked on the west side of the bridge toward Stanley. We had to triage the trauma, load the ambulance, and clear the bridge to get to the hospital in Sun Valley. The man who took the lead was Bill James, the tobacco-chewing and balding head of the recreation program for the Forest Service's Stanley District. Bill's priority was to get Mr. Harris out of the crushed van and then tow the two wrecked vehicles off the bridge. On that day, Bill worked miracles.

"Bill used a handyman jack and a tow chain," Dave recalled. That first summer, we had no other extrication equipment to pull people out of wrecked vehicles. "We pulled a door off the van to get to the driver." As we lifted him from the crushed van toward the ambulance, Mr. Harris was thankful and downplayed his injuries. "Once we got him out," Dave told the courtroom under oath, "people towed the vehicles, clearing the bridge." Unfortunately, Mr. Harris was a big man. It took several of us to lift his gurney into the back of our '58 Pontiac ambulance.

"I want an LDS doctor for my husband," Mrs. Harris insisted. Although frantic, her injuries were less severe. Nevertheless, she walked through the crowd, calling, "Are there any Mormons who can help me with my grandchildren?" Fortunately, one of our local ranchers at the accident scene, Jay Neider, was an LDS bishop and stepped forward to help.

Dave drove the ambulance with Mrs. Harris in the front passenger seat. In the back, I was monitoring Mr. Harris on the gurney. We headed up the Valley toward Sun Valley with lights flashing. Although the ambulance was old, the engine was surprisingly powerful. Dave accelerated on the highway's straight stretches.

Dave reached into his shirt pocket and pulled out a tin of chewing tobacco. He took a pinch and placed it between his cheek and gum. Then Dave turned to Mrs. Harris. "Would you like a pinch?"

Mrs. Harris just stared at Dave. Then, after a long pause, "No, thank you," she said.

We drove through Ketchum to Hailey and the ER at Blaine County Hospital. In 1972, the Hailey doctors were my preceptors, so we transported Mr. Harris to Hailey. Dave pulled into the ambulance bay. The nurses came out and spoke with me. "We can't handle that patient here, Marie," the charge nurse said. "You'll need to take him to Sun Valley."

Dave turned the key in the ignition to restart the ambulance. Nothing happened. The ambulance wouldn't start. Dave tried again and again. He jumped out and ran across the highway to the gas station. We were lucky: The attendant came over and jumped the ambulance battery. We were off, retracing our route to Ketchum, before pulling into the ambulance bay at Moritz Hospital ER in Sun Valley.

We off-loaded Mr. Harris and his wife, and Dave and I got back into the ambulance to return to Stanley. Dave turned the key in the ignition — and just like before, nothing happened. The Blaine County sheriff was at the ER and helped us jump our ambulance battery a second time.

Rarely did our patients or their families end up in court. The Stanley Clinic, the ambulance crew, and I avoided malpractice lawsuits. The head-on collision at the Steel Bridge was Dave Kimpton's first ambulance run as a volunteer EMT, and, unfortunately, he got called to the witness stand two and a half years later for a lawsuit over the death of Mr. Harris.

When we left Mr. Harris at Moritz, he was stable. However, the evaluation in the ER confirmed what we knew: an open femur fracture. Not long afterward, Mr. Harris went to the OR to reduce and stabilize his fracture. In 1972, surgeons weren't anticoagulating hospitalized patients to prevent thromboembolic disease. The mortality rate following hip fracture surgery is four to seven percent without anticoagulation. Mr. Harris did well in the OR and post-op recovery. Later, he sat in a chair in his hospital room, stood up, fell over, and died from a pulmonary embolus.

Mrs. Harris insisted that the pickup truck driver was responsible. Consequently, she filed a lawsuit against the driver. Dave recalled the events of his first-ever ambulance run on the witness stand. Testifying in a federal courtroom has a way of making memories indelible.

But that was only the first ambulance run that day.

On our way back from Sun Valley to the Stanley Clinic, we were passing over Galena Summit when Dave's Forest Service radio came to life. In those first years, we didn't have an EMS radio so our communication depended upon donated CBs and Forest Service radios.

"Stanley Ranger Station to Dave Kimpton."

"Kimpton."

"Hey, Dave. You and Marie have another emergency call just past Smiley Creek near the Beaver Creek Store."

"10-4."

Dave put down his radio, turned on the flashers, and headed off Galena Summit into the Sawtooth Valley. We passed Smiley Creek and, about a mile later, came upon a Ford Bronco flipped upside down on the opposite side of the road. The impact had caved the top of the car, a wonder that the driver survived. We weren't the first ones at the scene, but close. Other people had gathered to look but not help. The two occupants were still inside.

York Recovers From Crash: Gratitude to Stanley People

With feelings of gratitude to the 47 people of Stanley, Wayne York, Idaho Education Association executive secretary, now is on his way to recover from injuries received in a car accident.

On Aug. 5, York, 4101 Glencoe Place, was returning to Boise from the Idaho School Administrator's Conference in Sun Valley by way of Galena Summit, Smiley Creek, and Stanley.

His four-wheel-drive vehicle went out of control when the trailer it was pulling whip-lashed, causing both vehicles to roll, York said.

Within minutes Stanley emergency care nurse Marie Osborn was on the scene to administer first aid to York and his wife when they were removed from the vehicle. [The Stanley] ambulance whisked the Yorks over the mountains to Sun Valley, where York could begin diagnosis and treatment for a cracked vertebra....

Collete Wilde, *The Idaho Statesman*. August 18, 1972

I looked at the driver. I knew that man: Wayne York, the head of the Idaho Education Association. Not long ago, I met with him about Idaho's public schools as the PTA lobbyist at the legislature.

"Marie!" Wayne said. "Marie, I need to get up."

"No, you're not," I replied. "Not with your neck. You might have a broken neck." You could look at him and know he had a cervical fracture.

"I'm fine. I need to get up."

"Don't be stupid — listen to me," I pushed back. "If you have a broken neck and move, you could end up paralyzed or dead. You are not moving. We've got braces; let us do the work. We'll move you when it's safe. You do not move."

The car crash victim was a prominent man in Idaho. Although I was a short, middle-aged woman, I was wearing my white lab jacket and stethoscope, which changed the power dynamics.

Dave and I carefully placed our patient into a back brace that ran from head to buttocks. We first saw a brace like this at one of our EMT classes when a state instructor demonstrated it. Unfortunately, the price was high, and we couldn't afford it, so a talented transplant from New York, Dubie Dubendorf, built one using the commercial brace as a model. We used Dubie's homemade brace for Wayne.

Once we splinted and protected Wayne's spine, Dave and I lifted our patient onto the gurney and into the ambulance. The ambulance started this time, and we returned to the Sun Valley ER. Cervical spine x-rays (we didn't have CT or MRI in those days) showed a high cervical spine fracture. We had called it correctly in the field, saving Wayne from a spinal cord injury. He was lucky.

We returned to the clinic in time for our third emergency of the day: two teenage boys in a motorcycle accident. Their two families had been camping near Pettit Lake. The motorcyclists were riding toward each other, coming up over a rise in the road. They couldn't see each other until it was too late. The two fourteen-year-old motorcyclists collided at high speed.

One of the boys had a neck injury. The father, a doctor, had never had trauma training. He lifted his injured son into the back of the family station wagon without stabilizing the boy's broken neck. When they arrived at the Stanley Clinic, his son was dead. There was nothing we could do except console a grieving parent and wait for the coroner.

That was Dave Kimpton's first day as a volunteer EMT. Later, in the quiet of the clinic, Dave turned and looked at me. "I'm not sure I want to be an EMT if this is how it will be," he said wearily.

It was not a good day, and not many of us slept well that night. In the summer of 1972, before Idaho EMS, people scooped the injured and ran to the ER. The father didn't know. When I think about that boy dying, I still cry.

Dave Kimpton helped open the Stanley Clinic in 1972, rode our first ambulance, and dug snow to uncover the foundation for our new and current clinic building. A half-century later, Dave continues to volunteer — first as an EMT and now on the board of the Salmon River Clinic, often serving as president.

Stanley's first clinic and first ambulance. Trauma, notably head and spine injuries, marked that first summer in 1972.

DAVE KIMPTON, IN HIS OWN WORDS

Before Marie, emergency calls mostly came to the Forest Service. Many of us in the agency had advanced first-aid training. These were the Vietnam War years, and several combat veterans continued their service by joining the Forest Service. I had been on Army attack helicopters. Occasionally, we moved wounded soldiers. We had training on stopping bleeding and stabilizing soldiers until we could get them to a field hospital.

When I joined the Forest Service, the agency arranged my first-aid training before arriving in Stanley. In 1971, when I first arrived in Stanley, if someone was hurt badly and in severe pain, we administered Demerol. When we were up against it, we loaded people in the back of one of the agency's green station wagons and drove them over the hill to Sun Valley.

One example is a mule that turned on its owner. The owner and mule were between a propane tank and a wall, a tight space of about five feet. The owner couldn't escape when his mule started biting and stomping on him. We injected Demerol into the badly trampled mule owner and loaded him into the green station wagon for transport. He was still alive when my predecessor, Ranger Tom Kovalicky, pulled up to the ER in Sun Valley.

Kovalicky complained to the regional office in Ogden about all the car wrecks the Forest Service was handling. The RO responded, "Just do what you have to do" while the RO provided the Demerol. Local Forest Service staff did what we could when people needed emergency care.

When Marie appeared, it was "Hallelujah!" Tom and I discussed how we could help her. The Forest Service had to get out of the EMS business.

Tom directed me to work closely with Marie to establish the Stanley Clinic and Stanley Ambulance service. Before Marie, emergency care in the Sawtooth country was by the seat of your pants.

Dave Kimpton, Stanley Ranger Station, 1972

In the mid-1980s, Marie was out of the Valley when Stanley's EMTs got the emergency call: "Challis Dispatch to Stanley EMTs. Two cars collided at the intersection of Highway 75 and Highway 21. Seven people injured." When I arrived, the two wrecked vehicles were in the intersection. The premed intern came from the clinic, panicked and yelled, "Don't panic! No one panics!" When I trotted over, our eyes met. "Dave, thank God you're here!"

With EMTs on the scene, we began triage. We had seven injured patients with broken arms, legs, and head injuries. One woman complained of neck pain, worrisome for a cervical spine fracture. We began to splint, brace, and prepare all the patients for transport, when suddenly a man in his mid-40s arrived, approaching the ambulance and addressing the team.

"I'm a doctor," he said matter-of-factly. "I'm in charge now." As EMTs, we ceded control of our seven patients to the doctor.

The doctor asked me about our triage. I described each of our cases. He walked first to the woman with the probable cervical fracture. We stabilized her neck with a cervical collar and placed her on a scoop stretcher. The doctor knelt, took her head in his hands, and rotated her head side-to-side, asking, "Does this hurt?"

I was so shocked I didn't know what to say. I finally blurted out, "Stop! Stop what you are doing! We think she has a broken neck!"

The doctor stopped his manipulation, and we loaded her into the ambulance. The x-ray confirmed our field assessment at the Sun Valley ER: She had a cervical spine fracture. What that doctor did could have severed her spinal cord, leaving her a quadriplegic or killing her.

Marie recalls how this same doctor from Boise showed up at two more accident scenes. Again, he informed everyone he was a doctor and was in charge. Finally, he showed up by the bridge to Jay Neider's ranch for a car wreck. One of the injured was a suspected cervical fracture. As before, this doctor insisted on taking charge and rotating the head. That third time, Marie grabbed a cervical collar and stopped him.

That third episode did it. If this were happening in Stanley, it would happen all over Idaho. Doctors without training were preempting first responders and risking our patients in the field.

Marie went to the legislature and demanded change, carrying the message that someone would end up a quadriplegic or dead. People in charge at an accident scene must have training. Being a doctor doesn't mean you have trained as a first responder. The legislature responded.

Today, the senior EMT on the scene is in charge. They can disregard orders from a physician, except for physicians in their chain of command. EMTs must establish and maintain patient care control in an emergency setting.

The Stanley Ambulance's longest run — over fourteen hours — began as darkness fell in late November. The emergency call came by radio and phone from the Diamond D Ranch north of Stanley. Hunters had rolled their Jeep, and the driver was severely hurt. That was the nearly snowless winter of 1976-1977.

One blessing and curse of a low snow year is that back roads remain open. As a result, hunters drive into places that they probably shouldn't. One hunter had gone to the Diamond D Ranch on the Loon Creek Road, then up to the Lookout. Coming down from the Lookout, he hit ice and rolled his Jeep off a ledge.

Marie and I left Stanley at 5:30 pm. We knew it'd be a long night — and it was. We were up all night trying to save that hunter's life, nearly dying in the process.

We headed downriver to Sunbeam, then turned up the Yankee Fork. It was darker than hell. At the Yankee Fork dredge, we missed the turnoff to Loon Creek Road, realizing our mistake when we arrived in the ghost town of Custer. We retraced our route and then turned west toward Loon Creek Summit. Still today, the road can be treacherous with multiple steep hairpins. In a ModVan ambulance in winter on a pitch-black night, the Loon Creek Road over that 8,686-foot summit to the Diamond D Ranch was nearly impassable.

The ambulance lights illuminated a sheet of ice covering the road ahead. The ice sloped steeply, ending in pitch blackness. We parked and got out our flashlights. We turned the light beams downward, with the sinking realization that the ice sheet sloped into an abyss about 300 feet down. If we drove across that ice, we would slip off and plunge to our deaths. The ice field was only thirty to forty feet long but pitched at a horrible angle. So, we dug a trench across the ice to hold the tires, covering it with dirt and gravel for added traction. Then we climbed into the ambulance, prayed, and started inching forward.

About halfway across the ice field, we suddenly felt the ambulance begin to slide sideways. Oh, God. We slipped again. Driving the ambulance, I had turned the tires up too high in the ice trench. When the tires dropped back into the track, the ambulance slid sideways. It was almost enough to poop your pants.

We crept forward in total silence. Afterwhat felt like hours, we finally made it off the ice and back onto bare earth. We arrived at the Diamond D Ranch to find the hunter nearly dead. Marie got an IV into him, started fluids, and returned to Loon Creek Summit. When we arrived at the ice field, we put more dirt on the ice and inched our way across without sliding. Transporting that injured hunter from the Diamond D Ranch to the Sun Valley ER made for a long night.

We finally returned to Stanley as the sun rose over the White Clouds, more than fourteen hours after we set out for the Diamond D. We wore out a lot of protective angels in those years.

5

"I'M HAVING CHEST PAIN"

At the same time Ranger Dave Kimpton was experiencing his first days as a volunteer EMT, John Roskelley, who would become an internationally acclaimed mountain climber, was in the White Cloud Mountains trying to manage someone with an acute MI.

John's experiences straddled the rural healthcare divide in 1972 when emergency services first came to Idaho's rugged Sawtooth country.

White Cloud Mountains overlooking lower Warm Springs Creek

JOHN ROSKELLEY, IN HIS OWN WORDS

My family is from Challis, but I grew up in Spokane, Washington. My mother was British and moved to Spokane with my dad, who became the outdoor editor for the Spokane newspaper. Not surprisingly, as the son of an outdoor editor, I grew up hunting and fishing, but my passion is climbing. I have climbed mountains throughout the world. But, like my father before me, I'm also a writer.

My other passion is Joyce. We married in January 1972. Two months after our wedding vows, the United States Bureau of Mines hired me to work out of its regional office in Spokane. My new job would take me back to Custer County.

I started in Spokane processing field samples, separating gold from amalgam mercury and black sands. One of the geologists and mining engineers at the Bureau of Mines, Bob Evans, learned that my family was from Custer County. The Bureau of Mines was to determine whether the White Cloud Mountains in central Idaho were suitable for federal wilderness protection because of mining activities over the years.

Bob Evans was a full-blooded Paiute. His family lived on a reservation in northern California. He knew the challenges of driving a government rig in rural areas. So, when Bob was assigned the mineral analysis of the White Clouds, he wanted someone who knew the families in that region of the Salmon River. I was Bob's Custer County connection — along with helping with the mineral analysis. So, in late spring 1972, Bob and I packed up and drove out of Spokane for Challis.

Bob liked working with horses. None of the other mining engineers or geologists wanted near them, but with his Native American upbringing, Bob used horses whenever he could. Arriving in Challis, we leased horses for the summer from a ranch outside town. We loaded the horses into the back of the pickup, which had a cage. We then headed upriver to our camp at the base of the East Fork of the Salmon River.

Bob also had an old trailer. He used the roof to dry salmon rather than the more traditional sticks. In those days, salmon were still returning to the Salmon River.

Castle Peak is the White Clouds' highest point at 11,815 feet. At Castle Peak's base are streams and lakes, including Frog Lake. Underground is a significant deposit of molybdenum. ASARCO owned the mining claim. Bob and

John Roskelley, who later became an internationally acclaimed mountain climber, preparing to collect mineral specimens in the White Clouds in 1972. He faced a medical emergency in the high country.

I were there for the US Bureau of Mines to collect samples. We packed our horses, headed up the trail, and camped at Frog Lake. The following day, after breakfast, we started collecting samples. Then, about midday, everything changed.

We were on the hillside above the lake when Bob suddenly stopped and sat down. He was having trouble catching his breath.

"John, I don't feel well," Bob said. "We need to leave. I need to get to a hospital."

Bob was a man of few words, never one to complain. He wasn't clutching his chest, although he complained of chest pressure and arm pain. Earlier, Bob had disclosed he had heart trouble, so I knew. Now, at 9,000 feet elevation, far from the road, Bob was having a heart attack.

I helped Bob down off the slope, broke camp and packed the horses, and helped Bob up on his saddle. Then, we trotted down the trail on one long ride back to our pickup on the East Fork Road.

At that moment, with Bob at risk of dying, all I knew was I needed to get Bob to a hospital. What to do? Fifty years ago, few people lived along the East Fork, so I didn't stop. When I got to the highway, I turned upriver heading toward Sun Valley.

I drove past Stanley. In late June and early July 1972, the Stanley Ambulance, NP Marie Osborn, and Stanley's team of volunteer EMTs had been responding to emergency calls for only a few weeks. I wouldn't learn of Marie and Stanley's EMTs until years later when I met Marie's son, John. All I knew was the hospital in Sun Valley, so that's where I headed.

Castle Peak is the highest peak in the White Cloud Mountains. Controversy over a proposed open pit mine and the valley's real estate development helped establish the Sawtooth National Recreation Area in 1972. The Salmon River Emergency Clinic opened that same summer.

Bob and I didn't have a radio, and anyway, it would be years before EMS radio networks were in place. So, we were on our own, arriving at the ER in Sun Valley unannounced.

Bob survived, was hospitalized for several weeks, and eventually returned to Spokane. We reviewed maps in his Sun Valley hospital room, and Bob instructed me on collecting samples from mining claims.

After Bob's heart attack, I worked out of Smiley Creek with the horses. Following Bob's directions, I collected mineral samples in the White Clouds and drove them to Spokane every ten days.

My wife of six months, Joyce, joined me at Smiley Creek. With the approach of autumn and the school year, she returned to Spokane to start teaching.

Smiley Creek in 1972 had just a half-dozen cabins. Few people lived there, even in the summer. The stream flowed between the cabins. Joyce and I enjoyed walking across the bridge to the cabins and looking into the stream.

Smiley Creek was chock-full of bright-red salmon that had returned 900 miles upriver to spawn. That phrase, "There were so many salmon you could walk across their backs," was how it was that summer of 1972 in Idaho's Sawtooth Mountains. The full impact of the four Lower Snake River dams in destroying the salmon runs would come later.

We took risks and didn't consider the lack of EMS in those years. In that summer of '72, the Bureau of Mines also sent me to work collecting samples on the Salmon River's North Fork. To get to mining claims, I floated across the river — alone. I kept my dog with me all the time. As I went to get out of the boat, I nearly stepped on a rattlesnake. If I'd gotten bit, what then? I'm on the other side of the river with no one to help and no radio. Who's going to come to get me?

Horses are an accident waiting to happen, an injury opportunity. Joyce and I had horses on my farm near Spokane for twenty-seven years. I was injured more often when hunting and packing with horses than I ever was climbing mountains. You can be back in the wilderness, make one mistake, and have a broken leg or shattered arm. In 1972, when the Stanley Clinic and Stanley Ambulance were starting, we didn't have backup emergency care working for the government or know any better.

My dog, Sam, was insurance. If I didn't show up at Smiley Creek, I hoped people would eventually come looking and find my dog. He was a muscled Doberman and Labrador mix, a survivor in a rough land. Sammy would wait at the entrance to the underground mine, where I was required to obtain samples. Some of these 100-year-old mine adits were thousands of feet above the remote valleys that led up to the peaks of the White Clouds. I figured if I was injured collecting samples in those mines, Sammy would faithfully remain standing sentry at the mine adit. Eventually, someone would come looking, see Sammy waiting, and find me. Fortunately, we never had to see if this assumption would actually work.

We were lucky and got by without emergency medical services. Not everyone was.

White Cloud Mountains from Shaw Mesa at sunset

PART TWO

FROM KENTUCKY NURSE ON HORSEBACK TO IDAHO NURSE PRACTITIONER ON SNOWMOBILE

Caulfield & Shook Collection, Photographic Archives, University of Louisville

A nurse from the Frontier Nursing Service in rural Kentucky, 1932. During the Great Depression in Appalachia, the Kentucky Nurses on Horseback provided healthcare to underserved communities.

Marie with granddaughter, Ashley. Growing up in Depression-era Kentucky and Indiana, Marie dreamed of becoming a Kentucky Nurse on Horseback and caring for patients in Appalachia.

6

BSN

I was born in Russellville, Kentucky, on May 18, 1931, during the depths of the Great Depression. My parents, Parnell and Alma, named me Alma Marie Clark, but I prefer "Marie." I was the first of six children.

We were poor. My dad was desperate for work, and driving a Coca-Cola truck part-time was not enough. So, the Clark family moved from Kentucky to Indianapolis.

Dad walked the streets of Indianapolis looking for a job in the cold and pouring rain. His shoes had holes, so when he came home, Mom and I would put dry newspaper in them and remove the wet. Some days, Dad found day labor for twenty-five cents an hour. We survived.

The Clark family moved to Daleville, Indiana, where the cost of living was cheaper. We lived in a dump of a house. Our kitchen had a hand pump for water and an outhouse in the backyard. To help keep food on the table, Dad planted a huge garden. I hated weeding, though I loved gardening later in life. I also lost my tonsils in Daleville.

Two tonsillectomies for the price of one? Nancy, my younger sister and the second of six children in our family, had terrible tonsils. Nancy occasionally asked me to look in her mouth when she was having pain. A surgeon from Indianapolis who also did primary care in Daleville advised Mom that Nancy needed her tonsils out. Since we had so little money, the doctor offered to do Nancy's tonsillectomy for the regular price and mine for free. But I didn't have tonsil problems. Mom, fearing that I would eventually, agreed. In a doctor's office in Daleville in the 1930s, using ether for anesthesia, the doctor performed tonsillectomies on the two Clark daughters. Lucky for us, neither had serious bleeding complications. Otherwise, we could have bled to death there in the office.

Dad finally landed a job in Muncie working for Acme-Lees, eventually becoming a highly skilled die maker. Dies, made of steel, require precision workmanship. Dad was knowledgeable and understood more about steel than many experienced metallurgists.

Marie graduated with her BSN from Ball State in Muncie, Indiana in 1953

My parents never finished high school because they were so desperately poor. Quality education for the Clark children took priority. In choosing a house in Muncie, Dad's only criterion was that we had to live in the best school district. For Muncie in the 1930s, the best was Burris Laboratory School, associated with what was then Ball State Teachers College, now Ball State University.

We were lucky enough to rent a nice old house with indoor plumbing across the field from Burris and Ball State. Burris and Ball State were in an affluent Muncie neighborhood, and wealthy people sent their children to Burris. My classmates' fathers included bankers, lawyers, and doctors who were mostly Republicans. The Clark family was certainly not affluent. Dad was a union official, and my parents were Democrats.

Dad asked me to join him for a walk in my senior year. Dad was not a walker, and I could feel something wasn't right.

As we walked together across the field, Dad said, "Marie, I can get you through high school. But you're the oldest of six. There's no way I can get you through college. We don't have the money. I can't do it."

My father, an emotional stoic, was nearly in tears. He knew that Burris pushed its students to go to college, and he could not deliver as a parent. My dad, the talented die-maker who loved mathematics, never had a chance to graduate from high school. Neither did my mother. They both worked hard to make sure we all graduated from high school. But with six kids, they couldn't afford college for me. The memory of his pain still makes me cry. Eventually, I received a scholarship for teacher education, although even then, I knew my future was in nursing.

Already, I had been saving money for college. Through my Sunday school class in the sixth grade, I volunteered as a candy striper at the hospital. I loved helping care for people. By the time I was a freshman in high school, I was getting paid thirty-five cents an hour working as a nurse's aide. Also, I sang soprano, loved music, and got work singing for organizations, usually solo but sometimes with a choir.

During the 1940s, Muncie's synagogue hired me to sing in Yiddish at the Jewish Reform Temple on Friday nights and high holidays. The rabbi was a kind and gentle man. He had escaped from Germany, where Nazis had killed his wife and children in concentration camps and burned his library. The rabbi knew or spoke sixteen different languages. The last language he learned was English when he fled to the United States.

Before becoming a nurse, I did think about becoming a doctor and told our family physician, Dr. Tucker, who said, "Marie, you're too feminine to be a doctor. You should go into nursing." Furthermore, medical school was and still is expensive. Despite saving money from singing, nursing, and babysitting, I couldn't afford it. As a young woman with few means and no connections, I had to look elsewhere. In life, some doors open, and others remain closed.

Getting accepted into nursing school wasn't a problem. I had excellent grades and good references. When I graduated from Burris Laboratory School in 1949, third in my class, my future lay across the field from our home at Ball State, where I began a four-year degree program to graduate with my Bachelor of Science in Nursing (BSN).

Fear of polio pervaded the sweltering summer of 1949 after my high school graduation. Our county was quarantined. I spent that summer working as a nurse's aide at Ball Memorial Hospital. We weren't the first nor the last to live during contagion, spending our days caring for the afflicted.

We had no air conditioning on the polio wards in the heat and humidity of Indiana summers. We wore personal protective equipment of gowns, gloves, and masks on top of our heavily starched nursing uniforms and caps. We hot-packed and bathed our polio patients in hot water to relieve pain and relax muscles. Eventually, nursing administration allowed us to wear white shirts and pants. I sweated through that polio summer with a team from the National Polio Foundation through the March of Dimes.

Would I carry polio from the hospital and infect my sisters and brothers? The medical board for Ball Memorial Hospital, including the director of nursing, didn't want me to live at home. My neighbors didn't want me living with them, either. Everyone was afraid. When people found out where I was working, they slammed doors in my face. Eventually, Dad converted the back porch into a bedroom, so I remained separated from my family but still had a place to sleep when I wasn't caring for polio patients.

As fall neared, polio cases declined. I walked off polio wards and into first-year classes at Ball State. The seniors put on a "hop" to welcome the first-year students. I met this handsome young man, a senior. As a lowly freshman, I was

Folger Brown, IU Health Ball Memorial Hospital

Ball Memorial Hospital, 1950s

thrilled. We danced every dance. When he came to the Clark home and knocked on the front door, my parents didn't like him immediately. Years later, Mom revealed she feared I'd get married, get pregnant, and not finish nursing school.

During my first year, money was tight, so I continued to sing. I lived at home to save money. During the second year, the nursing program required that I live in the dorm — two blocks from home. As my hospital ward duties increased, my singing career ended. By then, Dad had been promoted into management and was making more money.

That first year was filled with classes and studying. During our sophomore year, we formally entered nurses' training with the three-year, non-degree nursing students who would become RNs. We were all freshmen in the three-year nursing program, although those on the four-year BSN track were sophomores at Ball State.

At the beginning of our sophomore year, we were called "probies:" on probation for six months. After those six months, we celebrated with a traditional tea ceremony, where we received our nursing caps and capes. Our families gathered at Mariah Bingham Hall, the nurses' dorm. In a darkened room, all the nursing students held little Florence Nightingale lamps in a candlelight procession. After the director of nursing spoke, one by one we stepped forward, and she placed our nursing cap on our heads: the "capping ceremony." It was solemn and spiritual, almost a religious ceremony. My cape was beautiful and warm, dark blue with gold lining.

BSN students learned nursing on the wards and liberal arts in the classrooms. Ball State required certain courses to complete the baccalaureate program while also permitting electives. Walking across campus during the bitter cold of Indiana's winter wrapped in a nursing cape, then sitting in an overheated classroom, listening to droning monotone lecturing on sociology, was an invitation to nap. Like a jolt of caffeine, "Greek and Roman Mythology in Translation," taught by Dr. Magoon, a huge man with a booming voice, was an electric elective, more psychology than mythology, and unforgettable.

Too many patients, insufficient hospital beds, and few nurses are perennial problems. Polio aggravated a nursing shortage. Then, as now, reserve and resiliency in the health-care "system" are inadequate for surges from epidemics and other crises. In Muncie, patients overflowed into the three hospital solariums. When protecting patient privacy, make-shift curtains are poor substitutes for walls.

Nursing-short teaching hospitals used student nurses rather than closing down patient wards. At Ball Memorial in the early 1950s, nursing students in our junior year worked night shifts and filled in on the obstetrical ward. Working nights, we functioned as charge nurses. For backup help, an RN "floated" between the medical building and the main hospital. Working alone helped prepare me for the Stanley Clinic.

While I walked through the graduation line in June 1953, three more months of work still awaited me to finish my BSN program. I missed time because of pneumonia and then joined my family to share the last days of my grandmother, Mother Tatum, in Kentucky and then attend her funeral. I also took time off in June for my honeymoon.

With my honeymoon over, I returned to the wards in late June. I overheard an angry conversation about me between the director of nursing and the ward's charge nurse. I had taken time off to get married without asking permission from the nursing administration. Nursing students during their senior year could marry if "the Gods" (the director of nursing) gave permission. Instead, I eloped without the administration's permission. I asked the Gods' permission to move out of the dorm to live with my new husband. The nursing administration delayed my request, then eventually gave approval. My reward was working nights all summer to complete my three months and my BSN degree.

To become an RN, you must first pass the state board exam. Cal and I moved from Muncie to Seattle in September. Rather than take my state board exams in Indiana, I took them in Washington State. In the fall of 1953, with Cal working part-time at a hardware store and attending the University of Washington, financial pressures mounted. Although pregnant in my third trimester, I was hired as a nurse at Harborview Hospital. The nursing administration agreed to allow me to work until December 1, with my baby due on January 15.

In 1953, we didn't have many specialty wards like ICUs or CCUs. At Harborview, I worked in a medical ward where physicians were using experimental drugs for cancer and some heart problems. At the end of November, with my last day looming, one of the nurses abruptly left. Frantic efforts were underway to replace her. I volunteered to stay another week.

"Marie, no," the head nurse retorted. "You are not having your baby on this ward!" As it turned out, I would be pregnant during much of the 1950s and early 1960s, and not working as an RN on hospital wards.

7

MUNCIE, MARRIAGE, AND MOVING WEST

Carpe Momento!

Cal Osborn 1928 – 2014

Cal Osborn, formerly located at Hamilton Air Force Base, California, has been honorably discharged from service. On Monday, he will go to Danville, Ill., where he will return to his former position with Conron and Co. He has been on military duty for the past two years. He is the son of Mrs. Carrie Osborn, 923 W. Sixth St.

Chronicle, Marion, Indiana, 1953

Our Stanley motel room was dark and quiet. Our marriage needed this time together. We had enjoyed dinner at a local restaurant and now a motel's anonymity. Our bodies together, husband and wife.

BAM. The door kicked open. "What the hell?"

"Marie! Marie! We need you. Now! The Piva boy has an allergic reaction. His throat's swelling! He's having trouble breathing!" It was Judy Uresti, Stanley's schoolteacher.

Calling a "code" comes in different forms: code pagers, hospital PA systems, and phone calls. In Stanley that night, the code blue came with kicking open a door.

I threw off the covers and mumbled, "Cal, I gotta go. Sorry. I'll be back." I threw on clothes and ran out the door. Our romantic night together in Stanley, Idaho? The Piva boy did fine. But, for Cal and me, our night together ended badly.

We were both famished. Cal had just arrived from Boise after a week at the IBM office. On Friday, driving those curvy roads on Highway 21 that wind through Idaho City and Lowman, all the slow-moving camping trailers caused long lines of traffic. For me, the clinic had been busy, so I didn't have time to eat lunch.

Cal and I met at the clinic and walked across the street to the Kasino Club for dinner. We were seated, looked at menus, and ordered. Cal sipped a beer. We caught up on our kids and traded stories about IBM and the Stanley Clinic. We planned projects for our new Sawtooth cabin and Boise home on Hillway Drive.

Then, this guy walked up to our table.

"Marie?" he asked, pulling up a chair and joining us without an invitation.

"Yes."

"Marie, I have this rash. It started on my legs and has spread to my back."

Cal stared at me from across the table.

Cal managed IBM's Office Products Division for southern Idaho and eastern Oregon. On Friday afternoons, he left work early, made the rounds in Boise picking up pharmaceuticals and medical supplies, and then drove 130 miles of curvy mountain roads to the Stanley Clinic. We tried to spend the weekend together if there were no emergency calls, but there were always emergency calls.

One Friday, Cal stopped by the clinic. The front door was locked. He headed upriver to our family cabin. As he neared the Redfish Lake turnoff, he saw the cars. Cal pulled over and parked. Two vehicles had collided at the intersection. I was on my hands and knees trying to stabilize one of the trauma patients who was screaming with pain. I looked up. There was Cal.

Our eyes met. He turned around and walked toward his car. I turned back to try and help my patient.

Without my husband, Cal Osborn, there would be no Stanley Clinic.

Without the Stanley Clinic, our marriage likely would have endured.

How do you resolve competing duties to your family and patients as a sole healthcare provider? How many school programs can you miss?

Our spouses and partners don't walk in our shoes. We come home from clinic or ambulance runs. "Pass the pepper, please. He was vomiting huge amounts of bright red blood. We couldn't get it stopped." Or, "He had this huge boil. I lanced it and got a bucket of pus. Honey, this is great pasta sauce!" Your husband, wife, kids, and friends don't want to hear it. "Stop! I'm trying to eat dinner. That's gross!"

At the end of a shift in a clinic, ER, or hospital ward, we close a door literally and figuratively: "What happens in Vegas stays in Vegas." Not really. We carry home what we saw, smelled, heard, and touched with our patients. When caring for others, we must be able to decompress. Who do we talk to? Information must also be protected, especially in a small town like Stanley.

As the sole rural healthcare provider, my office hours might come to an end, but emergency calls continue. "Shifts" never really end. We remain on call unless we leave town or retire. Our patients know us at the grocery store, post office, gas station, bar, and restaurant. "Hi, Marie, it's great to see you. Oh, by the way, I have this pain ...." Now try adding in a marriage.

From 1953, Cal and I found ways to resolve our marital problems. But once I started the Stanley Clinic, there was no off-ramp. Eventually, however desperately needed and professionally fulfilling, my patient care work brought an end to our marriage.

Endings can be beginnings, as it was for Cal, me, and our five children. Time can heal. As a mother, I don't want to minimize the pain and disruption of our divorce. But I can hear Cal even now, "When God closes a door, he opens a window."

Cal became a "host" on cruise ships and danced the seven seas on over seventy cruises. "Some people walk on water. I dance on water," he laughed. Cal re-met Cory Thiebert, the former wife of another IBM-er who had wired our cabin on Shaw Mesa. Cal, a leading "Boise Booster," and Cory danced at Boise's "Alive After 5" street events. Almost to the end of his life, Cal worked to convince community leaders to protect his beloved Boise from the risk of upstream dams failing, drowning thousands in a catastrophic flood.

Cal loved life. He brought me from Muncie, Indiana, to Stanley, Idaho, via Seattle, Bellingham, and Boise. Our marriage was not perfect — none is — but we had a great run, including bringing five children into the world who survived while losing two in childbirth. The Stanley Clinic — its role in creating the nurse practitioner profession and rural EMS — arose from our marriage and the Osborn family.

Muncie, Indiana

The phone rang. "Hi, Marie."

"Oh, hi, Dick!" It was Dick Worth, my boyfriend. His father owned a lumberyard in Muncie. "Marie, I have this buddy just out of the Air Force. He asked if I could fix him up with a date. Do you know anyone?" I did and volunteered my best friend and classmate. That night we double-dated with the Air Force veteran Cal Osborn.

We danced a lot that night, Cal and I. He kept looking down and commenting on my bust line. "This guy is crude," I thought. I didn't care for him at all; still, he was a great dancer. Cal was your typical military service person, just out and wanting to "play the field" and party.

Cal was born in Ft. Wayne, Indiana, and was the only child of Earl and Carrie Osborn. He grew up camping and canoeing, fishing, hiking, and hunting. "My church starts on the other side of the windowpane," Cal liked to say, sitting around the campfire after a day of fly fishing with one of his sons.

Air sickness washed Cal out of pilots' training in the Air Force, so he worked in cryptology, decoding messages from the South Pacific. After separating from the Air Force, Cal returned to selling for Conron Hardware out of Danville,

Cal Osborn in the U.S. Air Force uniform with his parents, Earl and Carrie, who divorced shortly after Cal was born.

Illinois. He also stayed in Muncie, calling on hardware stores to sell them tools. Cal was a salesman, storyteller, and jokester.

"Hey, have you heard my duck call?" Cal asked. He picked up a flip-top from a beer can and held it to his lips: "Calling all ducks! Calling all ducks!" Cal would laugh until tears rolled down his cheeks — each time.

In the spring of 1953, Cal and I had a couple of dates, but not that final one. My roommate, June, fell hard for Cal. I warned that he was up to no good. He only wanted one thing: to get into her panties. June and Cal went out a few times. One night, the dorm room phone rang. "Hi, Marie. This is Cal. Are you available? Can we get together? Just to talk." We had an unwritten rule in the nurses' dorm: You do not date your classmate's boyfriend. June really liked Cal. "Just to talk" seemed safe. He was going to tell me he really liked June, I presumed.

Cal and I returned to the same place as our first date, the 67 Supper Club on Highway 67 outside of Muncie. In 1953, it was a nightclub that served food and always had live music. All evening, we sat and talked — no dancing. From then on, it was just Cal and me. We were together, never anyone else.

After getting to know each other for two months, we decided to marry. "No," said Mom and Dad. Mom, who married at age eighteen, was particularly adamant. "Marie, you are too young." I was twenty-two! Mom also wanted me to have the traditional wedding but couldn't afford it. Clark family finances were tight with the added expenses of Mother Tatum's recent death and funeral. I didn't want to add to my family's financial burdens. Cal and I decided to elope.

"Have you ever been camping, Marie?" Cal asked.

"No, never," I replied. "I know nothing about camping."

Cal said I should ask one of my scouting friends what to pack. An Eagle Scout, the son of the organist who accompanied me when singing at the Jewish temple and the Baptist church, wrote up a long list. I showed my camping equipment list to Cal. He looked at it and tore it up.

Cal and I married on Father's Day, June 21, 1953. Even before we decided to marry, we settled on that date for Cal to introduce me to his father, Earl. We would meet near Angola at a little state park and camp and celebrate Father's Day with introductions. Later, we decided to marry on that

Marie and Cal married on Father's Day, 1953

day — without telling our parents. Lucky for us, Angola was the elopement capital of Indiana in the early 1950s.

Those days before we married were frantic as we tried to pull it all together. Then, as Sunday approached, everything fell into place.

The state required blood tests before issuing marriage licenses. On Thursday, we sought out the lab director at Ball Memorial, who had been one of my instructors and who Cal knew from Toastmasters. After the lab closed, he met us, drew our blood, ran the test with negative results, and handed us the completed form.

Cal and I had our results in hand when we showed up on Friday at the county courthouse, went to the Bureau of Marriage Licensing, and picked up our marriage license for the minister to sign at our wedding.

On Saturday afternoon, Mom and Dad hosted a hamburger fry for my friends from nursing school. Cal came. My parents knew we were dating and liked Cal. After hamburgers, we drove to the gravel pit to swim. I dived — not far enough to miss the rock outcropping — and hit my right second toe and broke it.

My foot hurt like hell. Saturday night, I was scheduled to work as the charge nurse at the hospital in Newcastle, Indiana. I was working during my vacation, hired as a graduate nurse (not yet an RN), and trying to make money for my wedding dress. In Newcastle, one of the doctors who came in to check on a patient taped my broken toe so I could hobble around. That was a long night shift.

My wedding dress was a beautiful pale blue with matching three-inch heels. A friend at the Jewish temple bought clothes for me on her buying trips to New York. She brought home my wedding dress and shoes. I would wear those heels for the wedding ceremony. But oh God, my toe hurt.

Our nuptials on Sunday began at the state park outside of Angola with Earl Osborn. I slept under a tree after working all night. Cal woke me up.

"Hey, Dad. Great to see you. I want to introduce you to Marie Clark. And we have a surprise for you this Father's Day: We're getting married today!"

Earl, the first of our four parents to know, was thrilled. He was a short, thin man, not much taller than me at five feet, who bought his clothes in the boys' department. Earl was afflicted with "short man syndrome" and picked fights. Earl loved his only son.

Around noon, Earl, Cal, and I drove into town searching for a minister. Church was just over. Congregations had gone home for Sunday dinner. We couldn't find a minister. "Let's just go camping and not worry about it," Cal suggested.

Earl shot back, "Absolutely not. You two are getting married today." Earl wouldn't let his son back out just because he couldn't find a minister. So, Earl and Cal kept looking. I was sleep-deprived and along for the ride. Cal and I named our firstborn "Calvin Earl Osborn," knowing that we might have gone camping instead of marrying without Earl along.

We walked into a church decorated beautifully for a wedding later that day. White flower bouquets were at the end of each pew. We walked down the flower-lined aisle toward the altar and a bank of white flowers. Lovely floral scents filled the church. Someone had spent a fortune on our wedding ceremony, but not us. We had no money. I hadn't even finished nursing school.

The minister arrived. Earl handed me a bouquet. Cal and I recited our vows, placing gold wedding bands on each other's ring finger. The minister signed the marriage license. Next Cal signed. Then I signed. We were married.

After the ceremony, we found a telephone booth, and I called home.

"Hi, Mom. I've got some huge news! Cal and I just got married!"

Silence.

Mom started crying. I could hear her saying something to Dad. Dad wouldn't talk to me. We ended that painful call. I was the oldest of six. Eventually, Alma and Parnell Clark would share in their other children's weddings. My younger sister, Nancy, had a huge church wedding wearing a drop-dead-beautiful white dress. My parents grew wiser

The Clark Family. BACK ROW, LEFT TO RIGHT: *Marie, Bud, Susie (Rider), Nancy (Smith), Betty (Hunt)* FRONT ROW: *Parnell, Alma, Jerry.*

with each of their six children. Years later, when my sister Betty and Tom eloped, my parents helped find the minister, attended the ceremony, and then went on their honeymoon.

Next, Cal called his mother, Carrie. Unfortunately, that phone call would be more painful. Cal was an only child of a Jewish mother. Earl was a Methodist who never attended church. At birth, Earl selected the most non-Jewish name he could think of for his son: Calvin. However, when Carrie's mother proposed middle names, Earl refused. As a result, Calvin would go without a middle name. Earl and Carrie divorced after eighteen years of marriage when Cal was eighteen months old.

Cal grew up hitchhiking back and forth between Indiana and Michigan, between mother and father, two different people, one Jewish and one not.

When Cal and I met in the spring of 1953, he wanted what he had never known: a stable marriage and a large family.

Cal's mother was a controlling force in his life. She lived in Marion, thirty miles from Muncie. Carrie had a friend on the local draft board. When her son's number came up during the Korean War, she fixed it so that her son could join the Air Force. Carrie supplied her son with stamped, addressed postcards to write to her daily (Cal negotiated to write to her every week).

In Air Force pilot school, flying was misery for Cal. He even used uniform caps as vomit bags to avoid cleaning the cockpit. Given his unrelenting airsickness, when he was slotted into cryptography, Cal wanted an overseas assignment with his eye on Japan. His mother said, "No."

"My mother always used the 'he is my only child' to keep me stateside," Cal recalled. Cal was stuck, managing to make the best of it in Sheridan, Wyoming, and then in San Francisco.

While you marry into families, I'm not Jewish. Anyone Jewish living in Indiana in the 1950s and attending temple knew prejudice.After the war, the Nazi's Holocaust horrors came to light. From my years of singing in temple, I heard the stories.

Even my Kentucky grandmother, Mother Tatum, whom I never heard say one word of prejudice, let slip one day, "Marie, you can never marry a Catholic, a Jew, or a Black person."

Cal drove me to Marion to meet Carrie and his Aunt Blanche. Blanche was warm and welcoming, but Carrie was not. Her son brought home a *shiksa*, a non-Jewish woman. Our meeting was frosty. And then came the telephone call after the wedding. "You did what?" Silence. "Oh, my son. You married a *shiksa*. And you didn't even invite your mother! My only son. My only child."

Cal stepped out of the phone booth. The telephone conversation with his mother was transforming. His big grin was gone.

Cal's father stood there with me, waiting to take us to dinner. Emotionally, Cal moved on. We both did. We had to. We were married now.

Our wedding dinner was fifty miles to the north at Schuler's Restaurant in Marshall, Michigan. Earl called ahead. "Mr. Osborn, you want a wedding cake for newlyweds? Today is Sunday, almost four o'clock — the bakeries are all closed. We'll try, but no promises." Schuler's staff came through, and celebrating with a cake made our wedding day more delicious.

I was still in my wedding dress and heels, fading fast from champagne and our wedding and working all night at the hospital.

For our nuptial night, Cal found a nice hotel in Marshall. We needed sleep. My broken toe hurt so bad; getting those heels off was a relief. Ahead of us was our honeymoon camping trip.

In our lives together, we did things I'd never dreamed of doing. Until I met Cal, I had never camped out and gone fishing. I'd never been out of Indiana except to see family in Kentucky.

"We've met before," said John Corriveau years later, an IBM-er and great guy from Mercer Island in Seattle. "I'm sure we have, Marie. Where could it be? Wait. It's coming back to me now. It was ... at Sleeping Bear Dunes. Yes! Only you weren't wearing anything on top!"

I was stunned. Cal burst out laughing. For the two honeymooners, Sleeping Bear Dunes was our first stop. And no, John Corriveau had never been to Sleeping Bear Dunes. Sleeping Bear Dunes was sunny, warm, and a delight.

The next day, we went to Traverse City, wandered through town, and then headed north to Mackinac Straits. We parked the car to save money, walked onto the ferry, and rode back and forth across Lake Michigan. A full moon was rising, and the moonlit water was beautiful.

We headed further north to Lake Superior. We approached Batchawana Bay in Canada, about thirty miles north of Sault Ste. Marie, and the weather changed. On Batchawana Bay was a fishing camp where Cal had spent summers during high school. He loved the place. This fishing site was historically significant to the Ojibwe.

After we arrived at the fishing camp and set up our lean-to, threatening rainclouds appeared in the sky. Since we didn't have a tent, the fish house became our nighttime shelter. I slept well once I got used to the smell of dead fish.

The following morning, the people at the resort ushered us aboard their boat and then took us to a beautiful little island Cal knew. We off-loaded our food and gear. Here we were, just the two of us, honeymooning on a lovely small island in the expanse of Lake Superior. What could possibly go wrong?

We arrived about noon and were setting up camp when I asked, "Cal, is that a storm?" Clouds, big and black, headed toward us. We hurried through our lunch. The thunder got louder. "Marie, don't worry about washing dirty dishes. You can wash 'em later. Just put them in the water there by the ledge. The suckers will clean 'em." What's a sucker? I didn't know. The plan sounded reasonable. After all, Cal was an experienced camper.

The storm moved over Honeymoon Island, first, breezes and gusts with sprinkles, and then a full-on gale pouring rain by the buckets. Lightning flashed, and then thunder exploded over the sounds of rain and wind. Cal and I crawled under our lean-to. We got soaked. As quickly as the storm hit, it passed, and sunshine returned to the island.

We scrambled to the shore to retrieve our dishes, pots, and pans. Wind-whipped waves had taken everything. Our cooking utensils, plates, and silverware were gone. We scoured the tiny island, finding only an old, discarded bean can and a rusty wire rack. We had our canned goods and supplies, just nothing to cook and eat with.

"Ahoy there!" We saw a boat loaded with well-dressed tourists visiting from Detroit. "We've come to see the honeymooners!" the pilot yelled over the water. When the vessel came closer to shore, Cal told them we lost our cooking supplies in the storm. "Do you have anything we could use?" From then on, a parade of boats came to see the honeymooners on this island who had lost all of their kitchenware. We got lots of supplies — and lots of gawks, too. We felt like animals in a zoo.

We had a great week fishing from the island. Our honeymoon was my first time fishing. Beginner's luck: I caught a really nice-sized bass, bigger than Cal's. Kind-hearted people brought us replacement utensils, probably better than Cal had scrounged.

After a week, the resort boat came to pick us up. We said goodbye, leaving behind our original cooking utensils while taking away honeymoon memories.

We went along the shores of Lake Huron to Windsor, Ontario, the city across the lake from Detroit. Finally, we crossed the border and entered Detroit. Cal had relatives

Honeymooners on Lake Superior, 1953

who welcomed us, dirty and bedraggled after camping. A shower felt so good.

Honeymoon over: For me, it was back to Maria Bingham Nursing Dormitory and the wards of Ball Memorial Hospital. To graduate with my BSN, I had nearly three months of required training hours to make up for my absences. For the nursing administration, I was free labor on the wards at night. Cal and I found an apartment, and I moved out of the dorm. He drove me to work every night and picked me up every morning. During the day, Cal worked selling hardware.

The West had captured Cal's imagination. He talked about Seattle, the Pacific Northwest, and attending graduate school at the University of Washington. When the Air Force stationed Cal near San Francisco, he traveled up the coast to Puget Sound with a barracks mate. On a sunny, clear day, Puget Sound can be one of the world's most beautiful places: islands, blue water, beaches, and lush green forests leading up to the picturesque Olympics, Cascades, Mt. Rainier, and Mt. Baker. Cal, an Indiana boy, knew he had to return.

In early September 1953, I finished my nurse's training and my BSN degree. Cal's father loaned us money to buy a little teardrop trailer. On Labor Day weekend, 1953, we finished packing. Saying goodbye to my family, I sobbed. I had never been away from my family before. I just kept crying. As we were heading out of Muncie, Cal pulled the Ford and trailer off to the side of the road and turned off the engine. "Marie, look, we don't have to go to Seattle. We can go back and make our lives in Muncie."

I was still blubbering. I stopped, looked at Cal, and said, "No. Let's go."

So, we headed out West on our big journey together. When you take that first step, you never know how big a country can be or what's ahead in life.

Heading West

Cal wanted to go West, and I was going where he went. As a twenty-two-year-old pregnant woman, I knew nursing could provide work wherever we went.

Wouldn't the University of Washington be ideal? Cal had his BA from Indiana University and wanted a master's degree in international business. Moreover, Seattle was a major seaport. Surely, the UW would have an extensive course selection in international business.

Today, with the web and cell phones, information is easily accessible and sometimes accurate. Not in 1953. Our major life decision to leave Indiana for Washington State assumed facts not in evidence. UW's graduate program in international business was thin: two graduate-level classes.

"Little Shit" was the name Cal gave our new traveling home. We had looked all over Delaware County for a small trailer to pull with the Ford. Unfortunately, Little Shit had no bathroom. For cooking, it had a two-burner, hot-plate-like gas stove. Our trailer had a sink with a tank to store water. It had built-in benches doubling as a bed and a table folded against the wall. Cupboards had to be closed securely for traveling. When we arrived at the University of Washington, we planned to park our trailer at a veterans' mobile home park, assuming all major public universities had mobile home parks for veterans.

While packing our trailer, my brother Bud appeared. "Hey, Marie, I thought you could use this." He brought us a lovely baked ham, which Cal thoroughly enjoyed. How better to say "Bon voyage" than with a ham?

Our only deadline was the start of classes at UW. We had two weeks. The early fall weather was delightful, and we took our time traveling West.

Cal could navigate us from Indiana to Yellowstone. He had worked at the national park, hitchhiking the route we would follow across the Midwest and Great Plains.

Beyond Yellowstone, we would head toward Spokane, then on to Seattle. On our first night, we camped on a riverbank somewhere in southern Illinois. Mosquitoes welcomed us.

Swarms of mosquitoes stormed our camp. The smoky fire Cal built didn't get rid of them. That night, mosquitoes covered our food as soon as we served the macaroni and cheese on paper plates. You'd brush them away so you wouldn't eat them. They just kept coming back. Finally, we fled into the car to eat. That night, we slept in the car.

We had one near miss with a trailer fire. I was fixing breakfast. Pregnant and leaning over the stove, I wore a fuzzy flannel robe, black and green houndstooth-checkered. "Oh my God, I'm on fire! Cal!" Cal grabbed the robe and put out the fire with his hands. Neither one of us was hurt. The robe was a total loss. We moved on.

What I saw for a girl from "Middletown, USA" was entirely alien to my Indiana upbringing. I was not in Muncie anymore. The Wall Drug Store in South Dakota featured a giant "jackalope" and this amazing, old-fashioned soda fountain. Further west, the Devil's Tower in Wyoming, sacred to tribes of the Northern Plains, rose above the land. Burma-Shave signs on fences along the highway announced cute little rhymes advertising shaving cream.

Most wonderous of all was Yellowstone.

Geysers, hot pools, bison, bears, and elk: Yellowstone is a marvel. In mid-September 1953, we had the park mostly to ourselves. Kids were back in school. The cabins were locked. Aspens were beginning to turn vibrant colors. Days were sunny and warm; the nights frosty. Autumn's beauty had come to Yellowstone.

On a Friday morning, we unhitched our trailer and drove the sixty miles from Yellowstone's South Entrance to Jackson Hole. Along the way, we stopped at Jenny Lake. The lake's surface perfectly reflected the Tetons on that still autumn afternoon.

We arrived in Jackson Hole, and Cal took me to the Elks Club. The guys at the bar helped Cal celebrate our being newlyweds, celebrate a newly discharged veteran, celebrate a Hoosier coming West, and celebrate a fellow member of Elk-dom. Cal didn't buy a single round. By the time we left the Elks Lodge, Cal felt no pain. I didn't know how to drive.

A harvest moon rose to light our way. We stopped again at Jenny Lake. Watching the full moon and Tetons reflected in the water felt like a second honeymoon. There were no other cars on the road that night. The moonlight turned landscapes into fairylands. Later that night, we returned to Yellowstone and our sleeping bags.

A week later, we were driving across northern Idaho. Passing through the Silver Valley with mining towns and industrial buildings, I remember the water: The river was such a strange, dirty-dough color. I didn't know about Idaho's mining pollution. I remember thinking that nothing could live in that water.

Years later, my kids would compete in ski races at Jackass Bowl Ski Area, above these barren hillsides deforested by sulfuric acid. One of my children would work for years to support the Coeur d'Alene Tribe's efforts to clean up the mining pollution.

Near Spokane, entering eastern Washington, rain began to fall. It was Saturday, and a Huskies football game was on the car radio. The rain fell harder after we crossed the Columbia River and drove up into the Cascades toward Snoqualmie Pass. In the pass, the clouds hung low. Windshield wipers at full speed could barely keep up. Rocks were down on the rain-slicked road. In 1953, there was no interstate freeway; we drove on the old two-lane highway. Until then, except for the Badlands in the Dakotas, the Ford hadn't labored much pulling the trailer. We listened to the football game and finally got over the top. We pulled over, stopping to rest the steaming Ford.

Then, we started down. The clouds closed in, darker, drearier. The rain came down harder and harder. I began to cry. The harder it rained, the harder I cried. As we drove into Seattle, it was still raining. And it was still raining when we drove to the University of Washington campus to park the trailer at the veterans' trailer park. Only, there was no trailer park for veterans, no veterans parking, no married housing, nothing.

Cal spoke with someone who suggested we could find a trailer park on Aurora Avenue and gave us directions.

In the drenching rain, we finally found a trailer park. Cal unhitched Little Shit in the mud. With no bathroom in the trailer, we squished through yucky mud to the community bathrooms. With darkness, the rain increased. Cal said we needed to go to church the following day.

We found a cafe on Aurora near the trailer park. The menu was in Cal's price range for my ever-frugal husband, later fondly known as "Coupon Cal." It was the greasiest of greasy spoons, plain awful. After dinner, I cried more. We got into the Ford, drove around the University District, and saw various churches. We liked the Christian Church. Then we returned to our trailer and mud.

The next morning, we got up and went to church. We walked in the door. "Welcome! You look like you're new here." The church greeters took us in hand, introducing us to the congregation. We met many people and had coffee and rolls; it was so amazingly warm. The rain stopped, and the sun came out. One of the church members invited us to their home for Sunday dinner that afternoon.

I knew then we had come to the end of our journey West. We had finally arrived.

Marie and "Little Shit" heading west, driving across the Rathdrum Prairie from Idaho into Washington, September 1953

8

EMERGENCY CALL: THE MIRACLE

Life is not a matter of holding good cards,
But sometimes playing a poor hand well.

Jack London, "*To Build a Fire*"

What I cared *about* was caring *for* patients. Below is one of the great life-saving stories in the Sawtooth country recounted by Dave Kimpton in his book, *Mountainous Events*. You might want to wrap yourself in a warm blanket before you start.

In rural America, saving lives is about volunteering, training, properly working equipment, availability, and showing up. The injured and sick survive because of Good Samaritans. Dave Kimpton is one.

An EMT, Dave volunteered often. Dave was compact and solid, not big but strong. In those first summers, Dave and other volunteers hand-carried people out if something bad happened in the backcountry. A good friend, Dave, listened. When I was frazzled after a clinic day packed with patients, we might walk over to the Kasino Club for a beer or rum and Coke and talk. Also, for my nightmares, Dave was a dream interpreter. He had nightmares of his own from the Vietnam War.

Soft-spoken and fun to be with, Dave could talk about many things, not just Forest Service or ambulance runs. We talked politics, a touchy subject in small-town Idaho, especially with men. On the other hand, he never complained of all-night ambulance runs. Dave knew how to use his "self-edit button."

In the 1980s, we had massive amounts of mountain snow. Snow piled up until reaching rooflines, and still, the snow kept falling. At my cabin home, I had to cut steps into the drifts to climb up to my snowmobile. The weather forecast? Another massive snowstorm was heading our way. That was when the two young women went missing.

FROM *MOUNTAINOUS EVENTS* BY DAVE KIMPTON

The will to live is an incredible force which taps the deepest power of the spirit. Total focus eliminates peripheral functions, freeing the mind to concentrate on only one issue: survival.

The storm was a monster stretching from central California into Canada. For five days, record-breaking snowfall had buried the Sierras, Cascades, and northern Rocky Mountains.

It was my birthday, and I watched the storm's fury as I relaxed in a cafe in the small village of Stanley, chatting with friends and drinking coffee. I felt warm and secure in the belief that I would not have to venture out into this raging maelstrom of blinding snow and wind, other than to eventually make my way home riding my vintage snow machine. Little did I suspect that I and six others would soon be exposed to the storm's full fury in a desperate attempt to rescue two young women who were missing and presumed dead.

At the onset of this severe weather event, the morning of February 15, 1987, Sherrita Benham, nineteen, and her sister Lydia, eighteen, left Boise for Stanley, 130 miles distant. They planned to visit friends and work at one of the restaurants in town over the President's Day weekend. At Lowman, fifty-seven miles away, it was raining and a sign warned that the road ahead was closed due to heavy snow. After calling a friend in Stanley, however, they were encouraged to continue their journey. Ahead of them lay Banner Summit at 7,200 feet in elevation, now enveloped in what would become one of the heaviest snowstorms and worst avalanche conditions in memory.

As the two sisters started up the grade on the south side of the summit, the falling snow rapidly deepened until they could neither proceed further, nor turn their car around. By this time the storm had intensified into a furious blizzard. After a brief discussion, the two women made the fateful decision to continue on foot. They hoped for a break in the weather and that friends would meet them near the summit, about six miles away.

They struggled through the deep snow for hours until waves of exhaustion nearly overpowered them. Each step now became a painful effort as they tried to press onward against the relentless and deepening snow. It soon became apparent that they were not dressed appropriately since their cotton jeans rapidly absorbed moisture and their other clothes were inadequate to keep them warm. A lack of food and drink added to their trauma and eventually, after a valiant struggle, exhaustion overcame both of them. They summoned enough strength to dig a snow cave which would serve as a crude sort of shelter against the storm. With only a wet blanket and soaked clothing, they crawled into the snow shelter where they curled into each other's arms and fell into a fitful, terrifying sleep. They had struggled uphill for a remarkable five miles through the deep snow and violent wind. They now faced the horror of being buried alive and slowly losing the fight for survival as the blizzard raged unabated above them.

As the storm intensified during the next several days, all access roads into Stanley were closed by deep snow, with the exception of State Highway 75 from the northeast, where highway crews struggled to keep the road open to one-way traffic. Sometime during February 17 and 18, massive snow slides tore at the slopes in hundreds of locations throughout this mountainous area. Some of these slides ripped out huge trees that were 150 to 200 years old. Other slides, some in the vicinity of the missing women, were sixty feet deep, four hundred yards wide, and thousands of feet long. Additional smaller slides continued to cascade off the steep slopes as new snow built up. Clearly, any extended travel under these severe conditions would be extremely hazardous to those involved. After numerous close calls, the state snowplows withdrew back to Stanley since conditions were too dangerous to attempt to keep any highway open. All roads into Stanley were now blocked by deep snow and massive avalanches.

When the sisters awoke the next morning in the icy darkness of their snow cave, they hoped that the storm was over and that they could continue their journey and find help. To their dismay, they found that snow conditions were even worse than the prior day. They now attempted to return to their vehicle. However, due to extreme weakness, the cold, wind, and deepening snow, they were forced to dig another snow shelter after only a very short period of struggle. Snow slides now buried the road within fifteen feet of where they huddled, wrapped in each other's arms, terrified that they were now going to die. The snow continued to fall, burying them in a living tomb, blending them into its whiteness.

On February 18, concerned relatives called the Boise County sheriff's office to report that neither sister had arrived at work the Tuesday after the holiday. This was the first time that anyone knew they were missing, since they lived alone in a Boise residence and had been vague as to whether they were going to drive to Stanley or not. A search party was then organized, but the sheriff decided not to leave until the following morning due to the extreme conditions and lateness in the day.

By the third day, the young women started having hallucinations, especially Sherrita. During lucid periods she talked to her sister about dying, asking her sister to tell their parents that she loved them. Lydia was horrified at this new development and desperately tried to encourage her sister not to lose hope, even though she realized that with each passing hour the chance of rescue was waning, especially since she could still hear the storm in full force above their snow shelter. By now they were nearly sitting on the pavement due to the melting of snow under them caused by their body heat. Suffering from lack of water, dehydration was now a major problem, even more than hunger, and they clawed at the icy walls trying to eat ice and snow to alleviate the awful thirst.

After leaving the restaurant and returning home the morning of my birthday, I was contacted by Mike McGowan, a local businessman and friend, on behalf of Deputy Parkhouse to determine if I would participate in a rescue attempt. After explaining the situation to me, I readily agreed. We both knew that travel would be extremely hazardous due to a high probability of triggering a snow slide. The very lives of the searchers would be in jeopardy with only a very small chance of locating the missing women, either alive or dead.

I returned home and packed essential survival gear, enough to permit me to survive several days in case the worst happened, and the searchers also became trapped. With permission from Deputy Parkhouse, I contacted Joe Leonard who had extensive backcountry experience and who also owned a European Larven, an over-the-snow machine similar to a small snowmobile, that was steered by skis worn by the operator and was especially good in deep powder snow. Mike owned a Thiokol Snow-Cat that was designed to travel through deep snow and had a heated cab, a crucial asset in case any survivors were found. Additional local volunteers, with their own snowmobiles, were Don Cutler, Darrell Brown, Gary Gadwa, Brad Bever and Jim Funderberg.

Our search party started out at 1:35 pm. We all felt that the possibility of finding the two young women alive after four days exposed to the storm was slim, but a rescue attempt from us must be made on the chance that they still survived. Clearly, if alive, time was running out for the two sisters, but we were optimistic that maybe a miracle would still occur.

Meanwhile, the Boise County Search and Rescue Team had found the young women's car, but had encountered extensive avalanches and blizzard conditions. Due to the constant threat of new avalanches and because snowmobile, ski and snowshoe travel was exhausting and nearly impossible, especially over the new avalanche deposits, the team was forced to give up their rescue attempt during the morning of February 19. The sheriff then contacted the two sisters' parents, who were visiting friends in California, and informed them of the situation and that it was very unlikely that either daughter had survived the ordeal. They were informed of the Boise County failure to reach the women and of a last, desperate attempt being made by the Custer County search team to locate them. The parents informed the sheriff that they'd return to Boise on the soonest available flight.

By their fourth morning, both women were still alive, but a feeling of despair and hopelessness engulfed them. Their situation was grim, and they suffered from frostbite and severe dehydration. Their fingers were cut, and the skin was shriveled and white from clawing at the sides of their dark icy prison in an attempt to obtain critical moisture. Their wet, cold clothing pulled crucial heat from their bodies no matter how close they clung to each other. As hypothermia took its toll, they both lapsed into long periods of semi-consciousness and hallucinations.

On the other side of the summit, our search team was encountering very difficult progress. The snowmobiles eventually bogged down and we were forced to wait for the Thiokol which was traveling at a slower pace behind us. We all knew that if the Thiokol could not make it, our search effort would have to be abandoned. Unknown to us, the snowcat had broken down. McGowan worked desperately to find the cause, knowing that time was critical. Mike eventually located and repaired a faulty fuel pump and rejoined us. After Mike arrived, we all took up positions behind the snowcat which was breaking trail; although at times, the snow came up over the headlights to the bottom of the windshield. Mike would then back up and make another try. Only Leonard, with his Larven, had been able to go ahead without assistance from the snowcat. Near the summit, we met Leonard. I asked Joe how the terrain was ahead of us. He replied that the avalanche conditions were so severe that he had turned back since "he did not want to take a chance of being buried alone."

We arrived at the summit around 5:00 pm and daylight was quickly fading. Ahead of us lay the most severe avalanche terrain we would encounter, which would be especially hazardous to traverse in the dark. We briefly discussed the possibility of turning back and starting our search again at dawn. However, it was still snowing heavily and we realized that if Sherrita and Lydia were still alive, we were their only hope. Dominating my thoughts was how I would feel if faced with spending yet another night in the snowy wilderness. I could imagine the agony the women must be experiencing if they were still alive.

The others must have experienced similar thoughts since we all seemed to receive renewed vigor and determination to continue the search. We handed out snow shovels stored in the Thiokol to each team member and spread out so that only one person at a time risked being buried in a snow slide and silently pressed on.

Led by the Larven and snowcat, we started down the summit and immediately crossed numerous small snow slides fifteen to twenty feet deep. At a little over a mile down from the summit, Leonard nearly ran into an unusual depression in the snow. He stopped and backtracked to investigate at about the same time that the Thiokol and several snowmobiles arrived at the site. The Thiokol stopped just short of driving over the depression.

Sherrita and Lydia drifted into consciousness at the sound of a distant, low rumbling. Sherrita was dreaming that the sound came from her father who was riding a motorcycle and had come to rescue her. Lydia thought it was an avalanche, but somehow it sounded different. As the sound grew louder, it was suddenly apparent that rescue machines were making the noise. Sherrita cried out but was too weak to rise. Lydia summoned all of her strength and shakily stood up, but could not reach the top of the cave, now completely covered with snow. She jumped as high as possible and was able to stick her hand through the top of their snow cave and wave frantically. She only realized she was not hallucinating when she saw Leonard looking down at her.

Both women started crying uncontrollably as they were lifted, soaking wet and half-dead, from their icy tomb. We quickly replaced their wet clothes with dry blankets, administered warm water, treated them for hypothermia as well as conditions permitted, and loaded them into the snowcat. Deputy Parkhouse radioed back to Stanley with the incredible news that, against all odds, we had found both girls alive, but that they were in poor condition, suffering from life threatening exposure to the elements. Later we learned that state highway personnel had scrambled all available equipment in a desperate attempt to reopen Highway 75 so that the patients could be transferred to an ambulance from Salmon, Idaho, 120 miles downriver; the closest available hospital. They also risked their lives to reopen the highway to one-way traffic.

After the snowcat left with its precious cargo, I reentered the icy snow cave to retrieve their few belongings. I estimated that over seven feet of new snow had fallen from February 15, when their ordeal began, until now. The shelter was round, over ten feet deep, and three feet in diameter. The walls had frozen into very hard, clear ice. I found that considerable assistance was required to get out of the pit due to its depth and icy, vertical walls.

The patients were transported to the Stanley medical facility operated by Marie Osborn, the resident nurse practitioner. Both women were briefly treated and stabilized, although Sherrita's heart rate soared dangerously high and both women were in danger of lapsing into a coma and dying.

Both were transported downriver until the Salmon ambulance was met where they were transferred and driven to the hospital. Both women suffered from the effects of hypothermia, frostbite of the toes, feet and buttocks and dehydration. Their physical condition was so serious that it is unlikely that either sister would have survived another night buried beneath the icy snow.

Today both sisters are fully recovered, but Sherrita experienced pain in her feet for years after her ordeal.

Returning home, I finally enjoyed a belated birthday dinner. In the warmth of my home and surrounded by family, I thought of the elation we had all felt when we discovered that the two sisters were still alive.

Against the full force of nature, they had tapped the necessary will and strength to survive. We all agreed that "somehow they were meant to live."

I cannot recall a more joyous birthday!

As the sole nurse practitioner, I had to be prepared to treat cold injuries and hypothermia, especially during cold-weather months.

Alive after being buried for four days in the snow, the two girls arrived at the ambulance near dark in a raging storm. We were parked on Highway 21 beneath a high wall of snow, eleven miles west of Stanley. That was as far as the snowplows could go. From the parked ambulance to Banner Summit was another fourteen miles. Once we knew the two women were alive, we radioed Stanley to let the world know.

The young women wore their soggy denim jackets, light sweatshirts, and tennis shoes when found. They dressed for a party and dancing in Stanley, not survival. The sisters expected the guy in Stanley who had invited them to meet them at the Summit. Instead, four days later, a team risked their lives to save the sisters.

Stanley's volunteer EMTs placed the young women on blankets, stripped off their wet clothing down to underclothes, wrapped them in blankets, and loaded them into the snowcat. The EMTs gave sips of warm water from thermoses before transporting the women to the Stanley Ambulance.

The sisters were in bad shape. In the ambulance, I worried they would slip into a coma. Instead, after four days buried in their snow prison, they were amazingly resilient — and extremely lucky. Accessing veins for IVs was a challenge because they were so dehydrated. We had warmed Gatorade at the clinic and filled thermoses before heading out in the ambulance as part of the search team. We spoon-fed the warm Gatorade to our two patients until they could drink on their own. They remained alert and quiet. They answered all my questions. They wanted their parents to know they were alive and okay.

Their feet were so cold and blue, with toes purple from frostbite. We wrapped their feet in cotton to protect damaged tissues.

Their feet reminded me of a frozen body we had retrieved from the Yankee Fork. Unlike the girls, he walked into a bad winter storm and never made it. He was dressed better than the sisters, in heavy-duty overalls, a heavy jacket, and a cap with earflaps. In the spring, they found his body after he'd been missing for several weeks. He was still frozen when they brought him into the Stanley Clinic: the color was good, cheeks were rosy — he didn't look dead. Without a morgue in Stanley, we put him in the garage.

Thankfully the mortician arrived within two hours, even traveling over Galena Summit in the snow. A miracle that the girls survived. He didn't.

Avalanches had closed all roads to the Sawtooth country except downriver, where the plow opened a single lane. The girls went to the hospital in Salmon, 120 miles of curvy river road to the north. The Salmon and Stanley ambulances met about halfway to transfer our patients. During the ambulance journey, one of the sisters became unresponsive. Later she revived to become more alert and oriented. I called the ER at the hospital to speak with the doctor. I provided him with the girls' history, my physical findings, and a description of all the interventions that were taken after their rescue.

"Thanks, Marie," he replied. "I've never taken care of anyone with frostbite and cold injuries before. Guess I'll read up on it before the ambulance gets here."

The Sawtooth Mountains from Marie's home on Shaw Mesa

9

IBM: SEATTLE TO BELLINGHAM

From December 1, 1953, when I waddled pregnant out of Harborview Hospital, until the fall of 1971, when I began reorienting to nursing in Boise, I was a mother to five kids and wife of an IBM executive.

Being pregnant was birth control before birth control. Calvin was born on January 13, 1954, and Jerry on December 31, that same year. Eighteen months later, in 1956, John was born. Then I lost twins, born prematurely. Melinda was born in 1960, and Debbie in 1964. It was the '50s and early '60s. Birth control and family planning were still in their first trimester.

When we lived in Bellingham after Cal took a job selling typewriters for IBM, I met with the religious sisters at St. Joseph Hospital about teaching. Before I could even sign a teaching contract, I ended up pregnant. With three little boys running around the house, working outside the home was impossible.

When my children or husband were in the hospital, I would don my nursing uniform, cap, white hose, and white shoes and be at their bedside. That was the only way I could keep my hand in nursing. I continued to maintain my nursing license and my membership in the American Nurses Association.

IBM — "I've Been Moved" — sent Cal and Marie from Seattle to Bellingham and Boise. Cal lived under constant pressure to meet his quota selling IBM typewriters: "We live by the numbers." He became one of the corporation's top salesmen. FROM LEFT TO RIGHT: *Cal Jr., Marie, Jerry, Melinda, John, Debbie, and Cal*

The phone rang. I was at our home in Bellingham. Our three sons were in school, but Lindy, two years old, was home with me.

"Marie, I'm calling with some great news!" It was Cal, calling from the IBM regional office in Seattle. He was meeting with an executive leadership team from Armonk, New York. "Honey, I've been promoted! I'll be the new branch manager for IBM's operations in southern Idaho. So, we'll be moving to Pocatello!"

Pause. Laughter in the background.

"Where the hell is Pocatello, Idaho? Cal, have you been drinking?"

"Marie, honestly, we'll be moving to *Boise*. I'll be IBM's new branch manager for southern Idaho. Isn't that just great?"

I realized Cal wasn't joking. IBM was promoting him. We were moving to Idaho. After ten years in Bellingham with so many friends, this was a bombshell. Cal later laughed about being with his bosses, trying to look like his wife was thrilled while she was on the phone having a meltdown.

Cal returned to Bellingham and then headed to Boise almost immediately to start his new job. I remained behind with the kids to orchestrate the move. With a telephone call in February 1963, the life we had built in a beautiful place ended.

For most of the twenty-four years Cal and I were married, IBM was integral to our lives. IBM (International Business Machines) also stands for I've Been Moved. IBM moved us from Seattle to Bellingham and then to Boise.

IBM may be a corporation, but it was also a whole community. We had many good friends with IBM, including John and Char Sailors and their three children. IBM moved John seventeen times in thirty-seven years. While we lived in Boise, IBM wanted to promote and move Cal. We discussed it, but Cal said, "No," that he wouldn't accept the offer because of what moving would do to his children. You only did that once with IBM. After that, IBM never again offered Cal a promotion.

IBM helped establish the NP as a profession and make advances in rural EMS. After all, IBM sent us to Idaho and introduced the Osborn family to the Sawtooth Mountains at Redfish Lake. And it was through IBM that Cal and I co-hosted the National Lieutenant Governors Association meeting in Sun Valley in July 1971, setting the stage for my fateful conversation with John Hutchinson. Finally, our IBM "family" of close friends enthusiastically supported Cal and me in opening the Stanley Clinic. Without IBM, the Stanley Clinic would never have opened in 1972.

Cal and IBM met in November 1953 at the University of Washington. It started when Cal saw a job fair posting on a UW bulletin board. Cal was looking for work partly because he was disappointed in the UW graduate program in international business. Meanwhile, Cal worked at a feed store in south Seattle to make ends meet with a pregnant wife.

At the UW job fair, Cal walked up to the IBM table. Cal could sell, and he sold himself as a salesman to IBM. Almost overnight, we went from Cal slinging 100-pound feed bags to working for IBM's Electric Typewriter Division.

When IBM hired Cal, I was twenty-two years old and seven months pregnant. We couldn't afford health insurance, which IBM provided to new employees only after a six-month probation period. Shortly after Cal started, IBM's president, Tom Watson Jr., announced medical benefits for all employees effective immediately, including maternity care. Our worries about how to pay for our firstborn vanished.

Cal was not your typical IBM employee in the mid-1950s. Yes, he was a white man in a white shirt, tie, and well-polished shoes. But Cal, who grew up in the Midwest, hitchhiking between his divorced parents, fishing, and hiking, didn't like sitting in an office behind a desk. Cal liked being out. He often came home from the office with suit pants rolled up, feet sandy and wet from wading in Puget Sound "cuz I felt like it." Once his feet were wet and his suit wrinkled, Cal couldn't call on anyone to sell typewriters. Nevertheless, he was devoted to IBM and a top salesman. Cal brought who he was to his job — we all do.

IBM was a company driven to succeed — and profit. Management pressured employees to sell, meet quota, and excel. For Cal, with kids and a wife, those pressures to perform and conform were immense and, inevitably, they came home with him from the office. So, before coming home after work, Cal became a regular at the YMCA, swimming laps and working out stress. Through it all, Cal Osborn excelled as an IBM salesman.

IBM rewarded success. Cal met or exceeded one hundred percent of his quota for most of his thirty years with IBM, rewarded with a trip to the company's annual convention, the "100 Percent Club." For top salesmen and managers, IBM's reward was the "Golden Circle," sending employees and their wives to an all-expense-paid trip to a first-class resort hotel. Our first Golden Circle was in Hawaii. These week-long affairs were a much-needed break for me with three, then four, and finally five kids to look after.

Men had a dress code at Golden Circles and other IBM functions in the late 1950s and '60s. Wives did too: heels and hose, white gloves and hats with our dresses. At IBM's Golden Circle at Palm Beach, I decided to walk downtown from the Princess Hotel. I'd never seen Palm Beach and wanted to see the shops. Cautioned that IBM wives should remain in their outfits, I didn't change into shorts. For a girl born into the Great Depression in Kentucky, taxis seemed extravagant, and I couldn't bring myself to hire a cab. So instead, I walked two miles in those high heels, white gloves, lime-green silk dress, and white-straw hat. In that humid heat, I was a vision.

I looked forward to the Golden Circles. For weeks in advance, I'd look at patterns and then sew my dresses. Later, I bought dresses after seeing what other IBM wives were wearing. Finally, Cal and I would pack, give last-minute instructions to the kids and their babysitter, and head for

Cal and Marie at IBM's 1968 Golden Circle, Honolulu

All smiles at Palm Peach, IBM's 1969 Golden Circle

the airport. Then, we were off for one of the great times of our lives.

When IBM promoted Cal to manage its southern Idaho operations in Boise, I found myself staring at the prospect of being a social director, planning parties and joining the country club to golf and play bridge. That didn't work for me. With five kids, I didn't have time or interest to be IBM's office social director. So, instead, I was a mom and became active at the Idaho Legislature to improve public education. I could never have known that my relationships with lawmakers would prove critical during the founding years of the NP profession.

Seattle, 1953–1954

Our life with IBM started in Seattle in 1953. Compared with Muncie, Indiana, Seattle was a big city in a stunningly beautiful location.

To become an RN, I had to take and pass the state board exam in nursing. I postponed taking the exam until we arrived in Washington State. The exam was in Seattle, lasting the entire day with a lunch break. It was hard, but I passed. My last hurdle crossed; I was now an RN.

When Harborview Hospital hired me as an RN, I didn't drive. Instead, Cal drove me to and from work, or I took the bus. My last day working on the wards was December 1. Eighteen years later, in February 1972, I returned to Harborview for trauma training, preparing to open the Salmon River Emergency Clinic.

Cal and I settled into a small rental house in Seattle's Ballard district overlooking Ray's Boathouse, Puget Sound, and the Olympic Mountains. After the holidays, I waddled as Cal joined me for an evening at the theater to see the newly released *From Here to Eternity*. During the scene where the Japanese attack Pearl Harbor, I felt a 3/10 cramping pain in my lower mid-abdomen. It went away, but a few scenes later, I felt it again.

With the film credits rolling, we left the theater, went home, and Cal went to bed. I stayed up, showered, washed

Harborview, 1931. Image courtesy of University of Washington Library Special Collections, UW23514

my hair, and dressed. "Cal, you need to wake up. I'm having contractions. I'm in labor."

Cal sprung out of bed almost manic, dressed, helped me into the Ford, and drove to the emergency room at Virginia Mason Hospital. It was early in the morning of January 13. In contrast to Ball Memorial's open maternity ward with rows of beds separated by curtains, Virginia Mason had semi-private rooms with two beds. Nurses helped me to bed, although I was up frequently helping the laboring mother in the adjoining bed with her bedpan.

Each pain got slightly stronger; the time between pains was shorter, like a tightening spiral. Gradually, contracting, cramping pains escalated to 8/10, extending into my lower back. With my cervix fully dilated four hours later, nurses moved me down the hall to a delivery room. Cal came in from the waiting room as the anesthesiologist administered a caudal anesthetic. The pain stopped. At around six am, I gave birth to our first baby, conceived in Indiana, born in the Pacific Northwest, a boy we named Calvin Earl.

Mothers and their newborn babies stayed in the hospital for a week, a luxury compared with today. I shared a room with a new mother, and we talked and shared what we were going through.

My first dozen of five dozen red roses arrived at my bedside: IBM management sent roses for each of my five babies. The new mother and father's tradition was to go out for dinner at a nice Seattle restaurant while the nurses looked after the newborn. After our son's birth, an Arctic blast hit Seattle. Ice covered the streets. Cal's car froze. My houseplants in Ballard froze. The Arctic blast canceled our night out. However, I did paint my toenails after being unable to touch my toes for several months. The Osborn family numbered three when we returned home to our Ballard house.

The week after I returned home with our new baby, IBM sent Cal for training in Poughkeepsie, New York. Cal was on the other side of the country, and I was home alone. I didn't know anyone in Ballard. I knew a few people from church, but they were miles away in the University District.

Breastfeeding was not foreign to me. After all, I watched my mother breastfeed my siblings. When I trained as a nurse, I helped new mothers with breastfeeding on the hospital wards. For my infant son, breastfeeding went well until one of my nipples started to hurt. It turned red, and the redness spread. I didn't feel right and was achy and tired. Fevers and chills began. The chills became rigors — teeth-chattering, bed-shaking chills. Mastitis hurts. I put my baby in the bed next to me. I knew my fever was high. The phone rang. I was too weak to answer it.

Someone from the church called to check on me. They knew my husband was away, and I was alone. When I didn't answer, they called and met the police at the house. The police managed to unlock the door. I was in bed with a high fever next to my son. The police called an ambulance — before Seattle's Medic One, probably a black hearse with white crosses. I ended up in the hospital on IV antibiotics. My Ballard neighbors, whom I didn't know, took my baby and bottle-fed him for the first time. When the doctors released me from Virginia Mason, I went home with the people from the Presbyterian University Church, not returning home until Cal returned in early March.

In March, IBM moved us to Bellingham. Cal's first posting was to sell typewriters and time clocks in a vast, sparsely populated sales territory stretching from the King County line north to Canada, and from the San Juan Islands east to the crest of the North Cascades.

Bellingham, 1954–1963

When we moved to Bellingham, we rented a house seven miles from town on Lake Whatcom. Our son, Calvin, was six weeks old. Cal might be gone all week selling for IBM, traveling up and down a beautiful coast. On weekends, Cal wanted to stay home. Since I didn't drive, we worked it out so Cal would drive me to town to shop.

I needed to learn how to drive. First, my dad tried to teach me, but that didn't work. Then, Cal offered to teach me, and that definitely didn't work. Both men "mansplained,"

talking to me like I was in kindergarten. I got angry and hurt Cal's feelings. Sitting at home with one baby and another on the way, I finally opened the phonebook's Yellow Pages and called a drivers-training course. The instructor came to Lake Whatcom and taught me how to drive.

As a young woman of twenty-three, I needed to learn how to drive, so I did. Later, in my eighties, macular degeneration took my vision and forced me to stop driving. During those sixty years behind the steering wheel of a car, I drove for groceries, took my kids to football practice, dance classes, and ski races across the Pacific Northwest, and eventually, sped along mountain roads responding to emergency calls. Driving is bound up with our freedom of movement. We take driving for granted until we are forced to stop. At that point, the loss of freedom becomes almost unbearable.

After John was born in June 1956, we bought our first home and moved into Bellingham, just south of the Fairhaven district. Our first house was a new three-bedroom rancher with a kid- and dog-friendly, big backyard in a new neighborhood.

I was pregnant six times. Five of my children survived childbirth; my twins did not. My first two sons are "Irish twins:" Calvin Jr. was born in January; Jerry was born on the last day of 1954.

Not long after John was born, I became pregnant for the fourth time, and I was due in mid-June 1957. By February, my belly was more prominent than it should have been.

Cal Jr., Jerry, and John in Bellingham

"Dr. Zoet, I'm awfully big," I said. My OB, Dr. Zoet, was a big, lovable, plain-spoken family doctor. He was of Dutch descent, as were others in the nearby town of Lynden, where he grew up.

"Just be glad it's not an insect, then you'd have six legs kicking you," Dr. Zoet said reassuringly.

At seven months, I felt contractions. Our neighbor, a tough-as-nails yet soft-as-silk former WWII Army nurse, Jane Rideout, came over. She called Cal at work. The contractions became regular. Cal was in the bedroom when Jane called my OB from our phone. "She can't be; it's too early."

"Well, I can see a foot coming out," Jane responded. I delivered twins in the hospital. We were so thrilled. The first was a girl — our first daughter! The second baby was a boy. But the twins were having trouble. The nurses took them away to the nursery.

The next morning, the janitor, while mopping the floor, told me my baby girl had died. My son died twenty-four hours later. If there had been a neonatal care unit in Bellingham in 1957, my babies probably would have survived.

The death of the twins was a loss both Cal and I took pretty hard. Even with three little boys at home needing us, we had a rough time. We had planned a cruise to Alaska with Cal's dad and stepmother, Ella. Once on the ship, I only wanted to hide and watch the water. With time and distance, raw grief and severe depression subsided. The open wounds closed, but the scars remained.

With a child's loss, "what if?" questions linger forever. Years later, a toddler, wanting her mother, darted across Highway 21 at the Boundary Creek turnoff. When I arrived at the scene, I knew those heart-wrenching sobs. I held that little girl's body. In comforting the parents and starting them on their grief journey, I knew. With the loss of our twins, I, too, had "walked through the shadow of the valley of death."

After losing the twins, we waited four years to try for another child. In those years before ultrasound, we had to wait until the birth day to know whether it was a girl or a boy. The twins' due date was June 14, and my mother's birthday was June 12. On June 10, 1960, my obstetrician sang and whistled during my labor. He was singing when I delivered ... a girl! After three boys, we celebrated having a baby girl and named her Melinda Marie.

In late 1963, Cal and I got a babysitter and spent a few days together in Lowman. Nine months later, on August 10, 1964, our second baby girl came into the world. We named her Deborah Anne.

When I was in the sixth grade and making my parents' bed, I lifted the mattress to discover a weirdly shaped rubber balloon on top of the box springs. I held it up, wondering how I could blow up the balloon. At that moment, my mother walked in and saw her daughter holding up her husband's condom. She struggled with answering my questions, even after giving birth to six children. Mom did the best she knew how: She replied by assigning me to a time-out.

In 1957, after my twins died and with the nuns in the hallway, Dr. Zoet closed the door to my room at the Catholic hospital and spoke to Cal and me about birth control. Dr. Zoet didn't want me pregnant for another four years.

For birth control in the 1950s, men could use condoms but often didn't. Cal, like many men, did not like condoms. Some couples used the "rhythm method," avoiding intercourse during the mid-part of the menstrual cycle when women were more likely to be fertile. Others avoided intercourse altogether to avoid pregnancy. While using female hormones (estrogen and progesterone) is commonplace today, well-tolerated birth control pills were unavailable until the 1960s, and IUDs even later.

The first hormones I tried were in the form of a vaginal estrogen suppository inserted before intercourse.

Later I tried the first birth control pills when they became available. Unfortunately, the high estrogen level made me feel like I had morning sickness. Eventually, Dr. Zoet discussed one of us having a sterilization procedure to prevent further pregnancies.

Two psychiatrists had to approve a woman having a tubal ligation or other sterilization procedure in Washington State during the 1950s. For men, vasectomies in the 1950s — and still today — are straightforward. Men walk into their doctor's office and walk out with a sore scrotum, no longer at risk of impregnating their female sexual partner.

After Debbie was born in 1964 — after six pregnancies and five living children — I decided to proceed with a tubal ligation. My OB no longer required psychiatric clearance. One of us had to act, so I did. I didn't think there'd be much pain when I agreed to the procedure. In the 1960s, tubal ligation was a substantial abdominal surgery. So, not surprisingly, my pain was intense when I awoke from the anesthesia.

Family and friendships interweave with who we are. While in Bellingham, our next-door neighbors, Barney and Sue Stewart, were close physically and socially. The Stewart and Osborn families, their three kids, and our kids were inseparable — until IBM moved us to Idaho.

The American Osborns adopted the Canadian Tod family. Nursing helped unite these two families: "Aunt Rachael," an R.N., holds Marie's daughter Debbie, a future R.N.

Cal brought home a delightful man with a heavy Scottish brogue: Bob Tod. Both men belonged to Kiwanis International and met at a Kiwanis convention in Bellingham. Bob's wife, Ray (Rachael) had trained at the Florence Nightingale School of Nursing in London. Bob and Ray were from Edinburgh, Scotland. They married, survived the siege of London during WWII, and eventually found their way to Canada, then West Vancouver.

The Tods wanted children but had none, and we had no relatives in the West, so they became Uncle Bob and Aunt Ray to our three sons. We headed north to West Vancouver, and they came south to Bellingham. We were family. Both Ray and I were RNs, which was part of the strength of the bonds between our two families. Then, the Tod family grew when Ray gave birth to Tosh Tod. Even "I've Been Moved" would not end the close relationship between these two families.

With three little boys and a girl in the late 1950s and early '60s, our ten years living in Puget Sound were terrific. We explored our new world, from the North Cascade Range to the San Juan Islands, from Seattle's World's Fair to Vancouver's Stanley Park. We took trains to visit our adopted Tod family in West Vancouver and gazed out over the lights of Seattle from the top of the Space Needle. We sailed and crabbed in Bellingham Bay and harvested oysters from Chuckanut Drive's beaches. We hiked the North Cascades, rode ferry boats, explored the San Juan Islands, and skied at Mt. Baker.

Fifty-three feet of snow — 641 inches — is the average annual snowfall for Mt. Baker's ski resort, the unofficial world

Marie at Mt. Baker and her first real experience with mountain snow. The three boys started ski racing through Komo Kids.

record-holder. So, for a girl from Kentucky and Indiana who would spend nearly thirty years in Idaho's Sawtooths, our ski trips to Mt. Baker proved a valuable introduction to deep snow and mountain weather.

Winter weekends became increasingly busy when our three sons started ski racing with Komo Kids at Mt. Baker. I'd set the alarm, get up early, pack a family lunch, and fix breakfast. Then we'd drive fifty-four miles from Bellingham to the ski lodge parking lot, depending on the weather, a little over an hour. The final miles of road on that volcano curved through walls of snow 200 inches and higher.

After IBM called, we packed up our memories of the San Juan Islands and took them with us from Washington to Idaho. Two islands, Macia and Soucia, gave their names to our Idaho horses. CalMar, our Puget Sound sailboat, became our Idaho canoe, which remains at the Sawtooth cabin near the woodpile. It has become a ship of memories that is no longer seaworthy, now dented by years of heavy Sawtooth snow.

In February 1963, after Cal left for Boise to start his new IBM position, I stayed in Bellingham to arrange our move. I arranged for our three sons to end school in one place and start in another. I also contacted movers and began to let our Bellingham friends know. And I cried.

Cal returned for the big farewell party. Saying goodbye to our many close Bellingham friends was moving, and deeply painful. The life we built for ourselves after moving from Muncie to Puget Sound ended.

On a cold rainy night in mid-April, our neighbors Barney and Sue Stewart drove my three boys, Lindy, and me to the bus station. Sobbing, tears flowing, and raindrops splashing, we hugged each other goodbye, and I ushered the kids up the stairs onto the bus. Then, the bus pulled out of the Bellingham station, heading for Seattle and, eventually, SeaTac Airport.

On April 18, 1963, our plane landed in Boise. Cal met his family at the airplane with a huge smile and hugs, a genuine Cal Osborn "Welcome to Boise!" that would greet his family and friends at the Boise airport for another fifty years.

On that April day, the sky was gray, and the wind was gusting. It was cold, dreary, and spitting snow. I didn't know anyone. As we drove toward Boise from the airport, we saw pasture and sagebrush with tumbleweeds blowing across the roadway instead of today's commercial and residential districts. I thought, "This is such a woebegone country." I had just left one of the most beautiful places on earth and come to this God-forsaken place.

So began our lives in Idaho.

10

IBM – BOISE

Boise's population in 1960 was 35,000. In 1963, when we first arrived, passenger trains still came to Boise. Standing at the Boise Train Depot, you could look down the hill onto Capitol Boulevard and see the white-domed state capitol building towering over Boise, dwarfed by Shafer Butte and Bogus Basin Ski Area. Idaho's capital "city" was surrounded by sagebrush and farmers' fields.

Today, banks and other high-rise buildings obscure the state's capitol building. Boise's landmark depot is mostly quiet after passenger train service ended. Across Idaho's Treasure Valley, sprawl has mostly merged Boise, Eagle, Meridian, Nampa, and Caldwell.

Going back to the 1960s and early '70s, Boise was a great place to raise our family. In 1963, on a warm, sunny day in late winter, IBM sent Cal and me from Bellingham to Boise to pick out a house. As with my parents deciding where to live in Muncie in the 1930s, school quality was the crucial factor determining where in Boise we would live.

Cal and I settled on a wood-and-stone, two-level house in the Boise foothills overlooking Treasure Valley at 3015 Hillway Drive. For fifty years, "3015" would remain the family home and then, after our divorce, Cal's refuge until he died in 2014.

Cal loved walking with the kids in Boise's North End in the fall, smelling the leaf smoke and reliving his Indiana boyhood. The first snowflakes in the valley were beautiful and exciting for the kids, a harbinger of snowball fights and inner-tubing. For the boys, snow meant shoveling off 3015's steep through-driveway and back sidewalk.

Idaho Power Company inquired about showcasing our all-electric home, which was heated with baseboard heaters. I did my hair for the photo shoot, dressed up Lindy, selected my dress, and put on makeup, jewelry, and high heels. The company's advertisement shows a perfectly dressed daughter handing clean clothing to her perfectly dressed mother next to a tidy washer and dryer — your typical, everyday laundry scene in Idaho.

Cal and the Mighty-Mite ski racing team from Bogus Basin at an event in McCall, Idaho. The Osborn's Travelall could carry over 20 pairs of skis, luggage — and 11 small racers.

Missing from the Idaho Power Company's advertisement was the harried housewife and mother with stacks of dirty clothes, a house to clean, and meals to prepare. Later, when I started as an NP in Stanley while continuing as a housewife in Boise, I struggled to keep the family and professional balls in the air.

The seven Osborns sat together for breakfast and dinner at 3015. In the mornings, by 7:45, Cal needed to leave for IBM and the kids for the bus stop. That meant my getting up early, preparing breakfast, waking up Cal and the five kids by

Idaho Power

7 am, and having breakfast on the table by 7:15. Our family sat together for breakfast and dinner and talked, with no TV.

If the kids missed the bus, then I drove them to school. Otherwise, silence settled on 3015. If I didn't have meetings at the school or, later, at the legislature, I'd clean up the kitchen and get started cleaning the house, doing laundry, and other wifely things you do with a family of seven. Before wash-and-wear fabrics, clothes wrinkled. So, ironing was part of my housewife chores. While ironing stacks of freshly-laundered clothes when Cal and the kids were skiing, I turned on the TV and started to watch football. Hooked ever since, I'm a football fanatic.

"Only dull women have immaculate houses!" Cleaning was a constant: dusting, vacuuming, washing windows, cleaning toilets, sinks, and showers for a husband and five kids. Southern Idaho's dust storms meant windows must be closed in the afternoon. I expected my five children to make their beds, although I changed their sheets weekly, much as my mother had insisted in Kentucky and Indiana.

I came to love Boise and our family home at 3015. Cal had no use for air conditioning in the house or car. During summer's heat, we closed the windows and drapes by mid-morning to keep the house cool, reopening 3015 to the cooler night air. Today, with climate change and increasing numbers of triple-digit days, going without air conditioning during Boise's summers would be stifling. Then as now, people escaped to the mountains, including Stanley.

Honeysuckle, syringa, and lilac filled my kitchen with a sweet fragrance in the spring. We planted Concord grapes vining into the grapestake fence, and petunias along 3015's steep driveway. In 1963, a small oak tree in the backyard attracted our dog, who chewed and nearly girdled the tree. We dressed the dog bite wound with electrical tape. The oak survived, growing into a massive, beautiful tree by the time our kids sold 3015 after Cal's death a half-century later.

Easter Sunday, 1964, with the Osborn family at "3015" before church. LEFT TO RIGHT: *Cal Jr., Marie (pregnant with Debbie), Melinda, Jerry, John, and Socks. Boise's foothills are behind.*

Gardening in Boise and Stanley is different. Boise's elevation is 2,700 feet, while my home on Shaw Mesa in the Sawtooths is nearly a mile higher, at 7,100 feet. Gardening in the high country, where snow can fall on any day of the year, is limited. I planted lilacs and iris that held on and still bloom in late June, delighting me in my nineties. My Sawtooth flowerpots, once an impressionist's palette of vibrant colors, now grow a few weeds on bare dirt.

Before I learned to sew lacerations at the Harborview ER, I sewed clothes as a girl in Indiana and then for my husband and kids. I sewed my daughters' dresses, shirts for my sons, Halloween costumes for the kids, and matching pajamas for Cal and the three boys gifted under the Christmas tree. I tried pants, but they are hard to do.

"You wouldn't use an old treadle sewing machine to sew in this day and age — you'd have a nice electric one," was how Cal started his sales pitch to secretaries. "Well, you shouldn't be using the old manual typewriters; you should be using a nice electric typewriter." Cal never mentioned that his wife was still using "an old treadle sewing machine" to sew clothes at home. Ever-frugal Cal eventually bought me an electric sewing machine.

Whether sewing clothes or suturing lacerations in a small-town clinic, you will likely see your handiwork. Your sewing skills may be the leather uniform your oldest son is wearing leading a marching band down the field, or your patient's suture scar at the grocery store. My advice? Do it right and be proud of your work. Patients will wear your suture job for a lifetime. Whether on a homeless veteran or a baby's face, if the wound is more than you can handle, know your limits and ask for help. Know and respect your sewing skills.

I loved sewing to create clothes and to close wounds. Still, years have passed since I gloved to suture a wound. Today, over fifty years after opening the Stanley Clinic, my sewing machine and all those spools of thread in rainbows of color remain upstairs in my Sawtooth cabin home, gathering dust. I quit sewing for the same reason I stopped seeing patients and, eventually, stopped driving: I was going blind from macular degeneration.

Marie sewed Halloween costumes for Debbie (LEFT) and Melinda long before she sewed human skin.

In 1963, Highlands Elementary was new. I walked into the library, a beautiful, open, and airy space — with almost no books. In my childhood, I set out to read every book in the library at Burris Laboratory School in Muncie. To walk into a school library with near-empty bookshelves, open a half-day a week, just shocked me.

Student access to books drove me to join the PTA and organize volunteer staffing for the library. Parents stepped up and volunteered to keep the school library open full-time. Seeing kids reading was our reward.

Cal and I remained active in PTA for Highlands Elementary School and North Junior High during the 1960s. We were co-presidents for several years. Then, PTA members elected me to serve as the state lobbyist (no one else would do it). PTA's lobbyist at the time, Hope Kading, took me under her wing and taught me the ropes at the Idaho Legislature. Hope, who had been a personal assistant to singer Peggy Lee, was a beautiful, talented, and progressive woman. Hope later ran for lieutenant governor in 1974 as a Republican and worked to pass the Equal Rights Amendment.

When the legislature was in session, we would meet every morning and wander the halls of the capitol building until the legislators convened in their chambers. Once lawmakers were seated, Hope and I sat up in the gallery, observing the legislature at work.

"Marie, even if nothing interesting is going on," Hope instructed me, "you always carry a legal pad and scribble away taking notes." So, while legislators conducted their business on the floor below, we sat above them, busily writing notes. You should've seen all the legislators who came upstairs to the gallery to talk to us during a break.

"Ladies, you're sure taking a lot of notes," one legislator commented. "Can we answer any questions for you?" Several legislators tried hard to see our notes, and we kept our tablets covered. Hope Kading was right: Taking notes was a great way to learn the legislature.

If it had not been for the opening of the Stanley Clinic, I might have continued with PTA, lobbying the legislature to improve public education in Idaho. My legislative experience and relationships, built on public education advocacy, later proved invaluable to defending my NP work at the Stanley Clinic.

During the 1960s, Marie's work at the Legislature advocating for public education prepared her to defend the Stanley Clinic and Ambulance against attacks while helping to create the nurse practitioner profession and rural EMS.

At 3015, we displayed our kids' ski-racing trophies below the portraits of Debbie and Melinda in our living room.

Our kids grew up on skis. Before Bogus Basin, our boys started racing at Mt. Baker through Komo Kids. We could see Shafer Butte and the Bogus Basin Ski Area when we arrived in Boise. Cal and I drove the kids to dryland training in the fall, the sixteen miles of curvy road from Boise to the ski area on weekends, and races, including Mt. Hood's Government Camp, Crystal Mountain near Seattle, and Mt. Spokane.

Wherever our kids raced, we drove. Eventually, our kids became part of the Bogus Basin Ski Team, traveling to ski races by bus across the Pacific Northwest.

Cal and I joined parents across the Northwest who made ski racing possible for their kids. In Boise, ski-racing families included the Porters, Johnsons, Vandenburgs, Naylors, Rowles, and Carters. Through ski racing, Cal and I came to know Bob and Leanne Carter and their two ski-racing kids, Noah and Leslie. Noah was a top racer, knows our family, and describes the connection between ski racing and starting the Stanley clinic:

> "In 1984, at the winter Olympics in Sarajevo, Yugoslavia, ski-racing twins Phil and Steve Mahre from White Pass, near Yakima, Washington, won gold and silver in the slalom and Bill Johnson from Boise won gold in the downhill. Those Olympic games were a pinnacle of alpine ski racing success for the United States and especially the Pacific Northwest. Those three ski racers stood on the awards podiums with the national anthem playing. Unseen and unacknowledged by reporters were the hundreds of parents who volunteered to make ski racing possible in the northwest.
>
> My parents joined Marie, Cal, and so many others in supporting ski racing programs. Our parents helped pay for equipment and ski passes, drove young racers to training and competitions, served as gatekeepers and timers, and raised money for ski teams and coaching. Through the lens of volunteerism, you can better see Marie standing all day in freezing temperatures as a ski-race gatekeeper or timekeeper, then turning around and volunteering to open the emergency clinic in Stanley.
>
> Much has changed about ski racing since the 1960s. The equipment, the training, the money required to race, and climate change impacts on snowpack. What must not change is people's willingness to volunteer in support of their community.
>
> That's true on the ski slopes, and that holds for EMS also. We owe a debt of gratitude that we need to pay forward."

The Osborns were among many ski-racing families in the Northwest during the 1960s and early 1970s.

In the early 1970s the Carter family joined us at the cabin for a weekend of stream fishing. Fifty years later, Noah Carter, the father of two ski racers, is a talented carpenter who works with one of his sons, Adam, to help maintain my Shaw Mesa home and patch my leaky roof.

My first forty years prepared me for my second forty as an NP. As a ski-racing mom, I learned to better budget time and finances, whether for packing lunches, getting the family fed and out the door for Bogus Basin, or driving the Travel-all filled with ski racers all over the Pacific Northwest. We could stuff eleven kids inside (including my youngest, Debbie), twenty-two pairs of skis on top, snacks, and luggage into that big white car. I barely skied, so the time I spent shivering as a gatekeeper prepared me for jumping on a snowmobile in forty below weather to pull a kid out of the Salmon River.

Before the internet, I picked up the phone and made motel reservations in racing destinations, including Spokane, Government Camp, and Bend. For all those kids, I learned to arbitrate and intercede. Then, on those long drives home with racers asleep, I kept my eyes open to deliver those kids home safely.

With five active kids, inevitably, bad things happened. You learn.

Debbie, a toddler in a diaper, wandered alone down the steep driveway on a hot summer day. Where were her brothers, who were supposed to be watching her? The gas company had completed a repair on the road and finished with hot asphalt. The crew left for lunch. Debbie, barefoot, walked out onto the still-steaming asphalt. Screaming, she fell forward, burning her hands, then stood and fell backward just as a neighbor caught her. The deep burns on her hands and feet eventually healed, but the memories of my burned baby never went away.

While at an IBM Golden Circle event, we stayed at the Honolulu Hilton Hotel and took three of our kids. In the elevator, Debbie fainted. We watched her in the hotel room, and she did fine. Later, on our flight to Maui, Debbie pulled down the front of her shirt, "Mom, what's this spot?" It was chickenpox. Eventually, sores covered her body, including her hands and soles. With Debbie contagious, we stayed in quarantine for an extra week on Maui. Darn.

I learned how not to manage earache pain from my older daughter, Melinda. We were staying in Idaho City's hot springs and pool. To escape Boise's heat during the summer, we rented a rustic cabin near the pool. One night, Lindy started crying. Her ear hurt. She kept crying over the next two hours and started screaming with pain. We had baby aspirin, so I tried that without relief. Finally, around midnight, while Cal stayed with the boys and Debbie, I drove Lindy to the ER at St. Luke's. "We're concerned your daughter might be septic," the ER staff said frantically, looking at her flushed cheeks.

"I'm sorry, but my daughter was screaming," I disclosed. "The only anesthetic we had was whiskey, so I made her a hot toddy." We were in Idaho City, there was no medical care, and I had nothing except aspirin and alcohol, so I tried using what I had. "I probably should not have given her the alcohol," I said. Lindy screamed as the doctor lanced her bulging eardrum. Gradually, the pain subsided, and we returned to Idaho City at early dawn.

My youngest son, John, underscored the importance of ambulance transport in the mid-1960s. John had followed his oldest brother, Calvin, to the diving board at the Idaho City hot springs. Calvin, the ever-graceful athlete, had done a perfect inward dive off the end of the diving board. John was next.

John walked to the end of the board, sprung up, turned inward, and came down just as his oldest brother had done. Only John didn't clear the diving board. Instead, he struck his head and shoulder, tumbling into the water. With blood in the pool, Calvin dived to help his little brother. Together, they climbed out, blood flowing from a large laceration in John's scalp.

I placed a pressure dressing on John's head, positioned him on the car's back seat, and headed for St. Luke's ER. While driving that curving highway to Boise, I called, "John, how are you doing?" He didn't answer. Oh my God, my son with a head injury wasn't responding! So, I drove even faster — the fastest I've ever driven on that winding canyon highway.

John couldn't respond because I had put the pressure dressing on so tightly, he couldn't move his jaw. I couldn't hear if John mumbled: the car windows were down because Cal didn't want air conditioning. We arrived without incident at the ER, where we met our family physician, Dr. Swartley. He sewed John's laceration, x-rayed his left shoulder, and diagnosed a left scapular fracture.

And finally, Calvin, my oldest son, went from being one of the nation's top ski racers to the operating room for a leg amputation. He was on the US Junior Nationals team and was among the top fifty ski racers under seventeen.

Then, during the winter after I opened the Stanley Clinic, Calvin was training for a downhill race, lost a ski going sixty mph, and crashed into a creek filled with logs. As the orthopedic surgeon told Calvin, "Imagine going down the freeway at sixty mph with a heavy ski and boot. Ahead is a roadside post. You collide with the post between your right knee and ankle. You'd expect to lose your leg."

The ski patrol realigned and splinted the fractured leg, gently moving Calvin into the toboggan. My husband drove Calvin to St. Luke's ER in Boise, where I met up with them "Mom and Dad don't worry; it's just a broken leg," my son said. We knew otherwise.

"Calvin, we're concerned about possible gangrene," Dr. Gardner said two days later. He was Idaho's first sports medicine orthopedist and Boise State University's first football team physician.

When you walked into my son's room, that awful smell of dead tissue filled the room. Calvin had been to the OR once when Dr. Gardner reduced the fracture. There was swelling, bleeding, and loss of blood supply to the right leg and foot.

Dr. Gardner planned to return my son to the OR for an amputation. We didn't tell our son.

Fifteen years later, with Cal's help, Calvin sought out Dr. Gardner to thank him for saving his leg.

"In the OR, after injecting saline, we suddenly saw your right little toe turn pink," Dr. Gardner recalled. "Then the other toes started to turn pink. You could hear a pin drop in the operating room when your great toe also turned pink. People stood still. Then some cheered. Others cried."

As a mother and an RN, I learned from my children.

When we opened the Stanley Clinic in 1972 with our 1958 Pontiac ambulance, I was forty-one years old, Cal's wife, a mother, and Idaho's first nurse practitioner. My life in Muncie, Seattle, Bellingham, and Boise had provided me with a unique preparation for the adventures that would come next.

Calvin Osborn Jr., airborne, during a jumping competition. Marie and Cal supported their five children as ski racers. Cal Jr. was one of the top racers when an accident during a downhill training run nearly led to a leg amputation.

11

FATE'S FINGER

Steve Lipus

The Finger of Fate is a dramatic spire of granite

Two decisions, one in a gravel pit and the second after a hailstorm, led to the opening of the Stanley Clinic and Stanley Ambulance, launching the NP profession in Idaho. And, like mothers everywhere, I lived in fear of my children getting hurt, especially in the Sawtooth country where there was no healthcare. When the Osborn family camped at Stanley Lake, my two older sons went missing on McGown Peak. On another Stanley Lake camping trip, a hiker fell in the wilderness and needed help. Still later, four teenagers were hurt in a car wreck at Galena Summit. The final straw occurred in 1971 when one of my sons nearly fell to his death while climbing a granite spire, the Finger of Fate, near our cabin. Someone needed to do something.

"I'm worried," I told Cal. "Oh, God, I hope they're okay."

"Marie, it's almost dark. If they don't return soon, I'll go to Stanley and try to find help."

All three sons, ages fourteen, thirteen, and twelve, had headed around the lake. John, the youngest, returned to camp by midday. The sunny morning turned overcast and gray by afternoon, threatening rain by nightfall. My two oldest sons were missing on McGown Peak, looming above Stanley Lake.

"We got ourselves into some pretty hairy ravines," Calvin recalled. "Jerry and I climbed snow fields in the cracks going up McGown. Then, once on top, we could run down the backside. We got back to camp late. Mom and Dad were freakin' out. McGown, though, was nothing like the Finger of Fate."

Calvin recalled, "At both McGown and Finger of Fate, we scrambled up in tennis shoes without food or water, with no idea where the cliffs would take us. There is a point, especially when you don't have ropes and protection, when

IBMers canoeing the CalMar. IBM's annual campout at Redfish Lake first brought the Osborn family to Idaho's Sawtooth Mountains.

you realize you can't go back the way you came. Even now, while I don't wake up in the middle of the night in a sweat, I sometimes shiver when I think about Jerry dangling from that ledge by his fingertips. I could've looked over the edge at his body on the rocks a thousand feet below. Jerry didn't die on the Finger of Fate. I'm so grateful."

Our first IBM family campout in the Sawtooth Mountains at Redfish Lake's North Shore Picnic Area was in 1963. On a Friday, Cal drove the six of us (Debbie wasn't yet born) and our camping gear over three mountain passes on Highway 21, a gravel road between Lowman and Stanley.

While several IBM men hauled power boats to the annual Redfish Lake office campout, we brought our canoe, the CalMar. Our canoe glided quietly on the crystal-clear, blue-green waters, over sunken logs and trout of Redfish Lake.

The annual IBM campout was a passing kiss that blossomed into a full-blown Sawtooth love affair for the Osborn family. At first, we lingered a few extra days at Redfish Lake to camp. Then, during the 1960s, Cal added more IBM vacation days; we stayed longer and eventually found the solitude and beauty of Stanley Lake.

Our favorite was Stanley Lake's Inlet Campground. The boys cooked just-caught rainbow trout over our campfire. Cal took the kids hiking in the Sawtooth Wilderness, sometimes carrying the more tender-footed. Occasionally, we went to Stanley for breakfast at the old Stanley Club to break from campground cooking. Then, to clean away the camping grime, we waited in line at the Stanley Bathhouse until we could soak in the enclosed, natural hot water pool between Stanley and Lower Stanley — girls first.

We fell in love with the Sawtooth Mountains.

With Cal as our driver, the Osborn family explored southern Idaho. But increasingly, we returned to the Sawtooths.

One summer, after the Redfish Lake campout, we joined another IBM couple, Dave and Patty Carr, and their kids, pulling our rental camping trailers to Williams Lake near Salmon, Idaho. The lake road was rough, and we couldn't pull the trailers to the campground. Instead, we parked the trailers and pitched tents in a gravel pit. Patty and I had fixed a big spaghetti dinner with salad and garlic bread for everyone. Cal and Dave had gone to the lodge to check things out, which meant inspecting the bar. We waited. Finally, we fed our hungry kids and went to bed.

In the dark, we could hear singing, getting closer. Cal and Dave were swacked. Patty and I boiled more spaghetti, fixed a second big salad, and set the table for our husbands. The salad sat under one of those hanging gas lights with its burning wick — the blinding bright light attracted flying insects. I noticed pepper on top of the salad — only it wasn't pepper. We served hot garlic bread and spaghetti with the salad.

The Osborn family fell in love with Stanley Lake, often camping at the Inlet Campground. This beach would be the site of a terrible drowning, then collapse into the lake during an earthquake.

The following day, we packed and said goodbye to the Carr family. We had planned to drive to Vancouver, B.C., to visit our Canadian family, the Tods. But instead, we canceled our Canada trip and returned to the Sawtooths and Stanley Lake. That was a pivotal decision: afterward, our summer vacations were in the Sawtooths.

Our final family campout was at Alturas Lake. Cal had a superintendent of schools meeting in Sun Valley and changed from camping clothes to his IBM uniform — a tie, white

Debbie and Melinda fishing and camping at Stanley Lake. Near the CalMar canoe, the mornings still water mirrors McGown Peak

shirt, suit, and polished shoes — then headed over Galena Summit. Unfortunately, a beautiful morning gave way to thunderstorms. When the storm hit, all the kids returned to camp — except for John.

John had been fishing in his bathing suit, standing in the sunshine and icy stream where it flowed into Alturas Lake. Then, when the weather turned with thunder, lightning, and hail, John reluctantly waded to shore. He walked across an inch of hail in his bare feet to the closest shelter he could find: an outhouse. We found him with teeth chattering, shivering, barely able to talk, dressed only in a wet bathing suit, standing on cold concrete, barefoot.

How do you treat hypothermia? Whiskey? That's the wrong answer, but I thought whiskey was the remedy. We didn't pack whiskey because of the kids. We bundled John in sleeping bags, and I ran frantically through the campground, trying to find whiskey. Campers at Alturas that week were nondrinkers. Without whiskey, John survived anyway.

Meanwhile, the kids stood and held up the top and walls of our tents so the hail would slide off and not collapse them. Inside the tents, sleeping bags and clothes were damp, some sopping wet. Our firewood was wet. Even worse, the deluge had flooded our food tent. Our dry goods, including pancake flour, were a yucky mess. We tidied up, piled into the Travelall, and drove to Sessions Lodge in Obsidian for dinner.

When Cal returned to camp days later, we talked. "Cal, we love this place. But I can't do the camping; not in this weather. If we're going to spend time here, we're going to look for property."

Our realtor took us to Shaw Mesa, twelve miles south of Stanley, on the White Cloud Mountains side of Highway 75, between Fisher Creek and Fourth of July Creek. You can see Galena Summit in the south and the Twin Sisters in the north from Shaw Mesa. When you look west, the Sawtooth Range stands above the Salmon River, lined with willows. To the east are the White Cloud Mountains' peaks with aspen groves. You feel like you are standing on top of the world in one of the most beautiful mountain valleys. On that day in 1969, the grass was up to my shoulders, waving like a golden sea in the afternoon mountain breezes.

Cal and I were anticipating the kids' future college expenses, so we weren't naïve about the finances. We had come close to buying land in the San Juan Islands, only to pass it up with lifelong remorse. This time was different. We weren't going to let this go. So, to take one last look before we decided, the seven Osborns drove to Stanley, staying at the historic Sawtooth Hotel.

Planting trees on Shaw Mesa. LEFT TO RIGHT: *Cal Jr., John, Melinda, and Debbie*

The Sawtooth Hotel is a great, rustic, western historic building with grand views and creaky floors. One community bathroom down the hall served the upstairs guests.

The kitchen and dining room are on the main floor, while upstairs and out back are hotel rooms. Grates in the floors help move the wood-stove-heated air into the cold spaces above. In the morning, the aromas of bacon, coffee, and pancakes wafting upstairs are incentives to get out of bed and seize the day.

Cal and I walked the ground with the kids several times to decide which land parcel to buy. We wanted a mountain refuge where we could get away from telephones, TVs, radios, and people. We wanted a mountain retreat for the family. Finally, Cal and I bought 16.5 acres on Shaw Mesa.

We spent the summer of 1969 excited about where and how we would build. We imagined different architectural styles, bought books, and lingered over issues of Sunset Magazine. However, knowing that a national park or recreation area was coming, we also wanted a building that fit central Idaho's rustic, western style. So, we settled on a log cabin. And we built it, hiring the Dugan brothers out of Jerome.

When I drove from Boise with John to the US Senate hearing in Sun Valley, the Dugan brothers had placed the log walls on the cabin's main floor. The Congressional public hearing gathered testimony on mining threats to the White Clouds, real estate blight in the Sawtooth Valley, and options to protect the area. For decades, the question had lingered: should this part of America the Beautiful be protected as a national park? Finally, the dual threats of an open pit mine and real estate development forced the issue.

The packed public hearing in that early summer of 1970 was at the Sun Valley Lodge, chaired by Senator Frank Church. Church invited people in the audience to speak. John got in line and then testified in favor of protecting the White Clouds and Sawtooths.

Afterward, John, fourteen years old, talked with a spokesman for Kennecott Copper Company about open-pit mines and the fate of the White Clouds. "You must mine the minerals where they are. We all need molybdenum. This mine means jobs and income," said the spokesman.

"The dam will fail and pollute the Salmon River," John responded. The proposal was for a 400-foot-high dam creating a tailings "pond" 1.75 miles long at the 9,000–10,000-foot elevation at the base of the White Clouds' tallest mountain, Castle Peak. Eventually, the "moly" mine drove Congress to act, creating the Sawtooth NRA.

After the Senate hearing, we stopped in Ketchum for dinner when we saw two men fighting. I stepped between the two. They stopped slugging, continued cursing, and then went separate ways. For me, the decision to act is instinctual, not a weighing of risks.

Later at dusk we arrived at our new cabin. What fun it was to brush my teeth and spit out the window — or where the window would be. We rolled out sleeping bags on cots without a roof, looking up at the Milky Way. The Osborns spent their first night on Shaw Mesa.

While the Dugan brothers built the cabin's shell of log walls and roof, my oldest son, Calvin, did most of the interior finishing work. Calvin turned out to be meticulous and gifted with his hands. Over the next several summers, the family worked hard to finish the cabin and build a fence to keep the horses in and the cows out.

Drilling our well was expensive. The well driller's wife used a forked willow stick to witch for water. "This is where you need to put the well." While her husband drilled down for water, day after day, Cal and I would go to bed each night praying for water. We ended up with the deepest and most expensive well in the Valley. Years later, the well went dry, and I had to drill a second well, taking out a mortgage to pay for it. Today, new homeowners on Shaw Mesa use sprinkling systems to water their landscaping with precious groundwater from our shared aquifer.

Although we had a well, we didn't have electricity. Instead, we drove three miles to Sessions Lodge and filled water containers until we had electricity to pump water from the well. Oh, how I looked forward to a stove and oven, washing machine, hot showers, and a flush toilet rather than an outhouse.

In the summer of 1971, John Thiebert, who worked out of IBM's office in Twin Falls, volunteered to wire the cabin. John brought his wife, Cory, and their kids for the weekend. I cooked for both families using our two-burner Coleman stove. After a weekend of wiring, we had electricity. (Yes, the same Cory who, years later, Cal met when both were divorced, and who ended up sharing his life for nearly thirty years.)

Our cabin was the second home on Shaw Mesa. The Stanford family cabin was first. Lyle and Lottie Stanford were from Caldwell, where Lyle was the head of the biology department at the College of Idaho. Dr. Stanford, a polio survivor with eyes that sparkled, and a big smile framed by a white goatee, walked with the help of forearm crutches and leg braces. He was also an artist who painted the Sawtooths and White Clouds using watercolor. Dr. Stanford convinced John to attend the College of Idaho as a premed student. Later, in 1974, Dr. Stanford said "yes" to John's request to start the premed internship program at the Stanley Clinic.

After we built the cabin, Ernie and Lois Day built their view home on an exposed point overlooking the Valley.

Ernie was a landscape photographer, conservationist, and realtor. In 1969, as head of the Idaho State Park Board, Ernie Day followed Governor Don Samuelson at a Forest Service hearing on the proposed open pit mine at Castle Peak. Governor Samuelson testified in support of the mine. Ernie stepped to the microphone and resigned from the Samuelson Administration: "I don't see the sense of being part of a team which doesn't have enough regard for our resources to better differentiate uses." Ernie then took the issue to the Sierra Club's wilderness convention in San Francisco. Conservation publications nationwide published stories on the White Clouds controversy.

Ernie, the realtor, was part of a group that bought land on Shaw Mesa and subdivided the land into lots called the "White Clouds Subdivision." Eventually, Ernie stayed true to his conservation values and did not move forward with developing the full subdivision. Still, some on-the-edge view lots were sold with houses visible from the valley's floor.

We shared information about Shaw Mesa with our friends and Boise neighbors, Jim and Mary Mitchell. Jim worked for Boise Cascade Corporation, and the Mitchell family would also become Shaw Mesa neighbors. Jim was behind Boise Cascade's help in donating materials for the new Stanley Clinic.

The Sawtooth Mountains dominated the view across the valley from our new cabin on Shaw Mesa. In the summer of 1971, we used our family telescope to examine geologic formations more closely, including the Arrowhead and the Finger of Fate, a granite pinnacle over a thousand feet high.

As it turns out, the Finger of Fate is aptly named — where I nearly lost a son.

"That Sawtooth day was beautiful and cloudless," Calvin recalled. "I was a teenage carpenter in charge of finishing the cabin's interior, including the paneling. I worked as a short-order cook at Sessions Lodge when not working at the cabin. I was lonely and probably depressed. Mom and Dad were thrilled to have us out of the cabin that day. A day off from work! I got to play. Jerry and I looked across the valley at the Sawtooths and the Finger of Fate. We didn't leave the cabin with a purpose. We just set out to set out."

"Calvin and I didn't know anything about climbing," Jerry said. "Hiking from the cabin to the Finger of Fate was something we just decided to do that morning."

There is no established route up to the Finger of Fate. First, climbers hike from the trailhead to Hell Roaring Lake.

The Finger of Fate is across the valley from the Osborn's family cabin. Marie's second son, Jerry, nearly died on the Finger. With five kids, Marie became increasingly concerned about the lack of emergency services in Idaho's Sawtooth country.

"Looking up from the lake," Calvin said, "this granite finger looms like the middle finger of a man with a broken knuckle." Next, climbers walk the shoreline on a fisherman's trail and take off up scree slopes and over boulders to the base of the granite pinnacle. "As we got closer," Calvin recalled, "we knew we were going to climb this mountain, and that's all there was to it."

"Jerry went first when we came to a steep boulder. He stretched far enough to get a handhold as his feet came from underneath him. After that, Jerry had to climb up or let go and fall. Once up, he reached down, took my hand, and helped me up. After that move, we knew we couldn't ever go back down this way. There's no foothold. We'd fall."

"Calvin and I hadn't studied or scouted anything. We'd never really climbed before. Then, near the base, a couple of tricky moves convinced us that once we started, we couldn't go back down using this same route. We learned that going up was as much about finding an alternative way to get back down again. One thing I've learned about climbing is that going up is easier than coming down. So, that day we just kept going up."

"Jerry and I came to this giant cave. The rock was too steep on either side, and we had no ropes. We had no day-packs or climbing gear, just blue jeans and tennis shoes. 'Let's just see where this cave goes,' we told each other. It got darker and darker until the very end, where there was light and an opening."

"Calvin and I came out onto a wide ledge that kept going up. At first, it was easy, and we walked. Then we climbed and, finally, scrambled. The ledge narrowed, then ended. In front of us was a sheer cliff dropping into space on our right. Looking up, we saw the cliff rising upwards, broken by a wide crack or 'chimney.'"

Jerry described the crack as twenty-four to thirty inches wide. "To climb a chimney, you crawl into the crack, wedge your body, then move up. You do this over and over: wedge, move up. We faced into the crack going upwards, without any idea of what we'd find at the top of the crack. We knew this: it was easier to go up than down."

"Calvin and I climbed out of the chimney, realizing the summit was close. Next was a summit block, or huge boulder, wedged atop the Finger of Fate."

"Jerry's right. You cannot see from the valley floor that a giant, triangular boulder sits atop two crags on top of the Finger. Underneath that granite triangle was enough space for us to sit. Years later, when pine pollen had turned the air misty, Jerry and I were hiking at Hell Roaring Lake at sunset. The sun's angle was just right, and light shone through the Finger of Fate's top, through that space beneath the boulder. That light beam streaming through the Finger of Fate was a spiritual moment."

"To reach the summit, Calvin and I had to make a mantle move, like trying to climb onto a table higher than you. You reach up your arms and lunge with your feet, moving your foot up to replace your hands. The summit block was easily chest high, at an angle with lots of exposure. We were just a couple of kids in blue jeans, cotton shirts, and tennis shoes. We were cutting it close and just went ahead and did it."

Calvin was scared. "We're looking over a thousand-foot vertical cliff, and we had to shimmy up this exposed area somehow, get one leg up, and get up on top. We did it. Jerry and I stood together on top of this triangular boulder. There was not much room for both of us. Surrounding us was nothing but space. We were on top of a granite needle, the tip of Fate's Finger."

"Now what?" Jerry asked. "Calvin and I talked about it. We knew we couldn't get down, certainly not the route we came up. We also knew Mom and Dad would grow worried and send out a search party. Afternoon shadows were falling. We had no warm clothes or gear for spending the night. We didn't have food. So, we reversed course. Down we went, first off the summit boulder, then down the chimney."

Calvin recalled his descent into the chimney. "The vertical crack in the rock was about chest wide. We would not slide down the crack if we took a deep breath. If we leaned out, we'd fall out of the crack into thin air, a thousand feet to our deaths. So down the crack we both went: breathing in to stop, breathing out to shimmy down."

"Going down a chimney, you face out instead of facing in," Jerry explained. "Below you are a thousand feet of nothing as you wedge and move down. It's scary. Finally, Calvin and I lowered ourselves onto the narrow ledge. We started down the traverse. We still had this concern, bordering on irrational fear, that we could not reverse our first couple of moves that got us onto the Finger of Fate. We were freaking out. We had to find another way down. I started looking for an alternate route."

"Jerry was ahead of me. We were carefully moving across this granite face. It's slippery. There were no handholds. Walking on granite wearing tennis shoes can be risky. Then, suddenly, I heard Jerry sliding. He screamed."

Jerry had only seconds.

"I probably slid about twenty feet. Heading downward, I clawed at the granite for anything to stop the fall. In those few seconds, my life really did pass before my eyes. Then, I bounced."

"My tennis shoes hit rock, and I stopped. My fingers were bleeding. I was numb. I didn't feel anything. I was in disarray. To this day, I'll never know how I stopped. I was on a narrow ledge. Below me was nothing, space, a thousand feet of emptiness with boulders below."

"Jerry was crouched on the ledge when I looked down. The rock between us was steep, not vertical. The ledge that saved Jerry was only a few feet wide, sticking out, probably ten feet long. In the granite was a small crack shaped like a 'V.' When Jerry fell, he fell into the V, clawing and clinging to life with his fingertips. Once stopped, he used that crack to scramble back to where I stood. Jerry had peeled off the ends of his fingernails and the tips of his fingers. He was bleeding. That little ledge and crack saved my brother. Jerry was alive."

With adrenalin pumping and heart throbbing, Jerry now knew what he wanted. "'Screw it! We're going back down the way we came up.' Coming so close to death changed me. No longer 'happy-go-lucky,' I took control. 'Calvin, we're getting the hell out of here.'"

On the outside, Calvin remained calm, as Jerry remembers. "Calvin kept his cool. We would have been in trouble if either of us had lost it. Instead, Calvin was solid when I needed him the most. To this day, I'm amazed by that. You know that expression, 'cool as a cucumber'? Well, that was Calvin on the Finger of Fate. His calming effect kept us in the game and got us off that mountain."

What Jerry could not see was the impact on his oldest brother. "Watching Jerry slide toward his death, I became as scared as I have ever been scared. I just wanted Mom. I just wanted my mommy. You hear of grown men in foxholes, crying out for their mom? I was there.

"Moments after Jerry and I continued our descent, we had to jump across a tiny crack from one rock to the next. It was no big deal. I couldn't do it. I was petrified. I was nearly in shock. Yet, it was Jerry who almost died. I'm the oldest, who got in fights and beat up my younger brothers. No, not now; I was humbled: Jerry got me off the mountain. Jerry led, and I followed. I could not have gotten off the mountain alone. With my brother's help, we came down together."

"Calvin and I returned to where we had made our ascent and continued down. Finally, we came to the rock that had freaked us out. We both started laughing when we realized how easy these sections were. I had nearly fallen to my death worrying about these sections that were, in reality, easy. One of life's lessons is what looks impossible often isn't. The converse of that is true, too.

"It was getting dark when Calvin and I finally stepped off the Finger of Fate. God, we were relieved to be off. We knew Mom and Dad would be worried. We found our way back to the trail. We hiked to the trailhead, went across Decker Flat, made our way up Shaw Mesa, and at last walked in the door of the cabin. 'We're home!'"

"Mom and Dad were pissed!" Calvin remembered. "And I recall saying, 'Well, you practically kicked us out of the cabin, so how can you be mad that we came back late? We did what you wanted us to do, which was to disappear for the day.'"

"Calvin and I, born in the same year, brothers and competitors, didn't talk much about what happened up there. But, although our lives went independent ways, what

The Osborn family cabin on Shaw Mesa in 1977, with the Finger of Fate visible to the right of the chimney. With funding from the Robert Wood Johnson Foundation, Idaho EMS installed the antennae, enabling Marie to respond to emergencies by car or snowmobile. To stay warm, she heated her cabin with wood. For Marie to see patients at the Salmon River Emergency Clinic meant traveling nearly two miles to the highway and then twelve miles to Stanley.

happened on the Finger of Fate played on us intensely. We both grew up on that day — in different ways." Of my two oldest sons, Jerry became the mountain climber.

"I decided I wanted to climb, and so I did, learning to climb safely and responsibly. Next, I became an Outward Bound instructor in the Sawtooths. From there, I created and ran the Outdoor Program for the College of Idaho, paying my tuition and completing a college degree. After graduating, I guided in the Tetons. I've returned to the Finger of Fate several times, all the wiser. Eventually, I got a scholarship for further studies at Western Illinois University. Illinois, unlike Idaho, doesn't have many mountains." Jerry's life journey led him to becoming a Seattle architect, married to Hanane, father to three children.

For fifty years, Calvin never climbed again until, in his late sixties, he and his wife, Dia, trained to ascend Idaho's highest peak, Mt. Borah. After watching his brother nearly die on the Finger of Fate, Calvin eventually became a teacher of transcendental meditation in Boise.

In 1971, as an RN with five kids putting down roots in an isolated area with no emergency services, I knew that someone needed to do something.

PART THREE

BEACHHEAD

Sawtooth Mountain Star

FULLY-EQUIPPED AMBULANCE is now available at Stanley, following fund drive. Community also has emergency treatment center. (SMS photo)

12

EMERGENCY CALL: STEVE & TERESA LIPUS

It's been forty-five minutes; each minute seems like a week. You'd been driving Highway 21 west of Stanley around midnight. Suddenly, a deer stepped into your headlights. No time. Reflexes. You swerve. Oh God, you can't control the car. Spinning. Rolling. Deafening are breaking glass and tortured metal. Then ... quiet.

Pine branches poke into your face. Warm blood is trickling into your left eye. But it's your left thigh — Oh God, 10/10 pain. "Oh, help me!" you yell over and over. You are hurting, bleeding, and wrapped around a steering wheel.

Then you hear a distant siren. Louder, louder. Then, quiet except for muffled voices and slamming doors. Red lights flash. You hear that soft, gentle, firm human voice: "I'm an EMT with the Stanley Ambulance. Can I help you? Where are you hurt?"

Steve Lipus, a Forest Service employee, was a stalwart EMT volunteer for the Stanley Ambulance from 1975 until 1998. As a member of our "Goat Patrol," along with Gary Gadwa of Idaho Fish and Game and Phil Coonts of the Forest Service (and later Idaho Fish and Game), he combined EMT training and knowledge of the backcountry to help people and save lives.

The Forest Service recognized that part of Steve's job in law enforcement was serving as an EMT and in search and rescue operations. His supervisor, Bill James from Challis, knew rural trauma well and was a valuable mentor for Steve.

Steve grew up in Flushing, Queens, New York City, leaving the city in 1968 and heading west to earn his BS in Wildlife Management from Utah State.

His thirty-two-year career with the U.S. Forest Service spanned the Sawtooth NRA's dedication in September 1972, to include firefighting, recreation management, and law enforcement.

Steve met his future wife, Teresa, in my 1977 EMT class. For ambulance runs, we were staffed with two EMTs and a driver. You might get two EMTs with one call: Steve and Teresa were one of Stanley's first-responder couples. Teresa remained active as an EMT until she became pregnant with their first child, Tim.

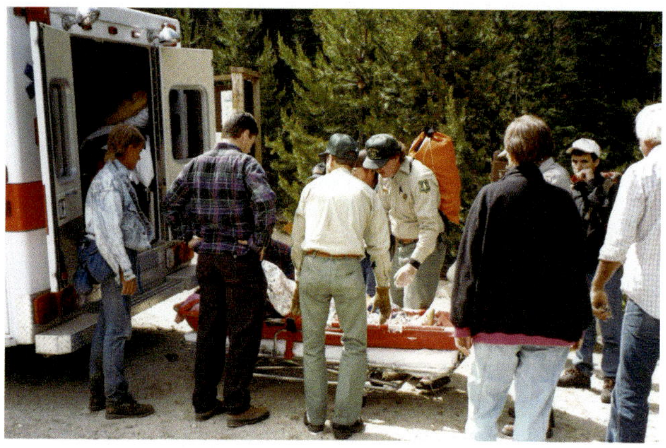

EMTs loading a trauma patient into the Stanley Ambulance. Note the U.S. Forest Service uniforms. Until Marie opened the Salmon Emergency River Clinic in 1972, emergency calls went to Forest Service staff. Agencies have an ongoing and critical role in staffing and supporting rural EMS.

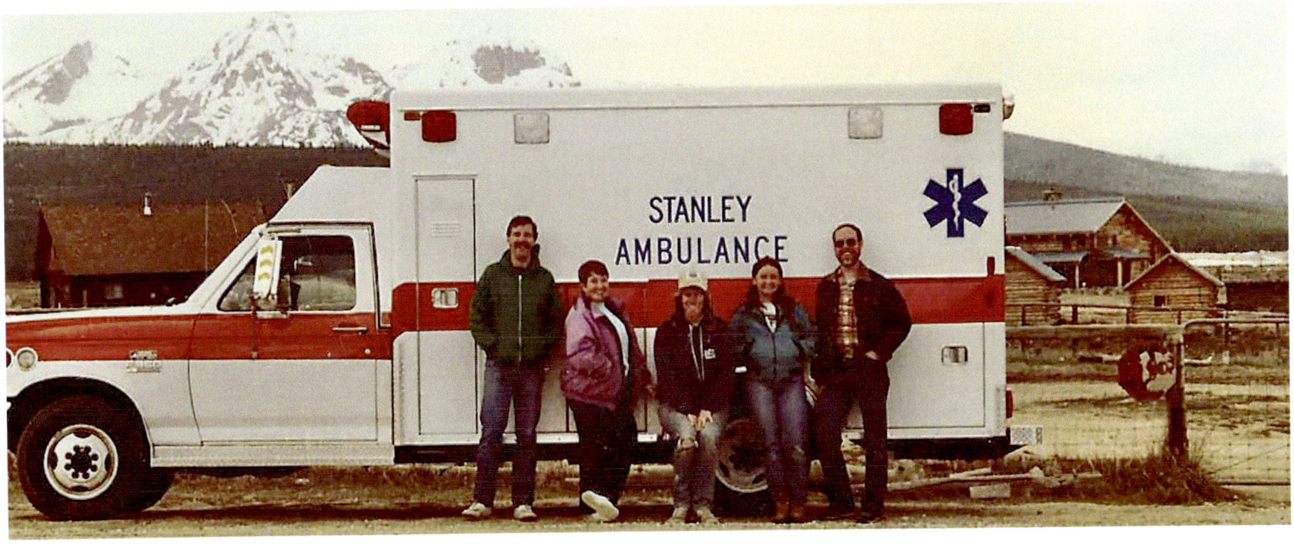

EMTs and the Stanley Ambulance. Steve Lipus is on the far right.

STEVE & TERESA LIPUS, IN THEIR OWN WORDS

An injured hawk introduced me to Marie. It was fire season, and a Forest Service crew had put out a lightning-strike wildfire northwest of Stanley. Returning to the Clayton Ranger Station, we encountered an injured hawk on the side of the road. We built a cage at the ranger station, trapped mice, and fed the injured raptor. Someone suggested taking the hawk to the new emergency clinic in Stanley, and I volunteered.

I carried the injured hawk inside a box and walked into the old log cabin clinic.

"What do we have here?" Marie asked. When I explained, she said, "Let's take it back to the lab." When we opened the box, the angry hawk was on its back with talons raised and ready.

Unfazed, Marie handed me a roll of gauze, "Steve, you need to secure those talons before I can examine the wing." Marie's physical exam revealed the diagnosis: a broken wing. Marie provided splinting materials and instructions.

I met Marie helping a hawk and ended up as an EMT.

They were both young: He was perhaps twenty, and she was barely a teenager. She was camped with her family at Redfish Lake and stepped away from a picnic. She was too young to die.

The curves in the road at Redfish Lake will mean nothing to you. For us, the memories don't go away.

Being young and feeling indestructible with testosterone, alcohol, and a motorcycle makes for a deadly mix. The motorcyclist picked her up. She sat on the seat behind him. Neither was wearing a helmet. To show his masculinity, he drove fast — too fast. The young man lost control and missed the curve by the bridge over the outlet at Redfish Lake. The motorcycle went airborne. Meanwhile, her family's picnic was underway nearby.

We got the emergency call and got there as fast as we could.

He sustained a fracture of his leg. The girl did not respond to voice commands or sternal rub. She was not breathing. She had no pulse. We started CPR and continued for a long time. For kids, you don't want to stop. In your patient's face, you see your child. You don't stop.

Marie directed us to end CPR. The girl did not move. Marie checked for a pulse and listened for heart and breath sounds. "She's dead," Marie said.

The girl's father and brother saw the commotion and came over from the picnic.

"Don't tell me I offed some broad!" the teenager yelled with the dead girl's father standing there. Imagine hearing these words as you look down and see your daughter not moving. Moments ago, she was alive.

The young man smelled of alcohol. He was angry and awful. He also had a broken leg. "We're going to have to cut your pants," I said. "If you cut these pants, I'm going to kick you," he slurred.

We ambulanced the motorcyclist over the hill to Sun Valley and transported the dead daughter's body to the clinic. She was so young. She had her whole life ahead of her. I still get teary-eyed thinking about that emergency call.

When terrible things like this happen, you have to be able to talk about it. For the Stanley Ambulance EMTs, we held debriefing sessions. Those who have run codes in hospitals know what this is about. Especially if you stop CPR, end the code, and the patient is dead, you take a moment as the whole team to check in with each other. It is not just a "check the box" review on whether you correctly followed BLS and ACLS protocols; this is about how each team member involved in trying to save a life is handling the tragedy at an emotional and spiritual level.

In urban settings, counselors are often available for first responders. In Stanley, we had help from Sharlene Stahl for a short time. Sharlene brought her counseling experience from California when she moved to Stanley. She helped with some of our first debriefing sessions. Otherwise, Stanley's EMTs, like first responders in other rural communities, had no counseling support for coping with bad outcomes.

After the body was gone, we met in the reception room at the Stanley Clinic. What we said in those meetings never left the room. Each of us talked about what we had done, and a lot of emotions would come out. We'd ask questions such as, "What could I have done better or differently? Would it have changed the outcome?"

Talking was the first step toward healing. Marie helped with the debriefing and consoled us. Marie was more than our EMT instructor. She was a teacher in so many other ways. A lot of the long-term EMTs would do anything for her. She came to see these debriefing sessions as essential for the mental health of Stanley's EMTs. That Marie was so drawn to this work stayed with me. Mine was dedication to Marie and the cause.

In the end, you do your best. You do all you can do. Haunted by memories of emergency calls? Debriefing helps, but the memories remain.

They were two brothers from Clayton, Idaho, out for a hoot on New Year's Day, riding their snowmobiles on the north side of Railroad Ridge in the White Cloud Mountains.

Avalanche near the Rocky Mountain Ranch

They'd come up through French Creek to near the Hermit Mine at the head of Silver Rule Creek. The brothers must have been having a great time, driving their snowmobiles far up into the beautiful winter wonderland of the White Cloud Mountains.

Snow and wind build cornices, overhanging walls of snow along the ridge. The vibration of the snowmobile, perhaps even joyful hooting and hollerin', reached up to that overhanging wall of snow. A crack would have started along the ridge, triggered by that tiniest vibration. In the blink of an eye, cracks grew into a giant fracture line ten feet deep and about 300 yards wide. Then, with gravity's unrelenting pull on that massive snow wall and weight, the cornice broke free into an enormous slab avalanche. Down plummeted a wall of snow, split by a ridge, creating a debris field over 500 yards long.

At what moment did glee turn to horror? One brother turned to see the other following him, and then, on the next glance back, he saw the remains of a massive avalanche where his brother had been.

So full of life and just having fun. Then ... everything gone, crushed beneath tons of avalanching snow. Watching a beloved brother buried.

Gary Gadwa and I got the emergency call that day. The brother had snowmobiled out eight to ten miles to report the incident. We pulled together a search and rescue team, about ten of us, locals and Forest Service staff, joined by the brother. Gary and I took turns breaking trail with our snowmobiles. Finally, we arrived at the debris field. The brother showed us where he last saw his sibling alive, and we focused our search there.

Meanwhile, winds whipping across Railroad Ridge were rebuilding the cornice.

You need people probing the snow to find someone buried in an avalanche. My Forest Service avalanche kit contained four-foot poles that, screwed end-to-end, create twelve-foot probes. We established a line spaced an arm's length apart with our volunteers. "Probes down." "Probes Up." The line stepped forward. "Probes down." "Probes Up."

You hope your probe hits something, but ours didn't even meet the ground. The avalanche debris field was probably twenty-five to thirty feet deep in spots.

"Probes down." "Probes Up."

A MAST (Military Assistance to Safety and Traffic) helicopter brought in several more search and rescue volunteers. As the helicopter departed, we suddenly heard a "POP" like it had backfired. The pilot headed downslope, landing at Yankee Fork Ranger Station along the Salmon River. Mechanical problems eliminated our helicopter support.

Quiet returned to the debris field except for the wind and blowing snow. We were on our own.

"Probes down." "Probes Up."

Dusk was deepening toward darkness. Temperatures were dropping well below zero with increasing winds. Night would come early, just ten days past the winter solstice. Getting off Railroad Ridge in a winter storm at night was unsafe, so we spent the night at the old miner's cabin. We all crowded into the shack, crouched and cramped with the mice to await the dawn. Winds howled through the night.

Two Air Force helicopters brought in more search and rescue volunteers the following day. Volunteers arrived from the Galena Patrol's specially trained Ski Mountain Rescue Team (a unit of Blaine County's Search and Rescue). Some of these volunteers stationed themselves on the ridge to monitor the cornice. Other volunteers were from adjacent county search and rescue teams. Again, we organized ourselves for the continued search.

Winds picked up as the search continued for most of the second day, and the snow fell harder. Above us, the Galena Patrol team advised that the quickly rebuilding cornice above us was unsafe for the search to continue. We had to leave the search area.

No longer a rescue effort, we reached a consensus that the brother buried in the debris field was dead. Ours was now a recovery mission with worsening weather and rebuilding cornices. We could not risk the living to recover the dead. The volunteers headed out. "I'm not leaving," the surviving brother told Gary and me. "I can't leave my brother."

Gary and I weren't going to leave him there. The Galena Nordic Ski Patrol leader gave the surviving brother a mini-avalanche course to help him understand the danger.

Sawtooth Avalanche Center

Avalanche deaths have prompted heightened vigilance. This includes the Sawtooth Avalanche Center, founded in the 1990s, to provide avalanche and mountain weather information.

We waited. Finally, the living brother understood that we couldn't leave him behind, and his staying put our lives at risk, too. We left behind a brother buried in the debris field below Railroad Ridge.

Spring brings longer, warmer days. Snowmelt in the high country uncovers many things. Deputy Sheriff Jim Parkhouse, who had joined us on the New Year's Day search and rescue mission, returned to Railroad Ridge and will describe what he found further in this book.

Pregnant, Teresa decided to stop volunteering as an EMT for the Stanley Ambulance in the spring of 1985.

Marie was adamant that Teresa not give birth in Stanley. "If you have any problems, you must be close to a hospital — not in Stanley."

Early Easter Sunday, Teresa went into labor. We headed for the Moritz Community Hospital at Sun Valley. A nurse examined Teresa, "Everything's fine." It wasn't.

Shift change: a new nurse examined Teresa, "Your baby is having trouble, Teresa." Fetal distress. The nurse paged Dr. Stone in choir practice rehearsing for the Easter Sunday service. Dr. Stone arrived in a few minutes. Off Teresa went to the OR for an emergency C-section. When Dr. Stone delivered our baby, Tim, he wasn't breathing. Our newborn was intubated and transported by air ambulance to Primary Children's Hospital in Salt Lake City. Marie's wisdom and insistence saved our son: a pregnant woman needs to be near a hospital before her due date to handle possible complications.

Marie was concerned about our second baby. We were past the due date, and Dr. Stone was leaving town. "I could just see what was going to happen," Marie later told us. Marie worked with Dr. Stone to schedule a second C-section. Adam was born healthy in 1988.

Marie even offered a Lamaze class to help us and others prepare to give birth. We attended all the classes Marie offered before her other responsibilities took priority.

Through it all, Marie was our primary care provider, including for our dog.

"And the cat's in the cradle and the silver spoon
Little boy blue and the man in the moon
'When you coming home, dad?' 'I don't know when'
But we'll get together then
You know we'll have a good time then"

Harry Chapin

You might have experienced this dilemma: Do I respond to another emergency call or spend time with my spouse and kids? I have skills that can save lives, yet I have responsibilities to my family.

When Teresa and I volunteered together as EMTs for ambulance runs, decisions were more straightforward. Adding kids and a job promotion, continuing my public service as an EMT and with Search and Rescue while keeping balls juggling in the air got more challenging.

In 1984, I attended the Federal Law Enforcement Training Center in Georgia to become the first Forest Service Law Enforcement Officer (LEO) assigned to the Sawtooth NRA. My patrol area was immense: the Sawtooth NRA, Ketchum Ranger District of the Sawtooth National Forest (NF), and parts of the Challis NF and Boise NF west of Stanley.

As an LEO, my primary responsibilities were protecting natural resources and people working on and visiting within my patrol area. If people were hurt, my job was to help. I was a volunteer EMT with search and rescue experience.

Long-term Forest Service staff in Stanley, like Bill James, knew how essential it was for Forest Service law enforcement to take emergency calls. Bill knew the realities of trauma before Marie opened the Stanley Clinic and began training EMTs. Behind Bill's big smile lurked some dark memories of trauma. This powerhouse of energy and work ethic was my mentor, and I followed in his footsteps. Anyone getting hurt? It was my job to help. My Forest Service supervisors had my back.

National regulations to protect wilderness values prohibit motorized equipment and equipment used for mechanical transport. Yes, but what happens when a mountain climber is injured, or a middle-aged backpacker has chest pain? Medical emergencies are exceptions to the rule. The Forest Service has a protocol for using helicopters in wilderness areas. After Bill James retired, I became the search and rescue coordinator in the Sawtooth NRA.

Seasonal workers with the Forest Service became pillars of the volunteer EMT team staffing the Stanley Ambulance. Gretchen Koberness, Joe Miczulski, Ken Hartz, Roland Miller, and Danny King, to name a few, all took Marie's EMT class, graduated, and shared in handling emergency calls. My supervisors and I, as an LEO, supported my staff becoming EMTs, helping the community while providing relief for me. "Many hands make light work."

The Forest Service helped in other ways, too. For example, our radios had an EMS channel to connect to Idaho EMS and StateComm. My supervisors supported me in buying equipment for my jump kit. We purchased a portable oxygen tank and regulator. As the federal agency had done before the Stanley Ambulance, we used Forest Service rigs to respond to emergencies, including my marked law enforcement vehicle. Agency staff — Dave Kimpton and I — served on the Stanley Clinic's board of directors to interlock the Forest Service and the Clinic.

Let's face it: The U.S. Forest Service has a vested interest. If the clinic and ambulance go away, Forest Service staff, many without first-aid experience, will again be fielding emergency calls. And not just the Forest Service: Idaho Fish and Game also has "skin in the game." Fish and Game staff Phil Coonts at the Sawtooth fish hatchery and conservation officer Gary Gadwa carried the state's water in responding to many emergency calls starting in the 1970s.

Marie likes to say that Gary and I were joined at the hip — her "senior EMTs," mountain goats who knew the backcountry like no other. The "goat patrol" competed to see who could be first on the scene. Gary was the winner most times.

Sometimes, you must say, "No, sorry, I can't do this ambulance run. If you really can't find anyone else, call me back."

Once, Teresa had just pulled a leg of lamb out of the oven, and we had dinner guests. Dispatch got a "yes" from Sparky and Maryellen Easom, and Roland Miller. What a relief. We sat down to dinner as the ambulance transported a patient over Galena Summit to Sun Valley.

Hours later, around ten pm, in the pitch black of night, red lights flashed through our front windows, startling us, and then we heard from the ambulance PA, "Steve Lipus, we know you're in there. Come out with your hands up!"

In the Sawtooths, those two months from the Fourth of July to Labor Day are a 100-yard dash. I spent time with my sons when I was off duty. During mid-week, we sometimes went camping. And yet, the calls for help never stopped. People got hurt, and sometimes they were dying. Put yourself in my shoes: You can help. What are you going to do?

One time, I was home when the emergency call came: "Steve, we need you. There's a car wreck out on Highway 21. We need an EMT. Can you help?"

I grabbed my pack. I reached for the door. Still today, I am haunted by that child's voice of my oldest son calling to me across the room. "Hey, Dad, thanks for stopping by!" That hurt. I ran out the door, heading for my patrol vehicle and the car wreck.

Climbing steep alpine trails at high altitudes with lower partial pressures of oxygen is a cardiac stress test. Most hearts pass the test, but not all.

Summertime in the Sawtooths, tourists poured into the Valley. "Where's a good place to hike in the Sawtooth Wilderness?" was a question frequently asked.

If you don't mind crowds, the trail to Alpine Lake and then to Sawtooth Lake is quintessential Sawtooth Range: cascading streams, meadows abloom with wildflowers, and forests — sunny lodgepole pine and shady Douglas fir. At the end of your long uphill journey you are rewarded by those beautiful lakes.

But there is a cardiac stress test part: The distance from Iron Creek Trailhead to Alpine Lake is 3.9 miles, with an elevation gain of 1,173 feet. From Iron Creek Trailhead to Sawtooth Lake, the length is 4.8 miles, with an elevation gain of 1,730 feet.

"We have a middle-aged male with chest pain and shortness of breath. He is down on the trail to Sawtooth Lake. Are you available to respond?" Gary Gadwa and I grabbed our jump kits and the portable oxygen tank. We hustled up the trail without chest pain or palpitations. Unfortunately, our patient was not so fortunate.

We found him on the ground with his family. Shake and shout? No response. Check the carotid artery for a pulse. None. "Start CPR." Chest compressions, count out loud. There is no AED to turn on, followed by reassuring instructions, "Apply pads to the chest. Stop CPR. Analyzing rhythm. Shock."

"Switch!" Gary and I took turns every few minutes between doing compressions and breaths.

People gathered. Someone stepped in to help with chest compressions. We were on the radio to Marie with the ambulance at the Iron Creek trailhead.

"Marie, we have a middle-aged male who had chest pain. His friends said he was on the trail and not moving for about an hour before we arrived. When we arrived, he had no pulse and no respiratory effort."

"How long have you been doing CPR?"

"About thirty minutes. Still no pulse. Not breathing."

"Steve and Gary, we should call the code. Are you okay with that decision?"

From both of us: "Yes."

"Stop CPR."

There is a profound stillness, a quiet when you stop CPR, step away, and acknowledge a life has ended. Your best efforts won't change death as the outcome. You gave it your all. But, your "all" didn't change the inevitable.

Maybe in a hospital setting with this same middle-aged male with multiple cardiac risk factors who collapsed during a cardiac stress test, a code team might succeed where we failed. Not here. Sudden cardiac death on a wilderness trail in the Sawtooths is far from a code cart and cath lab.

Now what? We had a moderately obese body a long way from the road. "Hey Marie, we're considering asking Jeff Bitton to send in a pack horse." Jeff was an outfitter and guide who, with his wife Debbie, ran the Mystic Saddle Ranch. Their pack horses helped move the dead and injured out of the backcountry, especially before Life Flight.

Slinging a large body across a horse is no easy task. The visual had to be unforgettable for hikers passing us on one of Idaho's busiest wilderness trails. "Howdy, partner. Welcome

Roland Miller

The Sawtooth country's "Goat Patrol": Gary Gadwa (LEFT) and Steve Lipus, EMTs, Stanley Ambulance.

to the Wild West," doesn't really capture the solemnity of transporting the dead by horseback. People stepped off the trail, staring as we passed. Law enforcement at the trailhead stopped people from coming up, but we couldn't do much about people already on the trail to Alpine Lake.

As we approached Iron Creek Campground, we were joined by other EMTs walking up the trail to help. Concerned about appearances and respect for family and friends gathering at the trailhead, we transferred the body off the horse to a Stokes stretcher and hand-carried him the remainder of the way.

Climbing accidents and fatalities happen in the Sawtooths. Carrying out the injured by stretcher is an ordeal.

We got the emergency call: A mountain climber had fallen off the Finger of Fate. This granite spire near Hell Roaring Lake in the central Sawtooths rises over 1,000 feet, a magnet for climbers.

On that day, one member of a climbing party had fallen feet first. The impact of his landing resulted in compression fractures in both lower extremities. However, another climber got down safely and came out for help.

EMTs answering the call included Roland Miller, Gary Gadwa, and Ken Hartz. We hiked the trail to Hell Roaring Lake, then headed cross-country toward the Finger of Fate in steep terrain. Finally, we got to the injured climber at dusk. He was awake and in severe pain. We splinted his fractured lower extremities, immobilized his cervical spine, and moved him onto a Stokes stretcher. Now came the hard part.

Most people don't realize what it takes to carry a patient in a Stokes stretcher out of the backcountry. You need eight stretcher-bearers: three on each side of the stretcher and two to spell the others. You must also be careful when carrying an injured patient, especially at night: don't drop.

At the bottom of the Finger of Fate is a steep scree slope. Pea gravel was like walking on ball bearings: treacherous. In the dark, we began to carry the immobilized climber in the stretcher and then belayed the loaded stretcher down the steep slope with three people on each side. As we approached Hell Roaring Lake, the trees became so dense that we turned the loaded stretcher ninety degrees to squeak between trees.

Our all-night ordeal ended when we met with a fire crew about halfway between the trailhead and Hell Roaring Lake. The new team took over, carrying the climber the rest of the way to the waiting Stanley Ambulance. Exhausted, we returned home.

To transport the injured out of the backcountry by stretcher takes a husky team — a big team — especially when helicopter transport is not available.

"We have an elderly man unresponsive at Stanley Lake." I grabbed my emergency jump kit and headed to the ambulance at the Stanley Clinic. Marie wasn't in the valley. She was returning from Boise.

When we arrived at the campsite, a tidy, small, elderly, white-haired woman was hunched over, weeping.

"Hi. I'm Steve Lipus. I'm a Forest Service law enforcement officer. We heard there's a problem with your husband."

She led me to their pretty little camping trailer. I stepped up the trailer's steps and turned the corner. Her husband's body lay in the small bed.

"Are you okay? Can I help you?" No response. No movement. No respiratory effort. I reached over the bed and began my assessment. No pulse. No heart sounds. No breath sounds. The limbs were stiff and cold. He had been dead for a few hours. Rigor mortis was setting in.

I exited the trailer and walked a few steps to put my arm around the dead man's wife. "I'm sorry." I was only confirming what she knew. They were both in their eighties. Yet, they stayed faithful to their wedding vows: "Til death do us part." Once two, now one, she struggled with the loss and being alone. Death may be inevitable, but so is grief's pain for those left behind. She sobbed in my arms. For EMS personnel at a death scene: Remember and respect the living.

"Steve Lipus to Marie Osborn," I spoke into the Forest Service radio.

"Marie here. Steve, I'm at Banner Summit. Unfortunately, it will be a while before I can get there." Marie was monitoring the radio traffic while driving up Highway 21 from Lowman.

"Marie, I have a deceased individual." Silence.

"You'll have to pronounce and then move the body," she replied.

"Marie? Uh, how do I do that?"

"Steve Lipus, I deputize you as deputy coroner for Custer County. Go ahead and move the body to the clinic. I'll meet you there."

I pronounced the man dead and used the time of the radio transmission as the time of death. How do we get him out? He's inside this little trailer offering very little room to maneuver. Spatial skills are needed! We brought in a Stokes stretcher and strapped him in. We almost had to stand him straight up, tilted to angle him around the corner and down the trailer stairs. Finally, we got him out of the trailer, loaded, and off to the clinic.

On a warm Sawtooth summer day with no morgue, we pulled the ambulance out onto the street and placed the body on the garage floor's cool cement. I stayed with the deceased man until Marie arrived.

Today, when I travel Highway 21, certain places trigger memories that can be pretty tough. I'll drive through beautiful meadows and forests with the Sawtooth peaks as a backdrop. Then, memories flash back like a switch flipped by a specific location or highway mile marker. Suddenly, I'm reliving the trauma.You never forget those people. The memories remain of those you saved and those you lost.

Steve Lipus was one of my "senior" EMTs until he and Teresa moved from Stanley in 1998. During Steve's twenty-four years in Stanley, he was an EMT and Forest Service liaison for search and rescue operations. In addition, Steve served on the board of the Stanley Clinic and as a volunteer Hunter Education Instructor for the Idaho Department of Fish & Game.

In 1998, the Forest Service promoted Steve to be the Law Enforcement Patrol Captain in Boise, managing the program for nine LEOs in southwest Idaho on the Boise, Payette, and Sawtooth National Forests.

Steve had applied for the position because there was no high school in Stanley. As a result, Steve, Teresa, Tim, and Adam moved away from Stanley and began a new chapter of their life in southwestern Idaho.

When asked about highlights of his career in public service, Steve replied, "I witnessed the first four wolves reintroduced to Idaho on January 14, 1995. In 2002, I was part of the Utah Olympic Public Safety Command for the downhill ski races. Best of all? Working with folks doing search and rescue and EMT responses within the Sawtooth NRA."

Steve retired from the Forest Service in 2007. He now volunteers with Idaho Fish and Game to help restore critical wildlife habitat after damaging wildfires and restore streamside habitats in southwest Idaho.

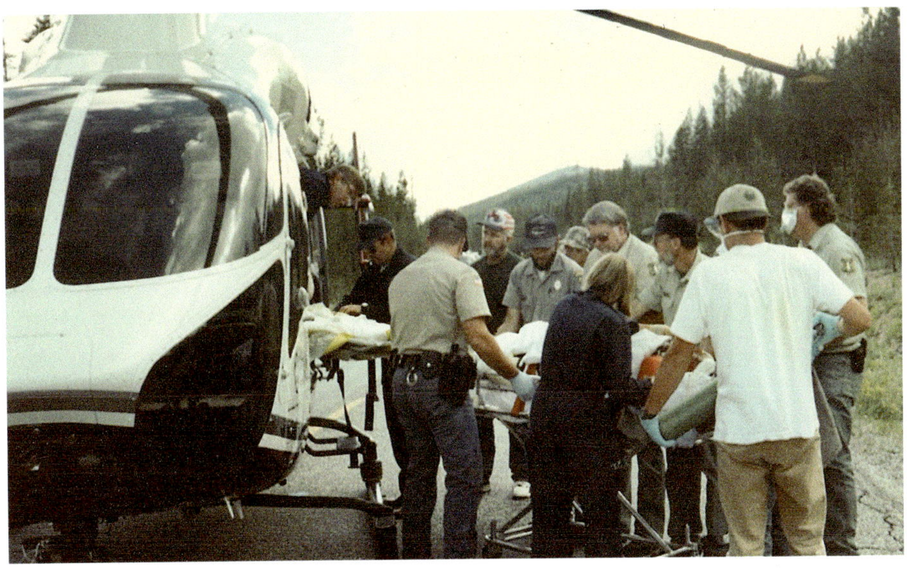

Stanley's volunteer EMTs CENTER: *Gary Gadwa (Idaho Fish & Game) and to the right in US Forest Service uniforms are Ken Hartz, Steve Lipus, and* (FAR RIGHT) *Roland Miller.*

13

EMS FOUNDATIONS: DR. MICHAEL COPASS

University of Washington Medicine

Dr. Michael Copass, Director of Emergency Services at Harborview Medical Center and Medical Director of Airlift Northwest

The Doctor with the Iron Hand

Commanding over the tiled trenches of Harborview Medical Center's emergency room is a doctor who, according to many, has done more for the health of King County residents than any other person.

Michael Copass is a juggernaut in a sweater vest, a man likened to a mix of Albert Schweitzer and General George Patton, with four pagers and a radio strapped to his belt.

He has presided over the state's busiest emergency room for twenty-seven years, and helped design Seattle's Medic One system, which became an international model. Copass fills so many roles that he can frequently seem a one-man majority, observers say, and a few begrudge his sway over the emergency medical and trauma systems.

A professor of neurology at the University of Washington, Copass grew up in Seattle. He took over Harborview's emergency department in 1973 at age 34. The city had already started a novel paramedic program that would rush aid to people suffering heart attacks. Copass expanded the system to apply to other emergencies, training select firefighters to be the "long arms" of doctors.

He also established a rigorous paramedic-training program that requires roughly 3,000 hours of education. As a result, the program "60 Minutes" once called Seattle the best place in America to have a heart attack.

Copass helped launch Airlift Northwest, which transports patients to Harborview from around Washington, Idaho and Oregon, and from as far away as Alaska and Wyoming. He helped shape the trauma system that cares for people injured in car accidents or falls, by burns, bullets or knives.

"It's hard to speak about him in normal human terms," Tom Gudmestad, the operations-medical-services officer for King County Medic One, once said of Copass.

Chris Solomon, Susan Kelleher, *The Seattle Times*. March 7, 2000

From 1973 to 2008 — thirty-five years — Dr. Copass was the Director of Emergency Services at Harborview Medical Center, a central figure in creating one of the world's leading trauma centers. He founded and became the medical director of Airlift Northwest. Dr. Copass was also the medical director of Seattle Medic One and the director of paramedic training. He was a neurologist who saw patients in the clinic. Michael Copass may have been married to EMS, but he was also married to Lucy and father to Cloantha, Mike III, and Catharine.

In the winter of 1972, Dr. Copass agreed to be one of my teachers. He was the Chief Resident in Neurology at Harborview. The last time I'd been on the wards at Harborview was December 1, 1953, as a new RN in my third trimester of pregnancy. When I returned five children later in 1972, Harborview was part of the University of Washington (UW) system.

When I arrived in Seattle, UW had no NP training program or materials, so we made it up as we went along and created an NP training checklist. I trained in the ER, attended classes with paramedics, and rode the Medic One cardiology unit. I needed the Harborview emergency medicine training because, once back in Stanley, I would be responsible for teaching EMTs, opening the Salmon River Emergency Clinic, and staffing the Stanley Ambulance on 24/7 emergency call. In addition, from Stanley, we would send our worst burn and head trauma cases to Harborview and Salt Lake City.

When I first met resident physician Dr. Copass at Harborview on Seattle's "Pill Hill," I didn't know his commitment to EMS and his understanding of rural realities. I asked Dr. Copass if I could join his neurology teaching rounds on Saturday mornings. He paused, looked at me, and said, "We've never done this before." He paused again, "Okay, we'll try it."

Dr. Copass was an excellent clinician and teacher, and the spectrum of neurologic disease on the hospital wards was astonishing. On rounds, Dr. Copass asked questions: If you answered wrong, he would cut you down to two inches — or less. You wanted to disappear.

Friends brought in a young male patient one Saturday night at the Harborview ER. He was unresponsive after overdosing on Valium. Dr. Copass said, "Marie, it's time you learned to do a gastric lavage" — pump the stomach. I'd seen it done, but I'd never done it. I inserted the tube into the patient's nostril down to his stomach. Then, I filled a large syringe with saline, inserted the syringe barrel into the tubing, and pushed saline into the stomach through the tube. Next, using the syringe, I withdrew pill fragments and other stomach contents. Eventually, I used thirty-six liters of saline to empty my patient's stomach of pill fragments.

Jean Sherrard

Harborview Medical Center, Seattle, 2018. In 1953, Marie worked briefly as an RN at HMC during the third trimester of her first pregnancy. Nearly twenty years and five kids later, Marie returned to Harborview in 1972, with support from the Idaho Board of Nursing, preparing to open the emergency clinic in Stanley, Idaho.

Dr. Copass walked in. He stared at the empty bottles and blurted, "You used all those?"

"Yes," I replied defensively. "You told me to pump until it came back clear. That's how many it took." He didn't say another word about the lavage. Then, with the patient marginally responsive on the gurney, Dr. Copass stated, "He's gay."

"Do you know him as a patient?" I asked.

"No."

"Well, how do you know he's gay?"

Dr. Copass replied, "The Seattle Police Department and I decided anyone wearing colored underwear and socks is gay."

Sometimes, I should keep my mouth shut. "Well, I buy my husband's underwear and socks and always buy the colored ones."

"You'll see," he said and walked out.

When the patient regained consciousness, I asked. He was gay.

About eight years later, Dr. Copass visited Boise for a conference sponsored by Idaho EMS. I attended as an EMT instructor and Stanley's NP. The two of us met and talked like old friends.

Lucy Copass recalled that her husband's support for rural healthcare, including EMS, is long and deep. Every summer through high school and college, Mike Copass worked at hard-core farm jobs in rural and remote parts of eastern Washington. In addition, as a young physician, Dr.

Copass traveled and taught for several years as part of the UW medical school's WWAMI faculty team.

Dr. Copass co-founded Southeast Regional EMS in Alaska and was an active board member until 2013, when a stroke forced him to step away. In the 1980s, he pushed to establish Airlift Northwest. That air ambulance service supported medical personnel in small towns and rural areas to transport trauma and burn patients to capable facilities and care teams. In Idaho, we now have Life Flight and other air ambulance services based on the same foundation laid by Dr. Copass and other EMS pioneers.

When Dr. Copass and Lucy made weekend trips to hike in the Olympics, it was Dr. Copass' practice to first swing by the Harborview ER to pick up backboards left by fire department medic units from small communities. Then, driving westward, Dr. Copass and Lucy would return the backboards to home fire stations in those tiny towns on the Olympic Peninsula.

Have you ever taken an EMS radio into your bedroom at night? When you are on emergency call 24/7, that radio goes wth you, even to bed. It contributed to the breakup of my marriage with Cal. For Dr. Copass, carrying radios and pagers, the stories are legion of him monitoring and occasionally intervening in EMS radio traffic.

"It's hard to speak about [Dr. Copass] in normal human terms," the Medic One director for King County told The Seattle Times.

But in the end, we are human. Who we are is what we do until that day when we can't do our life's work anymore. We transition from one side of the stethoscope to the other, from caregiver to patient.

For Dr. Copass, a neurologist, that shift came abruptly with his stroke in 2013, a decade before his death in 2024.

EMS history is inseparable from the personal story of Dr. Copass. So, the next time you hear the sirens, see the air ambulance helicopters flying overhead, receive patients from paramedics, or meet people who have survived terrible burns, trauma, or cardiac arrest in the field — pause for just a moment to thank those EMS pioneers, including Dr. Copass — and remember to thank their families, too.

DR. MICHAEL COPASS, IN HIS OWN WORDS

I grew up straddling both sides of the Cascade Mountains. While growing up in Seattle, I also worked farm jobs north of Pasco during high school and college summers. This part of eastern Washington is dryland wheat, big farms, scarce water, and self-reliant farming families. People had no medical care and didn't think they needed it. They didn't mind helping others if it didn't cost too much. But they'd always taken care of their own.

About sixty miles from the farmhouse was a physician in Connell. If something terrible happened, people sought emergency care in Pasco. My idea for a response program was to give one of the women a radio and use the telephone party line. When a tractor rolled over and crushed someone or a farm worker caught an arm in a thresher, you'd have some basic emergency communication system.

Loen Baile, a rancher/farmer for whom I worked, got his hand caught in a v-belt, the rubber belt used for driving mechanisms in an engine. It cut off the tips of his fingers. I didn't know what to do. Loen's wife drove a hundred miles per hour on back dirt roads to get him to emergency care in Pasco. The surgeon tucked Loen's fingertips into his abdominal wall to give partially amputated digits time to heal. Eventually, Loen could tap his fingers without excruciating pain.

In dryland wheat country, there were no organized emergency services. Farmers had an aid car between Pasco and Connell in Mesa, and a physician was in Connell. However, the area lacked any system for responding to emergencies and no ambulance. Responses were up to each farming family. People were mainly on their own; you take care of yourself.

An extensive injury went south to Pasco. And that hasn't changed much with time. In the 1950s and '60s, there was no EMS radio system, no 911, no ambulance, and no helicopter air ambulance. People operated by the seat of their pants using homemade first aid.

During the 1960s, we used to say wounded soldiers in Vietnam had a better chance of surviving battlefield trauma than citizens with highway trauma here at home. Training medics, deploying helicopters for transport, and staffing field hospitals for trauma improved the soldiers' survival chances. Thus, saving wounded soldiers in Vietnam helped drive the evolution of EMS to save lives at home in America.

I graduated from Northwestern University Medical School in 1964 and completed my internship in the Northwestern system in 1964–1965. Then, the Army drafted me. I did basic training in Texas during the summer of 1965. After that, I served at the US Army hospital and other medical facilities in Frankfurt, Germany, 1965–1967, and then at an Army outpost in Berchtesgaden, Bavaria, 1967–1968.

In Germany, during the Vietnam War, people called the military police for emergencies. So, we trained MPs. We got called to help with a Green Beret climbing exercise. A soldier fell and was severely busted up. We went in with MPs, loaded the soldier in a body bag, and transported him out. That prompted requests for more training for MPs. German soldiers wanted what the US soldiers got, so we trained German soldiers, too.

While in Germany, I helped train soldiers assigned to transportation, including mechanics. How do you manage injuries like cutting off a finger? What do you do if an arm gets cut off? One of our EMT students was a Romanian soldier. He survived Stalingrad. He didn't need a brash young American telling them how bad things could be. He damn well knew.

Soldiers could be trained as combat medics to start IVs and manage wounds. By the time combat medics returned home, they were trauma experienced. Given the shortage of doctors, we needed these skills here at home. In 1969, the University of Washington opened the MEDEX program, the nation's second-oldest training program for physician assistants. Today, the MEDEX Northwest Physician Assistant Program is part of the Department of Family Medicine at UW Medicine.

Helicopter pilots who survived combat in Vietnam were incredibly talented and experienced. Some of these pilots flew the military's air ambulances, a model for civilian air ambulance services that came later. The pilots flew with the 54th Medical Detachment (air ambulance) based at Fort Lewis, now Joint Base Lewis-McChord or JBLM. Those pilots were utterly astounding.

Under Geneva Convention rules, the unarmed Huey helicopters of the 54th were marked with a red cross, evacuating wounded from the battlefield. These military air ambulances provided onboard medical care while transporting injured and sick to field hospitals and trauma centers, often under enemy fire. Stateside, people raised money to transform these Hueys for civilian transport, adding equipment like isolettes for transporting high-risk newborns. Military air ambulances depended on people on the ground to prepare patients for transport.

Medic One Foundation

Dr. Michael Copass, former Medic One Paramedic Training Program Director and Medical Director for Seattle Medic One. Marie trained under Dr. Copass and attended classes with the newly-established paramedic program.

Even as the UW MEDEX was underway, a chiropractor from Spokane elected to the legislature supported nurses doing advanced practice. William Day, known as "Big Daddy" for his imposing size and political acumen, championed the UW nursing program in the legislature.

Big Daddy led the effort for advanced practice nursing in Washington State, enabling nurses to order X-rays and write prescriptions. Harborview explored how we might involve nurses more with patient care in the ER.

In the ER, we have two kinds of problems: acute cases that come in by ambulance, and walk-ins, who are usually less sick. We trained six nurses to handle chief complaints like a sore toe or productive cough. With the excitement in the rest of the ER, it didn't take long for those nurses to move over and get involved with the higher acuity cases. With nurses making initial assessments and ordering labs,

ER physicians had more time available to manage higher acuity cases.

These nurses became a great asset in the ER. The nurses worked as part of the team for the major trauma cases. We trained nurses in trauma physiology, closing wounds, calculating IV fluid volumes for severe burn patients, performing peritoneal lavage, and even placing chest tubes. If we sent nurses into the field, we trained them.

In a trauma center like the Harborview ER, if you could be depended on to get the work done, then the work came your way. Marie was one of those who was dependable. As with our other students, the more Marie did, the more she learned. The harder students work, the more they put in, the more they get out. Soon, they were managing the patients themselves. Marie started out as an R1 (first-year resident) and became an R3. That is a compliment.

Roland Miller

MAST helicopter from Mountain Home Air Force Base taking off from Fourth of July Work Center (formerly Sawtooth Valley Ranger Station), Sawtooth NRA. Vietnam War pilots transporting wounded soldiers helped create a foundation for EMS.

Airlift Northwest, part of UW Medicine

Dr. Copass was driven to create Airlift Northwest after, lacking air transport, three children died from burns in a housefire in Sitka, Alaska.

Time before arriving at the hospital is vital for patients. First, EMS staff have to stabilize the patient. You must anticipate catastrophe. Are you prepared if the pressure drops from volume loss? Are you ready for a pneumothorax if your patient took a gunshot to the chest? Whether your patient lives or dies may depend on whether you anticipate a catastrophe.

We prepared our students for acute care in the field so that patients are alive and stable when they arrive at the hospital. Using EMS, we pushed the work we do in the ER out into the field. Training is key. The pioneers in EMS, like Paul Anderson of Idaho, were deeply committed to training, a commitment that is eroding over time.

Air ambulances began with the military. Medevac helicopters transporting injured soldiers in Vietnam served as models for civilian operations. The military-to-civilian air ambulance bridge was MAST (Military Assistance to Safety and Traffic). This program enabled military medevac helicopter crews to gain additional training while helping civilian communities respond to emergencies. In the 1970s, we had MAST support here in the Seattle area. In central Idaho, Marie depended on MAST helicopters based in Mountain Home Air Force Base for moving trauma and burn cases out of the mountains.

Time is key. In the 1970s, we began looking at Harborview and Children's Hospital ambulance arrivals. Then came the catastrophe in Sitka. In 1980, I got a call from Sitka's surgeon, George Longenbaugh, after giving a lecture in Sitka. There had been a house fire, burning three children, and George needed help. We needed to transport those badly burned kids from Sitka to Harborview's burn unit. I was on the phone begging for charter aircraft. I was finally able to get a plane from Oregon. We loaded a twelve-year-old girl into the aircraft. She died on the flight.

Why is a doctor using precious time calling around to find air transport while kids are at risk of dying? Instead, there should be one number you call for readily available air ambulance transport to the hospital.

Losing those three children in Sitka never left me. Their deaths led to Airlift Northwest, a Harborview and University of Washington program. We started in 1982 with fixed-wing and added helicopter transport. Airlift Northwest became our response to calls for help from the field, the region's first critical care air ambulance service. "One call does all." That was our motto.

To advance EMS in Alaska, George Longenbaugh, MD and I collaborated during those years. Dr. Longenbaugh completed his surgical residency at Johns Hopkins and moved with his family to Sitka in 1963. Dr. Longenbaugh struggled to help trauma patients in Southeast Alaska's isolated communities. His work was instrumental in helping establish EMS in Alaska. He trained workers in floating logging camps, and commercial fishermen, to manage the severely injured. In his honor, Alaska gives the "Memorial Longenbaugh Award" to a physician who exemplifies leadership and dedication to the state's EMS systems. Mount Longenbaugh near Sitka is named for him.

Another physician was Jack Davis, MD, who practiced internal medicine and cardiology in Kalispell for thirty-five years. Dr. Davis took action in 1975 after a twenty-six-year-old logger was crushed in an accident near Hungry Horse Reservoir. Without an air ambulance, a Forest Service helicopter transported the trauma patient dangling in a wire basket. Unfortunately, the young man died in flight. In response, Dr. Davis helped create a hospital-based helicopter ambulance service called ALERT (Advanced Life-support and Emergency Rescue Team).

Dr. Davis served as ALERT's medical director for seventeen years and then for another ten years on its board. ALERT was the first of its kind to serve rural America and the second in the nation. Building that air ambulance system from the ground up took a lot of work by many people. Firefighters and rescue units also get credit for using and supporting the air ambulance.

Air ambulance started as a public service and evolved into a money-maker for hospitals, losing its glamor. Ultimately, hospitals won't support a public service unless they get paid.

The public takes EMS for granted. Until the 1960s and '70s, there was no EMS. Once people have it, they expect it. Today, if you were to take away EMS, people in rural and urban communities together would scream at the legislature. Unfortunately, few political leaders were willing to advocate for excellent, reliable, affordable EMS care. One who saw EMS as a public service was King County executive Ron Sims. Sims promoted EMS and campaigned on it.

Fire chiefs have incentives to include EMS in their operations. Fire stations get calls to help older people who fall, are on the ground, and are too weak to get off the floor without help. You take care of those older adults. Do you know what older people do? They talk to their friends and family. Positive stories spread like wildfire. Positive stories bring public support.

My OB clerkship in medical school took me to Chicago's South Side, where there was a lot of poverty. Women, some of whom had no prenatal care, would get referred to the maternity clinic. A nurse-midwife and medical student staffed the clinic. The midwife knew pregnancies and deliveries. Those pregnant mothers were in the good hands of the midwife — and so were the medical students.

When nurse practitioners first started at Harborview, they had a good fund of knowledge. They were RNs. Some, like Marie, knew from their life experiences of being pregnant, giving birth, and raising kids. In the ER, Marie and other NPs could bring their life experiences to bear to help our patients.

Intervening to better a patient's life might be "Meals on Wheels" or a bus ticket to a shelter. Some ER patients may need nursing home placement. In the ER, you apply your medical knowledge and your knowledge of systems to help and advocate for your patients.

In training others, you look for students who want to work hard, take direction, be responsible, and hold themselves accountable. Personal accountability is critical. Healthcare providers are not born accountable. During training, you watch students like a hawk. Once you find people willing to work hard and be accountable, giving them responsibility is easy. You start with an eager soul like Marie, desperate to learn and looking for new responsibilities. As she demonstrates competency, you give her responsibility. Let responsibility be her teacher.

In EMS, women can do the same job as men. Women will have hills to climb, the "teasing hill" for one. Keep at it. Former Navy SEALs staffed Fire Station 28 in Seattle's Rainier Valley. The men put up a sign taunting women: "If you can't do the work, ring the bell and leave." The next day, there was no bell — just pansies. I was there in the 1970s when women went into EMS. Men accepting women was the norm.

For women, getting started in EMS was challenging. Many of the women were as strong as the guys. They steeled themselves to be as tough as any man. These are people, women and men, who enter burning buildings, putting their lives on the line by running toward a crisis. At first, when women sought work in fire stations, men pushed back. Men didn't want the liability of protecting a woman while also trying to survive. Women come to EMS work with valuable knowledge. Many have raised a family. They know what it takes. They still end up having to prove themselves. We all do.

Training is a forever commitment in EMS. Create societal incentives so that people want that training. For example, becoming an EMT in the workplace could be a condition of employment or extra pay. For school bus drivers, city bus drivers, and taxicab drivers: train them. Be creative. Make EMS apparent everywhere.

People stay engaged if shown they're successful. Do the metrics: EMS did how many thousands of runs? EMS provided care for how many thousands of lives? What was the survival rate? Collecting and crunching the numbers are vital. People in EMS who are making a sacrifice need to know that the metrics support them in making a real difference in the lives of their community.

You need survival and morbidity metrics to prove the system is working. Measure response times: How long did it take to reach a guy who caught his leg in a mowing machine, bleeding to death? Or the hand that came off in a bailer? Or the logging truck driver who didn't tighten the chain, and a log rolled on his chest? How long did it take to get to these people?

Beyond the metrics are living, breathing outcomes: the woman who survived two broken legs and is walking. The baby, burned in the house fire, who is starting school. And that baby's mother? She tells her baby's story and how firefighters and EMTs saved her child and comforted her and her family in the worst moments of their lives. She will never forget — nor will you.

Accept all the help you can, use that help, and make people proud of what they are doing.

EMS is a community responsibility. Doctors locally have to buy in for quality control and to participate actively. Law enforcement has to buy in, too. The guys drinking coffee at the local "liars' club" must be supportive. Local businesses have to buy in. People walking past businesses will come upon one with a sign, "Defibrillator located here. We're ready for catastrophes." Support those businesses. Walk on in.

Funding EMS is a challenge. We will tax ourselves for fire protection services based on assessed property value. The same holds for emergency medical services, so lump fire and EMS together: two-for-one pricing. Fire chiefs are wise to combine the two to build community support. With community support comes budgets for equipment and personnel.

When a farmer gets hurt in Franklin County, family and friends need EMS to work. First, you train everyone to know how to use the equipment. Then once a month, you bring people together for part training, part social events. Organize and be prepared to save lives. After all, it may be your own, or the life of someone you love.

14

CREATING THE NURSE PRACTITIONER: DRIVEN BY THE REALITIES OF THE UNDERSERVED

In April and May [1972], the Board of Medicine and the Board of Nursing formally adopted the rules and regulations for the expanding role of the registered professional nurse. It might be of interest to you to know that Idaho is the only state in the Union that has developed this type of approach to legalizing the practice of nursing within the expanding role.

Memorandum, Board of Nursing, Dept. of Law Enforcement, State of Idaho, June 16, 1972.

The Impossible Dream

"On February 7, 1972, a group of farseeing dedicated people of the Stanley area met at the Rod and Gun Club with Gary Steinbach of the Idaho Hospital Association to discuss the possibility of providing nurse, ambulance, and clinic services for this area. The unit to be known as the Salmon River Medical Center.

Emergency medical training for ambulance attendants, provision for a nurse practitioner, building site, building plans, and methods of financing were also discussed. The requirement for two doctors to support the clinic was met by Doctors Packer and Gwinner volunteering their services.

Marie Osborn, our nurse practitioner, was at this time taking an Emergency Medical Nurse Practitioners course at the University of Washington followed by an internship in the emergency room and lab of St. Alphonsus Hospital in Boise. Since that time, she has completed the Family Practitioners Program at the University of Utah followed by 800 hours [of] internship at Blaine County and Sun Valley Hospitals plus one month of independent study specializing in lab training and radiology. The residents and visitors of this area are indeed fortunate to have someone with such exceptional ability and dedication to staff our clinic...."

Dedication of the Salmon River Emergency Clinic and Open House, Stanley, Idaho, June 15, 1975

I didn't know what I was getting into. Advanced practice nursing was new to me. I had never met an NP except for pediatric NPs in other states. Dr. Copass, other Harborview staff, and Seattle's new paramedics helped prepare me for what was to come. In May 1972, two months after the completion of my Harborview training, I saw my first patient at the Stanley Clinic. We celebrated the clinic's opening on Father's Day.

Our first clinic was a small log cabin across the street from the Kasino Club, one of Stanley's three bars. During the school year, we shared our small rental house with Stanley's sole teacher, Judy Uresti. The living room doubled as the clinic reception room and makeshift morgue, the bedroom was our exam room, and the kitchen doubled as a lab and pharmacy. My daughter, Debbie, walked the short distance from the schoolhouse to the clinic kitchen for lunch.

When we had dead bodies in the clinic kitchen or reception/living room, I'd call Judy so she could stay away until we moved the body, usually to the mortuary in Hailey. Judy was gracious and a great gal from a long-time Idaho ranching family.

Our landlord, Marvin Larson, a Forest Service retiree, was also the president of the clinic's board. Marvin and Fern Larson donated the cabin rent-free so that we could open the Stanley Clinic. But we also had to name the clinic.

Ever have trouble naming a baby? Try naming a clinic. Salmon, Idaho, already had its "Salmon River Clinic." In 1972, as we planned the clinic, we wanted to avoid the political minefield of "medical" and emphasize "emergency." Finally, on April 5, 1972, community leaders agreed to "Salmon River Emergency Clinic." After I retired from the Stanley Clinic in 1999 and was unavailable for emergency calls, the clinic board dropped the word "Emergency." Today, a half-century later, the clinic sign says "Salmon River Clinic." I mostly call it the "Stanley Clinic."

We tried to handle animals on the front sidewalk, which is where I was, on my knees wearing my white coat and cowboy boots, pulling porcupine quills, when I looked up to see the head of the Board of Nursing, Eileen Merrell, looking down at the dog and me.

I finished de-quilling the dog on the sidewalk, gathered the quills, and picked up the bloody sheet. The dog's owner thanked me as Eileen and I walked into the clinic together. Eileen never once mentioned the dog.

Eileen, representing the Board of Nursing, helped troubleshoot challenges. One was my title: what would I be called?

In 1971, Eileen and I talked about my title in conversations at the state capitol's Hall of Mirrors. By then, articles in nursing journals had described the groundbreaking work of Loretta Ford, RN, and Henry Silver, MD, training RNs in Colorado as NPs to provide pediatric care in underserved areas. My work in Idaho's Sawtooth country would focus on emergency medical services.

After lengthy discussions, we settled on "Nurse Practitioner" as the title for advanced practice nursing in Idaho.

Sounding close to "practical nurse," Eileen and I knew "nurse practitioner" was not ideal. Why would an RN train to become an LPN (licensed practical nurse) with less training?

"I'm Marie Osborn. I'm a nurse practitioner," is how I introduced myself to my patients and healthcare colleagues. If patients called me "doctor," I corrected them: I am not a doctor.

There was no well-traveled trail to becoming a nurse practitioner. As the first licensed NP, I saw no trail at all. We created the profession as we went along, driven by the authentic need to provide medical care for people living in and visiting the Sawtooth country of central Idaho.

At a time when almost all doctors were men, when asked to explain my new profession, I responded, "A nurse practitioner is not a mini-doctor. She's a super nurse."

In 1971, the US Secretary of Health, Education, and Welfare, Elliot Richardson, recommended expanding the scope of nursing practice and enabling nurses to serve as primary care providers. For Stanley, Idaho, lacking another option, the healthcare solution was creating an NP position.

That same year, 1971, was when I had that fateful conversation with John Hutchinson of the Idaho Hospital Association, and he assigned his intern, Gary Steinbach, to help me set up a clinic in Stanley. Gary was a mix of an energizer bunny and a miracle worker.

Gary tried to interest the doctors at Moritz Hospital in Sun Valley in serving as preceptors in July 1971. They were the closest physicians to Stanley, and it just made sense. I met with the doctors. The Sun Valley doctors, led by Ivan John Gustafson, MD ("Dr. Gus"), said, "No."

The Sun Valley physicians would only support an NP position in Stanley if it was year-round. However, at the time, we assumed that healthcare services in Stanley would be seasonal. After all, only about thirty to sixty people lived in Stanley during the dead of winter. In contrast, hundreds of thousands of tourists visited the Sawtooth country during the summer even before the National Recreation Area designation. Financially, providing year-round medical care would not pencil out. Further, I was an unlikely prospect as a forty-year-old woman who hadn't worked in nursing for eighteen years, and whose husband and five kids were in Boise most of the year.

Gary next talked with two family physicians in Hailey, Dr. Robert Gwinner and Dr. Aldan Packer. While most of the people in Stanley got their medical care in Ketchum-Sun Valley, a few went to Hailey. Gary set up a meeting with the Hailey physicians. At the time, this meeting seemed like a "pig in a poke." I didn't know them. I drove up from Boise and walked into the meeting, knowing they'd say "no" just as the doctors in Sun Valley and Ketchum had.

Dr. Packer and Dr. Gwinner were very different men in personality and appearance. Dr. Packer was a Mormon bishop, tall and thin, wearing glasses, and with a well-hidden sense of humor. Dr. Gwinner was shorter, often smiled, had a good sense of humor, and had a reputation for being easier to work with.

We met at the Blaine County Hospital in Hailey. Standing at the nurses' station desk, we talked about the project. I spoke of the desperate need in the Sawtooth country and asked for their help.

They looked at each other. "Sure, Marie, we'll do it," Dr. Packer said. I was stunned. As I reflect on their decision, I know the project would have stopped right then and there without those two physicians. They were our last hope.

Once the two Hailey physicians said yes, doors opened. Gary sent out a flurry of letters to build support for the project. The Idaho Boards of Medicine, Nursing, and Pharmacy agreed to support establishing a nurse practitioner position in Stanley. All three boards agreed to jointly promulgate rules and regulations for the Stanley project as the first NP position for the state of Idaho.

At our cabin on Shaw Mesa, communication wasn't available: Telephone and EMS radio were years away. Still, when people were in trouble and needed help, word came. I got called to see one poor fellow with severe COPD on oxygen living in a sheepherder wagon. One of his mules kicked him in the chest, sending him into respiratory distress.

Another case that scared the bejeebers out of me and underscored my need for more training involved an allergy shot. My oldest son, Calvin, was cooking at Sessions Lodge about four miles from the cabin. A woman came in and shared that her eight-year-old daughter needed an allergy shot. Calvin, who had been volunteering his mother to help others, provided the mother and daughter with directions to the cabin. Thankful for the help from this lovely young man, they arrived unannounced at the cabin.

I hadn't given a shot in eighteen years, and never an allergy shot. The mother didn't have syringes for the allergy shots, just the medication. I had some standard sterile syringes — not TB syringes that we used for allergy shots. I calculated the dose. I gave one injection. No problem. But as I injected the second, I realized my calculation was wrong, and I was giving twice the dose.

I disclosed my error to the mother and daughter and kept that child and her mother at the cabin for an hour. I was sweating, scared that I had hurt the child, that if she had a complication or went into anaphylaxis, I had nothing available: no antihistamines, corticosteroids, or epinephrine.

The daughter did fine, but I didn't. That was one of the scariest moments of my life. In that "come to Jesus" moment, I knew I should not have given that injection. More than any other experience, that day burned into me the need for more training if I was going to provide care for people. And so began my put-together training to become Stanley's NP.

Gary worked magic with his letters. My first training was to reorient into nursing at Boise's two hospitals, St. Luke's and St. Alphonsus ("St. Al's"). St. Al's had just opened its new building with a new emergency department.

After so many years out of nursing, I was struck by how hospitals had changed. Specialty units like the coronary care unit (CCU) were entirely new to me. Other services, notably the delivery rooms, remained unchanged with time. The two hospitals agreed to coordinate to avoid duplication of costly services and diagnostic equipment. St. Al's took major trauma and neurology, and St. Luke's did obstetrics and pediatrics. At both Boise hospitals, I reoriented and spent time in the ERs and specialty wards.

"Mrs. Osborn will start her month's experience in Seattle at Harborview Hospital on February 14, 1972. ... Mrs. Osborn has been keeping a record of the procedures and experiences she has had to date at St. Luke's Hospital, Boise, as well as other observations and educational (formal) opportunities. At the present time, she is auditing the first two weeks of our coronary care training program.

The experience at Seattle will be primarily under the direction of the Nursing Department in a program worked out conjointly with Mrs. Osborn and Mrs. Lucke, and also with Dr. Eugene Hessel, the attending physician. You indicated that Dr. Hessel is interested in the nurse's "expanded role"—a fortunate coincidence, we feel."

Letter from Eileen Merrell, R.N., Western Interstate Commission for Higher Education
to Hilke Faber, R.N., Washington/Alaska RMP, February 1, 1972

While I reoriented to nursing in Boise, Gary worked with the Idaho Board of Nursing to secure funding for me to attend an emergency training program at Harborview Medical Center in Seattle.

The grant paid for part of my travel expenses and an apartment that, while filthy, was close to Harborview and cleaned up nicely. I returned to where I'd started working as an RN. In those two decades, from 1953 until 1972, Harborview, once a county hospital, had become part of the University of Washington and a teaching hospital. Today, Harborview is the state of Washington's sole level 1 adult and pediatric trauma and burn center.

When I arrived at Harborview in February 1972, it had paint peeling in the hallways and looked like another run-down county hospital. Harborview had teaching staff, resident physicians, and interns, but I was its first nurse practitioner student.

We created that first NP training program as we went along, based on what the teaching faculty thought I would need to care for patients in rural Idaho. We would discuss what we thought I should try to see and do. Next, the Harborview teaching faculty would provide that training.

While I loved to sew and embroider clothes, I hadn't sewed human skin. One of the Harborview ER doctors showed me how to inject local anesthetic and suture. "Marie, the next one who comes in will be yours."

The "next one" was this poor fellow in the Harborview ER, probably homeless. He was severely alcohol intoxicated. His left cheek was ripped open with an extensive, ugly, spiculated laceration. With more experience, I would have referred that facial wound to a plastic surgeon. "Here you are, Marie," said my attending physician. "Fix him."

I cleaned the wound with betadine and injected lidocaine into the wound margins. As the patient snored, I tried to determine how much lidocaine to use. However, the alcohol was serving as general anesthesia, and the patient was oblivious as I began to suture. Two hours later, the wound was closed. Like delicate embroidery, that carefully sutured cheek was a lovely piece of stitchery.

One of the first Harborview doctors who taught me about suturing said you always assume that eventually, you will meet your handiwork walking down the street towards you. Looking at my patient still snoring, I was proud of my first suture job. Others were impressed, too. Several ER staff came to look. After that, lacerations came my way.

Harborview teaching staff wanted me to learn emergency airways, a handy skill in rural Idaho. If you can't intubate and are out of options, performing a tracheostomy can save a life. To my procedure list, the faculty added "emergency tracheostomy."

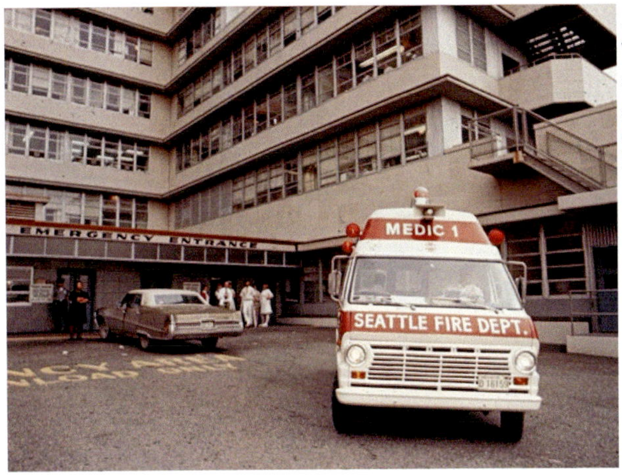

Medic One Foundation

Seattle's Harborview Medical Center, with its newly created Medic 1 paramedic program, was on EMS's leading edge when Marie arrived in 1972.

An ER attending physician stopped me in the hallway and told me that a patient needed a tracheostomy, and it was my turn. He and I walked into the room and found the woman in severe respiratory distress. Her neck was markedly swollen. She never opened her eyes. The ER doc quickly concluded this was not a teaching case, paged the surgery team, and moved her to the OR for an emergency tracheostomy.

In my nearly thirty years running the Stanley Clinic and Stanley Ambulance, I never performed an emergency tracheostomy. However, during those years, more airway options became available, for which I was thankful.

The nursing superintendent for Harborview set it up for me to audit classes for training King County Medic One's paramedics. During the day, I'd see patients in the ER; then, I trained with paramedics at night. Paramedics walked me back to my apartment near the ER late at night.

I really needed trauma training and experience. In 1972, a trauma unit for Medic One was just up and running. When I asked to ride the ambulance, the response was no: trauma ambulances were unsuitable for a woman. Eventually, I would ride a trauma ambulance in Chicago's South Side, but not Seattle.

As a woman, I was allowed to ride an ambulance for cardiac emergencies. One emergency call came on a Friday evening, around five o'clock. With Puget Sound rain pouring down, we drove the viaduct downtown to Frederick and Nelson Department Store and ran up the escalator carrying equipment into the "women's lounge," where we found our patient with chest pain.

At the end of my Harborview training in 1972, the University of Washington issued a certificate listing the procedures that I had done. The Idaho Board of Nursing then issued my emergency NP certificate, a first, to place on the wall at the Stanley Clinic.

The Idaho Board of Nursing issued NP licenses, and I received number "2;" there is no NP license number 1.

In Idaho during the early 1970s, nurses could become NPs based on experience, a bachelor's degree in nursing or better, and attending an approved NP training program such as the University of Washington's at Harborview. In 1972, there were few bachelor-degree nurses in Idaho.

Initially, the legislature placed control of NPs under the joint supervision of three professional boards: Medicine, Pharmacy, and Nursing. The Board of Medicine insisted on its involvement in overseeing NPs as a condition for legislative support.

The Idaho Board of Nursing retained responsibility for ensuring NPs followed the regulations promulgated by all three boards. At a practical level, the Board of Nursing drafted regulations and sent them to the other two boards. Unfortunately, the draft regulations were not well received, particularly by the Board of Medicine, stretching out the approval process.

Once approved, the three boards sent the rules they expected me to follow. These included having an Idaho-licensed physician as a preceptor with whom I would consult. The three professional boards also requested that I write out and submit all of my treatment protocols.

At a practical level, two to three times a year, I would take a representative number of charts (an armful, perhaps twelve of my more challenging cases) over Galena Summit to Hailey and sit down with Dr. Packer or Dr. Gwinner. They would review each chart, perhaps write a comment, and countersign and date my note.

The rule from the three boards also required that my physician preceptor visit the clinic once a week and see patients with me. However, given the distances, mountains, and weather, this proved onerous.

Rural Idaho's realities quickly upended the rules and regulations written in Boise. The boards relaxed requirements for weekly chart reviews. The required weekly in-clinic presence of a physician preceptor soon became every two weeks instead, and, in the wintertime, once a month. Eventually, an NP legislator, Senator Sheila Sorensen, led the Idaho Legislature in ending the requirement for physician preceptors altogether. Today, in Idaho, NPs are "LIPs": licensed independent practitioners.

When I picked up the phone at the Stanley Clinic and made calls for my patients, hostility might answer the phone. While most physicians, nurses, and pharmacists were supportive, not all were. One night I rode an ambulance to Sun Valley. The hospital's nurse supervisor was working that night. "I'll never take an order from you," she said coldly. I replied calmly, "That's okay, because I'll never give you an order."

For some older nurses, doctors were men and nurses were women. However, younger nurses were generally more supportive of advanced practice nursing.

Today, when you see an NP, you probably don't think twice. You don't stop to ask yourself, "Now, what is a nurse practitioner?" When I introduced myself, saying, "I'm Marie. I'm a nurse practitioner," the usual response was a blank stare or questioning look, or the question, "Excuse me, Marie. What is a nurse practitioner?" Even Stanley community members wanted to know and probably had doubts. We made it up as we went along, responding to rural realities.

"I'm a super-nurse, not a mini-doctor," became my trademark tagline.

Alone and facing major trauma and other emergencies, I longed for the education that medical doctors receive. I was not able to attend medical school and residency training. Besides, small rural communities can be a good fit for an advanced practice provider — an NP or PA — but not a physician. Still, when people's lives are in jeopardy, you want to be ready.

We formally opened the Salmon River Emergency Clinic on June 14, 1972, Father's Day. An Idaho Falls physician, Dr. Cutler, a general practitioner and ENT, had read about our effort to establish the clinic and, upon retiring, donated his office equipment. Some of the items were museum pieces, even wrapped in newspaper from 1918. Unfortunately, one of his exam tables was unsafe: If patients sat too close to one end, the table would tip. Still, Dr. Cutler's gift was a great kindness that got us started. He donated all his instruments, including an obstetrical stethoscope and calipers for pelvic checks, an old EKG machine, office furniture, and even his black bag. And Dr. Cutler came for our grand opening.

We interrupted cookies and punch for an emergency: A dog had ripped open its abdomen running through the brush, and I sewed it up.

New at "U": Nursing Program Aids Doctorless

SALT LAKE. Improved primary healthcare for thousands of residents of the Intermountain West is the goal of a new program in the University of Utah College of Nursing.

Registered nurses living in underserved and rural and urban areas will learn to function as family nurse practitioners who will work in clinics, physician's offices or remote from the physician in very small communities which have no readily available health services.

The nurses will be prepared to assess and handle common illnesses in emergencies and provide health maintenance programs for families and individuals, according to Dr. Madeline Leininger, dean of the College of Nursing....

Eagle Advertiser, Murry, Utah, September 26, 1974

When the head of the Board of Nursing, Eileen Merrell, found me de-quilling that dog on the sidewalk in front of the Salmon River Emergency clinic, she came with a message. The Board of Nursing wanted me to enroll in the first NP class at the University of Utah.

"Marie," Eileen started, "Your training at Harborview was for an emergency nurse practitioner. So, you're fine if someone comes in with an acute sore throat or earache ready to rupture. But you're not legal to manage blood pressure or follow up on your emergency call."

I'd been doing school physicals for the kids attending Stanley's Quonset Hut schoolhouse. "Technically, Marie, you're not legal to do physicals by the Nursing Practice Act," Eileen said.

In the eyes of the Boards of Medicine, Nursing, and Pharmacy, if you were dying and I provided emergency care, that was okay. But if you just needed your blood pressure managed or a routine pelvic or prostate exam, I wasn't legal.

The Board of Nursing actively supported my attending Harborview for training to become an emergency nurse practitioner. Next, the board required me to complete a certified program as a Family NP. Unfortunately, the closest training program was in Salt Lake City at the University of Utah.

By 1974 you could become an NP in two ways. One was a traditional master's degree program in nursing that lasted about two years and, once completed, would allow you to teach and see patients.

The second was a certificate program involving graduate level training, lasting about one year, and preparing NP graduates to see patients. My objective was to staff the Stanley Clinic, not to become a teacher, so the certificate program was the better choice. Still, I became a teacher of rural healthcare for EMTs, NP students, premeds, medical students, and a few resident physicians.

The certificate program lasted one year: three months of lectures and labs at the University of Utah and the remaining nine months in an internship, capped by writing a thesis. The Board of Nursing helped find a scholarship, but funding was limited and only covered lodging, travel to Salt Lake City (but no budget to return home), and books. My husband, Cal, was generous and covered the rest of my expenses.

This first-ever NP class at the University of Utah consisted of twelve to fifteen women: all female nurses, generally thirty to forty years old. Several were physicians' office nurses from southern Idaho. A few were from Utah. Whereas I had been working as an emergency NP doing suturing and other procedures, none of my classmates had sutured.

Lectures and labs dominated our days at the University of Utah. For hands-on clinical experience, one of our assignments was working in a nursing home. We also trained in the emergency room at St. Mark's Hospital in Salt Lake City. In contrast to the hands-on training of the Harborview ER, at St. Mark's, we stood and observed doctors doing patient care. For suturing practice, we used cadavers.

NPs were a new profession, and many Salt Lake City doctors were unwilling to help train us. Only one dermatologist was willing to work with NP students. Diagnosing rashes is challenging in primary care, so I pushed for this training with our instructors. Rashes in the flesh look different than on the page.

"I don't want you intimidating my office staff," the dermatologist warned during our orientation. His office staff were all women, and he'd trained them. None had a nursing background or other official training. The doctor's warning made us uncomfortable. Our group of professional women would not engage in that sort of behavior. As the University of Utah's first class of NPs, we were trying to make our way. Ours was a new program, and he didn't know what to expect and was probably apprehensive and aggressive. Nevertheless, we were grateful for his teaching.

After three months in Salt Lake City, I started an eight-hundred-hour internship while juggling my work at the Stanley Clinic and my family responsibilities at home in Boise. Rural clinics need to run basic labs and take X-rays. Part of my internship was at the lab and radiology departments at the new St. Alphonsus Hospital in Boise. I also saw patients in Hailey at the emergency room and office practice of Dr. Packer and Dr. Gwinner. When those doctors left Hailey, I covered their practice and, at night, slept in a chair in Dr. Packer's office.

When you step into a new professional role, having patients accept and trust you as their caregiver is not a given. Patient relationships take time. Patients expected to see male doctors.

A truck driver had requested a vasectomy. Dr. Packer was in the middle of the procedure when he asked me to enter the room and help hand the instruments. This sizeable man with his genitals exposed was appalled that a woman was in the room. "Don't worry," said Dr. Packer, the Mormon bishop, to put him at ease. "She's seen it before."

Packer and Gwinner ran a small clinic in the farming community of Fairfield, located between Hailey and Mountain Home. The clinic was staffed part-time with a physician assistant, who flew his plane from Hailey's airport, landed, and saw patients. As part of my NP internship, Packer and Gwinner thought the Fairfield clinic would be a good experience while giving the PA a break.

In the Fairfield clinic, once an old-fashioned drug store, time stood still. Drugs in the back room dated from the early 1900s. Arsenic was one old medication that caught my eye. The bathroom was a tiny room that had been added; you walked up to the toilet. It was like sitting on a throne, looking out over the old drugstore. The curtains were heavy, royal blue velvet.

On my first afternoon, nobody ventured into the Fairfield clinic.

Nobody came in on the second afternoon.

Two days later, I returned to sit alone in a clinic with no patients. Then, I heard someone walking into the clinic. Standing before me was one of the tallest people I've ever seen, well over six and a half feet. He was a huge, older man who came for his tetanus shot. He was a county commissioner who also came to check me out. It must have been a good tetanus shot, because after that, I was busy.

The Fairfield clinic was the second time I passed inspection with a tetanus shot. In Lower Stanley, Jerry Funderberg, owner of Jerry's Country Store, insisted that while the Stanley Clinic was fine for tourists, locals didn't need it and took care of themselves. Jerry carried weight in the community, and voters elected him as a Custer County commissioner for many years.

Then came that day when he needed the clinic. Jerry was tearing down a shed in the back of his store when he ripped his arm on a rusty nail. The wound didn't need suturing, but Jerry hadn't had a tetanus shot for years. That meant closing his business and driving 120 miles round-trip. Instead, Jerry wanted care at the Stanley Clinic.

In those first years the cabin had no telephone or emergency radio. Our clinic's first board president, Marvin Larson, who lived on the valley floor, looked up at Shaw Mesa for my orange VW beetle, then came and got me.

When Jerry called Marvin about needing a tetanus shot, Marvin became excited. Of all the local naysayers who now wanted to use the clinic, Jerry was a breakthrough. Almost overnight, Jerry became an ardent supporter of the clinic, serving on the clinic board and, later, as board president.

With eight hundred hours of internship completed in Hailey, Fairfield, and Boise, I submitted the paperwork to the Board of Nursing. After my Harborview training, I was certified as an Emergency Nurse Practitioner. After completing the University of Utah program, I was a Family Nurse Practitioner and "legal" to provide primary care. But still, I wanted more trauma training. Next up was the Cook County ER and Morgue in South Side Chicago.

When I arrived for three months of training in 1976, Cook County Hospital was one of the largest hospitals in the world: a capacity of 4,500 beds with almost 100,000 admissions each year. Cook County Hospital's emergency room was renowned for excellence in trauma care. I wanted that experience to prepare me for trauma in wild Idaho.

Similar to Seattle's Harborview, with trauma and burn cases being flown in from adjoining states, at Cook County, major trauma cases came from surrounding areas, including Indiana. In addition, Cook County Hospital served South Side Chicago.

Advanced practice nursing was still in the future in Illinois. Staff nurses were not used to seeing a nurse practitioner suturing patients. Still, I had a valuable educational experience; people were friendly and supportive.

Tunnels connected all the buildings at Cook County Hospital, so people didn't have to walk out on the street. Most nurses felt safer on the streets than in the tunnels, which were big enough to drive a car through. With lighting dim and security sparse, they were spooky. I didn't walk alone; I usually traveled with someone else at the shift change.

While working in the ER, I slept across the street at an old dorm for nurses as part of a former nursing school. My room was on the third floor. There was a TV, and I thought, "Great, I can watch football!" Unfortunately, the TV didn't work.

Like Harborview in Seattle, Cook County was a county hospital with a teaching mission. Ambulances brought patients, and so did the police. In 1976, patients packed the ER. Ambulances delivered people with gunshot wounds, stabbing wounds, and overdoses. So many of South Side Chicago's failings ended up in the ER. While some people abuse the system, emergency rooms are places of last resort and a lifeline for many people at the margins.

On the first floor were the ambulance bays and treatment rooms. The triage nurse met everyone at the front door. Severe trauma, including life-threatening gunshot wounds or stabbings, rolled into the stat elevator for the trauma team on the third floor. The trauma team was the most synchronized I'd ever seen, almost beautiful in the choreography of physicians, nurses, technical support staff, and others. From the trauma room, patients headed to an OR.

The ER staff were kept busy with alcohol intoxication and withdrawal, liver cirrhosis, mental health disorders, and drug overdoses. Chicago's finest delivered a homeless man with ongoing seizures. The resident physician ordered Valium, stopping the seizures. I needed to pull off the man's cowboy boots to complete my neurologic exam. I tugged and tugged to get a boot off, finally succeeding. The sockless foot and distal calf were crawling with maggots.

Before coming to Cook County, I served as a deputy coroner and then Custer County coroner. The ER's charge nurse heard of my background and facilitated a training rotation through the Cook County Morgue. I spent two weeks in the morgue working with pathology residents doing autopsies. In Illinois, all unattended deaths required an autopsy. In Chicago, many people died alone.

"I ran out of money and couldn't buy my medications," I heard repeatedly from patients with diabetic ketoacidosis, COPD exacerbations, and hypertensive emergencies. Welfare checks were a lifeline for people with low incomes,

Cook County Health

both urban and rural. Yet, those public monies also fueled problems for people in poverty.

Patterns of pathology in the ER linked to the timing of the welfare checks. After welfare checks arrived, we saw an uptick in battery and suturing. What a horrible way to live: you wait all month for your welfare check, you finally have some money in your pocket, someone stabs you, beats you over the head, and you end up in the ER or the morgue. And your money is gone.

In the mid-1970s, most healthcare professions were dominated by white men, including firemen and the first paramedics. In South Side Chicago, I had the honor of integrating the ambulance staff by being the first woman to ride ambulance.

As in Seattle, I wanted the ambulance experience to prepare for emergency calls in rural Idaho. The nursing director arranged my experience at Harborview and Cook County. Chicago's fire department ran the ambulance service with paramedics based at fire stations. The men were firemen first and paramedics second.

The firemen told me exactly how they felt about having a woman in their fire department. I gave right back. Their fear for my safety was a constant. Perhaps the nursing staff had warned the firemen and paramedics not to let anything happen. They were great guys, despite the firemen's sexist jokes trying to get my goat. In the end, we worked it out, and another door began to open for women. The Cook County staff, those women who set up my training at the fire station, were thrilled. The firemen and paramedics didn't know that a woman had already been assigned to the fire station and would start in a few weeks. So, I was there partly to break the ice.

Ambulance crews came to work each shift with highly polished shoes and perfectly pressed uniforms. By the end of their shifts, they looked like hell. The fire station was near Cook County Hospital and high-rise public housing projects. Many of our emergency calls came from the

Projects, including Cabrini-Green. I couldn't imagine trying to raise my five children in this kind of place. So many people here were destitute, and almost everyone was Black. These pathetic buildings were nearly all they had.

The sheer poverty was unreal. You'd walk into these tenements and elevators reeking of urine — if there was an elevator or one that worked. Then you'd walk down a poorly lit hallway, knock on a door, and enter a packed little apartment. Almost invariably, these apartments were spotless. As you entered, looking back at you were the faces of small children and teenagers, parents, and grandparents. In Chicago's Cabrini-Green, multiple generations lived together, crammed into apartments.

I was born into rural poverty in Kentucky during the Great Depression. Still, South Side Chicago's urban poverty was eye-opening.

After my first month, I was "gung-ho." During the second month, my gung-ho had diminished. By the third month, my gung-ho had got up and gone. I was homesick for my Idaho mountains. I was tired of the noise, confusion, and poverty of living in a big city. I wanted to return to caring for my patients in Stanley again.

After working in ERs and riding ambulances in Chicago, Seattle, and Boise, I was better prepared for trauma in wild Idaho. That's not to say that trauma training in inner-city ERs is perfect for managing rural and mountain trauma.

The Stanley Ambulance trauma calls tended toward car and motorcycle crashes, bicycle and rafting incidents, and climbing accidents. In the mid-1970s, Chicago's South Side ambulances responded more to ODs, epileptics who stopped their anti-seizure meds, mental health crises, gunshot wounds, and stabbings. In Stanley, while we did have gunshot wounds, they were usually minor hunting accidents involving a hand, foot, or buttock. Stabbings were more likely to occur during a bar fight or hunting season when sportsmen were dressing out their elk or deer. We also saw few overdoses, unlike what came barreling through the doors of the Cook County ER.

Trauma's nexus for South Side Chicago and rural Idaho is this: People die unless we train, are prepared to act, and receive our community's support. The same organs are injured, although injury mechanisms and skin color may differ. People bleed, blood pressures drop, heart rhythms flat line, or patients become unresponsive, and we respond to save lives.

After three months, I returned from Chicago to my home in the Sawtooth Mountains of Idaho. Coming into the Valley, you take a deep breath that fills your entire body: the mountain air is so clean and fresh. On moonless nights, a billion stars fill the sky. In the stillness, you can hear the Salmon River from miles away. I'm a mountain girl at heart.

One of my Ketchum preceptor doctors had relocated to LA after a difficult divorce and offered me trauma training at Los Angeles County General ER. Although the scenery would be better in LA than Chicago and the weather warmer, I thanked him and said, "No." Stanley's summer tourist season was coming, and I'm not sure I could ever work in a big inner city. The city surrounds you and fills your lungs. You can't get away from it. To work in an inner-city ER, you live close to your work or commute. I couldn't live where I would see one broken-down building after another.

After five years of training as an emergency and family NP, I was ready to remain in my mountains, seeing patients and responding to emergency calls. I wanted to be home. My home was now in Idaho's Sawtooth Mountain and Salmon River country.

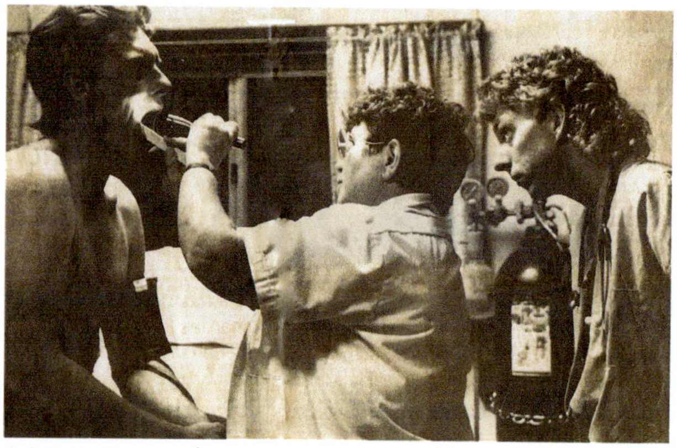

Paul Peck

Marie examines a throat as one of the premed interns from the College of Idaho looks on. From "At the Salmon River Clinic, interns discover the joys of frontier medicine" by Tony Huegel for The Post Register, Idaho Falls, Idaho, July 12, 1987

Portrait of a Distinguished Citizen

Marie Osborn

The Idaho Statesman

Marie Osborn, her husband Cal and their five children divide their time between Boise and the Stanley area. She noticed the lack of emergency medical care facilities in the Stanley area so she used her nurse's training to organize the Salmon River Emergency Clinic. It provides volunteer emergency treatment to anyone in the area needing treatment. A graduate of Ball State University and Ball Memorial Hospital School of Nursing in Muncie, Ind., Mrs. Osborn and her family have lived in Boise and Stanley since 1963. She has been active in the Pacific Northwest Ski Association, a former member of the Bogus Basin Ski Club board of directors and a co-host to the national lieutenant governors conference at Sun Valley in 1971. With the help of the Idaho Hospital Association, the town of Stanley and Drs. Alden Packer and Robert Gwinner of Hailey, she began the pilot Salmon River Emergency Clinic project.

Since that time Mrs. Osborn has taken advance medical training as an emergency nurse-practitioner at St. Luke's Hospital, a coronary care course sponsored by Nampa's Mercy Hospital and has attended the University of Washington Medical Center's emergency nurse practitioner course. She started an emergency [medical] technician's course at Stanley that has trained 20 Stanley residents to maintain the center. Mrs. Osborn has also been active in PTA functions, having served as past president of Highlands PTA, member of the Boise PTA council, District Eight PTA president and a member of the Idaho PTA board of directors. Born in Russellville, Ky., Mrs. Osborn was a member of the National Honor Society both in high school and college. Mrs. Osborn, her husband Cal and their children, Calvin, Jerry, John, Melinda and Debbie reside at 3015 Hillway Drive in Boise and in Stanley.

The Idaho Statesman. March 4, 1973

15

CREATING EMS: SAWTOOTH COUNTRY

State's First Nurse Practitioner Retires

The clinic first purchased a 1958-vintage Army surplus ambulance.

"You could see the highway through the floorboards, but it did its job," Osborn recalled.

From those humble beginnings, Stanley is on its fourth ambulance — a 1999 fully equipped model with a $93,000 price tag, covered by money set aside by the clinic board.

Barb Newlwert, *Times-News*, Twin Falls, Idaho, 1999

Bev Angel has taken the ambulance to Boise to have the electrical system checked and repaired. As of April 11, we are in for $400.00. The situation was becoming dangerous with lights going out, ambulance not starting, etc.

Salmon River Clinic — Hospital District Board of Directors Meeting, April 11, 1986

The ambulance broke down the Thursday before the Fourth when a bolt sheared off, hit the fan, and went into the radiator. Challis EMS loaned their backup ambulance for our use during the usually disaster-prone Fourth. Our ambulance was back 40 hours and $700 later, however, so it was not necessary to use the Challis ambulance. Thanks was expressed to the Challis group ....

Salmon River Clinic — Hospital District Board of Directors Meeting, July 10, 1986

Looking like an orange and white hearse, our first Stanley Ambulance was the '58 Pontiac. Hearses used to do double duty, transporting the living to a hospital, then returning to retrieve the dead. Our first ambulance saved many lives and, fortunately, didn't kill anyone.

With no money, we found a workaround with property declared "surplus" by the Armed Forces. After putting out feelers, we got a call that the US Army had a surplus ambulance. Fourteen years old, it was painted in military colors. In the back was a single gurney stretcher.

The Bishop Volkswagen Dealership in Boise volunteered to paint the ambulance orange and white with "Stanley Ambulance" stenciled in navy blue on the side. That ambulance looked so beautiful with new paint and mats on the floor. Unfortunately, those mats covered substantial holes in the floorboards.

On the return trips after dropping off patients at Sun Valley and Hailey, the more adventurous would remove the floor mats. While transporting patients, the mats stayed in place because you didn't want to scare anyone. Lifting them, you'd watch the blur of pavement. While the hole by the front passenger seat was big, the holes by the gurney in the back were small. Those holes probably explained the exhaust fumes inside the vehicle. Then, too, the ambulance floor got uncomfortably hot. With the gurney anchored in the middle, EMTs sat to the side and with more than one patient, we placed stretchers to keep people off the hot floor.

In the wintertime, though, the hot ambulance floor wasn't so bad. One mid-winter night ambulance run to Sun Valley, it was forty below zero. First, the windshield wipers stopped. Then the headlights went out. We kept going. Wearing gloves, I held a flashlight out the passenger side. Bob Fisher steered with his right hand and held a flashlight out the driver's side window with his gloved left hand. With both front windows open, and flashlights replacing headlights, we drove over Galena Summit with a patient having an acute MI. He lived, and so did we.

The Sawtooths are a lonely part of the world in the wintertime, and we were lucky that night driving over a mountain pass at forty below with no heat, no lights, no windshield wipers, no radio communications, and no law enforcement backup. Stanley sorely needed an ambulance that could be relied upon.

Indeed, our inaugural ambulance run did not go well. A boy was playing Tarzan, swinging from a tree. He fell, landing on a staub that pierced and embedded in his shoulder. I wasn't called; instead, Stella Critchfield and her daughter, Judy Smith, staffed the ambulance. The driver was Dubey Dubendorf, a retired engineer from New York.

Stella and Judy knew from their training to leave the staub embedded in the shoulder. They dressed the wound, anchoring the staub. People at the scene cut the branch to load the boy and gurney into the low-ceilinged Pontiac. They lifted the gurney and rolled it into the back of the ambulance. Then the problem arose: Stella and Judy didn't know how to lock the gurney into place to keep it from rolling.

The women positioned themselves on either side of the gurney and held it. Dubey headed for the hospital in Hailey. All was well until Dubey entered the curves over Galena Summit. The wheeled gurney began to roll back and forth. Stella and Judy tried but couldn't hold it. That poor kid was in agony.

Sawtooth Mountain Star

FULLY-EQUIPPED AMBULANCE is now available at Stanley, following fund drive. Community also has emergency treatment center. (SMS photo)

With lights flashing, Dubey drove past Ketchum-Sun Valley to Hailey. He went to Blaine County Hospital because my physician preceptors were there. Not knowing where the ER was, Dubey parked at the hospital's front door. As Judy and Stella began to offload the patient, the nursing supervisor marched out the front door. "What are you doing? You need to drive over to the ambulance bay."

Dubey replied, "I got him here; now, you take him." They did. After the rolling gurney incident, the board of directors for the Stanley Clinic directed me to staff all ambulance runs.

The '58 Pontiac was our starter ambulance. It did help people realize that the Sawtooth country needed an ambulance with EMTs. In the early 1970s, Idaho EMS (Emergency Medical Services) was still on the drawing board. Funds for an ambulance were not available. So, we put out donation jars at Stanley businesses and sent letters to our patients and clinic supporters. Dollar by dollar, we raised the money to buy our first new modern ambulance and retire the orange hearse.

New ambulances can be exciting — and intimidating. To help me retrieve our new ambulance, Jimbo Funderberg volunteered. Jimbo worked at Jerry's Country Store in Lower Stanley. Together we headed for Spokane, 450 miles away. Jimbo climbed into the new ambulance at the dealership, drove it back to our motel, and parked. He turned the key to turn off the engine. But, the ambulance kept running. Jimbo stepped out and held up the key.

"Hey Marie, I can't get it to stop."

"Jimbo, let's drive it back to the dealer."

"No," Jimbo said. "We're not going back. There has to be a way."

Jimbo was flustered. I certainly didn't know what to do. But I opened the driver's door and pulled myself up. Then, probably a force of habit, I stepped on the brake. The engine stopped.

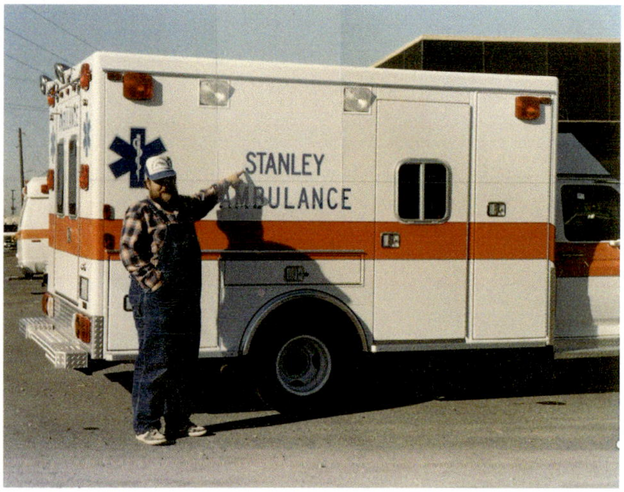

Jimbo Funderburg and the Stanley Ambulance

At the end of our trip, when Jimbo drove the ambulance into Lower Stanley, he turned on the siren and flashing lights. I'll never forget the grin on his face. He was so proud, and so were the people of Stanley. None of us thought we could do it. Ambulances are not cheap, and we raised $18,000 through donations plus help from Idaho EMS. Unfortunately, costs for a new ambulance have increased astronomically by 2020 to ten times what we paid in the mid-1970s.

Jimbo never did become an EMT. He loved driving the ambulance and took good care of the equipment. He set up a program to teach volunteer drivers including to avoid "hot rodding." We learned the hard way when people drove the Pontiac on dirt roads like they were driving freeways, twice breaking the axle. Blaine County loaned us an ambulance while ours was in the shop.

The first ding in Stanley's new ambulance happened one night while transporting a trauma patient. The intoxicated man fell down the boat-launch ramp for the Middle Fork at Boundary Creek.

Fred Dauber with the Forest Service remembers that ambulance run along with his wife, Marilyn:

> Marie, Marilyn, and I had made the ambulance run to Boundary Creek. After Marie stabilized the man, we returned to Stanley, let Marie off at the clinic, and continued to the Sun Valley hospital. Near the Idaho Rocky Mountain Ranch, a big bull elk ran across the highway, got confused, and ran back smack into the passenger side door.
>
> When we parked in the ambulance bay in Sun Valley to unload, the main doors in the back wouldn't open, probably a new-vehicle glitch aggravated by the rough road to Boundary Creek. So, to get the patient out, we tipped the stretcher onto its side with the dude strapped in and skidded him out the side door.

Even newer ambulances can have electrical problems. On a night run with a coronary patient in the back and his wife sitting up front, the ambulance lights went out at Fisher Creek. We still had a long way to go, and out came the flashlights in place of headlights.

Yet another time, the lights went out, and the family was following behind. We stopped, transferred the patient into the family car, and left behind the ambulance with the family.

What if avalanches closed Galena Summit during heavy winter snow? Except during winter, you could drive 129 miles to Boise on Highway 21. With snow, avalanches usually closed the canyon just beyond Banner Summit. Air ambulance? During bad winter storms, helicopter medivac wasn't an option, either. The only option was driving the river road 116 miles to the small hospital in Salmon, or 200 miles to Idaho Falls — in bad weather. For unstable patients, this could be a long, scary ambulance ride for everyone. And if the river road below Stanley was also closed, you were out of options and waited.

When we started the Stanley Clinic and Stanley Ambulance in 1972, some rural communities were using hearses to transport patients. Before our '58 Pontiac, the closest ambulance was in Hailey, seventy-five miles away, over Galena Summit.

We planned on replacing our ambulance every ten years because of the wear and tear created by the distances, terrain, and backcountry road conditions. And everything ambulance-related seemed to increase dramatically except for the gas mileage: notably weight and cost. Our first "mod van" ambulance got four miles to the gallon, far worse than our Pontiac.

To help with buying the next ambulance, Idaho EMS set up a grant program, but to qualify, we had to raise part of the cost (hence the donation jars).

In 1977 Bonnie Hansen created a local service organization, the Sawtooth Mountain Mamas, whose annual Arts and Crafts Fair helped fund community projects. The Mountain Mamas spent winters quilting, then auctioned the quilts to help fund the Stanley Ambulance. Many people reached into their wallets or wrote checks to support EMS in the Sawtooth country. Idaho EMS would help us, too, starting in the mid-1970s under Paul Anderson's leadership.

Imagine you're trapped in a mangled vehicle, covered with shards of glass, smelling gasoline, and fearing your wrecked car might explode. If you're lucky, you'll see flashing lights and hear sirens coming to help you. In Idaho's Sawtooth country, ours were the faces and voices you saw and heard, your first responders.

During the early 1970s, law enforcement was thin in the Sawtooth country. The newly established Sawtooth NRA attracted tourists with their motorcycles, cars, bicycles, and snowmobiles. Visitors needing medical care learned that Stanley now had a clinic staffed by a nurse practitioner and an ambulance staffed by volunteer EMTs.

More than staffing the Stanley Ambulance, our EMTs became an extension of the clinic — and of me. I was on 24/7 call in the Valley, and I couldn't be everywhere. Most EMTs packed a complete first aid kit and carried radios whenever they responded to emergency calls.

We could — and did — have major traumas in different places simultaneously. Our EMS system needed redundancy and reserve to move beyond being a "one-deep" operation. Most of our service area was rugged mountain wilderness where hikers, climbers, and boaters got into trouble. EMTs might be ten or fifteen miles or further from the Stanley Clinic and Stanley Ambulance, who could start emergency care when they arrived on the scene. Ours was a region-wide safety net of EMTs anchored by the Stanley Ambulance and the clinic.

One Sunday afternoon, two bad car accidents happened almost simultaneously. We needed the Life Flight Network to medivac the injured. At one of the wrecks, I was standing in the highway borrow pit after putting in an IV. Word came over the radio: Life Flight was responding to a call in Eastern Oregon and was unavailable. I had that sinking feeling in my gut. Then, the weather turned bad. EMTs stabilized the trauma cases from the first car accident, loaded the patients in the Stanley Ambulance, and transported them over Galena to Sun Valley.

At the second car accident scene, I stayed with the EMTs. We waited. Radio update: Life Flight was on its way. Then we heard that distant *chuff-chuff-chuff*. At long last, the helicopter arrived. We loaded the second set of trauma cases, then headed back to Stanley with Life Flight airborne for Boise. Walking into the clinic, we got a radio call: a plane crashed at Stanley's airstrip. We arrived to find a father and son — uninjured.

Responding to multiple simultaneous traumas in rural America is nothing one clinician can handle. It takes training and a well-functioning team. And, on that day in the Sawtooth country, the first-responder system performed beautifully.

Stanley was one of the first communities in Idaho to have an organized EMT training program. Our first EMT instructor, Sandy Cottrell, was an RN and Director of Nursing Services at McCall Memorial Hospital. Even before we had an ambulance and opened the clinic, we started training Stanley's EMTs.

Sandy drove 320 miles of river road each weekend for eight hours of instruction on Saturday and Sunday. I attended the program's first half, then went to Harborview, where I audited paramedic classes. When I returned from Seattle, I took over from Sandy and finished teaching Stanley's first EMT class.

Our first class was a shocker. Nearly the whole community turned out. Stanley's year-round population in 1971 was thirty-seven. About twenty-five to thirty people, including ranchers and Forest Service personnel, took the course. Locals wanted to volunteer.

The EMT book we used in 1971 was written for students at the seventh-grade level. Some of Stanley's old-timers who enrolled in the EMT class had made it through school in Stanley, which only went through the eighth grade. The EMT book had terminology many older students had never seen. For them, the class was challenging, but they stuck with it.

The EMT class lasted eighty hours. To become EMT-certified, students had to pass a multiple-choice test and demonstrate core skills, as well as complete ten hours of observation in an ER. One of my students from Smiley Creek, while training in an ER, was asked to swab blood out of a scalp wound. He passed out into a sterile suture tray. Eventually, he became an excellent EMT.

Teaching mouth-to-mouth breathing was an anesthesiologist from Salt Lake City, Dr. Will Chamberlain. Will was a CPR instructor, spent time in the Valley, and helped build our new clinic. His view was that the teaching manikins for CPR are made to somebody's concept of an average face when, in reality, faces differ. As Will pointed out to our EMT class, "You have bearded faces, clear faces, people with beautiful dentition, and others without teeth. You have young, old, skinny, and obese people. Faces differ, so you need to train on different faces." Will instructed the class to choose a partner and practice mouth-to-mouth.

The EMT courses needed a sponsoring agency. Since Idaho EMS did not exist until 1973, the state's EMT training program was placed under the Department of Education. When I returned from Harborview, I was duly appointed an official EMT instructor for Vocational Education.

In Stanley's first EMT class were Ted and Phyllis Williams. Phyllis was the school teacher when the school building moved back and forth on skids between Stanley and Lower Stanley. Ted was a rancher and outfitter. If ever you got hurt in the backcountry, you would want Ted Williams there. CPR? Ted was the best. Fracture? Ted instinctively knew how to splint and could improvise from almost anything. But take a written test? Ted knew the material backward and forwards. But he choked on multiple-choice tests. Still, Ted helped in many ways, taking his pack horses to rescue people before we had helicopters and helping establish the training program for our volunteer ambulance drivers.

In the summer of 1972, when we opened the clinic, we held our second EMT class — or tried. We'd start lectures, and there'd be an emergency call. I'd have to suture someone or scramble into the '58 Pontiac for an ambulance run. The lesson was clear: Summers were too busy to instruct an EMT class.

An ambulance requires unending commitment to maintain trained personnel. Ultimately, I taught a course nearly every year in Stanley, and also taught in Challis and Ketchum. Altogether, with support from Idaho EMS, I trained and recertified over five hundred EMTs during my nearly thirty years at the Stanley Clinic.

When telephones first came to the Valley, landlines were prohibitively expensive. As the region's sole healthcare provider, having a phone at my home would greatly help. Unfortunately, I couldn't afford it. I made less than $1,000 a year in my first years as an NP. To run a telephone landline two miles from the highway to my cabin would cost $2,000. One day in the mid-1970s, I was stunned to see the telephone company laying the telephone line up from the highway to my home. Frantic, I drove to town and called the telephone company. "What are you doing? I don't have the money to pay." I was almost in tears. The company reassured me. An anonymous donor was paying to put in my telephone.

Even with telephones, radio was our first line of emergency communication. We desperately needed radio communication to link the Stanley Ambulance to the clinic, and also to ERs in Sun Valley and Hailey. Without an effective communication system in the field, the risk to our patients increased substantially.

Our emergency radio network "beachhead" consisted of donated CB equipment. Before casino magnate Bill Harrah began buying up parts of Stanley, the town's Mountain Village Motel was owned by Val Black. Val was a pilot who used a souped-up radio system with reception in much of the Valley. He offered his CB at the motel office as our radio base station.

For 24/7, the motel's office staff did double duty serving motel guests while facilitating emergency radio communications for the Valley.

At Smiley Creek, below Galena Summit, lived another CB radio operator who owned a Twin Falls furniture store. He donated the use of his radios.

That loaned portable radio became "Unit 1," my constant companion moving from charger to charger in my bedroom, car, and clinic.

Night and day, CB radio traffic was ongoing, from Mexico to California to Canada, fishermen swapping stories to housewives sharing recipes. Emergency calls often came on weekends when my husband, Cal, joined me at the cabin. We'd get in bed, turn off the light, and ... listen to CB radio chatter.

The price was right for our put-together CB radio network since we had no money. It wouldn't have been financially feasible to buy those CB radios. But, amazingly, people stepped up, loaning or giving us equipment and volunteering time. A team of generous locals emerged from out of thin air and patched together our first radio network.

Within a few years, Idaho EMS would establish a statewide radio communications network.

Radio communications and mountains aren't a good mix. We could cover most of the valley. But the more massive the mountain range, the less reliable the radio range.

"Marie, this is Mountain Village base station. Are you there?" Just past midnight, I had turned off the lamp and snuggled into bed when the voice boomed from the CB radio beside my pillow.

"This is Marie."

"You are needed at the Beaver Creek Store, at Dirty Dora's. There's a young woman who is unconscious."

"Okay. We'll need an ambulance dispatched to the Beaver Creek Store. I'm on my way." Ending the radio call, I dressed and grabbed my black bag.

"Mom, I'm going with you." John was staying at the cabin that night. It was the first year of the premed program with the College of Idaho. The other premeds, Ken Harris and Mike Nowling, were at the clinic.

Raging over the Sawtooth Valley was one of the most intense thunderstorms in our memory. Flash-boom. Flash-boom. Rain blew in torrents. John and I raced for the car, soaked when we jumped in.

I put the radio in the charger. We were off, headed down the hill. The windshield wipers on high speed couldn't keep up. Headlights showed curtains of rain and streams of water starting to gully the dirt road to the highway.

"Ambulance to Marie."

"This is Marie."

"Marie, this is Ken. We've left the clinic and are headed for Dirty Dora's. We should be arriving in about fifteen or twenty minutes."

"Okay, we'll be there."

I turned onto Highway 75, heading south towards Beaver Creek. The rain falling in sheets made it hard to see the sides of the road. Although standing water on the road risked hydroplaning, I pushed on the gas pedal, hoping not to lose control.

As we pulled into the Beaver Creek Store, the thunderstorm let up. Dora Schlunegger was waiting for us. Dora was born in Switzerland in 1907 and immigrated as a young bride to North America in 1928. She and Conrad had five kids. In 1938, the couple settled in Ketchum. Unfortunately, Conrad's gambling ended their marriage in 1948. To support her children, Dora worked as a maid and seamstress.

In 1958, she bought the Beaver Creek Store. Dora's earthy humor, including nearly every dirty joke ever told and her collection of "peters" displayed on the property gave her prominence in the Sawtooth's panoply of colorful characters.

Dora loved mushroom hunting. Rain was plentiful that summer, providing just the right conditons for an abundant supply of wild mushrooms. In July, Dora went mushrooming with a young couple from Switzerland who had rented one of the cabins behind her store. Their foraging was successful; the couple added mushrooms to their dinner. The young woman feasted on mushrooms. Her boyfriend, uneasy, ate only a few.

Hours later, Dora anxiously led us to the cabin. The woman was lying on the bed. "Can you hear me?" I asked. No response. I ground my knuckles into her sternum. No response. Giant bubbles of saliva frothed from her mouth. I examined the young patient and questioned the boyfriend about her medical history. She had no medical problems, including no seizure history and no history of drug use. Her vitals were stable, and a quick neurologic exam showed no focal findings. We placed mushroom poisoning at the top of the possible explanations list.

Our ambulance arrived, and we loaded the young woman onto the gurney and into the ambulance. MAST helicopters didn't fly at night, especially with thunderstorms moving through the mountains. We used Dora's store telephone since our CB radios wouldn't reach the Sun Valley ER. After I described the patient to the physician in the ER, he acknowledged he didn't know anything about mushroom poisoning. Also, he was concerned she might be having a stroke, although she was in her early twenties. At around two in the morning, the Stanley Ambulance headed out with lights flashing.

At Moritz ER, the physician did his initial evaluation. He didn't have a definitive diagnosis and remained concerned about a stroke. So, the physician called Blaine County ambulance for transport to Boise. During the ambulance ride on a curvy stretch of highway, she vomited. Up came the mushrooms, and she woke up. We had sent the bag of mushrooms with her. Once in Boise, the ER staff sought help from a mycologist to ID the mushrooms. Among the mushrooms were Death Angels — Amanitas.

Later that same day, with the sun shining and the storms passing, our mushroom poisoning patient returned to the Sawtooth Valley and came to the Stanley Clinic to thank us for saving her life. And, she was missing a pen and wanted to know if we had it. We did. She got her pen back but never paid her ambulance bill.

Using CBs to anchor an emergency communications system was a gamble. When Bill Harrah bought the Mountain Village Motel, our put-together emergency communication system was in trouble. Harrah's attorneys in Nevada were afraid of the liability.

And it wasn't just us. Throughout Idaho, rural communities were struggling without the security of a stable, coordinated emergency communication network that could be relied upon.

Death by trauma in the early 1970s wasn't just a problem in Idaho. Nationwide, trauma was the leading cause of death between infancy and adults in their late thirties. To help, the Robert Wood Johnson Foundation (of the Johnson & Johnson family) committed funding to improve emergency communications, including a national 911 emergency medical response system. In addition, the foundation gave a grant to the newly established Idaho EMS for a statewide emergency radio communication network. Subsequently, EMS radios replaced our CB equipment for communication in the Sawtooth country.

In August, 1977, Idaho EMS chief Paul Anderson walked into a small room at St. Alphonsus Hospital in Boise. He turned on a newly installed, two-way radio system connected statewide through mountaintop microwave base stations. For the Sawtooth country, in five years we'd gone from no radio communication to being part of a statewide network centered in the Idaho State EMS Communication Center, known as "StateComm."

In concept, the new EMS radio system would connect the Stanley Clinic and Stanley Ambulance to the Sun Valley hospital and other ambulance services. Our new EMS radios had three channels: two local channels and one for StateComm. Tall radio antennas were installed at the Salmon River Emergency Clinic, my cabin on Shaw Mesa, and Smiley Creek. In addition, Idaho EMS installed mountaintop repeaters to aid in transmissions, including at Basin Butte, west of town.

Amazingly, we could now talk to Boise. Unfortunately, the mountains blocked our communication with Sun Valley, even with our new EMS radios. Sometimes the radios worked, sometimes they didn't. Only specific locations gave you consistent radio reception with StateComm. We could reach StateComm from the clinic; the best reception in the valley was just down the road at the intersection of Highways 21 and 75. Radio reception was hit-and-miss on the ambulance heading from Stanley to Sun Valley. Moving up the valley toward Galena Summit, the Stanley Ambulance and Stanley Clinic could always communicate. However, going over the summit, the ambulance entered a radio dead zone. Reception was out until we passed the Sawtooth NRA headquarters north of Ketchum.

When the radio went off in the ER in Sun Valley, we depended on someone hearing our call. If nurses were elsewhere, they might not know that the Stanley Ambulance had tried to reach them. So, we always telephoned the Sun Valley nurses' station from the Stanley Clinic to tell them an ambulance was on the way. That way, a doctor was more likely to be in the ER when the ambulance arrived. Dr. Stephen Luber, a pediatrician for eighteen years at the Mollie Scott Clinic in Sun Valley, was outstanding about waiting for us to arrive: He'd always be standing at the door.

In 1977 we had glitches. With lightning and thunder pounding overhead, I walked into my bedroom. A blue light danced around the radio base station at the head of my bed just above my pillow. A few days prior, Idaho EMS had installed a fifty-foot antenna outside my bedroom, running a cable from the antenna through the logs to the radio charger. My telephone sat next to the radio charger with the dancing blue lights.

As lightning flashed and thunder crashed, I panicked, picked up the telephone, and called Dave Kimpton. "Dave, what do I do?"

"Unplug the charger!"

I reached through the dancing blue field and pulled the plug. The blue light stopped. After the storm passed, I plugged in the charger. The system still worked.

The following day, I called Paul Anderson at Idaho EMS. Paul reached the engineer who had installed the radio antenna at my cabin. That day the engineer drove from Boise up to Shaw Mesa to inspect the system. "Marie, I found the problem. Apparently, I didn't ground the antenna." He grounded it, and that antenna remained standing for over twenty years until 1999, when I retired as Stanley's nurse practitioner.

Radios were expensive, and Idaho EMS could only provide a few. One radio passed from volunteer EMT to EMT, whoever was on call for emergencies. The Forest Service boosted our radio coverage by adding an emergency channel to agency radios. Many of our leading EMTs were also Forest Service staff who carried radios wherever they went.

We also set up a local 911 system for the Valley, Idaho's first. Locals had numbers that all started with "774." When people dialed 911, the Mountain Village Motel staff picked up the call. The motel was our first CB radio base station and dispatch. Later, the calls would go to the sheriff's office in Challis.

People injured in these rugged mountains need first responders who know the country. In the 1970s, three young men from the Forest Service and Idaho Fish and Game enrolled in my EMT classes: Steve Lipus, Gary Gadwa, and Phil Coonts. They knew the backcountry like nobody else. Steve and Gary, in particular, became our "Goat Patrol" because they could get almost anywhere, anytime, often faster than the helicopter. They knew the shortcuts and how to get around in the mountains, even at night and during stormy weather. The Goat Patrol spent many long nights helping people, including one night on the Middle Fork when one river rafting adventure turned tragic.

In late June 1985, rafters launched their boats on the Middle Fork of the Salmon River at the Boundary Creek put-in. With spring melt, the river was running high. About seven miles downriver, the rafting party floated around a bend and encountered a fallen tree. With barely enough space to get the rafts under the tree, everyone ducked down — with one exception.

As the raft swept under the tree, a young man dropped his head but was blocked by a gear box. The tree pinned the head against the box, ripping open his jaw. With bleeding and swelling threatening the boater's airway, the rafting party got to shore. Rafters hurried up the river trail to the put-in, in search of help.

It was after dark when we got the emergency call for the Middle Fork rafting accident. Gary Gadwa, doubling as Goat Patrol EMT and Idaho Fish and Game's conservation officer, volunteered to go. But Gary couldn't do it alone. Who else? As fate would have it, my son John, now a resident physician, had just arrived from Spokane. He was joined by another resident, Dave Burica, who would practice internal medicine in McCall for more than thirty years. John and Dave were in Stanley for a backpacking trip into the White Cloud Mountains. They agreed to help Gary with a nighttime emergency hike into the Middle Fork.

We rendezvoused at the clinic, added IV supplies and airways to the packs, and Gary and the two young doctors headed to the trailhead. The team walked the river trail for three hours using headlamps, arriving around two am. They found their patient near the river, able to respond to questions despite a swollen tongue, oral cavity lacerations, and severe facial trauma. He also was suffering from respiratory distress and low blood pressure.

Dave and John worked together by flashlight to clear the airway and start an IV. The rafter's blood pressure improved, and his breathing normalized. Then, everyone waited for daylight.

EMS StateComm worked through the night to line up helicopter transport: a Bell 206 staffed with a doctor from Challis. By early morning, the rafters and rescuers heard the helicopter's saving chuff-chuff-chuff above the noise of river rapids in that steep canyon. Unfortunately, there was no safe place to land.

Two men jumped out with a chainsaw as the helicopter hovered over the river's edge. First, they dropped small trees to create a safer landing zone. Next, the pilot lowered the aircraft until the skids gently settled onto a boulder poking above the water and the shore. Finally, a doctor hopped out and walked across the skids to the shore when the blades stopped rotating. Like the Marlboro Man, the doctor lit up a cigarette and puffed while John and Dave reported on the patient's status. Next, he insisted that the rescue team place a Foley catheter before transport.

Helicopter loaded, the gifted pilot lifted the Bell 206 out of the canyon. Stanley's rescue team hiked back to the boat launch. The boating party — minus one — was left to pull themselves together and finish their Middle Fork adventure.

As with our Army-surplus ambulance, the military provided the first air ambulance services for the central Idaho mountains. The Department of Defense (DOD) was part of America's revolution in EMS. The Vietnam War was ongoing: wounded soldiers helped by medical corpsmen and helicopter air ambulances were more likely to survive than motorists injured on America's roads. Lessons from Vietnam informed decisions to start paramedic programs and EMS helicopter transport. In 1970 DOD piloted MAST at five military installations, including Mountain Home Air Force Base in Idaho.

The MAST helicopter airlifting our patients was a Huey (nickname for a Bell UH-1 Iroquois), a utility military helicopter deployed extensively during the war. It was huge, seating up to thirteen passengers. The Air Force outfitted the Huey for medevac. Unfortunately, pilots couldn't fly at certain times of the day and usually not at night. Altitude was also a problem — a real challenge for us when we needed MAST to medevac climbing injuries in the Sawtooths. The pilot would land the big ship where he could, and we'd carry the patients to the waiting MAST team. The Stanley EMTs sometimes had to carry patients up to a half mile to load them into the Huey, still a big improvement over hand-hauling patients miles out of the wilderness.

Huey helicopter at the Forest Service's Sawtooth Valley Work Center

Doctors on the MAST helicopters were not always trained for the job. For example, we needed a severe burn patient to go to Salt Lake's burn center during one transport. The physician on the helicopter was a pediatrician with no burn experience. Eventually, in 1972, the American medical establishment recognized emergency medicine as a specialty, integral to the revolution in EMS underway during the 1960s and 1970s. We lived through that transition as more and more emergency medicine-trained physicians did emergency medicine.

Helicopter pilots could be incredibly talented, having spent years transporting wounded soldiers during the Vietnam War. We'd be standing along the highway at the scene of some horrible car accident, waiting for the telltale sound. When we first heard the *chuff-chuff-chuff* coming over the Sawtooths or down the valley, it was the most incredible relief; the sound of a helicopter meant our patients had a chance.

Duct tape and baling wire were how we first put together medical evacuation in Idaho's Sawtooth country: training a team of volunteer EMTs, establishing Stanley's Salmon River Emergency Clinic, and seeking help from the US Air Force and Forest Service. It worked.

When we started, the helicopters didn't have lights for night landings. EMTs would gather at the clinic and head out for all-night rescues, waiting for daylight medevac. Where we could, at the airport or along the highway, we'd park cars to shine headlights and give helicopters a safe place to land at night.

The first time we used a helicopter at night in the Sawtooth Wilderness was to transport an injured hiker. You would have thought Santa Claus had arrived when the pilot turned on that big landing light.

We never lost a helicopter during an emergency medical transport in Idaho's Sawtooth country.

We don't get do-overs in life. If only we could.

Nothing was out of the ordinary at the clinic that summer Sunday afternoon. On weekends I might do laundry at my Shaw Mesa cabin. As a child of the Great Depression, I still used clothes pegs to hang wet laundry to dry in the mountain breezes. From my clothesline, I could see the stunning Sawtooth peaks, including El Capitan. That granite half-dome is unforgettable and was about to consume my day.

An emergency call came over the radio, and I headed for town.

While finishing up with my patient, I was called to the reception room. A high school student with a sunburned face streaked with dirt and sweat looked distraught. He spoke matter-of-factly, describing a climbing accident at El Capitan earlier that morning.

The student had traveled to the Sawtooths from North Carolina with his climbing partner and teacher, Tom Brothers. Both were experienced climbers, using ropes and helmets. They did everything right. They were about three-quarters of the way to the summit when they paused to stand on a ledge and admire the incredible view of Alice Lake and the Sawtooth peaks. Then, under Brothers, the ledge gave way.

The student climbed down to the base of El Capitan's sheer face, finding his climbing partner still alive. Marking the spot with their backpacks, he headed down the popular hiking trail, scrambling the four miles of switchbacks and stream crossings to the trailhead at Petit Lake. Campers brought him to the Stanley Clinic, but at that point several hours had passed since the fall.

We sent out the emergency call, and EMTs gathered at the clinic. The Forest Service dispatched a helicopter, changing its status from fire-fighting duty to medevac. The pilot flew us to Alice Lake, then circled the base of El Capitan, searching for the injured climber. Finding him took time and fuel. The pilot couldn't land. As we hovered several feet above the ground, we opened the door, stepped carefully onto the skids, then jumped. The pilot headed back to ferry more EMTs.

We looked up a steep talus slope to the base of El Capitan's sheer wall, where the injured climber had landed. With our equipment, we climbed the slope, breathing hard from the exertion and altitude. When we got to the patient, we saw he was young, with a severe traumatic head injury, and not responding. We stabilized his neck, then examined him for fractures and found none. I got an IV in, and we moved him onto a stretcher.

Transporting the patient was a long carry, although the pilot had landed as close as possible. We had a crew of EMTs ferried in by the pilot. When one EMT tired, another would take over. Carrying the injured climber down the talus slope to the helicopter was an amazing feat of work by our EMTs. It's not only weight: you cannot stumble and risk dropping your patient. We arrived at the helicopter, then hoisted and buckled the injured climber into the back seat.

Space was limited inside the helicopter, enough for the pilot, the injured climber, and me. So I sat up front next to the pilot. On the trip from El Capitan to Sun Valley, the pilot skimmed the tops of the trees and buildings. It's the one time I've ever been scared in a helicopter. The helicopter was gone soon after we landed and got the patient onto a gurney. I was in the ER when Forest Service staff walked in. That was when I learned that we had almost run out of fuel. No surprise, thanks to a hot summer day in the high country, trying to locate the injured climber, and shuttling EMTs up to the base of El Capitan. The pilot had skimmed treetops and housetops to save fuel.

The mountain climber was sent by ambulance from Sun Valley to Boise, where he died three days later. They were experienced climbers. One climber lived, and the other died. If only we could turn back mortality's clock. But we can't. Instead, we live forward with memories.

If your community is too small to support an ambulance, one option is to create a Quick Response Unit or "QRU." At the southern end of the Sawtooth Valley is Smiley Creek. We had EMTs staying at Busterback Ranch and working at Smiley Creek. To better respond to trauma at that end of the valley, the EMTs asked me to help set up the Smiley Creek QRU, one of the first in Idaho.

One appeal of the QRU program is the training. The time commitment was about half the time required for EMT certification. The EMT course was eighty hours, with classes three or four nights a week. QRU training was shorter, while still including extrication for car accidents, CPR, fracture care, and other rural trauma basics.

Instead of an ambulance, QRU volunteers collected a cache of emergency care equipment used while waiting for ground or air ambulance transport. Later in the 1970s, Idaho EMS helped rural communities create QRUs statewide, strengthening rural EMS networks.

Lowman, on the Payette River's South Fork and about midway from Stanley to Boise on Highway 21, was another small community that wanted a QRU for responding to trauma. Given the distance, I could not teach that QRU course and the state provided an instructor. Eventually, Lowman got an ambulance staffed with volunteer EMTs, and their unit now responds to a surprising amount of vehicular trauma.

Clayton, a small mining town on the Salmon River about halfway between Stanley and Challis, also needed help in the 1970s. Ambulances from either Challis or Stanley could be called. Response times from Challis were shorter because the highway is better. In the summer, the Stanley Ambulance could be stretched over 100 highway miles from Grandjean on the Payette's South Fork, Clayton on the Main Salmon, and Galena Summit. Creating Clayton's QRU helped offload some of the pressure on the Stanley Ambulance.

Through all these emergency calls and ambulance runs — the horrific, miraculous, and mundane — were the EMTs. We were a team. Sometimes we just celebrated. For one of our first EMT classes, we held a graduation party at Robinson Bar Ranch on a warm summer afternoon.

Robinson Bar Ranch is downriver from Stanley, located where Warm Springs Creek flows into the Main Salmon River, still within the Sawtooth NRA. Joe Leonard was ranch manager and part-owner before selling to Bruce and Pat LaFavour in 1975, who then sold to Carole King. The Leonards invited the graduating EMT class to the ranch, including to swim in the hot springs-fed pool.

As the EMT course instructor, I wouldn't miss the graduation. I was wearing my new cowboy boots and my new watch for the event. After the steak fry, I stood next to the pool, chit-chatting about the EMT course and life in the mountains.

Suddenly, I felt myself being lifted up and then flying through the air ... splash! Warm and everything wet: my new cowboy boots, wristwatch, and clothes. My final initiation as an EMT instructor? Being tossed into the pool by her students. A ruined watch and wet-leather cowboy boots are small things in an otherwise memorable graduation.

Stanley's volunteer EMTs pulled people out of wrecked cars and off rivers, hiked with headlamps through the dark to find the injured, and staffed the Stanley Ambulance. Sometimes they carried patients on stretchers up to ten miles out of the wilderness. We'd send second teams so people could get a break, avoiding EMT exhaustion.

The trauma and long hours burned out some volunteer EMTs. Others moved away. One of our EMTs was a college graduate working as a summer seasonal employee with the Forest Service who stayed the winter. When he registered for the course, he added, "Marie, in the wintertime, the EMT course is the only thing to do in Stanley." He became one of our outstanding EMTs until the Forest Service transferred him.

Although EMTs on call or responding to emergencies cannot drink, after EMT classes during the winter, we'd bundle up and head for Stanley's only open bar. The Kasino Club stayed open just for us. Our EMT classes were a bonding experience for this tiny, isolated rural community.

Maryellen was a teacher. She'd teach all day and then get called at night — and go. These were not ten-minute ambulance runs. Some of these runs for hunting accidents or car wrecks went all night. We might head out at sunset and not pull into the ER in Sun Valley until sunrise. Don Sessions would gas up the ambulance at Sessions Lodge in Obsidian, and the ambulance would head out again with a fresh crew. Exhausted EMTs would return to their daily duties. Trauma happens, and we don't control the timing.

A point I want to emphasize: These EMTs were all volunteers. These rural residents were willing to put it on the line to help others, day or night. They didn't get paid a penny. Some were at work when the emergency call came. Sometimes they'd go all day without eating.

After a couple of EMTs went hungry, the clinic board created a pizza fund to feed hungry EMTs on those long ambulance runs. A favorite for Stanley Ambulance crews became Louie's Pizza in Ketchum. The Stanley community also held potluck dinners to honor EMTs.

Ideally, Stanley's EMTs would be paid as they are in urban ambulance units. Challis provides a small payment. Lowman is all-volunteer. If you don't have the tax base, you either rely on volunteer EMTs or go without and gamble with death. Death usually wins.

People traveling through rural America are oblivious to emergency medical services — until they need them. When you hear the sirens, see the flashing lights, and hear EMS-trained professionals ask, "Are you okay?" remember that those EMS networks exist because good-hearted people have made time to train, obtain equipment, and connect to EMS systems of care.

16

CREATING EMS: IDAHO

Paul Anderson

Rural Ambulence Key Ceremony. Rural EMS leaders gather at the Capitol steps to receive keys — and funding — for badly needed ambulances in rural Idaho. Governor Andrus, Dr. David Boyd (national EMS director) and Paul Anderson are among the people who are involved. Marie Osborn, ARNP, representing the Stanley/Sawtooth area, is on the right.

Should a woman training for trauma care in rural Idaho be allowed to ride the Medic One trauma ambulance in Seattle? "No, Marie. The trauma ambulance is no place for a woman."

In February 1972, when I arrived at Seattle's Harborview, the paramedic program was getting underway. I trained with Medic One paramedics and Dr. Michael Copass, who, along with Dr. Leonard Cobb and Seattle Fire Chief Gordon Vickery, created and built Medic One into an international model in pre-hospital emergency care. After leaving Seattle and returning to Stanley, I responded to multiple trauma calls that first summer of 1972 — as an NP and a woman.

I was wading into a man's world. Think about changes that occurred in the last half of the 20th century. I grew up during the Great Depression and WWII with typewriters, rotary dial telephones, telephone operators and party lines, telephone booths, and phone books. You may have grown up with the internet, home computers, and smartphones. With revolutionary changes, the unimaginable becomes commonplace, accepted, and expected. What was once unreachable for women, EMS and the nurse practitioner profession are now the norm.

In the 1970s, in putting together the Stanley Clinic and Stanley Ambulance, we lived through — and helped create — revolutionary changes. Of course, we didn't set out to be revolutionaries. Nevertheless, for me to provide patient care in Idaho's Sawtooth country required revolutionary changes. In other words, saving lives in rural communities forced us to develop new care systems. I emphasize "us" because many people in Stanley, Boise, and far beyond were involved. One was Paul Anderson, a central figure in creating Idaho EMS.

While visiting Boise to get help for the Stanley Ambulance and radio communications, I stopped by the newly created Idaho Emergency Medical Services (EMS) office and its first director, Paul Anderson. I blurted out, "How do you find anything in this mess?" Paul smiled. After that, Paul's desk was pristine when he knew I was stopping by.

Paul had a good way about him. He never seemed pushy; he got things done. Maybe it was Paul's history riding ambulance. Because he had walked in our shoes, he was committed to helping us. From creating an EMS radio communication system to finding funds to replace our aging ambulance, Paul was a doer and a friend.

"Stanley to Unit 1. We need you, Marie." That EMS radio, Unit 1, my constant companion in my car, clinic, and bedroom, was the work of Paul Anderson and Idaho EMS. Idaho EMS asked the Robert Wood Johnson Foundation for funding, and they donated generously. Our new EMS radio system in the mid-1970s was a big step forward, connecting us to the network of Idaho State Communications or "StateComm."

1971 is a pivotal year in Idaho's history for rural healthcare. The legislature and newly elected governor, Cecil Andrus, connected Idaho to a regional medical program, WWAMI. In addition, Idaho enacted policy reforms to license NPs, the first among the fifty states. State agencies also supported our first EMT class at Stanley. Idaho's support for rural healthcare and EMS comes from its elected representatives, including Idaho's governor.

The Idaho governor's office door was open when we needed help for the clinic. Cal and I had known Governor Cecil Andrus through our advocacy work in public education. Our kids went to the same Boise schools, and my oldest son, Calvin, had dated his daughter. On September 1, 1972, two months after we opened the log cabin clinic in Stanley, elected officials gathered at Redfish Lake to dedicate the Sawtooth National Recreation Area. Governor Andrus was there, having arrived in a limousine from Boise, and said, "Marie, I want to see the clinic."

At the time, I was driving my VW Beetle. My orange "Bug" fit my height well, but not so much for the tall governor. "I don't think you'll fit," I told him. But Andrus folded himself into the passenger seat, and we were off.

"Hey Marie, lose my escort." I looked at the governor and thought, "There's no way," but I tried, knowing I could probably talk my way out of a speeding ticket.

We toured our log cabin clinic, which was mostly equipped with hand-me-downs. Governor Andrus looked at every room and asked about equipment, including the anesthesia machine.

Later, when I needed help and stopped by the governor's office, Andrus would pick up the phone, and things would get done for the clinic.

In 1971, Governor Andrus created a task force to develop a statewide EMS plan. Over the next two years, the task force identified specific problem areas and proposed objectives to improve EMS statewide. In 1973, the legislature created Idaho EMS, the third in the nation after Maryland and Illinois started statewide systems for trauma and EMS. Andrus placed responsibility for Idaho EMS with Paul Anderson.

In 1971, rural areas in Idaho had almost no emergency services. Some rural communities were still using hearses to transport patients. Paul Anderson and Idaho EMS opened doors when we needed them to. Paul took us out of the dark ages and into the light.

Paul's work statewide, from 1973 to 1992, and our work in Stanley to establish EMS in the Sawtooth-Salmon River country went hand in hand. He oversaw a long list of Idaho EMS initiatives:

- Development of the statewide EMS communication system;
- EMT and paramedic training;
- The MAST helicopter program;
- The poison control center;
- Funding for new ambulances, and much more

On July 13, 2019, another Idaho governor, Brad Little, declared Paul B. Anderson Day for Paul's service in advancing EMS.

Paul was a young, eager leader in the 1970s, a man on a mission. He visited every community in Idaho that had an ambulance, helping locals and encouraging the legislature to support rural EMS better. During those formative years, Paul was the best administrator that Idaho EMS could have had.

PAUL ANDERSON, IN HIS OWN WORDS

Stanley's volunteer ambulance service is based in one of the smaller towns in Idaho to have an ambulance service. Today, the sign on the highway coming into Stanley lists the population as sixty-nine. Each year, tourists log over a million visitor days in the Stanley/Sawtooth area, mostly during summer. But when tourists and locals get hurt and need help, who will respond? That is also the larger question for rural America: Who among you will respond to the call for help?

A child in a pool of blood: that's a formative memory. I was riding my bicycle when I was six years old. A crowd of gawkers gathered near an alley. A police car drove up. Then came the black hearse that doubled as an ambulance. The attendant scooped up the injured boy, loaded him in the back of the hearse, and drove away to the ER with white flags flapping. Vehicles doubling as hearses and ambulances — for the dead and the living — didn't have sirens or flashing lights then.

Using hearses as ambulances has logic: bodies fit in the back of hearses. You can open the back door, lift in a gurney with an injured patient, or slide in a coffin. White flags and red crosses over each front fender cued the destination, the dead going to a cemetery and the living to a hospital. But, when used as an ambulance, hearses didn't carry dressings, splints, oxygen, or medical equipment. Until the 1960s, the standard of emergency care in the United States was scoop and run. The funeral-home era of ambulance service in America lasted from about 1900 until the 1970s.

Even at age six, I thought there had to be a better way.

At age seventeen in 1956, I rode a bicycle through Europe between my junior and senior years in high school. I sailed on a steamer from Montreal, disembarked in Southampton, rode my bike through London, then the continent — from France to Norway — before returning from Germany to Canada. Besides visiting tourist sites like the Eiffel Tower, I stopped by ambulance services and fire departments. I met London's ambulance service supervisor at the city's central dispatch center. While talking, a call came in on the 999-emergency number for police, fire, and ambulance for a multi-fatality accident on the edge of London. The supervisor headed out by ambulance. That ambulance was not a hearse. Instead, by the 1950s, London's ambulances were white and modular, tall enough that you could stand inside. You could see the flashing blue (not red) lights and hear that distinctive London siren, "nee-naw, nee-naw."

Why were London and Europe generally far ahead of the United States in EMS? The wars inflicting massive civilian casualties are part of the answer. Mass bombings of WWII killed 40,000, injured up to 140,000, and destroyed two million homes, mainly in London. Out of the ashes emerged new strategies for responding to people needing help.

Dorothy Carpenter Medical Archives, Digital Forsyth

This 1938 Packard Limousine doubled as a funeral home hearse for the dead and ambulance for the living in Forsyth County, North Carolina. Image courtesy of Wake Forest University School of Medecine.

London Ambulance Service NHS Trust Historic Collection

London ambulance in 1949, Daimler JXP63. Two world wars with massive civilian casualties forced EMS advancements in Europe.

As I traveled Europe in the summer of 1956, I took note of ambulance services being separate from funeral homes. Instead, dedicated ambulances, not hearses, arrived at accident scenes to transport the injured.

When EMS crossed the Atlantic Ocean to North America, whole new systems of emergency care emerged: EMTs, paramedics, air ambulance services, and more. Today, EMS is diverse. Physicians and nurses sometimes staff ambulances, helicopters, and fixed-wing aircraft. In rural America in places like Stanley, Idaho, communities rely on volunteer EMTs and ambulance drivers.

Calling for an ambulance also changed. That, too, started in Europe and moved to America. Today, we have 911: one number to call for emergencies. Where did that start? In 1937, the UK was the first to use a single telephone number, later adopted by other nations. Eventually, the European Union settled on 112. In the US, until the 1970s, you had to pull out the phone book and "let your fingers do the walking" until you found an ambulance service. Idaho did not have a 911 system anywhere until the mid-1970s. Stanley, Idaho, was first.

Two days after graduating from high school in Grand Forks, I tried to get an ambulance job in Minot, where I had relatives. I checked in with Schram Ambulance Service, which was not connected to a funeral home. "I don't use help, Paul," the owner said. "I run the ambulance myself." Minot, a town of 20,000, had three ambulances (converted delivery trucks) with a one-man staff. Mr. Schram told me he hired extra drivers and attendants when local racetracks and sporting events paid for standby ambulances. That was a few hours on weekends. The rest of the time, he alone responded to ambulance calls.

What this meant in reality was that the owner left the ringing telephone for a coffee shop a block away. He apparently did this often, according to a local police officer. On one such occasion, police arrived in need of an ambulance for a boy hit by a car west of Minot.

I left Mr. Schram's and hitchhiked toward Grand Forks.

Ninety miles west of Grand Forks, my ride dropped me off in Devils Lake. I walked over to the fire station. "You got any work?" I asked.

Devils Lake was the sole fire station in North Dakota that operated an ambulance service. Floyd Reardon was the assistant chief. A couple of years earlier, when our family drove between Grand Forks and Minot, we stopped and got an autographed photograph of the ambulance. Floyd remembered that. Also, my timing was good: the day before I arrived, a firefighter left his position, so Floyd needed help. "Sure, we can use you," Floyd said. "You're hired for the summer."

That summer, I lived at the fire department, slept in the dorm, and slid down the pole. There was no EMS training. I learned on the job as a firefighter and an ambulance attendant. On my first night at the Devils Lake fire station, around two in the morning, came an emergency call: a car accident with one person dead and two injured badly.

A week after my first ambulance call, the fire station phone rang, and I picked up. "I need help," the woman said frantically. "My husband is having chest pain. He can't breathe. He is covered with sweat." So off we went for the 50-mile trip to help a man having a heart attack. We arrived, found the man still alive, and started oxygen. We had nothing to offer except a ride to the nearest hospital. EMS in the 1950s and '60s was primitive.

I paid for my college education working on ambulances from 1957 to 1967. When the massive F-5 "Fargo tornado" struck the Fargo and Moorhead, Minnesota, area on the evening of June 20, 1957, I had been on the job for only two weeks. We drove from the Devils Lake Fire Department to Fargo to help. Unfortunately, the F-5 and four other tornadoes killed ten and injured over a hundred people. The 1957 Fargo tornado sparked my lifelong interest in how we better prepare for mass casualty incidents. Two years after the Fargo tornado, the 100,000-person Fargo-Moorhead (FM) area got its first independent ambulance service, and funeral home hearses no longer doubled as ambulances. In 1962, the F-M Ambulance Service hired me. Before hiring

Sanford Health

The Fargo-Moorhead Ambulance Service began in 1959 with a small fleet of Cadillacs. Paul Anderson was hired in 1962.

with F-M Ambulance Service, I worked on two ambulance services, one operated by a fire department, the other by a hospital. I had been on several hundred ambulance runs. During my years at F-M, I responded to several thousand emergency calls.

We would arrive at car wreck scenes thirty to forty miles from Fargo. Since we didn't have EMS radios, we could not inform others if we needed more help, additional units, or rescue and extrication equipment. Later, when Governor Andrus appointed me to head Idaho EMS, we quickly established a statewide EMS radio communication system. Idaho learned from North Dakota.

Revolutionary changes in EMS were underway. When I started in 1957, we were a scoop-and-run service. Then came cardiopulmonary resuscitation (CPR), the pioneering resuscitation work of Drs. Kouwenhoven, Safar, and Jude. These physicians created CPR by combining mouth-to-mouth breathing with chest compressions. (Dr. Peter Safar, a Jewish anesthesiologist who survived the Nazis and emigrated to the US, is a crucial figure in the history of EMS and critical care medicine.)

Paul Anderson

This is the first cardiac ambulance, entering service in 1967 in Belfast, Northern Ireland. Cardiologist Dr. Frank Partridge started this specialized ambulance as an extension of the Coronary Care Unit at Belfast's Royal Victoria Hospital.

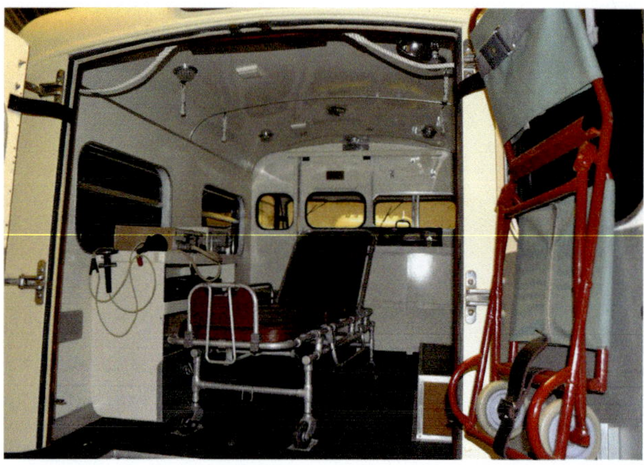

Paul Anderson

Inside the world's first Mobile Coronary Care Unit (MCCU) is the first portable defibrillator. The unit weighed about 150 pounds, including two auto batteries.

CPR came to Fargo in 1962. Instructors limited our first CPR training to ambulance crews and medical personnel in an evening session. Two days later, we got the call. One of our pharmacists had collapsed while mowing his lawn. His wife called for help. We started CPR within four minutes, transporting him to the hospital. In the ER, he was hooked to a monitor, and we saw ventricular fibrillation.

We couldn't shock the pharmacist using an external defibrillator; they didn't exist. The only defibrillators were internal. You had to crack the chest and directly defibrillate the heart. The patient had to be in a hospital ER or on an operating table with a trained surgeon to open the thorax and expose the heart. An orthopedic surgeon who had just finished training in critical care came to the ER and performed an emergency thoracotomy, and we attached the leads to the heart. We placed paddles on the non-beating heart and started shocking. Despite multiple shocks, he was dead, and we stopped. We needed an external defibrillator.

In 1965, Dr. Frank Pantridge, a consulting physician at the Royal Victoria Infirmary in Belfast, Northern Ireland, invented the first portable external defibrillator. That first "portable" defibrillator weighed 150 pounds (70 kgs) and was powered by two car batteries. Just carrying the machine would give someone chest pain. But with time, defibrillators became more portable.

Today, you will see portable cardiac defibrillators in many locations. Look around airports or other public spaces. If someone collapses, you simply need to grab this device, an "AED" or automated electronic defibrillator, and push the start button. A voice will instruct you on what to do next.

In 1968–1969, the United States had five paramedic training programs: New York City, Columbus, Miami, Los Angeles, and Seattle. People from all over the nation tuned in to the TV program "Emergency," based on the Los Angeles program. Television got people thinking about EMS, leading to upgrades. The nation's first defibrillation in the field happened in Miami. The first paramedics trained in Seattle, soon to be joined by Marie, preparing for trauma care in Idaho's Sawtooth country.

The Seattle paramedic program kicked into high gear in 1970, responding to cardiac and trauma calls. Seattle became the best place to have a heart attack, an international model for EMS. Paramedics with whom Marie trained in early 1972 staffed Medic One ambulances responding to cardiac emergencies and trauma. From out of UW's Harborview Hospital and Medic One came public education about CPR and the need to move fast to call for help: "Time is heart." Today, we build on those earlier systems of care for stroke emergencies: "Time is brain."

We'd driven out to see Yellowstone and the Tetons. Then we headed to Idaho Falls, the only big town, along with Pocatello, in eastern Idaho. I'd heard that the Idaho National Laboratory (then the "National Reactor Testing Station" or NRTS) was hiring, so I applied. Later, I flew from Fargo to Idaho Falls for the interview, and they offered me the job. NRTS hired me as a specialist in occupational health and toxicology.

The federal facility covers nearly 900 square miles in eastern Idaho's high desert, between Arco to the west, Idaho Falls to the east, and Atomic City to the south. The NRTS had several test sites with nuclear reactors, including a naval reactor at the north test site, a reactor at the central site, and a University of Chicago-run reactor at the east nuclear reactor. My colleagues were mostly safety engineers. In addition, the NRTS had four fire stations that also operated ambulances.

We had a problem with the ambulance service in Idaho Falls. When an emergency call came, the Idaho Falls ambulance would head out. The answering service would take down information if other calls came in. The answering service would advise callers with heart attacks or other life-threatening conditions to be patient: "The ambulance will be there as soon as possible. They are out on another call right now. You'll have to wait your turn." As a result, emergency calls might stack up. After waiting fifteen to twenty minutes for the ambulance and talking with the answering service one or more times, callers would grow desperate and dial the Idaho Falls Fire Department. The fire department would dispatch their rescue truck, arriving within a few minutes. Remember, this was before 911. Police and the fire department were unaware of the emergency call unless the call came to them directly.

The Idaho Falls mayor and chair of the Bonneville County Commissioners appointed me to lead a study that included surveying people who had used the ambulance service. The study was not part of my official federal duties; instead, it was a service I volunteered to do based on my years of EMS experience in North Dakota. Working with the Idaho Falls Fire Department, we completed the study in December 1969. Our study validated reports from firefighters and emergency callers that the ambulance service was atrocious.

In early May 1970, I got off the bus from the NRTS around 5:30 pm, walked into my home, and picked up the ringing phone. "Paul? Paul Hovey here." Hovey was newly appointed to the Idaho Falls City Council to fill a vacancy. "Can I meet you at the fire station in twenty minutes?"

We met at the fire station and a nun, the administrator for Sacred Heart Hospital, joined us. Hovey shared the news that the ambulance service operator had announced he would quit at midnight. "We're not going to have an ambulance service after midnight unless we put one together," Hovey said. "We need your help." The Catholic sister promised that the hospital would provide us with bandages, splints, and a shopping cart of supplies to equip a couple of ambulances. When we returned to the fire station after picking up these supplies, a loaner ambulance had arrived from the NRTS. For our backup ambulance, we equipped the battalion chief's station wagon. At two minutes to midnight, we got our first emergency call. Idaho Falls had a new, working ambulance service.

Physicians went to Governor Cecil Andrus with a message: We needed EMS to save lives. Idaho's governor and legislature responded, and Idaho became a national leader in emergency medical services.

With so much vehicular trauma in America, President John F. Kennedy had declared, "Traffic accidents constitute one of the greatest, perhaps the greatest, of the nation's public

Paul Anderson

Idaho Governor Cecil Andrus (LEFT) and the first Chief of Idaho EMS, Paul Anderson.

health problems." The National Academy of Sciences issued its report, *Accidental Death and Disability: The Neglected Disease of Modern Society*, also known as *The White Paper*.

During the hearse era of America's ambulance history, *The White Paper* underscored that the quality of ambulance services varied widely and was often unsatisfactory and unregulated. There were no standards, and everyone was on their own.

In 1966, Congress responded to America's highway carnage, enacting laws that established standards and created agencies. Congress later reorganized federal highway safety and EMS into the National Highway Traffic Safety Administration.

Federal highway safety laws promoted state involvement in advancing EMS. In 1973, President Richard Nixon signed the EMS Systems Act, establishing three hundred EMS systems in the US and providing partial funding.

In the context of this national EMS awakening, on May 2, 1971, Governor Andrus appointed a task force to write a statewide EMS plan. Dr. Fred Graber, a Boise physician, headed the EMS task force of nearly two dozen members. He pulled in people with health planning from the state's Department of Health and Welfare, Idaho Hospital Association, and Idaho Medical Association. Graber wanted rural and urban hospitals on the task force and asked cities and counties for recommendations. Andrus appointed me to the EMS Task Force after I resurrected the Idaho Falls ambulance service.

The state EMS task force had five-person study committees. Our task force finished in early 1973. Dr. Graber and the task force leadership team presented our recommendations to Governor Andrus.

Meanwhile, I continued working as a federal contractor employee with the NRTS. In March 1973, a task force member took me aside. "Paul, the governor's going to call you. He wants to meet with you about heading up Idaho EMS."

"I have a job in Idaho Falls," I responded. Several days later, Governor Andrus did call and invited me to his office. I don't remember word-for-word what was said in our meeting. But one thing stuck with me: "Paul, EMS will be my top priority in the coming year." I knew he was committed to EMS and would have my back. So, when I walked out of the office fifteen minutes later, I had said "yes" to heading up Idaho EMS.

My initial plan was to take a year's leave of absence from the NRTS position to give me time to get the EMS system up and running. But instead, I would head the agency for the next nineteen years.

Idaho EMS launched on July 1, 1973, in a ceremony at noon on the State Capitol steps.

Finding funding to start Idaho EMS within the Idaho Department of Health and Welfare (DHW) was one of our first challenges. The federal EMS Act of 1973 partially funded Idaho EMS. The federal funds helped with ambulances, radios, and rescue equipment, but not salaries.

For EMS, this was an exciting, creative, and building time. In creating Idaho EMS, we learned from people on the front lines elsewhere. In 1973, several of us, including Idaho Falls surgeons Donald Bjornson and Thomas Higgs, went to Illinois to meet with Dr. Boyd at Cook County Hospital. On the day of our meeting, Dr. Boyd apologized for being late. He was a surgeon, delayed by multiple shootings in Chicago's South Side. When we shook hands, I couldn't miss all the blood on Dr. Boyd's surgical scrubs. The following year, Dr. Boyd became the national EMS director.

Fears of being sued after providing advanced life support in the field led to legal protections. Terry Crapo, Speaker of the House, introduced the Idaho Paramedic Bill modeled on liability protection in Washington and California. For many legislators, the first time they ever heard of EMS was when considering Crapo's draft bill. The legislature gave liability protection to trained and certified EMS personnel who operated under a medical/physician director.

Other legislators supported EMS, too. A state senator from Blackfoot was also a funeral homeowner and director. He was instrumental in helping EMS ambulances. I remember the senator speaking in hearings about using hearses to pick up patients and how frightened people were about being hauled away in a hearse.

Soon after moving to Idaho, I learned about the challenges for EMS in the central Idaho mountains. Coming to work at the NRTS one Monday morning in the late 1960s, I heard a coworker had been in a severe motor vehicle crash that weekend. Two cars collided on a narrow metal bridge on the Ketchum-to-Stanley Highway, a short distance from the Redfish Lake turnoff.

My coworker said the injured waited more than ninety minutes for a station wagon "ambulance" to arrive from a funeral home in Hailey, seventy-five miles away. No one had rescue equipment to extricate the other automobile's driver properly. Rescuers used a wrecker to free the driver.

The man suffered life-threatening injuries, dying in the Sun Valley hospital a week later.

Several years later, Marie Osborn, an advanced practice nurse, opened the Salmon River Emergency Clinic.

While our EMT class in Idaho Falls was probably the first in the state, Stanley's EMT class was not far behind, and Marie would continue to instruct this class for nearly three decades. Marie's EMTs were a critical EMS link for Idaho, staffing the Stanley Ambulance and helping with backcountry rescues.

Other communities also started ambulance services in the early 1970s. In the spring of 1973, Ketchum's fire chief, Bill Brand, contacted me. "Paul, our only ambulance is the funeral home in Hailey," Bill lamented. "Hearses and station wagons are fine, but we need an ambulance service in Ketchum and Sun Valley." Bill also had his eye on EMS that would help beyond the Wood River Valley and into the central Idaho mountains.

"Paul, they have a little red log cabin clinic in Stanley," Bill noted. "The town has a nurse, Marie Osborn, who provides emergency care. She has also set up a volunteer-staffed ambulance as part of the Stanley Clinic." I made a mental note to introduce myself to Marie after we launched Idaho EMS on July 1. Later that summer, I drove Stanley's dusty dirt roads, parked in front of the red log cabin across from the bar, and stepped into the Salmon River Emergency Clinic, where I introduced myself to Marie.

What was happening in Stanley regarding the clinic and the volunteer ambulance squad was truly impressive. However, I was not impressed with the old military surplus ambulance parked in front of the clinic. Marie told me the stories of holes in the floorboards, exhaust fumes, the superheated floors next to the gurney, and the failing electrical system with lights going out while transporting patients over Galena Summit.

"Marie, you have to replace that ambulance." I couldn't help but notice the new ambulance donation jar. Like other rural communities, Stanley struggled to create and sustain ambulance services. I would soon meet with Senator Frank Church of Idaho about the need for a reliable ambulance for Stanley and, using Stanley as a teaching case, ambulances for communities throughout rural America. Here is Senator Church's statement from the floor of the US Senate about the Stanley Ambulance:

November 20, 1975 **CONGRESSIONAL RECORD — Senate 37587–37588**
By Mr. CHURCH

S.2714. A bill to amend the act of May 27, 1930, to expand the emergency authority of the Secretary of Agriculture regarding persons who are lost, seriously ill, injured, or who died within the National Forest System, and for other purposes. Referred to the Committee on Agriculture in Forestry.

Mr. CHURCH. Mr. President, the campgrounds, shelters, waters, and trails of the national forest system are rapidly becoming the most intensively used recreational facilities within the Western United States. Each year, during the summer months in particular, a large number of visitors utilize these unique, and other remote attractions.

The remoteness of these areas, while helping to enhance a sense of retreat from the pressures of urban life can quickly turn a serious injury or illness into a nightmare of giant proportions. These scenic areas are often many miles from adequately staffed and equipped medical facilities.

To anyone who has driven the steep, winding roads which often lead to the most spectacular parts of these areas, the need for dependable, high-quality emergency ambulance operations is obvious. Presently, however, serious deficiencies are often common to the ambulance operation which served these predominantly federally owned areas. Another is the lack of ambulance-to-hospital communications equipment. As Mr. Paul B. Anderson, Chief of the emergency medical services of the Idaho Department of Health and Welfare has said:

The dedicated personnel (of the existing local ambulance operations) can not provide dependable, high-quality emergency service with inadequate, undependable vehicles lacking (radio) communications capabilities.

A case in point is the volunteer ambulance service provided by the small township of Stanley, Idaho. Stanley, with a population of 47 permanent residents, is located within the boundary of the Sawtooth National Recreation Area. Over a million tourists visit the immediate area annually, most during the summer months. The closest hospital and physicians are located in Sun Valley, 60 miles and a major mountain pass away from Stanley. Before 1972, however, it was necessary to summon an ambulance from Hailey, which is 75 miles away. Needless to say, this meant that the area essentially had no emergency ambulance service during this time period. In 1972, the residents of Stanley decided that someone had to accept some responsibility to improve the situation.

Therefore, they formed a volunteer ambulance squad and acquired a 1958 Army surplus ambulance with the assistance of the Idaho Civil Defense Office in the State Department of Environmental and Community Services. The current situation with an old, often unreliable vehicle—the windows must be kept rolled down to prevent the ambulance filling up with carbon monoxide—is undoubtedly better than no service at all. However, it seems to me that an isolated community, surrounded by rugged terrain and 60 miles from the nearest hospital has a greater need for consistent ambulance service than most small towns.

Mr. President, I ask unanimous consent that an editorial from Safety Signals, titled "Stanley's Ancient Ambulance," which presents a vivid description of the situation as it now exists in Stanley, and details the need for ambulance service there and other such remote areas be printed in the RECORD.

There being no objection, the editorial was ordered to be printed in the RECORD, as follows:

From Safety Signals, October 1974

STANLEY'S ANCIENT AMBULANCE

A patched emergency vehicle serving 1.25 million people whose closest doctor lives a mountain away is causing a lot of talk in the West—but so far nobody has come up with a new ambulance.

The permanent residents of Stanley, Idaho — numbering 47 — are holding their breaths. And the reason is that 1¼ million tourists move into the Sawtooth National Recreation Area between Memorial and Labor Day dragging their tents and their cameras and inevitably some collide on the snaking mountain roads, slip over drop-offs or get fishhooks in their eyes before they go back home.

The wounded are brought to a three-room red log cabin to be treated by Marie Osborn, the only emergency nurse-practitioner in hundreds of miles and one of the few in the country. Marie, who skis in winter to treat gunshot wounds, fractures and burns, has pleaded in vain for a replacement for Stanley's 1958 Pontiac ambulance. A year ago, Marie thought that one of the victims of an exploding propane stove would be lost before they got a helicopter because intravenous feedings could only be administered in the ambulance to one patient at a time. One victim was on the floor and another on the stretcher while they raced to make contact with a helicopter.

What does the 42-year-old mother of five do at a time like that? "We drive as fast as we can," Marie says. Not long ago a woman was shot in a hunting accident and Marie was not certain the vehicle would survive the fast race over rocky mountain roads. The woman got emergency treatment but the Pontiac front frame actually did fracture from metal fatigue and had to be welded before it could be put back into daily service.

Part of the problem is the terrain. Stanley's closest mountain raises 8,700 feet in Galena Pass between Stanley and Sun Valley shoots up to 10,000 with drop-offs that earn it the name of "Swiss Alps."

"Any ambulance has to be able to stand the curves," Marie says.

The people in Stanley are reluctant to pay thousands of dollars from their own pockets to care for 1¼ million vacationers from other states.

The Federal EMS Act (through HEW) has appropriated $185 million including some for emergency vehicles but "we cannot shake it lose" according to Paul Anderson, Chief of Emergency Health Services, Idaho Department of Health and Welfare. Paul went to Washington (D. C.) with a proposal to get 75 percent funding for an ambulance to meet DOT standards, but failed. Meanwhile, Ms. Pat Ehrlich's office (Idaho Traffic Safety Commission) has tried breathing new life into the project by keeping the present ambulances equipment in shape. The Commission's philosophy is to spend current money on a statewide emergency network instead of pouring funds into just one or two communities.

Marie gives extensive care with telephone aid from two doctors beyond the mountain. If helicopters are needed, MAST (Military Air Safety Transport) at Mountain Home Air Force Base, Idaho, supplies them. On routine days, Marie takes care of lines of people outside the log cabin, teaches emergency training or instructs two ambulance technicians.

How did a housewife land such a job in the first place? "I complained to the head of the Idaho Hospital Association that rural areas of the state weren't getting a fair shake in advanced medical technology," the wife of an IBM employee in Boise remembers. Idaho offered Marie not a job — but a mission. She went to the University of Washington and added an emergency nurse practitioner's certificate to her college degree and RN credentials.

A New York Times travel article appeared on January 7, 1973, describing her as "one of the first (nurse practitioners) in the nation. Twenty-five people wrote inquiring letters. Soon, somebody started a move to build a small clinic. "Our new facility is to be opened soon," Marie says.

As this newsletter goes to press, the new clinic is in operation, but a new ambulance is still a dream.

Mr. CHURCH. Mr. President, the volunteer ambulance squad from Stanley and in other small communities throughout the West which operate in the midst of federally owned land simply do not have the capital necessary to purchase modern, dependable vehicles equipped with ambulance–hospital radio communications gear. It seems to me that the Federal Government should accept at least partial responsibility for funding emergency ambulance service in areas that are predominantly federally owned. For that reason, Mr. President, I am today introducing legislation which would help alleviate some of the current problems. This bill would authorize the Secretary of Agriculture to incur such expenses as may be necessary in:

- Providing emergency medical services for persons ill or injured in the National Forest System, and while in transit to the nearest medical facilities;
- Transporting persons ill or injured to the nearest medical facilities or to interested parties;
- Transporting persons who die within the national forests to the nearest place where the body can be transferred to interested parties, or local authorities; and
- Searching for persons lost in that National Forest.

This bill would also allow the Secretary of Agriculture to cooperate with State and local officials, and to enter into written agreements with these authorities to provide such services. I ask unanimous consent that the text of this bill be printed in the RECORD. *[S. 2714—a bill introduced by US Senator Frank Church to provide expanded emergency medical services to predominantly federally-owned areas.]*

"It seems to me," Idaho's senior senator said, "that an isolated community, surrounded by rugged terrain, and sixty miles from the closest hospital, has a greater need for consistent ambulance service than most small towns."

Senator Church and Idaho EMS teamed together to work on rural EMS. Eventually, funds from the 1973 Emergency Medical Services System (EMSS) Act were added to those ambulance donation jars.

After several years came the day on the capitol's steps when Governor Andrus stood with Dr. David Boyd, the Chicago trauma surgeon and national EMS director, to award keys for twenty new ambulance vehicles to Idaho communities. One of those new ambulance keys went to Marie Osborn. The photo of that event and those dedicated to rural EMS is one of the favorites of my tenure as Idaho EMS chief.

Later, Dr. Boyd returned to Idaho to observe the start of paramedic programs in Idaho Falls, Canyon County (Nampa-Caldwell), and Boise (Ada County). He watched Backcountry Medical Rescue Team (BCMRT) personnel from southwest Idaho and North Idaho demonstrating rescue techniques.

Marie's son, John Osborn, MD, described the advances in EMS and rural healthcare in the 1970s that his family lived through as "frenetic, rich, and transformational." He is correct. For EMS, those were revolutionary years.

When Idaho launched EMS to create a statewide system in 1973, there were many holes. However, one pressing void in the state was already filled with Marie in Stanley. Because of Marie's knowledge and skills in emergency medicine and Stanley's EMT program, Idaho EMS used Stanley to anchor EMS in that part of Idaho, better enabling us to create a statewide emergency response system.

Between Boise and Stanley, in the mid-1970s, there was nothing if people needed emergency help. Marie and Stanley's EMTs were trying to cover from Lowman to Challis while struggling to staff their clinic. Most small communities had no Marie Osborn. Getting local EMS units started in Idaho's small towns — to serve vast areas with mountain highways, hiking trails, and rivers — required time and effort from our EMS staff. We worked to support volunteer-based EMS units in Lowman, Idaho City, Garden Valley/Crouch, and elsewhere in Idaho.

Our 1973 Governor's Task Force recommendations identified a statewide EMS communication system as a high priority. In emergencies, you have to be able to communicate. Think about what that means in a state with Idaho's boundaries and landscapes. Mountains dominate the state from Canada to the Snake River plain. In the mid-1970s, Idaho's rural communities had no dedicated emergency radio channels.

"StateComm," a mountaintop radio communication network networking the entire state, was our response to that. In 1974, the Robert Wood Johnson Foundation awarded Idaho a $400,000 grant to develop that system.

Eventually, microwave links connected remotely controlled mountaintop stations to regional hospitals and the Idaho Statewide EMS Communication Center (StateComm). We worked on networking with all Idaho hospitals, ambulance services, QRUs, and rescue units.

In August 1977, I entered Idaho's new EMS communication center and turned on the radio console equipment. Various colored status lights came on, and the audio speakers came alive with radio transmissions from all areas of the state. A motor vehicle accident in north Idaho, a heart attack in central Idaho, and a motorcycle accident in eastern Idaho were all in progress.

Suddenly, Idaho EMS staff in that room heard radio transmissions from an ambulance crew traveling to a hospital about a hundred miles north of Boise. Unfortunately, what we heard was not good. The ambulance was transporting a thirty-year-old male who had accidentally shot himself while hiking in a forest.

The ambulance tried several times but could not make radio contact with the hospital. The ambulance crew occupied a location within a rugged, mountainous area, out of radio range for the local hospital twenty miles away. Although we knew that StateComm was not yet officially open, we jumped on it and relayed information to the nearby hospital.

"You have a young male with a gunshot wound in hemorrhagic shock headed your way with an ETA of thirty minutes."

"Okay, we'll have a physician ready and waiting. Thanks!"

Next, we started coordinating air transport and alerting St. Al's in Boise that we might need a surgical team.

So began Idaho's StateComm, which provides 24-hour networking support and coordinates resources to respond to emergencies statewide.

Even in those first years, the center handled 30,000 emergency responses yearly. As Idaho's population has grown, so has the number of emergencies and the importance of StateComm.

In 1977, sitting down to those blinking lights on the radio console, we helped respond to mountain rescues, chemical spills, difficult rescue extrication situations, critical patient transfers, and more. Today our work continues supporting and coordinating an EMS team that is big and diverse, spread across Idaho's challenging geography.

Marie's retirement celebration was held at the Redfish Lake Lodge in 1999, and on that day I reflected upon how much one person meant to her community and far beyond. Marie showed the nation what one competent and skilled advanced practice nurse could do in a rural and remote community tucked into the central Idaho mountains. (Marie came late to her celebration, splattered with mud and blood after an ambulance run and a fatality.)

Marie is an iconic figure. She may be the world's first licensed nurse practitioner. For nearly thirty years, Marie-provided 24/7 emergency services and healthcare to a town of roughly fifty year-round residents and over a million summertime visitors across 6,000 square miles of backcountry. She was a Rock of Gibraltar for the Sawtooth–Salmon River country for emergency care and rescue when someone's life was in jeopardy.

Thousands of people have served and continue to serve, standing ready to respond to emergencies. In EMS, each of us has a job as part of that team.

Marie may have helped create the EMS team, but she also had her work as part of that team. Marie was just doing her job covering the wild country of central Idaho until she was nearly seventy years old. And she still would if she could.

In 1999, Idaho StateComm heard Marie on the radio for the last time.

"Marie Osborn, Unit 1, over and out."

PART FOUR

BUILDING

Digging snow to unbury the new clinic's cement foundation, March, 1974. Building the Stanley Clinic was a slow-motion community barn-raising, with labor and materials donated by locals and people throughout Idaho and beyond. The new clinic took several years to complete, opening on Father's Day, 1975.

17

EMERGENCY CALL: PHIL COONTS

Phil Coonts was there when you needed him most. His handyman skills were packaged with his being the biblical Good Samaritan.

Phil is an Idaho farm boy who became a fisheries biologist. His wife, Karen, was one of two special needs teachers in Custer County. Together, they raised three lovely children: Mark, Allyson, and Ellen. Unfortunately, while living in Stanley, their infant son, Mark, reached from his crib, pulled down a philodendron leaf, and started chewing. For children, these houseplants are toxic. Karen, scared, called the clinic.

I contacted the Poison Control Center. "Marie, do you have syrup of ipecac? You need to make the baby vomit."

I pulled the ipecac bottle off the clinic shelf, jumped in the car, and headed to Phil and Karen's apartment. As I walked in, Karen was holding Mark and sobbing. I dosed Mark with ipecac, and he vomited. After that, Mark did fine — and so did Karen.

At times, Phil almost seemed like my guardian angel. When the rain turned to snow around Halloween, and my car was snowed in at the house, Phil helped me get the car to the highway. Phil repacked my snowmobile track after snow and wind erased my trail. Otherwise, how would I have gotten out through several feet of drifting snow when the emergency calls came?

Sawtooth winters can be brutal. Phil Coonts, EMT, packed Marie's snowmchine trail so she could commute from her home to the highway for emergency calls and clinic patients.

With ground blizzards or bitterly cold temperatures at 7,000 feet elevation, a lot can happen between the highway and my cabin, especially in the dark. Phil and Karen would call the house to ensure I had arrived safely home. Then, during the night of a ground blizzard, Phil and Karen knew something was wrong when I didn't answer the cabin phone.

PHIL COONTS, IN HIS OWN WORDS

I'm from Wilder, Idaho. My dad worked for a farmer. My high school buddy wanted to go backpacking. "We're going to the Sawtooths."

"Never been there," I replied. "Don't know anything about them."

I'll never forget the jaw-dropping moment I experienced when we drove over Galena Summit and saw the beautiful Sawtooth Valley opening up below us. To this day, driving over Galena Summit and coming into the Sawtooths still gives me goosebumps.

After high school, I eventually was hired by the Forest Service, a dream job.

During my first summer as a Forest Service seasonal, I worked on a recreational crew stationed at the Fourth of July Work Center. When Karen was pregnant with Mark, Marie insisted Karen deliver with Dr. Bryan Stone at the hospital and not in the Sawtooths with her. Marie was unyielding, worrying about complicated deliveries. Better to give birth in a Sun Valley hospital than in a car pulled over on Galena Summit. Dr. Stone, not Marie, delivered Mark, who came fast for a first baby.

We needed a place to live. Unfortunately, the Forest Service wouldn't let us room at the Fourth of July Work Center. So, instead, we rented an apartment at Sessions Lodge in Obsidian. While living at Sessions in 1980, I took the EMT class from Marie.

Living off the highway one winter, Karen and I drove two old snowmobiles. The machines wouldn't start unless you brought the carburetors inside to stay warm. I drove the snowmobile, and Karen rode in the sled with the kids, bundled with tarps and blankets to keep off the blowing snow.

I loved horses, and Forest Service teams were forever coming in and heading out with stock. During my second summer I worked on a trail crew, and I returned year after year. In the summer, wilderness trail work kept me away from Karen and the kids for ten-day stretches.

Finally, after twelve years, Karen put her foot down. So, I applied to the new Sawtooth Fish Hatchery, located six miles south of Stanley on Highway 75 and run by the Idaho Department of Fish and Game. I worked as a fish culturist. My job year-round included feeding fish, cleaning raceways, trapping mature returning salmon and steelhead, and caring for them until we could harvest eggs. In addition, the fish hatchery hired temporary employees during the spring, summer, and fall. I worked with them, teaching and learning skills. Working with young kids starting in life was one of the best parts of my jobs with the Forest Service and Idaho Fish and Game.

My oldest, Mark, hit high school age but did not want to take the bus to Challis or board out. The Stanley school only went to eighth grade. There was an opening at Mackay Hatchery in 1995. Karen and I moved the family to Mackay, where I worked for the next twelve years. Eventually, in 2008, I returned to the Stanley hatchery. I worked until retiring in 2018.

We lived in Custer County, which covers just shy of 5,000 square miles. The county's population was 4,275 by the 2020 census — or about one person per square mile.

Stanley Ambulance EMTs: Phil Coonts (LEFT), Maryellen Easom, and Steve Lipus

Marie's commute to the clinic and for emergency calls started here, snowmobiling two miles to the highway and then driving twelve miles to town.

Karen taught kids with special needs in Stanley, Challis, and Mackay.

We loved Stanley, but winters can be brutal. You can lose depth perception in the dark with blizzards blowing snow sideways. Before the snowpack gets hard, getting a snowmobile stuck in December and January is easy. We worried about Marie in her fifties, living alone on Shaw Mesa, two miles uphill from the highway. When the emergency calls came, Marie had to go. I kept her snowmobile trail open.

Anytime there was a storm or wind, I made a point of breaking trail to her house, 3–4 snowmachine-widths wide. Then, I'd shovel the drifts at Marie's home and snow off her roof. Marie was always so thankful. I was a Marie "groupie." I'd do anything for her.

That fateful night, the weather was miserable. Marie passed me on the highway in the blizzard, heading home after seeing clinic patients. Waiting ample time, I called her cabin to ensure Marie had made it home. The phone rang and rang, then flipped to message mode. She should have been there and picked up. I waited and tried calling again. No answer.

"Karen, something's wrong. Marie should be home by now. I'll need to check on her," I said, while grabbing my snowmobiling clothes, hustling out the door into the darkness and blowing snow.

I parked the car at the Fisher Creek Road turnoff, started up the snowmobile, and headed up the hill. The snow was blowing hard, and I couldn't see any tracks. The wind-driven snow covered the trail I had packed earlier. When conditions deteriorate to that point, you move by muscle memory.

My headlight didn't pick up a stuck snowmobile or Marie. At the same time, when the snow is that deep, you can't just wander around in a blizzard at night and risk getting stuck in deep powder. Still, I saw no tracks anywhere before arriving at her house. Marie wasn't home. I turned around, went back to the highway, then tried again. With the wind-blown snow, you couldn't see anything. Even along the mesa's crest, the trail disappeared in the wind. Marie had vanished in the blizzard and darkness.

Battling rising fear, I headed back to our apartment, intending to call for more help. After shaking off the snow, I walked in the door. "Phil," Karen said, "Marie's okay. I just called the clinic. She's there." Marie missed a corner on the mesa's crest in the blizzard and dark, plunging over the cliff with her snowmobile. Unhurt, she climbed back up the steep snowy slope, then waded through the snow to her car parked at the highway.

Lessons learned: Marie never again tried to get home in dangerous weather, instead staying at the clinic. Marie could have died. That night also encouraged the clinic's board to approve living quarters for the College of Idaho premed students — and Marie.

For seventeen years, I volunteered as an EMT for the Stanley Ambulance. Marie was gone when I got one of my first emergency calls, a young woman at Smiley Creek contemplating suicide. Steve Lipus and I went.

The woman was twenty-four or five years old. When we entered, she was wearing a robe. "I don't want to live," she said. Winter had caught up with her, isolated and alone for too long. Now, it was mud season, especially tough to get out. Unfortunately, our EMT training had not prepared us for responding to mental health emergencies like suicidal ideation.

We sat and listened. Our patient talked about her family. Gradually, we were able to connect. She called a friend who promised to come and help her get care. The young woman committed not to kill herself and agreed to a safety plan. And she promised to call us both two to three days later.

In those years, none of us really talked about mental health and suicide. There was no crisis line. Two days later, as promised, the young woman called. She was doing better and had started seeing a counselor in Ketchum. Trauma and bleeding might have been easier for one of my first emergency calls. Still, I think Steve and I made a difference in this woman's life.

In a world of EMS champagne and horseshit, I do have some horseshit memories.

We got an emergency call once when Marie was on another emergency and unavailable. If Marie had known how bad it was, she would never have let the EMTs go it alone. But she didn't know. None of us did.

Not far from the Grandjean turnoff near Warm Springs Creek on Highway 21, a van — a driver and her three kids — crossed the centerline. Going in the other direction was a Winnebago motorhome. Behind the Winnebago, a husband and wife were riding a motorcycle.

The van with the kids hit the Winnebago head-on. The motorhome burst into flames. The motorcyclist and his wife plowed into the back of the motorhome.

StateComm called for backup assistance for Lowman. The Stanley Ambulance responded, along with the Custer County deputy sheriff and Forest Service Law Enforcement Officer and EMT Steve Lipus, and Forest Protection Officer Ken Hartz. Steve and Ken ran code (lights and siren) through the Valley and over Banner Summit, arriving a few minutes after we did. StateComm also dispatched two helicopters, National Guard and Life Flight, landing on Highway 21.

For the Stanley Ambulance, it took us 35 minutes to get to the trauma scene. When our three EMTs stepped out of the ambulance, nothing had been done. We were the initial first responders on the scene of several burning vehicles. The flaming wreckage blocked the highway. Bystanders had pulled the kids out of the car. One of the two kids who eventually survived, a girl perhaps twelve or thirteen years old, was screaming. The other was unconscious.

While Lowman first responders attended to one of the kids, we focused on the other. As Steve Lipus recalls, "Our patient was a young man with a femur fracture and possible cervical/spinal injuries. We were concerned about the possibility of significant internal blood loss with that type of injury. We attached a Hare traction splint to the injured extremity, gradually applying traction. When you use the proper traction for an injury, you can see the relief on your patient's face."

The first helicopter transported the patient who received care from the Lowman ambulance. We stabilized and loaded our patient onto a second helicopter for transport to Boise.

With flames extinguished, the highway still smoked for days. Burn marks remained on the pavement for a long time. Every time I saw that spot, it was like a Vietnam vet hearing the *chuff, chuff, chuff* — it took me right back. A lot of people died there.

Had we somehow gotten there sooner, might it have made a difference? Knowing that these kids waited while nothing had been done still weighs on me.

Girl killed in Lowman wreck identified

LOWMAN, Idaho Authorities have identified the ten-year-old Marsing girl who died in a fiery chain-reaction accident on Idaho Highway 21 near Lowman that left five people dead.

Boise County Coroner Larry Abbott says Julie Cahill was killed in the Friday morning crash which claimed her mother's life and sent the girl's sister and brother to the hospital.

Idaho State Police say 40-year-old Kathy Cahill was driving a van about 18 miles northeast of Lowman when she crossed the center line and hit a motor home driven by 75-year-old Robert Coon of Boise.

Cahill and Coon were killed in the crash.

The motorhome struck a motorcycle carrying 54-year-old Fred Hart and 49-year-old Dianne Hart of Green River, Wyoming. Both died at the scene.

Two other passengers in the Cahill van, 12-year-old Tonya Cahill and 18-year-old Stanley Cahill remain hospitalized at Saint Alphonsus Regional Medical Center in Boise. Tonya is in fair condition, but Stanley is in critical condition.

Associated Press. August 18, 1991

"Did Marie cover this in EMT class?" you ask yourself. Book learning and practical, hands-on training help but will only prepare you for some emergency calls.

"StateComm to Stanley Clinic. Car rollover seven miles west of Stanley on Highway 21 at the Park Creek overlook." I drove my vehicle on this run since the ambulance had already left for the scene.

Parents and their two sons were driving west in two vehicles. The new driver, their teenage son, was at the steering wheel of a Suburban with his younger brother in the passenger seat. Following behind were their mom and dad, watching.

The teenage driver lost control of the Suburban. It rolled. The younger brother wasn't wearing his seatbelt and was ejected from the rolling vehicle. The Suburban came down on his head.

The parents watched the wreck and the death of their son. The ambulance transported the surviving teenage boy to the Stanley airstrip for helicopter transport while the parents drove to Sun Valley. The teenage driver had some injuries but nothing serious.

Along Highway 21 at the accident scene, I picked up pieces of brain and placed them in an emesis bag. That was hard. But I didn't want car tires driving over the child's brain and skull pieces. Magpies were already starting to gather. So I was there for a long time, cleaning up. When I finished, I moved the child's remains to the clinic.

Picking up the brains of a child who had been alive just a short time ago forced me to think about "what if." In death's wake, "what if" questions can linger a lifetime. Meanwhile, at the clinic, we waited for the mortician, Russ Mikel, to arrive from Hailey to transport the child's remains.

When teaching us in our EMT classes, Marie could not have anticipated what I would be called to do. As with so much in life, you learn as you go. When kids are hurt, processing can be hard, especially when you have kids about the same age. Your mind substitutes your child for the child who is sick, injured, or dead. "There, but for the grace of God...."

"Sometimes, you do everything you can possibly do, and nothing works," Marie would say. "You try everything you can think of. But, it's their time."

On my first run as an EMT, Marie was at the clinic when the emergency call came. Marie picked me up in the Stanley Ambulance at Sessions Lodge. A car had wrecked down by Smiley Creek. There's just something about that stretch of Highway 75 between Beaver Creek and Smiley Creek, almost like some Bermuda Triangle, with so many accidents and deaths.

Driving the Stanley Ambulance, we could see the car ahead of us, upside down.

The driver had lost control of his hard-top sports car. He wasn't wearing a seatbelt, and his buddy wasn't either. The driver was thrown free. His buddy was still in the passenger seat — not responding, not breathing, no pulse. The driver was up and walking around alive. They had been in the car together, just two feet apart. Now, one was alive. One was dead. He was the first dead body in my life.

As a volunteer EMT in rural Idaho, I offer driving advice: Do not swerve for any animal. If you swerve, you risk losing control of your vehicle, rolling, hitting someone else, or even dying. Marie hit a herd of elk in her Subaru on the highway at night on icy roads. Swerving on black ice might have been fatal for her and not changed the outcome for the elk.

The right extrication equipment can make all the difference for people trapped in wrecked vehicles.

Near Fourth of July Creek, a logging truck driver fell asleep at the wheel. The truck left the highway and rolled. When we got to the driver, we saw his foot wrapped around the brake pedal. He was stuck. I could smell diesel but wasn't too worried.

I worked for forty-five minutes and still needed help figuring out how to free him. The foot was broken, and maneuvering the foot caused the driver to yell. I didn't have the equipment to cut the brake pedal. I'm good at figuring things out, so I was frustrated that I couldn't find a solution. It was simple yet complex, and that fractured foot wouldn't budge. The injured driver was stuck in his wrecked truck.

Eventually, the Blaine County Fire Department arrived. With their jaws of life — hydraulic cutters, spreaders, and jacks — we could move the pedal out of the way, free the driver, and get him to the hospital.

That ambulance run underscored that the equipment must be available and in working order at the scene. Fortunately for that driver, Blaine County drove over the hill to help. But they are an hour away, if the roads are good. Later, Idaho EMS facilitated cooperative agreements to improve coordinated responses from EMS units. Still, for some accidents, time can mean life or death; we learned from that episode and ordered additional extrication equipment for the Stanley ambulance.

Getting cutters, spreaders, come-a-longs, and other extrication equipment onto an ambulance along with ropes, stokes litters, and wood cribbing is a tall order. Therefore, many EMS units work with their fire departments to carry equipment and train crews in extrication procedures. Many rural EMS units partner with their local volunteer fire department using a team approach.

I believe in people's fundamental goodness. If you ask people for help in a life-or-death situation, they will help.

A pickup between Lowman and Stanley lost control on Highway 21 and launched over a cliff. The accident was horrendous and had witnesses.

Lowman got the call but could not get the driver out. StateComm called the Stanley Ambulance for backup. Gary Gadwa rappelled down by rope, put the injured driver in a stokes basket, and we roped him up the hillside. We had practiced rappelling off buildings in Boise, and our EMS training helped save that pickup driver's life.

People stopped along the highway. No bystander said "No" when we asked them for help with traffic control and keeping the scene safe. For first responders, our challenge is knowing when to ask for help and using that help in the safest and best way to care for our patients.

In the mid-1980s, a car wrecked near Sessions Lodge. The woman driver was alone, and no other vehicles were involved. We arrived by ambulance and were able to extricate her from the car. However, until clinicians completed her ER evaluation and ruled out a cervical spine fracture, we had to protect her neck.

I held traction on her neck the entire time. Squares of glass from a side window had embedded in her head. I was wearing latex gloves as part of universal precautions. Continuing with traction as we moved her onto the spine board, I could feel those pieces of broken glass shredding my gloves. Glass cut my hands. Blood began seeping into what remained of my gloves.

Marie called after I returned home from transporting the woman to Sun Valley.

"Phil, I got a call from the ER staff at Moritz. That woman you transported told the ER physician ... I hate to tell you this. She has HIV. Until we know more, you must treat yourself like you have HIV to protect Karen and the kids." An HIV diagnosis was a death sentence in the mid-1980s. Effective therapy wouldn't become available for another ten years, in 1996. I had three kids and a wife. I couldn't go out this way. How could I be punished by dying of AIDS for helping someone?

Back at Moritz Hospital in Sun Valley, our patient was tested for HIV.

She was negative.

Epidemics and pandemics touch all our lives. European explorers were vectors for smallpox, measles, and other microbes that wiped out an estimated ninety-five percent of indigenous populations — some twenty million people. In more recent times, polio, HIV/AIDS, and COVID have all sparked fear and conflict, bringing out the worst in people. Yet, epidemics have also evoked compassionate care, bringing out the best in people, too.

On a frigid winter afternoon, a trapper walked through a foot of snow on a trail downriver from Stanley. The trapper was about a quarter mile from the road when he saw a man on the ground. The man was under a wet blanket, curled in a hole created by a tree's root ball left after a blowdown. The trapper drove to the nearest phone and called the clinic for help.

We parked the ambulance, headed up the trail, and found the man. He appeared thin and ashen with a scraggly mustache. We asked him questions, and he cooperated as much as he could. However, he was unable to move, barely able to whisper.

"I...have...AIDS."

Our AIDS patient had come to the Sawtooth country to end his life by freezing to death. He would not have survived another night if the trapper had not found him.

The young man's body was shutting down, past shivering. We started feeling around. His calves were hard like wood, frozen solid. We carefully moved him into the stokes basket and then carried him to the ambulance.

He was dehydrated, hypothermic, and needed warmed IV fluids. Marie tried getting IV access, but even using a heating pad, she couldn't get a vein — and she's a borrow-pit pro under pressure.

We didn't talk much during the ambulance transport to Sun Valley. He shared that lying there, freezing to death, he changed his mind and did not want to die.

"My greatest fear was the little critters would eat my body and get AIDS. Then they, too, would die." He struggled to get back to the highway for help when the cold finally stopped him.

Who am I to second-guess their decisions when someone faces a terminal diagnosis? Instead, I worked with Marie to stabilize and transport another human found down with severe hypothermia.

While serving as a volunteer EMT for seventeen years was an honor, I didn't look forward to the emergency calls. But, as you've heard from other EMTs, having Marie as part of our team was a security blanket. With Marie on our side, we knew that things would go as well as they possibly could.

At first, I could do what people asked of me. Then, with experience, my confidence grew as a first responder. Eventually, I could line out the troops. With Maryellen and Sparky Easom, Steve Lipus, and Gary Gadwa, we had solid leaders and a team that meshed well together. I hear that some EMS units have ego problems. The Stanley Ambulance didn't have that. The crew is a team of exceptional people. We were friends before and friends afterward.

We came to rely upon each other to help those in need. When we rappelled steep cliffs from road to river, we depended on and trusted each other. Over the course of every ambulance run and backcountry rescue we shared, we learned and grew together.

And Marie? I'd do anything for Marie. Nothing she ever asked of me was out of line. She was a special person in a special place at a special time of our lives. And she took good care of my kids.

Phil Coonts retired after thirty-two years with the Idaho Department of Fish and Game, and Karen also retired from teaching kids with special needs. Their three kids have long since grown up and left Stanley. Mark Coonts is a public defender for Gem County, Allyson Komori is an internist and cares for patients at St. Luke's, and Ellen Johnson works at the National Interagency Fire Center in Boise.

In all the years, I don't recall once that Phil ever said "No" when we needed him, nor did any other EMT volunteers. When the emergency call came, they responded.

> But a Samaritan, as he traveled, came where the [injured] man was; and when he saw him, he took pity on him. He went to him and bandaged his wounds, pouring on oil and wine. Then he put the man on his own donkey, brought him to an inn and took care of him.
>
> *Luke 10:25-37 NIV*

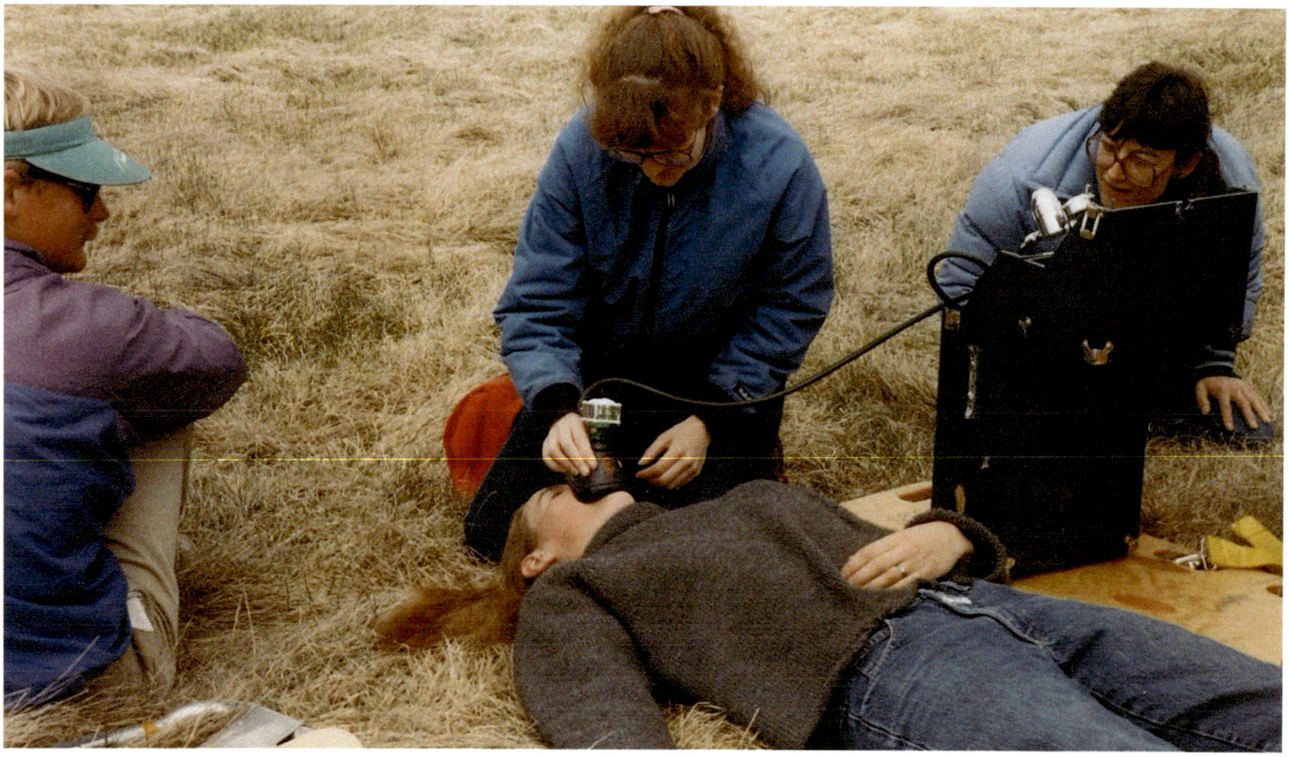

Training for the emergency call

18

THE IMPOSSIBLE DREAM

In October 1973 the foundation for the clinic was poured. Then Old Man Winter intervened with foul weather and deep snow... The weekend of March 15 the volunteer laborers, using a bulldozer, loader, snowblowers, and snowplow, discovered there was still a clinic foundation under all that snow. With construction leadership centered in Jerry Funderberg and Gerald Nicholson, and with the help of practically every able-bodied man and woman in the community, visible progress was made. The women of the community are to be commended for the excellent meals provided for these hungry workers.

The Impossible Dream. Dedication of the Salmon River Emergency Clinic and Open House in Stanley, Idaho, on June 15, 1975

Annual Report, January-December, 1993
Salmon River Clinic – Hospital District

	1993	1994
TOTAL ENCOUNTERS	2098	1954
People	2062	1923
Animals	36	31
AMBULANCE RUNS	44 (46 patients)	23 (28 patients)
EMERGENCY CALLS	183	159
HOUSE CALLS	30	25
HOURS (MARIE)	2312	1920

Be sure to clamp the cord! I remember that vivid dream just a week before the delivery. In my dream, a hippie couple in a converted school bus rushed to the clinic. She was in labor. We put her into the second treatment room where she delivered. I awoke in a sweat: I had forgotten to clamp the cord. I told the EMTs and the premeds about the dream. "Whatever happens, just remind me to cut the cord."

Barely a week later, that dream became an emergency childbirth reality. One of our premed students, Craig Pierce, tells that story:

I was a summer intern in the early 1980s, a student from the College of Idaho in Caldwell. At the time, Marie lived south of town, and two premed interns covered the Stanley Clinic in her absence. We assisted Marie during the day and slept at the clinic to be available at night until Marie could arrive. Most of our days were routine: there were lots of cuts to clean and fishhooks to remove. As interns, our background was largely premed, and we were taking a first-hand crash course in rural healthcare at the clinic. Marie was training an EMT group while we were at the clinic, and I studied along with the group.

My favorite memory of my time at the Stanley Clinic occurred one beautiful Sunday morning. I was alone then, and it was early, just after sunrise. I heard some noise from tires on the gravel in the clinic parking area. I went outside to find an old, rusted hulk of a school bus parked. As I approached the bus, I was met by a wild-eyed gentleman, likely in his mid-thirties. He kept saying, "It's my wife. It's my wife."

After calming him down slightly, I asked where his wife was because I didn't see any movement on the bus. He led me to the back of the bus and opened the emergency door I remembered from childhood. Once the door swung away, I saw the man's wife looking at me with a determination I will never forget.

Her words to me: "I'm going to have this baby ... right now."

You have to realize that I was the rookie on the team. My clinic intern partner had been there the year before, but she was away for the weekend. I was an Idaho farm boy and familiar with the general process, but with no experience of a moment like this.

I left her husband to keep her occupied while I raced to the phone to call Marie. She was twenty-five minutes away, and it was early. I explained the situation to Marie and returned to the bus to find the woman with even greater determination that the baby would be on the scene any moment.

I enlisted the husband to help me get her into one of the clinic exam rooms and position her. I noted the stirrups and helped her into what seemed a reasonable birthing position. It seemed like the couple were veterans of previous deliveries.

Not wanting to appear as unprepared as I felt, I excused myself, claiming I needed to check Marie's progress or something equally professional. I ran into Marie's office and pulled down a copy of our EMT study manual. I flipped to the chapter on emergency childbirth and did my best cram session for an exam for which I was woefully unprepared. When I returned to the examination room, the baby's head began to crown. I ran to the sink, scrubbed quickly, and put on gloves, knowing I was beyond committed.

The woman was beginning to push, and I was doing my best baseball "catcher" impression when Marie came through the door with KT Fisher, one of the young, recently minted physicians who had interned at the Stanley Clinic.

Marie coolly moved in to relieve me of my duties and delivered the baby without a hitch. I think I went out to the lobby and felt like passing out.

Mom was fine. Baby was fine. And a new life came to be at the Stanley Clinic.

The mother delivered a beautiful baby boy within five minutes of my arrival. It was as if she was just waiting for me to get there so I could take off my coat and catch her baby as he entered the world.

My nightmare of forgetting to cut the cord was barely a week old. After the delivery, with the baby and placenta in the treatment room, Craig Pierce and KT Fisher reminded me, "Marie, be sure to clamp the cord." I did.

"Why don't you name him 'Stanley'?" I asked the mother. She looked at me, smiled, and said, "No." I was disappointed.

Main Clinic Building

That clinic building you see in Stanley has a story to tell. But, since buildings don't tell their own stories, I will. A community clinic is a structure, but it's also a symbol. When I look at the Stanley Clinic, I think of all those locals putting on the roof with the Sawtooth Mountains as a backdrop. Just about everything in that building was volunteered or

donated. It is as close to an old-fashioned barn-raising as you can get in healthcare.

After we moved into our first building in 1972, we realized we had to have a larger facility. With the Sawtooth NRA dedication scheduled for September, that first summer was a busy season for tourists and sadly, also for our makeshift morgue. In the first few years, there were an ungodly number of car wrecks and motorcycle accidents. A father and son both died in an awful motorcycle accident. Their bodies remained in our clinic for hours, waiting for the mortician to arrive from Hailey.

Once we began the Stanley Ambulance service, we parked the orange and white hearse in front of the clinic. The morning we found tacks under the ambulance tires, we decided we needed a secure place for the vehicle. Also, while the log cabin clinic was fine for seeing a few patients, it was too small to handle major trauma, multiple fatalities, and increasing demands for primary care services.

Form follows function. We needed a building to support both emergency and primary care (including women's care), and our service area was enormous. Community leaders and the clinic board agreed our three-room log cabin clinic was inadequate. A local family, the O'Connors, owned a lot they offered to sell for half price. We launched a donation drive, raised money, and started the process of building a new Stanley clinic.

Cement for the foundation arrived in October 1973, donated by the King family, who owned a concrete business in Salmon. Dan King was a volunteer EMT. Unfortunately, heavy snow in November buried the clinic foundation.

March 15, 1974, was a sunny, late-winter day in the Sawtooths. The sky was deep blue and cloudless. With the Sawtooth Mountains as the backdrop, the people of Stanley gathered, bringing shovels, snowblowers, a snowplow, and their collective commitment to rural healthcare. Townspeople dug through six feet of snow, exposing the foundation. Work commenced to create a crawl space. People brought food and pots of coffee. Volunteers worked shoulder to shoulder. Clinic construction got underway on that glorious March day in the Sawtooths. Once the townspeople excavated the foundation, building the clinic with volunteer labor and donated materials still took over a year — a barn-raising in slow motion.

Many hands were involved. Jim Mitchell worked for Boise Cascade and was a neighbor who helped build the clinic. Later, he flew missions in Africa, Asia, and elsewhere, working with Doctors Without Borders and other disaster relief organizations. For sixteen years, Jim also served on the board of Air Serve International, including four years as board chair. Jim recalls his role in building the Stanley Clinic:

> I worked for Boise Cascade from 1966–2000. In Boise, the Osborns were our neighbors, and over dinner, we first heard about Shaw Mesa. My wife, Mary, and I bought eleven acres on the Mesa. While we've moved several times in the Treasure Valley, we've never left Shaw Mesa. This place is home to the Mitchell family.
>
> In the early 1970s, Stanley needed a clinic, but the town had no money. At the time, I was running Boise Cascade's trucking company. Cal and Marie asked if I thought I could get plywood for the clinic.
>
> I drove to our Boise Cascade plant in Emmett, met with Wayne King, the manager, and told him the story. "How much do you need, Jim?" Wayne asked.
>
> "All of this," I replied, and we loaded up a 45-foot flatbed with studs and plywood.
>
> Boise Cascade was a big supporter of the Stanley Clinic, and many people within the company helped. Our company donated most of the materials: the coated paneling in the hallways and treatment rooms and the walnut and mahogany wood paneling in the reception room and Marie's office.
>
> Stanley often lost power in those years, so Boise Cascade donated the wood stove and stonework. For the clinic's exterior, we also donated the cedar shakes for the roof and the wood siding.

While I was procuring materials, John Fery, then Boise Cascade's CEO and board chair, asked to meet with me. "Busted," I thought. Instead, Mr. Fery carried a different message. "Hey, Jim, I understand you're helping with the Stanley Clinic. You just make sure they get whatever they need."

We had drawn a floor plan of the rooms we wanted. Our volunteer builders looked at the plan, said, "Okay!" and got to work. The new clinic took shape: rough around the edges, but it worked.

Memorial Garden

As you walk up the steps of the clinic, on your right are aspen trees, part of a garden planted in memory of an angelic child.

Jesse was a precious baby. The perfect child with golden curls and big blue eyes, he was the first child of my recently married good friends, Joe and Sheila Leonard.

After Jesse's first birthday, Joe and Sheila brought him to the clinic. Something was wrong: his startle reflex was off, and he didn't react normally.

I sent him to Dr. Ben Katz in Twin Falls, an excellent pediatrician, past president of the Idaho Pediatric Society, and member of the Idaho Board of Medicine. Still, with no answers, Joe and Sheila took Jesse to the University of Utah. No one could diagnose what was wrong.

As Jesse turned two, he kept getting worse. For days and nights, he would scream painfully. We could do nothing but soothe the child and support Sheila and Joe. Shortly after turning two, he died.

To remember Jesse, we planted a memorial garden of aspens. The aspens are still there, on the north end of the clinic at the corner of Highway 21 and Niece Ave.

Joe and Sheila Leonard had another son, who thankfully did well.

The other parts of the Stanley Clinic—the garage, main building, and apartment — all have funny stories. Not the clinic's memorial garden: There is nothing funny about losing a child.

Reception and Stocking the Clinic

When entering the clinic through the front door, you walked into the reception room and stepped onto plush, beautiful red carpeting donated by Thornock Brothers Carpet out of Boise. Eventually, the company donated all clinic flooring: heavy-duty commercial carpeting for the hallway and linoleum tiles for the treatment rooms and the lab.

Boise's Intermountain Surgical, whose owners snowmobiled in the Sawtooth Valley, gave me carte blanche to take any supplies needed for the clinic. I used it. Opening the new Stanley Clinic was an "impossible dream" that came true because of the Stanley community and our many supporters in Idaho and beyond.

Stocking the clinic was easier: We packed up the old clinic and moved the contents two blocks. Linens, dressings, instruments, lab equipment, books, medications, and more walked down the street.

The clinic has two big treatment rooms, a lab-pharmacy combined, an extra-wide hallway for moving gurneys and wheelchairs (and for mass casualty incidents), room for an X-ray machine, two bathrooms, and an office. Learning from the log cabin clinic, we built extra-wide doors to unload the ambulance gurney and move patients into the treatment rooms. A Boise electrician donated the wiring and his services.

We built a room for the X-ray machine donated by physicians in Idaho Falls. The state inspector assured us it was usable and safe — just keep it pointed toward the parking lot when not in use.

Eventually, I said "no" to doing X-rays in Stanley. I had minimal training in taking and reading X-rays. What if I misread an X-ray? What about the liability? If I suspected a fracture, the safer option was to send the patient over the hill for an X-ray read by a qualified radiologist.

For safety, Idaho state staff removed the X-ray tube from the machine and out of the clinic. The machine had lots of lead, so we found a buyer and made a few bucks for the clinic.

Ambulance Garage

The clinic's garage is tall but barely wide enough to house the ambulance. Soon after the new clinic's opening and after a night ambulance run, I drove the vehicle out to

gas up. I should have stayed in bed that day. Next to the ambulance was a donated exam table. As I drove out, the ambulance bumper caught the exam table, pushing it into the garage door frame. The impact knocked the entire wall off the foundation. Thank God the whole wall didn't collapse.

I couldn't believe what I had just done. Down the street, a construction crew was building the new Mountain Village supermarket. I drove to the construction site.

"Guys, I've got a little problem. I just knocked the clinic wall off the foundation and can't get it back on." They came to the clinic, laughed about the "typical woman driver," and then bolted the wall to its foundation. After that, we moved the ambulance with care, bordering on fear.

Unfortunately, we did not have enough land to expand the garage and add a second door. The Stanley Clinic nearly fills the lot, especially once we built the apartment for premed students.

Lab and Pharmacy

If you frequently unzip for painful urination, you might have a bladder infection. If your throat is sore, is that strep throat? You might need basic lab work, such as a complete blood count (CBC) or chemistry. We needed a lab in Stanley to handle these basics.

Our combined lab and pharmacy were sandwiched between the two treatment rooms in the new clinic building. At first, we used a lab service for urine and throat cultures. Sending out added two or more days before we had results.

Timing a patient's blood and urine for commercial lab processing is key. Specimens must arrive within a specific time, sometimes twenty-four hours or less. In Stanley, if you put a specimen in the regular mail, the postal service would take it to Challis, Pocatello, and then Boise — definitely more than one day. We got around this by working with the post office staff.

Patient specimens were dropped into a bag marked "Boise" and then sent by special contract mail carrier to Hailey and Treasure Valley Lab in Boise that evening.

Results were printed out in the clinic using a dedicated line into our printer. If lab results were markedly abnormal, the lab techs would call the clinic. With help from the postal service and lab staff, we had a faster turnaround than many doctor's offices in Boise.

At first, we used an old microscope that had been donated to us. We obtained an incubator and bought petri dishes with growth medium. Treasure Valley Lab advised us on what supplies and equipment we would need. In time, we were able to add a number of valuable lab services to the Stanley Clinic.

You count the dollars and pennies with rural clinics to keep the doors open. One of our patrons, Dan Mahoney, publisher of The Palm Beach Post, The Palm Beach Daily News, and The Miami News, donated $20,000 to help with the lab.

We bought a small countertop Coulter counter to do our CBCs. The equipment required calibration every day, periodic inspections, and special chemicals. It wasn't cheaper than sending a vial of blood to Boise, but it was valuable for emergency cases, such as an acute abdomen, when knowing the CBC is useful.

Lab results are more likely to be valid because of quality control measures. In the 1960s, errors reading PAP smears prompted regulatory reforms: the 1967 Clinical Laboratory Improvement Amendment (CLIA), which was expanded in 1988. CLIA is a national lab quality control program administered by the states. Once a year, state CLIA inspectors visited Stanley to assess our lab for cleanliness and to ensure we followed procedures. At least quarterly, we were required to run tests with controls, usually urine. Periodically, we received unknown specimens that we had to test and send our results to the state for verification. Our lab received high marks on inspections and testing, and we always passed.

Lab personnel are helpful in a busy rural clinic. At the Stanley Clinic, summer college student interns brought helping hands, new perspectives, lots of questions, and energy. Our college students were premeds from the College of Idaho in Caldwell. Many of our students started their internship already comfortable with culturing microbes, Gram stains, and microscopes. They quickly learned the Coulter counter. Some students learned how to draw blood, starting with my veins. I was an easy stick, even for a first-time nervous premed student.

An autoclave was necessary to sterilize instruments. Our first autoclave was tiny, donated by Dr. Cutler, a retired ENT from Idaho Falls. A small suture pack would barely squeeze into the six-inch-wide autoclave. While good for his practice, it was too small for Sawtooth trauma. So, we turned to patients and clinic supporters for donations to purchase a countertop autoclave large enough to serve our needs.

Our lab became a significant part of clinic operations. Tourists converged on the clinic with urinary tract infections, sore throats, and wicked-looking infected wounds. I used the lab at least a dozen times a day.

For College of Idaho premeds, the microscope became their third hand. Indeed, the laboratory was essential. If diagnosis is the first step to treatment, then history, physical exam, and lab are necessary for diagnosis. I was lucky to have students from the College of Idaho, especially on the microscope. Even though we were working with CLIA, it was good to feel confident that we were not getting false positives or negatives.

Students learn medicine at Stanley Clinic

The accident victim had tried to descend a steep, shale rock slope when she slipped and fell, breaking her leg and jaw and leaving blood on the rocks behind. Fortunately, local emergency medical technicians were able to reach the accident site and stabilize the victim. They also cleared a landing site so that she could be airlifted to a Boise hospital.

"It looked like a completely hopeless situation," said the College of Idaho's Katie James, one of more than 30 rescue and medical personnel involved in the effort. "But it turned out to be a dramatic emotional turnaround from desperation to 'we've got it solved.'"

James, a senior from Grangeville, and classmate Mary Barinaga, a senior from Cambridge, spent a busy 10 weeks this summer living and working at the Salmon River Emergency Clinic in Stanley. The two C of I premed students are part of a 16-year-old program which is designed to provide the students with some first-hand experience in rural medicine.

The clinic is the only licensed health care provider for more than 6,600 square miles of rugged central Idaho.

Gregg Koller, *Challis Messenger*, Challis, Idaho, September 13, 1990

PreMeds Housing

One warm summer night, rare in Stanley, one of the male premeds, Kelly Mutch, answered a knock at the clinic door wearing only his briefs. At the door was Freda Nicholson with an armload of clean clinic laundry. Freda, the staid owner of the town's laundromat, served on the clinic board. But for Freda, near-naked premeds greeting patients would not do. She insisted the clinic board take action and build living quarters for our students. The second reason the board added living quarters was so I had a place to stay during storms, a lesson from my near-fatal snowmobile mishap, recounted earlier by Phil Coonts. Here is my version:

My last patient had kept me late at the clinic. Driving the twelve miles to Fisher Creek, I could barely make out the highway in the blizzard. Driving slowly in the whiteout, I made it to the Fisher Creek turnoff, parked, donned my helmet, fired up the snowmobile, and drove into blowing snow and night. My dog ran behind.

Willow. branches, placed to mark my trail, had disappeared with the ground blizzard. Wind pummeled me with snow. I kept trying to wipe snow off my mask. In the blizzard and without snow markers, I missed the turn and careened over the edge.

I held on, then bailed off, and watched my snowmobile continue downhill, lights on. It crossed an irrigation ditch, then bogged down in deep snow. The engine kept running, headlight on. Above me, through the howling storm, my dog barked.

Wind had swept much of the snow from the steep hillside. I pulled myself together and crawled uphill toward the barking. Panting and sweating in my snowmobile suit, I was welcomed back to the top of the cliff by my dog, probably wondering why I had done such a stupid thing. Together, we slogged through the blizzard back down the trail to my car parked on the highway. We got in my car and drove back to the clinic, still barely able to see the road through the blowing snow.

Word travels fast in a small town. The board of directors, all locals, heard what happened. The clinic board was already discussing whether to add onto the existing clinic to provide living quarters.

Marie's cabin in winter. Sawtooth winters are beautiful and treacherous. When Marie went missing during a ground blizzard at night, Phil Coonts came looking for her.

The new clinic needed an apartment. When we originally designed the new clinic, we didn't plan for students. During busy summer months, the premed students lived at the clinic, slept on the floor, and cooked on a hotplate behind the ambulance in the garage. They slept wherever and, with multiple ambulance runs, whenever they could. My son, Jerry, a budding architect, drew the plans for the students' apartment.

The College of Idaho was and is successful in placing premed students into medical schools. We needed help at the Stanley Clinic, but we had no funding. My third son, John, who helped open the first clinic, spoke with our Shaw Mesa neighbor, C of I professor Dr. Lyle Stanford, about creating a clinic internship for premeds. Dr. Stanford turned to the head of the college's Snake River Regional Studies program, Donna Parsons, for help.

In what would become the college's longest and most successful student internship program — which continues to this day — Dr. Stanford, Donna Parsons, and John created the clinic's premed internship to start in the summer of 1975. Donna found funding to provide stipends for three students.

John was among the first four students and started his premed internship working nights to stain the new clinic molding before our grand opening in June. He passed on the premed stipend, instead making money cleaning Forest Service campgrounds. As other premeds would do, John also worked part-time at Stanley's Armada Café as a short-order cook — good preparation for ERs.

Ken Harris arrived next. Ken, who would become a physician in Challis and then Twin Falls, set the standard for the Stanley Clinic's premed program, working 24/7 when needed to keep the clinic running. Next arrived Mike Nowling, who later directed the Heart Institute in Spokane. Patrice Gibson also joined the premed team and stayed at my cabin.

The summer of 1975 is never to be forgotten; it was full of compelling cases, some horrible. The premeds were smart, fast learners, and motivated. By first practicing on each other, they learned to collect vitals: blood pressures, pulses, and temperatures. That summer of 1975, everything was new: the clinic, the ambulance, and even our rural medicine premed program.

Premeds wanted the rural medicine experience. Getting into medical school was intensely competitive. The Stanley Clinic experience was special, focusing on rural medicine and EMS, improving the premeds' chances of getting into medical school.

Who would choose which students should work at the Stanley Clinic? I wanted nothing to do with that decision. Selection was left to Donna Parsons and later Sheri Robison, a biology professor at the college. Other premeds from other schools desperately wanted to come to the Stanley Clinic. But this was a College of Idaho program from the start.

We eventually settled on two students for a better teaching experience. On ambulance runs, one premed teamed

Anne Palmer

Marie's dog Mousse and fourth-year medical student Doug Langrock. Rural healthcare training for premeds, medical students, Advanced Practice Providers, and others became part of the Stanley Clinic's mission. Image from "Nurse Patches Up Small-Town Void by Staffing Rural Medical Clinic," Salt Lake City Tribune, September 2, 1986.

with EMTs while the other remained at the clinic to help with incoming patients. After transporting patients, the students slept in the ambulance on the return trip. When they returned to Stanley, more patients and more ambulance runs awaited them.

Eventually, in 1983, the era of hot-plate cooking and bedpan salads ended when we added living quarters to the clinic: two bedrooms, a private bathroom, a kitchen, a living room, and a laundry. A little deck opens onto a beautiful view of the Sawtooths.

> Betty [Rember] wanted to know why it was necessary to have a stove with a self-cleaning oven [for the students' new apartment]. Marie said that since they were boys, they usually left the oven in a deplorable condition, and it would be a great time saver to have one that cleaned automatically.
>
> Salmon River Clinic-Hospital District Board of Directors Meeting, November 10, 1983.

Medical Students

Rural clinics can go hungry for student help, while urban medical centers enjoy a relative abundance. Premeds, medical students, residents, and fellows fill the rungs of the training ladder in cities like Seattle and Boise.

In the 1980s, Stanley Clinic's rural healthcare education programs expanded beyond premeds to include medical students and nurse practitioner students.

In 1979, the WWAMI program accepted my son, and he would become one of twenty medical students from Idaho. The Idaho WWAMI medical students spent their first year at the University of Idaho in Moscow, sharing classes with medical students at Washington State University in Pullman.

In their second year, all 180 medical students from multiple states moved to the University of Washington in Seattle. Medical students spent their third and fourth years doing hands-on patient care called "clerkships" in the multi-state region.

John began to ask the question: why not a clerkship in rural medicine at the Stanley Clinic? John found his way to Dr. Gabe Smilkstein at the UW Department of Family Medicine. Gabe was committed to community-based education and to providing healthcare services to the medically underserved. Gabe and John set up WWAMI's first clerkship at the Stanley Clinic in July, 1982. When John needed an attending physician to help supervise, Dr. Stone volunteered for the position.

John saw patients at the Ketchum Medical Clinic with Dr. Stone and at the Stanley Clinic with me. Ann Stone opened their home to John and other medical students who followed.

We all agreed that medical students would need to complete clerkships in emergency medicine and surgery before coming to Stanley. John had completed these, including training under Dr. Mike Copass in the Harborview ER, as I had done ten years earlier.

I have to tell you a story about Dr. Smilkstein. He was a marvelous person. For the medical school to approve the Stanley Clinic for a clerkship, Gabe had to do a site visit. It was early spring, and in preparation for Dr. Smilkstein's visit, we cleaned that clinic until it sparkled. On the inspection day, the clinic board convened for a special meeting so that they could meet Gabe, and he could meet them.

No Gabe.

He didn't show, and he didn't show. Finally, the phone rang. It was Dr. Smilkstein.

"Marie, I'm not in Twin Falls. You'll never guess where I am."

"What do you mean?"

"Marie, I'm in *Great* Falls, Montana." Instead of making a flight reservation for Twin Falls, his assistant made the reservation for Great Falls.

In a leap of faith, he approved the paperwork for the inspection, boarded the plane, and returned to Seattle. The clinic board members went over to the bar for a drink.

And so began a second major program in rural healthcare and EMS, for medical students completing their final year before receiving their MD degree. For many, this was the first time being on their own without other students, residents, and fellows.

The Stanley clerkship for medical students was rewarding in the day-to-day care of patients and managing acute medical problems and trauma in a rural setting. There was plenty of major trauma in Stanley, but not all happened during office hours.

Dr. Stone and I became clinical associates of Family Medicine at the University of Washington to oversee the medical students and we were part of the WWAMI teaching program.

At UW Seattle's Family Medicine office, John's vivid photograph of the Sawtooth peaks at sunset with a thunderstorm approaching and a helicopter airlifting one of our trauma patients provided a dramatic greeting for visitors.

The Board of Regents of the University of Washington has appointed Marie to the position of Clinical Associate of Family Practice. She's pleased that she has a parking sticker for the campus!

Salmon River Clinic-Hospital District Board of Directors Meeting, November 11, 1986

You should never mix pills in the same bottle. While John was doing his rural medicine clerkship one evening, the clinic door burst open. A woman was frantic that her friend needed help. The two women hiked into the Sawtooth Wilderness and camped at Sawtooth Lake. Her friend needed Tylenol and reached into her bottle of medications. Unfortunately, the bottle included a mix of penicillin and Tylenol tablets. After taking what she assumed was Tylenol, her throat swelled, and she had trouble breathing. Her friend ran down the trail for help, made it to the trailhead before dark, and drove to the Stanley Clinic.

We assembled the EMT team, John grabbed medical supplies, and everyone headed for the trailhead with headlamps. They walked up the wilderness trail through the night, arriving at the campsite with the first morning light. Would she be dead from anaphylaxis or alive? At dawn, they arrived at Sawtooth Lake. Coming around a bend in the trail, they spotted their patient — smiling and drinking her morning coffee.

Becoming a physician or advanced practice provider attracted almost all my students for the right reasons. Caring for patients is a lifetime commitment to giving and caring for others. Caring for others is a calling.

Some of my students took several bites at that apple. They first came to the clinic as premeds, and some even returned for a second summer. Once accepted into the WWAMI program, these same students would sign up for the fourth-year rural medicine clerkship at the Stanley Clinic and put themselves through it all over again. One of my students is now my physician, Dr. Katie Reynolds. She spent two summers at the Stanley Clinic. I noticed that even then, other premeds asked her questions before they would ask me. And Katie knew the answers. "This woman is sharp," I concluded. So, when Katie graduated from medical school, completed her residency training, and set up practice in Boise, I decided that's who I wanted as my doctor. If others could ask her questions, then I could, too.

The premed internship and WWAMI rural medicine clerkship were a chance to "pay it forward:" helping students as others helped me become a nurse and then a nurse practitioner.

Nearly a half century after the program started, in early 2020, John and I met with the College of Idaho co-presidents Doug Brigham and Jim Everett, who informed me that the premed internship program was still going strong and was the college's most valuable internship program. More recently, the college set up the Marie Osborn Internship Fund to provide stipends for the premeds at the Stanley Clinic. The WWAMI rural medicine clerkship and nurse practitioner preceptorships did not survive my leaving Stanley. However, the College of Idaho premed internship in rural medicine endures and remains vibrant. We'll never know the full impact of the Stanley Clinic's teaching programs. But, far more than helping run the Stanley Clinic and caring for people in the Sawtooth country, these programs opened doors for students searching for fulfillment as caregivers. The Stanley rural healthcare teaching programs touched students' lives and thousands of patients' lives in rural and urban communities in Idaho and far beyond.

Step by step, we created a rural clinic at the center of a healthcare system. Many people came together to make it happen. Everything was donated: Companies donated big items and materials, while kids donated their nickels and dimes. Others donated thousands of dollars. People also donated their time and skills. The grown-ups showed up to

Lara Antonello

The Stanley Ambulance crew, marking 50 years of service to Idaho's Sawtooth country, 1972 – 2022.

shovel snow and later to frame and build. If they couldn't hammer, they pushed brooms and swept.

Building the Stanley Clinic was an incredible shared effort, a community's labor of love. At the clinic's grand opening on June 15, 1975, those who made it possible were proud.

Our new clinic in Stanley was the "Impossible Dream" that became a reality. These rural community clinics are a legacy of people working together, neighbor helping neighbor, and caring for those in need.

Amy Klingler

The Salmon River Clinic as it appeared in 2022. In October 2022, the Stanley community joined with physician preceptors, past and current, and EMS leaders to celebrate 50 years of rural healthcare.

19

TO MY PHYSICIANS: THANK YOU

"Primum non nocere; First, do no harm."

Hippocratic Oath, a pledge taken by new physicians

> Amends existing law to remove physician supervision requirements applicable to certified nurse midwives, clinical nurse specialists and nurse practitioners; and to require peer review for renewal of license.
>
> House Bill No. 659, Idaho Legislature, becoming law July 1, 2004

Having a baby in the Sawtooths is a life event some young women want to experience. My view? Delivering a baby in Stanley is risky. Everything always goes right until it doesn't; it's a nightmare. If the mother or baby dies or the baby suffers harm during childbirth, what's the point of delivering in a beautiful place?

What if the mother starts bleeding, and I can't stop it? What if there is fetal distress? The closest operating room is sixty miles away over Galena Summit. If the roads are good, transport time is an hour, plus another thirty minutes to pull together our volunteer ambulance crew.

I never lived the horror of losing a viable fetus, although I did deliver nonviable fetuses.

A young couple came to the clinic. The pregnant woman was less than seven months along and had contractions. As soon as we got her onto an exam table, she delivered. I placed the dead fetus and afterbirth in a pan. The mother could hardly talk. The father sobbed.

I carried the fetus into the lab. He followed me, sobbing. I gently placed the fetus by the sink, and the man and I hugged each other and cried together. They were so young and to lose a baby is so hard. I know. I lost my twins.

Some women waited too long, went into labor, and scrambled to get over Galena Summit. Most made it, but

Bryan Stone MD

Bryan Stone, MD, with staff from the Ketchum Medical Clinic. LEFT TO RIGHT: *Susie Werner RN, Rown Brons RN, and Julie Watson RN, ARNP. Dr. Stone served as Marie's physician preceptor for nearly 20 years.*

not all. I got the call that a woman was delivering in a car. I spotted the vehicle where the highway leaves the valley heading up Galena Summit. The father had delivered their baby in the car. You can imagine the scene in the front seat, the screams, "It's coming, it's coming!" The father had enough wits to bring a suction bulb to clear the newborn's nostrils and mouth. We radioed the on-call physician in

Sun Valley and took the baby back to the Stanley Clinic for the initial evaluation. Once cleared, we sent the proud but shaken parents and their baby over the hill

My physician preceptor, Dr. Bryan Stone, loved bringing kids into the world. A popular family practitioner, Dr. Stone did a lot of OB and teamed with the two obstetricians in the Wood River Valley. All three physicians were great about working with an NP. If there was a problem with my pregnant patients, or I was worried, they helped day or night. Dr. Stone and I created a prenatal program at the Stanley Clinic, saving pregnant women 120 miles of driving. Once monthly, Dr. Stone saw OB patients in Stanley, and that clinic grew large. If a woman had a problem, she could call me for a check-up. During their last trimester, they saw Dr. Stone once and me twice monthly, increasing to once a week during their last month.

As pregnant women approached term, we encouraged them to relocate closer to a hospital. When they started dilating, I'd call Dr. Stone to make a recommendation. If a multiparous woman was dilating, she usually went over the hill to see Dr. Stone.

During my nursing education in the 1950s, I learned to check the cervix during labor by inserting fingers into the rectum. I could feel the cervix, whether it was effaced and dilated, and by how much. Not until my last year of nursing training did practice patterns change to allow vaginal exams for women in labor.

Women have looked after women through the ages. Indeed, the NP profession has deep roots: In medically underserved places, nurses may not have had licenses for "advanced practice nursing," but they did what they had to do to care for others, especially women and children.

Physicians like Dr. Stone opened doors for me to become an NP. Most physicians knew the grueling pace of 24/7 calls and the realities I faced. Especially during the chaos of multiple emergencies, when I needed physicians to help, they were there for me: "Hello. This is Marie Osborn, the nurse practitioner at the emergency clinic in Stanley. I need to speak with one of your ER doctors." A physician would pick up the phone and help, day or night.

I first met Dr. Stone after he started at the Ketchum Medical Clinic and volunteered to help another clinic after a physician there had a major heart attack.

We met in a packed waiting room at Blaine County Hospital in Hailey. He walked into the reception room, saying, "Excuse me. I'm Dr. Stone. I'm covering for Dr. Packer. I'm sorry, but I'm running behind. If you need to leave, we'll schedule you for tomorrow or as soon as possible. I'll stay tonight until everyone is seen." Most stayed. Dr. Stone worked until 7:30 that evening, until everyone was seen. I'd never seen that before. I was impressed.

Dr. Stone had scrubbed in on many surgeries in Africa, during the course of his medical missionary work for the Methodist Church. To prepare for that, he completed a one-year rotating internship and a four-year surgical residency.

Originally headed for the Congo, he, his wife Ann, an RN, and their two sons Quin and Greg were diverted to Rhodesia by the Methodist Mission Board, arriving in early 1971. Their first posting was at the Mutambara Mission Station Hospital near the Mozambique border.While Dr. Stone attended to patients, Ann supplemented Quin and Greg's education, worked with the women's groups at the mission, and revamped the hospital pharmacy. (She even chased a cobra out of the laundry room.)

Leaving Rhodesia (now Zimbabwe) after his medical missionary work, Dr. Stone and Ann sought a safe place to raise their two sons. In 1974, the Stone family moved to Idaho's Wood River Valley.

Dr. Stone had trained for family practice, emphasizing OB and general surgery. He eventually joined Ketchum Medical, on the banks of Trail Creek.

With a great team of physicians and nurses, lab, radiology, and administrative staff, walking in the door felt good. It was after he joined the Ketchum Medical Clinic that Dr. Stone agreed to be my preceptor.

My patients, who had been going to the clinic in Hailey, transitioned to the Ketchum clinic, a welcome change. Ketchum was closer than Hailey and driving sixty miles over the hill from Stanley meant shopping too.

Moritz in Sun Valley became our go-to ER for the Stanley Ambulance. I also had my cancer surgery at Moritz. Moritz was better staffed, more up-to-date, affluent, and demanding. Blaine County was more comfortable and laid back, more rural. Each hospital gave you a different feeling.

Today, NPs practice independently in Idaho, and physician preceptors are not required. But for the first three decades, physicians like Dr. Stone were pivotal figures — not just as preceptors but as advocates for NPs and our ability to care for patients. Sometimes, these doctors got in trouble with the state's professional boards for supporting NPs (Dr. Stone certainly did).

Dr. Stone and Ann were active in their community. Ann worked as a receptionist, nurse, and bookkeeper in the

Ann Stone with the head surgical nurse, Mozambique's Chicugue Hospital. In 1993, Bryan and Ann moved from Ketchum to Emmett, Idaho, and promptly returned to Africa as medical missionaries with the Methodist Church. Ann served as assistant head of nursing while teaching English to nurses. Dr. Stone's surgical cases included victims of exploding landmines, TBIs and spinal cord injuries from people falling out of trees trying to pick cashews, and severe burns requiring skin grafts. Transferring patients for medical care the 300 miles to the capitol city, Maputo, was nearly impossible.

Ketchum Medical Clinic, at the Ketchum Library, for the American Red Cross Bloodmobile, and did much more.

In 1974, when Dr. Stone joined the Ketchum clinic, he became the seventh physician in the Wood River Valley. Twenty years later, in 1993, the Wood River Valley had thirty physicians, and Dr. Stone was the most senior.

With their sons grown, in 1993 Dr. Stone told Ann about a newly formed community health clinic in Emmett.

"Where the hell is Emmett?" she quipped. But within three months of arriving in Emmett, their lives changed once again.

The Methodist Mission Board asked them to return to Africa, this time to the Chicuque Mission Hospital in Mozambique. AIDS had come to Africa since the Stones had worked in Rhodesia. In the 1990s, the leading industry in many rural communities was coffin-making.The people of Mozambique had lived and died through years of revolutionary war against colonial Portugal and then civil war and communism.

Land mines exploding in rural Idaho is not a worry, but it was in rural Mozambique. The hospital had 135 beds, with 40 in the surgical ward for which Dr. Stone was responsible.

Ann's primary duties were as an administrative nursing assistant for the entire hospital and as a backup for dressing changes for overwhelmed nursing staff.

In his Mozambique operating room, Dr. Stone amputated limbs and removed shrapnel lodged in abdomens, consequences of exploding land mines.

Then, without neurosurgery backup, Dr. Stone treated traumatic brain injuries, commonplace for impoverished people falling from trees while picking cashews, pecans, and coconuts.

Basic medical supplies we take for granted were scarce. Children came with burns when their clothes or bedding caught fire while sleeping near cooking fires.

After completing their second four-year assignment in missionary medicine, Bryan and Ann returned home to Idaho.

For the next seventeen years, Dr. Stone continued to see patients in Emmett's community health system. He retired from medical practice in 2015, at age eighty-three, but remains active in serving his community. Tragically, their son Quin died earlier, in 2006, while piloting a helicopter on a wildfire. Ann died in December 2020.

All of us caring for people carry memories. Some we cherish. Others are dark. For Dr. Stone, tears come when he tells the story of a four-year-old boy badly burned in Mozambique.

In Stanley, we'd transport to a burn unit. There were no burn units in Mozambique at that time.

Dr. Stone removed old dressings from burns to do wound care. The pain was awful, and kids would scream and cry just being carried into the room for their dressing changes, because they knew the ordeal that was about to begin: unwrapping, cleaning. Screams pierced the room.

Dr. Stone told one little boy, "Repeat these words: 'I have strength. I have courage.'"

The four-year-old recited these words all during his agonizing treatment. Despite everything, the boy died of his wounds.

Dr. Stone was my physician preceptor for twenty years and an enduring friend. One commitment we shared was providing care for those in need in rural Idaho.

BRYAN STONE MD, IN HIS OWN WORDS

Right from the start in Idaho, I had 115–120 deliveries in my first year. That's a lot of OB for a general practitioner.

OB and pediatrics were three-fourths of my practice. For my OB patients, I was always on call. "Don't call me until she's crowning" was not me. I would not walk in at the last moment and "catch the baby." Instead, I was in the room if my patient was in labor. Often, the husband was there, too.

Insurance companies were dead-set against home deliveries. I did a few. They're risky. If labor becomes complicated, you could usually move the mother to the hospital, but not always. You might only have seconds to save the baby.

Insurance companies threatened to cut me off from malpractice insurance because of home deliveries. I objected. "You are forcing me to abandon some of my patients!" Didn't matter.

While I did my own C-sections, when it came to general surgery, I often assisted one of my colleagues, Dr. Gustafson, in the OR. Maintaining surgical skills while in Idaho would later help me in Mozambique.

I saw primary care patients in the clinic when I wasn't in the OR. Healthcare is a team effort: we had a great team during those years at Ketchum Medical Clinic. Patty Provonsha was my nurse; Marie doing OB checks on my pregnant patients in the Sawtooth area was a huge help. In that last trimester, you need to be looking at the cervix. How much is it effaced? Will the delivery be premature? When does your patient need to move close to the hospital?

We saw our OB patients at least once a week as the due date neared. Marie and I worked closely caring for pregnant women in Stanley, Challis, and Salmon.

In saying "yes" to becoming a physician preceptor for an NP, I didn't know Marie, and she didn't know me. But Marie called me, and I agreed to serve.

In the mid-1970s, all three professional boards — Medicine, Pharmacy, and Nursing — oversaw Idaho's nurse practitioners. So, my name went to the three boards for approval as Marie's physician preceptor. I insisted that I could only be at the Stanley Clinic one day each month to precept Marie, not one day a week as was required then. The boards approved the change.

For nearly twenty years, I drove over Galena Summit to Stanley once a month. Ketchum Medical Clinic paid the fee to the boards to precept Marie, so she didn't have to pay.

"Could I see your driver's license?"

"Of course, officer."

"Mr. Stone, you exceeded the speed limit by fifteen miles per hour."

"I'm sorry. I'm headed to the clinic in Stanley to see patients."

Once you dropped off Galena Summit onto the valley floor, those long straight stretches of highway, a heavy foot, and no cruise control meant trouble.

"You work with Marie?"

Marie worked closely with law enforcement on many emergency calls and coroner cases in central Idaho.

"Yes, I'm Dr. Stone. She and I work together, and I'm scheduled at the Stanley Clinic today."

"Dr. Stone, slow down. Drive the speed limit. I'll give you a warning — this time."

Law enforcement always let me off because I was working with Marie. Her name was a golden ticket to avoid a speeding ticket.

Galena Summit could avalanche in, closing the highway. The 1980s were big snow years. Sometimes the weather conspired against you, and you'd reschedule.

I looked forward to going up there every month — without reluctance. Others might grumble, "Oh, I have to go up to Stanley again." For me, there was no burden, only joy. Before leaving Ketchum, I rounded on my patients in the hospital, saw patients in the clinic, put out fires, and headed out to Stanley.

Marie would call the patients if the weather turned bad or the pass closed. For women driving from Salmon, sometimes they were already on the road.

When I walked into the Stanley Clinic, pregnant patients and kids lined the packed reception room benches. Marie put out extra folding chairs. It may have been snowing all the way to Salmon, but my OB patients still came. "Hi, Dr. Stone!" "How was your trip?" "So great to see you." I arrived in a room filled with warm greetings. Marie would pull me away from the warm welcomes to get me into a treatment room.

On the walls were dozens of postcards, cartoons, and photos of wrecks. I always checked them out, chuckling at the cartoons. Car wrecks and plane crash photos: trauma care in rural Idaho. Thank God for this clinic and all the folks who help when needed.

Pregnancy planning is vital to avoid pulling off the highway in labor and delivering your baby on Galena Summit. It happens, especially the "multips" (women who'd given birth multiple times), but you don't want it to. I was always amazed by women traveling from Salmon to Ketchum to have their babies.

For new patients, I wanted an hour, and for revisits, fifteen to thirty minutes. I saw my OB patients each month and then each week during the last month. We started seeing patients at noon and hoped to be done by five pm, but that rarely happened. Marie made use of every minute, and I always ran behind.

People are not widgets: when they need you, you take the time it takes. And the clinic is not an assembly line: clinicians are not automatons meeting performance measures. We care for human beings in all their complexity. I wanted to know how my patients were doing. Marie would break away if an emergency walked through the door, and we'd adjust treatment rooms and schedules. Otherwise, Marie was in the room with our female patient and me, just as any RN would be with a male doctor, especially when doing a pelvic or breast exam.

As Marie's physician preceptor, I was required by the boards to review charts and count narcotics with Marie. In the era before electronic medical records, we used paper charts. Fortunately, I could read Marie's handwriting. That made it easier! We shared our OB patients, so I reviewed Marie's charting as we saw patients. Each time the board changed the rules, we adjusted the review process to comply with them.

Narcotics — opioids — have to be watched like a hawk. Precise documentation is a must. Marie opened the safe and counted pills and vials daily, updating her records. As allowed by the boards, she had one morphine vial for acute myocardial infarctions and one Demerol vial for trauma cases.

Marie opened the safe, pulled out those little black trays of tablets and injectables, and together, we'd count: Vicodin, Tylenol #3, Demerol, morphine. Marie would record the numbers in a green-covered logbook she kept in the lab near the safe. With the count completed, she signed, and I signed.

Once we finished the narcotic count, we were done with Stanley Clinic day. Unless...someone else walked in.

"I'll see you on the telephone," was my usual goodbye. Who would've thought you could video conference on your phone? Ann would call Marie if we ran late ("Where is he?").

Marie would be left picking up toys and cleaning the clinic for nighttime emergencies while I headed back over Galena Summit.

The Board of Medicine tried to limit Marie's ability to care for patients by removing her ability to write prescriptions. That really pissed me off.

At one hearing with the Boards of Medicine and Pharmacy, they asked me about Marie filling medications at the Stanley Clinic.

"How do you expect her to treat people?" I objected. "Why are you blaming her for transgressions before they occur? You need to trust her."

Our concern was treating patients. Their solution was impractical for isolated places like Stanley with no pharmacy. They decided to have a licensed pharmacist pre-fill medication bottles, and then Marie could dispense a few days' supply of medications. I disagreed and made my position clear, but their decision stood.

Marie and I worked with Gene Steiner at Chateau Drug in Ketchum's Giacobbi Square. Gene was a super guy. Unfortunately, Chateau Drug got in trouble with the Board of Pharmacy for its procedures in prepackaging medications, and Gene got hauled to yet another hearing in Boise involving the Stanley Clinic.

Marie and I were also sanctioned under the boards' ruling and accused of improperly handling medications. We both ended up on probation.

That mark against me remained on my record until I returned from Africa to Idaho in 1998. Sometime around 2000, after nearly twenty-five years, my probation ended.

Whether in Africa or Idaho, those responsible for patient care work together as a team. We're not one better than another. We have different skills, and we need each other. We are equals, doing different jobs and trying to help people. There is no hierarchy. Each is trying to do the best for our patients.

With Marie, I didn't feel like I was "precepting." Once I started going up to Stanley, we were colleagues and equals. Marie was always formal with "Dr. Stone." I always called her "Marie." However, the boards viewed precepting differently. I had to follow the rules: reviewing Marie's charts, counting pills, and watching her manage patients.

Caring for our patients is a calling, not a job. I trusted Marie. She had good clinical instincts. She knew her abilities and limitations, and so did I. Sometimes, she called because she really needed help. At other times, she might call for liability protection: "Case reviewed with Dr. Stone." She never got sued, and she didn't call me that often. I never had any criticism of Marie's handling of a case.

In 1982, Marie's son John was the first WWAMI medical student to work with us at the Ketchum Medical Clinic. Ann and I hosted him at home — easier than commuting from Marie's cabin daily. Giving medical students experience in rural medicine is invaluable. Of course, they might enter into a practice in a small community. But even if they end up in an urban area, and most will, they will at least have a better understanding of the realities we face.

Marie had a really tough road to recovery after her cancer surgery. I was away, and didn't scrub in on her surgery. After she was back seeing patients, Marie asked if I would help with John's graduation from medical school. His last clerkship was in a Presbyterian mission hospital in Thailand, and he was delayed getting home. So rather than graduating in Seattle at the University of Washington, the Stanley Clinic hosted John's graduation. I was asked to recite the Hippocratic Oath at the town ceremony. The Hippocratic Oath is ancient, a rite of passage for doctors and an early statement of medical ethics. Passed from generation to generation, the oath is probably 2,500 years old. "Do no harm" are three riveting words you know from that oath.

The day of John's graduation in June 1983, the clinic's reception room was packed for the ceremony. After I read the oath, we moved to Redfish Lake Lodge for a community party. Marie gave John his black doctor's bag. Amazingly, not a single emergency call or ambulance run interrupted that day.

Dr. Stone was a doctor cut from a different pattern. We never argued. As he put it, "We adjusted." Ours was a great relationship. If Dr. Stone was leaving Ketchum, he'd let me know who to call for coverage. At night, he always took calls, drowsily after midnight.

Starting in 1972 with Drs. Packer and Gwinner, I drove the 140 miles to and from Hailey with charts for their review. Time was money, and that reality drove decisions in private practice. Precepting an NP took time. They came to the clinic only once: Dr. Packer's son had a fishbone stuck in his throat, and he needed instruments to remove it.

Before the legislature changed the law in 2004, I had other physician preceptors. Dr. Peter Gannon, who was smart as a whip. He moved back to California and asked me to join him. The money would have been better, but I couldn't leave.

"I wrecked my new truck on Galena." That long-distance telephone call came from Dr. Joe Jensen when he didn't show for clinic. Snow and ice on Galena Summit can be treacherous. Dr. Jensen lost control of his rig, spinning 360 degrees off the highway. He called the clinic to let me know he was canceling. Dr. Jensen wasn't hurt, thankfully, but his new truck was. In 1992 he left Ketchum for Twisp, Washington, beloved by his community there, where he saw patients until 2015.

In 2004, Senator Sheila Sorensen, a nurse practitioner, led the legislative effort to amend the Nurse Practice Act to establish NPs as licensed independent practitioners, no longer requiring a physician preceptor. By then, I was in my early seventies, no longer at the Stanley Clinic but seeing patients in Idaho City, Horseshoe Bend, and Emmett. I wasn't active in the legislature and didn't need to be. The nurse practitioner movement was blossoming, with younger NPs stepping up. Our new healthcare profession was coming into its own. The Boards of Medicine, Nursing, and

Pharmacy could see that. Senator Sorensen helped the Idaho Legislature see that, too.

For night emergencies in the Sawtooth country, my physician preceptors mostly had an easy time of it. I usually called ER physicians in Sun Valley or Boise for emergencies. Only a few times did I wake up Dr. Stone, usually for his OB patients. Here's a secret: I didn't need a preceptor as I grew as an NP. You get good at what you do if you do it long enough. In the late 1970s, the Board of Medicine proposed that I be required to call my physician preceptor for just about everything. Imagine if the Board of Medicine succeeded:

"Hi, Dr. Stone. This is Marie. Sorry to wake you up."

"Marie, what time is it?"

"1 am. The bars just closed here in Stanley, and we had another fight. It spilled into the street. I wanted to let you know I've got two patients with lacerations. I'll suture their wounds. They'll both get their tetanus boosters."

"Okay. Thanks, Marie."

Two hours later, my physician preceptor's phone rings again. "Dr. Stone, sorry to wake you again."

"Huh?" Pause. "Oh, just a minute, Marie. Let me get out of bed and go into the other room so I don't wake Ann." Pause. "Okay, go ahead."

"Dr. Stone, a vehicle collided with an elk after the bars closed. The two people in the car were drinking and headed to their campground, neither wearing seatbelts. Both went through the windshield. They have multiple lacerations. The female probably has a closed femur fracture. We've splinted her injury and we are and are transporting both patients by Stanley Ambulance to the ER at Sun Valley."

"Okay, Marie. Thanks for letting me know. By the way, what time is it?"

"Three-thirty in the morning. Thanks again, Dr. Stone. Hope you get some sleep."

Why punish my physician preceptor with multiple phone calls that add little to patient care? Of course, I'd call Dr. Stone when appropriate, but not otherwise. I knew my limits and picked up the phone to ask for help when needed.

At the same time, I was also well aware that there was no time to call the physician preceptor just to "check the box" and satisfy the boards under high-pressure, high-stakes circumstances.

With Senator Sorensen in leadership, the Idaho Legislature at last amended the Nurse Practice Act to reflect this reality: Nurse practitioners would work independently. I certainly did because I had to.

Hanging out wet laundry to dry awaits snowmelt: clothesline and single clothes peg at Marie's Sawtooth cabin.

20

DOCTORS AND RURAL HEALTHCARE

The only doctor living in Custer County left in June.

His reason for leaving was the same as others before him: One doctor in a county this large is on call 24 hours a day, every day. The workload wears them down and after one, or two, or three years they leave.

Custer County stretches nearly 100 miles from border to border at points, holding 4,933 square miles of forests, mountains and the meandering Salmon River. The 1990 Idaho highway map lists seven towns in the county; 5,200 people in an area almost five times larger than the smallest state, Rhode Island.

Yet Custer Country, especially the western portion that includes the Sawtooth Valley and the Sawtooth National Recreation Area, attracts thousands of visitors a year. They can be a long way from help in case of an emergency.

Since the doctor left, the primary and emergency medical care falls on the only two clinics in the county, one in Stanley, the other in Challis. But this is not new. The clinics have been here many years for residents and tourists alike.

Marie Osborn, a nurse practitioner, opened the Salmon River Emergency Clinic in 1972.

"I didn't really know what I was getting into at the time," Osborn said of opening the clinic.

"In Custer County, emergency help can be 'a fur piece off'." *The Times-News*, Twin Falls, Idaho. August 21, 1990

For my premed students from the College of Idaho, I wrote many recommendation letters to medical schools. Most students wanted me to write about six letters, although one asked for fourteen. The College of Idaho premed program started first and took priority, but I also mentored NP students from Gonzaga University, Idaho State University, and other programs.

Each one of my students was changed by the Stanley experience. The clinic was a place of growth and transformation. For most students, helping care for patients in a rural setting gave clarity, reaffirmation, and direction to their life's journey. Premed students also came to the Stanley Clinic for the experience, which was a positive addition to their resumés.

As the College of Idaho premed program has endured a half-century, some of our first Stanley-trained physicians are now retired from medical practice. Our first class of premeds was in 1975, three years after we opened the Stanley Clinic. Dr. Ken Harris was in our first class.

Ken was from Caldwell, Idaho, and graduated from Caldwell High School. He stayed close to home, enrolling at the College of Idaho in 1972 and graduating in 1976.

Ken applied to several medical schools but was not accepted (although he made the alternate lists at the

University of Washington and the University of Utah). After those disappointing rejections, Ken strengthened his resumé by taking two semesters of biochemistry at Boise State University and working as an orderly at St. Luke's Hospital in Boise.

In 1977, Ken reapplied, and both the University of Washington and the University of Utah accepted him. That fall, he enrolled in Salt Lake City as one of ten Idaho medical students under a cooperative program between Idaho and Utah.

In the first year of medical school, Ken married his college sweetheart, Sarah Richards, the daughter of Hailey dentist Arthur Richards. Like my family, the Richards family was an Idaho ski-racing family. Sarah was a competitive racer in both high school and college. Her father, Dr. Richards, never said no when I asked him to provide dental care for my patients from Stanley, although some could not pay. In addition, Dr. Richards believed in community service. He became a certified EMT and volunteered for ambulance calls until Hailey hired full-time first responders.

Ken's medical school experience was traditional: medical students spent their first two years mostly in classrooms and their final two years in clinical rotations called "clerkships." That third year, when medical students began hands-on patient care, was intense and grueling. The fourth year consisted primarily of clerkships designed to help prepare students for their next training phase. After graduating from medical school, almost all new doctors enter a residency program that provides further training in specific fields of medicine.

Deciding on a residency program may be the most important life decision a doctor will make, other than who to marry. Yet, fourth-year medical students choose their specialties based on brief clinical experiences during third- and fourth-year clerkships. Medical students then list their desired residency programs, while residency programs list their desired applicants. Connecting medical students with residency programs occurs on the third Friday of March: "Match Day."

On Match Day, medical students gather with intense anxiety at 155 medical schools in the United States. In 2017, 36,000 medical students competed for about 32,000 residency positions, leaving 4,000 who did not match.

With Sarah's support, unending patience, and tolerance, Ken graduated from medical school in 1981. Ken and Sarah worked through the difficult process of choosing a specialty and a residency program. Ultimately, Dr. Harris returned to Idaho to specialize in family medicine.

KEN HARRIS MD, IN HIS OWN WORDS

Getting into medical school is competitive. As a premed working at the Stanley Clinic, I could see if I was cut out to be a doctor, experience rural patient care, and get a leg-up on other premeds. Also, if I did well, I counted on Marie to write me a favorable letter of recommendation. Good letters of recommendation were probably more important to medical school acceptance committees than GPAs and Medical College Admission Test (MCAT) scores.

When I was considering the premed program in Stanley, I worked swing shifts helping severely intellectually disabled persons at the Idaho State School and Hospital in Nampa. Choosing between the Sawtooth Mountains' fresh air versus the odious odor of the sugar beet plant in Nampa wasn't hard. While my work in Nampa was meaningful, the Stanley Clinic offered significant opportunities to further my professional goals.

When I arrived in early July, I first stayed with Marie and her son, John, in the cabin on Shaw Mesa. Like me, John was a premed at the College of Idaho. After a few weeks, John and I moved into the clinic, sleeping on the floor and storing our sleeping bags and clothes in an unused room. With that move, the premeds "staffed" the clinic 24/7 for the rest of the summer. We used a hot plate in the ambulance garage for cooking. Our culinary clinic specialty was the bedpan salad: lettuce, cucumbers, and tomatoes, tossed with a Caesar dressing and croutons and served from a reusable green plastic bedpan. We poured morning coffee from the coffee pot in the lab.

Our day started early, making coffee, gobbling cereal, and stashing sleeping bags. Next, we cleaned the clinic, sweeping and vacuuming, wiping exam room sinks and countertops, and cleaning the bathrooms. The clinic was then ready for patients when Marie walked through the door.

We were the first premeds in a novel teaching program in rural healthcare that has remained vibrant for a half century. Later that summer, two more interns joined us:

Mike Nowling and Patrice Gibson. Patrice could beat the pants off her fellow interns on the tennis court, but I do not know where life took her after graduation from the College of Idaho. Mike's path led to medical administration, and he ultimately became the administrator for Spokane's Heart Institute. In the summer of 1975, Mike joined John and me sleeping at the clinic, and Patrice bunked at Marie's cabin.

Marie taught us to do Gram stains and to prepare and read urine and throat cultures. After Marie sutured a patient, we cleaned the instruments, repacked the suture kits, and sterilized them in the autoclave. Next, we checked the defibrillators and made sure they were ready. When the ambulance returned from a run, we cleaned off the blood and other bodily fluids, wiped surfaces with bleach, cleaned the floor, restocked, checked the oxygen tank, and recharged the heart monitor.

When patients arrived at the Stanley Clinic, our job was to greet them and begin the registration process by filling out the patient encounter forms: name, date of birth, home address, phone number, and billing information. Next, we obtained vitals and took a clinical history. When an exam room opened up, we escorted the patient back and briefly summarized the patient's concerns to Marie. Finally, we helped with evaluation and treatment and then helped arrange for aftercare if needed. Before the College of Idaho started the premed internship, all these tasks fell to Marie. Marie and the premeds forged a team.

Marie "debriefed" us on the medical aspects of cases as time allowed. Her teaching often proved to be the best part of the workday. Inside those Stanley Clinic treatment rooms, we began to learn about medicine.

After Marie left the clinic in the evening, we usually had downtime. What better way to spend time without a TV or radio reception than studying for the Medical College Admissions Test (MCAT)? We reviewed textbooks and MCAT study guides and tested each other using flip cards for vocabulary and organic chemistry, both components of the MCAT.

When we heard footsteps on the porch followed by knocking on the door, our study reverted to emergency response, often culminating in an ambulance ride over the hill.

The Stanley Clinic's reception room doubled as our bedroom and classroom. Marie expected the premeds to complete her EMT class along with Stanley-area locals. After completing an eighty-hour course, passing a written test, and demonstrating proficiency in core skills, we became certified as EMTs. The premeds joined the community's EMTs on ambulance runs and other calls, coming to know and respect Stanley's first responders.

One duty as premeds was answering the phone, an actual telephone with push buttons and a pig-tailed cord. In 1975, our premed internship's inaugural year, Idaho EMS's mountaintop radio system was still two years away. Eventually, Marie would carry her EMS radio with her. But in those first years, if Marie wasn't in the clinic, the premeds located her by phone. She also carried a donated CB radio. During emergencies, we learned to communicate salient information to Marie and initiate a plan of action while she was speeding toward the clinic. With Marie's telephone orders, we could begin initial care. As premeds, while we could not provide medical advice over the phone, we were often able to triage situations and provide helpful information to both Marie and patients. That made life easier for Marie during those hectic summer months.

"My dog got into a porcupine. There's no veterinarian available, so we came here hoping you could help."

Marie was Stanley's "doctor" and its "vet" too. There was no one else. She enjoyed helping animals, maybe more than people. We used the clinic's front porch as a veterinary procedure room. We put down a clean sheet on the porch floor, wrapped the dog's snout with roll gauze to prevent biting, and then used hemostats to yank out quills, one by one. As a result, the Stanley Clinic's front porch saw a lot of porcupine quills and many remorseful dogs.

On Friday nights, Stanley would go nuts. On Thursdays, you might see two cars drive by the clinic. Then came Friday, with hundreds of cars arriving on the two highways leading into town. The town filled with hikers, bikers, river runners, cowboys, hippies, and tourists. Many came for the "Stanley Stomp," to drink and dance the Western swing at the three local saloons. For those who came looking for solace in the wilderness, they did not find it on Friday and Saturday nights in Stanley. The premeds staffed the clinic on those weekends, occasionally joining in the fun and listening to live music. By Sunday noon, lines of cars, many with hungover occupants, fled the town on Highways 75 and 21. By Sunday night, quiet had returned to the Valley for another five days.

In medicine, common things are common. In addition to providing primary care at the Stanley Clinic, we saw what you'd expect to present to an urgent care clinic: sore throats, urinary tract infections, skin rashes, and soft tissue infections. We also saw numerous lacerations, campfire burns, sprains, and fractures. My favorite malady was a fishhook stuck in a finger, ear, or eyelid. Marie's technique for flipping out barbed hooks I used for the rest of my medical career. In those years before AIDS, the Stanley Clinic was also the only place to buy condoms.

One July night in 1975, around midnight, we unrolled our sleeping bags and turned off the lights. Then, we heard footsteps coming up the porch steps, followed by a knock at the door. I opened the door and saw a middle-aged man clutching his chest. We had trained for this moment: a probable heart attack. We quickly escorted the man back to a treatment room, got his vitals, started oxygen, and radioed Marie at her cabin.

As I attached leads for an EKG, Mike stepped into the garage, got into the driver's seat of our new ambulance, and drove it out of the garage to park in front of the clinic for ready access. Unfortunately, in all the excitement, Mike snapped the key in half when turning off the engine. In his hand was the bow of the key. The rest of the key remained in the ignition.

Stanley had only one ambulance, now incapacitated. Mike ran into the clinic to let us know. John grabbed needle-nose pliers and succeeded in extracting the key fragment. He also knew where his mother kept the spare key; the Stanley Ambulance was back in business.

Marie arrived from her cabin; her twenty-minute drive had seemed much longer than usual to her trio of premed interns. After coming down from the ceiling when she understood the ambulance was still functioning, she calmly reviewed the EKG, confirming an acute myocardial infarction. She controlled the man's chest pain with nitroglycerin and started an IV. We loaded the man into the ambulance and transported him over Galena Summit to Moritz Hospital in Sun Valley. This chest pain patient was my first acute heart attack — and he lived. That night, our team did well. Sadly, years later, the man had a second heart attack. Although the Stanley Ambulance crew got him alive to Sun Valley again, he died in the hospital several days later.

Marie's black medical bag carried miracles in that isolated place. In the dead of night, during my first week on the job, we got an emergency call for an elderly man struggling to breathe. He lived about eight miles from town, so off we went.

We arrived, and Marie hooked him up to oxygen as she took a history and did her physical exam. She diagnosed congestive heart failure and phoned his cardiologist. Then, Marie put in an IV, reached into her black bag, and pulled out a vial of Lasix (furosemide). After Marie administered the drug IV, our patient started to pee. And pee. Throughout the rest of the night, he urinated two to three liters as Marie and I checked vitals and urine output.

Finally, with sunrise and our patient breathing easier, we returned to Marie's home to clean up and prepare for our day at the clinic. That was how I learned the power of Lasix — and Marie's black bag.

Over the decades, the Stanley Clinic's premed interns have seen emergency childbirth, death, and almost everything in between. Our teacher was a dedicated, confident, caring, and skilled nurse practitioner at the helm of the community's healthcare system. She was breaking a trail that we could follow.

My premed experiences at the Stanley Clinic convinced me I wanted to specialize in family medicine and practice primary care. During my final year of medical school, I applied to several family medicine residency programs and wound up where I wanted to be: Boise's community-based Family Practice Residence of Southwest Idaho.

Sarah, Ian, and I moved to Boise for the three-year program with eighteen doctors-in-training. After completing my three-year residency training and passing my board exams, I became a board-certified physician in family medicine. My next step returned me to the mountains of central Idaho — a step with strings attached.

Medical student debt impacts major decisions for future physicians. Sarah and I decided to minimize long-term debt by joining the US Public Health Service (PHS) in my second year of medical school in Utah. A PHS stipend meant we didn't accrue a large debt. But, when I finished my residency program in Boise, I owed three years of service to the PHS in an underserved community, the Indian Health Service, or the Federal Bureau of Prisons.

Sarah and I fortuitously landed in the Idaho mountain town of Challis, population 758, just sixty miles downstream from Stanley on the Salmon River.After working as a premed and medical student under Marie at the Stanley Clinic ten years earlier, I viewed the Challis assignment as a homecoming of sorts.

Challis is the county seat of Custer County. The county has about 5,000 residents and covers about 5,000 square miles, the size of Connecticut. Idaho's tallest peak, Mt. Borah, sits east of Challis in the Lost River Range. The county also includes parts of the Sawtooth Range and White Cloud Mountains. Idaho's River-of-No-Return, the Salmon River, flows through it. Challis is isolated, surrounded by rugged, beautiful mountains.

Although Challis didn't have a hospital, its locally elected hospital board governed the community-owned clinic. Shortly after I arrived, the internist abruptly quit and set up a competing practice. Fresh out of residency training, I walked into a new community and clinic without a physician to show me the ropes. I was sixty miles from the nearest hospital in Salmon, 120 highway miles from Sun Valley, and a million miles from my comfort zone.

Thankfully, there was Jim VanArk, a physician assistant who trained in Michigan and found his way to Challis. Jim had weathered two or three previous PHS assignees before my arrival. He knew everyone in Challis, had trained all of Challis' EMTs, and even worked out a system for transporting critically ill patients utilizing a talented Vietnam-era helicopter pilot.

Jim had working relationships with doctors in Salmon, Sun Valley, Idaho Falls, and Pocatello and knew where to send patients for specialty care. Of course, he knew Marie in Stanley. Jim knew almost everything in the clinic and was likely the best clinician I have ever worked beside. Jim figured out how to survive in a remote rural setting and enthusiastically shared what he knew.

Physicians with urban and suburban practices are unfamiliar with rural realities. For example, when the roads were good, patients often drove two to four, sometimes six to eight, hours one way for specialty care. However, when the roads were bad or closed in winter, patients might be stuck and unable to get the needed care.

Being on call for patients can take a toll. "Call" involved at least two to three phone calls each night. If I couldn't comfortably handle the problem by phone, I met the patient at the clinic.

Jim and I both responded to catastrophic emergency calls, especially when we needed to transport a patient.

In my second year, a second PHS physician joined our clinic duo. Shelly (Sheldon) Wendler was a family practice physician from Oregon who also owed the Public Health Service for three years of service. Shelly, Jim, and I shared calls, which meant I was only on call every third day and weekend.

In a small town, everyone knows your telephone number and where you live. I could count on at least one free medical consultation when our family went for dinner or skiing. The punishing schedule and sense of clinical isolation were stressful and difficult to overcome. I do not understand how Marie functioned so well as the sole healthcare provider on 24/7 call for nearly thirty years. And I don't know how Jim did it, either. Both have something in their mental and emotional constitutions that I lack.

In remote rural areas, transporting ill or injured patients to hospitals can pose significant challenges. In Challis, as in Stanley, we utilized a ground ambulance staffed with EMTs (and sometimes a clinician) to transport patients to Sun Valley, Salmon, or Idaho Falls. Since Sun Valley doctors had our staffing contract, Sun Valley's Moritz Hospital was often our preferred destination. From Challis to Sun Valley, our ambulance drove the curves along the Salmon River, then the curves over Galena Summit before parking at Moritz's ambulance bay.

The hospital in Salmon was fifty miles away along the serpentine Salmon River road. Logistics meant most ambulance runs went to Salmon. I delivered a baby in the ambulance on such a run soon after I started in Challis. But, when patients were critical or the terrain was formidable, we flew.

We all owe a debt of gratitude to Vietnam helicopter pilots who returned after the war and continued to fly. Our

Gary Gadwa

LifeFlight at the scene of a flipped Jeep on Highway 21. Garay Gadwa served as Incident Commander for the crash. The driver, although ejected, survived the crash.

veteran pilot was Dan Odlum, who worked out of the Challis airport, mainly doing contract work for the Forest Service. Life Flight, based in Boise and Idaho Falls, was prohibitively time-consuming for air transport to Challis. So, we called Dan at the airport, a half-mile from our clinic.

Dan would land his helicopter in our clinic parking lot, we'd load our patient, and he was off. Most flights terminated in the parking lot of Moritz Hospital in Sun Valley some thirty minutes after take-off from the Challis clinic parking lot. While the trips into Sun Valley were often hectic, flights home were absolutely gorgeous. People pay big money to see those mountains from a bird's-eye perspective. We got to enjoy the view for free.

Two times, Dan flew me into Indian Creek Guard Station, an airstrip and campsite on the Middle Fork of the Salmon River. That area gets 10,000 or so "river runners" each summer who float the 100-mile stretch from the Boundary Creek put-in (forty miles from Stanley) to the confluence of the Middle Fork with the Main Salmon. Indian Creek, roughly thirty miles from the Boundary Creek put-in, was accessible only by air. On my first flight with Dan, we helicoptered out a Forest Service ranger with appendicitis. My second trip with Dan, the airplane crash, was unforgettable.

The night before the crash, a small single-engine plane flew into Indian Creek and landed on the backcountry dirt airstrip. The following morning, the pilot took off with three passengers. We'll never know, but we suspect the pilot mistakenly flew up the wrong canyon. Once committed, he couldn't gain the altitude to get out: the canyon was too steep and short. As a result, the plane crashed into the mountain.

The call came as Sarah, our two kids, and I sat down for Sunday breakfast. Rather than a rescue, this would be a recovery mission. All four in that airplane were dead. As the Custer County coroner, I had coroner duties to perform and headed to the Challis airport to meet up with Dan.

The morning helicopter flight into Middle Fork country was beautiful. But, as we approached the crash site, we could see the plane had crashed into a steep hillside, and there was nowhere to land. Dan nosed the helicopter's skids as close to the steep hillside as possible and said, "Jump, Doc!"

Clutching my black bag in one hand and body bags in the other, I leaped from the hovering helicopter and landed on the tilted earth. Dan flew away, landing at Indian Creek airstrip over a mile away. I did my work and helped Forest Service personnel place the four bodies into black bags, which we carried trudging and straining down the long, steep mountainside to the Salmon River and flatter ground. A fixed-wing airplane awaited to transport the bodies. Late that afternoon, Dan and I lifted off for Challis, returning home to my family. I've not jumped from a hovering helicopter since.

Small-town docs are called upon to perform duties we'd never undertake in cities. One such duty was a stint as Custer County coroner that began with a phone call that interrupted a busy day at the clinic.

"Dr. Harris, I represent the county elections board. Sorry to bother you. We'd like you to run for Custer County coroner."

In Idaho, the coroner is an elected position and, in 1986, not one that required any forensic pathology experience or training. Probably because patients were backing up in the office, I said "Sure," and continued my day.

During a break at lunch, I ruminated on what had just occurred and concluded correctly that the Custer County election board would list my name on the ballot as a Republican. After all, no one would run for any office as a Democrat in this county and be elected. However, my wife and I leaned left politically, along with a small handful of people in the county. If I ran as a Republican, I feared my wife would surely divorce me. I dialed the number the election board representative gave me and clarified, "I haven't changed my mind; I will run. But I will run as a Democrat."

After a considerable pause, the representative said, "Okay, I guess you can run as a Democrat."

A half-hour later, the election board representative was on the phone with my partner, Shelly, asking him to run for county coroner as a Republican — against me. Shelly laughed and declined, and I ran unopposed for the office of coroner as a Democrat and was duly elected. At the time, I was the only elected Democrat in Custer County, and I would not be surprised if I was the only Democrat ever elected in that county.

Why do we elect our coroners? I have never understood the logic. In 1986, once elected, I never received training or even a list of duties. The State of Idaho never contacted me on how to fill out a death certificate correctly, let alone appropriately assess a death occurring under potentially suspicious circumstances.

As a busy physician, I was then coroner of Idaho's third-largest county. I alone couldn't provide coroner services to the entire county. Instead, I worked with a team of deputy coroners who provided coverage in areas where they lived and worked. Marie served the Stanley area.

I traveled the sixty-mile winding road to Stanley if Marie wasn't available as deputy coroner. Close to Marie's cabin, on Highway 75 at Fisher Creek, a motorcyclist and his wife were enjoying the stunning views of the Sawtooth Valley when a local rancher's bull lumbered onto the highway. Idaho is a free-range state, so bulls own the right-of-way, and ranchers aren't responsible if their livestock are on public thoroughfares. The motorcycle collided with the bull, and both riders died. Marie was out of the valley. I took the call and drove to the scene, a trip of more than two hours, to pronounce them dead and perform my other coroner duties.

The deputy coroner in Mackay once called me to evaluate a possibly suspicious death at a group home. I made an assessment, wrote a report, and referred the case to the forensic pathologist in Pocatello. In Custer County, while we did many things, we didn't do autopsies. Instead, we referred to a forensic pathologist if we were suspicious about a death.

"Dr. Harris, I'm with the Forest Service in Stanley. We've found a boot near Redfish Lake. Unfortunately, the boot has a foot in it."

That call came on a busy clinic day in summer. A hiker had found the boot near the Elephant's Perch, a 1,200-foot golden granite face, the "ultimate rock climb," at the head of Redfish Lake. Law enforcement suspected the foot belonged to a climber who had gone missing the year before, and the foot was all that was left. Was the death an accident? Foul play? The more likely assessment was a fatal fall, then hungry wildlife scavenged the body. I placed the boot with foot in a plastic bag and then into the clinic freezer. As coroner, I wrote my report, then called the father of the lost climber.

"Yes, that's my son's boot," the father said after I described it. Since this was all that remained of his son, I considered offering for the father to come to Challis to claim it. But, since the death was unwitnessed, I was careful to "dot the i's and cross the t's," and sent the boot and foot to the forensic pathologist. For the climber's father, my decision may have added angst. Nevertheless, I never had to testify in court.

Dull, practicing medicine in rural Challis? Rarely. In my first week at my new job, Sarah and I were eating lunch at our rental home four miles from the clinic when the radio went off. That big, black, portable EMS radio told me the ambulance was responding to a call just two miles downriver from our house. Since we had only one car, Sarah drove me to the scene.

EMTs and the ambulance were already at the home of an older man. That morning, he'd been doing carpentry work. He dropped the spinning blade on his lap while sitting, cutting two-by-fours with his skill saw. Blood spurted: the spinning blade transected his right femoral artery. By the time we arrived, he was in shock from bleeding.

With EMTs vigorously compressing the area, we loaded him onto the ambulance and transported him to the Challis clinic. Since I was only a few weeks from residency training, I was still reasonably adept at starting a subclavian vein IV. The saline ran wide open. Unfortunately, it was all we had: we had no blood to transfuse. When the blood from his severed femoral artery was the same color as our IV fluids, we threw in the towel. He died on one of our two emergency room tables from an exsanguinating injury.

Welcome to rural healthcare.

The week after my patient bled out, I delivered a baby in the ambulance on the way to Salmon. I delivered one other baby in the clinic during my tenure in Challis. We made special efforts to get pregnant women to the hospital well before delivery, as we had no capability for complicated obstetrics or newborn care. I am proud and happy that every other soon-to-be mother made it out to their obstetrician for delivery.

What might start as a routine clinic day could turn upside down with a car wreck, a chain-saw injury to the face, chest pain, a really sick kid, a diabetic in ketoacidosis, or some other unexpected emergency that, in an urban area, would be taken care of in a hospital ER. But not in Challis or many small, isolated towns in America.

Just as Marie had a lab at the Stanley Clinic and taught us as premeds, we also had a lab at the Challis clinic. We could do throat and urine cultures, CBCs, urinalyses, everything else we sent out, and even basic chemistries. We had good X-ray capability only because we had a great lab and X-ray tech willing to be on call virtually every day.

Specialists sometimes came to help the Challis community. For example, about once a month, an orthopedist from Sun Valley, a urologist from Idaho Falls, and an optometrist from Twin Falls ran scheduled specialty clinics. We even had a pediatrician come up from Sun Valley two or three times. But, no obstetrician/gynecologist, cardiologist, pulmonologist, rheumatologist, or gastroenterologist came to

Challis to see our patients. Instead, all those specialists were faceless practitioners on the other end of the phone. Also, Challis did without many basic services, including child protective services.

Like spousal abuse, child abuse can occur anywhere, including in rural communities. When clinic staff suspected a mother was abusing her child and serious harm was imminent, we succeeded in removing the child from the home and transporting him to Salmon.

This was a big deal in a little town: law enforcement, a judge, state Child Protective Service staff in Salmon, and Challis EMTs were all involved in removing a child from parental custody.

It took this team hours of wrangling, but we got the child safely to Salmon. I had made the right call. Unfortunately, I didn't know that Idaho Child Protective Services had reviewed the child's case, failed to see a problem, and released the kid back to his mother the following morning without bothering to call me. In less than twenty-four hours, the child returned home with one irate mother.

The mother showed up at the clinic and came looking for me. The woman was large, strong, and mad as a hatter. She found me, grabbed me by my lapels, and threw me against the clinic wall. She suggested that, from now on, I stay out of her business. I remember the mother's name and have stayed out of her business ever since. As for the fate of that poor child, that is unknown.

My service to the people of Challis and Custer County ended when my three-year contract ended. The Sun Valley physicians who employed me were no longer willing to fund three clinicians, and my contract was first up for negotiation. The Challis Medical Group concluded they could only financially support two clinicians, despite needing three to avoid burnout.

In 1987, Sarah and I said goodbye to Challis and moved our family to Twin Falls. For the next thirty years, I cared for my patients in a "big-city" practice with a hospital and specialty-care clinicians. In 2017, forty-two years after I first walked into the Stanley Clinic as a premed, I retired as a physician. Much as Marie's deteriorating eyesight pushed her to hang up her stethoscope, my progressive hearing loss forced my decision.

Inspired by my work with Marie at the Stanley Clinic, my goal was to become a small-town doctor. However, my three years in residency training and then my three years in Challis caused me to reassess. I learned I needed a hospital, an emergency department, and a cadre of available specialists to practice medicine the way I wanted. Although I still wanted to provide medical care in a small community, Stanley and Challis were too small. Is my experience unique? Maybe. But, my story as a small-town doc underscores some of the challenges we face in providing healthcare in rural America.

For physicians, NPs, PAs, nurses, and ancillary medical personnel, stress levels can be high in small, isolated towns caring for our patients. Each of us has different tolerances for stress. I was never comfortable enough with that stress to endure as a small-town doctor.

Those who enter healthcare should look deeply into themselves, critically assessing their capabilities and limitations, both medically and emotionally. This is especially important before clinicians commit to the unique responsibilities posed by the rural practice of medicine.

I'll always have empathy and deep respect for those who take their patient-care talents into rural settings. My medical story started in Stanley, where my mentor was a nurse practitioner with the drive and courage to bring healthcare to a small community with none. She not only rallied a community to support and assist her efforts, but she did so when the general medical community viewed NPs as lacking the knowledge to provide medical care without direct, on-site physician supervision. Marie proved the medical community wrong and, in the process, created a new paradigm for nurse practitioners in Idaho.

Marie got a clinic built. She trained a horde of EMTs. Marie prevailed in battles with the Idaho Boards of Medicine and Pharmacy. She lobbied United States senators and representatives. Marie developed a premed internship that became a conduit for scores of future doctors' acceptances to medical schools. She raised five successful children. I will carry my gratitude, respect, and love for Marie Osborn to my grave. And, although I never got the opportunity to read it, the letter of recommendation for medical school that she wrote for me must have been good.

21

PAYING FOR RURAL HEALTHCARE

As Stanley's NP, I was the lowest-paid NP in Idaho by the late 1970s. One of my three sons earned more cleaning outhouses and fighting forest fires in three months than I did all year. You have to eat, pay your bills, and save for retirement. Being Stanley's NP was not lucrative, even if it was exciting. I stayed because I loved being Stanley's nurse practitioner.

Each of us has a relationship with money. Mine began at birth during the Great Depression in Russellville, Kentucky. In the depths of the Depression, Dad might find day labor for twenty-five cents an hour. We survived.

When I started my BSN program at Ball State University, academics took priority over work. By then, my father's income was enough to help me with tuition and related expenses. After completing my BSN degree and marrying Cal, I worked as an RN at Harborview Hospital until late in my first pregnancy.

Once I left the hospital wards, I didn't work outside the home again until 1972, when we opened the Stanley Clinic. During those nearly twenty years, I worked as a full-time mother and wife.

Soon after we married, Cal handed me the checkbook. "This is your job, Marie," he instructed. Cal didn't explain further. While I had a checking account in high school, my father balanced my account. I assumed running the home finances was a man's job. Eventually, I learned how to manage bank accounts and made peace with my finances.

Without Cal Osborn, the Stanley Clinic and Stanley Ambulance would never have happened. Cal supported the clinic and me during those first years. During the clinic's first summer in 1972, Cal looked after our house in Boise, and I lived at our new family cabin in the Sawtooths. I planned to keep the clinic open just during the busy summer tourist season, and then I would return to Boise for the other nine months with kids in school.

Spring wildflowers, Marie's home on Shaw Mesa

Cal's IBM income paid those first expenses for my training, as well as my orange VW Beetle, followed by my orange Volvo. But, more than just the financial support, Cal encouraged me. He was proud of what I was doing and remained proud and supportive, despite our divorce, to the end of his life.

Cal worked all week at IBM, crisscrossed Boise to pick up pharmaceuticals and wound dressings from warehouses, drove three hours on Friday night to deliver his carload of supplies to the Stanley Clinic, and then returned to IBM on Monday morning. Cal transported clinic supplies week after week, all summer long.

When Cal and I divorced, the rural realities of earning an income loomed large. My son, John, helped by sending money from his work fighting forest fires and some money he took out in loans to pay for medical school. For the Stanley Clinic, finances were tight. We counted our pennies to keep the doors open. We positioned a donation jar near the front door, hoping people would help, and they did. A dollar here and a dollar there, sometimes just a handful of coins, helped us buy wound dressings and other supplies from the wholesaler in Boise.

Today, payments for services we take for granted didn't exist when I started caring for my patients in 1972. Our state and federal governments lacked the mechanisms to fund rural healthcare and EMS. We filed our application with the IRS to create a 501c3 nonprofit corporation for the Stanley Clinic and then convened our first board of directors. The 501c3 status made donations tax-deductible. Donations opened the Stanley Clinic's doors and funded our $300 purchase of the Pontiac ambulance. Once we started, donations and fee-for-service kept us afloat.

THIS IS NOT A FREE CLINIC

Arrangement for Payment must be made before Treatment.

Posted in the Stanley Clinic waiting room, 1983

1. FEE FOR SERVICE

Many of our patients used Medicare or had health insurance. Unfortunately, Medicare did not catch up with the nurse practitioner idea and did not reimburse us for our services in those first years. Insurance companies didn't pay NPs either, because they based their reimbursement on Medicare.

In May 1972, my first patient walked in the door of the Stanley Clinic. My fee-for-service charge was $7.50, with fifteen percent going to my physician preceptors in Hailey.

The clinic board and I struggled with how much to charge. As Idaho's first NP, we had to create much of what we did as we went along.

Also, Stanley is between two very different communities: Challis, to the north, relies on ranching with some mining. Sun Valley and Ketchum, comparatively wealthy, are to the south. People in Custer County couldn't afford Ketchum prices. Furthermore, we didn't want to undercut the Challis clinic.

The board and I adopted our first list of charges. The cost for an office visit was $7.50, eventually increasing to $25 and then $35. The feedback the clinic received from our first patients was, "Wow, this is quite reasonable."

Shortly after we opened the clinic, a hardcover booklet arrived in the mail. It contained the usual and customary charges for all procedures, office calls, and everything used nationwide by insurance companies. Comparing the figures featured in the booklet with our own list of standard clinic charges was an eye-opener. The Stanley Clinic was vastly undercharging.

Although insurance companies became vital to the survival of the Stanley Clinic, we did not go by their allowable charges. Besides, years would pass before insurance companies would reimburse NPs. (That breakthrough happened from a fly-fishing accident in Stanley; story to come.)

When I started providing women's care in Custer County, the clinic board and I charged $35 for pap and pelvic, including a complete physical exam. I did a lot of women's care from Salmon to Ketchum. Although we didn't want to undercut other clinics, we needed to provide affordable healthcare, especially for women. It always irked me that medical professionals told me I had to have cervical cancer screening — in those years, it was a pap smear every year — and then charge $150 or $200. In the 1960s and 1970s, that seemed exorbitant.

In Idaho's rural communities, women couldn't afford cancer screening. Women who had *never* had a pap and pelvic came for care because they could afford it and wanted a female doing their exam. Eventually, I drove downriver to Challis and Salmon to run women's clinics at the request of the Idaho Department of Health and Welfare.

I filled out a little pink postcard for each of my patients who were due for an exam, and once a month, I took the stack of cards to the post office. Pink postcards became a hallmark of women's care in that part of Idaho. Everybody up and down the Salmon River knew those cards. Secrets are harder to keep in small towns, especially if your post office box has a glass door and a sizeable fraction of PO boxes have pink cards. People used to laugh, but it worked.

We did not lose money on pap smears because we did so many of them. The reward was that rural women who otherwise would not have gotten care now had healthcare. Women would bring in their daughters, too, for their first pap and pelvic. In a society where many people, especially men, take better care of their trucks than their bodies, pink cards encouraged women to think about better, affordable healthcare for themselves.

Paying Physician Preceptors

The Stanley Clinic paid my preceptor in two ways: a flat fee plus fifteen percent of clinic earnings from fee-for-service. The remaining eighty-five percent paid for the clinic's expenses, the ambulance, and my salary. Expenses came first; whatever was left was my annual income, often less than

$1,000 in those first years. Again, Cal's support allowed me and the clinic to continue and grow.

As our first preceptors, Dr. Packer and Dr. Gwinner invoiced the Stanley Clinic board during our yearly budgeting. Eventually, the physician preceptor expense increased to $2,000, a lot of money in the early 1970s, especially with clinic finances close to the margin. Cutting my income was the only way to keep the doors open. Later, Dr. Stone waived his fees, donating his time and services for twenty years.

Rules required physicians to come to the Stanley Clinic, which was not an easy 120-mile round-trip commute from Ketchum. That drive meant being stuck behind tourists, watching for deer and elk at night, and driving over Galena Summit, especially risky when roads were snow-covered and icy. Coming to Stanley also meant not seeing patients in Ketchum, so a loss of income. If physicians took any money for being my preceptor, and most didn't, they earned every penny.

To Pay, or Not to Pay?

> Marie opened the [Clinic board] meeting expressing her concern about insurance billings as well as Medicare billings, and the turning into the collection agency of delinquent accounts. Some clinic bills have not been paid.
>
> Salmon River Clinic – Hospital District,
> Board of Directors' Meeting, June 7, 1984

> Since you did not respond to our letter about your past-due account, we must presume you do not intend to pay this bill. Every courtesy has been extended to you regarding this account. Unless this account is paid within 15 days, it will be referred to our Collection Agency.
>
> Notice from the Salmon River Emergency Clinic

I always kept a handwritten log for all my patients: their name, address, telephone number, date and time of the incident, diagnosis, whether an emergency run, ambulance run, or regular clinic visit. That information helped with reporting, including for our monthly clinic board meetings.

We had no money to pay for help, so I also did the cleaning, stocking, and administrative work, including billing in those first years. I knew who paid their bill and who didn't.

A man in his early twenties stopped me in front of our first clinic on Stanley's main dirt road, Ace of Diamonds Street. He looked at me wearing my white lab coat and concluded I was a caregiver.

"Excuse me, are you a doctor?" he asked.

"No, I'm a nurse practitioner," I replied. "Can I help you?"

He lifted his left hand, covered with a dirty dressing.

"I cut my hand fishing in the Sawtooth Wilderness. It was pretty deep. I got the bleeding stopped. I used fishing line to sew up the cut. But I'm concerned it's infected. I'm having a lot of pain and swelling and draining pus."

"Well, I'll need to look at your hand," I said, pointing to the Stanley Clinic's front porch.

"I don't have any money," he said. "I can't afford to pay you anything."

Would you tell him, "Sorry, no money, no healthcare"? Would you risk him losing the use of his hand, or worse? Of course not. We went into the clinic's treatment room. I removed the fishing line suture, opened up the infected laceration, irrigated the wound, administered a tetanus shot, and prescribed and dispensed antibiotics.

"I'll pay you when I can," he said, thanking me as he left the clinic. Almost ten years later, the man returned to Stanley, came to our new clinic, showed me his fully functioning and healed hand, and paid his bill. He apologized profusely for not paying sooner. Instead of dirty jeans and shoulder-length greasy hair, he was wearing a white shirt, tie, and a gray suit with closely trimmed hair, looking out of place for Stanley

Too many patients didn't pay their bills. When fee-for-service income determined whether the Stanley Clinic and Stanley Ambulance survived, failure to pay was a disservice to everyone. Sometimes, I'd be angry and resentful, only to find out they couldn't pay. Others could pay but wouldn't.

At the clinic, I got a call from the Boise County sheriff. A member of a motorcycle gang called Brother Speed crashed and injured himself in an accident near Idaho City. He needed suturing. The sheriff was preparing to send the injured motorcyclist to an ER in Boise.

"Marie, Brother Speed wants his emergency care in Stanley," the sheriff told me. "They're on their way."

About ninety minutes later, Brother Speed parked their motorcycles in front of the Stanley Clinic. I like to sew, and the injured motorcyclist needed someone to sew. I cleaned, sutured, and closed his lacerations.

After his tetanus shot, the man asked me to send him the bill. After sending the bill several times, I stopped trying. Unfortunately, his payment has yet to arrive at the Stanley Clinic.

Blue Cross

For insurance companies paying NPs, one big breakthrough was a break involving an ankle.

In those first years, insurance companies did not reimburse NPs for their services. Many of our patients had health insurance through Blue Cross but paid out of pocket because insurance companies refused to reimburse NPs. A fishing accident in Stanley changed that.

In the late 1970s, a woman was fly fishing in Stanley on the banks of the Salmon River just off the intersection of Highways 21 and 75. The fishing was great that day — until she lost her footing, fell, and landed on rocks. In severe pain, she arrived at the Stanley Clinic.

On exam, she had a severely deformed, swollen, and ecchymotic left ankle. After splinting and stabilizing the presumed fracture, I gave her Demerol to manage her pain. Then, we transported her by ambulance to Sun Valley for X-rays and for orthopedic care.

"Marie, just send the bill to Blue Cross," she instructed me as we loaded her gurney onto the ambulance.

"Sorry, but that won't work," I replied. "Blue Cross doesn't reimburse. I'm a nurse practitioner. Insurance companies won't pay us."

"That can't be right," she said. "My son is the administrator for Blue Cross. Let me check with him about this bill." And with that, we said goodbye and closed the ambulance door, and she was on her way.

About a month later, we received an envelope from Blue Cross. It was a check for services — services provided by a nurse practitioner.

That mother and son changed the world for the Stanley Clinic, nurse practitioners in Idaho, and probably beyond. After that fly-fishing accident, Blue Cross had no problems reimbursing us. After Blue Cross, Blue Shield paid, too. Then, the following year, after Congress had acted, Medicare started reimbursing.

Medicare

Insurance companies defended their position of not paying NPs because Medicare didn't reimburse them. And because Medicare didn't reimburse NPs, Medicaid didn't reimburse either.

People on Medicare don't go out of their way to get sick or hurt. But when Medicare patients seek help, medical bills start arriving. For rural clinics increasingly staffed by NPs and PAs, Medicare's failure to pay puts financial burdens on rural residents and threatens the economic viability of rural clinics like Stanley's.

One workaround was to submit bills to Medicare through my physician preceptor, Dr. Stone, using Ketchum Medical Clinic. Eventually, Dr. Stone and I met with a lovely, gray-haired woman from Medicare.

"What you two are doing is illegal," she explained politely. "If you do this again, we will file charges against you for Medicare fraud. You won't be able to plead ignorance of the law. And you should expect a fine and probably time in prison." Rather than risk prison, we turned to Congress to expand Medicare reimbursement to cover NPs and PAs.

Reforming Medicare to reimburse NPs took a national effort. While Idaho was the first to license NPs, by the late 1970s and early 1980s, the nurse practitioner idea had by then expanded to multiple states. Congressional delegations worked together in what became a national effort enabling advanced practice providers to be reimbursed by Medicare.

In Idaho, NPs worked through our Board of Nursing and reached out to our four members of Congress. I wrote letters, as did clinic patients and friends. Dan Mahoney, a patron of the Stanley Clinic, owned newspapers and TV and radio stations, helping with news coverage and with public understanding.

Even back in the 1970s, a lot of folks depended on Medicare. When our patients got a big bill from our little clinic, and Medicare refused to pay because I was an NP, they got upset. And when people get angry, they are more likely to take action. People, not just in Stanley but across the nation, contacted their members of Congress.

"That can't be right," was a typical response when I explained that our Medicare patients had to pay out of pocket because Medicare wouldn't pay me as an NP. When enough people — especially those who are connected — insist, "That can't be right," change will come. Eventually, Medicare reimbursed. And with that, the other insurance companies followed suit.

The clinic board and I reviewed physician reimbursement rates to determine the dollar amounts to bill Medicare. Although the rates for physicians may be too low, they were high for our clinic, and I'd never charged that much. My intuition was that if the Stanley Clinic billed Medicare for NP services at the physician rate, we would open a can of worms.

We slowly increased my NP rates based on the clinic's finances and our patients' ability to pay. I submitted my list of general charges to the clinic board every year for approval. They also knew that some patients never got charged because they had no money. The board never called me on the carpet for giving a break to those in financial distress and poverty.

2. DONATIONS

Donations comprise a second leg of the three-legged stool that provides funding for the Stanley Clinic and Stanley Ambulance. Let's take a moment to reflect upon the donations from thousands of people and businesses that have made the Stanley Clinic and Stanley Ambulance possible since 1971:

- The Forest Service, seeking to exit its role as the primary provider of emergency services, donated staff time and resources to help start and sustain the Stanley Clinic and Stanley Ambulance.
- Locals donated their time to serve on the Stanley Clinic board.
- Attorneys donated time to help us become a non-profit corporation with the IRS.
- The president of our board, Marvin Larson, donated his rental cabin next to the laundromat so we could open our first clinic.
- Physicians donated their instruments and their office furniture.
- Bishop Volkswagen of Boise painted and serviced our first ambulance.
- The King family of Salmon donated cement and poured the concrete foundation for the new clinic.
- Boise Cascade donated most of the supplies to build the clinic.
- A licensed electrician from Boise donated his time and materials to wire the clinic.
- Residents volunteered their time to take the EMT class and serve as EMTs and drivers.
- Physicians and nurses in the Wood River Valley, Boise, Seattle, Salt Lake City, and Chicago gave their time to help me become a nurse practitioner.
- My physician preceptors and many others donated their time to take my calls and to assist our patients.

The list of donated time, money, supplies, and services continues on, but support cannot be a "one-off;" it must be perpetual. The Stanley Clinic and Stanley Ambulance must remain viable year after year.

Our gross income for the clinic from fee-for-service was a few thousand dollars in the early 1970s, so there was no cushion for buying new instruments and little else. In 1972, we faced the dual challenges of raising money to build a new clinic and replace the ambulance.

When we started fund-raising, we sent letters to everyone we knew who might use the clinic and ambulance. We raised the money that was needed, although not enough to pay me a salary.

Small and large donors have breathed life into the Stanley Clinic and Stanley Ambulance. However, I do want to acknowledge three donors in particular. Dan Mahoney was a Florida newspaper publisher with a ranch west of Stanley. He was a clinic supporter during the 1970s and early 1980s.

Dan walked into the clinic and handed me $2,000 in cash, saying, "Marie, they don't pay you enough. Here, I want you to have this."

"Dan, I can't take it," I said.

"Yes, you can, Marie.

"No, I really can't ... I can't ethically accept this gift," I said. "We'll put your donation toward replacing the ambulance." I wanted to accept the cash with Dan's good intentions and could have used the money. But it wasn't right.

Another notable donor is Teresa Heinz Kerry, whose foundation donated $15,000 in the 1980s to help replace our aging ambulance. Stanharrah Corporation was another major donor.

The Mountain Mamas auctioned off a quilt each year to benefit the ambulance fund or other worthy community projects. You could join the group if you knew how to quilt. Bonnie Hansen, who helped start the group, was an excellent quilter and an all-around good person. The quilts represented long winters and women gathering weekly around the quilting frame, laughing and sharing stories. We started at Bonnie's home, then moved to the Community Center when it opened. The Mountain Mamas created one quilt a year, although occasionally, we added a baby quilt.

We also asked tourists to donate. We put out ambulance donation jars at the clinic and distributed them among several local businesses. As soon as we bought one ambulance, we needed to raise money for the next. Raising money to keep the Stanley Ambulance on the road became an activity of daily living.

We couldn't get oxygen delivered to the Stanley Clinic, so I drove to Twin Falls, dropped off smaller empty tanks at our oxygen supplier, Norco, and loaded up as many tanks as possible. Norco delivered the big tanks used in the clinic and ambulance to Ketchum Medical Clinic. Jimbo Funderberg and other locals donated time and trucks to haul the big green oxygen tanks over Galena Summit.

Of course, none of this is allowed today: a car wreck could turn oxygen tanks into missiles. But back then, with the effect of Stanley's elevation on those with cardiopulmonary disease, we did what was needed to make oxygen available for our patients.

A significant focus of our fundraising was the ambulance. After paying $300 for the Pontiac, costs skyrocketed: By the 1990s, a new ambulance cost over $100,000. Our board figured we'd need to replace an ambulance in ten years because of distances and terrain. We added an "ambulance replacement" line item to the clinic's annual budget. Stanley is not alone in maintaining an ambulance service. The high cost of EMS, especially ambulances, challenges rural communities everywhere.

We received financial help through grant writing to foundations. The Robert Wood Johnson (RWJ) Foundation was a pivotal supporter, having paid for our EMS radio communication system. The RWJ Foundation made a significant grant to Idaho EMS to help rural communities pay for their ambulances. What a generous and meaningful gift that was.

3. GOVERNMENT SUPPORT

Early on, I would pick up the phone and call people who might donate. We'd talk about the Stanley Clinic's equipment and supplies, the cost, and why we needed people to give financially. Many responded, "Oh, I thought the government supported the Stanley Clinic." Out-of-staters were especially amazed that we had no government funding, assuming that the federal government ran the clinic — far from it.

Counties do fund healthcare. In 1971, when I started training under Dr. Packer and Dr. Gwinner in Hailey, they staffed Blaine County Hospital. Later, I trained at two other county-funded institutions: Seattle's Harborview Hospital and Chicago's Cook County Hospital. County facilities were underfunded and understaffed, but the doors remained open.

Knowing that counties sometimes funded healthcare, we approached our own county. The Custer County commissioners said "No" to funding the Stanley Clinic.

The town of Challis, the county seat where most of the county's residents live, needed a clinic, too. However, the county's tax revenues come substantially from the Stanley area, and the county's finances couldn't afford one clinic, let alone two. What little money the commissioners appropriated went to opening the Challis clinic. That decision added to the perception that Stanley pays Custer County's bills but doesn't receive services other than a deputy sheriff and court system.

When Idaho EMS designated me as an instructor, I taught two classes in Challis. Both courses were excellent and well-attended. Still, it was a long drive on that winding river road in winter, traveling at night while worrying about black ice, losing control, and going into the river. I finally said no: the drive was too risky.

Starting in 1976, my son John contacted congressional offices to pursue options for federal funding for the Stanley Clinic and Stanley Ambulance.

John contacted Senators Frank Church and Jim McClure of Idaho, then worked with the staff of Senator Magnuson of Washington state, who chaired the Senate Appropriations Committee. We explored designating that part of central Idaho as a Health Manpower Shortage Area.

Ultimately, a vote of local property owners creating a local tax district preempted John's pursuit of federal funding.

Twenty years later, when the clinic board and I were in the throes of trying to hire my replacement, we pursued federal funding a second time. Physicians from the Wood River Valley helped by writing letters of support. But in the end, the Stanley Clinic and Stanley Ambulance muddled through without federal aid.

Polarization over the federal government in rural areas can turn federal aid for clinics into a political football, with elected officials opposing funding that would actually help their rural constituents. Federal funding also means more paperwork and administrative headaches.

I'm relieved we succeeded with the local funding option in the long run while knowing some rural clinics and hospitals can't survive without it.

4. LOCAL TAXING DISTRICT

Rural clinics must compete with urban clinics and hospitals to recruit and retain clinical staff. Generally, urban clinics and hospitals are able to offer better salaries, benefits, and call schedules.

By the late 1970s, the nurse practitioner profession was beginning to expand rapidly, mostly in urban settings. Meanwhile, in Stanley, I continued as the sole provider, seeing clinic patients and making a few thousand dollars a year.

But, of course, practitioners must have a livable income, even in rural communities. The remedy for Stanley proved to be establishing a local taxing district.

During the early 1970s, finances for many rural clinics and hospitals were marginal in Idaho, and rural facilities were folding beneath the burden. Stanley was not alone in depending on people to pay their medical bills to keep clinics and hospitals solvent.

In response, many small rural hospitals in Idaho sought legislation that would allow voters to tax themselves to support local healthcare. The Idaho Legislature made this a reality with a new statute that would enable rural areas to vote to establish "Clinic Hospital Districts," taxing themselves to support local medical facilities. The statute placed a three percent limit on taxing assessed value to protect property owners.

Stanley was not the first to vote in a taxing district. We watched as several rural hospitals sought support from local property owners.

In 1976, we began working on creating our own Clinic Hospital District. The Stanley Clinic board appointed a committee to set the district boundaries based upon our service area.

We were careful not to impinge on the Challis clinic and did not include the downriver town of Clayton. To avoid problems with Blaine and Custer Counties, we drew the southern boundary at the county line, even though Blaine County residents in Smiley Creek, at the upper end of the Valley, also used the Stanley Clinic.

We drew the western boundary at Banner Summit and included parts of Bear Valley. The northern part of our clinic hospital district included the southern reaches of the Frank Church River of No Return Wilderness and extended eastward into the White Cloud Mountains.

The roughly 1,400 square miles included within our hospital district boundary is far less than the area we actually covered, given county boundary lines.

The Custer County commissioners approved our proposed boundaries in 1978.

> Petitioners state as follows:
>
> 1. The name of the proposed District shall be "Salmon River Clinic Hospital District."
>
> 2. The general purposes of the formation of said District is to provide a tax base and public corporation status for the existing Salmon River Emergency Clinic in Stanley, Idaho, which is presently operated as a non-profit corporation.
>
> Petition to Form Hospital District, 1978

Property owners voted 98–2 to establish our hospital district. Because we had to wait two years before accessing tax monies, we kept the doors open by doing what we had from the start: using fee-for-service and donations.

Once we could access the taxing district funds, each year our clinic's board and I went through a budgeting process that projected expenses and income, including fee-for-service and donations. We then estimated what we needed from the clinic hospital district. Finally, we submitted a request to the county commissioners, who budgeted for each taxing district: cemetery, library, school, and the two clinic hospital districts in Custer County. We were cautious about our requests. We did not ask for the maximum tax allowable and risk a tax revolt; we asked for about one percent, rather than three percent.

The clinic hospital taxing district saved the Stanley Clinic. Eventually, the clinic went from not knowing whether we could keep doors open to a sound financial footing, including the ability to pay me a livable salary.

The vote hugely in our favor underscored that residents were willing to tax themselves to support and access local healthcare. At a time when I was being summoned repeatedly to Boise to defend my work as an NP and the work of the clinic and ambulance, I was surprised and proud that local people voted their faith in what others considered too radical. That vote turned the corner on the survival of the Stanley Clinic.

5. DEPARTURES NOW ARRIVING

When you are younger and in good health, you think more about beginnings than endings. But, as you age, "what if" questions start creeping in. I loved my work at Stanley. Still, as I entered my sixties, pressure increased to plan and prepare for my departure by hiring my replacement. No one lives forever. What if my cancer came back? What if I got hurt or died suddenly? Our failure to secure the transition would have been a bad outcome for everyone. The clinic board and I had to strengthen the position, hoping that an advanced practice provider, nurse practitioner or physician's assistant, would continue the work I had started.

After nearly thirty years as the clinic practitioner, I knew we had to offer a competitive salary or at least a package of benefits if we found another clinician to take over. During the battles with the Idaho Board of Medicine, our Chamber of Commerce president, Marvin Webb, described the situation in a letter published in the Twin Falls Times-News on January 4, 1979:

> One of the benefits of small-town life as it is lived in the Stanley-Sawtooth area is the capacity of the residents to pull together for the common good as the history of the Salmon River Emergency Clinic attests. The clinic building was constructed by the Valley people with no federal or state funds.
>
> All clinic personnel aside from our certified registered nurse practitioner are volunteers and our practitioner's earnings are half that of the lowest paid NP in the state. The medical services provided by our NP are beyond measure — without her, we would have to go 60 miles south to Sun Valley or 60 miles north to Challis for all medical problems.

While I had multiple job offers at multiples of my salary, I would never leave so long as I could do the work physically. When one Boise physician offered me a job, he said, "You can handle eighty-five percent of my practice, giving me the time to delve into the fifteen percent of patients that need me."

"Yes," I responded, "you would see all the interesting cases and leave everything else for me. No, thank you." I stayed at my post in Stanley until I was sixty-eight years old and physically pressed to continue doing the work.

> Marie requested her salary be increased to $19,000.00. She stated that she had agreed to take a lesser salary a few years ago with the understanding that it would be increased $1,0000 per year until it reached $20,000.
>
> Salmon River Clinic – Hospital District Board of Directors Meeting, August 11, 1983

Starting in 1979, my salary under the taxing district jumped. That was a massive increase for me, but less than half what NPs made in Boise. In the seven years after I started, NPs were certified in surprising numbers, many in Boise working with doctors. While I didn't make what the NPs in Boise made, the taxing district secured a livable income — but never adequately provided for my retirement. The clinic board funded a few annuities but could not afford a pension. My son John, who helped with the Stanley Clinic and Stanley Ambulance, committed to my financial security.

The law giving rural communities the option of establishing clinic-hospital districts also limited how much we could increase our taxing budget, partly to protect taxpayers. Consequently, we could never write the total amount we needed into the clinic budget and then raise it on taxes. Still, clinic and ambulance funding increased slowly as tax assessments increased each year. More people moved to the valley and built more homes. Each year, my salary went up in hopes that we would eventually be in a salary range acceptable to my replacement. While I never did get that salary, the clinic board was able to offer a competitive income when the time came.

People might want to work in Stanley, but it's not an inexpensive place to live. So that brought up other line items that we added to the budget, including housing for the next practitioner. A new person coming in, especially if they were not too long out of school and had debts, likely would not have the funds to buy property in the Stanley area.

The clinic has living quarters used for premed interns and medical students, and by me when storms made it impossible for me to make it home. However, clinic living quarters are not a substitute for a home. The next practitioner and their family would need a home.

We started a program to buy property within walking distance of the clinic. No more fourteen-mile commutes for emergency calls. Someone helped with a partial donation, and we purchased the property.

Eventually, the clinic board bought a three-bedroom manufactured home. With that, we could provide housing within walking distance of the Clinic for an incoming practitioner.

We became increasingly desperate to find that practitioner as we approached the end of the 1990s, and the clinic board could not hire my replacement. We again considered the option of federal funding and support. Eventually, the community and Amy Klingler, PA found each other. Although the transition was bumpy, the Stanley Clinic and Stanley Ambulance survived mainly because of her.

"Support proposal to raise money for emergency medical services." Bill Foxcroft (Idaho Rural Health Coalition president) and Marie Osborn, coalition board member and EMT Instructor.

The Idaho Statesman, Boise, Idaho, February 27, 1997

After several years of lobbying, Marie Osborn finally convinced the Legislature to provide money [to support rural EMS]. Beginning July 1, drivers will pay an additional $4 to renew their driver's licenses; this money will go directly to grants for training, vehicles and equipment for emergency medical services.

"State's First Nurse Practitioner Retires." Barb Newlwert, *Times-News*, Twin Falls, Idaho

Today, nurse practitioners may know little of the sorts of early struggles with poverty-level income that I faced, because of our successes in obtaining insurance payments for NP services and clinic taxing districts. Our wins have had profound consequences, including that NP- and PA-staffed rural clinics can continue caring for our patients. When we started, that was still in the future. Now, it is history.

6. FUNDING RURAL EMS?

About eighty percent of all emergency responders in this state are volunteers serving small units in some of the most isolated areas imaginable. Many units are having difficulty finding individuals willing and able to shell out the money, spend the time in class, commit to further training to maintain skills and be willing to respond at all hours — all for no pay.

Monies allocated by the legislature and augmented by federal funds and foundations have not adequately funded rural EMS. Keeping ambulance services running and staffed is expensive.

To help, I had an idea. What if two or three dollars from every speeding ticket went to EMS? After all, speeding contributes to motor vehicle accidents that require EMS. What if we used speeding ticket money, just a tiny part of the fine as a "user fee" to help fund the EMS? That would benefit all the rural ambulance services in the state.

I took the proposal to Idaho legislators who had a record of supporting EMS. Unfortunately, an idea that seemed practical to me turned out to be a legislative nonstarter. Traffic ticket fines are a sacred cow, with revenues supporting courts and judges. They weren't about to share. Legislators told me the proposal didn't have a chance to go anywhere. "Sure, Marie, we can bring it to a vote, but it will just get voted down."

The public must understand how costly new ambulances are and how difficult it is to staff with first responders and drivers. When people are hurt or dying, there is a public expectation that emergency services will respond.

"I need help. I hit a deer and rolled the car. My children are hurt, and I can't get my wife to respond. Please, we need help."

We need to fund rural healthcare and rural EMS.

Roland Miller

Ticket to Better Care
Nurse Practitoner Lobbies for Funding to Upgrade Rural Emergency Medical Service

Marie Osborn got a $53 speeding ticket recently. She wishes it had been $56.

That's because the nurse practitioner, a pioneer in Idaho back-country medicine, has been lobbying to get a $2 or $3 fee tacked on to fines for traffic violations. The money would be spent on training and equipping emergency medical teams.

"I would have gladly paid more, knowing that if I'd done something more stupid than speeding, there would be someone there with decent training to respond," Osborn said on a visit to Spokane.

Emergency services are, she said, "a vital part of the medical system, especially in places like Idaho, Eastern Washington and Montana, which have large rural areas."

Rural healthcare has consumed Osborn's life for 25 years, nearly 24 hours a day.

She helped found and continues to run the Salmon River Emergency clinic in Stanley. It faces all of the logistical challenges of rural healthcare. [...]

And she lobbies.

In the 1970s, she supported a bill that would allow for the development of clinic-hospital taxing districts. Its passage was, she said, "one of the great accomplishments of the Idaho Legislature."

Stanley residents voted [98-2] to tax themselves. The ambulance the clinic bought was a military surplus 1958 Pontiac. Pavement was visible under the seats, Osborn said.

The clinic is ready for its fourth ambulance. Osborn expects it will cost $90,000.

Federal emergency services dollars have dropped off dramatically, and she doesn't know where all the money will come from.

The state isn't likely to help. Last year, 143 ambulance units requested help replacing their rigs, but only one received help, and that was $5,000, Osborn said.

She is determined to change the situation before she retires in 1999. Last spring, she worked for the passage of legislation that would increase traffic fines.

The bill was sponsored by the Idaho Rural Health Coalition.

Julie Titone, *The Spokesman-Review*. October 21, 1997

22

THE DEAD

For everything there is a season, and a time for every matter under heaven: a time to be born, and a time to die ...

Ecclesiastes 3:11 (ASV)

Pryor Man Succumbs

STANLEY, Idaho (AP) - A 69-year-old Pryor, OK, man has died of an apparent heart attack as he stood in a shallow stretch of the Salmon River looking for a fishing pole.

Alvie Ramsey died about 8 pm Wednesday northeast of Stanley, where he was on vacation, said Custer County deputy coroner Marie Osborn. She said bystanders were not able to revive him.

The Oklahoman, Oklahoma City, August 15, 1992, 12:00 am

Births in the Sawtooth country were far exceeded by deaths. In 1972, I could not legally diagnose (or "pronounce") death or sign a death certificate. As the sole healthcare provider in an isolated area, I needed to be able to complete those tasks. The workaround for me was becoming a deputy coroner.

Birth and death are such contrasts in the human experience. Pregnancy has its due date with months of growing celebratory expectation, then "It's a girl!" or "It's a boy!" Death's hallmarks include grief and loss.

Life's bookends, birth and death, also share features in common. Some discomfort usually marks both: labor pain for the mother giving birth and for the dying, a full spectrum of pain possibilities. Both also require medico-legal documents, notably the birth certificate and death certificate.

For the dead, how we respond differs depending on whether it occurs in an urban, suburban, or rural setting. Let's begin with the death of a fictitious patient, George Smith, in an urban hospital. George has end-stage prostate cancer, is a "no code," and is in the hospital awaiting placement after a pathologic hip fracture. The nursing staff find George unresponsive, and they page you, the hospitalist working the night shift. It's three in the morning.

"We need you to 'pronounce' George Smith in Room 534."

You check in at the nurses' station before walking down the hall to Mr. Smith's room. When you arrive, Mrs. Smith sits in the room, crying softly.

Your diagnosis of death must be accurate. We've all cringed when reading the newspaper stories, "He looked dead," only to have the patient wake up in the body bag, morgue, or worse.

You speak to the body. "Mr. Smith, can you hear me? Close your eyes." He continues staring ahead without response. Radial or carotid pulse? None. You blow on the eyes and look for blinking or any eye movement. No response. You place your stethoscope on the chest and listen for heart and breath sounds, more than a perfunctory few seconds. None.

Your diagnosis? "Mrs. Smith, I'm sorry for your loss. Your husband is dead."

It's now 3:30 in the morning, and death demands documentation. While completing your work, you respect the dead and are compassionate toward the living: you type your death note and complete the necessary forms. Someone else will stop by to slip Mr. Smith into a body bag, move him into the hospital's refrigerated morgue, or to a funeral home. Tomorrow, the administrative staff will pursue you to complete the death certificate.

Next, try this in a Forest Service campground at Redfish Lake in the Sawtooth NRA.

You get the "emergency" call: a seventy-four-year-old male, dead, found by his wife. You drive to the campground and park your car. People are standing around picnic tables. A few are crying. Inside the camper, the dead patiently awaits you. "George had metastatic prostate cancer. He wanted to die in the Sawtooths. He so loved these mountains," his softly crying wife says.

Mr. Smith appears cachectic from end-stage cancer. He is lying on the camper bed, eyes and mouth open. "George, this is Marie." No response. You reach for his hand, white and cold. You place your fingers on the side of his neck to check for a carotid pulse: no pulse. You blow in his eyes; he does not blink. Finally, you place your stethoscope on his chest and listen: no breath or heart sounds. Your diagnosis? You turn to the wife. She already knows. You hug her and say, "I'm so sorry." But wait, there's more.

"Mrs. Smith, I need to ask you some questions." Death demands documentation.

Now what? Welcome to the complexities of dying in a Forest Service campground — or rural America generally. Who has the authority to pronounce the patient dead? Where does the body go, and what are the laws about transporting the deceased across jurisdictional boundaries? Don't delay: the sun is rising. In a sun-warmed camper or tent, dead bodies begin to putrefy.

In 1971, when we started planning the clinic and ambulance service, we focused on emergency care and life, not death. Stanley doesn't have a morgue. When the dead arrived at the Stanley Clinic, I had no idea what to do. My first summer as an NP was horrendous because of an exceptional number of major motor vehicle accidents. We also had what were essentially hospice deaths. We used our first clinic's kitchen for a morgue, occasionally overflowing into the reception room. I couldn't pronounce these people dead — by state law, only a physician, coroner, or sheriff could do that.

Dead bodies in bags could and did wait for hours, even over a day. Forest Service old-timers remembered that moving a body out of the Sawtooth Valley could take days. The delays are understandable, given the jurisdictions and regulations. Yet in the summer's heat without refrigeration, if you cannot move a body, that's a problem.

I needed the Custer County coroner, who was sixty miles away in Challis, to pronounce death, move the body, and sign the death certificate. Custer County is the size of Connecticut — only with mountains and fewer people. The closest funeral home was south, in Blaine County, which involved the administrative headaches of transporting a body across county lines.

We had no refrigeration for the dead. We couldn't leave a body inside the ambulance because it gets hot in the summertime and putrefaction accelerates. Moreover, the days were gone when ambulances doubled as hearses. Ambulances are for the living, not the dead.

When we opened our new clinic in 1975, we kept bodies chilled by moving the ambulance out of the garage and placing the body on a stretcher on the cold concrete. During clinic hours, you didn't mention to your patients that the dead were on the other side of the door.

The only requirements for being elected coroner in Idaho are being a county resident and twenty-one years old or older. Medical training is not required. A county coroner could appoint deputy coroners. For the dead in Idaho's Sawtooth country, the easier path was for me to get appointed a deputy coroner for Custer County.

I spoke with the County Clerk, Ethel Peck, and asked if I could become a deputy coroner. Ethel relayed my offer to the coroner, who liked the idea. The Custer County coroner, an elderly man living in Challis, was trying to cover a vast county. For him to travel to Stanley could take hours, and until he arrived, we were stuck.

"Congratulations, Marie. You're now a deputy coroner," Ethel told me over the phone. I could now pronounce someone dead and move the body within Custer County. The following spring, the county judge swore me in.

Moving a body across county lines remained a problem, nor was I to act as coroner or deputy coroner over county lines. Instead, I would turn the body over to the county coroner in the county to which I was moving the body.

The closest funeral home and mortician were seventy-five miles away in Hailey, in Blaine County. Conveniently, the mortician, Russ Mikel, also happened to be the Blaine County coroner. Russ was invaluable in arranging funerals or further transport of a body for autopsy or final disposition.

The phone rang at the Stanley Clinic.

"Hi, Marie, Ethel Peck here. How are things up in Stanley?" As the county clerk for Custer County, Ethel was a fabulous gal and a treasure trove of information. I turned to Ethel for help with Idaho state law, how things ran in Custer County, or who to contact.

"Marie, the county commissioners met last night and want you to be county coroner."

I knew of the vacancy; surely, the county would hold an election for a new coroner. "Ethel, I'm honored. But I'll have to say no." Challis is just too far from Stanley. Also, I knew nothing about being a coroner.

Ethel didn't give up. "Most of the coroners in Idaho know nothing about being coroners." She filled me in on legislative requirements. The county paid its coroner $2,000 a year and reimbursed for mileage. As deputy coroner, I was already making a small amount, and the remuneration did not seem worth the trouble. I thanked her for the additional information, and we said goodbye.

Ethel called back. "Marie, please, would you reconsider and become coroner?" She added, "You know, Marie, the coroner is the only law officer who can arrest the sheriff." Really! The sheriff and I had been on the outs several times that summer. And with that, I agreed to become the Custer County coroner.

Most county sheriffs and I worked together well, but one sheriff and I never established rapport. Whether intended or not, he was painfully paternalistic, verging on misogynistic. After I became coroner, he and I seldom met. Instead, I worked with his deputies. I needed law enforcement's help, and, as I had done as deputy coroner, I worked to establish professional and cordial relationships.

The coroner needed to respond to every death in Custer County. As coroner, I investigated unattended and suspicious deaths, determined the cause of death, and completed the death certificate. The coroner investigated all suicides. There was no crematorium or mortician in that part of Idaho, so we shipped bodies elsewhere.

In addition to examining the body, a coroner's investigations might include interviewing witnesses, first responders, law enforcement, family, personal physician, and others; ordering drug screens and other lab studies; and obtaining medical records. I ordered autopsies if our investigations were inconclusive or unearthed suspicious or criminal circumstances. I didn't want to end up in court trying to explain to the judge or jury why I didn't order an autopsy.

If questions arise, the coroner can impanel a jury to conduct a "coroner's inquest" using subpoena power to call witnesses. Only once did I initiate an inquest, at the scene with the body present. I didn't want to have people return later as witnesses under threat of subpoena. If my investigation raised concerns of a crime, I contacted the prosecuting attorney and sheriff.

Custer County was too big and rugged for one person to cover the whole county. In Stanley, I was already on 24/7 emergency call and seeing patients in clinic. I told Ethel, "There's no way I can handle the whole county. I've got a

Custer County is rugged, covering about 5,000 square miles with 5,000 people. For coroners, responding to deaths across this landscape poses a formidable challenge. Marie's training at the Cook County Morgue under Robert Stein, MD, helped, but covering Custer County as coroner was a steep learning curve.

clinic to run and must be here for emergencies. I can't drive from here to Mackay, spend a couple of hours there, and then drive back and hope nothing has happened."

I proposed to appoint deputy coroners to resolve the geographic issues, and the Custer County Commissioners agreed. We assembled a great team of deputy coroners: Jim VanArk, the PA in Challis; a mortician in Arco; and Russ Mikel, a mortician in Hailey and Blaine County Coroner. Two deputy coroners didn't live in the county but helped cover Custer County deaths anyway.

In the 1970s, I was on a steep learning curve for trauma, primary care, and caring for the dead in a rural, isolated part of America. As a coroner, I wanted more training in forensic pathology. That training came from Chicago's Cook County Morgue.

When I trained at the Cook County Morgue in 1976, Custer County had a population of about 4,000, while Cook County had 5.4 million. I studied under one of the world's leading forensic pathologists, Robert Stein, MD, who was the newly appointed Chief Medical Examiner.

Dr. Stein was a transformational figure for whom the Cook County Morgue is named. Born in Russia, raised in Brooklyn, and graduating from medical school at the University of Innsbruck in Austria, Dr. Stein was appointed Chicago's first medical examiner, serving from 1976 to 1993.

Before Dr. Stein arrived, Cook County, like Custer County, had an elected coroner, and medical training was not required. A public referendum replaced the coroner with an appointed medical examiner, board-certified in pathology. Dr. Stein oversaw autopsies and, during his career, investigated more than 20,000 deaths. His forensic investigations included serial killings and the 1979 crash of a DC-10 jetliner near O'Hare International Airport that killed 279 people. Dr. Stein was known to say, "My work is for the living."

Mornings in the Cook County morgue started with the smell of formaldehyde and twelve bodies covered in sheets. In this big room, curtains separated the gurneys. Twelve pathologists stood at twelve bodies with twelve assistants to open the bodies. The autopsy team carefully pulled back the scalp, sawed open the skull, removed the brain for examination, and opened the chest and abdomen. All body parts removed were weighed and measured, carefully examined by the pathologist, described and documented, saved, and stored in formaldehyde. Each autopsy took about an hour. When complete, the assistants wheeled out the body and wheeled in the next. Autopsies continued all day. Every unattended death in Chicago was autopsied — and many people died alone in Chicago.

You learn about disease states and the human condition when you can see and feel inside. In 1976, we wore hospital gowns over street clothes with shoe covers. For the few women in the room, our hair was up and covered. When Dr. Stein entered the room, chit-chat ended, replaced by quiet, intense dissections and organ examinations.

Dr. Stein was brilliant, a dedicated pathologist with firmly held views, and was sometimes blunt. He was adamant that coroners should be medical examiners. To avoid problems when I started, the ER nursing director cautioned, "I'll handle the introductions." She introduced me as the coroner of Custer County, Idaho. She didn't mention that I was a nurse practitioner. Dr. Stein likely assumed I was a physician.

Near the end of my two weeks working with Dr. Stein, a pathologist from Germany joined us. He traveled to Chicago to learn about Chicago's novel medical examiner system. Dr. Stein introduced me to him in the morgue, saying, "This is Marie Osborn. She's a physician and coroner from the state of Idaho."

Wanting to avoid deception, I replied to the two men, "Nice to meet you. Just to be clear, I'm not a doctor. I'm a nurse practitioner. And yes, I am also a coroner in Idaho."

Silence settled on the autopsy room. Dr. Stein looked at me. He never again spoke to me or even made eye contact. He moved on, and after a few more days in the morgue, I moved on too, resuming my training in the Cook County Hospital ER's unending stream of overdoses, knifings, and gunshot wounds.

You can understand Dr. Stein's position on coroners: appointed medical examiners trained as forensic pathologists are preferable to elected coroners without medical expertise. Cook County, Illinois, with over a thousand times more people than Custer County, Idaho, had an over-the-top need and the resources to meet the need. Dr. Stein's transformative work in Illinois, especially Chicago, was remarkable and historic. As a nurse practitioner and coroner, my training at the autopsy table in the Cook County Morgue was invaluable and unavailable in Idaho.

Dr. Stein's take-home message? Truly look at the body: the victim, your patient. Before you touch, take your time and absorb the scene in front of you. Stop before you start pulling or tugging on a body. Ask yourself: what does the scene have to tell you? Most of the time, deaths are benign, not warranting suspicion. Then, a case that raises questions and needs scrutiny will come. Don't assume. Look actively, and you will see.

Coroners should have a medical background. I'm not saying they must be doctors, but they must have medical knowledge. In rural Idaho, replacing elected county coroners with pathologists appointed as medical examiners wasn't doable. In Custer County, we didn't have enough doctors for the living, let alone the dead.

Transporting the dead involves complex regulations. Dead bodies triggered a process that involved Stanley Ambulance's EMTs, law enforcement, coroner, funeral home — and me doing paperwork.

My first Sawtooth death was on a sunny, warm day in May. In the Sawtooths, spring comes late and is glorious. High mountain meadows turn green and explode with wildflowers. Mountain peaks with snow and jagged rock against the blue sky are dramatic. On that spring day in 1972, the call came: a body at Beaver Creek in the field across from Dirty Dora's Beaver Creek Store. EMTs joined me at the Stanley Clinic. We loaded into the Pontiac and headed out.

Across the highway from Dirty Dora's was a middle-aged man sitting with his back against a tree. We assumed that he had had chest pain, moved into tree shade, and died from sudden cardiac death. Cool shade became warm sunshine as the day passed. I knew the funeral director in Hailey would take at least two hours, and we couldn't leave the body in the sun. We loaded the body into the ambulance, transporting it from the Beaver Creek Store in Blaine County to the Stanley Clinic in Custer County: we moved a body across county lines.

Wyethia blooming on Shaw Mesa. In the Sawtooths, spring comes late and is glorious.

When you drive between Ketchum and Stanley, you probably never notice those small signs, "Entering Blaine County" and "Entering Custer County." You wouldn't think about the county line unless you were transporting a body.

Years later, Idaho EMS StateComm occasionally messed up on the county line, radioing me for a Blaine County death: "Marie, you have somebody who has expired at Smiley Creek." At times, Blaine County would authorize me to act for them because they had no one available to drive over the summit in a timely manner. With multiple deaths, demands can quickly outstrip coroner resources.

"The closest mortician is in Hailey. His name is Russ Mikel. I've called Russ." When a loved one dies, people are upset and need help processing arrangements. I'd let survivors know when Russ would likely arrive — trying to give them a sense of the wait time.

Russ our closest mortician, was in Hailey in Blaine County. Russ is the gentlest, sweetest man. He'd come to Stanley as soon as possible, although if conducting a funeral in Hailey or Picabo, it could be a wait. When I began Blaine County's EMT training program in the Wood River Valley, Russ became an EMS instructor and occasionally helped me with classes in Stanley. Russ also became deputy coroner in 1984 and was appointed to fill the coroner vacancy in 1986. Voters have elected Russ as Blaine County Coroner ever since. As a mortician, Blaine County Coroner, EMS instructor, and friend, Russ was invaluable during my Stanley years.

Families, especially from big cities, might not understand the difficulties of moving a body out of Stanley. We kept them busy with paperwork, providing patient history, and other tasks, then suggested they call their family, be with them, or get a cup of coffee. If they wanted to stay with the body, that was fine, too.

Russ would handle much of the paperwork. "Sign here. Sign here." His soft, gentle voice was soothing after a long wait with the dead. More than once, we had problems with regulations, completing forms, and moving bodies across county lines. "Don't worry, Marie. We'll deal with it." And Russ always did.

Downriver of Stanley, the closest mortuary was in the town of Salmon in Lemhi County. If a family wanted to transport a body from Stanley to Boise, mortician services were unavailable in that 130-mile drive along rivers and over mountain passes. "Do you really want us to arrange to move the body to Boise?" Moving bodies can be expensive, as someone must pay for time and mileage. If it was a criminal case, then the body was transported 215 miles to a forensic pathologist in Pocatello, an expensive final trip.

Families would ask if the Stanley Ambulance could transport their loved one's body to the funeral home. We could transport a patient to a hospital but not a mortuary. Further, why tie up the sole ambulance covering that part of Idaho to transport a dead body when the living need the ambulance?

With the body cooling in the body bag on the clinic's garage floor, Russ Mikel would drive up in a station wagon or a hearse. After transferring information and responsibility, we'd watch Russ drive away. The dead finally leaving Stanley was closure for family, and for those of us who had responded to the emergency call.

Some campers came, year after year, to the Sawtooth Valley's stunning mountains and lakes. Then would come the dreaded words of a terminal diagnosis with not much time left: "I'm sorry to have to be the bearer of bad news." In life's trajectory, there comes a time to stop aggressive treatments, instead focusing on quality of life and comfort measures. Facing a terminal illness, why not end life peacefully in one of the most beautiful places on earth? Some did, traveling to the Sawtooths to die. Not suicide, just peacefully dying in a place they loved.

Elderly campers who came to die picked campsites that were easy for them to get to, and therefore, it was easy for us to get to them. Their decisions about their death were generally deliberate and well-thought-out. But they and their loved ones don't usually think about all the steps that must be taken after someone dies, especially in a small, isolated town like Stanley. Most visitors are from urban and suburban areas and assume the mortician will be on call to retrieve the body. Unfortunately, it didn't work that way. As first responders, we often found ourselves with a body and an audience of one or more upset people: spouse, child, lover, partner, close friends, campers, and gawkers. The living may have been unaware that death was imminent. For them, a profound event has occurred in a campground, an isolated place where no services exist: no morgue, mortician, or mortuary. The family will have no idea of the problems they're about to encounter. We were there to help the living and the dead.

Some campgrounds feel almost sacred because of what I know happened there. We'd get the emergency call, arrive, and find someone dead from a terminal illness, usually an elderly male. At one campsite, we drove up to find an older fellow sitting in his camp chair. He'd risen early, built a fire, and fixed a pot of coffee. He poured a cup and sat down in his folding chair to enjoy the peace and quiet of that Sawtooth morning. We found him dead by his still-smoking campfire, facing the morning sun with a smile, still holding his cup of coffee.

His wife knew of his terminal diagnosis. She had crawled out of their tent and found him. She was crying. There were times during those first years when we had so many deaths in both counties that we ran out of body bags. We were out when we responded to this call.

Russ came, loaded him into a body bag from Hailey, and took him over the hill.

Determining the cause of death is necessary to completing the death certificate. Information at the scene can provide answers. For example, family or friends might have a telephone number for the deceased's clinician. The physician, NP, or PA often knows the patient well enough to help you determine the cause of death. Rarely, a clinician would not want to be involved, and we would have to jolly them along to get the information. I would order an autopsy when we had to know with certainty the cause of death, such as when the death was unwitnessed or suspicious.

Autopsies can be hugely valuable in providing answers. Clinicians sometimes attend autopsies to learn one last time from their patients, although this was not a viable option in Stanley, given the time and distances. Autopsies are highly invasive of the dead and expensive. Families sometimes asked for an autopsy, and coroners sometimes ordered them. I had to keep a hawk eye on the budget.

Infants dying of SIDS, suspected murder, or unattended deaths without a reasonable cause prompted me to order autopsies. One possible murder that troubles me still, despite an autopsy, occurred up the Yankee Fork.

On a beautiful Sunday, my day started with a call from Deputy Jim Parkhouse: "Marie, I need to talk with you at the clinic."

"Jim, what's going on?"

"I can't tell you over the phone. But when you get to the clinic, I'll let you know what's up. You'll need to wear comfortable shoes. Don't wear sandals." Odd. When I arrived at the clinic, Jim shared what he knew.

"A Forest Service helicopter checking for fires spotted a body on a mountainside up the Yankee Fork. The sheriff's there now and radioed me. The guy's from Chicago. Right now, that's about what we know. Oh, and he's dead."

When I got in Jim's vehicle, I was wearing new white tennis shoes, a new pair of jeans, and my white coat. After several ambulance runs, being neat and clean felt good. We headed down the Salmon River, turned at Sunbeam, and headed up the Yankee Fork River road.

The sheriff and a deputy sheriff from Challis were waiting for us. The sheriff's rig was near a station wagon parked along the dirt road facing the wrong way. A Forest Service officer was there, too. Greetings came from the sheriff: "Hey Marie, good to see you. Sorry to bring you out on a Sunday. But we got ourselves a coroner's case."

A vehicle drove by kicking up dust, probably anglers looking for promising pools and riffles. This road gets a lot of use in the summer. Although many people drove by, no one stopped, no one was curious about this station wagon parked the wrong way. Had it not been for the Forest Service helicopter spotting the body, days or weeks might have passed before we were notified.

The dead man's car wasn't locked. The windows were down. Inside was high-quality camera equipment and an expensive fly rod. Nothing in that car was cheap.

"Nobody from Chicago would leave that kind of expensive equipment in an unlocked car," I noted from personal experience. "They just wouldn't."

Wearing my new white tennis shoes and white coat, I climbed up the mountainside with the sheriff, two deputies, and the Forest Service official. White shoes turned brown. The sheriff had on dress Oxford shoes, scuffed and dirty after surveying the death scene before we arrived. On that sun-exposed steep slope, I was hot and sweaty when we came upon him.

The body was cold, not yet putrefied. The man probably left his car early in the morning and made it about halfway up the hill when the shot was fired. The long gun was beside his body.

Law enforcement concluded this was a suicide, a "natural" death. The dead man had climbed up the hill, sat down, put the long gun barrel under his chin, and pulled the trigger. He slid feet first down the mountain until a boulder stopped him.

For me, it just didn't add up. The firearm was a double-barreled shotgun. It seemed hard to pull the trigger. There was no suicide note. Later that day, I spoke with his sister. The family was unaware of depression or suicidal ideation. And then there was the unlocked car filled with expensive camera equipment. For a guy from Chicago, that was not right. You lock your car when you live in a big city, especially Chicago. It's just habit. The death was weird. There was no evidence of a second person, but it was hard to tell with that terrain. My instincts were to do the autopsy.

The body went into a body bag, and we transported it to the Stanley Clinic. Russ Mikel came from Hailey. The body went to Boise for autopsy, then to Chicago for final disposition.

The forensic pathologist concluded that he died from a gunshot wound. And yet, still, I'm left wondering who really pulled the trigger.

Hunting accident or murder? I got the call to investigate a death up the East Fork of the Salmon River. Two young men, no older than twenty, were out hunting. They were close friends. Both were carrying guns in their arms, held in front of them. Walking down a steep hillside, one of the young hunters lost his footing. He fell. His gun fired. The shot killed his hunting partner and friend.

The sheriff went over — and over — the course of events with the shooter. Then, we all walked up the hillside and asked the shooter to re-enact what happened earlier that day.

After repeated questioning and the walk-through, law enforcement and I assessed the story as accurate: everything the friend told us checked out.

The family of the deceased? They didn't buy it and insisted that their son's best friend murdered him.

Because it was a gunshot wound death, we sent the body for autopsy. We signed off on the case as a hunting accident, not murder.

In another Sunday death near Galena Summit in Blaine County, the body was among the trees. Law enforcement arrived, gathered information, and left. Then, the family left. I was the last living person at the scene.

In Blaine County, I lacked the authority to move the body, yet I didn't feel right about walking off and leaving him. You can't just walk off and leave a body in the woods.

The man was leaning against a tree. I sat and leaned on the other side of the tree, and fortunately, I didn't get called for a trauma case while waiting.

After three hours, Russ arrived from Blaine County. It was good that I waited: the body bag's weight took both of us to move it down the hillside and hoist it into the hearse.

Walking in unprepared and finding someone dead is hard. It's not something you ever forget.

The emergency call came from the owners of Stanley's Sawtooth Hotel. One of the young girls working as a maid had walked into a motel unit behind the historic hotel. It was early summer, and the tourist flocks had not yet arrived. Not all of the motel units were rented.

The guest from Boise had specifically requested one of the units in the back. "It's quieter back there," he explained.

The young maid opened the door.

The man was dead. There was the pistol. A pillow, too, that he had apparently held to his head to muffle the gunshot. Indeed, no one heard the shot.

In filling out the death certificate, I estimated the time of death after midnight, considering his check-in time and movements in town.

A briefcase was in the room. One of the College of Idaho premeds opened it. Inside was a sugar-like crystalline substance that filled the briefcase loosely, not in bags. Cocaine? We all assumed it was cocaine, including the deputy sheriff, Carl Ellis. It wasn't cocaine. It was white sugar: a briefcase full of sugar.

I telephoned the wife. "Okay. Thank you for letting me know." She didn't seem terribly upset.

"How did he die?" I explained to her how we had found her husband.

"What kind of gun?" I described the pistol. "Yup, that's his gun."

I asked about his medical history and whether he was treated for heart disease. Stroke? Cancer? "No. He'd been down and depressed. But otherwise, in good health," she answered matter-of-factly.

The wife had no idea why he was carrying a briefcase full of sugar. He did not have diabetes. That suitcase of sugar at the suicide scene remains a mystery. Why do you carry a briefcase full of sugar and then shoot yourself in the head? He had planned well: came early in the season, rented a room well away from Stanley's main street, and used a pillow to muffle the sound.

For those of us who get the call for suicide, we usually bring training and experiences that help protect us from what we see. Unfortunately, the young girl who found him was unprepared when she opened the door to clean the room. She was young, starting a new job, and walked into that. How does she cope with a truly awful experience? As first responders and coroners, we try to help those left behind.

The Fourth of July holiday marks the start of the summer tourist season in Stanley. It can be wild. This last case was not a coroner's case — thanks to God's grace, it wasn't.

Early in the evening, the front door to the reception room opened at the Stanley Clinic. A couple of hikers assisted a disheveled young woman wrapped in a blanket. We took her back to one of the treatment rooms. We picked up a clipboard with patient history forms to get the story from the hikers.

They had been near Stanley Lake west of town and had taken one of the side roads up to the top of Elk Mountain. Suddenly, they come upon a woman. She was naked, wandering, and in extreme distress. She was bleeding from multiple cut marks. They wrapped her in a blanket, tried to console her, and brought her to the Stanley Clinic.

After asking the males to leave, with one of the female students, KT Fisher, present, I asked the woman to tell us what had happened to her.

She and her female friends from Boise had driven up for a weekend of the Stanley Stomp: live music, dancing, bars, and lots of fun. The women had started at the Kasino Club.

When her friends headed down the street to the Rod & Gun Club, she stayed behind to talk with a cowboy she had just met. He managed a big ranch north of Stanley, downriver near Clayton. He looked like a cowboy with a big belt buckle, jeans, cowboy hat, and boots. However, he failed to disclose that his wife and daughters were back at the campground at Stanley Lake.

She excused herself to join her friends, and the cowboy offered her a ride to the Rod & Gun Club. She said, "Sure," and got in his truck. That was nearly a fatal mistake.

He locked the doors and started driving, not to the bar nearby. Instead, he drove out of town. First, he turned at the Stanley Lake turnoff. Then, approaching the Inlet Campground, he turned up the road to the top of Elk Mountain.

He raped her, took his knife to her, cut marks into her body, and then drove away, leaving her naked and for dead.

She managed to crawl and walk until she saw hikers, a fortunate encounter saving her life. They brought her to the Stanley Clinic.

At the time, I was not qualified to do a rape exam. We were on the phone with the Sun Valley ER, and they had a physician on call who could do the legally-required exam and testing. Unfortunately, the volunteer EMTs on call that night were all male.

One of our female students, KT Fisher, went with our patient in the back of the ambulance. Later, the physician telephoned me to confirm it was a rape, and to let me know they'd admitted her to the Sun Valley Hospital.

The Fourth of July is the wildest weekend in Stanley, making it busy for the Stanley Clinic. That year, the weather in Boise and Twin Falls was hot, sending even more people to the mountains.

During the evening of the Fourth, the sheriff and several deputies joined us at the clinic to follow up on the rape. They were also preparing to arrest one of our patients: an underaged, obnoxious, intoxicated young man destined to spend the night at the Challis jail, to be picked up sober by his mother the following day.

The front door opened. A cowboy-looking guy came walking in and sat down. He didn't say anything at first.

"I need some cough syrup for my kid."

"Well, I need to see your child," I replied. "I just don't give out cough syrup."

The first thing was the smell. My son, John, was struck by the odor of stool. For me, it was more like the smell when you gut a deer. Then I could see blood on his jeans, the way some hunters wipe their knife blades across their thighs while gutting a deer. But, of course, this was not hunting season.

I looked at him. He didn't act right, although he had kids in his vehicle.

The sheriff was sitting there. I motioned for him to walk with me into the hallway. I whispered, "This guy's the one you're looking for. He's the one who attacked the woman." The sheriff replied, "Oh, Marie, he wouldn't just walk in."

"It's him."

"Why don't you come on back to one of our treatment rooms," I said. The "cowboy" did, and the sheriff came, too.

I looked at his hands. Blood covered his nail beds and caked under his nails. I scraped the blood and collected specimens into a test tube. He complied.

Next, the sheriff handcuffed him, moved him into the patrol car, and transported him to the jail in Challis, where he admitted to the rape.

While raping, brutalizing, and mutilating this poor woman, his wife and kids were waiting for him at the campground. He had told them he was going into town to get something. But, when he didn't come back, they grew concerned.

Later that night, he walked into the clinic to get cough syrup for one of his kids.

The mutilation of the victim prompted the sheriff to ask for the maximum sentence. The case went to a jury trial in Challis. With postponements, the proceedings took about two years. I testified in court three times, and the final time was for sentencing. The jury convicted him, and the judge sentenced him to forty-seven years in prison.

This case, and so many others, underscore the importance of law enforcement. When bad things happen, you really need their help. Those who work in ERs or as first responders know the value of police being present, supporting and protecting you when things go wrong. I was sure glad they were at the Stanley Clinic that night.

After two years, I concluded that serving as Custer County coroner wouldn't work. With the Stanley Clinic so busy in the summertime, I couldn't cover the rest of the county and do an adequate job. I resigned as coroner and continued as deputy coroner for my part of the county.

I had more medical experience than many coroners. Coroners do make medical decisions. Coroners also make decisions with a price tag: if a coroner orders an autopsy, as with SIDS deaths, the county foots the bill. Failure to order an autopsy may carry consequences, too, including possible lawsuits.

After Russ came and left with a body and I signed and dated the paperwork, I returned home to my cabin overlooking the Sawtooths and the White Cloud Mountains.

These words often come to me when I'm struggling with death and loss: "For everything, there is a season, ... a time to be born, and a time to die."

Something I learned as a girl, perhaps on the polio wards at Ball Memorial Hospital in Muncie: You owe each patient, the living and the dead, the best you have to give. They deserve your best. Maybe they don't deserve much else, but that's for others to decide.

The cases I've mentioned have stayed with me through the years. Some of them I continue to struggle with, wonder about, and lose sleep over.

I still wonder about that briefcase of sugar. I wonder about the man from Chicago who drove to Stanley and was found dead next to a long gun: suicide?

Death leaves behind the living. Our white coats, surgical scrubs, and stethoscopes are not firewalls to loss and grief, nor should they be. We are the ones who pronounce death and then try to comfort a sobbing spouse, child, or friend.

We are all in this universe together. While we may draw strength in caring for others, we are all still touched and diminished by death, as so insightfully captured by John Donne: "No man is an island, entire of itself...Each man's death diminishes me, For I am involved in mankind..."

No man is an island,
Entire of itself.
Each is a piece of the contintent,
A part of the main.
If a clod be washed away by the sea,
Europe is the less
As well as if a promontory were.
As well as if a manor of thine own
Or of thine friends were,
Each man's death diminishes me,
For I am involved in mankind.
Therefore, send not to know
For whom the bell tolls,
It tolls for thee.

John Donne

El Capitan (CENTER LEFT, GRANITE FACE) *above Petit Lake, from Shaw Mesa.*

PART FIVE

PUSH BACK

Nursing Regulations Stir Debate

Nurse practitioner Marie Osborn is Stanley's medical lifeline, residents say, and provides the only medical service for 60 miles.

That is why some people from the small mountain community are upset about proposed regulations governing nurse practitioners. The more restrictive regulations, they said, would impair Osborn's ability to provide medical care.

They said the regulations threaten the efficiency of the Salmon River Emergency Clinic, which is staffed by Osborn and volunteer emergency medical technicians from the community. The privately funded clinic was built in 1972.

Marvin Webb, president of the Stanley Chamber of Commerce, said that without some of the medical services Osborn provides, residents would have to go 60 miles south to Sun Valley or 60 miles north to Challis for medical attention.

Even Osborn's supervising physician, with whom she communicates by phone or radio, is 60 miles away Ketchum, he said. …

The state medical and nursing boards must agree on the proposed regulations. However, the two groups have differing views on prescription writing and the delivery of medication.

Under the heading of "Prescriptions prohibited," the medical board proposes a one-sentence guideline: "Nurse practitioners shall not be authorized under any circumstances to prescribe legend drugs." Pharmacists dispense "legend drugs" – medications with possible side effects – such as barbiturates or penicillin.

The state nursing board list 22 types of medication that nurse practitioners should be able to prescribe, including antibiotics (such as penicillin), topical and local anesthetics (such as Novocain) and anti-nauseants (such as Dramamine). …

The medical board proposes to allow nurse practitioners to administer medication only after authorization of the supervising physician. …

Some Stanley residents said they will protest the proposed guidelines at a public hearing scheduled for 1 pm Thursday at the east conference room of the Hall of Mirrors.

Bruce Spence, *The Idaho Statesman*. January 27, 1979

Roland Miller

23

EMERGENCY CALL: SPARKY & MARYELLEN EASOM

"Oh my God, I've got to stay here," Maryellen told herself after a ten-day backpack in the Sawtooth Wilderness. Her dream was to teach in a one-room school, and Stanley had that. While washing dirty clothes at the laundromat in Stanley after her backpacking trip, Maryellen met Sheila Leonard, who offered her a job at Leonard Expeditions. The Leonards guided cross-country skiers from hut to hut, ski touring through the backcountry in the still of winter. Maryellen hired on. She never left.

Weeks after Sparky and Maryellen met, they started their first EMT class together. After six years of ambulance runs (and much more), they married on a bluff above Crooked Creek meadow overlooking the Sawtooth Mountains. These two people are a special couple. Sparky and Maryellen are among Stanley's "two-for-one" couples for emergency dispatch: you get two volunteer EMTs with one call.

To make ends meet, Maryellen cooked at the Kasino Club, shoveled roofs, drove river shuttles, scooped ice cream, prepped food, did logistics for The River Company, taught kindergarten in Challis for a year, and more. Good things come to those who wait: eventually, Maryellen became Stanley's schoolteacher.

Maryellen met Sparky during their first winter in the Sawtooths. Sparky was a river guide from Colorado who came to Idaho to run the Middle Fork of the Salmon River. He got a job as a boatman for Eldon Handy, who tragically drowned in a boating accident. Eldon's son, Dave, took over the business and offered Sparky housing for the winter: a bedroom, not quite an apartment. The toilet didn't flush, and Sparky had to haul water. The kitchen sink drained to a bucket. But the price was right.

Sparky's college degree is in conservation biology. He was a certified cross-country ski instructor; a field technician on the central Idaho wolverine study in the early 1990s; and "headmaster," principal, and sole staff member of Stanley's high school in the early 2000s.

After thirty-four years of riding the Stanley Ambulance and touching many lives, Sparky and Maryellen retired as volunteer EMTs. However, Maryellen continues to serve on the clinic board.

SPARKY & MARYELLEN EASOM, IN THEIR OWN WORDS

Maryellen: There's not much to do in Stanley in the winter. In 1982, I unintentionally dropped by a QRU (Quick Response Unit) class that Sparky attended at Smiley Creek. Marie met me at the door and said, "Sign in here, Maryellen." So, I did. That's where it began.

After completing the QRU course, I started working on the ambulance. The following year, I completed the EMT class. Sparky and I often headed out the door together when emergency calls came. Here are some of the calls that stayed with us over the years.

Looking at Stanley Lake with McGowan Peak reflected in the water is sheer joy. Stanley Lake is iconic in Idaho; it is quieter, smaller, and colder than nearby Redfish Lake. That cold water is stunningly beautiful — and deadly.

It was a June day, ice was off Stanley Lake, and snow had receded towards the Sawtooth peaks. With the sun shining and blue skies, it was a perfect day for a horseback ride. Three sisters in their twenties borrowed horses from a friend. They invited a sixteen-year-old boy to help wrangle the horses for them. The party saddled up by Highway 21, and the four horses with four riders headed toward Stanley Lake.

At that time there was no human-made trail around the lake, only game trails. The riders made their way through deadfall and willows along the lakeshore. Eventually, they emerged onto the big sandy delta deposited by Stanley Lake Creek as it flowed into the lake. The beach dropped steeply into the lake: no wading here. The old Forest Service campground was just upstream, and the sandy area was big enough for big recreational vehicles to turn around, boats to launch, cars to park, and people to fish. Unfortunately, the sandy delta was unstable, and actually collapsed and disappeared into the lake during the March 31, 2020, earthquake. The horses and their riders walked onto the unstable beach sand that lovely day in June.

The four horseback riders paused along the lakeshore. Suddenly, the beach gave way. One of the sisters tumbled with the horse into the ice-cold, deep water. She got out while the horse, confused, started swimming toward the lake's center.

Wearing chaps and boots, the young man dived in and started swimming toward the horse. He began having trouble in the cold water, struggled, and finally disappeared. One of the three sisters dived in to try and save him. She, too, started having trouble, then disappeared. A second sister dived into the lake to save her sister.

We got the emergency call and arrived with the Stanley Ambulance at the delta. We saw a crowd of people and four horses. Two of the sisters were in an emotional state beyond words, one soaking wet.

Other than comforting the living, there was little we could do. During the ambulance ride to Sun Valley, one of the sisters could talk a bit about what happened.

Nearby, people watched with increasing horror at the unfolding events. Finally, a quick-thinking bystander jumped into his boat and got to the still-struggling second sister, pulling her up out of the frigid water.

Minutes before, all four had been gazing at the lake on their horses. In the blink of an eye, the world forever changed, and the sixteen-year-old horseman and one of the sisters were dead.

We had multiple EMTs show up, and that was good. Once the call came, people rolled down the windows in their cars or picked up a phone: word traveled fast, and people scrambled, heading for Stanley Lake. Others saw the ambulance pulling out of the clinic.The Stanley Ambulance pulled over, and EMTs climbed in. It all worked.

Sparky and Maryellen Easom

Finding those two bodies took several days. Eventually, a professional diving team found them at the lake's inlet. A large cavity under the sandy delta held the bodies.

Maryellen: The crew completed the EMS Run Report at the end of an ambulance run. We used spiral-bound notebooks to record the information, then handed our notes to Marie, who wrote the formal reports. Over the years, reporting became digital, and we filled out a Patient Care Report (PCR). Practitioners who came after Marie were horrified that they would be responsible for these reports. Our thanks go to Marie; we had no idea of the work involved.

Reporting requires you to fill in the location. For that, we relied on our ambulance drivers. As EMTs, we were in the back of the ambulance and didn't track highway mile markers or landmarks. One example was a nighttime emergency call responding to a car wreck on Banner Summit.

The couple wore nice clothes, heading for a recognition dinner. Their toddler was in a car seat, sitting beside the family dog in the back. The car veered off the highway and hit a tree. In the Sawtooth country, especially at night, you can wait a long time for another car. The wrecked vehicle was far off the road. With darkness, tree cover, and distance, no one zipping by on Highway 21 would ever know. The father, terribly injured, crawled back to the side of the road. That someone drove by just then was a miracle. The car stopped, left him at the roadside, and drove hell-bent to Stanley for help. The emergency call went out.

We responded in the Stanley Ambulance, driving in the dark with lights flashing, headed west out of Stanley. We got to the injured man by the road, and his wife was still in the car. We stabilized both adult patients and loaded them into the Stanley Ambulance.

We assessed the baby, and she was okay. We kept her in the car seat and set her in the front seat of the ambulance for warmth. This baby's lesson to all of us adults: Maybe everyone in a moving vehicle should travel in a baby's car seat!

Sparky: That baby had just survived unscathed a significant car wreck that nearly killed both parents. We didn't want anything to happen to that baby during transport. But where do you attach a baby's car seat in an ambulance? The ambulance's jump seat in the back won't work. So, we ended up putting the baby, secured in the carrier, in the front passenger seat, and Maryellen sat on the floor without a seatbelt between the baby and the driver. Maryellen tended to the baby while the other EMTs tended to the baby's seriously injured parents.

We offloaded the parents into the care of the ER staff at the Sun Valley ambulance bay. No one knew what to do with the baby. After multiple calls, a social services agency finally stepped in to help.

The deputy sheriff walked to the ambulance while we cleaned up the blood. "Oh, by the way, there's a dog," he said. In the aftermath of emergency calls, sometimes you open your home and heart to people and their pets in need.

Maryellen: They were a young couple driving the highway at night. Suddenly the deer jumped in front of their car. He was wearing his seatbelt; she wasn't. The car rolled.

We got the emergency call. Marie was in the middle of it all. The young woman was injured badly, and helicopter transport was her only hope of living.

Knowing that life depends on that helicopter, those in EMS get anxious, which only worsens with waiting. Then you hear it, barely at first, from far down the valley, "Whoop, whoop, whoop." Hallelujah! The aircraft landed, and the flight crew stepped out. We prepared the young woman for transport.

A helicopter flight nurse called out to Marie, "She's circling the drain."

She didn't make it.

The man who survived the car wreck was devastated. He wanted to go to a hotel, but Stanley had no rooms that night. Besides, will you leave someone alone in a hotel room after what happened?

He was dazed and distraught, emotional in the extreme. So, we took him home and showed him to our spare bedroom. The rest of the night, he walked around the bedroom. Finally, in the morning, he called a friend who came to Stanley and took him home.

Sparky: We didn't bring people or pets home after ambulance runs often, but it happened. Helping others in the worst moments of their lives is part of the EMS effort, yet you don't find that in the EMT training manual. Caring for your patients is more than splinting fractures and binding wounds: you treat the whole person and, sometimes, surviving family and friends.

Sparky: The Sawtooth Valley and Stanley Basin have long highway straightaways. After driving on curvy roads over mountain passes, motorists hit the valley floor and "put the pedal to the metal." Drivers ignore speed limit signs, throw caution to the wind, drive too fast, and embrace the freedom of the road. Watch out!

Coming off Galena Summit, you drive past the tiny town of Smiley Creek and then enter a curve just before the Beaver Creek Store. Unfortunately, too many drivers pay no attention to speed limit signs, and some pay the price.

"Pregnant woman on the ground." We got the emergency call for a one-vehicle accident near the Beaver Creek Store. With our lights flashing, we headed south from the Stanley Clinic.

Two EMTs evaluated the pregnant woman and prepared her for transport to Sun Valley. The husband was up, walking around, and okay.

I went over to him to obtain information. One of the questions I asked was, "Do you have any idea how fast you were going?"

"Yes. Sixty-eight." It's a fifty-five mile per hour curve.

"Really, how do you know it was sixty-eight?" I asked.

"When I came off Galena and hit the flat, I set the cruise control for sixty-eight."

Maryellen: Should we transport the pregnant woman? She was in pain and pregnant. As Marie repeatedly pointed out, you transport if there is any question. We decided to move the woman to Sun Valley. Fortunately, she did not lose her pregnancy.

Maryellen: For me, the scariest ambulance runs are the kids. I've seen some gory trauma cases, but when kids can't breathe, that's terrifying. They're so young with their whole lives ahead of them and all that potential. They compensate and compensate, and then suddenly, they decompensate. Things can go bad so quickly.

We got an emergency call to Sunny Gulch Campground for a toddler in respiratory distress. We arrived at the campsite to find frantic parents and a one-year-old toddler, a baby boy, struggling to breathe. We loaded the mother and toddler into the ambulance and hightailed it to Sun Valley.

We watched every breath the toddler took for an hour on the trip over Galena Summit. The baby was inconsolable. We held oxygen to his face, and he'd push it away. The mother held the child until we arrived at the ER.

He wouldn't let anyone else get near him or even let an oxygen mask touch him. I sat across from them, holding a mask as close to his face as he allowed. He started wheezing and struggling for breath again, and I started moving the mask closer.

When he came around a little, he pushed the mask away again. I'd slowly move it forward again. It was a dance. I have seldom been so relieved to have the ambulance doors open with ER staff waiting.

Marie has been on ambulance runs with CPR in progress, trying to save babies who have arrested. No one ever wants to call the code on a baby. You don't give up a child. Those resuscitations went on for a long time: usually, the hour to get from Stanley, over Galena Summit, to Sun Valley. Doing CPR on an infant for an hour can seem like an eternity.

Bill Leavell — another Stanley EMT — and I did CPR on a man who stopped breathing as we headed up Galena Summit. This run was the first time either of us had done CPR on a person rather than a training mannikin. We continued to the hospital. After the ER doctor declared the patient dead, he took us aside.

"Although the patient died, I want you to know his blood gas was excellent," the doctor said. "You did a good job with the CPR. Next time, consider stopping CPR sooner and save yourself the stress." Even if we could call a code on an adult, I know I could never stop CPR on a child.

Sparky: You learn by doing. You study the EMT text, attend the classes, and pass the exams, but much of the learning begins when you are with a patient for the first time. For my first emergency call, I was the only EMT available.

Alcohol withdrawal can be fatal. One of our locals was going through severe alcohol withdrawals and needed ambulance transport. In a town of fifty people, you pretty much knew most folks. My first patient was a good fellow with a quick smile but too quick to reach for a drink. When the Stanley Ambulance arrived, the fellow was in rough shape, shaking badly and hallucinating, known as delirium tremens or "DTs." We loaded him onto a gurney and headed for the Sun Valley ER.

My patient's eyes suddenly rolled back, and his body went rigid. Then his arms and legs started flailing in rhythmic, jerking movements. He was seizing, his teeth clenched, turning blue, making awful guttural noises. It was too late to place an oral airway. The seizure stopped after about three minutes, but it seemed like three hours. We didn't arrive at the ER ambulance bay soon enough.

Reading the book, going to class, and passing the written test and the practicum is one thing. But you learn to be an EMT by being an EMT. Responsibility becomes your teacher. In class, when you train, it's controlled. No one is going to die. But, when you get into that ambulance, somebody might die. You learn fast how to apply what you learned.

Our patient? He returned to Stanley — and returned to drinking.

Maryellen: On my first run as an EMT, I got the call to help Ida May Decker.

I'm unsure where she went in the winters, but she spent her summers in the Sawtooths. Her hair was steel gray, and you never saw her with her hair down. Ida looked like a retired schoolmarm. She was trim, articulate, and well-dressed — always.

The 911 emergency call came for a "woman in excruciating pain." Riding the Stanley Ambulance, we arrived at Ida May's home. We walked onto her porch and knocked on the door.

"Come in."

We opened the door. Ida May was sitting at the dining room table. She was dressed perfectly with her purse in her lap, all ready to go. Next to her was the overnight case that she had packed. Ida was in 10/10 pain and she couldn't move. We brought the gurney into her kitchen, apologizing while rumpling her clothes. Ida May had probably struggled in pain through the night, waiting until office hours to call for help. She was prim, proper — and in pain.

Ida May Decker never returned to Stanley.

Maryellen: We were eating dinner at the kitchen table near dusk. We could see up Crooked Creek. It was autumn, night came earlier, and we could see headlights coming down the Crooked Creek road. The vehicle was driving way too fast. We continued our dinner. A few minutes later, the phone rang.

"We have a male with an arrow in his chest. EMTs needed." We scrambled to the car and headed for the clinic.

Rushing into the clinic, we heard Marie's voice and hurried to the back treatment room to help. We walked in to find our patient lying on the gurney, wearing camo with green and black face paint. As I walked in, Marie asked, "Maryellen, will you get the stethoscope out of the drawer?" Then, she turned to the patient, "Don't worry, Luke. Your mom will be here in a minute."

Luke? Luke McCoy? Marie's action was perfect because otherwise, I would have lost it. The distraction gave me time to compose myself before I turned around and faced one of my students with an arrow protruding from his chest.

Luke had been hunting up Crooked Creek calling in an elk. He bugled, and the elk bugled back. After calling back and forth, Luke realized that the bugling was not an elk but another bowhunter. Luke stood up to let the other hunter know. At that moment, the hunter became the hunted. Seeing motion and assuming he had his elk, the other bowhunter let fly an arrow ... into Luke's chest.

Sparky: The hunter who shot Luke was a big man. After his original stupidity, the bowhunter did everything right. First, he did not pull out the arrow. Instead, he stabilized the arrow in Luke's chest with a game bag. Since Luke had walked from his home to go hunting, the bowhunter drove Luke to the Stanley Clinic and carried him in.

The arrow had entered the right side of Luke's chest in front of the ribs at about the nipple line, slipped along, and hit the sternum, where it fractured before exiting the other side. It looked like the arrow had gone through the chest but never penetrated the thoracic cavity to pierce Luke's heart and lungs.

Maryellen: Marie and I rode the ambulance to the Sun Valley ER. Luke's mom, Jane McCoy, followed behind in her vehicle. As bad as it was to have one of the local kids with an arrow stuck in his chest, as far as we knew, without an x-ray, it had not entered the chest cavity, marginally lowering everyone's anxiety during patient transport.

Maryellen: Luke returned to school after taking the arrow in his chest. We're still friends and neighbors with Jane, his mother. People don't forget when you help them during those terrible times. As a volunteer EMT, it's different when you know someone.

Sparky: Being an EMT is about serving your community. Maryellen and I had no desire for the adrenalin highs. With two to three ambulance runs a day, I have to be honest: sometimes, I'd resent the tourists. Still, helping people you don't know when they are in trouble, or dying, is right. Being there for your neighbors, people you may see every day, when they need you is essential.

Providing emotional support on those bad ambulance runs is such a valuable service. Sometimes, it's easier if you don't know these people. But, if someone is dead or badly hurt and the family is distraught, to be able to say something, touch, or hug them can mean so much.

One of Stanley's EMTs, Bob Downing, was especially good with people. Bob was a Baptist minister, married to Lois, and had four children. Bob was such a gentle soul with a loving demeanor. He also served as an ambulance driver and chaplain. Every time we had a fatality, we were thankful that Bob was there to help the living with spiritual and emotional needs. We often focus on EMTs and overlook the essential services chaplains provide. Bob had that gentle touch with our patients and our Stanley Ambulance. One day in Stanley, Bob walked out his back door and died from a heart attack. Bob, we miss you. Thank you.

Maryellen: Stanley must have an ambulance service and trained people to staff it. Despite the genuine need, Stanley struggles to recruit and retain people to support EMS, like many rural towns in America. The flip side of "many hands make light work" is that an essential public service is falling on fewer and fewer people, risking burnout.

There are several reasons why people are no longer stepping up to volunteer as EMTs. First, living in the Valley is expensive now. People with little or no money trying to make a go of it struggle to make ends meet. There's no place to live. Wealthier people are buying houses for short-term rentals for out-of-valley residents, eliminating those places as housing for locals. Caretaking homes used to provide low-income locals a place to live, but owners don't need caretakers because they rent to tourists year-round.

Sparky: Local workers used to camp for the summer. The Forest Service changed regulations for dispersed camping, so you can only stay in one place for ten days and then must move thirty miles or more. For locals who depend on camping to avoid the high cost of housing, the new Forest Service regulations have had a huge impact. Workforce housing is a problem that needs serious solutions.

At the same time, the cost of a new ambulance has skyrocketed. Even with Idaho EMS support, Marie and the clinic board were engaged in dogged efforts to raise money to keep an ambulance on the road and teach EMT classes year after year.

People with means have and continue to help fund the Stanley Clinic and Stanley Ambulance. EMTs who once volunteered are now paid to be on emergency call and for ambulance runs. One EMT recently chose to forego a second job to make ends meet and instead signed up to be on-call for emergencies. These donations can make the difference between life and death.

The Forest Service, as the federal agency responsible for the Sawtooth NRA, also should help shoulder the financial burden of maintaining viable EMS services. Moreover, national leadership needs to step up to provide better support to rural communities.

Tourists are loving the Sawtooth NRA and River of Return Wilderness to death. One way to reduce demand for EMS services is to reduce visitors using a permit system: fewer tourists, fewer injuries. But that would also mean less money for local businesses.

Stand back when greenhorns pick up a hatchet, pour gasoline to start a fire, or binge drink and drive. If we can prevent people from doing stupid things, maybe we can reduce the demand on our limited capacity. An ambulance run in Stanley can take five hours or longer. If our one ambulance is in Sun Valley transporting a patient and you're having your widow-maker heart attack, or your child can't breathe, it's a problem.

People have to step up. The Stanley Clinic and Stanley Ambulance drove so many changes for the nurse practitioner and rural EMS. We need to find solutions to head off a worsening crisis in rural EMS — for Stanley and a lot of small towns across America.

24

RX FOR CONFLICT

In Idaho during the early 1970s, inducing dogs to vomit fishhooks opened the first battle over whether NPs could write prescriptions. The outcome? Now they can, including writing prescriptions for controlled substances such as opioids.

In rural areas and urban too, being able to provide medications is an essential part of what we do in caring for our patients. What happened at the Stanley Clinic drove outcomes for NPs statewide.

Stanley has three bars but no pharmacy. I asked Stanharrah Corporation to open a part-time pharmacy in our "supermarket" that wasn't very super by most standards, but it wouldn't pencil out. In the winter, a pharmacy in Stanley might fill one prescription a day, if that. Stanley's summer population dwindles during the winter to thirty to fifty people, not enough people to support a pharmacy. When patients needed medications, such as an antibiotic for a urinary tract infection, I could telephone the closest pharmacist sixty miles away, and the pharmacist would mail the medication. It could take four days on holiday weekends before the prescription arrived in Stanley.

One option was to have medications available at the Stanley Clinic when needed. Before I left for training at Seattle's Harborview in early 1972, I received help from the Chief Pharmacist at St. Luke's, Donald Ness, who wrote up a list of medications I would need. With Don's list, my next step was to purchase medications. In those pre-computer days, we used phone books listing personal and business telephone numbers. I opened the Boise phonebook, flipped to the yellow pages of business listings, and located the section on wholesale pharmaceutical supply businesses. I called and then stopped by the pharmaceutical wholesaler.

Snow drifts from Marie's bedroom window.

They very nicely set up an account for the Stanley Clinic. It went through fine, no questions asked. I used Don Ness's list to place my first medication order with the wholesaler.

Pills and syrups must move from large bulk containers into small dispensing bottles to fill individual prescriptions. The clinic was on the list with the Idaho Surplus Property Agency, which is used by government agencies and nonprofits. They gladly donated boxes of pill bottles to help us out.

I found lick-and-stick labels for the bottles at one of the local stores in Boise. You'll notice on your pill bottles the nicely printed name, address, and phone number of the dispensing pharmacy. Unfortunately, we didn't have pre-printed labels. So, I hand-wrote our clinic's name, date, patient's name and birth date, medication, amount, and dosage.

Buying drugs in bulk meant containers with 500 to 1,000 pills and giant jugs of cough syrup. If a patient needed ampicillin, I would pull down the stock bottle, count out the pills, and put them into a small bottle. Dispensing medications from the Stanley Clinic was easy and cheap. Most importantly, patients avoided driving 120 miles round trip over a mountain pass to pick up a prescription at the nearest pharmacy in Ketchum, or 150 miles to Hailey, or 240 miles of river road to Salmon.

"This is the cheapest medication I've ever had, bar none," my patients commented, especially those from California. I followed the advice of a pharmacist and doubled the wholesale acquisition cost. Penicillin and tetracycline were dirt cheap in bulk. Even doubling the cost, my patients were amazed at the low price. We made a little money for the clinic through the pharmaceuticals, which worked just fine — until it didn't.

"I think my dog swallowed a fishhook. Can you help?" was a plea heard more than once inside the clinic. Fishermen gut their catch, leaving entrails and occasionally fishhooks. Dogs gobbling fish heads and fish guts risked embedding fishhooks in their throats. Sticking your hand into a dog's mouth, especially a big dog with big teeth, always seemed risky. Tom Bulgin, a licensed veterinarian who helped at the clinic in the 1970s, encouraged me to use apomorphine. This drug, a morphine derivative, induces vomiting in dogs. Tom asked me to order the drug and keep it on hand.

I called the pharmaceutical wholesaler and ordered over the phone. I should have driven to Boise, walked into the office, and personally picked up the apomorphine. I didn't. I couldn't leave Stanley with patients in the waiting room, and ambulance runs to Sun Valley. The wholesaler agreed to mail. Only, he didn't ship the apomorphine to the Salmon River Emergency Clinic in Stanley. Instead, the apomorphine arrived at the Salmon River Medical Clinic in Salmon. We both had accounts with the same wholesaler. Concerned physicians in Salmon contacted the Board of Pharmacy.

The horseshit was about to hit the fan.

On a busy afternoon at the Stanley Clinic, one of the premed interns walked into the lab. "Marie, an investigator with the Board of Pharmacy is in the waiting room. He is asking to talk with you." We met in my office. The agent looked like one of Cal's IBM salesmen dressed in a suit, white shirt, and tie that were out of place in Stanley. He showed me his credentials. I was shaken.

"I would like to see your facility," the agent said. "Show me where you keep your narcotics and how you record them." He was not impressed with our flimsy, locked narcotics drawer. Later, after that inspection and a robbery, we purchased a safe for all our controlled substances. I also showed the agent our logbook: the detailed information we kept on each controlled substance used. He turned out to be a charming and helpful man. Over the years, he would stop in the Stanley Clinic to say hi, conduct his reviews, offer suggestions, catch up on local happenings, and ask where the elk were hiding before hunting season.

Next came the summons to appear at a hearing of the Board of Pharmacy and Board of Medicine. I was unaware that under the Idaho Board of Pharmacy rules, only a licensed pharmacist could pour liquids or count pills from a stock bottle into a dispensing bottle to give to a patient. Likewise, only a pharmacist could fill out and lick a pre-printed label. So off to Boise I went.

Unfortunately, Dr. Stone, my preceptor, also received a summons.

At the hearing were five to seven men, all sitting at a long table representing the Idaho State Board of Pharmacy and Board of Medicine. Not at the table but also in the room were several women representing the Idaho Board of Nursing. We started with formalities, a welcome and introductions. Then came the questions.

"Marie, how did you know what to order for stock drugs?" asked a pharmacist I didn't recognize.

"Oh, I had help from a friend who was a pharmacist. I had worked with him at one of the hospitals. He was supportive of the Stanley Clinic. He prepared the medication list he thought my patients would need from a rural clinic." I did not point to the pharmacist in the room who had helped me.

The Board of Pharmacy and the Board of Medicine viewed what I was doing, ordering pharmaceuticals at the wholesaler and writing and filling my prescriptions, as completely illegal, and the two boards directed me to stop.

I felt like a criminal awaiting sentencing. I had to promise not to count pills and not fill out and lick a label. Finally, the board members moved to other topics, excusing me from the hearing.

The fallout from that hearing was lasting. The Idaho Board of Medicine placed Dr. Stone on probation for nearly twenty-five years, sending a warning to other physicians precepting NPs. At the same time, the Idaho Board of Pharmacy took steps that impacted small rural clinics in towns without a pharmacy.

That hearing ended my ability to buy drugs from a wholesaler, stock medications, and dispense them to my patients. Instead, the boards agreed that NPs could issue "emergency" prepackaged bottles filled by a licensed pharmacist. The amount in those bottles was for twenty-four hours.

While that might work for Boise, it would not work for Stanley and other rural communities without pharmacies. When my patients walked out of the Stanley Clinic, they might be leaving for a whitewater raft trip, or heading out for a wilderness backpack or hunting camp. The twenty-four hours of medications wouldn't get my patients very far.

Here is how it worked when we first started the new prepackaging system.

You wake up with a severe sore throat. Is it strep throat? You get out of your sleeping bag and find your way from your campsite to the Stanley Clinic. Sitting on the exam table, you open wide and stick out your tongue. I use a tongue depressor and flashlight to look. Sure enough, you have little pus pockets. To confirm the diagnosis, I swab your throat, plate the specimen onto blood agar, and place the petri dish into the incubator. Next, in the 1970s, I reach into the cabinet for a pill bottle of prepackaged antibiotic: penicillin, unless you are allergic. The standard course of therapy for Strep throat was ten days. The emergency prepackaged bottle contains a one-day supply of penicillin. Do you see the problem? Remember, the boards ruled I couldn't lick a label. The prepackaged bottles had labels from Broyle's Pharmacy in Hailey. After Ted Broyle retired in 1980 and the family pharmacy closed, I worked with Chateau Drug in Ketchum.

Now look at the label on your one-day supply of penicillin. You'll see the pre-printed label with Broyles pharmacy/address/telephone number and PENICILLIN V. If you're an adult, you'll also see my handwriting for your name, take 500mg twice daily, and the quantity: four pills. You'll need thirty-six more pills to complete your ten-day course of antibiotics. Here are your options: — it's a long trip to Hailey and back.

Under the new system, for mail delivery of your penicillin, I place a long-distance call (before cell phones and costing the clinic) to Broyles Pharmacy to fill the remaining nine days of your medication. The mail carrier is a contractor. She stops by the Ketchum pharmacy at nine in the morning, Monday through Saturday, then drives over Galena Summit and drops medications at the clinic by noon, including your penicillin. Remember: no mail on Sundays, federal holidays, or if winter storms close the highway.

Your penicillin arrives in the mail at the clinic. Where are you? Remember, cell phones are decades in the future, and reception in the mountains is spotty anyway. If you are camping at Grandjean, Rough Creek, or Alturas Lake, you'll make a long trip back to the Stanley clinic to pick up your nine-day supply of penicillin. For some campers, I sent the clinic's premeds to the campgrounds, checking tents or trailers to find patients so they could get their medications.

Stanley's summers can be a three-ring circus. Weekends could turn into one massive street party, almost a riot, attended by what seemed like a thousand partiers. Drunken brawls kept our suture trays busy until the wee hours of the morning. Law enforcement eventually had to shut it down as year-by-year Stanley got ever crazier. The new twenty-four-hour prepackaged emergency dispensing medication system imposed by the boards nearly crippled the Stanley Clinic.

Picture a three-day weekend over the Fourth of July with the Sawtooth Valley campgrounds packed and the Stanley Clinic's waiting room full. Add in a couple of car accidents or perhaps a drowning at Redfish, Stanley, or Alturas Lake. How workable is the one-day supply of prepackaged medications for my patients?

"Here is your one-day supply of pills. Because it's a holiday weekend, you'll need to drive 150 miles round trip to Hailey for the rest of your prescription."

Boise is not Stanley. A straightforward solution for a city can be unworkable in a small town. And that's what we faced.

The boards and legislature took pity on us, acceding to rural realities, and changed the standard so we could provide three days of prepackaged medications. I ended up prescribing multiple prepackaged bottles for some patients. Meanwhile, the days of me buying medications in bulk at wholesale prices, handwriting labels, and filling free surplus pill bottles were gone. We were now paying a licensed pharmacist to prepackage medications. Drug costs went up, which hurt our small, rural clinic teetering at the financial margins.

We billed the patient or insurance company for the bottles we got from the pharmacies. Sometimes patients and insurance companies paid their bills, and sometimes they didn't. Pharmaceuticals had been a small money-maker for us. We lost money when people or their insurance companies didn't pay.

When your clinician writes and hands you a prescription, you might not think much about those little pieces of paper. You should. In America, where we have a pill for everything, prescriptions are your ticket to the pharmaceutical universe. Even in our electronic era, handwritten prescriptions remain part of patient care. Rural realities eventually dawned on rule-makers. As a result, the boards again adjusted the rules, allowing us to prescribe and issue entire courses of medication. Today, NPs write prescriptions for their patients. Before prescriptive authority, some physician preceptors co-signed stacks of blank prescriptions for their NPs to use when seeing patients. Dr. Stone and I spoke with Medicare staff about pre-signing blank prescriptions, and federal employees cautioned us that we risked Medicare fraud charges, so we didn't go there. Prescriptions were printed with both our names and our license numbers. If Dr. Stone saw his OB patients at the clinic, he would use the clinic's prescriptions. I alone signed the prescriptions I wrote. He never co-signed my medication orders. I was more afraid of Medicare than repercussions from the boards, especially after all we went through to become Medicare-certified. If you lose the ability to bill Medicare, you may as well close.

A visiting pharmacist was at Chateau Drug in Ketchum, saw a big bag of pharmaceuticals, and inquired. Ketchum pharmacy staff would have explained that the big bag of drugs held prepackaged medications destined for Stanley that had no pharmacy. But the visiting pharmacist filed a complaint with the Idaho Board of Pharmacy, accusing the pharmacist in Ketchum of jobbing out his pharmacy business to Stanley.

We had to go before the Board of Pharmacy again and defend the whole system of prepackaged medications, explaining that Stanley had no pharmacy and no pharmacist. Finally, after more hearings in Boise, the prepackaging medication system got put to rights again, and Stanley could get prescriptions through Ketchum. That was one of our last battles over dispensing medications from the Stanley Clinic.

In caring for patients, NPs must be able to write prescriptions. Of all the battles fought by NPs to be accepted and licensed, the most challenging was prescriptive authority.

Before the Stanley Clinic, ordering medications in Idaho was exclusive to doctors writing prescriptions and pharmacists filling them. Turf and tradition within pharmacy and medicine put the brakes on needed change. Opposition to advanced practice nurses writing prescriptions was often clothed in arguments of patient safety. Rural realities told a different story. The desperate need for healthcare in Idaho's rural communities drove the evolution of prescriptive authority.

Not once, but over and over, we were called before the boards in Boise. Especially during the first decade, the Idaho State Boards of Medicine and Pharmacy intensely opposed NPs writing prescriptions. (However, the Board of Nursing's support was unwavering.)

Our patients lived the consequences. They showed up, too, traveling to Boise year after year to testify for rural healthcare. The legislature convenes in wintertime when driving can be treacherous. Yet, Sawtooth locals risked black ice and avalanches to show up and defend their healthcare.

The hearings on prescriptive authority for NPs were well-attended from both sides of the debate. We had to prove that NPs could care for patients in rural communities like Stanley. Our patients and the people of Stanley offered evidence by telling their stories and defending our practice.

When the Boards of Pharmacy, Medicine, and Nursing summoned me to testify, it was a learning experience. Of course, we didn't always agree, but there was a sense of comradery. I knew people on the boards, and they knew me and the challenges I faced.

Legislative hearings were different. Legislators with no medical background and those from more urban districts knew little about rural hardships. They might vacation in the Sawtooths but had little or no grounding in rural healthcare.

Step by step, year by year, entrenched opposition gave way to accepting NPs and our need for prescriptive authority. First, rules changed to allow us to write prescriptions for an emergency period. Then we could write full prescriptions, but with one big exception: pain medication.

The telephone call for help came on a winter night. Chuck Ebersole, the chief naturalist for the newly created Sawtooth NRA, was in terrible pain. He was passing another kidney stone. "God damn, Marie, I'm really hurting. I need something for the pain. Please, can you help me?" Chuck's wife, Brady, was getting ready to drive him from their ranch out Highway 21 over Galena Summit to the ER in Sun Valley.

"Chuck, tell Brady I'll meet you at the Highway at the Fisher Creek turnoff." I suited up, grabbed my pack with the Demerol, walked out into the night, started the snowmobile (there were no electric starters back then), and headed down the hill two miles to the highway.

Chuck was in misery. I asked him to stand in front of their headlights and drop his drawers. Snow was falling, but car headlights were brighter than almost any operating room, illuminating a white buttock in the darkness. Once I injected the Demerol, Chuck pulled up his pants, and Brady drove him to the ER. I got on my snowmobile and headed up the mountain for home and bed.

Demerol was the one opioid the boards allowed me to inject at first. The Sawtooth country has lots of trauma. I carried a multidose vial of Demerol, syringes, and needles. If I injected Demerol into a trauma patient out Highway 21, pain was returning by the time the ambulance pulled into

Sun Valley's ER. Demerol's duration of action is relatively short, metabolites are a problem, and it's less potent than morphine or hydromorphone. As a result, Demerol, the go-to opioid during the Stanley Clinic's first two decades, fell from favor starting in the 1990s.

To manage patient pain from burns or fractures, I prescribed oral hydrocodone or codeine with acetaminophen. For crushing chest pain from acute coronary syndromes not relieved with nitroglycerin, the boards allowed me to use injectable morphine — not at first, but later. Also, for bad burns accompanied by excruciating pain, I injected opioids if there was no risk of respiratory compromise.

One of the first bad burns I treated in the Sawtooths was a hunter camped in a trailer at the top of Fisher Creek road. Autumn came with deep blue skies and balmy afternoons changing into crisp, ice-on-water nights. The hunter had a small propane stove. He awoke, got out of bed, dressed, and turned on the propane for coffee. He lit the match, and the stove exploded. The fireball blew him out the trailer door.

The hunter had his keys to his pickup in the pocket of his burnt clothes. Despite a badly burnt face, he drove down Fisher Creek Road to the highway and then to the Stanley Clinic. He put on a new shirt over the burns to be more presentable because the explosion had so badly burned his shirt. When the hunter walked in the door, he was in terrible pain with at least partial-thickness burns on his upper extremities and chest and full-thickness burns on his face. I injected him with Demerol, dressed his burns with sterile saline and gauze, and arranged for transport to the Salt Lake Burn Center via the Sun Valley ER.

Weather and method of transport also influenced my opioid choice. Bad burns went to either Salt Lake or Harborview, depending on bed availability. For ground ambulance transport to Boise, morphine was the better choice. For air ambulance transport, I used either Demerol or morphine.

It seems crazy now, but during those early years, I was prescribing hydrocodone and injecting Demerol without a DEA number. (Prescribing opioids requires a DEA number issued by the U.S. Drug Enforcement Administration.) For oral opioids like hydrocodone and codeine, I bought them in bulk from the pharmaceutical wholesaler. The head of the wholesaler didn't have a problem with it. He kept records. I kept records. I didn't know I needed a DEA number. It may have been Ted Broyle, the pharmacist in Hailey, who first alerted me. Eventually, the three boards worked out that if I had extra training in pharmacology, I could be issued a DEA number. Taking pharmacology classes continued through my nearly forty years as an NP. For the Stanley Clinic, I stocked 20 ml multidose vials of morphine and 50 ml vials of Demerol. While I didn't use that much, I didn't want to run out of these drugs. To restock opioids for the clinic, I drove to Ketchum and met with Dr. Stone. He filled out the special opioid prescriptions, which I hand-carried to the pharmacist. With new vials of opioids, I drove to Stanley and placed them in a locked drawer at the clinic.

"Oh no. Please no. Oh, God!"

I opened the clinic's front door Tuesday morning after Labor Day weekend. Something was terribly wrong. Pink slips were strewn across the reception room, my office, and the hallway. I hurried into the lab. Someone had forced open the locked drawer where we kept the opioids and any cash. The shower of pink slips strewn across the floor were receipts. From the wrecked drawer, the money was gone, but not the opioids, thank God.

The front door was locked when I arrived. The burglar likely entered through an unlocked door to the premed students' apartment. The students had worked that Sunday, then left to return to Caldwell and college classes. The thief waited until the students were gone. It had been a hellishly busy weekend. In the drawer was about $500, a lot of money for the clinic.

Then I walked into my office and saw the old piece of gifted furniture with the secret drawer. Inside that hidden space was my jewelry. The drawer had been forced open. All of my jewelry was gone. My star sapphire ring, black diamond earrings given by Cal, and a star ruby bracelet John brought from Thailand after my cancer surgery: all gone. Keepsakes, each with special meaning, were lost to me forever.

The thief robbed the clinic of cash and me of my jewelry while leaving untouched the morphine, Demerol, hydrocodone, and codeine. That was the only break-in during my thirty years at the Stanley Clinic. That robbery, combined with an inspection by the Board of Pharmacy, prompted us to install a big iron floor safe. There, we kept all controlled substances and cash. We had no further break-ins. Unfortunately, I had no jewelry left to secure in the safe. As a consolation, I used insurance money and took my daughter Debbie to visit my son Jerry, studying art in Italy.

Looking back, I want to stress that in 1972, I did not set out to brazenly flaunt rules, nor did I set out to change the world. Instead, I aimed to provide emergency services and healthcare for a rural community that had none. With a lot of help from a lot of people, I succeeded — including being able to write prescriptions for my patients.

During those formative years, I ended up expanding some legal boundaries. Although at first controversial, those boundaries have been accepted with time. I did need good reasons to defend my actions in some unpleasant hearings with professional boards and the legislature. We have come a long way in a relatively short time. May it never happen again that a nurse practitioner is asked to help a dog who swallowed a fishhook. But don't bet on it.

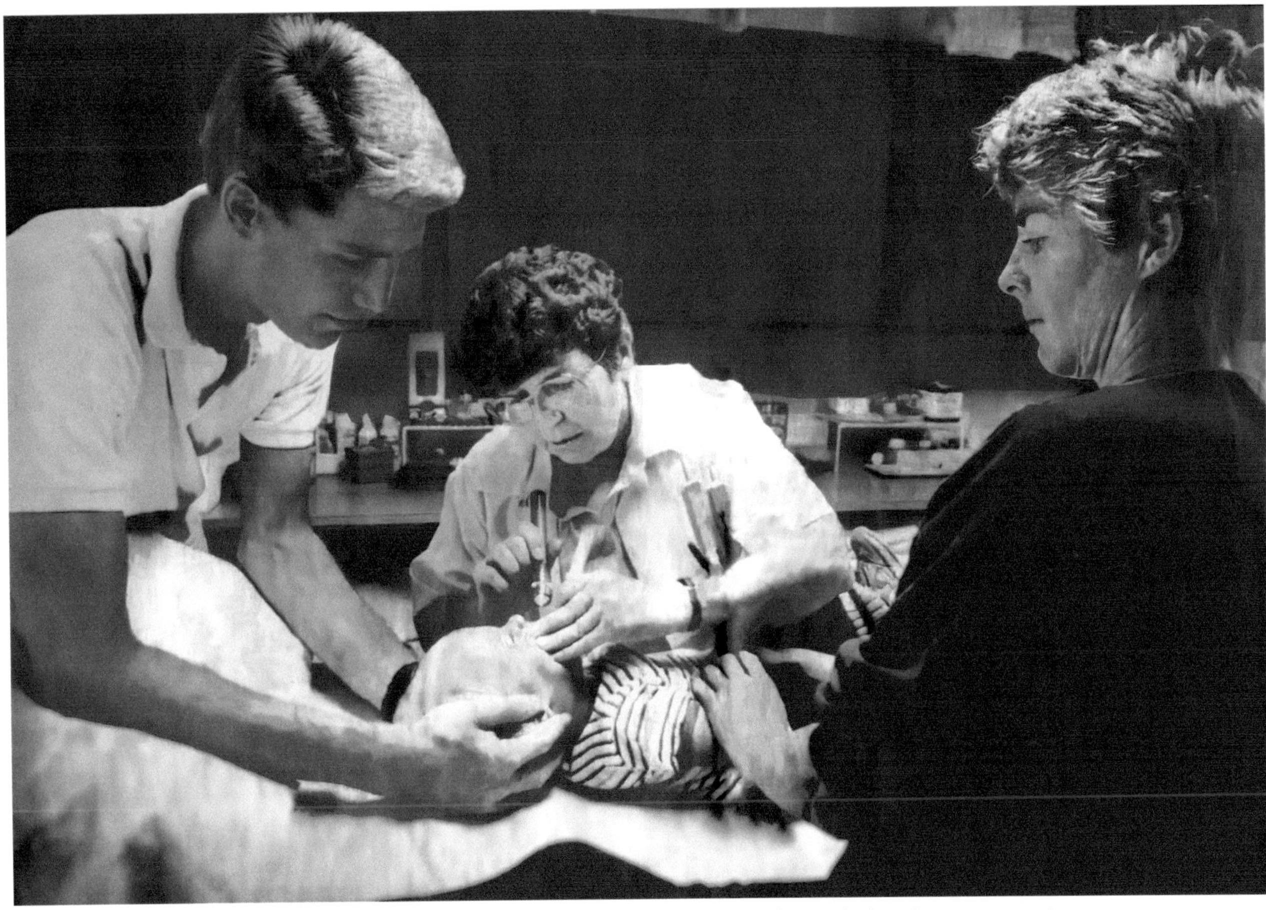

The Idaho Statesman, Boise

From "Mountain Nurse: she's a camper's best friend and lifeline." Article by Larry Gardner with photo by Teri Davis, August 7, 1987.

25

CROSSHAIRS

Rural America struggles with healthcare, a world apart from urban medical centers and high-tech diagnostics and treatments. Yet, by 1978-1979, the Idaho Board of Medicine sought policy changes that threatened to close the Stanley Clinic and other rural clinics statewide staffed by NPs.

At first, the three professional boards — Idaho's Boards of Medicine, Nursing, and Pharmacy — worked together to launch the NP profession. Nursing and Pharmacy mostly went along to get along with Medicine.

The Idaho Board of Medicine was always up in arms about something I was doing. "Marie is messing up again," was how they saw it.

If a doctor had concerns about me, he filed a complaint with the Idaho Medical Association. The complaint moved to the Idaho Board of Medicine, followed by joint discussions with the Board of Nursing. Finally, the three boards summoned me to a joint session.

Eventually, the three professional boards diverged. As the nurse practitioner idea took hold and began to flourish, especially in urban practices, so did controversies. Stakes over the future of the NP profession increased.

In the depths of winter 1979, nearly the entire town of Stanley traveled to Boise to defend their healthcare and nurse practitioner. The February 1, 1979, legislative hearing was pivotal in deciding the future of the nurse practitioner profession in Idaho.

Advanced practice providers, NPs and PAs, are needed where physicians can't or won't provide patient care. While Idaho was the first to license NPs, pay and working conditions were better elsewhere. Those who came and stayed often had community connections. Not helpful were the ongoing and increasingly bitter battles between Medicine and Nursing. The people of Idaho needed a single oversight board committed to building and safeguarding the NP profession.

The Idaho Board of Medicine and Idaho Board of Nursing engaged in quite the struggle. Who controlled nursing was the defining issue, and a political issue, too. The Board of Nursing insisted on control over nurses, including nurse practitioners. Both boards fought hard.

The battle over which board would control NPs was part of a larger effort by nursing to control nursing. Idaho's first Mental Health Nurse Practitioner, Marilyn Lamper, CNP, who practiced in Salmon, wrote to Representative Ray Infanger before a pivotal hearing held on February 1, 1979:

> Indications are, I am told, that the Board of Medicine wishes to have control over Nurse Practitioner Rules and Regulations through legislative change.... I have been reading national and state journals, newsletters, etc., regarding this issue and note that this issue seems to be a nationwide trend on the part of the American Medical Association. As you may know, it has been traditional in the past that physicians have enjoyed a great deal of power and authority over the nursing profession. However, in recent years the nursing profession has been asserting itself vehemently regarding its separate identity within the field of medical care. Pharmacists, hospital administrators, Laboratory

> Technicians, X-Ray Technologists, and other allied medical professionals all have their own well-defined professions, and even though they work closely with physicians there is no allowance for physicians to have any kind of voice in their professional Rules and Regulations, Licensure, Certification, etc., except as consultants, colleagues, advisors, etc. As I understand it, the nursing profession is striving for a similar interdependent and collegial relationship with physicians while doing what is defined by law as nursing care....
>
> The main point here is that the Board of Medicine opposes nurse practitioners ordering and administering any kind of drugs, using skilled nursing judgment, without immediately notifying his/her sponsoring physician. Sometimes this can involve much valuable time to say nothing of the expense of long-distance calls for small, scarcely funded rural health clinics run by nurse practitioners. Can you imagine what it might be like for a nurse practitioner in a remote geographical location to have an emergency requiring immediate lifesaving measures and have to spend critical moments trying to contact the sponsoring physician in order to administer a stimulant or pain medication immediately indicated? How would it be for such a well-trained person to have to hunt down the sponsoring physician for permission to suture a gaping wound or administer tetanus toxoid, etc.? I have an admirable nurse practitioner colleague running the emergency clinic in Stanley, Idaho, who has to deal with critical situations very often. I am afraid to think of the lives which could be lost or shortened if the residents of the Sawtooth Valley did not have her fine services. Such care takes much dedication and personal sacrifice. Evidently, she has the trust and support of her sponsoring physicians in Hailey and Ketchum as she has been doing her job for about seven years now....

By 1978, the Board of Medicine sought sole oversight authority over NPs, muscling out the Board of Nursing. Finally, the Board of Medicine went to the legislature to limit the role of NPs and effectively eliminate NP prescriptive authority.

Not until later did I understand how the Stanley Clinic figured into the battles between the professional boards over the future of the NP profession. The political vortex pulled in those of us trying to care for patients in the field, and often, we didn't even know it. The Board of Nursing strategically used the rural NPs to justify and create a new profession that today is mainly urban. Eventually, after leaving the Stanley Clinic, I became one of those urban NPs, serving low-income and uninsured patients until I turned eighty.

Within the Board of Medicine was a strong contingent who believed NPs were unqualified to do what I was doing. Among them was Dr. Dean Sorensen, a surgeon and president of the Idaho Board of Medicine. He was also elected to the Idaho legislature representing Ada County and quickly rose to a leadership position as Majority Caucus Chairman in the Idaho House of Representatives.

Dr. Sorensen was critical of my work almost from the beginning. It was inescapable that the Stanley Clinic was in the crosshairs as the poster child for the new nurse practitioner profession.

Dr. David Barton joined Dr. Sorensen in publicly challenging the new NP profession. Dr. Barton was a big man, an OB-GYN with a distinguished career, involved with the WWAMI program, recognized later by the University of Washington for his teaching excellence, and president of the Idaho Medical Association. Dr. Barton opposed the nurse practitioner idea and was scathing, combative, and belittling during hearings. With so much at stake, those were miserable hearings for me.

The Board of Medicine objected to NPs diagnosing and prescribing, raising patient safety concerns. NP supporters responded by criticizing the Idaho Board of Medicine as a guild protecting physician turf rather than helping meet the healthcare needs of rural communities.

The state's medical board proposed a one-sentence guideline: "Nurse practitioners shall not be authorized under any circumstances to prescribe legend [aka prescription] drugs."

For Idaho's rural clinics staffed by NPs, this meant no birth control, no antibiotics for kids screaming with bulging red eardrums, and no pain relief for people suffering from trauma.

In contrast, the state's nursing board listed twenty-two types of medications that NPs should be able to prescribe, including antibiotics and local anesthetics (lidocaine, for example, used for suturing wounds).

Two nurses, Eileen Merrell and Leola Daniels, led the defense of NPs and the Stanley Clinic. Both women served as directors of the Idaho Board of Nursing. They interfaced with Medicine and Pharmacy, doing their best to help me navigate the minefields.

Eileen Merrell, whose husband was a doctor, was highly supportive. You have to wonder what went through Eileen's mind when she drove to the Stanley Clinic in 1973 and got out of her car to find me on hands and knees in front of the clinic, pulling porcupine quills out of a dog's face. Leola Daniels was quiet, capable, and smart. She also wore gloves of steel and got things done. NPs today and into the future should celebrate these two women for making their profession possible in Idaho.

Out of the battles and rancor of the late 1970s, the Idaho Board of Nursing ended up with sole oversight authority of the NP profession.

During debates over the new NP profession, I became the public face, although talented NPs saw patients in other rural clinics in Idaho. Of the legislative hearings, the most tumultuous occurred in the Hall of Mirrors across from the state capitol building on February 1, 1979.

In the depths of that winter, nearly the whole town of Stanley traveled Highway 21 through the avalanche chute past Banner Summit to Boise. In that pivotal hearing, one person stood out with unforgettable testimony: Bud James.

Bud and his wife Rita, a nurse, were veterans of World War II and managed The Mountain Village Motel (formerly the Armada) in Stanley. They also managed our radio system's base station for the clinic and Stanley Ambulance. With a booming voice, Bud was on a mission to have the legislature hear him loud and clear. They did. No one had to turn up a hearing aid. Bud spoke passionately about the lives on the line in rural communities like Stanley, which are too small to support a physician. On that day, in that hearing, Bud helped save the Stanley Clinic, beating back efforts that would have crippled the fledgling NP profession.

Joining the Stanley community in testifying were premed students from the College of Idaho who had interned at the clinic. Premed Kelly Mutch, who later was a WWAMI student and then internist in La Grande, Oregon, spoke on behalf of premeds who had interned at the Stanley Clinic:

> During the last seven years, Marie Osborn has filled the need in the Stanley Basin competently and efficiently. This not only our opinion but that of Dr. Bryan Stone of Ketchum, her supervising physician. The medical contributions she has delivered are widely recognized and appreciated, and in Dr. Stone's words, "Several times they were lifesaving." If the proposed regulations are adopted, they will destroy her ability to administer these services effectively. They will reduce the standard of medical care now present in Stanley and similarly impact nurse practitioners and communities elsewhere.
>
> The authority to prescribe and dispense medications beyond the limits proposed by the Board of Medicine is essential to delivering effective healthcare in rural areas. The Board of Nursing's proposal would allow prescribing, provided the nurse practitioner can submit documented evidence of sufficient course work in pharmacology. The Board of Medicine, however, appears bent on establishing prescribing as a right belonging solely to physicians.... I have witnessed many occasions where people in the wilderness area needed medications, and the distance from a pharmacy is exceedingly long. As now practiced, the system allows the successful management of most minor illnesses and conditions. The ultimate and irrefutable justification for any method or system is whether it works. It *does* work, so why change it? ...
>
> These restrictions cause us to have two major concerns. Our narrowest concern is for the survival of the healthcare delivery system in the Sawtooth country of Idaho. In the areas of community and emergency medicine, this system has been a true blessing for the residents and visitors of the region. Our experiences at the Salmon River Emergency Clinic have been an invaluable exposure to rural medicine and awakened us to the problems faced in rural healthcare delivery. The experiences have also motivated us to reach our goals: four of us have been accepted to medical school, one is receiving his degree in hospital administration, and three others are currently applying to medical school. More importantly, enacting these rules could mean the closure of the clinic and the end of all the benefits that Marie Osborn has brought to the Sawtooth Mountain-Salmon River region.
>
> Our broader concern is that the restrictions will have the same effect on other small communities that fail to attract physicians. We have recognized nurse practitioners' role in meeting the demand for primary healthcare delivery in medically underserved areas. The need for adequate medical services is desperate in much of rural Idaho; to enact these impractical standards would be to neglect and deny a possible solution to this problem.

Several days before the hearing began, a letter arrived for me at the Stanley Clinic. I carried the letter with me to Boise and I was pleased to have the opportunity to read into the legislative record:

January 28, 1979

Salmon River Emergency Medical Clinic
Stanley, Idaho

To the Nurse-in-Charge:

The members of the Southern Idaho Sailing Association wish to express our appreciation for the rapid response and excellent care received during the emergency situation involving our club Commodore, Robert Wood, when he suffered a heart attack last August 6. We feel that if it had not been for your personal concern and your clinic's existence, an entirely different outcome may have happened.

We hope that this token donation can help your clinic in some way to help others when the need arrives. Each one of our many members would like to thank you personally as we are extremely pleased to know that such an organization does exist in the remote area of the Sawtooth Valley.

Thank you.

Al Jacobs
Commodore, SISA

"In the summertime," I testified to the legislators, "with the influx of summer residents, church and scout camps, and tourists (over 1.5 million estimated by the Forest Service last summer), the requirement to consult the supervising physician for every act of suturing, medication administration, etc., would produce chaos in the clinic and for the busy physician, as well as the unnecessary delay of treatment for the patient who should be the primary consideration of all healthcare providers." The proposed changes were draconian and unworkable. "The rules and regulations proposed by the Idaho State Board of Medicine would essentially close our clinic's doors in Stanley, Idaho."

The word "doctor" holds special meaning in patient care, and I am not a doctor. When my patients addressed me as "Dr. Osborn," I corrected them. "I am a nurse practitioner. I am not a doctor. Think of me as a super-nurse, not a mini-doctor." I did not have a doctor's training or background. However, as a sole provider in rural areas caring for the critically ill or injured, I did wish for better knowledge about anatomy, physiology, and pharmacology. People with PhDs should be careful not to be seen as medical doctors. When we had a possible anaphylactic shock case at Sawtooth Lake in the wilderness, a "doctor," drinking at the Rod & Gun Club, walked into the clinic and volunteered to help. Only later, while EMTs loaded gear for the night hike to the patient, did the "doctor" disclose he was a PhD in psychology, not a medical doctor. I believe this to be an abuse of the title "doctor," and to be avoided.

Despite my steadfast opposition to childbirth in Stanley, I delivered two babies. Unfortunately, one of those emergency deliveries landed me in hot water and a return trip to the Capitol's Hall of Mirrors for yet another hearing. The complaint filed with the Board of Medicine falsely accused me of scheduling baby deliveries in Stanley. The mother and I did not schedule that childbirth; instead, it was an emergency delivery, and any trained EMT would have done what I did. The complaining doctor, then in Challis, was no fan of the Stanley Clinic and my work as an NP. He used the opportunity to complain to the Idaho Board of Medicine. The boards summoned me to Boise for another hearing, and Dr. Stone and Stanley's townspeople joined me. Despite our view that the Idaho Board of Medicine wanted the Stanley Clinic closed and me censored, no action was taken, including no curtailment of my practice. Instead, without apology, the Board of Medicine unofficially told me that I was not to do scheduled deliveries in Sawtooth country. I had never done a scheduled delivery in Stanley and never wanted to.

After the powerful legislative testimony on February 1, 1979, with nearly the whole town of Stanley in attendance and the positive media attention, the attacks tapered off. Another factor was the growing number of NPs, especially in urban clinical settings. The NP profession would remain in Idaho — and flourish.

Today, the Idaho Board of Nursing oversees nursing in Idaho, including nurse practitioners. The battles over the NP profession occurred in a larger historical and cultural change context. Idaho, with the rest of America, was changing. So, too, were the healthcare professions changing, driven partly by the healthcare needs of rural America.

One of my major detractors, Dr. Sorensen, married Sheila Sorensen, the same Sheila Sorenson who, as a nurse practitioner and state senator, led the Idaho legislature in 2004 to change the law and allow NPs to be licensed independent practitioners, providing patient care without physician oversight.

Roland Miller

26

"ALL CREATURES GREAT AND SMALL"

"Help the needy
And show them the way.
Human kindness is overflowing,
And I think it's gonna rain today."

Randy Newman, Singer-Songwriter

"I could do terrible things to people who dump
unwanted animals by the roadside."

James Herriot, Veterinarian and Author

Most of my patients were human, but not all. Animals also needed emergency care, and there was no one else in Stanley to do it — just me.

We had an animal emergency on the day we opened the clinic. After we were done with the speeches and chatting over coffee and cookies, a speeding station wagon lurched to a halt in front of the clinic. The driver jumped out and bounded up the front steps. "It's my dog. She's hurt. Can someone help?"

The dog had been running through brush and ripped open her abdomen on a staub. The wound needed suturing. I love to sew, starting with clothes for my family and then my first suturing case, a facial laceration on an intoxicated man brought in by police to Seattle's Harborview ER. But... I looked at the dog, then looked at Dr. Cutler. "I've never sewed a dog."

"Marie, it's just like sewing a human," Cutler commented. "Go to it." So, I did.

The celebration paused while I cleaned the dog's wound and started suturing. I didn't use local anesthesia, and that beautiful Irish Setter looked at me and never even whimpered. Closing its abdominal laceration required many sutures. When I finished, the owner promised to follow up with his veterinarian in Boise.

Not all animals are so mild-tempered and agreeable. The next dog that arrived in the back of a car tried to bite me as I sewed. I wrapped roll-gauze around the dog's muzzle to avoid getting bitten while removing porcupine quills.

Animals do feel pain. I used a local anesthetic, lidocaine, when providing emergency care to animals. Whether a hurting dog or cat, or horse caught in a barbwire fence who ripped skin that hung almost to the ground, I used lidocaine. It was better to administer an anesthetic at the start rather than be sorry in the middle of surgery.

To keep dog hairs out of the clinic, we used old sheets donated by local motels. When I finished sewing wounds or pulling porcupine quills, I'd take the sheets outside, give them a good shake away from the clinic, and get rid of animal hair. One of our clinic's board members, Freda Nicholson, owned the laundromat with her husband, Gerald. Freda always used hot water when washing anything from the clinic. She wanted to make sure no germs got passed around.

For the occasional animal needing emergency care, I tried to treat them outside the clinic on the porch. During

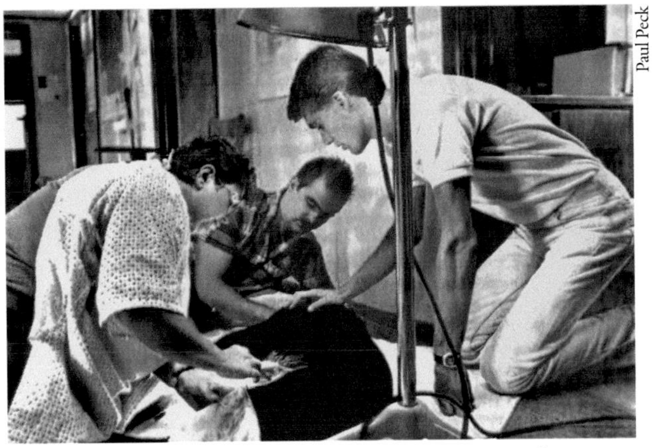
Paul Peck

Marie pulling porcupine quills. From "At the Salmon River Clinic, Interns Discover the Joys of Frontier Medicine" by Tony Huegel, The Post Register, Idaho Falls, July 12, 1987.

our first three years in the rental cabin, sometimes we had gawkers from the laundromat next door and one of the town's three bars, the Kasino Club, across the street.

I am a nurse practitioner, not a veterinarian. Still, things happen, and when they did, I provided the care, otherwise, the animals suffer. What are you going to do? But I did not want to get crosswise with the Idaho Board of Veterinary Medicine. As I tell you this, at ninety-three years old, I also don't want to go to jail for violating the Veterinary Practices Act of Idaho. "No person may practice veterinary medicine in the state who is not an actively licensed veterinarian, or the holder of a valid temporary permit issued by the board." An exception is allowed for emergency care. Indeed, laws regulating veterinary medicine are much stricter than those regulating the practice of medicine. If anyone from the Board of Veterinary Medicine is reading this: I never charged. I worked hard to comply with the law.

"Marie, I need you to come to see one of my horses." Piero Piva, a local rancher, was on the telephone, and he was really upset. "He's one of my best. He's dead in the pasture."

Piero raised Quarter Horses, and this was a prized stud colt worth thousands of dollars. Like most ranchers, Piero doctored his animals and kept a big jar of penicillin. He had not given penicillin to his colt. After all, in healthcare, we often live by the adage, "Diagnosis is the first step to treatment." Piero didn't know the diagnosis, and neither did I.

Piero and I walked over to the dead horse. Just looking, I had no idea what had killed the colt. There were no signs of injury, trauma, or that it had been sick. It was just dead. Back at the clinic, I called the Board of Veterinarian Medicine to see if I could get some help. Eventually, I got a return call from a veterinarian.

"Why didn't you do an autopsy?" the vet asked.

My mouth dropped. I'd never done an autopsy alone. I didn't perform autopsies on humans, let alone dead horses. The Board of Nursing would have been shocked to hear I'd performed an autopsy on a prized horse. I was not about to autopsy a dead animal.

Piero's dead colt launched a cavalcade of telephone calls about my providing emergency care for animals in Stanley, Idaho. The next call was from the head of the Board of Veterinary Medicine. That conversation did not go well, at least at first. He proceeded to lecture me on the rules.

"Marie, the law allows you to do emergency animal care. However, most of what you are doing is an emergency only in the eye of the owner, but not an actual emergency."

"Most of what I do is provide care for humans, not animals," I explained. "Occasionally, I do get called for emergencies that involve animals. My closest veterinarian, Dr. Beede, is in Hailey, nearly seventy miles away, over Galena Summit. Sometimes, I don't have options. It's just me or no one. Stanley doesn't have a veterinarian."

A pet is like a child for some people, and their owners will escalate and push back if they think you are brushing them off. Telling them, "Sorry, this is not a true emergency based on the Board of Veterinarian Medicine's ruling," when their beloved dog is in agony with a face full of quills doesn't work. I remember when my horse, Matia, broke out in hives. Her eyes swelled, and she had big bumps all over. I had no idea that horses even got hives. The vet was sixty-five miles away on the south side of Ketchum. While vets make house calls, that's a long house call. I described these rural realities to Idaho's lead veterinarian.

By the time our telephone call ended, the head of the Board of Veterinarian Medicine and I came to an understanding. I did not want to violate the Veterinarian Practices Act. However, with no vet in Stanley, people would call for me to treat the occasional animal needing emergency care.

One animal emergency call was for a deer tangled with barbed wire at the Jay Neider Ranch, suffering an extensive laceration on its abdomen. I sewed up the wound. Afterward, I sent the bill to the Idaho Department of Fish and Game to pay for supplies (I didn't charge a professional fee). The agency paid the bill. Enclosed with the check was a letter saying the agency's philosophy was to let nature take its course. However, "nature's course" includes humans destroying wildlife habitat. And when wildlife is injured, humans call for help.

Stanley is known as "Dog Town." Steve Lipus recalled, "When our young dog became uncharacteristically lethargic, we took him to Marie. After examining his belly, she said he likely had an intestinal blockage. Marie recommended getting him to the vet, so we did. Marie was spot on. Our dog needed lifesaving surgery to clear the blockage." The failure to diagnose and treat can mean agony and death for animals, just as with humans.

Cats were part of Stanley's animal population and also needed emergency care.

"Marie, our cat is delivering. One of the kittens is stuck in the birth canal." A difficult birth thrust Tom Angel, a longtime local, into kitty midwifery. "The kitten's head is hanging out."

"Tom, try gently pulling on the head."

"If I do that, I'm afraid I'll pull the kitten's head off. Marie, can you come over and help me?"

I gathered up supplies and headed over. The pregnant cat was in the loft, so I climbed the ladder. Sawdust covered the loft and the mother cat. A little kitten's head poked out of her in that mess. I applied gentle traction to the head, but no movement. We took the cat to the clinic. After assembling a makeshift operating room and anesthetizing the cat, I performed a C-section and delivered her kittens. Earlier, I had assisted veterinarians Tom and Marie Bulgin in their surgeries and C-sections, so I knew how to do it.

The Bulgins, a husband-and-wife veterinarian team, lived in Stanley during part of the 1970s. The Bulgins had come into the valley to caretake the Idaho Rocky Mountain Ranch. They volunteered to hold a veterinary clinic one afternoon each week at the Stanley Clinic and saw large animals at the ranch.

The two veterinarians treated animals in the clinic hallway, on the floor outside our two treatment rooms. They charged their regular service fee and donated the money to the Stanley Clinic, a gift that helped keep our doors open for human care.

The Bulgins got called for obstetrical emergencies. Because I was also helping caretake the Idaho Rocky Mountain Ranch during those years, I joined them on some of those emergency calls. One call involved a goat having a difficult delivery fifteen miles downriver at Robinson Bar Ranch.

"Marie, my goat's in labor, and she's not progressing. We think the fetus is stuck in the birth canal." On the phone was Joe Leonard at Robinson Bar Ranch. Joe couldn't see any part of the fetus.

We loaded our backpacks with instruments and supplies, figuring from Joe's description that we needed to prepare for a goat C-section. Although it was early winter, the snow was deep, and we couldn't drive into the ranch house. Instead, we parked on the highway, skied over the bridge, and then three miles to the ranch house. I am not a great skier, especially without a groomed trail at night, but we made it.

Joe escorted us to the goat. The vets began by examining the animal. After a moment of quiet, Tom stood up.

"Joe, this goat is not in labor. It's having gas pain."

At three in the morning, it was too early to ski back to the highway, so Joe put us up in the ranch cabins. I remember the bitterly cold wind coming through the uncaulked cracks between the logs. We got through the night, ate breakfast, and skied back to the highway. That turned out to be a practice run.

A month later, with snow deeper and temperatures colder, we got a second emergency call from Joe Leonard. The goat really was in labor; a kid's head was out, but the delivery wasn't progressing. Joe was afraid the goat was going to die.

We packed instruments, drove downriver, parked, and skied again into Robinson Bar Ranch. This time, the goat was definitely in labor, and we performed a C-section on the floor of one of the cabins, delivering two healthy kids. Afterward, we celebrated, and in honor of the two vets, Joe named the two kids Tom and Marie.

"See one, do one, teach one," Tom Bulgin said often. The Bulgins taught me a lot and gave me hands-on experience caring for animals. Long after they left the Sawtooth country, their willingness to teach endured through our ability to provide emergency animal care. Fortunately, I had support and help from other veterinarians, especially Dr. Bob Beede in Hailey.

"When you take a cat's temperature, Marie, you have one chance to get that thermometer in." Dr. Beede was right. Cats object to rectal thermometers and are not shy about letting you know. He advised me what to watch for when dogs and cats have high fevers.

Dr. Beede was warm and welcoming. He loved his work. When I had to board my dog, Mousse, during travels, he always took my dog home for a stay.

To avoid problems with the Idaho Board of Veterinary Medicine, I had a low threshold for checking with Dr. Beede or other veterinarians willing to take my calls. We would review my cases over the telephone, and they'd tell me whether they thought I should send the injured or sick animal over the hill.

A dog jumped a fence, caught a staub, and opened a wound from his chest across his abdomen. That laceration ran almost the entire length of the dog's underside. Fortunately, the staub did not enter the peritoneal cavity. I called the Wood River Valley vets, who said, "Sew it up." So, I did.

Another injured dog, a pretty toy poodle, arrived one Sunday morning and was carried into the clinic by its owners. They were near Lowman at a natural hot spring when the poodle fell in and got scalded. I touched the dog's silver-gray fur. Clumps of dog hair fell to the ground. I picked up the phone and dialed the vet on call.

"Just give it some pain medication, Marie. There's nothing more you can do. You can try sending it over the hill, but it won't make it." A few minutes later, the dog stopped moving and died in the clinic. There wasn't time to get it over the hill. The couple broke down sobbing.

When dogs are hit by cars and mortally wounded, all you can do is put them out of their misery. To euthanize an animal requires veterinarian support and medication. Because of distances, mountain passes, weather, and Stanley's isolation, the veterinarians provided opiates for euthanizing. To put down a horse or cow requires a substantial dose. A dog's dose is significantly less. I didn't want the animals to suffer, so I gave a dose of tranquilizer before giving the final injection.

Cats are abundant in the Stanley area. Every ranch has cats. Some are pets, and some are barn cats. Unfortunately, cats are prolific breeders, and ranchers controlled the cat population by castration. They put the cat's head down a cowboy boot and use a pocket knife or Buck knife to cut off testicles before releasing the bleeding, neutered cat. That upset me. Cowboy boot castrations were one of the most brutal things I'd seen.

Tom and Marie Bulgin castrated many cats using general anesthesia, local anesthesia with lidocaine, and sterile technique. After incising the scrotum, they carefully removed the testicles and closed the emptied scrotum with sutures. Neutering an animal this way was humane. Tom and Marie taught me how to fix male cats.

After the Bulgins moved to Boise to caretake a ranch in the Treasure Valley, locals continued bringing their cats for sterilization. I did a few, wanting to offer a humane alternative to the ranchers' cat castrations in a boot. And it was fun! Maybe it's a female thing, but I must admit there is a particular joy to popping those testicles out of there.

"Yes, I'm on rat poison," is how some patients answer when asked about their medications. They are referring to a blood thinner called warfarin or Coumadin. Blood thinners or anticoagulants prevent strokes in people with atrial fibrillation. They also prevent recurrent DVTs (clots) and pulmonary emboli in thromboembolic disease. Warfarin has a narrow "therapeutic index:" too much, and people bleed; not enough, and people stroke or develop clots.

Warfarin's bleeding complications found a commercial use killing rodents in a product called d-CON. But, as often happens, our industrial culture's creations have some unintended consequences.

"Marie, can you take a look at a cat? Something's wrong with the poor thing." That sweet and caring southern voice belonged to Brady Ebersole, animal lover and wife of Chuck Ebersole, the naturalist with the Sawtooth NRA.

Brady gently placed the sick cat on a sheet on the clinic's front porch. I could hear fluid sounds as the cat struggled to breathe. I started to collect vitals and do my exam before calling the vet. As I lifted the tail and inserted the thermometer into the anus, the cat groaned, stopped breathing, and died. I called Dr. Beede.

"I'm not sure, Marie. Why don't you freeze the cat and bring it over the next time you're in Ketchum? I'll do an autopsy." Dr. Beede was always so helpful.

When the weather cleared, I pulled the cat out of the freezer and dropped it off at the vet's office. Later, after the autopsy, Dr. Beede telephoned to discuss his findings. The cat's lungs were filled with blood, explaining the audible fluid sounds we heard.

Dr. Beede surmised the cat had been eating mice poisoned with d-CON. Everyone used d-CON because the barns were thick with mice. Cats and dogs would die unexpectedly, and I didn't understand why. Now I knew.

One night, at about 10:30, the animal emergency call came: a dog with porcupine quills.

I arrived at the clinic and met a young Mountain Home Air Force Base airman. He and his dog, a pit bull, had come to the Sawtooths to go camping. The dog saw a porcupine, ran after it, and caught it.

Most dogs hurt so badly from the quills that they back off. Not this pit bull, which had gotten into porcupines before. The quills enraged the pit bull, and it was out to kill it. A vet I had worked with shared that a dog learned after their first porcupine encounter or became so angry they saw red and wouldn't let go until they killed. That was the airman's pit bull.

I've never seen a dog with so many quills: in its nose, mouth, and ears, particularly in the mouth, back to the base of the tongue, along the teeth, and gum line; quills packed the oral cavity. It was a mess.

Before starting, I administered an anesthetic but didn't completely put the dog out. Putting it on a sheet covering the floor, I positioned the floor-standing surgical lamp to spotlight the dog's face, put on gloves, picked up the hemostats, got down on my knees, and started tugging on embedded quills. That dog just laid there, looked at me, wagged its tail, and let me pull quills for over two hours. That dog was remarkable.

While I didn't charge the airman for my time, I did ask him to pay for supplies. Being down on my knees on that hard floor for over two hours ought to be worth something, at least a beer. But charging a professional fee would have landed me in hot water. People were always so grateful when I cared for their pets, so that reward had to suffice.

Bambi lived with me one summer. Bambi was a Harlequin Great Dane whose owner was a college student working for the Forest Service. "Someone shot my dog near McCall," the owner explained. "I was patrolling, and she took a bullet in her neck. The vet got the bullet out. But I've got a problem. My job with the Forest Service will keep me in the field for six weeks, and I hope you might have a kennel."

Bambi's owner had heard about the Stanley Clinic and driven from McCall, hoping to find the help he could afford. Unfortunately, this college student probably had no money, and we didn't have a kennel.

Harlequin Great Danes are beautiful, with black patches on a sleek white body big enough to be a small horse. These dogs are big, affectionate, and loyal.

"I'm sorry. We don't have a kennel. Here's what I'll do. Bambi can stay with me at my cabin, and I'll look after her for the summer." And with that, Bambi became my companion.

I fell in love with that dog. I kept hoping the young man would never come back. Unfortunately, that fall, he returned to take Bambi home. I didn't cry — until after she was gone. Then, I sobbed.

Caring for animals (emergencies only) can be a unique part of being a sole provider in a rural, isolated community. You also meet people who love their animals as much as they would a child. Indeed, no one ever brought in an abused animal to me. People who abuse their animals or their children usually avoid seeking care for those they harm.

After the Bulgins left Stanley, I didn't have time to continue the animal clinic for a half-day a week. The two-legged animals needed the clinic and my full attention.

Without Tom and Marie, we couldn't offer the service, and I did not want to get crosswise with the Board of Veterinary Medicine.

27

EMERGENCY CALL: GARY GADWA

Rural America's social contract is fraying at the edges. Stanley is no exception: People, including those with wealth, are moving in. More people bring more demands and expectations of service, even as fewer people are volunteering to provide those services.

Stanley's volunteer EMTs and ambulance drivers struggle to keep their heads above water. Increasing pressure on fewer townspeople leads to burnout, more volunteers stepping away, and more demands on those remaining EMS volunteers.

Gary Gadwa, still climbing peaks to rescue people in trouble as commander of Sawtooth Search and Rescue, retired at age seventy-two after forty years of service as a volunteer EMT.

Gary is one of Stanley's fabled "goat patrol," courageous and committed to helping others. He is wiry, strong, and sure-footed like a mountain goat. He's a truth speaker even when the truth is uncomfortable.

Gary was an employee of the Idaho Department of Fish and Game for twenty-eight years. He twice earned recognition as Idaho Conservation Officer of the Year, the only law enforcement officer with this honor. Now retired, Gary personified how state and federal agencies can open doors to support rural EMS.

Gary and Laurii raised and educated their two children, Jodie and Cody, in Stanley, and have been year-round residents since 1979. Laurii has an impressive record of community service. Gary and Laurii remain active in the Stanley community, with Laurii serving on the city council and Gary on the Stanley Clinic and Sawtooth Interpretative and Historical Association boards.

If you were down, looking up and struggling to breathe, in and out of consciousness, or with severe pain from fractures, here are words that may have saved your life during forty years in the Sawtooth country: "I'm Gary Gadwa. I'm an EMT. I'm here to help. Where are you hurting?"

GARY GADWA, IN HIS OWN WORDS

Over the decades, we've witnessed the spirit of volunteerism on the decline. People are too busy working to pay the bills.

When dispatch calls for help, employers aren't as supportive and don't readily release their employees who volunteer as EMTs.

Old photos of Stanley EMTs show state and federal employees supported by their agencies. Our community remains steadfast in supporting the Stanley Clinic and Stanley Ambulance. For example, the Mountain Mamas still raise money to support our clinic. But without active involvement from federal and state agency staff, EMS is at risk, and community cohesion frays.

I particularly want to call out the Forest Service — and Idaho's members of Congress — responsible for the Sawtooth NRA. Serving as a ranger for the Forest Service used to be a long-term commitment.

We had a ranger here in the Stanley District for three years, and then, poof, suddenly that ranger was gone. Unfortunately, the federal commitment to the Sawtooth NRA's mission has eroded. Positions go unfilled. Budgets go begging.

Roland Miller

Gary Gadwa, "Goat Patrol"

We no longer have a full-time Forest Service law enforcement officer, as just one more example. Consider Steve Lipus and his many years as LEO combined with community service: law enforcement and responding as an EMT to emergency calls, which he and I partnered on many times. Unfortunately, Steve's law enforcement position has gone unfilled in recent years.

If the Forest Service doesn't hire, staff can't respond to 911 calls. Agencies need to build on, not retreat from, the legacy of community service established by Tom Kovalicky, Dave Kimpton, Bill James, Steve Lipus, Ken Hartz, Roland Miller, and Phil Coonts, among others.

The Cowan family story illustrates the incredible multiagency cooperation sometimes needed to make critical backcountry rescues.

Devin Cowan and his three sons, Ben, age ten, Alex, age nine, and Spencer, age seven, hiked the roughly five miles to Alpine Lake at 7,825 feet elevation. Alpine Peak, 2,000 feet higher, stands over the lake. Father and sons pitched their tent that Sunday and set up camp at the lake. Then, they headed out to hike and climb in the rocks above Alpine Lake. At about 8:15 pm on July 28, 1996, the father and sons took a shortcut to return to their camp.

Alex fell on a steep section about 500 feet above the southern end of Alpine Lake. Devin grabbed his son's arm but couldn't hold on. Both fell about thirty feet, landing on a ledge. Devin, an occupational therapist at St. Alphonsus in Boise who worked with back-injury patients, knew about backs and knew he had injured his. Alex had minor injuries.

Thirty feet above them, Ben and Spencer were together and could hear, but not see, their father and brother. Night fell. They kept each other awake in the cold without adequate clothing to avoid falling asleep and possibly falling to their deaths.

At first light, Ben took action and headed out for help. When he returned to their camp, he met two backcountry rangers, who radioed the Stanley Ranger Station. The Forest Service notified Custer County sheriff Joe Hess, who became incident commander and sent out the emergency call. Meanwhile, the weather turned, and rain began falling.

In Boise, the Life Flight helicopter crew went on standby until people could get to the cliffs and provide them with a status update.

Backing up Life Flight, a ground crew of mostly EMTs assembled at the Stanley Clinic and headed out to the trailhead at Iron Creek: Julie Meissner, Bob Griswold, Bob Downing, Roland Miller, College of Idaho premed intern Jake Clendenon, Scott Fish from the Sawtooth Hotel, Fish and Game conservation officer trainee Mark Rhodes, and me.

Bringing up the rear was a third team of six packhorses and a pack mule carrying rescue gear and food led by Dusty Bitton and Scott Moses of Mystic Saddle Ranch, joined by EMT Ken Hartz.

Ketchum Fire Department, Miles Canfield

Life Flight helicopter at Alpine Lake in the Sawtooth Wilderness

Ketchum Fire Department, Miles Canfield

LOOKING FROM THE HELICOPTER ONTO THE CLIFF: with the injured patient (MID-PHOTO) are the Life Flight crew and Gary Gadwa. Above them in blue is one of the Cowan sons who attempted climbing down to his father and spent the night in that spot. The crew at the top in red lowered a rope to bring the stranded son to safety. The helicopter delivered the rope rescue team, Ketchum Fire Department, to help move the patient to a pick-up point.

Ketchum Fire Department, Miles Canfield

Unloading the rope team. As captain and paramedic Miles Canfield of the Ketchum Fire Department recalled, "The helicopter would hover next to the cliff with the front of the skids at the cliff. Rescuers, one at a time, undid their seatbelt and stepped onto the skid. Next, holding onto the rain gutter, each walked the skid toward the front of the aircraft before landing on the cliff. Below us was nothing but open space.

Ketchum Fire Department, Miles Canfield

Looking down on the ledge with the first responders and the patient who has been moved from the upper left using ropes. For the pilot, Gary Brennan, and first responders from Stanley, Ketchum, and Boise's Life Flight crew, the challenges were formidable in this cliff rescue.

With Forest Service permission, Mark Rhodes and I headed out first on motorized trail bikes into the Sawtooth Wilderness. Mark had never ridden a trail bike, especially not into the Sawtooth Wilderness; he was a real trooper to follow me.

The backcountry rangers reached Devin and Alex while the ground crew headed in. The rangers looked at the cliffs and notified Sheriff Hess that the rescue needed a technical rope team. Hess reached out for help to the Ketchum

Life Flight

Spine stabilized, the patient was safe for transport. Among Stanley's first responders was Gary Gadwa, standing on the far right wearing the Idaho Department of Fish and Game uniform. He was communicating with the rescuers above to secure one of the boys.

Ketchum Fire Department, Miles Canfield

Pilot Gary Brennan had to hover the helicopter close to the cliff to load Devin Canfield onto Life Flight for transport to St. Alphonsus Medical Center in Boise. Rotors were inches from rocks and trees. Mountain rescues involving helicopters require a team effort with gifted pilots.

Fire Department's technical rope rescue team: full-time Ketchum firefighters John Rathfon and Miles Canfield and volunteers Tory Frank, Gary Robrahn, and Brad Mitchell responded. They arrived at the Stanley Ranger Station early that Monday afternoon.

With heavy rain, my radio shorted out. Once I reached the ledge with Devin and Alex Cowan, I tried Ranger Doolittle's radio, but the Life Flight crew circling nearby could not hear the Forest Service radio frequency. Finally, the Bell 206 set down on a rock ledge jutting into the lake. Paramedic Kevin Hudson clambered up from the lake carrying a fifty-pound pack of first aid supplies, reaching us on the rock shelf with our patients.

The youngest boy, Spencer, was still on the cliff above us. Life Flight ferried Julie Meissner and Bob Griswold with climbing gear to a landing spot above Spencer. Julie and Scott reached Spencer and moved him to the landing spot; Life Flight returned and carried them all off the cliffs. We also got Alex into the helicopter and off the mountain. Unfortunately, the rain continued, with the visibility dropping to about a half mile or less.

Devin was the challenge. We assumed he had a spine injury and was at risk for spinal cord damage and paralysis. We had to stabilize Devin's spine before moving him. On that ledge, we could not get him into the helicopter. Below the shelf, 200 feet down, was a rock outcropping that would work.

Life Flight ferried Ketchum's technical rope team from the Stanley Ranger Station onto the cliffs. First, team members jumped four feet from the helicopter skids to the rock outcropping. Eventually, the team members bracketed Devin, standing on the ledge above and the outcropping below. Once in place, the rope team and the paramedic used a belay system to lower Devin those 200 feet over the course of ninety minutes.

Tree branches at the rock outcropping risked the rescue effort. Helicopter rotors hitting branches would be deadly. So, I went to work using a bow saw to cut trees, making the zone as safe as possible for Life Flight to get in close.

The final step was moving Devin into the hovering helicopter. With blades spinning about five feet from the rock wall, the team bench-pressed and "hot loaded" the litter into the helicopter. Below us was a sheer drop of several hundred feet.

Life Flight landed at the Stanley Airport and offloaded Devin to the Stanley Ambulance, which was staffed with Marie and volunteer EMTs Maryellen Easom and Bob Downing. The helicopter returned to the cliffs to ferry the rescuers. By early evening, our team had reloaded Devin and Alex Cowan into Life Flight. The aircraft then headed for St. Al's in Boise, where Devin underwent surgery. I loaded Ben Cowan on my motorcycle at Alpine Lake and headed down the trail.

That talented Life Flight pilot was Gary Brennan. Helicopter Association International recognized Gary's life-saving work at Alpine Lake with its Golden Hour Award for advancing the use of helicopters in the vital mission of medical air transport.

In addition, Governor Phil Batt formally recognized and thanked those who responded to that emergency call to help the Cowan family.

"I...can't...breathe!"

We feel it to our core when someone can't breathe — whether in the field, ER, hospital ward, or ICU. "I...can't... breathe...help...me!" focuses our attention more than the retching sounds and smells of vomit, more than chest pain, stroke, and even most trauma.

Dispatch called for Stanley EMTs. "We have a young woman who fell mountain climbing at Iowa Peaks. She is in respiratory distress and has a lower extremity fracture." The emergency call came late in the day. We would be running out of light soon.

Mt. Iowa is an impressive summit of three peaks in the Sawtooth Range's north-central region. The trailhead near Redfish Lake Lodge to the top of Mt. Iowa is seven miles with 4,300 feet of elevation gain.

When a life is in the balance and time matters, Steve Lipus, the Forest Service's law enforcement officer, approved using my trail bike in the Sawtooth Wilderness. Onto my back went my pack, thirty to fifty pounds of first aid gear.

My emergency pack included two small oxygen tanks, each with about forty-five minutes of oxygen. Carrying weight on my motorbike requires extra care and caution on a wilderness trail with rocks and tree roots. From Redfish Lake Lodge, I headed up to Bench Lakes. Other EMTs followed on foot.

Getting the emergency call and mobilizing to save a life requires someone first to call for help. So often in these backcountry rescues, especially before cellphones, the heroes are companions who have the courage and stamina to go for help regardless of their age. The hero at Iowa Peak was an Air Force recruit. She knew her friend was in trouble and scrambled off the mountain, running most of the distance for help. Delay can mean death.

The two women and a male friend, all in their early twenties, had driven from Mountain Home to spend a day climbing. They scrambled from Mt. Heyburn to Iowa Peak and then took a shortcut. At cliff base is a steep scree slope: rocks the size of bowling balls, resting at the angle of repose. The hikers' shortcut took them onto that scree slope where our patient fell.

I arrived at Bench Lakes, parked my trail bike, and headed cross country toward Mt. Iowa. As I broke out of the trees, I saw a man standing and a body in the rocks.

"Help! Oh God, help us!" the young man screamed and cried out. For EMS personnel, keeping your wits about you when others have lost theirs has merit. This man was clearly out of control.

The young woman lying in a pile of rocks looked white to gray, was in moderate respiratory distress struggling to breathe and was in shock. I pulled out an oxygen tank.

Around midnight, I heard the faint *whomp-whomp* of helicopter blades. With a medical team on board, MAST had flown from Mountain Home Air Force Base to the Stanley airport, then headed straight toward Iowa Peaks. Marie had briefed them.

Over the radio came the voice of the helicopter pilot. "Gary Gadwa, are you there?"

"Yes," I replied. "I'm here with the patient."

"Can you see the Stanley airport?" I said I could.

"Turn on a flashlight so we can see you!" I turned on my headlamp.

"Hey, that's not a light. Here's a light." Suddenly, several thousand candle-power bathed the accident scene in the darkness with blinding, bright light from the hovering Huey helicopter.

Next, a medic jumped from the Huey into the rocks, dropping fifteen feet like an angel coming out of the heavens. The helicopter's downdraft felt like it would blow us off the mountain.

The relief I felt is hard to describe. Until MAST arrived, I was the sole first responder trying to help a young woman who couldn't breathe and her distraught companion. Then, suddenly, help and hope dropped out of the sky.

The Huey also dropped a big bag of medical gear before flying to Stanley's airstrip to await the first light of dawn. The medic took charge, and we placed a traction splint on the fractured leg. While the medic attended to the young woman, I attempted to calm the young man. Finally, with the slope nearly vertical, we roped in our patient for safety.

The Stanley EMTs, led by Steve Lipus, arrived downslope with mountaineer Kirk Bachman and outfitter Jeff Bitton, with his packhorses from Mystic Saddle Ranch. They were several hours behind me, having come on foot. With chainsaws and working through the night, the team created a helicopter landing zone as close as possible to the base of Iowa Peaks.

At first light, under Kirk Bachman's leadership, we belayed the injured climber about 200 yards over the rocks and then carried the litter another quarter mile to the makeshift landing zone. The Huey returned and transported the injured climber to the horse corrals near the trailhead, where Marie was helping coordinate rescue efforts. After Marie evaluated the injured climber and updated the medical team at St. Al's, MAST lifted off one last time for Boise.

Marie was good about providing updates to the EMTs. The young woman had multiple rib fractures complicated by a pneumothorax and a closed lower extremity fracture. Her young life was one we were able to save.

I want to do a "shout out" to the helicopter pilots. Pilots are vital members of our EMS team. Over the decades, we have worked with some genuinely talented "hot-shots," including Gary Brennan and Dan Odlum, who were Vietnam pilots. EMS personnel in the field caring for unstable patients know the relief they feel when they hear the first faint noises of a rescue helicopter. We are forever grateful to you, the pilots, for flying those missions of mercy.

Three doctors without a first aid kit climbed to the summit of Castle Peak in the White Cloud Mountains. On the way down the peak's south side, they glissaded a steep snowfield about 150 yards long. None of them had ice axes to arrest their glissade. At the bottom of the snow were rocks that abruptly ended the glissade with a head injury for one doctor. Another hiked out and found a wilderness ranger who radioed for help.

I was first on the scene, having come in on a trail bike, parked, and scrambled up the mountain to the bottom of the big snowfield and the injured doctor. Next, Blaine County Search and Rescue and Stanley EMTs hiked in from the Fourth of July Creek trailhead. As twilight gave way to pitch-black night on Castle Peak, out came our headlamp flashlights.

The injured physician was in and out of consciousness. In addition to a head injury, he had an ankle fracture and possibly other internal injuries. As the first responder on the scene, I did an initial assessment and radioed my findings to Marie at the trailhead and others on the emergency radio band.

In the stillness of the night, suddenly I could hear *whoop whoop whoop* — faint at first, then louder — as the Life Flight helicopter approached. That night, Gary Brennan was pilot. Over the years, Gary became a familiar radio voice for backcountry rescues requiring helicopter support.

Dropping supplies on a steep high-elevation mountainside in the pitch black was hair-raising. Gary's only light was a spotlight. This rescue was years before Life Flight supplied night-vision goggles for their pilots. Like manna dropping from the sky, IV fluids landed nearby.

Who is in charge: EMS or doctors who happen to be on the scene? The correct answer is EMS. In Stanley, we learned the hard way — no offense — that you can't trust that people at the scene who say, "I'm a doctor," know what they are doing or are even real doctors. EMS has to retain control and is responsible for the patient.

Although two doctors were at the scene, Marie ran the show using her EMS radio from her car at the trailhead. One of the physicians placed the IV and started fluids, coordinating with Marie.

Kirk Bachman, the founder of Sawtooth Mountain Guides and a Sawtooth Search and Rescue volunteer, helped get our patient off the mountain.

Our focus was on stabilizing and moving the injured physician, but this was before helicopter hoists. We waited until dawn, then moved our patient by litter down the mountainside.

It took sixteen of us to carry the doctor off of Castle Peak. Our footing was tricky and risky, and we all took turns scouting the route and carrying the litter and supplies. The Castle Peak rescue brought together Stanley EMTs, Sawtooth Search and Rescue, Blaine County Search and Rescue, and Life Flight. At a small flat spot near Upper Chamberlain Lake, we lifted the patient into the helicopter bound for St. Al's in Boise.

Quiet returned to Castle Peak. Those of us who still had energy left climbed back up toward the accident scene to pick up first-aid supplies scattered by the helicopter rotor downwash.

Why, you ask, do EMS personnel not defer to doctors who happen to be at an accident scene?

Dispatch on the radio: "Stanley EMTs. Motor vehicle accident on Highway 21 Mile Post 109. One injured." The Stanley Ambulance and EMTs arrived at the scene near Banner Creek Summit along the highway. Our male patient was unresponsive just off the pavement, thrown from his rolling car.

Marie was on the ground with the patient, doing her initial assessment and placing an IV, when a car slowed and stopped. Out stepped a man wearing white scrubs, a doctor's white lab coat, and a stethoscope draped over his neck. As Marie remembered vividly, he was wearing white shoes but no socks.

"I'm a doctor. Can I help?"

The doctor took control, and we allowed him to. After all, he said he was a doctor, and he looked like a doctor. Marie had started an IV. "That was a good thing to do," the doctor said approvingly.

We loaded the patient into the ambulance and headed toward Lowman. Partway, our Stanley Ambulance rendezvoused with the Lowman ambulance, eventually transporting the patient to St. Al's in Boise.

We returned to Stanley, cleaned the ambulance, and parked it in the clinic garage for the next emergency call. Then, Marie got a call from St. Al's in Boise.

"We're missing the patient's wallet and some belongings."

"I don't know where it is," Marie said. "We'll check the ambulance and get back to you." We searched the ambulance, but no wallet. At the accident scene, the doctor had asked for the wallet to check for medical information and identification. He never returned the wallet to the patient.

Truth revealed, and lessons learned: the surgical scrubs-wearing "doctor" was an orderly at a hospital. When he came upon the accident, he must have changed quickly, probably explaining why he was not wearing socks. He had some medical knowledge and looked like a doctor. As bad as it was, it could have been worse had the "doctor" tried to treat the patient.

We all learned from that awful experience. From then on, we trusted no one. EMS is in charge. I've lived by that rule my entire EMT career.

A Pontiac was one of many vehicles driving too fast on curvy river roads. It missed a curve and careened into the Salmon River on a particularly deadly stretch known as the Narrows across from Robinson Bar Ranch. The passenger was a young woman who bailed out and survived. After scrambling up the bank, she flagged down a driver who brought her to my home in Lower Stanley. I called 911 and reached dispatch, who sent out the emergency call. Among those who responded was Deputy Jim Parkhouse.

I headed downriver in the Idaho Fish and Game truck, parked, pulled out my flashlight, and scanned the riverbank: no wrecked car. Then, the Stanley Ambulance arrived with Marie and EMTs, joining Deputy Parkhouse and me in the search. We turned our lights onto the river. In the distance, we saw four tires and the Pontiac's undercarriage breaching the water's surface.

We searched the riverbank, hoping to find the driver alive. Near the river's edge, I came upon a three-inch piece of skull with fresh blood. Thinking this was significant evidence, I picked up the skull bone, clambered up the cliff to the highway, and showed Marie. Marie was also our deputy coroner; I assumed she would want documentation that the driver was deceased.

"I didn't need to see that, Gary," Marie said dryly.

We searched for the rest of the driver's body all night, eventually finding him a half-mile downriver. Deputy Parkhouse and I pulled the body from debris below whitewater rapids that make the Narrows a thrill for boaters.

Someone has to remove the dead from the backcountry. Emergency dispatch called: "A person is missing after a boat flipped above the Dagger Falls launch on the Middle Fork."

We headed west on Highway 21 and turned onto the Boundary Creek road to Dagger Falls, where thousands of boaters start floating down the legendary Middle Fork of the Salmon River. A rafter met us at the campground and guided us about half a mile upriver.

When we arrived, we spoke with members of a sizeable rafting party. Early in the season, the Middle Fork runs high and cold from snowmelt.

The party launched at Marsh Creek and floated downriver until whitewater flipped one of the boats, drowning a woman. After a prolonged search, the rafters found the body floating in the river and pulled it to shore. She had been unresponsive for well over two hours before we arrived.

As the senior EMT, I checked for vitals and examined the body: no pulse, no respiratory effort, no breath sounds, and no heartbeat.

I decided not to attempt resuscitation; it had been too long. Later, I got Marie on the radio, and she supported the decision I'd made.

Then, the rafters pointed me to the husband. "Do whatever you want with her," the husband said nonchalantly. "I'm done with her." I was stunned. His response was relief, not grief.

With help from six EMTs and river runners, we placed the body into one of our black body bags and onto a litter. Next, we carried the body up from the riverbank and loaded it into the back of my Fish and Game truck. I was not used to hauling deceased women in the bed of my pickup. Despite the strict rules that govern transporting a body across county lines, we didn't wait for authorization and moved the body across county lines anyway. In these parts, sometimes you do what you have to do to help the living — and the dead.

"Gary," I heard on my radio scanner, "this is Deputy Stewart. I have a young woman who overdosed on LSD. She's totally out of control and in my patrol car. I'm bringing her to your house."

The underage girl had gone to Stanley's Rod & Gun Club, where someone had slipped the drug into her drink. When she became psychotic, the bartender called Deputy Steve Stewart.

Steve was a muscular, huge former Army Ranger. The sixteen-year-old girl was petite at five feet, four inches, and barely 115 pounds, but transformed by LSD into a linebacker: "The wild one," we called her later.

The deputy sheriff arrested the wild one, placed her in the patrol car, and headed toward the county jail in Challis. Unfortunately, she went berserk, prompting the radio call and detour to my home for backup law enforcement.

In my driveway, Steve slammed on the brakes. The wild one, without handcuffs, flung open the car door and ran from the patrol car. We coaxed her into our house. She came in, then decompensated. She cracked our ten-gallon aquarium in the chaos, tearing apart our living room. We tackled her and tried to hold her on the floor. She took a deep bite into the deputy's right nipple. The three of us — the deputy, my wife, Laurii, and I — couldn't contain her. We sat on top of her, and she threw us off. Eventually, Laurii calmed her down slightly.

"I have to go to the bathroom," the wild one said quietly. Laurii showed her to our bathroom but kept her foot in the door.

The deputy hurried off to the clinic to get Marie. When Marie arrived, we were trying to be firm but polite. "We don't want to hurt you," we reassured her. The wild one bit the deputy sheriff's leg and returned to ripping apart our home. Marie grabbed the patient, took her to the ground, pulled down her pants, and injected Valium. A few minutes later, the wild one was sleeping.

We moved the sleeping girl to our couch. I began to take her vitals. She appeared to be sleeping, but suddenly, she grabbed my hand in a death grip.

Marie and the deputy began calling, trying to find a place for the girl. She had a relative at Sunbeam.

We transported her, still sleeping, downriver to her family: far better for this girl to wake up with family than in a county jail.

The deputy ended up being treated prophylactically for hepatitis. He investigated how the drugs ended up in this girl but never uncovered any evidence.

Fourteen EMTs responded after two pick-ups collided carrying Boy Scouts near Camp Bradley Scout Camp. EMTs dropped what they were doing and turned out in droves whenever kids were hurt.

When kids died, as happened at Camp Bradley, we struggled. You can't just pack the pain and carry it on your back. Instead, we experienced the value of debriefing after these incidents. We made it up as we went along, like many other things at the beginning. Now, debriefing is a formal policy.

Some EMTs become hardened, and others become emotional. We all have life experiences that may include military, family, or previous EMT runs. As EMTs, we bring who we are to what we do. People are impacted differently by death, especially that of a child.

We lost three or four EMTs who quit because the emotional toll was too heavy. After a particularly horrific ambulance run, closure is critical. We may be unique as individuals but we share many awful experiences as first responders. For closure, we gather in a circle, get things out so we can live with ourselves and move on.

For kids, we might do CPR for an hour in the ambulance over Galena Summit to the Sun Valley ER. When the doctor in the ER called the code, we stopped compressions and then came the silence. Our child patient was dead. That was so hard. Debriefings enabled us to bring closure so we could at least sleep at night.

Lessons on the importance of debriefing that we and others learned in those early years of EMS have become formalized as Critical Incident Stress Debriefing. These are more standardized, facilitator-led groups held after a traumatic event. But the concept is the same: for first responders, a life-long commitment to helping others requires protecting your mental health.

You need to know one thing about Marie: Marie was always there for us. She went on most of the ambulance runs and was on the radio helping us when she wasn't with us.

Marie will point out that she and Stanley's EMTs grew up together. Marie led the EMS team as our nurse practitioner. Teamwork is the essence of emergency care.

For me, what I do is who I am. I've volunteered as an EMT and for Search and Rescue for forty-three years. Some lives we've lost, others we've saved. I am just grateful to have been able to help others in need.

PART SIX

LIFE

Cal and Marie at IBM's Golden Circle in Honolulu in 1974. Without Cal Osborn's support, Marie could not have opened the clinic in Stanley. Neither anticipated the outcome. The Salmon River Emergency Clinic, including Marie's 24/7 call, ultimately ended their marriage in 1977.

28

EMERGENCY CALL: BEV ANGEL

Stanley is not the city. What does it mean to volunteer for your community? In a city, you pay your way to anonymity. First responders, including law enforcement, firefighters, and ambulance crew, are hired. After your emergency, you're not likely to see your rescuers in the grocery store or the bar.

But, in a small town, it's different. Small-town budgets are small; money is scarce, so you depend on volunteers or go without.

Unlike the city, there's not much anonymity. You come to know and rely on people. And, when they're gone, their absence can leave a gaping hole in the fabric of your community. Unlike a city where people come and go with little disruption, essential services can be "one deep" in small towns with little or no reserve. Stakes are high to recruit, train, and retain first responders for community resilience. These volunteers have a half-century of institutional memory of the Stanley Clinic and Stanley Ambulance. One of these is Bev Angel. Bev came to the Stanley area in 1973, working downriver at Robinson Bar Ranch before moving into Stanley in 1975. The following year, she signed up for one of my EMT classes. As a first responder in the Sawtooth country, Bev Angel has never looked back.

BEV ANGEL, IN HER OWN WORDS

I enrolled in Marie's third EMT class to keep myself busy in the middle of winter and further my education. I took Marie's class, passed the test, and became a volunteer EMT with the Stanley Ambulance.

I grew up in the San Francisco Bay area and lived at Lake Tahoe for two years. A friend described Robinson Bar Ranch, and that conversation nagged at me. Later, when I was traveling through Idaho with a friend, as we prepared to return home, I said, "We've got to find this ranch."

On a Sunday afternoon in August, we hiked up Warm Springs Creek upstream from Robinson Bar, a guest ranch in those days. When we returned, we met and talked with Joe Leonard, who offered me a job. The ranch was shorthanded, with staff returning to college. My friend was still in high school and had another week before she had to be back. She stayed a few days longer, but I never left.

In October, I returned to California, got my stuff, and moved to Idaho.

Bev Angel (STANDING) after a snowy Stanley Ambulance transport with EMT Quincy Heithecker in 2023.

From 1975 to 1985, to stay in Stanley, I did anything and everything I could. I worked in the woods, as a bookkeeper, and doing maintenance for Stanharrah Corporation. Anything that interested me and helped with income, I did. For working people who call Stanley home, life financially can be marginal.

In time, I paid off all of my debts. I worked constructing custom homes and building the fish hatchery, where the pay was good. Also, I had a divorce settlement. I am frugal and don't incur significant expenses. Eventually, I was financially secure enough to become a river guide.

Summer, when the tourists arrive, is everybody's busy season. As a volunteer EMT, when the emergency call comes, you go when you can and don't when you can't, but you do your best to be available.

In the mid-1970s, we didn't have EMS radios and cell phones, so emergency calls usually came by landline telephone. Sometimes, the emergency call arrived by word of mouth. The person getting hold of me and other first responders was our dispatcher, Bud James, at the motel. Bud ran the telephone tree. During an emergency call, my home phone would ring.

"Hello?"

"This is Bud at the motel. We have an ambulance run." Click. That's all we got.

When EMTs got to the clinic, Marie was almost always there, and we climbed into the ambulance and went. Once inside the Stanley Ambulance, we'd have time to share what we knew and prepare. But Bud's priority was getting EMTs to show up at the ambulance, not to give out information.

Locals who volunteered as EMTs are more available in the off-season. But most emergency calls come during the peak of summer's tourist season.

In the 1970s, EMTs asked Marie to use a schedule, but that didn't work. So, without a schedule, it could be feast or famine as to who responded to emergency calls. It's still that way today, almost fifty years later. Our clinician, Amy Klingler, has an on-call system for which you can sign up but don't have to.

On some ambulance runs, five to six EMTs might show up at the clinic. On a few runs, you're sitting alone, saying, "Okay, what do I do now?" With fewer people willing to volunteer, we have a backup plan with Ketchum Fire. If no one is available, we use a mutual aid agreement, and Ketchum Fire will come over the hill and help us — if they can.

Dispatch has moved from the motel in Stanley to the sheriff's office in Challis. Challis Dispatch sends out emergency tones over our EMS radios and cell phones. I carry the radio; that's what I'm comfortable with. When we hear those unique tones over the airwaves or cell phones, we know we're needed.

Challis Dispatch couldn't write our names fast enough, so we started using numbers. I'm number 309. When the emergency call comes, I say, "309 responding." The call might be for fire or ambulance; many of Stanley's first responders are cross trained for both. I listen for who does what. If I'm needed on the ambulance, I say, "309 responding to ambulance." If it's for fire, I say, "309 responding to fire."

Overall, the communication network has improved since the 1970s. You hear the emergency tones, then dispatch: "Stanley Ambulance. We have a motorcycle accident at mile marker 109 on Highway 21." If we need more information, dispatch can often help. What hasn't improved is the number of trained volunteers showing up as first responders.

What if no one responds? Dispatch will send out emergency tones multiple times. For a fire call, if no one answers, dispatch calls the Sawtooth Valley Rural Fire Chief. If it's a medical emergency and no one responds, dispatch calls the Stanley Clinic for Amy Klingler, our PA.

I've heard dispatch tone out four times. Once the tones stop, our radios keep beeping. If you're outside getting firewood, and you come in, and your radio is beeping, you know you've missed a tone out. Next, you get on the radio, asking, "Is there an ambulance run or fire call? I missed it. What is it?" Dispatch will let you know.

Dispatch will tone out multiple times for Stanley's emergency calls because some of us don't call in until we drive to town. I have to change clothes if it's morning and I'm in sweatpants. Or, I may have to take something out of the oven and get my shoes on. I may not respond to that first tone out.

There's no bathroom in the ambulance. With lights flashing, speeding down the highway, you can't just ask the driver, "Hey, I gotta pee. Can you pull over?" When the pressure is off on return trips, it's a lot easier for the guys who can stand behind the ambulance door. Overall, starting an ambulance run with a full gas tank and an empty bladder is best.

I volunteered as an EMT for eighteen years, from 1976 to 1994. After taking a break from the Stanley Ambulance, I returned in 2001 as an Emergency Medical Responder ("EMR"). The training and recertification are less stringent than the EMT.

After Marie retired from the Stanley Clinic and saw patients in Idaho City, she returned to teach our first EMR class in 2001. Many ambulance drivers are now EMRs, too, and can better help at the scene. We have EMRs in the front and EMTs in the back.

I'm coming up on fifty years as a volunteer for the Stanley Ambulance. I'm still working as a river guide on the Middle Fork and Main Salmon Rivers during the summer, just not full-time. Those are six-day trips in an oar boat, ensuring people have a good time and are safe, well-fed, and well-taken care of. You set up and take down camp and cook all the meals.

When I'm not on the river and hear dispatch's emergency tones? I try to respond.

"Somebody's having a baby," Bud said on the telephone and hung up. It was winter in the Sawtooths and snowing to beat the band.

I headed for the clinic along with nearly every certified EMT and the valley's two retired nurses, Betty Rember and Rita James. Rita was a first lieutenant in the Army, a nurse, a survivor of the Bataan Death March, and a returned P.O.W. Rita was one of the "Angels of Bataan," honored with seven military medals, including the purple heart and bronze star.

A young pregnant woman from Challis and her husband were driving to Sun Valley in terrible winter weather. They reached Stanley and pressed on until they saw barricades at Fisher Creek, closing the highway.

When heavy snow risked avalanches on Galena Summit, the Highway Department stopped plowing and closed Highway 75. Unfortunately, the woman was already in labor.

The couple turned back to town and sought help at the Stanley Clinic. Of all the times Marie was away, this was one of those times we needed her most.

Having the mother in stirrups helps when delivering a baby. Unfortunately, the woman was on the treatment table without stirrups for this emergency delivery. So, I became one of her stirrups, holding a leg. Another EMT became the other stirrup.

After considerable pushing and screaming during that hellacious winter storm, out came a beautiful baby, born into a room of first responders and two retired nurses. Betty Rember delivered the baby, supported by Rita James. On the phone was the mother's doctor in Ketchum, Dr. Stone.

The baby came out with a big blue streak across its chest and didn't breathe. The room went quiet. Then, suddenly, the baby started to cry.

At that point, we all knew the baby was fine, and we all felt like proud parents — or just about. We transported the mother and baby by ambulance over the hill, following the snowplow.

While screamers may draw your attention at a trauma scene, keep your eye on the quiet ones.

The emergency call came over the radio: "Male motorcyclist and female passenger down on Highway 75 near Sunbeam." We arrived on the Stanley Ambulance, pulled up to the wreck, and Marie and the EMTs got out. The woman was in the borrow pit, screaming with pain. Later X-rays confirmed a closed femur fracture that we suspected at the scene. Marie attended to our screaming female patient while I went to the motorcyclist.

The young man was right on the edge of the pavement, and I knew we needed to move him. But something kept telling me, "Don't move him. Don't move him. You're by yourself. Don't try to do something you know you shouldn't do." Instead, I kneeled over him, asked questions, and gathered information, waiting while Marie and other EMTs stabilized the femur fracture. I tried to remain calm, instructing the man, "Don't move until we have your back protected."

Marie had a message in our EMT classes: In trauma care, develop that "sixth sense." And here we were on the highway with one patient screaming and the other lying quietly, not saying anything. Eventually, I stood, walked over to Marie, and asked, "Hey, Marie, how much longer are you going to be? I'm concerned about a spinal injury."

"We're almost ready," Marie replied. After loading the woman into the ambulance, we worked together on the man to do a proper log roll maneuver and then stabilize his spine. Two hours later, in Sun Valley, diagnostic imaging confirmed my fears of a spinal fracture. At that point, I realized I had lived that "sixth sense:" Don't move him.

Sometimes, it's hard to sit and wait for more help. Listen for your sixth sense, especially in the chaos of a trauma scene. Once you do, you'll never forget.

The snowmobilers traveled from McCall to Stanley, making it as far as Bear Valley by afternoon. With worsening weather and losing light, the snowmobilers were traveling fast when one of the riders, a woman, lost control and hit a tree. On impact, she lunged forward, and her chest landed on the handlebars, resulting in severe chest injuries.

Winter weather in the central Idaho mountains can be treacherous. By the time we got the emergency call, it was nearly dusk. Marie called for helicopter support, and the Mountain Home Air Force Base dispatched a MAST Huey helicopter with a medical team on board. Meanwhile, we loaded into the Stanley Ambulance and headed west out of Stanley toward Boise on Highway 21. We got as far as the Boundary Creek turnoff and parked. The snowmobilers, including the injured rider, were several miles to the west. We needed that helicopter if the woman was going to survive.

The pilot navigated the Huey by following Highway 75 over Galena Summit and down the valley to Stanley. He then turned west, following Highway 21 towards Boise. When the pilot saw our ambulance with red flashers parked at the turnoff to Bear Valley, he was on the radio.

"I can see your ambulance. Now, where do I go?"

Flustered about how to give directions, Marie finally blurted out, "Turn right!"

That huge MAST helicopter wouldn't have been able to land on the highway because the snowbanks were too high. Instead, the aircraft flew overhead, turned the corner at the Stanley Ambulance, and headed up the snow-covered Boundary Creek road toward our patient. Snowmobiles encircled her, shining lights onto her and helping direct the pilot. He landed the Huey in a snowfield, and our EMTs lifted the injured woman to the helping hands of the military medical team. The gifted pilot got the patient through the winter storm to the trauma team at St. Al's in Boise.

responders. That's sad, not just for people in crisis who rely on a dwindling number of volunteer first responders for help. It diminishes the entire community. We are all less for it.

With better helicopter support, our ambulance runs are usually shorter. We don't hesitate to call for air transport. And standards have changed, too. When Marie started an IV, she could hand off the patient to the EMTs, and they'd monitor the IV during transport over the hill. Not anymore: If you start an IV, somebody trained in IVs must be with the patient. We only have a few people with that training. If a patient needs pain control, the days are past when Marie administered Demerol, and then EMTs transported the patient over the hill.

Our workaround is to do more paramedic intercepts, transferring patients from the Stanley Ambulance to a paramedic-staffed ambulance en route to an ER.

Marie's successor, Amy Klingler, faces the same dilemma that Marie did, juggling emergency calls and a busy clinic. And often, the Stanley Clinic is busy enough that she's unable to leave

Amy is an incredible resource for our region, but she can't be in two places at once. If you're sick or hurt enough to go on the ambulance, you probably need an IV or pain control, requiring ambulance staff with special training.

In rural communities, people roll up their sleeves and volunteer to help their neighbors and community. In urban areas you mostly pay for those services, but in rural areas, the resources just aren't there. And yet, that flame of volunteerism is diminishing.

When I moved to Stanley in the 1970s, nearly everybody volunteered, including the city council, mayor, clinic board, and Mountain Mamas. Everybody volunteered to better their community. Marie made the Stanley Ambulance team feel like family. She would have dinners at her cabin on Shaw Mesa for all the EMTs and drivers. You knew in your heart you were in the right place. Volunteering as an EMT was mostly fun and incredibly rewarding.

People's expectations have changed. Although there were no emergency medical services in the Sawtooth country before 1972, people now expect the service without a second thought. If they whip out their cell phone and call 911 (assuming they have cell coverage in the mountains), they expect somebody to show up and save them.

The Valley is gentrifying, and the people buying the property are seldom willing to train and volunteer as first

After nearly fifty years as a volunteer, I'm proud of the Stanley Ambulance and the Stanley Clinic. A tiny community created and sustained a valuable healthcare system. In doing that, Marie's dedication was a role model for all of us.

Soon after I became an EMT in 1976, one of my friends, Linda King, asked me to help her with billing for the clinic. We helped Marie handwrite all of the invoices to send to patients. That was two years before the community voted in the hospital district to fund the Stanley Clinic. Marie's income was based on the professional fee she charged as a nurse practitioner. When Linda and I wrote out the invoices, we wrote in Marie's professional fee: $7.50.

"Marie, what's this?" I asked.

"Oh, that's how much money I make," she said.

My response was, "Whoa, this can't be right." But Marie always made it clear that she wasn't in it alone. "Cal's helping me." Those close to Marie knew how much Cal helped her and the Stanley Clinic financially.

Eventually, Marie raised her professional fee to $25 and then to $35. She kept charges low for pap and pelvic exams for women because so many rural women otherwise didn't have access to healthcare and cancer screening. Marie wanted women to get medical care.

To this day, when the emergency tones go off, there are times I really don't want to go. But then, in the back of my mind, I hear, "Get off your fanny and go." It all comes down to helping others, some who might die if you don't show up. That dedication didn't just appear out of thin mountain air. It came from a role model. It came from Marie.

EMT trauma training

29

MARRIAGE, HEALTHCARE, DIVORCE

Carpe Momento!

Cal Osborn 1928 – 2014

Becoming a nurse practitioner and opening the Stanley Clinic came at a cost. Cal and I were married for nearly twenty-five years and raised five kids together. We lived in a gorgeous home in Boise and had a great family cabin in Stanley.

Most people would've thought we had it made. Except — I became an NP and set out to prove that an RN, with training, could provide rural healthcare. Once I started, I couldn't go back, only forward. No one would take over if I failed.

The Stanley Clinic drove many early decisions about healthcare in rural Idaho. The nurse practitioner as a profession flourished, and the Stanley Clinic and the Stanley Ambulance endured. My marriage with Cal did not.

The Osborn marriage and family felt solid. We could not have foreseen that opening the Stanley Clinic would change everything.

Cal and Marie at Stanley's first emergency clinic in 1972. Cal managed IBM's operations in southern Idaho. Cal and Marie worked together to open the Salmon River Emergency Clinic, never anticipating the impact on their marriage and the Osborn family.

With Cal's enthusiastic support, I began treating my first patients at the Stanley Clinic in May 1972. That summer was deadly, with one horrific accident after another.

It seemed like I'd return home from one ambulance run to Sun Valley, only to discover that yet another person was hurt badly or dead. Our family was living at our cabin that summer, with Cal coming up from the IBM office in Boise on weekends.

That year, Cal and I decided to have one big celebratory dinner instead of doing separate birthday dinners for our kids. That summer I was so absorbed with work at the clinic, I wasn't able to make it home for my kids' birthday party.

Cal worked while I was a stay-at-home mom. I looked after the kids, sewed, and took care of the house. In November 1963 at our Boise home, our family watched and wept at the televised funeral procession of President John F. Kennedy. In August 1974 at our Sawtooth cabin, we watched President Richard Nixon resign. Between one president's assassination and another's resignation, America changed. I was part of that change, going from an IBM family to training with paramedics and breaking new ground for women to provide rural healthcare. I was the public face of a new profession, but behind the public face were my marriage and five kids. No firewall divided and protected my family life from my rapidly evolving professional life. Even when I closed the door and left the Stanley Clinic, I remained on call for emergencies.

In 1971, the Stanley community couldn't reach a consensus on healthcare: some wanted only an ambulance, while others wanted a clinic. We did both. I agreed to staff the clinic only through the end of the summer of 1972, planning to return to Boise when school started in the fall. Community leaders came to the clinic at the end of my first summer and asked me to keep it open year-round. What should I do?

Years after the divorce, Cal and John became fishing partners, rebuilding their father-son relationship. It became an annual ritual for them to meet for a long fly-fishing weekend after Labor Day. For twenty-five years, they fished Idaho's trout waters. After a day of fishing, they would sit around the campfire and retell family stories. Cal had stopped drinking; John sipped whiskey while tending to the campfire.

"I just should have said 'Stop,'" Cal said. "'No more, Marie. Come home to Boise. You have to come home.' But I couldn't do that." He paused, "Marie became a legend in her own time."

In reality, Cal is just as responsible for the creation of the Stanley Clinic as anyone else. Without his approval and support, financial and otherwise, I could never have trained to become an NP, much less opened the Stanley Clinic. In those first years, Stanley did not have a delivery service other than the US mail. My husband was the clinic's delivery service, keeping the clinic stocked and open. Without him, we would have been up a creek getting medications, wound dressings, and other supplies.

Cal did everything he could to help. He even brought up IBM photographers. Our IBM friends would stop by the Stanley Clinic. What we were doing was big in IBM.

Caring for patients can be hard on a marriage, especially in small and rural communities. Personal lives take a back seat, and, especially with emergencies, patient care comes first. Unfortunately, this is an all-too-familiar experience, including for my physician preceptor.

"I was away from Ann so much of the time," anguished Dr. Stone, speaking at his wife's memorial service. "I was delivering babies all night, living in the emergency room," With remorse and sadness, he continued, "I wasn't there with Ann much of the time. So, I want *you* to tell *me* what she meant to you."

Ann was a top-notch RN. A shared dedication to patient care brought her and Dr. Stone together as husband and wife and helped hold their marriage together. In any marriage, in healthcare or otherwise, each partner brings the strengths needed to withstand stresses that can destroy it.

Although Cal married an RN when I was working nights at Ball Memorial Hospital, neither of us could have imagined the impact of the Stanley Clinic on our marriage and family. If you care for patients, you know the tensions. Somedays, Murphy's Law rules: what can go wrong will go wrong. And after spending your best hours with your patients, you go home. You walk in the door, put away your stethoscope, and put on an apron.

Talking about your day with a nonmedical spouse, you learn quickly to hit the "self-edit button." Here's an example of a showstopper at the dinner table:

"How was your day, honey?"

"It was tough. Could you pass the salt and pepper? A toddler ran across Highway 21 at the Boundary Creek turnoff. The driver never saw the little girl until it was too late. There was nothing I could do. All I could do was carry that dead child back to the clinic, cry with the parents, and wait for the coroner. When I walked into the clinic holding the dead child, a guy with a tick on his butt demanded I do something."

However much your spouse may love you, asking them to listen to these stories is a non-starter. Still, you need to be able to talk it out. Who will you talk with in a town of fifty people where confidentiality is essential? Cal hated negativity, however proud of his wife he might have been. Who wouldn't? Cal didn't want to hear about these horrific cases or patients with diarrhea or vomiting.

For me, quitting time at the Stanley Clinic was not five o'clock. If I was in the Valley, I was on call. When I finished charting, billing, and getting the clinic ready for tomorrow, I'd close and lock the front door, get in my car, and head home. Then came the emergency call: "Dispatch to Unit One. Marie, we have a motor vehicle accident at Idaho Rocky Mountain Ranch. A car hit a cow. Three people are badly hurt." Some days, I hated that radio.

In contrast, at five o'clock Cal headed to the YMCA to swim laps to work out stress before coming home, and he wanted me to turn it off at five, too, come home, and be a housewife and mother. Yet intellectually, Cal understood that I had to go when emergency calls came. I imagine him lying in our bed at the cabin, checking the clock, wondering where I was — especially when I had to go in the ambulance over the hill to Sun Valley. I tried to get word to him so he knew what I was doing. Eventually, inevitably, resentment crept into our marriage.

My husband, home, and friends at the time were all in Boise, but, I had to be in Stanley, 130 miles away, to run the clinic. At the time, the nearly sixty miles of Highway 21 from Lowman to Stanley were gravel, not paved. Furthermore, today's convenient paved road from Garden Valley to Lowman was, back then, awful: unpaved, washboards, narrow, and with few guard rails in the canyon high above the Payette River's South Fork. That left the curvy road from Boise, through Idaho City, to Lowman. In all, those 130 miles took more than three hours. Winter's avalanches often closed the canyon between Grandjean and Banner Summit, forcing the four-hour trip through Mountain Home, Hill City, and Ketchum.

Cal would arrive in Stanley on Friday evening. He might locate his wife at a car accident scene with Stanley's EMTs trying to stabilize a trauma patient for ambulance transport. I'd look up, and there stood my patient husband, just looking down. He'd tell me he'd meet me at the house, or he'd meet me at the clinic, or something. Most of the time, we'd meet for dinner, usually at the Kasino Club, where people thought nothing of pulling up a chair and sitting and talking about their medical problems. They interrupted a married couple who needed to talk about each other, about our kids and things that we had to do as a couple — or should do as a couple — or even a vacation. We needed to be a couple for a while, and it didn't work.

The clinic got busier and busier. Cal's traditional wife was the sole healthcare provider on call for 6,000 square miles of the Sawtooth/Salmon River country. Further, as Idaho's first nurse practitioner, I was committed to my core to show it would work. And if I failed, there was no one else to step in. The stakes were high.

With the growing demands of the Stanley Clinic, I found it harder to return to our Boise home. I intended to get home every week, but then it was every two weeks. After Labor Day, more would happen in Stanley, and I needed to be at the clinic, too. With the time away from each other, the closeness we'd always had began to slip away. We grew apart.

Another issue was Cal: he was different from the locals. The local men were rough and ready, could fix anything, and loved to stomp and snowmobile. On Friday nights, Cal would come in directly from Boise, often wearing his white shirt. Sometimes, he changed into jeans. Especially if I were out on an ambulance run, Cal would stop in the Kasino Club for a beer. Stanley was wild in those years, with bar fights, cowboys wanting to cut the hippies' hair, and Basque sheepherders mixing it up with highway workers. Stanley's three bars sent a lot of lacerations, broken hands, and noses to the clinic. Not many corporate executives from Boise in white shirts in those years walked into Stanley's bars, ordered a beer, and danced.

In the end, Cal and Stanley were not a good fit. I can't imagine Cal stuck at the cabin at forty below zero while I saw patients at the clinic. Cal would not have stayed; meanwhile, I couldn't leave. My work, especially the emergency call, was exhilarating if exhausting.

For twenty-one years, our gold wedding rings symbolized our marriage and commitment to each other. Eventually, our wedding rings — and the commitment to each other that they symbolize — came off.

We didn't talk to our five kids about our separation. We did not want our kids involved, although our break would impact each of them. We tried to protect them; we didn't want our children used to hurt each other. Our kids would talk later about their pain, not knowing our marriage was falling apart, that we kept the information from them.

Our separation lasted for three years. We discussed ways to continue, even in an "open" marriage. I said, "No." At the end of our marriage, we met for lunch in Boise. All I could do was bawl.

After three years of separation, we formally ended our marriage in 1977, signing the divorce papers and dividing our properties between Boise and Stanley.

Our experience was not unique. The wife takes a job at a rural clinic. It's wonderful, and she loves her work. But where does the husband fit in? Where does he work if he's not Fish and Game or Forest Service, or doesn't ranch or work construction? And if he doesn't work, he'll wait for his wife to come home from the clinic, or an ambulance run. He may wait more than twenty-four hours before she gets through with one or two or more emergency calls. Cal waited patiently, but not forever.

Above everything, I was out to prove that an NP could do what I was doing — and do it well. She didn't have to be a doctor. I was not going to give up, and in ending our marriage, I believed Cal would find someone to love,

Twenty years after our divorce, my experience of losing my marriage with Cal was foremost in my mind when I worked with the clinic board to begin the search for my replacement. So often, while you might hire a clinician, you also do what you can to make sure it's also a good fit for the spouse and children. Otherwise, you'll fail. The Osborn family knows.

"Leaf in the creek" is how Cal described life. There comes a time when you let go and allow life's current to carry you.

In 1976, a year before our divorce, Cal drove to the Boise airport to see John off on a trip. John was heading to Australia on a college expedition to Queensland and the Great Barrier Reef. For Cal, that moment at the airport was life-changing. Why wasn't he the one leaving to explore the world? He took a year off from IBM to travel internationally.

He started by taking our daughter, Melinda, on a PanAm Airlines "80 days around the world" excursion. On that trip, Cal began to keep a journal to hold himself accountable for his time on earth. Still today, Melinda wakes up on Christmas morning and starts the day by reading her dad's first journal of their round-the-world trip together. Eventually, Cal would leave his children an extensive collection of his journals.

On his year-long sabbatical, Cal visited our IBM friends, John and Char Sailors, in Hong Kong. Later, John wrote his remembrances of IBM's unique corporate culture of support that enabled Cal and me to do all that we did: "There may never be another corporate philosophy and culture that takes full responsibility for its employees and places community support so high in its priorities while maintaining profitability and industry leadership. ... The 75-year-old IBM culture, created by the Watsons, died in 1993 when IBM brought in its first CEO ever from the outside."

Even by the late 1970s, IBM was changing. When Cal returned from his year off, he was no longer in management. Instead, he was assigned a sales territory in eastern Oregon and southwestern Idaho. In the wake of our divorce, with his kids growing and leaving home, the pressures to meet his sales quota were receding. More and more, Cal was trying to hold on until he could retire with his pension.

In 1981, IBM confirmed plans to close its Office Products Division. Cal looked for an offramp from IBM, and it came in 1983 when IBM offered him early retirement. Later, during his hospice, Cal's eyes twinkled when he talked about receiving his pension for thirty years, a few months longer than the thirty years he worked for IBM.

IBM also gave retraining funds to employees who were leaving. Cal used his money for fly-fishing lessons. At age fifty-seven, he walked out of IBM into life's banquet with pent-up dreams of exploring the world.

That same year, 1983, he went skiing and ran into Cory Thiebert at the ski lodge. After skiing, Cal and Cory started their thirty-year relationship that lasted until prostate cancer overtook Cal in 2014.

"Carpe momento" — seize the moment — are two words that define Cal in his retirement. He retained a childlike fascination and energy for learning and exploring.

"If it's important, write it down," Cal advised his children. He followed his advice and wrote down life's most important lessons, placing them on his "business card." You may be one of the thousands who heard, "Hi. My name is Cal Osborn. Here, I want you to have my business card. I have a PhD — in audience and applause." Cal would be honored to have you read his card.

A divorce may not end a relationship, especially when kids are involved. Eventually, the pain of our separation and divorce receded in life's rearview mirror. Cal and I talked about the kids, 3015, the cabin, and each other. Cal, never bashful about seeking second medical opinions until finding one with which he agreed, often asked about his health issues.

And even after the divorce, Cal supported me financially.

Christmas remains an important family event for the Osborns. During our separation, those holidays were hard. Some of our kids would spend Christmas morning with their dad, drive through Mountain Home to Ketchum, and then into the Sawtooth Valley to spend Christmas afternoon with their mom. Some years, I didn't even decorate, and the kids would ski into the cabin, pull out the decorations, and keep our family traditions alive.

In the years after the divorce, as the Osborn family began to heal, the entire family shoe-horned into the cabin to celebrate a white Christmas overlooking the Sawtooths. Christmas was more stressful for Cal, as he had to choose between being with his kids or Cory. Gradually, each of our kids pursued their own Christmas celebration and traditions.

After I retired from Stanley in 1999 and spent more time in my Boise townhouse, most of the family gathered at my home for "premeal" on Christmas Day.

Late afternoon, Cal and Cory walked in the door singing, "We wish you a Merry Christmas." We'd share stories and catch up with each other's lives. Cal would fill the room with his jokes and laughter before he and Cory left for the Thiebert family dinner, and we sat down for the traditional Osborn Christmas dinner.

Cal did return to the Sawtooth country, usually pitching a tent and camping. On one camping trip in 1982, Cal was having prostate problems. Earlier in March, he had driven the AlCan Highway to Anchorage, tagging along with John and his friend, Sean Farley. The three awoke to Cal's many footprints in the snow on the morning after a snowstorm and with bitter cold in northern British Columbia. After drinking a few beers with the boys at the truck stop, he had been up all night.

Later, Cal talked to me about his prostate. I asked, "Cal, what does your urologist advise?"

That summer, Cal pitched his tent at Iron Creek Campground and drove to Stanley for a few beers. He returned to his camp and went to pee — and couldn't. He waited and tried again. Nothing. As mild discomfort became throbbing pain, Cal grew desperate.

Finally, he got back in his car and drove to Stanley. It was late, and I was closing the clinic when Cal arrived. He looked six months pregnant with his enlarged bladder.

Only once had I catheterized a male patient, then in an iron lung in the polio ward at Ball Memorial. Male orderlies, not female nurses, catheterized male patients. My ex-husband did not want his ex-wife catheterizing him. So, I gave Cal a Valium, and he tried lying on the couch.

No urine.

In those years, the clinic didn't stock Foley catheters, so instead, I reached for a catheter to do an "in and out" straight cath. The amount of urine was astounding, overflowing the bedpan. Cal's relief was immediate. After emptying the bladder, I removed the catheter and sent Cal to St. Luke's ER in Boise.

Cal was open about his cancer, even starring in a promotional video about hospice. He sought multiple opinions about what he should do, including mine and our son John's, then Chief of Medicine at the Spokane VA.

John began traveling to Boise to join his father at clinic visits and help him weigh treatment options. In the end, Cal decided against interventions. Cal, in love with life, did not want treatments that would risk his quality of life for the time he had left.

With the prostate cancer metastasizing to bone and Cal developing back pain, he entered hospice. Treated with Decadron, his pain resolved, and he blossomed. Cal so loved his hospice team. He'd sing for them and share stories of his world travels. Cal patched together care from his internist, Dr. Bollinger, with the Gold Team at the Boise VA. He and Cory continued to go out on Friday nights to dance and listen to live music. By December 2013, he could no longer dance.

On Christmas Day 2013, we met at Veterans Park. Children, their spouses, grandchildren, and Cory and I joined Cal in his wheelchair, pushing him over a walking bridge to a trail along the Boise River. Here was the Boise River Greenbelt that Cal treasured and one of the many trails he walked nearly daily. On those banks of the Boise River, the family dedicated a rock bench with a plaque, "Celebrating the life of Cal Osborn."

As Cal grew weaker, he wanted something in nature that his five children would see and remember him by. Cal was an Indiana boy who loved reading Hoosier poet James Whitcomb Riley and walking through piles of fallen leaves. Eventually, Cal asked his sons and daughters, "When you see falling leaves, will you think of me?"

Although they did not marry (getting married was something Cal would never do after our divorce: "When someone says 'marriage,' I break into a cold sweat"), Cal and Cory were a solid team. Cory allowed Cal to remain in her home during his hospice.

These were dark days for the entire family. Earlier in September, Cal's grandson Cameron Wilder, a seventeen-year-old beloved and talented teenager, died by suicide during the first week of school and National Suicide Prevention Month. As Cal struggled with the end of his own life, he grieved over the death of his grandson. "Why?" Cal sobbed, asking his son, John. "Why did he do it?"

Hospice, especially in life's last weeks, takes a team. Cal's and Cory's children gathered and took turns helping. Knowing his dad needed skilled nursing care, John called his youngest sister, Debbie, an ER and ICU nurse. Asking Debbie for help was not an easy call: She had just lost her son and was now losing her father. A few hours later, Debbie walked in the door.

On the night of January 9, we gathered at Cory's house to say goodbye. The cancer had emaciated Cal, and he was slipping away.

One by one, we said our goodbyes with tears and recitation, "I forgive you. Please forgive me. I love you."

The following day, as Debbie guided her older brothers Cal Jr. and John in gently bathing their father, Cal passed.

Like his father before him, Cal was a walker who, later in life, walked the Boise River Greenbelt nearly every day. Best of all, he loved the fall with its autumn leaves and deep blue skies. Cal, a life force and embodiment of carpe momento, left life surrounded by loving family.

To know the story of the Stanley Clinic and Stanley Ambulance and the history of the nurse practitioner in Idaho is to also know this man. Cal, thank you.

Best of all he loved the fall
the leaves yellow on the cottonwoods
leaves floating on the trout streams
and above the hills the high blue windless skies ...
now he will be a part of them forever.

Earnest Hemingway Memorial, Sun Valley

Sitting rock "Celebrating the life of Cal Osborn," along the Boise River Greenbelt near Veterans Park. Cal Osborn was a Boise booster who walked the river's Greenbelt nearly every day. Born a Hoosier who became an Idahoan, Cal — Air Force veteran, IBM executive, husband, father and grandfather, cruise-ship host, angler and walker, lover of life — helped Marie create the Stanley Clinic and Ambulance. On Christmas Day, 2013, family gathered here with Cal, dying from prostate cancer, to dedicate this memorial next to the river he so loved.

30

NURSING: DAUGHTERS & MOTHERS

I worked in a new part of the ED yesterday. Our longest non-intubated patient on high flow, non-rebreather mask got tubed before I arrived. He is young and has a wife and three young children at home. He was in the ED for 300 hours — with an approximate five percent chance of survival. He was replaced with another young man under my care. We set up a video call with his wife and toddler. That will probably be the last time he will get to say he loves them or see them.

When I left last night, there were eighty-five people in the ED and a line out the triage tent door. When I go back, it will be worse. The next wave of COVID is about to strike.

Deb's COVID Diary, May 4, 2020, Brooklyn, NY — Maimonides Emergency Department

Idaho Nurse Headed to New York to Help with Frontline COVID-19 Fight

BOISE, Idaho – Hospitals across the country are working hard to keep up with the coronavirus pandemic.

The reality is, some hospitals are just overwhelmed. To help those areas, doctors, nurses, and other healthcare professionals are traveling to the frontlines to help with the fight.

One of those places, the New York City area.

Idahoans like Debbie Wilder are on their way to help. Wilder is set to head to New York very soon...Wilder worked for 17 years in a Treasure Valley emergency room and intensive care unit. More recently she went to work at the Surgery Center of Idaho to do post-anesthesia care... "I anticipate there is going to be a lot of death," Wilder said. "I anticipate I am going to learn a lot about how to treat this virus because from what I've read up on, they aren't dealing with this like other viruses I've dealt with in the past."

New York City is a major coronavirus hot spot. Some have described it saying it's like a war zone. Wilder says it feels a little bit like that, but she knows she isn't alone.

"I know of a few nurses from Idaho who I've worked with in the ERs here that are headed there too," she said. "So, it's not going to be like I'm on an island by myself, there's going to be a lot of people that are swarming together to try and do the right thing."

Why does she want to help?

"I've always wanted to try and help when there is a problem," she said. "I have some knowledge, and I think I can be of benefit."

Across the board, Wilder has been encouraged by the response to the pandemic.

"I'm really impressed and excited with how many people are banding together to go fight something we've never fought before," she said.

Joe Parris, *KTVB-7*, April 9, 2020

My family knows pandemics. The 1918 influenza killed my grandfather, a prosperous Kentucky farmer. His death thrust his wife, Mother Tatum, and her children into poverty years before the Great Depression hit. I came of age in Muncie on the hospital wards caring for polio patients, including those in "iron lungs." My two children in patient care, Debbie and John, have each battled microbes. John directed the HIV/AIDS program for Veterans at the Spokane VA for twenty-five years until 2010. For Deb, an RN in ICUs and ERs, it was COVID.

When COVID hit in March 2020, Debbie and John were working in ERs. They gowned, gloved, masked, and put on shields. Deb saw the worst, first in Brooklyn, New York, and later in Los Angeles and southern Idaho. In Brooklyn, Deb walked into ER chaos: ambulances lining up, people in respiratory distress, ICUs overflowing into ERs, hallways filled with patients on ventilators and dialysis machines, and refrigerator trucks filling with body bags.

Debbie is every ounce of an ER and ICU nurse; she has a big heart with a hard-as-nails constitution. She has a low tolerance for abusive patients who scream demands, spit, punch, bite, or even throw urine and feces. Deb is strong and was so long before nursing.

My story as the first licensed NP is Debbie's story, too. Deborah Anne Osborn, born on August 10, 1964, made clear she would live her life on her terms. Debbie, the youngest of five, came of age in Stanley during Cal's and my separation and divorce. The daughter of Stanley's only healthcare provider, Debbie, grew up early. She had no choice.

In early August 1964, Deb and I missed the annual IBM campout at Redfish Lake, although Cal took our other four kids. Cal returned to St. Luke's in Boise, where I gave birth to Debbie. After five kids and losing the twins, Debbie was our youngest and final child.

Debbie in her nurse's uniform that Marie sewed for her, just as Marie's mother did for her.

Debbie went with me everywhere as an infant as I drove the ski team to races, lobbied for the PTA at the Legislature, or ran household errands. As a toddler, she brought her coloring book or a book to read. Mother and daughter came to an agreement that she would sit quietly during my

Debbie is with neighbor Brian Mitchell, as they learn to clean fish.

Debbie (LEFT) and Melinda at the Osborn's family cabin.

meetings, and her reward was a trip to McDonald's. She did beautifully.

One precious memory I have is sewing a nurse's uniform for Debbie when she was five years old, just as my mother had sewn one for me. Debbie loved her new white dress, blue and gold cape, and nurse's cap. Her uniform, including the cape, was modeled on my student nursing uniform at Ball State University.

When our daughters were young, Cal and I commissioned Boise artist John Collias to paint their portraits. Lindy wanted to pose in a red velvet outfit. She would sit for the artist a few minutes, then want an ice cream or Coke. Collias obliged, later recalling, "She was the original Eve." It took months to finish Lindy's portrait — not Debbie's.

Debbie wanted her portrait over with, so she sat in her little rocking chair until it was done. Debbie posed in everyday clothes she wore to kindergarten, refusing anything fancier — certainly not velvet. The artist captured Debbie's spirit.

In 1973, during our second summer at our cabin on Shaw Mesa, the girls were at the cabin, and I was seeing patients at the Stanley clinic when the phone rang.

"This is Marie."

"Is this the Salmon River Emergency Clinic?"

"Yes," I answered.

"Your daughter called on the CB radio. Something about your dogs getting into porcupines. She needs you at home."

In those years, the cabin didn't have a telephone or EMS radio. So, instead, Debbie reached for the donated CB radio we used for emergency calls. Debbie instructed a fisherman off the coast of California to call me at the Stanley Clinic. I headed home to dequill our three dogs.

What Debbie had done showed the value of emergency radio communications reaching hundreds of miles across Idaho, Oregon, and finally California. My eight-year-old daughter's level-headed response impressed me.

In our well-organized household in Boise, all seven of us — husband, wife, and five kids — sat together for breakfast and supper. At our family cabin in the Sawtooths, emergency calls blew up meal plans. Emergencies came first.

Four of my five kids grew up in Boise and attended urban public schools. Not Debbie. Although she started preschool and elementary school in Boise, when Cal and I separated, we agreed our youngest would live with me in Stanley.

When Debbie and I lived at the cabin on Shaw Mesa, Debbie had to travel two miles to the highway to catch her school bus and then ride twelve miles to town.

Some days, I drove her down the hill to the highway; other days, she rode her horse. Beginning around Halloween, the snow came, and we snowmobiled to the highway so Debbie could catch her bus.

Stanley's school in the 1970s was a two-room Quonset Hut. After graduating from the eighth grade, students left Stanley to attend high school.

None of the options were good in those years and still aren't great. Usually, Stanley's students went downriver to Challis, although some went to Ketchum or Boise. While many of Stanley's parents boarded their kids in Challis, other families left Stanley.

I decided for my daughter: She would go to Challis. A new molybdenum mine provided revenues to build new schools in Challis. More worrisome were illicit drugs in Boise and Ketchum, and I assumed Challis would be safer. Turns out, I was wrong. Drug problems weren't solely an urban or affluent affliction. "Oh, Mom," Debbie informed me later, "you can get anything you want in Challis, anytime you want."

As an IBM family in urban Boise, Cal and I had resources and support for our four oldest children: childcare, schools nearby, after-school sports, choir and band, and even vocational counseling.

In contrast, as a rural mother in Stanley, at times, I struggled. With Debbie in Challis sixty miles away, I was unable to provide a mother's supervision and support. When my daughter fell chasing rabbits, breaking both ankles, and couldn't get emergency care from the local doctor, she only reluctantly called her mother.

"I will never forget the look on your face when you showed up when I broke my ankles," Debbie wrote to me for my seventieth birthday, soon after retiring from the Stanley Clinic. "When you came through the bedroom door and looked at my feet, your face was priceless. You had the look of: 'What the hell did you do!' Ah, *the look* from my mother."

Eventually, Debbie dropped out of high school. That this young woman survived her teenage years in Challis is a testament to resilience.

Eventually, Debbie started nursing school at Boise State University. While in her first year, I telephoned her in the winter of 1983 to let her know I had colon cancer. Her immediate response was, "Mom, do you need help?"

But if Debbie left BSU to help me, nursing school administrators wouldn't let her make up the class time. Debbie's choice was to attend nurse training or nurse her mother. The morning the anesthesiologist wheeled me into the operating room in Sun Valley, Debbie walked beside me.

Debbie gave birth to two sons, Nate and Cameron, and then lost Cameron to suicide. Debbie was working as the charge nurse in the ICU when the social worker found her, "Deb, it's the police. It's your son." The hospital ICU was miles from her home.

Debbie ran out of the hospital to a waiting police car. Over the radio, the first responders, who Debbie knew from the ER, asked her permission to stop CPR. My daughter had to call the code on her son.

Tell it like it is: Debbie, the straight shooter, insisted on transparency starting with her son's obituary. She stood in front of TV cameras and walked the halls of the state's Capitol Building advocating that Idaho — with one of America's worst suicide rates — do better.

Deb's resilience enabled her to provide hospice nursing care for her father just four months after losing Cameron. She was instructing her brothers on bathing their father when he finally relaxed, stopped breathing, and passed. Deb's inner strength also powered her to hug family goodbye, board a jet at the Boise airport, and fly off to New York City during the nation's darkest days of the COVID pandemic.

From an early age, Deb ran toward trouble. Partly, she had no choice: I didn't have childcare, so she had to go on emergency calls with me. But it was far more than that. Who Debbie is to the core is to help people in trouble, not run away.

Debbie became Stanley's (and probably Idaho's) youngest ever EMT, riding an ambulance as a teen and helping at the Stanley Clinic. This independent daughter, who dropped out of high school yet completed her BSN graduating cum laude, would bring her life experiences to the bedside of her patients in ICUs and ERs from Idaho to New York City.

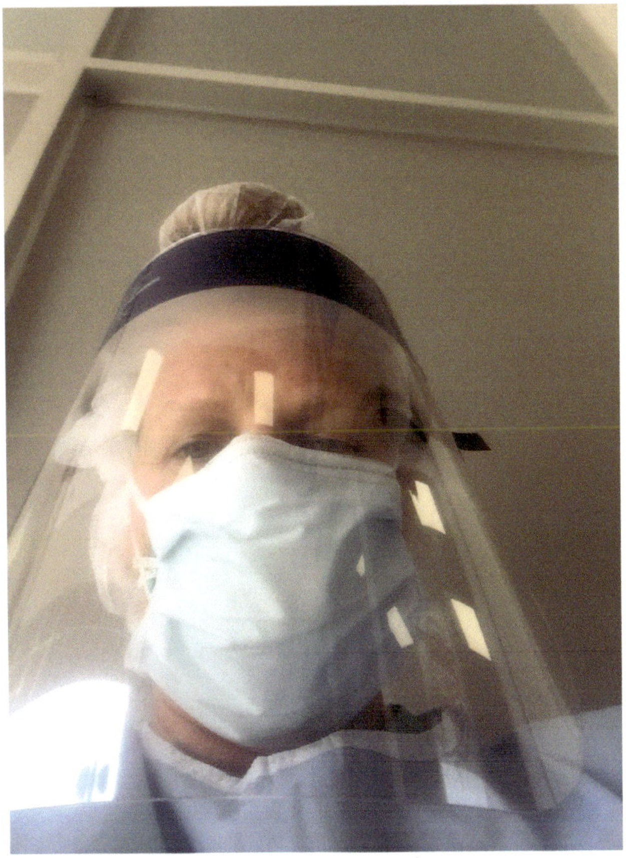

Debbie, Marie's youngest daughter and E.R. nurse, grew up in Stanley. During COVID, with New York City in crisis, Debbie responded to the plea for help and traveled from Idaho to help New Yorkers who were sick and dying.

DEB WILDER RN, IN HER OWN WORDS

I was still in the afterglow from my wonderful, supportive New York City neighbors and Idaho friends, and I got a huge boost from Idaho Candy Company, which sent Idaho Spud Bars to our ED in Brooklyn. But, even with all that, overcoming some of the things you see is hard.

I questioned the doctors about treatment, trying to understand what we do to our patients. Our "covids" (yes, that's what the ER staff calls them here) struggle to breathe. The body can't sustain breathing 30-40 times a minute for days. These folks are on one hundred percent oxygen using high-flow devices with nonrebreather masks. The mouth and throat dry, and sores develop even with humidifying the oxygen. We are running out of supplies: We have no mouth swabs, no glycerin swabs, no artificial saliva, and no washcloths. Sips of water? No. Oxygen saturations in the high eighties drop into the seventies after just a few seconds off oxygen.

"Excuse me, but why aren't we putting in central lines and giving our patients TPN?" I asked. The response? "We only keep our covids for 24-48 hours before they start eating."

Hello? Fuck no, these people aren't eating. Our patients burn up nutritional stores so fast that repositioning and turning these poor people drop their oxygen levels into the 60s or lower. Giving them a good bed bath or linen change? Forget it. Their oxygen levels desaturate to levels not compatible with life.

Deb's COVID Diary, April, 2020, Brooklyn, NY — Maimonides Emergency Department

I am the youngest of Cal and Marie's five kids. Birth order, genetics, fate, nurse practitioner history, rural EMS, and Stanley all help explain how I ended up nursing in Brooklyn hospitals during COVID-19's worst. Let's begin with Stanley, Idaho.

I'm a nurse who grew up in Stanley. Small-town hostilities have a way of making you thick- skinned and stronger. Also Mom didn't have childcare in Stanley. So, when I was with Mom and emergency calls came, I went with her. I saw death before I had a driver's license. With Mom, I grew up with the Salmon River Emergency Clinic, the Stanley Ambulance, and trauma. With Dad in Boise and Mom focused on keeping the clinic open and the ambulance running, I was on my own more than most kids.

Helping clean the clinic was one of my chores. As Mom instructed, I cleaned all surfaces with rubbing alcohol. My older sister, Melinda, and niece, Ashley, now clean the Stanley Clinic. So, the Osborn kids have cleaned the Stanley clinic for over fifty years.

Summertime in Stanley was a blast in the 1970s. Mom was busy at the clinic sewing up people, so parental supervision was minimal. There also wasn't any law enforcement. Things got wild and, as a preteen and teenager, you could get into all the trouble you wanted. Stanley's mayor, Gerald Nicholson, was always getting into fights. Mom and I attended a community potluck one winter at the Stanley Club that became a knock-down, drag-out fight with people thrown into the street. Some men hated each other, got over it, and were best buds — until the next time they beat the shit out of each other.

The near riots during the Fourth of July holiday forced the law-enforcement issue. Hundreds, perhaps thousands of people showed up. If not dynamite, then at least M-80s exploded in town. Each of the bars had live bands. People wandered from bar to bar, drinking on the streets. Dust from Stanley's street party hung over the town, mixing with marijuana smoke. With public drinking and even public fornicating, locals brought in law enforcement and ended it.

I became an EMT when I was fifteen. I might work with Mom in the ambulance when emergency calls came, transporting patients over Galena Summit to the ER in Sun Valley. Mom and I stayed at the clinic during blizzards and spring breakup. The new clinic had an office with a hide-a-bed couch and, later, an apartment for the premeds in the summer and Mom and me in the winter.

My school was a half-block from our first clinic. During the school lunch hour, I walked to the clinic. Mom might heat a can of soup in the kitchen that doubled as the lab. I loved those cans of Vienna sausages, although they congealed in the winter.

One winter's evening in the third grade, I came "home" to the clinic. As I opened the front door, there wasn't much light inside. At that time of year, mountain shadows quickly shroud the town.

"Hi, Mom, I'm here." No answer. "Mom?" She was probably off doing a house call. When I walked into the clinic, I could see a body.

Stanley doesn't have a morgue, so bodies ended up parked at the clinic. Eventually, the Blaine County coroner came from Hailey and hauled them away. The coroner might take four or five hours to get to Stanley from the Wood River Valley.

Eventually, Mom became a deputy coroner. But, at that moment, I was alone with a dead body. I was too young to understand and reached to touch the arm, "Hello?"

To keep the arms from dangling, someone had tied the hands together. The arm slipped and dropped as I touched it, releasing a big expulsion of air from the dead man.

"AAAAH!"

I've never gotten over that; it scared the hell out of me. My whole life, I've been afraid of the dark. Still, death was part of my life growing up in Stanley.

I was with Mom when she got called to a Redfish Lake campground. A girl had hopped on the back of a motorcycle, and the driver was drinking. He lost control as they sped through the campground, hitting a tree. The young girl didn't move — she was dead.

The intoxicated motorcyclist was yelling obscenities at us as we cut off his Levi's. At that moment, the girl's parents walked up, looking for their daughter.

Another time, I was with Mom when she got called to the highway curve between Stanley and Lower Stanley. In the cold of winter, a car probably hit black ice, lost control, and flipped into the river. That innocent-looking curve is near the old ranger station, now a museum. It's a Bermuda Triangle for tragedy, the same curve where one of Casanova Jack's wives ended up paralyzed.

As Mom drove up and parked, the woman, who survived the car wreck and got to shore, screamed hysterically at the river's edge.

"He's inside the car. He's in there. Please, someone, get him out. Oh, God. Where are the kids? Oh my God, my kids!"

Two white shoes stuck out from under the partially submerged car in the crystal-clear riffles of the Salmon River. Inside the vehicle were children's toys. "My kids, where are my kids!" I can still hear her screams. Stanley's first responders scrambled, heading downriver in hopes of finding the kids alive — but turned up nothing.

The tow truck arrived, and our local rescue team attached cables to roll the car. The white shoes still attached to the body floated with the current. After we pulled the dead man from the river, I remember it as the cleanest fatality I've ever seen. Mom, as deputy coroner, declared him dead, and we transported the body to the clinic. As it turned out, the kids weren't in the car when it plunged into the Salmon River. Those white shoes? A childhood memory that stays.

Stanley's a town where secrets are hard to keep, and stories make the rounds. Kids saw a lot, too. At school, another student might share, "So-and-so beat up his wife last night." Not surprisingly, with long winters and three bars, domestic violence was a thing in the 1970s. Kids know a lot more than adults give them credit for.

Attending Stanley's Quonset hut school was different than public schools in Boise. Walking into the hut, you entered a small, central room with a ping-pong table and bathrooms. The door on your left opened into the classroom for kindergarten through third grade; on your right, the classroom for grades four through eight. I was the only one in my grade until I started in the classroom for the older kids. In the fourth through eighth grades, three of us were girls. We'd go steady with one of the boys for a week, then suffer an emotional breakup. In Stanley's schoolhouse hut, we knew each other.

When Mom was called to the clinic for an emergency, I was alone at the cabin. As a little girl, I was terrified of the dark, although our dogs made me feel safer. Of course, knowing Bigfoot might be out there didn't help, especially in the winter, with wind driving snow: I was sure the wind moving the trees was the Yeti.

During the fall, I would ride my horse, Boots, to the bus stop, slap his butt, and send him back home. By Halloween, the horses were gone and Mom and I had to be ready for winter. Getting to the bus stop got harder. In the dark on subzero mornings, I straddled the snowmobile behind Mom and then boarded the school bus. We often stayed at the clinic during blizzards rather than trying to get up the hill from the highway. When snow turned to spring mud,

Mom and I gave up and stayed in town until we could drive the road to the cabin.

At first, we didn't have a television in the cabin. When we finally did, we had one grainy TV channel. So, when another Boise TV station broadcasted *Planet of the Apes* with Charlton Heston, I watched it with Dirty Dora's granddaughter, Heidi, at the Beaver Creek Store. How did we survive before cable, satellite TV, and the internet?

With both my parents largely unavailable, other adults were like family to me: the Armada Cafe's Maxine Baptiste and Joanne Shawl, Jerry Funderberg at the Country Store, and ranchers Piero Piva and Frank Heavrin. Frank gave me my first horse, Boots, and my dog.

Stanley's Armada Cafe became my home away from home. Maxine was like a grandmother. Walking to school from Maxine's cafe was far easier than getting from the cabin to the highway and riding the school bus to town.

At the cafe, I bussed tables and washed dishes. Working in cafes, especially during rush hour, prepared me well for ERs. You never know who is going to walk through that door. No matter the chaos, you maintain control and decorum. Also, there are times in restaurants and ERs when people overstep boundaries. At the Armada, Maxine asked the unruly and rude to leave.

When I attended high school in Challis, I had to catch the school bus on Monday at 5:30 am.

During the school week in Challis, I boarded out with whoever would take me. I worked to pay for my boarding, clothes, and a used car.

During my first year in Challis, an amazing family — a real family — took me in. They were so supportive. From there, it went downhill — eventually, I bought a fifth wheel and lived at the Saturday Mountain Mine in Custer County at 7,400 feet, driving back and forth to class. That didn't last, and I dropped out.

During COVID, working in city hospital ERs, I've cared for patients who screamed and yelled, threw stuff, and even threw punches. Sometimes I got hit. There were night shifts when the shit never stopped: You leave a patient who just died to care for another patient who curses you, "Goddammit, nurse, where's my blanket? I asked five minutes ago." Through it all, I try to keep calm, smile, and say, "Really? Tell me, how's your day?"

I am not my mother. I fought against being a nurse and said no to becoming a nurse practitioner.

Still, I couldn't escape it. My great-grandmother, Mother Tatum, was the nurse in her Kentucky community during the 1918 pandemic. Like Mother Tatum and my mother, I was called to nursing, especially emergency care. Sometimes in life, you take the more comfortable path. Blood and gore and smells don't bother me. I learned early. I had to. At the cabin one summer, we pulled porcupine quills out of our four dogs twenty-one times.

With time, our deepening wrinkles and graying hair, for those who still have hair, count for something in healthcare. New graduates fresh out of training may know the latest medical science. Yet, life can teach you a lot if you're willing to learn. You can look your patients in the eye: "I know what you're going through. I've been there."

Before I got on the plane for New York City during those first months of COVID, my son Nate and I had a long talk. "You need to know that these are my wishes."

"If I get infected, and I'm going to die, make me comfortable. Let me go." I'm an old ICU nurse. I've cared for patients stuck on ventilators for a long time. I didn't want to die caring for COVID patients in the ER, but you never know.

When I arrived in New York City from Boise and took my phone off airplane mode, I had a text from my son, Nate. "Mom, when we took you to the airport, I realized it might be the last time I see you. I love you."

Especially during those first pandemic months, chaos reigned in the city's ERs. Staffing and supplies couldn't keep up. Personal protective equipment (PPE) was in short supply. When I arrived in the ER, I got my N-95 mask, shield, and one yellow paper or blue nylon gown for twelve hours. You'd drip and sweat in the nylon; the paper was better. The shield made it impossible to hear. Other ED nurses hit you on the back to alert you when patients coded.

"Is that your patient?" another nurse asked as I walked by.

"No."

"They don't have a heartbeat! We need help over here!" Oh shit.

People were coding left and right. During those first months of COVID, it was nonstop "Code Blue" in the ED. You had to walk sideways after the triage staff crammed so many patients into those two giant rooms. The ICU was overflowing, and the ER became the ICU. End-stage renal disease patients infected with COVID couldn't dialyze at the hospital's dialysis center, so dialysis machines filled the hallways and ER. We only had two sinks.

Ambulances lined up outside the ER. With scary TV news updates, people refused to come to the ER unless they desperately needed help. So, by the time they called 911, many were already severely hypoxic and in acute respiratory failure. With so many dying, New York City couldn't handle the dead. We had big rigs parked out back, refrigerator trucks where the body bags were stacked. Ambulances in front brought in the living, refrigerator trucks in the back carted away the dead, and our ER team straddled both worlds.

Growing up in Stanley, I remember waiting hours for the coroner's arrival to haul away the dead. It was worse during COVID in New York City: The dead remained for days.

I'm an Idaho girl who had to find her way around New York City during the darkest days of the pandemic. I'd never used Uber in my life. At the airport, I schlepped all my stuff to the Uber lot. My son Nate set up the Uber application on my phone, so I hit the button. Nothing happened. Crap. So, I schlepped everything back to the airport and took a taxi. I was scared.

My first trip from the Maimonides ER in Brooklyn to my Central Park apartment was a disaster. I worked a grueling shift on April 22 and was too tired to take the subway home. The city was in lockdown, and everyone was afraid of everyone. I started by pulling out my phone and arranging an Uber pickup. I stood in front of the ER and waited. The Uber driver drove by me once, turned around, and drove by me again, looking right at me while driving slowly. He canceled my ride. Days later, another Uber driver disclosed that since I work in the worst-hit part of the city, some drivers were afraid after looking at me in my scrubs standing near a long line of ambulances.

So, after a horrible day in the ER, I found my way to the subway. With so many codes and people dying in the ER, I hadn't eaten all day and barely had time to go to the bathroom. I didn't keep count of the patients we body-bagged that day. After Uber abandoned me, I was even more "hangry" and emotional.

After finally getting on the subway, I felt confused and sensed I was traveling south, not north towards Manhattan. Almost in tears, I looked around the COVID-emptied subway car, to a woman sitting nearby. "Excuse me, I'm from Idaho, and I'm lost. I'm supposed to be going toward Manhattan. Am I going that way?"

"No, honey, you're going to Coney Island." So, I got off and onto the right train at the next stop. All the way back to Central Park, I cried. I was so downtrodden. However, once I figured out New York City's subways, although they freaked me out, that was a big accomplishment. Holy Christ, a girl from Stanley, Idaho, figured out how to use a subway with one of the world's great cities in lockdown!

New Yorkers with Idaho connections donated their apartment on Central Park, so I had a place to stay. On my second trip to Brooklyn, I stayed in a hotel closer to the hospital, a block from the One World Trade Center.

When I returned to Brooklyn after a break in Boise, I worked at Interfaith. Every ER nurse can identify with this: I was assigned eighteen patients on my first day and hadn't received training on the hospital's electronic medical record. I refused to go back. Instead, I worked in the ICU.

As a girl, I always wanted to do MASH. When Desert Storm happened, I was a nurse and wanted to go, but I had two young sons. After the Haiti earthquake, I had several friends in nursing who went to help. My passport was about to expire, and the timing wasn't right. During those first months of the COVID pandemic, Governor Cuomo was on cable news almost daily, pleading for help from nurses and other medical professionals.

I knew I had to go.

The last few days blended — surreal starts to seem normal. My mask is hurting my face: normal.
I can't hear because of my PPE and air scrubbers: normal.
I see people crammed into a 6x6' space: normal.
Two newly added refrigeration semi-trucks (six now): normal.
The smell of decomposition when the semi doors open to accept or remove a body: normal.

People in pain coming to the ED after falling and breaking a hip: not as normal but getting there. Seeing dementia patients in pain, more confused due to alarms and overhead pages for stat Respiratory Therapy and stat anesthesia: not as normal.

Tying masks on the faces of my dementia patients and taping oxygen tubing to their faces is not fun. Almost all get mitts, so they can't pull out their IV lines. Most are agitated and under-medicated because 99% have undiagnosed COVID, and resident physicians are timid with sedation.

Patients hit me three times this week. I turned in time to have the hits get my shoulder and back. One confused patient kicked me, but not hard. Here in the pandemic ED is another new normal: it's so noisy no one can hear you scream for help.

Deb's COVID Diary, April 28-29, 2020, Brooklyn, NY — Maimonides Emergency Department

Growing up in Stanley, there wasn't a lot to do except get in trouble. That's changed with the arrival of extracurricular activities and the internet, although kids still manage to find trouble.

"Deb, always remember: the road that takes you away can bring you home." When Jerry Funderberg spoke those calming words to me, he must have sensed how emotional I was. I was filling my car's gas tank at Jerry's Country Store, leaving Stanley behind for the first time. The road ahead would take me to my BSN in Minneapolis and a whole new life. Over the decades, Jerry's words have stayed with me: No matter what happened, I could come home.

"Oh shit! I grew up to be my mother!" Oh, I hoped that wouldn't happen. Some things I can't change. If you listen carefully when I speak, you can hear Kentucky and Indiana mixed in with Idaho. And there's the "the look:" Mom's pissed-off, penetrating look that could peel paint off the walls. I got that, too. Finally, Mom describes me as stubborn and independent. Okay, but what about her?

Mom loved rural medicine and emergency care. Me, I loved critical care and the ICU. However, nurses are hurt lifting patients, and I mostly had to give up the ICU. But like Mom, I am at home doing emergency care. And try running a hospital emergency department without experienced nurses.

"Why don't you get your nurse practitioner degree?" Mom asked. Why? Even before COVID, I did more hands-on patient care than an NP. I do emergency care. No matter how much COVID turns hospital ERs into war zones, I am at peace with being a nurse doing emergency care.

In honor of Mom's seventieth birthday, two years after she "retired" from the Stanley Clinic, I wrote a birthday message that holds true with the years:

Putting down my wishes for you on your birthday isn't easy. How does one write down the words to express how wonderful a mother you are? You managed through some difficult times and still raised five children, all who love you very much.

All the people you have touched in your life can never be as lucky as we are because we are your children. We have had you as a role model (and still do, for that matter), a friend, confidant, healer, babysitter, and mother.

Cal and Marie's love of Idaho's Sawtooth Mountains shaped and changed all five of their children. (LEFT TO RIGHT) *Cal Jr., Melinda, Jerry, Debbie, and John.*

31

WOMEN IN MEDICINE

"It is not easy to be a pioneer — but oh, it is fascinating!"

Elizabeth Blackwell (1821 – 1910), first woman in the United States to receive a medical degree, in 1849

"I decided that my mission was to care for and about people in compassionate and caring ways."

Loretta Ford, American nurse and co-founder of the first NP program, in pediatrics, in 1965

Women being subservient to men marks much of America's history: Women couldn't vote and had little or no control over finances, property, and even their bodies on matters of birth control.

The Declaration of Independence is notable for the absence of signatures of women (also those of Black and Indigenous leaders).

For women, our independence supposedly came with the women's suffrage movement and, later, the birth control pill and reproductive rights.

Still, even by the early 1970s, women were not considered equal to men. Young women may have thought they had achieved independence, but most men did not agree.

When, in the 1940s, I told our family physician, Dr. Tucker, also a man, "I want to be a doctor," he responded, "Marie, you're too feminine to be a doctor. You should go into nursing." Doctors were men. Nurses were women. That's just how it was.

Healthcare meant nursing for a female in the 1940s and 1950s. And that's just how it was. Even if a medical school had accepted me, my family had no money.

Nurses had to adhere to strict dress codes in the 1950s. I wore a white uniform, including white hose with seams up the back of the legs. In addition, we had to wear a white nurse's cap, which was our badge of honor advertising our school.

In those days when a doctor walked into the room, we, as nurses, stood and offered our chair to him, and he almost always sat in the warmed chair. Failure to stand up for the doctor could be reported to our supervisor, resulting in disciplinary action.

Today, when my son, a doctor, shares that story with nurses he works with in a Seattle ER, they laugh: "Really? Oh, come on. That can't be true." It was.

When I opened the Stanley Clinic, one of my clinic board members insisted that I wear the traditional white nursing uniform, cap, blouse, dress hose, and shoes.

Really? Imagine being on your knees in a ditch along a highway, pulling someone out of a wrecked vehicle. Whites don't work.

My NP uniform was a white lab coat, blue jeans, and cowboy or hiking boots.

Medical schools didn't start accepting women in significant numbers until the 1970s. Even then, females made up a small minority of each class.

Today, in most hospital emergency departments, you'll likely see women and men as nurses, paramedics and EMTs, pharmacists, NPs and PAs, and doctors.

> *"Matchmaker, Matchmaker*
> *Look through your book,*
> *And make me a perfect match"*
>
> Fiddler on the Roof

How do we match healthcare positions with providers? We recognize the value of long-term patient-provider relationships, especially in primary care.

On the one hand, this matchmaking involves the need for clinics and hospitals to staff with competent healthcare providers. For example, when I retired from the Stanley Clinic in 1999, the clinic board struggled to recruit and retain my replacement, eventually succeeding with another advanced practice provider, Amy Klingler.

On the other side of the match are those of us entering healthcare. "One size fits one;" each of us is unique. For example, I knew I wanted to care for patients as a young girl even before working in Indiana's polio wards.

My son John wanted to be a doctor by the time he was five years old. Amy Klingler walked into the Stanley Clinic as a young woman and knew, at that moment, that caring for patients was her destiny; she became a PA and has remained at the clinic. Others, like KT Fisher, realized later in life that their calling was patient care. No two of us are alike in healthcare.

Why is matchmaking so fraught, especially for rural clinics and hospitals? After reading this memoir, the list of reasons should be obvious: length of training, education costs, student debt, office hours and call schedules, marriage and childbearing, happiness of spouses, quality education for kids, quality of life, and adequacy of diagnostics and medical and surgical specialty support. Is it any wonder America struggles with rural healthcare?

One lesson from the Stanley Clinic is that NPs and PAs can staff rural clinics where physicians can't or won't. Still, one benefit of the Stanley Clinic's premed and medical student training programs is the experience in rural healthcare. Even if premeds end up heading an organ transplant program for the Mayo Clinic, they will have walked in the shoes of clinical colleagues struggling, with far fewer resources, to care for our patients in rural America.

Life is a fickle matchmaker. You start on a path in one direction, and life can take you entirely elsewhere. Regardless, caring for patients is a commitment grounded in medical science and steeped in history and ethics.

One of my students was KT Fisher. KT decided early on that she wanted to be a poet and, in college, also a writer of science books for children. But then, life intervened and took her down a different path. The summer after college graduation, the Sawtooth Mountains and her boyfriend being a premed student at the clinic attracted her to Stanley. The Stanley Clinic changed her life's path as it continues to change the lives of so many students.

KT FISHER, DO, IN HER OWN WORDS

Who wouldn't want to spend the summer in Stanley if they weren't entirely sure of their next steps in life? We had graduated from college. Now what? I was an aspiring writer; does a writer just start writing? Or go to grad school to delay adult decisions a while longer? And what about student loan debt? Some of the boys were heading up to work at the Stanley Clinic as premed interns for the summer. Some of their girlfriends tagged along. We got jobs working for Maxine at the Armada Café, waiting tables and washing dishes.

I had no intention of going into medicine. Born and raised in LA, as a student at the College of Idaho for a liberal arts degree, I had to take one science class. I took Biology 101 during my first semester and fell in love with

KT Fisher, who trained under Marie. KT and other women, encountering male-dominated healthcare programs and professions, created trails for women and men who followed.

biology. Envisioning a life of writing children's biology books (awakening to the reality that a poet might have trouble paying the rent), I kept my major in English while adding a second major in Biology and, later, a third, Human Ecology.

In Stanley, my premed boyfriend mentioned that Marie was starting an EMT class. Marie encouraged her premed interns to become EMTs and help with the Stanley Ambulance. Stanley's locals also signed up. I'd never taken a first aid class, but I signed up and became an EMT.

As a volunteer EMT, I went on ambulance runs. Also, I took training on how to drive the ambulance, although that terrified me. I preferred being in the back with the person trying to die. Marie took me under her wing, and I started spending more time at the clinic.

On Saturday night with the Stanley Stomp and the town's three bars, Marie did a lot of sewing. Those open wounds smelled bad to me. I wondered if gaping wounds had an odor or if it was the lidocaine. Marie wasn't sure what I was smelling; to her it all seemed normal. It turns out the vast majority of these weekend patients who needed to be sutured reeked of alcohol and tobacco, the combination of which was foreign to me until that summer.

When Marie realized what it was, she gave me that *look* over the top of her glasses that could have many meanings, this time meaning, "Girl, you have so much to learn."

Before my first Sawtooth summer, in 1976, even began, a prominent Idaho businessman, N.L. Terteling, recruited me to work for him. The Terteling Company, headquartered in Boise, is the parent company for Western States Equipment and Agri-Services. Mr. Terteling and I met during my graduation ceremony at the College of Idaho, where he served on the board and was a friend of my mother's North Idaho family.

Though itching to join my friends to celebrate graduation, my parents raised me to be polite and converse with my elders when invited. We had one of those graduation-day conversations: "Congratulations, young lady. What are you going to do with the rest of your life?"

"I want to be a writer. But for the summer, I'm going up to Stanley."

"Well, I want you to come to work for me."

"Thank you, sir, but I've already made plans to go to Stanley to be with friends." Young and naive, I didn't know a job offer when I heard one. "If there's still a job at the end of summer in Boise, I will come to work for you then." I knew my boyfriend was moving to Boise after Stanley, which helped my decision.

Later that summer in Stanley's Armada Café, the phone rang. "Hey, KT, someone on the phone for you!" yelled one of the other waitresses.

"Hello?" I said, a little out of breath after serving plates of food.

"KT, this is N.L Terteling." He had tracked me down, called the restaurant, and tried again to talk me into working for him in Boise.

"Gee, thanks, Mr. Terteling. Right now, I'm in Stanley working in a restaurant. But, if there's still a job in September, I'll take it." And when autumn arrived, I departed the Sawtooths for Mr. Terteling's office in Boise.

I hadn't thought much about what "office work" entailed. Mr. Terteling sent me to secretarial classes where I learned typing and shorthand. Years later, when I started medical school, knowing shorthand was a godsend.

Because he knew I wanted to be a writer and recognized I would be a lousy secretary, Mr. Terteling assigned me to research and write his family's history. It was a remarkable history, and I loved researching and interviewing retired company employees. After two and a half years, as I neared completion of the book, the company brought in a male author. When the company eventually published the book, the man listed as the author mentioned me — as helping with the research. That experience reminded me that doors remained closed to women.

While working for Mr. Terteling, I returned to Stanley on weekends during the summer of 1977. Marie needed help getting clinic supplies from Boise. So, on Fridays, I would swing by the medical supply stores in Boise, pick up her orders, and drop off supplies at the Stanley Clinic. I stayed with Marie at her cabin. When the emergency calls came, I went with her. I volunteered for ambulance runs as a driver or EMT. During my weekends in Stanley, I spent more and more time in the clinic.

Working at J.A. Terteling and Sons early on made me realize the business world was not for me. I remained in close contact with Marie and looked at her with her idealism and commitment to her patients and community. At the time, I naively thought the medical field was altruistic compared to the business world. So, I called Marie one day in 1977.

"Marie, what would I have to do to become a nurse practitioner?"

Remember that in the 1970s, after early support from the Idaho Boards of Medicine, Pharmacy, and Nursing, NPs were increasingly in the crosshairs. The Idaho Board of Medicine seemed driven to close the Stanley Clinic. Among Idaho's small number of NPs, Marie was the lowest paid. Indeed, it wasn't clear in Idaho that the NP profession would survive the 1970s. Given that context, Marie's response to me was unsurprising.

"KT, don't waste your time," Marie said. "Go be a doctor."

"No, no, Marie. I'm serious."

"No, I'm serious too. Go to medical school. You should be giving orders, not taking them."

That telephone call with Marie was an absolutely life-changing conversation.

To attend medical school, I would need physics, calculus, and organic chemistry courses. I juggled my full-time work writing the Terteling family history with taking premed classes.

Finally, two years later, in the fall of 1978, I applied for medical school.

My parents were ecstatic. "KT, you should come back down here to California." They inundated me with newspaper articles about the new osteopathy school near Pomona, where they lived. My mother had worked as an office nurse for an obstetrician who was a DO. I was born in the osteopathic hospital in Pomona. Also, the DO profession had always been more welcoming to women, even as early as the 1800s. So, becoming a DO rather than an MD became my path.

"I don't feel ready, and I won't get in on my first try, but applying now will be good practice," I told myself. So, I applied to just one medical school: the DO school in Pomona, College of Osteopathic Medicine of the Pacific, later to become the sprawling Western University of Health Sciences. The school invited me for an interview.

When the day came, I sat down with several male doctors for my interview. One question has stayed with me, not because of the question but because of my first-ever quick comeback.

"How come a girl like you isn't married yet?"

I could hear the unspoken question: "Why would a girl like you want to be a doctor?" I was, after all, at the ripe old age of twenty-four.

"Because I haven't yet met a man worth spending the rest of my life with," I replied. The men chuckled nervously, and we moved on.

The day my acceptance letter arrived, my trial run turned into the real thing. I was one of five women in my class of fifty-five medical students, and I would become Dr. Fisher, a physician, not a poet or writer.

After two years of classrooms and labs, my first clinical rotation was my elective. Clerkships had to be with physicians, not nurse practitioners, so that I couldn't return to the routine of the Stanley Clinic. Instead, I got as close as possible: I returned to the Sawtooth country to start my clinical experience with Dr. Stone in Ketchum.

Though he worked long hours, Dr. Stone and his wife, Ann, taught me how to balance life and work. A trained surgeon, Dr. Stone was a true rural physician who did primary care, obstetrics, and general surgery. In my entire career, I never met another physician as versatile as Dr. Stone.

When Dr. Stone got called out for emergencies, I tagged along. If he diagnosed a hot gall bladder in the clinic, I followed him to the operating room. When a woman was in labor, I met them at the hospital.On weekends, I drove over Galena Summit, stayed with Marie at her cabin, and went on emergency calls.

In a big teaching hospital, medical students are low on the ladder: below interns, residents, and fellows. As a medical student in those big hospitals during rounds at the bedside, you mainly observe. Not so in Ketchum and especially not in Stanley. In Ketchum, it was Dr. Stone and me; in Stanley, Marie and me.

Having made it through medical school, I faced the next hurdle: internship and residency. I had decided on internal medicine and was doing my residency in Portland, Oregon. Marie and I were still in close contact, and in my third year, she asked if I wanted to spend some time in her clinic. She had not had a vacation in a long time and wanted to leave the Valley for a week or two.

A third-year resident is a fully licensed physician and does not need a supervisor. However, I knew Marie handled more emergencies in a month than many physicians would ever see.

It was intimidating, but I agreed, knowing Dr. Stone was only sixty miles away. And, it was the off-season for tourists. It would be a quiet month. What could go wrong? I arranged to do a month's elective at the clinic.

The clinic was quiet, with only a few patients. But then, the phone rang.

"Salmon River Emergency Clinic. Dr. Fisher."

"We're calling from the Clayton mine. My buddy was pipetting cyanide and swallowed it. I don't know what to do. He's turning blue. I'm bringing him to the clinic." In caring for patients, when people have a bluish cast, we describe them as having "cyanosis." The word cyanosis looks a lot like another word: cyanide.

Bedside manner compels caregivers to be careful with communication. When working with Marie, you learn to be non-judgmental, wear a never-show-panic poker face, and speak calmly. So, I didn't blurt out what I thought, "Oh my God!" Instead, I responded reassuringly, "Okay, I'll see you when you arrive. Drive carefully." Then, my mind started racing.

My first call was to Poison Control. We didn't have internet back then, and the clinic's medical library didn't have treatment recommendations for cyanide poisoning. In those years, if you didn't have a book on the shelf, then you were on the phone searching for someone to help — if the phones were working. I picked up the phone and dialed with a life-threatening emergency headed my way.

When I heard the pickup on the gravel and the door slam, I opened the clinic's front door and helped the two miners back to a treatment room. Just saying "cyanide" will put people in a panic.

The miner calling me before heading to the clinic gave me time to panic calmly. After the patient arrived, his buddy was crazy anxious, pacing the clinic hallway. I had recently married, and my "non-medical" husband, who had come to Stanley with me, was responsible for corralling the buddy, especially keeping him away from the exam room.

I ran tubing from the oxygen tank to the patient, put a mask over his nose and mouth, and turned on the oxygen. Next, I called Dr. Stone in Ketchum.

The cyanide-poisoned miner sat tachypneic (abnormally shallow, rapid breathing), terrified, and motionless behind his oxygen mask. He was indeed cyanotic. I remember thinking, "How blue is blue?" I'd never seen true cyanosis. "Is he getting more blue, or is that the same shade of blue?" Mainly, I remember that deep blue around the miner's mouth and trying to assess whether he was getting better or worse.

Cyanide competes with oxygen and preferentially binds to oxygen receptor sites. Today, you might reach for a cyanide antidote kit in a busy, well-stocked ER. But in Stanley, in the early eighties, the treatment was supplemental oxygen and time.

In a teaching hospital, all kinds of experts converge at the bedside. In Stanley, it's just you learning by the seat of your pants. Calm and professional on the outside, scared on the inside, you never forget.

Dr. Stone said, "Keep giving oxygen."

"Shouldn't we load him into the ambulance and send him over the hill?" Please say yes, I thought.

"No, you're doing fine." Really?

It was good that Marie kept a full tank of oxygen at the clinic, because that big green tank kept my patient alive. After a long day, the miner left the clinic, less blue and breathing much easier.

Later, the miners invited us to take a grand tour of their operation. At the end of the gold extraction, they had a pyramid shaped block with gold at its point. We took pictures of ourselves holding a bazillion dollars in gold.

Roland Miller

A helicopter on Highway 75 near Robinson Bar Ranch and the Salmon River "Narrows." Downriver, at the scene of the mass-casualty event, the Stanley Ambulance crew triaged and stabilized patients before transporting them to the helicopter. The severely injured were airlifted to Boise. Agency staff were key. What are the roles and responsibilities of state and federal public land and wildlife agencies in providing and supporting rural EMS?

"That was one of the worst motorcycle accidents I've ever seen," Marie recalled later.

Motorcyclists, perhaps ten or twelve, were driving upriver from Challis. These were youngish bikers in their thirties and forties, some wearing leathers and others in T-shirts on that hot day. The bikers weren't a head-to-toe leather-clad "Hell's Angels" type of gang. They were just friends out for a ride.

At the same time, two local males, sixteen and twenty-one, were driving downriver.

Later, the local deputy tried to explain away what happened, that it wasn't their fault. Still, alcohol, testosterone, and poor judgment combined to place the pickup on the wrong side of the road, coming around a blind curve. The pickup collided with the motorcycle riders on that awful curve at the Salmon River Narrows just across from Robinson Bar Ranch.

We were at the Stanley Clinic in the early afternoon when the emergency call came. We ran for the ambulance and headed downriver on Highway 75. Forest Service EMTs arrived in agency rigs. Piling out of the ambulance, we saw bodies and wrecked motorcycles strewn across the highway. Groans and cries for help mixed with sounds from the river rapids below.

Marie was in total control. At least five motorcyclists were down. I still hear her voice: "You, take care of that person; you, that person. KT, take the woman in the ditch." Marie then began her assessments, placing IVs, starting fluids, and calling StateComm on the radio.

The woman in the ditch, wearing a short-sleeved blouse, looked dead. Having the least trauma experience of anyone, I assumed Marie had sent me to a body. But then, the woman opened her eyes. She looked up at me and whispered.

"Help me." And then, she was quiet.

"Marie, I need help over here." She was in shock when I first knelt beside her. So was I — and I knew enough to yell for help.

The woman's lower extremity, probably caught between the truck and her motorcycle, shattered at a weird angle. When we did a neuro exam, the biker was able to tell us she couldn't feel anything below her nipple line. We later learned she had multiple fractures involving her back and lower extremity. We placed a cervical collar and backboard to stabilize her spine, then a Hare traction splint to stabilize the lower extremity fractures.

Meanwhile, Idaho EMS StateComm launched helicopters from Boise while we ambulanced the woman to a nearby makeshift heli-spot for transport. She had to get to Boise quickly or die. She never would have survived ground-ambulance transport.

She lived, and so did the other bikers. Those who volunteered to take the call saved lives. We filled theStanley Ambulance to maximum capacity that day. The EMT volunteers, all trained by Marie, were the star players in a life-saving team.

When transporting by air ambulance, we preferred helicopters over fixed-wing aircraft. But, sometimes, you go with what you can get.

"My son can't breathe" is how that day started at the Stanley Clinic. The child, small enough to sit on his mother's lap, was wheezing and struggling with uncontrolled asthma. We moved him back to a treatment room. Despite everything Marie tried, including theophylline, she couldn't break the asthma attack.

"He's got to go to Sun Valley by air. He's too sick to go by ambulance." Marie was on the phone with Bob Danner and, in a few minutes, had a plane and pilot. Marie then turned and looked at me. "KT, I want you to go with the boy."

I was still a premed. And that plane? It was itty-bitty. At the Stanley airport, one of Idaho's premier backcountry airstrips, the boy's parents and I squirmed into Danner's airplane, and Marie handed us the boy on oxygen. He was doing better, and I concluded that Marie was sending me for the experience and to assure the parents, not because I could be helpful. Still, I thought, "Now, what if something happens while we're airborne?" And trying to remember what the EMT book taught us about asthma, what my mom did for my little brother's asthma, and...and...and.... I had several terrors. First was being in that little plane. Second was this little patient, still short of breath and wheezing.

Our pilot got us airborne, and we flew south down the Sawtooth Valley. The child was sitting and wheezing on his mother's lap. I kept my hand on the boy's back, counting respirations the whole flight and thinking, "Just keep breathing, just keep breathing." I may have seemed calm and controlled on the outside, but inside? I was terrified that the child would go into respiratory arrest while in that little plane.

We flew over Galena Summit and down the Wood River Valley before landing in Hailey. Helicopters can land and offload patients at a hospital, but airplanes need a landing strip. For Sun Valley, that meant landing fifteen miles and thirty minutes away at the Hailey airport. The Hailey ambulance was waiting for us on the tarmac.

After giving my report to the ER staff, I made a telephone call to Marie. "Hey, Marie. We got the boy to the ER. He's doing fine. I have a problem: I don't have a way to get back." Our plane wasn't returning to Stanley, and I was stuck. Marie sent one of the College of Idaho premeds to fetch me.

Sometimes, you have to wonder about doctors who should know better.

With Saturday night bar trauma, Marie often stayed at the clinic until after the last call for alcohol before heading home. Early that morning, she was at her cabin when a trauma case walked through the clinic door. The woman had been drinking and stumbled while walking back to her motel room, fell down a hill, and ended up with a minor scalp laceration behind her left ear. The premeds helped the woman back to a treatment room. With her was a friend, an anesthesiologist. In the morning, both women were heading out on a multi-day Middle Fork rafting trip.

We called Marie. She had just arrived home after a long day and evening at the clinic. After several summers interning at the clinic, Ken knew how to suture. And the laceration was small, on the scalp and behind the ear. Marie was deciding whether to drive back to town when our patient's companion interjected.

"I'm an anesthesiologist," the doctor said with authority. "I can sew her up if you give me permission." After a long silence, Marie gave the go-ahead. "But she'll need to come back in the morning so I can look at the wound," Marie said.

Ken and I provided a sterile suture kit, betadine, lidocaine, and suture material. When we asked about sterile gloves, the doctor said, "I take a size six. And I'll need a razor."

We were just premed students, and she was a real doctor. So, we stood back and observed, as we had with Marie. Only the doctor picked up the razor and began shaving her friend's hair. The doctor shaved the entire back half of her friend's head, not just around the laceration.

Ken and I looked at each other across the exam table. The now-exposed wound was maybe an inch long at the most. Unsaid, after watching the doctor shave her friend's head, we concluded she, too, had been drinking. After shaving half of her friend's head, the anesthesiologist placed a few sutures, and they left the clinic for the motel.

Marie has a way of saying a thousand words with one raised eyebrow, "the look" that could sink ships. Woe to the student caught in that stare. Marie was in the clinic the following day when the two women returned for the routine wound check. First, Marie stared at the hungover woman's half-shaved head and tiny laceration. Next, she turned to Ken and me, glaring over her glasses with that look that said, "What the hell were you thinking?" Finally, we explained that we were only observers and that the doctor had managed the wound.

The patient left for her rafting trip with half a head of hair. Marie was relieved that neither Ken nor I had done the deed.

The anesthesiologist? When she sobered up, the doctor may have been surprised by her wound-management skills.

There are times in healthcare when one needs to be especially sensitive and careful around women. Responding to rape is one of those times.

For years I had nightmares about a woman who survived a brutal rape mutilation at Stanley Lake. Campers found her and then transported her to the Stanley Clinic in the midst of a busy Saturday night. We moved her back to a treatment room.

When Marie and I walked in, we saw a woman in shock who had been raped, mutilated, and nearly murdered, her naked body covered with a sheet, surrounded by ten men: law enforcement and male EMTs. The men were stunned — and curious. I'm amazed at how insensitive the medical system was then on matters of rape, and sometimes still is.

"Not everyone needs to be in this room," Marie said. "All you men need to sit out in the waiting room."

The sheriff looked down on 4-foot-11-inches of Marie, considered, and retreated to the reception room while Marie and I completed the initial evaluation.

I was the only female EMT available for the Stanley Ambulance that night and volunteered. On the way to Sun Valley, the woman didn't want to talk. "You are safe now," I kept trying to reassure her. I didn't understand then that after a trauma like that, there is no "feeling safe," not then and maybe not ever. That was a long ambulance ride over Galena Summit.

I was there with Marie through her divorce from Cal and her second divorce from Tom. To help Marie heal after her second divorce, we went to Maui. Our tropical vacation didn't last long. Bearing down on the islands was Hurricane Iwa, which turned out to be the costliest and most damaging storm to hit the state up to that time. Marie and I caught the last flight out of Maui for Honolulu. In Honolulu, we had a suite on the fourteenth floor, but the hotel had no power. Our elevators didn't work, and the penthouse windows and balcony doors wouldn't open. Marie, in her early fifties, had trouble with the stairs. She did not mention the blood in her stool. Little did we realize Marie was becoming progressively anemic from the colon cancer growing within her.

I came of age during the late 1960s and '70s, excited because women could become anything they wanted. My daughter tells me how crazy I am to have thought that.

During my first year of residency training in Portland, my program had scheduled my surgery rotation at a community hospital.

One of my attending surgeons did his chart rounds in the doctors' lounge, which doubled as the men's changing room. The women's changing room was the nurses' lounge. I had a choice: miss chart rounds or attend while the men were changing. I decided, "Okay, I'm now a physician. I may be a woman, but I'm going in."

Male doctors were appalled. An ophthalmologist thought my presence was atrocious and stripped down in front of me. Other male doctors grabbed clothes from their lockers during chart rounds and stepped into the bathroom to change. I was the lone female physician, and the male physician establishment didn't know what to do with me. Conference rooms were available, but the attending surgeon wasn't about to mess with tradition.

Some male doctors seemed to save their dirtiest jokes during surgery when I was scrubbed in. You can't break scrub or talk back because, in a patriarchal specialty like surgery, you didn't.

While observing a coronary artery bypass surgery as a medical student in Southern California, I stood at the patient's head with the anesthesiologist. He was male and provided a stool so I could stand, look over the drapes, and watch. Throughout the surgery, the anesthesiologist kept touching my butt. In those years, you kept silent so you could watch and learn.

Finally, when the case was over, I stepped off the stool, turned, and my elbow "accidentally" nailed him in the face. "Excuse me," I said — with the word left unsaid: "Jerk."

Gender discrimination in the 1970s and '80s came in many forms, overt and subtle. With it came intimidation and embarrassment, intending to make you feel like you didn't belong. Marie didn't let it get to her; subsequently, neither did I nor many women in those earlier years.

As baby boomers, I don't think we fully experienced the gender discrimination our mothers faced. And we hope our daughters now won't experience the discrimination we felt.

At my medical school graduation, my mother shared a secret. She, too, wanted to be a doctor. When she was a nurse working for an OB-GYN, he offered to pay her way to medical school. It was the early 1940s. She had to choose: Go to medical school or marry my father. She married. That's what women did.

When I walked across the stage and accepted my diploma, becoming a doctor fulfilled my mother's dream. For women, doors that were long closed were opening.

My parents didn't talk about their lives before WWII when they were young, and my father never spoke about the war. Only later, after my mother had died and my sister and I were going through their old letters, did we discover that our parents had eloped during the war. Our family didn't talk about a lot of things. Then I met this woman, Marie Osborn, who was willing to talk about everything.

Marie ran toward trouble. She thrived on emergency calls. The more dangerous and challenging the situation, pulling people out of rivers or off mountains, the more she loved her work. For me, the more dangerous it got, the higher my heart rate went.

The Stanley Clinic taught me that I wanted to devote my life to medicine and helped me understand that there were types of medicine I didn't want to do. I ended up in internal medicine and teaching. I was more comfortable caring for complicated, multi-system diseases in middle-aged and elderly patients than a sick, unresponsive baby.

In Stanley, I learned how to dance. I learned that you could work on your feet all day as a waitress and then dance for hours at the bar at night. It was just a matter of endurance.

Something else that was a life lesson: Everybody in town told Marie their secrets. She knew about all the marriage problems, domestic violence, business problems, and more. Yet she never gossiped. People told her everything, and she shared nothing. It went into her head and stayed there. Keeping patient information confidential is an absolute. Sometimes people did try to extract information from Marie. "Hey, was so-and-so in the clinic?" Or, "Did my wife come to see you?" But, in the drama of that small town, Marie was tight-lipped.

Another lesson from Marie: She always treated people with respect, whether the sheriff or the drunks. She cared for people you would never want to spend time with, treating them respectfully when they walked in the clinic door.

Marie broke new ground for women. I didn't want to be a "Mrs." and "Miss" could sometimes sound condescending. "Ms." didn't feel right, either. I resolved all that by becoming "Dr."— all because of a phone call to my mentor and my friend, Marie.

32

CANCER

*"The days of our lives, for all of us, are numbered.
We know that. And yes, there are certainly times when we aren't able to muster
as much strength and patience as we would like. It's called being human."*

Elizabeth Edwards (1949 – 2010, attorney, author, and healthcare activitist)

On Friday afternoon, I sat alone in the radiology department waiting room at Moritz Hospital in Sun Valley. Periodically, one of the radiology techs would come out and try to reassure me, "We're just waiting for someone to come and read the x-ray." They explained that everyone was gone, and this was their slack time when staff left for vacation.

"Dr. Krielkamp will come to the hospital as soon as he finishes with the clinic," the techs reassured me. That Friday, Dr. Bernard Krielkamp, an internist, was the sole clinician seeing patients at Ketchum Medical Clinic. Unfortunately, that day, he was swamped. I resigned myself to sitting there, waiting.

"Marie, come on in here." Dr. Davis, the Chief Radiologist, had arrived. He was in the reading room, with my x-rays from the barium enema displayed on the viewing boxes.

I stood up, entered the reading room, and examined the X-rays. I saw it. The tumor looked huge and nodular, appearing to extend outside the wall of my colon. I knew what it was and told Dr. Davis, "Well, you know, a janitor could diagnose this." We talked for a while. He probably feared I would become hysterical and tried to calm me. I'm not the hysterical type. Still, Dr. Davis was especially friendly to me that day.

I got dressed and walked out the front door of the hospital. Coming up the walk was Dr. Krielkamp. He's a big bear of a man. He wrapped his arms around me, and I fell apart sobbing. It took me a while to stop.

I was scared. Looking at my x-rays and that cancer was like peering into the future and seeing my death. I finished crying, thanked Dr. Krielkamp, got in the car, and drove home to my Sawtooth Mountains, struggling with thoughts of life, death, and cancer growing within me.

Marie was unaware of her colon cancer and progressing anemia as she became increasingly weak and short of breath. Her home is at 7,100 feet, and she contended with a sled attached to her snowmobile during her commute to see patients.

In the summer of 1982, about eight months before my diagnosis, I started having constipation with bleeding. "I'm sure it's just hemorrhoids," I self-diagnosed.

Summer in Stanley is stressful, with 24/7 emergency calls, multiple ambulance runs, and no sleep. That summer of 1982 was awful, with many difficult accidents. Added in was the stress from going through my second divorce. Surely, these tensions were contributing to my bleeding.

I am not alone in running down the rabbit hole to hide from a potentially bad diagnosis. For my patients, I would have insisted on diagnostics. But for me, as the clinician, I disregarded the warnings. I personified "Do as I say, not as I do." My excuses seemed plausible at the time. Also, the bleeding stopped, and things seemed just fine. That fall, I traveled to Hawaii with former student KT Fisher. Except for Hurricane Iwa, we had a great time. While traveling, the bleeding started again. I blamed it on stress from the hurricane and its aftermath: being unable to find food, walking multiple flights of stairs without an elevator, and living in the building lobby in Honolulu without electricity.

When I returned to Stanley, the bleeding eased off. I managed to get through Christmas but wasn't feeling well and seemed to tire quickly. Usually, wintertime was my time to play. However, my home is at 7,100 feet, and I increasingly felt the altitude. Two miles of snowmobiling from house to highway made me increasingly short of breath.

In 1983, if I had a patient with rectal bleeding, I would start the diagnostic evaluation by scheduling a barium enema X-ray, a radiographic procedure replaced by colonoscopies. A barium enema begins with the technician inserting a tube with a balloon into your patient and inflating it to hold the tube in place. Barium liquid then flows through the tubing, filling up the colon. The radiology tech takes X-rays while you have this intense feeling that you really have to go to the bathroom, but can't until the technician deflates the balloon. It's miserable.

My barium enema was scheduled for a Wednesday. I started the bowel prep, diet, and laxatives. Unfortunately, a bad snowstorm hit the central Idaho mountains, closing Galena Summit on Tuesday night. Highway crews would take a day or more to clear the snow. The radiology department staff and I talked by telephone back and forth, and they suggested rescheduling the procedure for a week or two. "No," I replied. "Let's continue with the prep and do the barium enema on Friday. I know these guys up here. They'll have Galena open by Friday."

Looking south from Marie's home toward Galena Summit. Winter blizzards can close the highway to Ketchum. A bad snowstorm closed the summit the night before Marie's barium enema.

Most healthcare professionals will shake their heads, "Marie, how could you have waited eight months before getting studied?" I don't have a good answer. None of us is infallible, and my mistake nearly cost me my life. But one thing was sure: I had colon cancer.

I telephoned each of my five children. My last call was to John, who I spoke with at SeaTac airport. He was about to board a flight to Bangkok, heading for his final medical school clerkship at McCormick Hospital, a Presbyterian mission hospital in Chiang Mai, Thailand.

"Mom, I'm going to cancel my trip," John said, with SeaTac's PA system calling flights in the background. "Absolutely not," I replied. "You are going to get on that plane and finish medical school. I'll be fine." I spoke with optimism and reassurance, but I felt growing anxiety and fear. John departed for southeast Asia, and I prepared to head to the operating room.

The day following the barium enema, the phone rang at my Shaw Mesa home. It was Gus, my surgeon, telling me the OR staff had scheduled me for Tuesday morning. There were no alternatives at this point. Gus started me on antibiotics.

Gus is Dr. Gustafson, the surgeon on staff at Ketchum Medical Clinic. He was an excellent surgeon and a fine person. If the Stanley Ambulance crew needed a surgery team waiting in the ER, Gus would ensure the surgery team was there. He was caring and empathetic, had a feel for the body, and had great hands.

My relationship with Gus changed abruptly from colleague to patient with my cancer diagnosis. When healthcare providers become patients, we move from one side of the stethoscope to the other, from being in control to losing control and depending on others.

The colon cancer that nearly killed me also taught me how kind people can be and how much the little things count when you're on the receiving end of healthcare. Trust in your doctors is vital when you make life-or-death decisions. I trusted Gus.

On Monday evening, I drove up the Sawtooth Valley, over Galena Summit, parked at the hospital, entered, and walked to the nurses' station. Feeling unsettled and alone, I slowly walked down the hall and into my hospital room.

Flowers filled the room, not just a bouquet or two of roses. Facing colon cancer and major abdominal surgery, walking into a room of gorgeous flowers was overwhelming. The guy I was dating at the time had used some of his winnings from gambling in Jackpot, Nevada, to buy flowers for me. At the time, it was a beautiful gesture. Those flowers lifted my spirits and gave me hope.

On Tuesday, I awoke early. My youngest daughter, Debbie, was with me as the staff wheeled me into the OR. Debbie had enrolled in the pre-nursing program at Boise State University and drove up from Boise. Being with Debbie and thinking of my five kids was the last thing I remembered.

Before the surgery, I was adamant that I did not want a colostomy, a "poop bag." I developed an aversion to colostomies from my earliest years as a nurse's aide and then in nurses' training. "Marie, if we can avoid one, we will," Gus said. "It will depend on what we find when we get inside and how the surgery goes."

Eight hours later, I awoke from anesthesia and put my hands down on the dressing covering my lower abdomen while in the recovery unit: no colostomy. "That's right, Marie," the recovery unit nurse affirmed. "You made it through surgery without a colostomy." I was jubilant.

After the surgeons resected my cancer and part of my colon, they took the two ends of the colon and sewed them together, creating what's called a primary anastomosis. "Once you pass gas, your colon is working again," Gus said. "Then, you'll be out of the woods."

A day went by, and no gas — then two days and three days — then a whole week. In my entire life, I've never wanted to pass gas as much as I did then.

It's remarkable to consider the difference between major chest and bowel surgery. Those with coronary artery bypass graft (CABG) surgery have this amazing experience: The thoracic surgeon cracks your chest, stops your heart, uses grafted veins or arteries to bypass diseased arteries, restarts your heart, and then wires your chest closed. The next day, you are up walking and will go home soon afterward, barring any complications.

Bowel surgery is different. Watch out when you cut on the abdomen in major surgery. For some patients, recovery is uneventful; their bowels eventually open up, and they go home. For others, including me, the post-operative course is long and stormy, with complications that can be fatal.

My prayers to pass gas went unanswered. I cried. With no nutrition, I became weaker and malnourished, raising risks for nonhealing and infection.

Gus took me back to the operating room at the end of the week. When I awoke from anesthesia, I had a colostomy on the right side of my abdomen. I was devastated and tried to find comfort in it being only temporary.

The nursing staff used Gomco suction, attaching a tube for suction to my colostomy to reduce swelling and fluid build-up. Little had changed from when I was a nurse's aide in the late 1940s, caring for abdominal surgery patients with Gomco suction.

Gus warned me, "Marie, if you're still not passing gas after another week, we'll need to convert the temporary to a permanent colostomy." I prayed harder, "Oh please, God, let me pass gas."

That second week was so depressing. But on the seventh day, one day before returning to the OR, I passed gas. The relief, the joy: Finally, there was light at the end of this awful tunnel. After that, my recovery was long but uneventful. Eventually, I returned to the OR for a colostomy take-down procedure, my third and final abdominal surgery.

Gus discharged me from Moritz Hospital with a qualification: "Marie, I'll discharge you, but I can't have you returning to Stanley. I do not want you riding your snowmobile two miles up that mountain, and I don't want you seeing patients in the clinic."

For the next month, I continued my recovery in Ketchum. For the first week, Gus invited Debbie and me to stay at their family home. After that, we moved to Ketchum's Wagon Wheel Motel for another few weeks.

I want to take this opportunity to thank my daughter, Debbie. I don't know that I would have made it without her. She was my advocate in what were the worst moments of my life, running interference with the nursing staff, taking the brunt of my pain and despair, and staying with me nearly every step of the way. My daughter witnessed cancer stripping her mother of control.

I wash my hair nearly every day, but the nurses were adamant in those weeks after the surgeries: "You cannot wash your hair." Then, one night, when the nurses were busy elsewhere, Debbie rolled my gurney out of my room, down the hall, backed my head up to a sink, and washed my hair. I can't tell you how much that meant. To do something normal: Sometimes, the little things do make life worth living. For each of my five children, my cancer diagnosis had consequences. At a minimum, they each have had to undergo regular colonoscopies because my cancer increases their cancer risk. For Debbie, my cancer disrupted her pre-nurse program and life plans. Caring for me in Ketchum caused Debbie to miss classes at Boise State. She requested leave and the opportunity to make up missed classes later, but they said no, and she dropped out of school. Cal used to say, "When God closes a door, he opens a window." Debbie eventually completed her BSN in Minneapolis.

Word of my stormy post-operative course arrived in Chiang Mai, where John was studying. He was worried sick but was stuck. John had bought a one-way ticket to Bangkok to save money and was planning to buy a cheaper ticket for his return flight. On his second day, his traveler's checks were stolen while traveling by bus from Bangkok to Chiang Mai. Citicorp offered to replace the traveler's checks only after John returned to the United States. Catch 22: he couldn't return unless Citicorp replaced the traveler's checks.

Eventually, Cal interceded, and Citicorp replaced the traveler's checks in Thailand. John bought a ticket home, bypassed his medical school graduation, and came directly to Stanley. Citicorp later donated $500 to the Stanley Clinic to make amends.

People stepped up to cover the Stanley Clinic and Stanley Ambulance during my absence. Under Dr. Stone's supervision, WWAMI medical students and former College of Idaho premeds staffed the clinic and helped with ambulance runs. Steve Lipus taught my EMT course, and Stanley's EMTs pitched in. Still, I needed to get back to work.

With Debbie's help, I got stronger and walked further each day. Eventually, Gus approved my return home to Shaw Mesa.

Once home, I started riding my exercise cycle to regain strength. Soon after returning home, I got on the snowmobile and headed down the hill to see patients.

We got the emergency call. It was my second day back in the clinic. A power-company lineman had fallen off a pole up the Yankee Fork. Challis's first responders were already there when we arrived with the ambulance. We could see the lineman crumpled on the ground high above us on a steep hill.

"He's unconscious," one of the first responders said in giving me the report. "We need you up there to take care of him. What do you think? Can you make it?"

I looked at him and started to shake my head. I still had stitches in my abdomen from my third surgery. "I can't go," I said. "I'm sorry." I knew I wouldn't make it if I tried scrambling up that steep hillside. EMTs carried down the injured lineman. Life Flight arrived and transported him to St. Alphonsus in Boise.

On that day, for the first time, I felt incapable of caring for a patient. It's horrible when someone in trouble needs you, but you can't help them.

By the time John returned home from Thailand, I had regained some of my weight and stamina. Knowing that John missed his medical school graduation in Seattle, the community pulled together his graduation in Stanley.

Dr. Stone read the Hippocratic Oath with townspeople crowded into the clinic and out on the porch. John's

Dr. Stone reading the Hippocratic Oath at John's medical school graduation held at the Stanley Clinic in 1983 after Marie recovered from her cancer surgeries.

mother cried — a lot. Then, the town headed to Redfish Lake Lodge, where the owners, Jack and Patty See, served a delicious chocolate cake with strawberries for the community reception. Cal, John's father, joined us. It was the perfect small-town celebration.

Graduation is a time when you step into a world of challenges you could never have anticipated. Unexpected challenges awaited John. But on that June day in 1983, having survived cancer surgery but not knowing whether cancer recurrence was in my future, I watched with pride as my son reached a milestone: Doctor of Medicine.

Years later, when I talked to Dr. Del Pletcher, an orthopedic surgeon in Ketchum, he disclosed that Gus had stayed up much of the night before my surgery studying and preparing. "What do you mean?" I asked, surprised and dismayed. Had Gus not performed that surgery before?

"A good surgeon wants to be sure of what they're doing," Dr. Pletcher explained. "If necessary, they read, study, and practice before entering the operating room. If something comes up in my practice and I have any questions, then you bet I spend the night before knowing exactly where my hands will go."

Gus thought enough of me to ensure he was ready to walk into the OR and perform my surgery. Because of Gus and the rest of the Sun Valley team, and with support from my daughter Debbie, I survived colon cancer and never had a recurrence.

After I made a near-fatal mistake of ignoring my symptoms, they gave me the gift of life, which I paid forward in caring for patients for nearly thirty years.

33

OF MOUSSE AND MEN

"The odds are good, but the goods are odd."

Anonymous

"The more I see of men, the better I like my dog."

Anonymous

By convention, women change their surname when they marry. In 1953, when I married Cal Osborn, my surname changed from Clark to Osborn. When Cal and I divorced and I married Tom, my last name became Richardson. In 1982, when Tom and I divorced, I changed my last name back to Osborn because of my kids.

After Cal and I divorced, we thought the other would find someone to love. Cal did better than I did. One issue in Stanley is finding a compatible match. In a small town, pickin's can be slim and, to paraphrase the saying, the goods could be odd. As a former bartender and Stanley's sole healthcare provider, I also know that for a town with only fifty year-round residents, three bars, and long winters, alcohol is a problem.

Plus, my patient-care responsibilities would test any traditional marriage.

Tom Richardson seemed a good match for me. The Osborns knew the Richardson family in Boise, and our kids went to school together. Later, Tom was a hotel and bar owner in Yellow Pine, about eighty miles east of McCall, another town with fewer than fifty year-round residents. Tom was an excellent carpenter. He played in a band and was an outfitter, guide, and pilot. He volunteered for search and rescue and took my EMT class. Everyone thought Tom Richardson was pretty cute.

After we married, Tom and I began planning our retirement. I used my savings to buy a 160-acre ranch in the

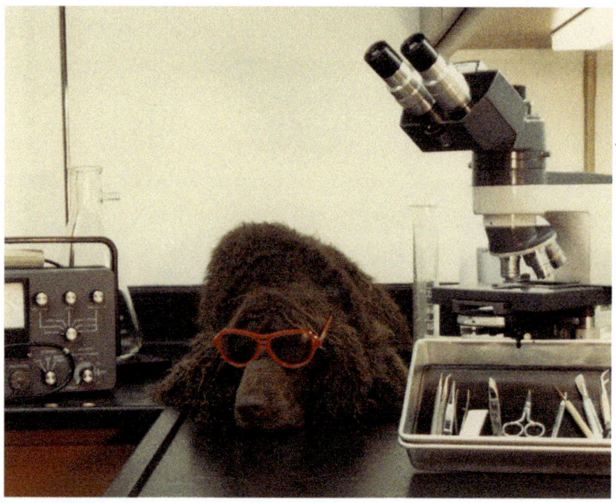

Robert N. Pierce DVM

"My Royal Chocolate Mousse" or just "Mousse," became Marie's closest companion after her two failed marriages. The dog welcomed patients to the Stanley Clinic. With Marie out of the valley, Mousse joined Bev Angel, Jim Funderburg, and Rob Pierce at the clinic lab and on the road.

Pahsimeroi River Valley northeast of Challis, and we moved my horse there. Tomas was a beautiful horse. Piero Piva, of Stanley and Challis, raised Quarter Horses, and had talked with me about working with Tomas to become a racing or rodeo horse. Unfortunately, it was not to be. Our caretaker failed to repair the fence, Tomas got out of the pasture, and a pickup hit him. Our caretaker called the veterinarian, who didn't show up until the next day. Waiting for veterinary care, Tomas bled out.

In a small town with rumor mills, gossip grapevines, and now social media, you must show good sense and be careful with information. Rumors of infidelity are but one example. In our town, friends protected me from the gossip, so I didn't see it coming.

In the summer of 1982, I came home from Boise after picking up supplies. I also picked up a case of cherries because Tom loved cherry pie. Tom was waiting for me on the deck when I got out of my car at the cabin.

"I want you to sit down," Tom said.

I was excited about the cherries. Still, something wasn't right. Tom was smoking a cigarette. He had quit when we married, so he had to be stressed. We sat on the deck.

After a long silence, Tom finally spoke. "I'm seeing someone else."

Tom was packed and ready to leave. He finished his cigarette and walked down the deck to the garage. "I want the butcher block," Tom said.

That old butcher block, made from hard maple and weighing several hundred pounds, had traveled from Challis to Boise before coming home to my cabin in the Sawtooths. How Tom intended to move it into the pickup was a mystery.

"No."

Tom left the garage, got in the pickup, and drove away from my home. Several months later, our marriage legally ended in a courtroom in Challis. With our divorce final, I sold the Pahsimeroi ranch.

After two marriages, no more. At fifty-one and for the rest of my life, I would remain a single woman. Besides, I always had my family and my mountains. They can be your salvation. The mountains never change; at least, not much. I didn't yet know that within a few months, I would be fighting for my life against cancer.

That winter evening in 1985 was beautiful. The White Clouds Mountains glowed pink in the setting sun. It was gorgeous, with the beauty that reached inside, held you, and made you happy to be alive. I was alone on Shaw Mesa except for my dog, Mousse, who had run after my snowmachine, chasing me two miles up from the highway.

I walked into my cabin. I never locked my doors. I removed my helmet and snow pants, put down my daypack with my medical equipment and supplies, and then walked past the wood stove to hang up my jacket. I saw something.

A man stood in the shadows at the bottom of the stairwell.

He was there for one reason.

Rape.

When he was done and zipping up his pants, he held up a gasoline can. "I'm going to burn down your house and kill your dog."

Just at that moment, the phone rang.

"This is Marie," I answered the phone, the man staring at me. The woman's voice on the phone said she was from Clayton. "My baby is sick. She has a fever, and I'm afraid. Marie, I'm sorry to bother you, and I know it's late, but can I bring her to the clinic to see you?"

"Your baby is really sick," I said slowly into the phone, looking at my rapist. "I'll see you in the clinic in thirty minutes," and hung up. I knew that if I didn't show up at the clinic, that mother would call someone. My rapist likely knew that, too.

"I have to go back to town. A baby is sick," I stated. He said nothing.

He followed me as I moved to the door. I climbed up the snowbank and started the snowmobile. He stood against the deck railing. He held my dog, Mousse, with one hand and, with the other, his can of gasoline.

As I snowmobiled away from my home, I felt violated and helpless, not knowing if I had seen my home and dog for the last time. On the ride down the hill to my car parked on the highway, I knew I'd lost control over the outcome. Once in my car, I refocused on getting to the clinic and the sick baby and mother waiting for me.

I walked into the clinic, examined my young patient, and issued antibiotics to the mother. After they left, I called the Fish and Game officer, Gary Gadwa, who was also in law enforcement. I told him what had happened. That night I spent in town with the Gadwa family.

We drove to Challis the following day, and I repeated what had happened to the sheriff.

"Are you sure you want to talk about this?" the sheriff asked. "Wouldn't you rather tell a woman?"

"No. You're the sheriff. I need to tell you what happened." After I finished, the sheriff started legal action.

The man who raped me — I knew him — had already left the valley, disappeared, never to return. Later that day, I returned to Shaw Mesa. My home still stood. At this point, I was afraid I'd never see Mousse again. A local rancher, Morgan Williams, found Mousse and brought him to the cabin. I cried.

Fortunately, Gary's spouse, Laurii Gadwa, trained as a child psychologist and worked with women in crisis. With Laurii's help, I got through it.

For a long time, I had trouble looking at the stairwell. I knew I had to check it but didn't want to. Over time, my fear and anxiety ebbed. As a woman living alone in the Sawtooth country, I kept a gun anyway, but after that, I locked my house.

My closest companion was Mousse, a gift from the Armada Café's Maxine Baptiste and Joanne Shawl. They'd gotten the dog as an award from their boss, but didn't want him. Mousse came home with me.

Mousse's full name was "My Royal," so I renamed him "My Royal Chocolate Mousse." Mousse was a papered American Water Spaniel, sired by Chocolate Charlie. His pedigree didn't matter. What mattered was that Mousse became my faithful companion.

Mousse loved to follow my snowmobile. If it was thirty-five degrees below or colder, he'd jump on the seat and ride with me until we got about halfway between the cabin and the highway, then run the rest of the way to my car parked at the highway. After clinic, Mousse would run up the hill when I got on the snowmobile at night. How many times I got called didn't make any difference; he'd run up the mountain.

When the weather was nice, Mousse would follow me in the car and run to the highway. In the pouring rain, he ran. We'd walk together if the snow was deep, and I couldn't operate the snowmobile. Mousse would run ahead and break trail until he got so tired he couldn't go any further. He'd turn around and look at me. Then, I'd break trail, and Mousse would follow until I was too tired to keep going. Mousse would come hopping to the front, and off he would go again. Eventually, we'd get home.

At the clinic, Mousse settled into the red-carpeted reception room and welcomed everyone to the clinic as the official greeter. He'd push his head against patients, demanding attention and pets.

During stormy winter days, he'd sleep in front of the wood stove until I finished charting.

Mousse was not allowed in the hallway and treatment rooms, although sometimes he would try to sneak down the hallway.

"Get back on the red carpet," I'd tell him sternly, and back he'd go. Visitors were amazed that Stanley even had a clinic, more so to discover we had a cute, curly-haired dog as a receptionist.

Only twice did Mousse bite someone. The first time, a boy ran through my office, and Mousse nipped him on the butt. My office was private and off-limits, and Mousse would protect it.

Mousse

A second time, I was getting groceries at Jerry's Country Store for Thanksgiving. Brett Wooley offered to help carry the groceries out to my car. Mousse was in the back seat where he always rode. When Brett opened the car door, he got bit. Brett came back into the store. "You know, your dog bit me. He didn't break the skin, but he bit me."

"Oh, Brett, I'm so sorry. I can give you a tetanus shot. You might need one anyway." Brett was known to get into fights in Stanley, and Mousse probably broke the skin. "That's the last time I'm carrying groceries for you, Marie," he said, and declined the tetanus shot.

At the cabin, Mousse slept at my bedroom door. He wasn't allowed into my bedroom. Then, one night, the cabin's outside door blew open during a terrible storm. In the morning, I opened my bedroom door to see my living room covered in snow. Throughout the night, Mousse had remained in front of my bedroom door, whimpering and shivering in the cold.

I nearly lost Mousse to drowning. One of my friends, Rob Pierce, who'd taken my EMT class, worked at the Sawtooth Fish Hatchery south of Stanley. Watching Rob as an EMT, I encouraged him to think about a future in medicine. Instead, Rob wanted to become a veterinarian. I had to leave the Valley one winter, and Rob volunteered to look after Mousse. Rob tells that story:

In a panic, we ran from the office of the Sawtooth Fish Hatchery towards the raceway, the watery concrete trough full of icy river water and juvenile chinook salmon. The Sawtooth sky was dark and heavy with snow. My awkwardly untied sorrels thumped on the crusty snow as I ran. I squinted against the stinging sleet while the laces of my boots clicked, threatening to snag and dump me into the slosh. I kept my strides long and wide.

Hatchery staff, including Jerry McGehee and Brent Snider, ran frantically beside me. Ahead was my golden retriever, Selway, who sat calmly in the storm, howling. Selway's red velvet muzzle pointed to the sky as he sounded his long and mournful howls. Where was Mousse? My heart pounded.

Two weeks earlier, Marie decided to leave for a vacation — something she rarely did. Late winter in Stanley is a nice time to leave. Because Selway was a noble and trusted beast of the Sawtooths, Marie asked me if I would take care of her dog, Mousse, while she was gone.

Without hesitation and with some sense of bestowed honor, I accepted. Mousse became my dog. He and Selway were buddies. Mousse was an odd dog for the Sawtooth Valley, an American Water Spaniel with a chocolate coat of curly poodle hair and long, floppy ears. Still, he was a mountain dog at heart, and he loved adventure. Mousse settled right in.

Never underestimate the power of a six-pack. Jimbo Funderberg, Bev Angel, and I concocted a plan for Mousse somewhere in the fog of beer and soaking in hot springs. We would create a photo album of "Mousse on Vacation" to surpass Marie's time away. We dressed Mousse in goggles and a scarf, posed him on a snow machine, and took him to the Lucky Peak Dam overlook for photos worthy of postcards. That dog was loaded and unloaded, dressed and undressed, and with Mousse's photo album complete, we came home to the Sawtooth Fish Hatchery, where I worked and lived.

Dogs, until fairly recently, were never watched closely. They waited by doors, met people, wandered a bit, and mostly lived their own lives. A simple whistle would bring Selway running. So when I entered the hatchery office that day, the dogs were outside. As we flipped through reports and sipped coffee, Jim Nixon, the facilities manager, wandered through, nodding and stomping snow. He offhandedly commented that he saw the damnedest thing driving back to the office.

"Selway was sitting in the snow by one of the raceways, howling," Jim said. That seemed odd and completely out of character.

"Did you see Mousse?" I asked, sitting up in my chair with a glance at Jerry, who also straightened.

"Nope," Jim replied. We leaped from our chairs, shoved damp socks into boots, and bolted into the storm.

When we arrived at Selway's howling spot, a glance into the raceway confirmed our fears: Mousse was in a death spiral, circling round and round in the freezing water. When he saw us, he stopped swimming and went to the bottom — he was done.

Jerry leaped into the frigid water, grabbed Mousse by his scruff, pulled the dog, dripping, into the colder air, and slung him to me. We then ran at full throttle to Jerry's house nearby. Mousse was limp and coughing. After submersions in a hot bath and vigorous towel rubs, Mousse recovered, was ready for dinner, and followed Selway.

From that day until Marie's return, Mousse was never out of my sight. We presented Selway with a Bronze Dog Star and two cans of Alpo, which he ate without chewing. We later presented Marie with a live dog and the photo album. She loved both.

Rob became a veterinarian after leaving Stanley, opening the North Idaho Animal Hospital in 1994. In 2019, the Idaho Veterinary Medical Association selected him as Idaho's Veterinarian of the Year.

Several years after the fish hatchery incident occurred, I took Mousse to see his veterinarian, Dr. Bob Beede, in Hailey for a routine check-up. "Marie, I hate to tell you this. Mousse has cancer." Dr. Beede thought it was probably colon cancer and described my two options.

"We can do major surgery. The other option is eventually, we can put Mousse to sleep. Not now, but the day will come."

I thought of Mousse and how much he loved to run. All those times he'd follow my snowmobile and car. I just wouldn't put my dog through major surgery. Instead, I took Mousse home.

My granddaughter, Ashley, was returning to Stanley to spend spring break with her grandmother as she did most years. I needed to go to Twin Falls to get supplies for the clinic. "Okay, we'll drive over and have a picnic."

As we were getting ready to leave, I heard Mousse. He was crying. Upon examination, I found a pork chop bone stuck in his mouth, and I got that out. But Mousse continued to cry. I put him in my car, and we drove over the hill to the vet. After examining Mousse, the vet said it was time With tears running down my cheeks, I agreed, and he injected Mousse.

I held Mousse as he stopped breathing and died. I don't know if my granddaughter fully understood why her grandmother couldn't stop crying.

We drove south from Hailey to pick up supplies in Twin Falls and have our picnic.

I, who had survived colon cancer, had lost my faithful companion to colon cancer. And that was it. Never again. I couldn't take on another dog. It's like you fall in love too much.

Years later, now blind and living alone in a facility in Boise far from the Sawtooth Mountains, I'm asked by my kids, "Mom, why don't you get a dog? You loved your dogs."

Across from where I sit, up on the wall, is a picture of a beautiful, brown, curly-haired American water spaniel: My Royal Chocolate Mousse.

"No," I reply. "I had Mousse."

Marie's home on Shaw Mesa, looking toward storm clouds over the White Cloud Mountains

PART SEVEN

LIFE IN A SMALL TOWN

Dean Conger

Stanley, Idaho, was known for the "Stanley Stomp" — three bars with live music, exuberant western swing dancing, and drinking. In March 1973, this photo opened National Geographic's lead article, "High-stepping Idaho."

34

THE STANLEY STOMP AND SHOOTOUT

Stanley's unpaved, rustic main street, Ace of Diamonds, was the setting for the Stanley Stomp. The spectacular peaks of the Sawtooth Mountains provided the visual backdrop.

The "Entering Stanley" sign at the edge of town posts a population of sixty-three, give or take a few. That's in the dead of winter.

On a summery Saturday night, Stanley's population swelled to hundreds or more and was often wild and crazy, as folks of all kinds, tourists and locals, converged on Stanley's three bars: The Rod & Gun Club, Kasino Club, and the Stanley Club.

All three bars had live music in the summer. Sometimes, old-timers showed up and played. The more people, the better the bands played. The Rod & Gun Club allowed smoking; the Kasino Club was smoke-free.

People stomped so hard at the bars that dust and sawdust rose through the floorboards. Dancing spilled out into the street. An empty lot between the Kasino Club and Stanley Clinic doubled as a makeshift dance floor, especially for underage western swing dancers. Marijuana smoke occasionally wafted among the dancers.

When all three of Stanley's bars were on the main street, patrons walked with glass in hand from one bar to another. On Sunday morning, bar owners got together and sorted out their glasses.

Thursday night was locals' night. On Fridays and Saturdays during the summer, tourists pack the bars. Urban cowboys mixed with locals at the bar and on the dance floor.

The Kasino Club hosted a Ladies' Night event when the town slipped into winter hibernation. Selma ("Cookie") Lamb, a ballet dancer from San Francisco, thought we should have a night just for women and dressing up. We had a ball, our private party with me bartending.

Given winter isolation, Ladies' Night helped women let off steam. After a few drinks, Stanley's women let off lots of steam. The bar owner, Bruce Brink, was the doorkeeper. His job was to keep the men out. Bruce showed off his new Stetson at one Ladies' Night.

"Bruce, look at your new hat!" They grabbed Bruce, pinning him on the floor. Off came the Stetson.

With dancing and laughing that pushed back the dark winter, the women transformed Bruce's Stetson into a sombrero for a Mexican Hat Dance. Dancing done, the women handed Bruce his hat, pushing him out the door into the snowy night.

Bartenders started clearing their patrons by one a.m. Bars had to close by two a.m. or risk losing their liquor license. One constant worry: state alcohol inspectors.

When I bartended at the Kasino Club to help ends meet (once the clinic got busy, I removed my bartending apron and put on my white coat and stethoscope), my ten-year-old daughter Debbie came with me. We had no childcare in Stanley. Debbie learned to shoot pool at the Kasino Club. My daughter was sitting on the bar when a man in a suit, white shirt, and tie walked in. His clothes were a hint: definitely not dressed for Stanley. Busted.

"Hello, I'm with the State of Idaho. I'm an inspector," he said, displaying his credentials. "Why's this girl sitting on the bar? She's underage."

"Her name is Debbie," I replied. "She's my daughter. I couldn't get a babysitter." Child care is challenging in small towns.

"Your daughter in this bar is a violation. Don't let it happen again."

He didn't cite me, but the bar's owner was upset. The Kasino Club could have lost its liquor license and we knew the state inspector would be back.

The Idaho Legislature's decision in 1972 to lower the drinking age to nineteen supercharged Stanley's Fourth of July celebration. July and August are make-or-break for

Stanley businesses, and July Fourth launches that frenetic stretch running through Labor Day.

As summertime temperatures climb in Boise, Twin Falls, and beyond, people pour over the mountain passes into the Valley. Add in a holiday weekend, alcohol newly legal for nineteen-year-olds, live music and dancing, and no law enforcement, and Stanley got crazy.

Year by year, more young people showed up until, by the mid-1970s, several thousand people clogged Stanley's dirt streets for the Fourth of July celebration. Stanley had become one massive street party.

Looking from the clinic to the Kasino Club, you'd see one big cloud of dust. People, mostly young, danced, drank, and whooped it up. Young men raced each other on the main street carrying women on their shoulders. Women went naked.

No one got hurt, although a cow wandered onto the highway near Lower Stanley and got hit. I did a "house call" on the cow the next day.

The throngs of revelers triggered a backlash. Local business owners and residents demanded control, and eventually, Challis deputies and state troopers showed up.

Long after law enforcement restored law and order in Stanley, the Idaho Legislature rescinded the new drinking-age law in 1987.

Stanley had no local law enforcement other than Forest Service and Fish and Game staff until the mid-1970s.

As Stanley got busier, Custer County posted a deputy for the summer. One of our first was "Bam Bam" (Carl Ellis). Carl was gung-ho getting grants for equipment, especially for guns.

Carl's wife, Fran, was eighteen years older. I first met Fran in the Post Office.

"I want you to know how much we appreciate your son," I said effusively.

"I'm Carl's wife," Fran said coolly. Fran forgave my faux pas, and we became good friends.

One young army soldier, not yet twenty-one, drank too much at the Rod & Gun and started threatening people at the bar. Casanova Jack pulled a gun. The two went at it, and the kid got the gun.

As the situation escalated, bar patrons fled. I got a call at the clinic: "Marie, we need you now. You have to sedate this guy before he kills someone."

In ERs like Seattle's Harborview or Chicago's Cook County, clinicians have the advantage of police backup, a trained hospital staff capable of a "show of force," injectable and oral antipsychotics, leather restraints, and locked seclusion rooms. In Stanley, we had none of those things available to us.

At the clinic, I did have Valium, but no antipsychotics like Haldol. When I got the emergency call, I drew up a syringe of Valium, put it in the pocket of my white coat, and hurried over to the Rod & Gun Club.

As I turned the corner onto Main Street, the crowd outside the Rod & Gun saw me.

The men walked toward me. "Thank God you're here. Don't worry, Marie. We're going to defend you."

"Oh, thank you."

I continued walking, and the crowd closed behind me. I got to the bar's wooden porch, opened the door, walked quickly into the bar, and then slammed and bolted the door. The bar patrons were outside pounding on the door.

I walked over to this young man — a kid, really. He had been pistol-whipped on the face, had abrasions and contusions, but was still agitated.

"You need to be sound asleep by the time the sheriff arrives," I told him. He was deathly afraid of needles. At first, he refused the injection, but relented.

The young man dozed on the bar stool, put his head down on the bar, then started snoring. He was sound asleep. I unbolted the door, pulled up a bar stool, and sat beside him.

By the time the deputy sheriff arrived, the soldier was sleeping peacefully.

"There's nothing for me to arrest him for. Besides, the jail in Challis isn't fit for anyone right now." The deputy got back in his vehicle and headed back to Challis.

Stanley's Rock Garage owner took the soldier home and sent him back to his army base the next day.

The soldier had shared his papers with me. I called his commanding officer. His response? "Service personnel assume no responsibility when their people are on leave. They are on their own."

The soldier wasn't AWOL; he just drank too much. Almost any place else, he would have ended up in jail.

In Stanley, the young soldier got tucked in, fed breakfast, and sent home. May he pay that kindness forward.

Dave Kimpton and I were sitting at the bar at the new Stanley Club, discussing how to raise money to replace our '58 Pontiac with a new ambulance. Suddenly all hell broke loose. Dave, the ranger for the Stanley District of the Sawtooth NRA, describes what happened next in this account adapted from his memoir, *Mountainous Events*.

DAVE KIMPTON, IN HIS OWN WORDS

A loud shot rang out from the deck of the Stanley Club, and almost simultaneously, the door crashed open. Two men, armed with a shotgun and a Thompson submachine gun, entered the bar, pointing their weapons at one of the occupants in the room, whose face turned ash gray and whose mouth gaped open. The target's two teenage sons, who were playing pool, suddenly became rigid.

A man and woman drinking beer stared. The man pushed the woman to the floor as they scuttled to the Stanley Club's rear door a few feet away. The bartender rapidly ducked behind the heavy serving bar out of the line of fire.

Today, we've become accustomed to America's weekly mass shootings. But in the 1970s, even in Stanley, Idaho, using guns to settle disputes was extreme.

I had just finished a refresher EMT class, feeling cocky and hoping for an opportunity to use my new skills. To celebrate with a brew and talk about replacing our old ambulance, I headed to one of Stanley's three bars with the EMT course instructor and our nurse practitioner, Marie Osborn.

As we walked into the Stanley Club, I saw the owner, Wayne, tending the bar as he did almost every day of the year. Wayne was a character, but being unique in Stanley is not unique. Locals march "to a different drummer" than people in more urban settings. Maybe it's the long, cold, and lonely winters, or the locals were so individualistic that they could only live comfortably on the outskirts of civilization.

After Marie and I greeted Wayne, I noticed a high level of tension in the room and took inventory after getting our beers. Behind the bar counter, Wayne stood off to the side and appeared ready to exit at a moment's notice. On the floor, partially propped up in the corner, was a somewhat battered local individual known as Pegleg.

Standing over Pegleg was a river runner. For simplicity, I'll call him Shelby. He was a physically large person who operated a river rafting company. Shelby looked intimidating and very angry. His face was beet red, and one large hand was balled into a fist a few inches from Pegleg's face, the other holding a whiskey. His two big teenage sons stood playing pool at the other end of the room.

After appraising the scene briefly, I asked Shelby what was happening.

Big, burly, and balding, Shelby was not someone to trifle with. His hands were twice as large as mine, and his arms were nearly as large as my thighs, the result of paddling an oar boat for many years. He struck me as an individual who constantly struggled to control his temper and had a "short fuse."

Approached respectfully, Shelby was cooperative and had a big heart for helping others less fortunate than himself. He was a successful, self-made businessman. Shelby often mentioned how hardscrabble it had been to build his family-owned whitewater floating enterprise into a financial success. He was proud of his achievements and commented that his father, if still alive, would have been proud of him.

Finally, Shelby relaxed and commented that he had been having a discussion with Wayne. He and his two sons, who were drinking soda beverages, were enjoying a private party when Pegleg arrived uninvited. Shelby told Pegleg to leave. Pegleg retorted that the open sign was up, and he would stay. Shelby "kind of lost it," grabbed Pegleg by the collar, dragged him behind the bar, and "gently beat him to rearrange his thinking!"

Pegleg Mac was an institution unto himself. He had drifted into the valley some years ago and managed several properties owned by absentee, wealthy individuals. He had finally saved enough money to buy a small piece of land south of Stanley and moved a small trailer onto it. He was wild-looking with a full beard and unruly hair, though he sometimes shaved, got a haircut, and surprised people by looking quite respectable. One of his ankles was mutilated, and he wore a brace to assist him when walking, but he still had a bad limp. One rumor was that Pegleg had accidentally shot himself while playing Russian roulette in the military. Another story was that he had purposely shot himself to avoid being shipped to Vietnam. The truth? We'll never know.

Pegleg drove around in a two-and-a-half ton, army surplus 6x6 military truck. Inexplicably, this truck blew up with the better part of a case of dynamite. The FBI investigated but never identified the perpetrator. Local scuttlebutt was that his brother Mel blew up Pegleg's truck after the two argued.

Neither brother got along well with the other, at least when living together. To hear them tell it, they squabbled, cursed, pushed, shoved, and hit each other on occasion when arguing over trivia. When living separately, however, they were best friends: visiting, joking, and bantering. One thing was absolute: If you criticized one of them, they were united and became closer than the proverbial "kissin' cousins," acting as one against the offender.

Pegleg and Mel fixated on firearms. They owned a small arsenal of pistols, shotguns, rifles, and several semi-automatic World War II vintage weapons. This interest probably came from their separate stints in the military.

Mel had to be taken at face value, and I never knew him to bluff or falsely try to intimidate others; he could be deadly serious in these instances. Pegleg, however, tended to bluff a lot, though it was hard to tell when he was acting or serious. A friend once said that Pegleg shot between his feet after he refused to leave the Pole Creek hot springs on private property that Pegleg was managing. Most locals avoided the brothers. That day in the Stanley Club, I decided to tone down the tension. I asked Shelby to release Pegleg if he agreed to leave the tavern. Pegleg readily agreed. Shelby came around to the customer side of the bar and started to sip his drink. His face had resumed its normal color, and his anger abated, though he and his sons jeered as Pegleg left the tavern. As Pegleg walked toward the door, I saw an intense rage.

Wayne sighed in relief and resumed bartending. Shelby was quiet, and his sons re-started their pool game. I went to the jukebox and selected my favorite record, hoping the music would lessen the prevailing bad mood.Marie and I moved to the end of the bar, close to the back door. Neither of us doubted that the drama was over.

I wondered what Pegleg would do now. Thinking like a law-abiding citizen, I decided he would file a formal complaint with the county sheriff. That would take time, so I concluded everything was okay, at least for the rest of the day.I ordered a second beer, and Marie continued sipping her rum and Coke. We discussed how we might get a new ambulance.

Then, a shot rang out, and the door smashed open. Mel and Pegleg entered the bar with weapons lowered. I pushed Marie out the back door, our heels blazing as we ran to the clinic.

We prepared to transport one or more patients with gunshot wounds to the Sun Valley Hospital, sixty miles away. We waited for more gunshots, dreading a disastrous outcome. Silence.

I wondered what was going on. Had the two brothers already shot Shelby? While Marie and I prepared our ambulance to transport gunshot victims, I didn't hear the firearm retort. Looking up the street, we saw Shelby and his two sons leave the Stanley Club by the front door, moving at a near run. Five or ten minutes later, Pegleg and Mel walked out. All was quiet.

I walked back to the Stanley Club, cautiously opened the damaged door, and walked in. Standing behind the counter, Wayne waved me in and said I should lock the door. I did. I nervously scanned the room. The combatants were gone. I walked to the bar, sat on a stool, ordered a beer, and drank it all in two or three swallows. I asked Wayne what had happened.

Wayne said the two brothers threatened Shelby and his sons until they virtually begged them not to shoot. Shelby pleaded for sanity: "It was all a mistake. I lost my temper. I'm sorry about roughing up Pegleg. I didn't know that he was crippled."

After a long pause, Mel said: "I am pissed that you picked on my crippled brother for no good reason. Maybe it is time to shoot all three of you f**kers!"

With a throbbing red face of anger, Pegleg screamed obscenities at Shelby and his two boys, shrieking, "My brother and I are going to set up along the river. When you float by, we'll pick you and your sons off one by one with a scoped rifle." He warned them, "Watch your backs! We may shoot anytime you're on the river. We'll try not to hit any of your guests!" Pegleg rushed them and shouted: "Get out of here before we change our minds and shoot you now!"

Grunting and cursing, father and teenage sons scrambled out of the Stanley Club, practically falling over each other. They moved down the street as if the hounds of hell were at their heels.

Pegleg and Mel apologized to Wayne for damaging the bar but stated, "Shelby had caused it, and this is what he deserved for his arrogance." After the brothers left, Wayne closed the door, put up the "closed" sign, and poured himself a stiff drink.

I thanked Wayne for the information, finished my second beer, walked to the ambulance, and returned it to the garage. I was relieved that Marie and I did not need our medical skills.

About a week later, Shelby humbly entered my Forest Service office, gently closed the door, and sat down, looking pale and worried. He briefly related what I already knew, especially about the threat to shoot him and his sons as they floated the river. Shelby commented that he and his sons were mostly confined to their house for fear of being shot. No one went anywhere unless at least two of them were together.

Other outfitters were also upset since they worried that Pegleg and Mel might confuse them for Shelby, inadvertently shooting them or their guests while floating the river. Shelby wanted my help. He wanted me to intercede for him and his sons and for Pegleg and Mel to withdraw the shooting threat.

"Have you considered filing a formal complaint with the Custer County sheriff?" I asked. Shelby turned pale. He worried that if he pursued legal action, the brothers would shoot him before law enforcement personnel could stop them. Shelby thought this was a terrible idea.

I paused and reflected upon his proposal. I was also very irritated. He was the one who beat up Pegleg. Now he was putting me, a nonparticipant, in harm's way with his request.

I let the silence linger until Shelby was visibly uncomfortable, squirming and fidgeting in his chair. Finally, I agreed to talk to the brothers to see if I could broker some agreement or understanding so that the threat, implied or real, could be eliminated.

Shortly after I met with Shelby, I drove to Pegleg's residence, parked, and walked down his road toward his shack. He met me at the door. I noticed his shotgun propped on the wall within easy reach. I told him I needed a cup of coffee. With freshly brewed cowboy coffee in hand, we sat down together.

Pegleg talked about the weather, his plans to get the Forest Service to condemn his property so he would not have to pay taxes, local gossip, and just about anything except the subject. I simply listened. I said nothing. Finally, he blurted out that Shelby was badly in the wrong when he had assaulted him. He added the gunplay, and threats were mostly bluffs intended to intimidate Shelby. Pegleg and Mel were willing to drop the matter if I would set up a meeting with Shelby and his sons for a formal apology.

I set the meeting for the next day. The boater and his sons apologized, and the two brothers accepted the apology. Everyone left the meeting feeling considerably relieved.

My reward? To remove the threat to his family and rafting business, Shelby offered to buy me anything I wanted, within reason. I was just relieved to end the matter. "Oh, just buy me a couple of brews at the Stanley Club." He phoned Wayne the same day, related what had happened at the meeting and how happy he was. Shelby set me up with a dozen brews to be consumed at my convenience. I don't know how he paid. Wayne told me years later that Shelby never came into the bar again.

While the Stanley Stomp was going on, I learned to stay at the clinic late, waiting to leave until after the bars closed. Staying late was was easier than driving in from my home for suturing after a bar fight or car accident — usually someone hitting an elk.

When I first opened the clinic, I might walk to one of the bars, listen to the band, and dance. Being out on the dance floor, letting loose to live music with so many others dancing, was fun. Now, in my nineties, the Stanley Stomp remains one of my life's champagne memories.

35

GRANDMA SNOWMOBILE

"There are no words; it's only music there."

Antonio Vivaldi, composer of "The Four Seasons"

What's life like for a middle-aged woman alone at 7,100 feet in a cabin looking out at the peaks of the Sawtooth Mountains? By the early 1980s, after Debbie graduated from the schoolhouse in Stanley and my second marriage ended, I lived alone with my mountains.

Living alone did not mean being lonely; far from it. My life was never dull, with patients to see in the clinic and on emergency calls. I also had chores: household duties, chopping firewood, and building fires in the woodstove to stay warm.

In the beginning, before the clinic caught on, I used to get up every morning, have tea, and then saddle the horse. In those years, we didn't have fences on Shaw Mesa; cattle were everywhere, and I'd scoot them back to their ranch. Mostly, I just loved to ride.

It's hard to stay angry with the world in the Sawtooth country. The Sawtooth and the White Clouds Mountains are spectacular, especially on cloudless days. And the universe opens up at night if you just look up, billions of stars marred increasingly by satellites.

If all else fails, a couple of hours swinging an axe and splitting firewood is a highly effective therapy for working out frustrations.

Unless I'd spent the night in the ambulance, I'd start my day with morning chores, half listening to the CB radio. Later, thanks to Idaho EMS and the Robert Wood Johnson Foundation, my constant companion was my EMS radio, "Unit 1," with emergency channels. Outside my bedroom the radio antenna linked me to StateComm.

The Stanley Clinic got busier as we became known. I started scheduling patients. My first opening was at ten am, and I usually worked until five or six in the evening. Avoiding

The Osborn family cabin became Marie's home in the Sawtooth country.

Mondays and Fridays, I'd schedule physicals, women's health, and regular checkups. Especially during the summertime, there was no time for lunch, so I ate on the run.

In the clinic's reception room, my scheduled patients mixed with people arriving with minor emergencies. The occasional crisis burst through the door. Other patients were the emergency calls: car wrecks, drownings, mountain climbing and river rafting accidents, chest pains, and more. With the drama of the human experience unfolding in the clinic's reception room, my scheduled patients were usually patient about waiting or rescheduling.

Sometimes, I didn't have time to go home, shower, and change clothes. I might be up all night with ambulance runs. We'd park the ambulance in the clinic's garage, and I'd walk into a reception room filled with patients.

From the Fourth of July through Labor Day, the campgrounds were full. At night, from Shaw Mesa, I could watch the lights from the line of cars driving into the valley from Galena Summit. There'd be thousands of people in the valley Is it any wonder the clinic and Stanley Ambulance were so busy?

After raising five kids with earaches, I couldn't say no to a parent seeking help for a child screaming in earache agony during the middle of the night. I'd rather get up, drive into the clinic, and relieve the child and parents. If someone is sick, they need to be seen. But, of course, getting an emergency call at one in the morning for painful intercourse is another matter. Some complaints could wait until office hours. I charted in paper until almost the end of my career, and I'd get caught up on my charting after the last patient had left the clinic. Controlled substances were of particular concern. Daily, I made sure to account for opioids.

Sandwiched between our two treatment rooms was a smaller room that doubled as our lab and pharmacy. I did my charting there on the lab's orange Formica countertops. Urine, pus from wounds, and throat swabs went on Petri plates and into the incubator in the lab's corner. Next to the Physicians' Desk Reference, the Colter Counter and centrifuge were handy for my patient's blood counts. I'd pack the autoclave with suture kits between patients or at the end of the day. There was always more to do to get ready for incoming patients.

> Marie said the autoclave she has used for the past 10 years has a bad short and is rusted out and cannot be repaired. The other one that was also donated has no instructions and she doesn't know how to work it. Bill James said he could loan one from the Forest Service while it was determined whether the one we have can be used or if it will be necessary to purchase one.
>
> Salmon River Clinic-Hospital District Board of Directors Meeting, October 3, 1983.

You never knew who might walk through the door. Chest pains, lacerations, fishhooks, earaches, premature labor, diarrhea, asthma flares, and more all mixed with my scheduled clinic patients. Others needed condoms or birth control pills before heading out for white water adventures on the Salmon River Middle Fork. Still others needed allergy shots.

Walking into the clinic might be David Hartman of *Good Morning America*, Burt Reynolds, or Jim Nabors (Gomer Pyle) staying down the street with Bill and Verna Harrah. Or, it might be Bill Harrah himself, bringing in his kids.

Sometimes, legislators or an inspector from the Boards of Pharmacy or Nursing would walk through the door.

After the Mt. Borah earthquake in 1983, StateComm asked me to check on the miners at the silver mine near Clayton. Idaho's history includes significant loss of life underground. The worst was in 1972 when ninety-one men died in the Sunshine Mine disaster in north Idaho. Like the Sunshine mine, the Clayton mine had deep shafts. StateComm was worried the earthquake had collapsed the mine, trapping and killing miners. I was walking out the door to Clayton when the Board of Nursing representatives arrived for a surprise visit. By the end of that day, the miners were okay — and the Board of Nursing was too.

You might think you have a day planned, only to get called for a motorcycle or car accident, a rafting or climbing accident, or even an earthquake. Something will mess up your schedule. Whatever life brings, you adjust and reschedule.

Stanley has a four-season climate dominated by winter. Providing care for patients in the Sawtooth country inevitably adapts to the seasons' rhythms.

Summer

In early June, you can wake up to rosy-colored Sawtooth peaks. Or, you can wake up to six inches of snow and blizzard conditions. With longer days, bluebirds return. Wyethia, with white daisy blossoms in green meadows, color coordinate with receding snow on the Sawtooth peaks. Fields of shooting stars and penstemon paint mountain meadows pink and purple. Snowmelt fills mountain streams and the Salmon River.

By the summer solstice, the snowstorms are gone. Summer's warm, long days are rewards for enduring winter's short, cold, dark days.

By mid-July, sunshine drenches the Sawtooth country, along with mountain weather's occasional thunderstorms. The July Fourth holiday reliably brings storms that drive wet, hungry campers into local restaurants and the laundromat. Mornings are quiet and still, giving way to breezes and then afternoon winds. Fields of timothy hay and wildflowers dance to the music of the mountain's wind instruments.

When we camped at Stanley Lake and Alturas Lake in the 1960s, we almost always had rain in early August. Rain and snow might come by early September, with willows turning yellow along the Salmon River. But the climate and weather are changing, and the late summer and early fall rains come later, if at all. By August 12, 2000, when my son, John, and Rachael married in a meadow behind the cabin, the air was amazingly clear. But forest fires were exploding all around, sending up plumes of smoke topped by cumulus clouds.

"The Sawtooth is the asbestos forest," John and others on the Stanley fire crew used to say in the 1970s. These forests never burned. Well, these forests are burning now. Bark beetles ate through lodgepole pine forests, killing many trees and raising the fire risk.

My granddaughter, Ashley, and I were at the cabin when a nearby landowner on Pole Creek burned trash on a dry, blustery September afternoon after weeks of no rain. What was he thinking? Flames caught and spread in the grass and sagebrush, then climbed into the forest canopy. Flames exploded up Fourth of July Creek behind my home. With a massive column of smoke billowing up from the burning trees, Ashley and I scrambled to pull a few precious things and evacuate. As the climate changes, fire risk is rising in the high country.

For everyone in Stanley, Labor Day looms like a finish line, when you can stop and catch your breath.

Fall

Before and after Labor Day is like day and night. By early September, mountain sunlight is less intense. The long, lingering sunsets and twilight of summer begin to shorten and hurry into the night. You feel the season changing as much as you see it.

Walking the streets of Stanley, quiet returns. You chit-chat with friends and strangers, taking time just to be neighborly and friendly. Whereas summertime is a hurried "hi" and "goodbye" while you run to get the mail, after Labor Day, the pace slows.

In the fall, before the first heavy snow, middle-aged and elderly local "snowbirds" would migrate south to Arizona and other warmer places for the winter. At the same time, Piero Piva and other ranchers drove their cattle down the highway to Challis, clogging the narrow river road. Retirees clashed with the West's ranching practices: Cowboys yelled and cussed at impatient drivers in their big recreational vehicles. Today, the cattle drives are mostly gone. Now, ranchers truck their livestock from the Sawtooths before the first big snow.

In autumn, emergency calls dropped, but I still got called. With the aspen turning yellow and orange, and Sawtooth peaks set against deep blue skies, the valley is stunning in the fall. Some people come to see the color, while others come for their winter wood. Unfortunately, chainsaws, axes, and hatchets can do terrible damage. Emergency calls were common for lacerations and traumatic amputations. Still, the call volume was less, a blessing for enjoying the fall weather.

Autumn was the first time I really experienced Little Redfish Lake. The Osborn family usually headed for the big lake. One autumn day, I thought, "It's too beautiful. Oh, the heck with it." I put the "closed" sign on the clinic door, drove upriver, and sat by the lake. The air was still, the water a perfect mirror for the Sawtooths and the deep blue October sky. I walked around the lake and then waded in. I had the lake to myself and my dog. Being there alone was delightful. Later, I discovered I wasn't alone: People on the shore were watching and wondering what I was doing. At least I didn't go skinny dipping.

After clinic or ambulance runs, I'd come home, turn on the TV to a football game, and gather up my crocheting. I watched lots of football and crocheted lots of afghans. For baby showers and newborns, I also crocheted baby blankets. Before giving away the afghans, I affixed my name tag. You might check to see if my name tag is still attached to your afghan.

Up until Halloween, autumn in the Sawtooth country is gorgeous. When Debbie was little, I'd take her trick-or-treating in town. After she was off to high school in Challis and then the University of Minnesota, I'd stay at the clinic. Just about every kid, EMT, and community member would stop by the clinic to trick-or-treat or just say hello.

After Debbie was gone, I'd leave the valley at the end of October. Most years, I'd drive to Hermiston and meet up with John. He'd schedule time away from his patients at the

VA hospital in Spokane. We'd go to Portland and check into a bed and breakfast.

The next day, we'd start our vacation at Powell's Book Store, have lunch at our favorite Greek restaurant, then travel west over the coastal range to Tillamook and the Oregon coast.

That first week in November was time for watching storms and election returns. Others might join us, including my son Jerry and John's wife, Rachael. Jerry, John, and I vacationed in the Canadian Rockies one November, including a night at Chateau Lake Louise. But, most years, we scheduled our week together to walk the beaches of the Oregon coast, read books, sit by the fire, and relax.

To leave the valley always left me uneasy. Yes, the EMTs were there and responded to emergency calls; I took comfort in that. But when you are the sole healthcare provider, it's different. I'd schedule time out of the valley during the slack season.

Autumn in the Sawtooths also means elk hunting season, both rifle and archery.

When I walked into the Kasino Club in late September 1976, the guys talked about hunting camp. "Hey Marie, you ever gone huntin'?" My dad didn't hunt when I grew up in Kentucky and Indiana. Cal and some of my kids hunted, mostly game birds, while I stayed home.

"No, never have," I replied. That year the local men at the bar invited me to hunt with them on the opening day of elk season.

Before opening the clinic in Stanley, I didn't know where the gun trigger was. In the Sawtooth country, most people have guns for hunting, even the minister. Except for the sheriff and deputy, locals didn't carry their weapons around town. If people wore guns into the bars, it was usually outsiders.

Piero Piva, and others encouraged me to get a gun and learn how to use it. I tried a 20-gauge shotgun, but the kick nearly knocked me over backward and hurt my shoulder.Al Sullivan, who worked for the Idaho Highway Department and sold guns on the side, recommended a .243 Winchester rifle. It was perfect. I learned to shoot, practicing in the weeks leading up to the opening day of elk season.

Word travels fast in a small town. "Hey Marie, I hear you're elk hunting with the boys," Jerry Funderberg said when I stopped for groceries at Jerry's Country Store. With a twinkle in his eye and chuckling, he added, "Hey when you get your elk, I'll even hang it for you." Elk has to hang and age before butchering, or it tastes gamey.

On the afternoon before opening day, I drove my pickup, hauling our horses, Sucia and Macia, about three miles up the Fisher Creek road near my cabin, and rode up the mountain to elk camp. The guys and I set up camp, enjoyed a great dinner, laughed, shared stories around the campfire, and then went to bed. With skiffs of snow on the ground and a universe of stars overhead, the night turned cold in those 8,000-foot meadows. Despite my heavy sleeping bag, I shivered and hardly slept.

Legal shooting hours are one-half hour before sunrise to one-half hour after sunset. We were up before dawn. The men staked me out on the hillside beside a huge boulder. I sat, getting colder and colder, shivering and wishing I were home next to my woodstove. On my head was my bright pink hat with a tassel that I had crocheted, and I pulled it down low over my ears to stay warm. Just before sunup, I heard gunshots.

All of a sudden, I heard the thundering of hooves. There was no mistaking: They were coming down the hill toward me. They stopped behind the boulder beside me, and I could hear them munching on grass. They grazed, not objecting to my being there, and I wasn't going to argue with them. When I finally stood up, the elk herd grazed just feet away. They just kept eating.

It finally dawned on me that maybe I should fulfill my duty as a huntress and shoot one. Shaking, I raised my rifle, aimed for the heart of a bull elk so he wouldn't suffer, and fired. He dropped. The herd scattered.

Now what? The men scrambled down the hillside. "Wow, Marie, you got your elk! Look at you! Congratulations!" I was stunned. I'd never done anything like this. The guys hoisted the elk onto my horse, Macia, securing it. I led Macia down the trail to my pickup; we backed her up to the truck bed and unloaded the elk.

Later that morning, I parked my truck at Jerry's Country Store, walked in, smiled at Jerry, and said, "Guess what, Jerry. I got my elk!" It wasn't even 10 o'clock on opening day.

Jerry stood still and stared. "You what?"

"I got my elk."

The look on Jerry's face was priceless, worth all the night's cold and misery.

I excitedly reminded Jerry that he had promised to hang the elk if I got one.

"Marie, I can't hang an elk here in the store next to commercial meat."

I had no idea what to do or how to hang the elk at home. Finally, Jerry decided to hang it in his cellar. Before Jerry hung the elk, the story was making the rounds in the valley.

After the meat had aged for a week, Jerry butchered and packaged it. The elk meat tasted good that winter for the first few months, anyway. Many families got their elk during that hunting season, and you couldn't give away the meat. Other years were lean for the elk herds. Hunters with families to feed need that meat to get them through the winter. I don't like killing. Getting my elk was the thrill of a lifetime, a champagne moment. But that first hunt? It was also my last.

Winter

Snowstorms paint the peaks white, highlighting their sawtooth features and creating the illusion that the mountains are even more massive and rugged.

After Halloween's rain, the snow arrives in earnest. I learned the hard way to park my car near the highway, walk up the hill in the rain, and move my snowmobile outside the garage door. Debbie and I made it a rule that we'd be ready for winter by Halloween. For the rest of the winter, until spring breakup, I snowmobiled, regardless of the time of the emergency call.

I tried cross-country skiing. During the day, skiing is fine. But, in the dark, with the mesa's wind-blown snow and the tops of the sagebrush catching my skis, I fell a lot. An injury alone at night was inviting disaster.

Snowmobiling ended up being my transportation of choice. When it is really cold, minus thirty or below, starting the snowmobile can be iffy. You pull the cord until you feel your shoulder will fall off, and still, the machine won't turn over. Although I lived alone on Shaw Mesa after Debbie left, I wasn't alone. People in the valley looked out for me, checking to be sure I got home, packing the snow on the trail to my cabin, and more.

In my morning commute to see patients, I'd park my snowmobile at the highway, put on the cover, and then walk over to the car. Depending on storms, snow might blanket my car. I started by brooming off several inches or even a foot or more of snow. Once in the car and turning on the engine, I might face a wall of snow if the snowplow plowed me in.

In the deep freeze of winter, cars don't always start. Using a block heater to warm the engine can mean the difference between getting to the clinic and returning home. Unfortunately, out on the flat next to the highway, there aren't any plugins. Fortunately, my neighbor, Ed Elliott, invited me to plug in my car at his home near the highway. He plowed the access road so I could get out. The Elliott's bedroom was on the far end of the house, so I didn't disturb them too much going in and out at night on emergency calls.

In the wintertime, I got called for some awful accidents. Cars hit elk on the highway. Drivers hit black ice, lost control of their vehicles, and went into the river. Occasionally, we'd get the call for a truck accident near the Yankee Fork, with the semi-truck jack-knifed or, worse, in the river.

After struggling to start the snowmobile one arctic morning, I pulled up to my car plugged in at Ed's house. I put the key in the lock, and it wouldn't turn. The lock was frozen. Rather than risk breaking the key off in the lock, I snowmobiled back to the cabin for the hair dryer, returned, and heated the car door lock until it thawed. Just at that moment, over my EMS radio, came an emergency call. "Marie, you're needed at the clinic." I got in the car and turned on the engine. The car wouldn't move: The wheels were frozen tight. I rocked the car back and forth. The wheels finally broke free, and I headed to town.

"That's my Grandma Snowmobile," my granddaughter, Ashley, described me. Her parents, Melinda and Mark, brought her up to the valley as a toddler. Ashley screamed on the snowmobile trip from the highway to the cabin. She hated the noise. Over the years, Ashley made peace with the snowmachine, which is now part of her life as a grown woman living in Sawtooth country.

In my nearly thirty years as Stanley's nurse practitioner, the coldest I remember was fifty-six below zero. When it's that cold, you wake up to crystal-clear air, no wind, and cloudless skies. Those arctic days were gorgeous but painfully cold.

In the 1980s, some winter storms brought snow up to the roof. Winds built snowdrifts 12-15 feet deep on the cabin's

south side. I used the hatchet to cut steps in the snowbank to access my snowmobile so I could climb up and get out.

In winter, Stanley was quiet until the snowmobiles discovered the valley. Then, it was as though the town woke up and discovered winter could be fun. Instead of snowbirding in Arizona, people stayed to snowmobile. Snowmobile clubs in Boise and Emmett would arrive. In recent years, curling has attracted people from all over the world to Stanley. People can drive into the Valley for winter recreation if the passes are open. Unfortunately, some visitors were real hell-raisers, drinking too much and driving too fast. That's when I got the trauma calls.

The Stanley community put on a 100-mile snowmobile race for several years. One local, Troy Spurgeon, set the course. It started at Smiley Creek near Galena Summit, came down the Sawtooth Valley to Stanley, then out Highway 21 in the Stanley Basin toward Banner Pass before circling back to the finish line in Stanley. Some locals were good riders, and Pat Cutler won the 100-mile race several years running. People registered and reserved every spare room in town. We had live music lined up, set the course, and planned a big town party. All the racers and their supporters showed up in town. Then, the storm hit. Heavy snows closed mountain passes and the road downriver.

Winters are long, from November through March and beyond. With time on their hands, townspeople organized a snowmobile poker run. Snowmobilers would stop, pick up a card, and take a drink. At the finish line, whoever had the best hand won. I always arranged for the ambulance, but never got a call.

Winter travel in and out of the Sawtooth country can be formidable. One November, on my way back from Boise, snow was sliding onto Highway 21 between Idaho City and Lowman.

When I arrived in Lowman, the deputy sheriff had parked his car by a barricade on the highway. "Sorry to tell you this, but you can't get to Stanley. Avalanches have closed the highway in the canyon just this side of Banner Pass."

It was possible to backtrack and enter the valley via Galena Summit, but that added nearly a hundred miles. And the road near Hill City could be treacherous with black ice.

"The road downriver is closed, too," the deputy added. "Bad rockslides that way."

"Okay, thanks. I'll head back to Idaho City," I said.

"No, ma'am. Too risky. We've just shut down that stretch of highway. Sorry. Looks like you're stuck here in Lowman." The deputy directed me to Lowman's South Fork Lodge. I was one of several waiting for a road to open.

By the next afternoon, bulldozers cleared the rockslide downriver, and we headed out on the Banks-Lowman Road to Highway 55 and then to Boise. Driving through Boise, I thought about calling my daughter, Melinda. Her husband, Mark, worked nights, and I didn't want to wake him with my call. So, I pressed on to Mountain Home, hoping to make it over Galena Summit. It was dark when I finally turned onto Highway 75 south of Bellevue. A flashing blue light suddenly appeared behind me. I pulled over. Was I speeding?

The deputy walked up to my car. I rolled down my window.

"Are you Marie Osborn?"

"Yes."

"Would you please call your daughter, Melinda?" He also informed me that Galena Summit was closed. The deputy added, "And you can't get to Stanley through Arco and Challis. That highway's closed, too."

I drove on to Bellevue and found the only pay phone in town. I called Melinda, who was frantic. I found the last motel room in Bellevue and slept like a log. Eventually, I got home.

When the passes shut down again, I drove the long way from Boise and made it as far as Ketchum. A friend, Tom Kovalicky, offered to let me stay at his house if Galena Summit ever closed.

That afternoon, I drove up towards Galena Summit. Cars had slid off the road, and barricades were up. I encountered a young woman, Jolene, who worked at the ranger station. She was upset.

"I don't have any credit cards. I don't have any money. Galena Summit is closed, I can't get home, I'm stuck, and I don't know what to do." Well, I had a credit card. But, at that time of year, motel rooms in the Ketchum-Sun Valley area are hard to come by.

"Don't worry," I reassured Jolene. "We can go to Tom Kovalicky's. Tom told me a zillion times that if I ever got stuck and he's gone, just get the key from the neighbor and make myself at home."

We drove to Tom's house and parked. Tom didn't answer the doorbell. I went next door, got the key, and we entered. By then, it was getting late. We put on our jammies, built a fire in Tom's fireplace, and sipped on Tom's beer. At that moment, in walked Tom — with his girlfriend.

You could cut the air with a knife.

Tom's friend was unhappy to see two females in their bedclothes, drinking, laughing, and having a good time in front of the fireplace. So, we excused ourselves and immediately went to bed.

At first daylight, we were out of there. Jolene and I enjoyed a long breakfast until the plows reopened Galena Summit, and we could return to Stanley. And Tom, I'm sorry, but I still laugh whenever I think of that night. I know we messed up your evening. But thank you.

While spring is dawning in lower elevations, winter still holds the high country. Often, the heaviest snow month was March. That month, I left the valley for a week to attend continuing medical education classes in Salt Lake City. The medical conference was for physicians, but organizers allowed nurse practitioners to attend.

Spring

On those first beautiful, clear spring days of April, people drive up to see the beauty of the Sawtooth Valley and Stanley Basin. They are glad and relieved that winter is over. But with spring comes mud.

Mud meant that snowmobiling from my home to the highway was ending. Muck and mud with sagebrush poking through snow don't work for snowmobiling. By my birthday on May 18, the last snowdrifts had melted enough that I could drive to my house. If you try driving too soon, you risk getting your car stuck in the mud. So, you walk.

For that first week, walking the two miles each way was trying for the soul, especially walking uphill after a day of seeing patients. Gradually, the hike got easier as my stamina improved. Then, too, you stop to enjoy the first spring wildflowers blooming through the snow. The walk became delightful, unless it was at night and an emergency call. Then, it wasn't much fun.

Eventually, the snow recedes off the valley floor and mesa, then the forests, and finally back to the peaks. Spring bursts forth in the high country. Just around the corner, summer returns with tourists and increasing emergency calls. Finally, after a long winter, you are ready.

Loneliness? Not really. With the Sawtooths outside your front windows, it's hard to be lonesome. There's an overlook of the Sawtooths as you drive up Highway 21, just past the Grandjean turnoff. When I drive around that curve and first see the peaks of the Sawtooth Mountains, I know I'm home. I feel that deep within me.

My professional life could be all-consuming. After two failed marriages, the one that endured was my marriage to my work caring for others. My EMTs and ambulance drivers were like family. The deputy sheriff, Jim Parkhouse, became a close friend and confidante, and we turned to each other to talk on Sunday mornings, talk therapy I treasured. Of course, I also had my family: my five kids, my five brothers and sisters, my parents, and even Cal. Beyond them, I had close friends in the Stanley community. I was part of the small Stanley community that shared holidays, loss, and life. Our civic lives included Thanksgiving and Christmas potlucks supported by the Chamber of Commerce. We also quilted together as the Mountain Mamas. So, was I lonely? I didn't have time.

For people who are alone, Christmas can be lonely. As a family, we tried to keep the season's spirit alive. Despite the divorce, the Osborn family skied and snowmobiled into the cabin to celebrate Christmas together. When I moved to Boise, Cal and Cory would drop by my townhouse on Christmas afternoons.

"Nothing in life is certain except death and taxes," Cal often said, quoting Ben Franklin. Age has replaced my snowmobile with an electric scooter. Hanging on the walls of my independent living apartment are photos and accolades. Still, sometimes I get bored and lonely. My oldest son, Cal Jr, and his wife, Dia, bring me coffee and non-institutional meals, and John calls nearly every day, and we discuss his ER cases.

Living in a facility for the elderly, a whole day can go by, and my phone never rings except for nuisance calls.

But in Stanley? The phone and EMS radio almost never stopped. And I always had my mountains. The mountains can be your salvation.

36

FIRST RESPONDERS: LAW ENFORCEMENT

I feel the earth move under my feet
I feel the sky tumblin' down
I feel my heart start to tremblin'
Whenever you're around.

Carole King

Someone was knocking at the door.

It had been another hellish Fourth of July weekend, and I was home at two am, dead tired. Driving home from the clinic, I saw a pitch-black night sky with a universe of stars silhouetting the Sawtooth peaks. As I drove up to the cabin and parked, my backdoor light was the only human light that night on Shaw Mesa.

Alone, I walked through the door to my bedroom, took off my white coat, undressed, put on my nightgown, snuggled under the covers, and dozed into sleep.

Knock, knock, knock.

Silence.

Knock, knock, knock.

I was alone on Shaw Mesa, a woman in my fifties, and scared. With my heart pounding and skin clammy, I opened the dresser drawer, feeling the pistol. With the gun in hand, I slowly walked to the back door.

KNOCK, KNOCK, KNOCK.

Aiming the pistol with my right hand, I unlocked the door with my left. I opened the door enough to target the gun at the level of my chin.

What do you want?" I croaked, my voice trembling.

"Marie?" I knew that voice.

"Jim!" Jim Parkhouse, our deputy sheriff, stood under the porch light in his uniform.

"Hi, Marie!" I lowered the gun that was targeting Jim's mid-abdomen.

An Idaho State Police officer accompanying Jim bent over with belly-busting laughter. That made me mad.

Gary Gadwa

The unsolved mystery of the ISP patrol car's broken window

"Jim! Why didn't you use your lights?"

"We didn't want to scare you."

Shit. "What did you expect me to do? It wouldn't have been a problem if you had your blue lights on." To this day, it still makes me tense. I could have killed Jim.

"Marie, you're needed at the clinic. The phones and radio are out in town, so we came to get you." I got dressed and followed the officers back to Stanley.

"I'm going to kill you."

The teenager was crying, his nose running. "I'm going to kill you. I'm going to kill both of you." A big-for-age sixteen-year-old male pointed the handgun at me as I, wearing my white coat and stethoscope, knelt over his father, whose chest was soaked in blood.

The emergency call came from Dirty Dora at the Beaver Creek Store after the son attacked his father. I was home, ran for my car, and sped down Shaw Mesa road. When I hit the highway, I turned south toward Sun Valley, pushing the gas pedal to the floor for the next ten miles. The deputy sheriff, Carl Ellis, would be rocketing up the Sawtooth Valley from Stanley, ten minutes behind me. Further behind was the ambulance crew.

I arrived first. There were able-bodied men inside the store staring out the window. The father was on the ground, bleeding. I knelt to do my initial assessment. Suddenly, a distraught teenager stepped from behind a tree, pointing his handgun at me.

He stepped closer. And closer. "Don't touch him. Leave him alone," he yelled.

Still kneeling over my bleeding patient, I looked up into the gun barrel. I was going to die.

It happened so fast. The patrol car slid to a stop. The deputy sheriff, Carl Ellis, leaped out. He grabbed the boy, took him down, and attached handcuffs. It was stunning how fast Carl moved. Carl, a stickler for rules and the frequent butt of jokes in rule-averse Stanley, saved two lives that day, the father's and mine. Actually, three: The messed-up teenage boy didn't die either. He might have been the first to take a bullet, pointing his gun, threatening to kill.

Whether in the field or ERs, we as healthcare providers need law enforcement. We are vulnerable. Helping our patients can place us at risk. Law enforcement must be there to support and protect us. Having law enforcement in Stanley is part of the saga of the Challis-Stanley relationship. During the 1970s, Stanley was a tax cash cow for Challis and Custer County, paying out taxes while receiving few services in return. Stanley's City Council and Chamber of Commerce sent a committee to make our case for a permanent deputy sheriff. After multiple meetings and escalating incidents in the area, the county sheriff acceded to Stanley's request. Finally, law enforcement came to the Sawtooth country. Placing a deputy sheriff in Stanley year-round went a long way to lowering the temperature.

Carl Ellis was our new deputy sheriff. On Mondays, when Carl was required to be in court in Challis, "the mice will play when the cat's away." Locals relaxed a bit and broke a few rules. But when you needed law enforcement, officers were there.

The locals' view of Carl was that Carl was rigid, strictly by the book. The Stanley community gossiped that he would have arrested his mother if she broke a rule. Carl wrote a lot of tickets, or at least that was what most folks thought. Carl became known as "Bam-Bam." Town gossip about Carl missed the truth about the human being under that crisp uniform. Beneath that all-official mask was a gentle, warm human being.

Carl actually got cross-wise with the federal government. Since Custer County didn't have money to invest in law enforcement equipment, Carl turned to surplus federal property offered to qualified units. The Stanley Clinic was qualified, too, and that's how we got exam tables, filing cabinets, and other equipment. Federal surplus was also available to county law enforcement. Carl took full advantage, but somewhere, he overstepped, and the federal government came after him, filing charges. I was summoned to federal court in Boise to testify.

I took my seat in the witness chair. Carl's attorney started by asking me to describe my role as the NP for the Stanley Clinic and Stanley Ambulance. Then he questioned me about Carl.

I knew Carl's attorney from Jerome. He had a dog named Stanley, who I had dequilled. The attorney was a smoker, and I had advised him to stop several times. "Marie Osborn, do you provide healthcare for Carl Ellis?" asked Carl's attorney.

"Yes, I do," I replied to the court.

"And does Carl Ellis always do everything you tell him to do?"

"About the same as you do when I tell you to quit smoking," I answered.

The courtroom erupted in laughter, including the federal judge. Fortunately, Carl was acquitted.

As Stanley's first deputy sheriff, Carl faced a challenge not unique to Stanley: a spouse who never felt at home in the high country with its harsh winters. "You can't eat the scenery," Fran would say. Carl and Fran had met when he served in the Navy's military police; she was older than he. As much as Carl loved his work in Stanley, the couple moved to Boise, where he continued in law enforcement, true blue by the book.

The brutal beating in their home of a good, giving couple I knew well one morning made me angry and sick. I got the call, went to the house, got them in my car, and took them to the clinic. After initial assessments and dressing wounds, I called the Sun Valley hospital to let ER staff know the young woman was on her way with facial trauma.

I drove to the Mountain Village Lodge's office to update our volunteer, Bud James, who operated our EMS radio base station. After updating Bud on the beating, I walked out of the office and looked up, surprised.

Above me was the new deputy sheriff, Jim Parkhouse, poised on the second-floor balcony overlooking the motel office entryway.

I turned toward my car, only to see the man suspected of the assault run past me. He was sprinting toward the passageway between the motel office and rooms. Muscular though not tall, easily angered, and quick to fight, the man was avoided by locals, especially when he drank, which he did too often.

The suspect never saw Deputy Parkhouse. Jim launched from the balcony. He landed on top of the suspect, knocking him to the ground in a puddle of mud.

When the two looked up, local military veteran Bud James stood there, holding a maul hammer.

"Deputy," Bud yelled, "If you let that man up, I'll kill him." Handcuffs on, the suspect headed for jail in Challis with Jim Parkhouse at the wheel of his patrol car. A day that started horribly with a brutal attack ended with Stanley a safer community.

Welcome, Jim Parkhouse, to Stanley, Idaho.

Jim was a good law enforcement officer: While you didn't mess with Jim, he also had compassion for people. In the chaos of trauma calls, Jim was calm and clear-headed. He was reliable: If anything went wrong or there was a problem, he handled it. For most of the 1980s, Jim was part of our Stanley community.

A southern Idaho boy, Jim was born in Wendell, raised in Soda Springs, and attended Idaho State University before joining the Army. His military service took him to Germany and Vietnam, but he eventually came home to Idaho. First, he drove heavy equipment, then worked in a couple of plants, where he also became an EMT. After getting to know the local sheriff and deputy sheriff, they offered him a job. And with that, Jim entered law enforcement as a career.

Custer County was looking for a deputy sheriff for Stanley, and it was a match. After one week in Challis, Jim sat behind the wheel of his patrol car and drove upriver to Stanley on New Year's Eve, 1981.

DEPUTY SHERIFF JIM PARKHOUSE, IN HIS OWN WORDS

Stanley welcomed me like I was coming home. Driving upriver from Challis, you come around a corner, and wow! The Sawtooth Mountains open up to you. White with snow, they seem even taller, more rugged. Part of joining the community was working closely with Stanley's EMTs and Marie. As an EMT before law enforcement, I could better walk in their shoes.

Who lives and who dies? We saved the two girls walking through deep snow to Banner Summit. We couldn't save the snowmobiler at Railroad Ridge. When that emergency call came, it was probably forty below zero in Stanley with a brisk wind. We started that New Year probing an avalanche, hoping for a rescue.

On our first night on Railroad Ridge, we were forced to seek shelter in a nearby miner's cabin. Our helicopter transport had mechanical problems shortly after dropping off a crew, and we were stuck on the ridge. The cabin lacked a few essentials: windows, doors, and, most importantly, the pipe connecting the wood stove to the ceiling. The wind whistled and shrieked as we huddled to stay warm.

The following day, we lined up, continuing to probe the avalanche field. If we found one piece of debris, we'd see the body alive, we hoped. Were we probing the right area? When that long cornice collapsed, a small ridge split the avalanche. We looked to the surviving brother to decide which side of the hill to probe. He was there when the snow torrent overtook his missing brother.

After a freezing, sleepless night in the miner's cabin, a second day of probing, with wind and snow increasing, temperatures dropping, and the cornice rebuilding, we abandoned the search.

In June, I returned to Railroad Ridge with my dog. I just needed to find debris, and I could locate the body. There, poking up through the melting snow, was about three inches of a snowmobile windshield. We had probed the wrong side of the ridge. Every place we had probed, hungry bears out of hibernation had clawed the snow, attracted by our scent.

Needing a tool for snow removal, I found a coffee can in the miner's cabin. I started digging. The snowmobile tilted, encased in the avalanched debris field. I kept digging, now down in a hole. Suddenly, my can hit something soft.

I set aside the can and used my hand. My fingers touched a boot with a leg.

Out of the hole, I lunged. This was an excellent time to talk to my dog.

Here was my dilemma: I couldn't leave the body because the bears would eat it. But I didn't have radio communication up on Railroad Ridge. I hunkered down, knowing that eventually, someone would send out a search party.

Chuf. Chuf. Chuf. Chuf. A Forest Service helicopter flew overhead. I stood, waving my arms and yelling. The ship kept on going.

Bored, I approached the cornice above the snowfield, melting in the warm afternoon. Standing on top, the view was incredible. I had a few things with me, including a plastic garbage bag. I sat down on the garbage bag and pushed off. Wow! What a thrill! I was faster than any sled. I barely stopped before I ran out of snow. I climbed back up to the top of the cornice for a second run.

Sitting on the garbage bag, preparing to push off again, I heard the *chuf, chuf, chuf.* A helicopter appeared over the ridge, flew up to the cornice, stopped, and hovered. I looked into the aircraft and waved at the pilot, deciding this was probably not the time for a second run.

The earlier Forest Service helicopter had reported to the Custer County sheriff. The sheriff dispatched a helicopter to retrieve the body and shuttle Stanley's deputy sheriff and his dog off of Railroad Ridge.

Marie received emergency calls day in and day out. She was the rock that held that community together. People who work in healthcare can see the worst. Unlike healthcare providers, we in law enforcement are less haunted by memories. We also get to do good stuff, like helping people get into their locked cars.

The mind can only take so much. In Stanley, emergency calls can come in threes: three this week, three next week, and three the week after. Calls don't come just during the day shift, either. Calls come at night. Just when you finish with one emergency, there's another. And another. With over a million tourists a year, you are lucky if you have any medical information when visitors get in trouble.

We had a transient living in one of the old buildings on Highway 21. In town, he spent time in the grocery parking lot. We booked him for a DUI. That's how we had information. A week later, he drank a gallon of Chablis and walked in front of a car on the highway between Stanley and Lower Stanley. On impact, his body knocked the car's top back over the trunk. People in the vehicle were horrified but unhurt. We did CPR on him for quite a while.

Marie arrived with the Stanley Ambulance and EMTs. We got a pulse and respirations back, then loaded him in the ambulance. We lost him again. This time, we couldn't bring him back.

He didn't die a "John Doe." Because of his DUI, we had information that eventually allowed us to notify the family.

His brother was an attorney. His sister was high up in California Highway Patrol. Our deceased patient? He had been a history professor in northern California.

He was intelligent and an alcoholic. He was so intoxicated the day he died that he probably didn't know until impact. He was in the wrong place at the wrong time.

And despite doing everything we could to save him, we lost him.

The old, white-bearded man kept saying, "Officer, I didn't see that car. Believe me, I really didn't see that car."

I was in Challis when the emergency call came over the radio. Pushing the patrol car, I drove fast upriver to Stanley and then west on Highway 21. The car wreck was west of Stanley on Highway 21 at the turnoff to Bear Valley and Boundary Creek.

By the time I arrived, the EMTs had already come and gone. No one was injured; incredible luck for everyone. According to witness accounts, the elderly man suddenly drove onto highway traffic from Boundary Creek Road. The speed limit is sixty-five, but drivers go much faster, a gold mine in traffic tickets.

I asked the elderly man to join me in the patrol car's front seat. He seemed confused.

"I didn't see that car," he said again.

"Hey, would you mind taking out your wallet?" I asked, thinking of my EMT training. He did and handed his wallet to me. There it was, the "Medi-Alert" card.

"Do you have a pacemaker?"

"Yup. It's not been working right."

I radioed Bud James at the EMS base station at Mountain Village Lodge.

"We have an elderly patient, confused, with a probable malfunctioning pacemaker. I need Marie to meet me at the clinic."

Don't shoot your gun across the highway. You could kill someone. And it's against the law. The call came in: "Someone in Lower Stanley is shooting across the road."

The suspects were sitting on the porch. I got out of the car.

"Hey Jim, how're you doing?" said Pat.

"Someone's shooting down the road," I responded. "I only give one warning. Are we done?"

Pat glowered at me. After a long silence, "Yes," he replied.

Pat and his friends Mitch, Terry, and Mac were a group of river runners you didn't want to fight with. Rowing boats all summer, they had muscles. They didn't mind mixin' it up.

Later, after sunset, I was in town patrolling because of the weekend Stanley Stomp. One of the West's biggest, meanest cowboys walked out of the Kasino Club that night. He was trouble incarnate and looking for a fight. Even with my gun, this was not good.

I grew increasingly uneasy as he walked toward me. Then I heard voices behind me on the street.

"When you get done whooping on the sheriff, we'll whoop on you. Around here, you don't whoop on local boys." The river runners Pat Silver, Mitch, Terry, and Mac stood behind me. Thank God for giving warnings instead of tickets. The river runners bordered on being a vigilante group, but they had a heart where it belonged.

Certain sounds can stop a crowd. I remember tangling with a bikers' gang, Brother Speed, in front of the Rod & Gun Club. Like a scene from Gunsmoke, I stood alone on Ace of Diamond Street facing the gang of bikers.

Then, breaking the silence, I heard this "click-click." That sound was a show-stopper. We all turned.

McCoy's general store and tackle shop was next door to the Rod & Gun Club. Sitting on the porch was Larry McCoy, holding his Remington 870 shotgun. Larry was a Veteran and former Fish & Game officer.

That slide going back and forth can be a magical sound in law enforcement when your life is on the line. It was for me standing alone, facing Brother Speed.

Should I move the body? The dead man was lying on the driveway about three feet from the garage door. It was three o'clock in the afternoon. Kids were starting to come home from school, walking on the sidewalk. Neighbors were driving by. The coroner was ninety minutes out. Inside my head, my inner voice kept saying, "*You never move a body.*" I turned to the paramedics, "Let's move him into the garage." Common sense prevailed, and the coroner was okay with my decision. My supervisor? Not so much.

Early morning on October 28, just before the 1983 Borah Peak earthquake, Challis Dispatch came over the radio, "Jim, you're needed in Robinson Bar Canyon. We have a truck overturned on Highway 75."

Already in my second year as Stanley's deputy sheriff, I was committing the river-road curves to memory. Entering Robinson Bar Canyon from Stanley-side starts with a blind, sharp turn to the left.

As I entered the canyon, an overturned truckload of lumber came into view. The downed vehicle was partially blocking the canyon highway.

"I'm Deputy Sheriff Jim Parkhouse. Could I see your driver's license?"

"Officer, it was a long night. I must've dozed off at the wheel," explained the trucker. For the truck driver, this was not his best day. It wasn't going to get any better for either of us.

"You're lucky. It's ninety-four feet down to the river. With those rapids, you wouldn't want to go in the river here," I noted, looking at the traffic backing up on the far side of the overturned truck. Robinson Bar Canyon's highway cuts into the steep, near-vertical mountainside for a quarter-mile.

My feet suddenly jolted as I felt the earth move under my feet. The noise of river rapids exploded into a roar. Imagine a fighter jet passing you less than sixty feet away. Small and large rocks tumbled onto the highway and into the river. Jesus Christ! Everything was falling. With the world falling apart, seconds seemed like minutes. After ten seconds, the earthquake stopped. The ground stopped shaking. Quiet returned except for river sounds.

The truck driver and I ran up the highway. One massive rock had landed, completely blocking the highway. It wouldn't take long for cars to back up.

Later that morning, we tried a boulder buster, which polished but didn't budge the rock. A crew from the Idaho Highway Department had to blast the boulder to reopen Highway 75.

Not long after the earthquake: Pow! Booming jet noise. Again! Aftershock? No, this time it was a fighter jet, two F4s flying low in the canyon, scrambled out of Mountain Home Air Force Base. Pilots were doing reconnaissance in the Salmon River canyon, heading toward Challis.

Two schoolchildren, Tara Leadon, seven years old, and Travis Frank, six, were walking to school when the earthquake collapsed a masonry wall of an old building, killing them.

ISP called. "Parkhouse, we need you to check out the silver mine at Clayton." EMS StateComm also called Marie to do the same.

There was a need to worry: Eleven years earlier, in 1972, ninety-one miners died underground in the Sunshine Mine up north in the Coeur d'Alene mining district.

What would a powerful earthquake do to the Clayton mine shafts, going down 1,100 feet and spreading out nearly 20,000 feet?

Closed spaces are not my thing. No way was I going down into that mine. One primitive elevator served the miners. When the earthquake struck, miners were at shift change and running late. The night shift had come up, and the day shift had not yet gone down. Miners were all standing by the open elevator shaft when the ground shook: pure luck. The Clayton miners were okay and accounted for.

My memories of the Robinson Bar Canyon were more than the Borah Peak earthquake, drownings, and car wrecks. There are good memories, too. They included a singer-songwriter named Carole King.

Carole lived at Robinson Bar Ranch. She's a celebrity, but down-to-earth and eventually just another local. Carole wanted me to see her greenhouse to ensure law enforcement knew she was not growing marijuana. After all, this was Custer County, Idaho, in the 1980s.

Carole was driving upriver when she got a birds-eye view of county law enforcement in action. Earlier that day in Challis, a couple of guys with empty wallets walked into a restaurant, ordered expensive dinners, ate well, and then walked out without paying. The "lobster boys" fled, speeding upriver toward Stanley with Custer County's sheriff in hot pursuit.

I stopped my patrol car on that narrow highway, flipping on my overhead lights. Coming down the road from Stanley was a dump truck with Pat Cutler at the wheel, his wife in the passenger seat next to him. I asked Pat to park his vehicle in one lane and then asked him and his wife to get out of the way.

I parked my patrol car next to Pat's truck, the two vehicles blocking both lanes, my lights flashing. I then walked out on the highway and stood with my gun.

The fleeing vehicle came into view, slowed, and stopped. Stanley law enforcement got the credit for halting the dine-and-dash duo.

Carole King, driving behind the Challis squad car, exclaimed, "I got to see news happen!"

Death can be so jarringly out-of-place in these beautiful mountains. Death is tough when you lose friends and family.

That morning, Marie walked with Dave Waite to the post office. After saying goodbye, Dave headed to the airport. The Waite family was a family of pilots: Dave's parents Dick and Joy, and his sisters, BZ and Marilyn. Marilyn married Brad Miller, who would also be on Dave's plane that day. The Waite family ran the River Rat Express Shuttle Service. Their office was next to the Stanley Clinic.

After saying goodbye to Marie, Dave started his plane and flew south to Twin Falls for a quick round-trip flight, flying back with Brad Miller.

Dave and Brad flew over Galena Summit and down the Sawtooth Valley toward Stanley on the return flight. Dave turned as he approached the Idaho Rocky Mountain Ranch. The 900-acre guest ranch has a great 1920s vintage lodge with a porch facing a fish pond and the Sawtooth Range. Dave wanted to buzz the lodge to let folks know he'd be making his date that night. He circled the lodge, tipping the airplane's wings.

It happened fast.

When wind shear hits a plane, sudden changes in wind direction can eliminate lift. Flying low eliminates time to take corrective action.

Dave's plane was just above the trees when he hit the wind shear. He and Brad never had time. The plane nose-dived straight into the ground in front of the lodge.

When I arrived, the plane was still smoking. The wing tanks had ruptured, leaving a sheen of fuel on the water. With three men from the ranch helping, we pulled Dave and Brad from the wrecked plane. C-collars and backboards were not needed. Both died on impact.

The Stanley Ambulance arrived with Marie, EMTs, and doctors. The physicians had been standing in the motel office when the emergency call from the ranch came to the EMS radio base station. They volunteered to help and got on board the ambulance with our EMTs. There was nothing they could do.

In 1987 I decided to leave Stanley to take on a new position with Ada County law enforcement. It was not an easy decision; Stanley was like home, and the community was like family.

In my last year in Stanley, we had eight fatalities. I knew all eight. These were locals, people I knew and cared for.

I found myself getting off work, going home, and crying. I knew I couldn't handle it anymore.

Shortly after starting work at my new positon in Boise, I was at a grisly death scene. "Jim, are you doin' okay?" asked the other officer.

"Sure," I said. "I'm fine. I didn't know them." Our job as law enforcement is to keep order and keep people safe. As Marie knows from her own experiences, healthcare providers can't look down the barrel of a gun while taking care of their patients. Marie and the Stanley EMTs would never have done what they did if they didn't care and care deeply.

I've always believed in leaving the world better than I found it. Through law enforcement, I was able to do that.

Sundays early, I'd arrive at the clinic. After a busy Saturday, there'd be suture kits to clean and autoclave, restocking, and more cleaning if there was blood or other bodily fluids on surfaces. Jim, seeing my car at the clinic, would stop in, "Hi Marie. How's it going?" And we'd talk – not gossip, but share our experiences. Or, if Jim saw cars parked in front of the clinic, he stepped in to assess for any problems, "Marie, you okay? Need any help?"

Talking can be therapy. You wear your white coat, stethoscope, and professional demeanor on the outside. Inside, you may be churning with the most recent drowning, mountain climbing accident, or car wreck. Talking through horrific cases can be a godsend when you're the sole provider in an isolated area. But who? You can't talk to anybody who walks in, or even your best friend.

In the 1980s, in Stanley, the person who understood and could keep confidence was Jim. We were in the same boat. Jim didn't have anyone to talk to either. With talking comes unburdening, reviewing your thought processes, problem-solving: so many good things. When spilling your guts, you just had to be sure the information didn't walk out the door into the community.

One Sunday morning, Jim shared his experience from the night before about kids setting off firecrackers right across the street from the clinic.

"Marie, you wouldn't believe it. One of those kids tried to set off firecrackers in the soles of my boots! I told them to get out of town and don't come back."

"Jim," I said with a wry smile. "Those were my kids." Jerry, John, and Melinda had come to town to enjoy the Fourth of July festivities. Wrong place, wrong time: One of them or their friends lit a firecracker just as Deputy Sheriff Parkhouse walked by. That night, it was not funny.

The following Christmas, Jim Parkhouse sent a package. The card read, "For the Osborn kids."Inside was a big box loaded with fireworks.

37

WHERE EVERYONE KNOWS YOUR NAME

Heart of Idaho

"Mighty pretty view of the Sawtooth Mountains,
Raging Salmon River running by my door,
Just seen an eagle fly by my window,
Yahoo, yippee oh — Idaho.

I'm never, ever going to leave the Stanley Basin.
This is the place I'm going to live my life.
Go down to the hot springs and do a little soakin,'
Build me a cabin for my babies and my wife."

The Braun Brothers

In a Town This Size

"In a town this size, there's no place to hide
Everywhere you go you meet someone you know
You can't steal a kiss in a place like this
How the rumors do fly in a town this size."

John Prine

Like towns and cities throughout civilization, Stanley has a beginning and history. Before Stanley, from time immemorial, the mountains stood and occasionally trembled, rivers flowed, salmon returned, and indigenous people lived and flourished. Still today, the upper Salmon River country remains the ancestral lands and waters of the Shoshone-Bannock Tribes.

University of Idaho Library Digital Collections

Cowboy in the Stanley Basin, Sawtooth Range, 1920. Image courtesy of Shipp Archival Idaho Photograph Collection.

Before Lewis and Clark, smallpox, measles, chickenpox, and other infectious diseases killed ninety-five percent of Indigenous people in the Americas. Humans living in the western hemisphere had no immunity. By comparison, the Bubonic plague's "Black Death" in Europe during the fourteenth and fifteenth centuries depopulated entire towns, killing about one-third of the population. Our recent experiences with influenza, polio, HIV/AIDS, and COVID pale in comparison.

On August 12, 1805, downriver of the future Stanley, explorers Lewis and Clark stepped out of the United States and into the Columbia River watershed, the richest salmon river on earth. Next came missionaries, fur traders, miners, and the US military. Explorers with the Hudson Bay Company entered the Sawtooth Valley in the 1820s, but beavers were scarce. Miners came later when, in 1863, Captain John Stanley led prospectors through the area.

In 1863, four months before the Battle of Gettysburg, Congress created a new territory, "Idaho." President Lincoln and Congress (the northern states only) federally chartered the Union Pacific Railroad in 1862 and the Northern Pacific Railroad in 1864. To build the "transcontinental" railroads, Congress conditionally granted about 200 million acres of Indigenous lands-turned-public domain to these federal railroad corporations. Eventually, the Union Pacific Railroad ran track up the Wood River Valley to haul out sheep and, later, haul in skiers to the railroad company's new swank resort, "Sun Valley."

Teddy Roosevelt used his presidency to thwart railroad-based companies and others from looting the public domain. With help from wrestling partner and America's first Chief Forester, Gifford Pinchot, Roosevelt dramatically expanded the National Forest System. In 1905, Roosevelt signed the law transferring control of the National Forest System land to the US Forest Service.

Protecting the Sawtooths as a national park took flight in the early 1900s. After decades of citizen protection efforts, in 1972, Congress established the Sawtooth National Recreation Area under the U.S. Forest Service.

The year 1910 opened with Pinchot attacking President Taft on the floor of the U.S. Senate as a traitor to conservation followed in August by the Big Blow-up that burned much of North Idaho and the surrounding region: three million acres in forty-eight hours. That same year, a mining company built a dam blocking the Salmon River's namesake salmon runs. The Sunbeam Dam powered a gold-mining dredge on the Yankee Fork. The dredge's front end consumed salmon habitat, extracted gold, and defecated gravel mounds at the back end for miles. To save the salmon, Idahoans blew up the Sunbeam Dam in 1934 — a year after the ceremonial first stake starting Grand Coulee Dam's construction. Today on the Yankee Fork, Shoshone-Bannock Tribes are leading restoration efforts.

Dams brought prosperity and devastation. The United States and Canada replaced the world's richest salmon river, the Columbia, with a machine: stair-stepping dams and slack-water reservoirs plugged into an electric grid. An engineering marvel was also an unmitigable ecological, cultural, and social justice disaster. Today, as with the Sunbeam Dam, Idahoans are working to breach the four Lower Snake River dams in Washington State that are destroying Salmon River salmon runs in Idaho.

Stanley eventually became a town in 1919 by surveying and recording its streets and lots. The town was incorporated as the "City of Stanley" in 1947. Stanley remains a gathering place with few year-round residents living miles from nowhere.

Like towns everywhere, Stanley's story has beginnings, endings, transitions, and change — and now facing climate change. With recent earthquakes and massive forest fires, even the Sawtooth Mountains are changing.

I met almost everyone I knew in Stanley when they walked through the clinic's front door. One new patient hobbled in with a sprained ankle. "Hi, I'm Bunny."

Bunny filled out the new patient form and handed back the clipboard. Her birth year was 1947, the same as the City of Stanley. What caught my eye, though, was her name: Khema Rani Kitselman.

"Kitselman?" I asked. "Are you related to the Kitselman family in Muncie, Indiana?" I had to ask. Kitselman is an unusual name.

"Well, yes."

Wow! If you grew up in Muncie, the Alva Kitselman mansion was too big and beautiful to miss. The estate covered several city blocks with gardens and swan-swimming ponds. My Muncie sorority made new pledges correctly count all the pickets of the wrought iron fence encircling the estate.

Bunny's father, Alva Kitselman Jr., or "Beau", was a mathematician, linguist, scientist, psychologist, and early computer code writer. While at Stanford, he studied oriental languages, transcribing Sanskrit into English. Kitselman named his daughter after a queen, or "rani", the beautiful and vain Khema. The Buddha helped her understand life's impermanence and Khema became Buddha's first nun and chief disciple. Her namesake, Khema Rani Kitselman, aka "Bunny," would become the mayor of impermanence: Stanley, Idaho.

Bunny was born on the Paiute Indian Reservation outside of Reno in 1947, where her father had a ranch, and later lived with her mother (and 7,000 chickens) in Rogue River,

Oregon. Bunny graduated from La Jolla High School during the Vietnam War. Close friends were drafted and died in the war. Tear gas, demonstrators, and black helicopters stopped Bunny, a political science major, from finishing her studies and taking her final exams. Frustrated, she fled college and California for Mexico, later returning to the United States, where she helped nurse her ailing father until he died in 1980.

That "mighty pretty view of the Sawtooth Mountains" pulled Bunny north. When thirteen, Bunny started spending summers in the Sawtooth Valley. At eighteen, she bought an acre of land near Stanley on Iron Creek. Bunny knew Stanley's Danner family as a teenager, and Bob Danner later built a log home for her in the Treasure Valley. Eventually, Bunny and Bob married.

In small towns, you marry into family and community. We knew Bunny not as a Khema Rani Kitselman, but as that strong woman who ran Danner's log-cabin motel and eventually became the mayor of Stanley.

BUNNY DANNER SIEMERS, IN HER OWN WORDS

"I hate women libbers." That was Jack Niece. Once Jack decided, he either didn't like you or you were all right. Jack was from one of the original mining families that homesteaded the Sawtooth Valley.

I didn't accept the insult. I was sitting on the lowboy after driving the backhoe. "My name is Bunny. You want a beer?"

"Sure. Never pass up a cold beer on a hot day."

Never underestimate the power of a cold beer: Jack and I got along. Besides, that's how locals welcomed newcomers in the early 1980s.

Jack would call me every morning to see if he could wake me. "You awake, rabbit?"

"Yeah." By six am, I'd be awake. Jack might come to the motel, pounding on the door, yelling, "Is that rabbit-ass in there?"

"Is that jackass out there?" And Jack walked in, joining me for morning coffee.

Jack was gruff and grouchy but also good and kind. During heavy snow, he volunteered to plow the clinic and school parking areas. He loved to watch wildlife and feed starving elk during brutal winters. Jack Niece loved Stanley but hated people moving in and changing the town.

"This is Custer County sheriff's office."

"Hi. My name is Bunny Danner. I'm co-owner of Danners Cabins in Stanley. We just dug up a body."

We were digging foundations so we could move cabins to create our motel when we came across human remains. The City of Stanley had condemned the old motel. It had a well, but no running water, and lodgers used outhouses. The old motel also had a restaurant until a propane explosion.

When Bob Danner and I married, I invested in the motel and became a business partner in Danners Cabins. Bob, my brother Glenn Kitselman and I shared ownership of Stanley Air Taxi. My business relationship with Bob lasted longer than our four-year marriage; that ended in 1989.

When we found the body, we were moving cabins to create an "L" configuration. The cabins faced our motel office, the Forest Service's first Stanley ranger station built in 1906. We moved in three cabins from the far side of the Rod & Gun Club, across from the Sawtooth Hotel. We jacked up those cabins, slid the lowboy underneath, and moved the three cabins one by one through town.

The backhoe unearthed human bones and clothing about three feet down while digging a new foundation. After I notified the Custer County sheriff, a deputy telephoned with instructions.

"Bunny, it's probably an old miner." The deputy explained that investigating and identifying the body would mean a trip from Challis, adding costs. "Won't change anything. Go ahead, rebury him."

We reburied the body under cabin 2, giving him our blessings. Then, we dug the hole, put him back in the ground, pouring cement on top. He got to hear what happened in that cabin every Saturday night, which was, too, a blessing.

Burying the dead during Sawtooth winters was no easy matter. The old ice house stored the bodies with the ground frozen until the earth warmed up for burial. Stanley has a town cemetery, but there are no vacancies. Old timers are buried outside the cemetery, including under cabin 2.

In the dead of night, the living might want a motel room. Running Danners Cabins, I was on duty 24/7. When receptionists at other motels wished to sleep, they turned on their "No Vacancy" sign. Not me. I always left on my vacancy sign. When customers stumbled in drunk from the bars, I'd answer the bell throwing a robe over my pajamas. "Just a minute! I'm coming!"

"Don't talk to me. Sign here. Give me your credit card. Here's your room key. See you in the morning." I was sending them to their room because I was returning to bed. Mostly, they were grateful. After all, what else were they going to do? The bars were closed, and they were probably too drunk to drive.

Strange people showed up sometimes. One evening, a man stumbled into the office with unzipped pants. "Go out and take care of that guy," I told the young girl working for me. Then, I glanced through the glass countertop and saw the problem.

"Never mind, I'll handle it." He was too drunk to put himself together. I handed him a cabin key. "Go to your room."

When we said "Welcome to Stanley," we meant it. We kept the motel open because people needed lodging. Vehicles break down, it gets cold, it rains and snows, and people need a roof over their heads. Even if there weren't a single motel room left in town, I'd still welcome room seekers, "Come on in. I'll get you blankets." And, they'd sleep in the office on the floor.

Sometimes, grateful guests returned with a gift bottle of wine. You'll find the light on and the door open in rural America at all hours. But if it's in the middle of the night, don't try to have a conversation with me.

We built Stanley. We had to: By the 1970s, the old town was falling apart. So, locals, including Bob Danner, Bruce Coburn, Fred Brubaker, and Don Cutler built their homes and businesses. It was not all work and no play. In the summer, Stanley had live music and dancing at three bars. So, we worked all day and danced until the music stopped.

C.A. Betts, University of Idaho Library Digital Collections

Stanley, Idaho, in 1931. Image courtesy of Bureau of Reclamation projects, Archival Idaho Photograph Collection.

Stanley's "Waldorf Hysteria" stood next to the Post Office, a visual feast for customers eating breakfast at the old Stanley Club. Two gals bought that old cabin, moved it, and added on. Eventually, the Waldorf became a summertime information booth for tourists.

Before electricity came to Stanley in 1954, people used diesel generators. At Danners Cabins, we had a small generator building that we wanted to replace with housing for hired help. Jack Niece found a home for the generator building and the generator. Everything that we could sell, barter, or give away got reused. We wasted almost nothing.

We built homes, businesses, and public places: the library, chapel, city park, fire station, and the Stanley Community Building. Rather than winter in Stanley, several townspeople worked in Antarctica.

The first of Stanley's community "barn-raisings" was the Salmon River Emergency Clinic. I hobbled up those stairs and into the waiting room with a sprained ankle to meet Marie from Muncie. We have remained friends ever since.

"Marie, I need drugs!" I announced loudly, knowing I'd get a reaction while walking into the clinic's waiting room packed with tourists. People looked up and stared.

Marie poked her head into the room with that look of "Oh God, Bunny!" Then, she treated my recurrent bronchitis. Marie told me for years to quit smoking. Eventually, I did.

I don't do blood well. A friend's son rolled his VW, so I drove the mom to her son's accident scene. He was bleeding like a stuck pig. I loaded them both in my car, went to the clinic, and got them to Marie in the treatment room. I walked back to the waiting room and nearly passed out. During a crisis with blood, I'm sturdy; afterward, not so much.

"Is this the clinic?" Standing before me was a man in his thirties, a mountain biker, with half of his face hanging and dripping blood.

"No," I choked with panic, "it's over there," and pointed. I helped him to Marie at the clinic. She and the EMTs stabilized his spine, dressed his facial wounds, and then ambulanced him over the hill to Sun Valley. Later, he returned wearing a halo brace for his broken neck and with a heartfelt message of thanks.

Marie held a special place in our community. So many people would have died without Marie and the EMTs, the clinic, and the ambulance. Marie was our tireless advocate for rural healthcare.

"I'm calling for Bunny Danner," said the voice on the telephone. I'd had a mammogram, and the office staff called me with the results. Recently, a friend had died from breast cancer, so I was on edge.

"This is Bunny."

After confirming my date of birth and then providing some general information, she added, "Your mammogram shows a calcification." My heart quickened as I felt fear's cold and clammy sweat on my skin.

"What do you mean, 'calcification'?"

"You might have breast cancer." She told me to talk with my doctor and hung up.

"Oh my God, I have breast cancer," I thought. I fell apart, sobbing not into a tissue but a towel. I called Marie. She came right over and sat with me. After I pulled myself together, Marie returned to the clinic and called the office.

"You never, ever call my patients in this valley, tell them they might have cancer over the phone, then hang up. That's information you deliver in person." That was Marie. You didn't cross her.

Another time, I had to go over the hill for a hysterectomy. The closer I got to the operating room, the higher my anxiety. My surgery was first on the schedule. At six am, before the orderly wheeled me into the operating room, Marie walked into my hospital room. She had driven over Galena Summit before the crack of dawn, to ensure the surgeons gave me hormone therapy before my surgery. That was Marie, always looking out for us.

Stanley has four seasons: tourist season, hunting season, winter, and mud season. Suppose you compare Stanley in January next to July: In January, the town is almost deserted, snow-covered, and shivering. In July, the sun is shining, people are pouring in, it's on high energy, and you're working your butt off.

Sawtooth winters are sunshine cold with beautiful blue skies and crystal-white snow. You learn to be happy playing outdoors wearing long johns and insulated overalls. Winters are for dinner parties, visiting friends, meeting at the bar and playing pool, cross-country skiing, and snowmobiling. Winter is about family and community while summer is about making money.

Winter storms with blowing, drifting snow close mountain passes, knock out power, and bury the town. Yet, bad weather has a way of bringing people together. Jack Niece and Don Cutler fired up their big cats and plowed, competing almost to the point of jealousy. "I plowed you out, Bunny, and just wanted you to know," Jack would remind me. Oh, I never forgot.

Mud season, or "thaw," follows winter. Near the end of your money, you go outside and work: paint the trim and spruce to entice tourists. You stand in the mud with cold winds blowing and spitting snow. With one hand, you clutch the paint can; with the other, the brush, and get to work. The days are longer, and tourists will arrive on Memorial Day. I painted, scrubbed, and cleaned to get ready, but on Memorial Day weekend, it rained. Stanley's streets were empty. A solitary cow wandered along the highway between Stanley and Lower Stanley. "That's our tourist!" Jerry Funderberg proclaimed.

Finally, around the solstice, the sun came out. Tourists were like summer storm raindrops: a few, then a downpour. The tourist season was on, and it was gung-ho. Running a business in Stanley, you made your money between the Fourth of July and Labor Day: two months.

Labor Day flipped the switch. Mountain shadows lengthened, nights got longer and colder, and tourists dwindled. Nevertheless, most businesses stayed open until the hunting season's end. When we still had salmon and steelhead runs, fishermen also helped keep local businesses afloat. And those time-immemorial salmon runs were so abundant that, even by the mid-twentieth century, locals like Craig Rember could recall, "There were so many salmon you could almost walk across the Salmon River on their backs." For Idaho, fishing and hunting hold a special place.

Idaho people know how to use guns, mostly. So, unless hunters were drinking, we didn't have problems in town. But then, I had a couple of hunters who didn't kill anything and, to entertain themselves, sat on my motel bed throwing hatchets at my log walls. After they left, I walked in to clean, and saw all their gouges. Those jerk hunters desecrated my cabins.

"These 130-year-old walls, this miner's cabin, deserve better," I thought, and was furious. After that, I never again stayed open for hunting season. The few ruined it for the many.

Women "kept the home fires burning" as the backbone of the Sawtooth Valley. Bob Danner's mother, a good Mormon woman, raised six kids and ran the motel and restaurant with a hand pump and wringer washer. After Bob and I rebuilt Danners Cabins, I ran the motel and finances.

Women ran many of the town's businesses, helped run the ranches, organized potlucks and fund-raisers, and cleaned up the messes. In the Sawtooth country, women are strong. They have to be. Despite women to "match my mountains," not a single peak in the Sawtooths or White Clouds is named to honor a woman, indigenous or otherwise.

We are all misfits up here in the high country, a community of characters, true outliers. People who came and stayed often escaped to a different life.

When you're in the Valley, life is different. Those mountain passes, winters, and isolation transform the valley into an island. The world's problems seem more distant.

But they weren't. Alcohol was a problem. For my new motel maids, I warned them to be careful, telling of Marie's patient who found herself a "cowboy" at the bar, only to be raped and nearly murdered at Stanley Lake while the "cowboy's" wife and kids were camping. Testosterone can be a terrible hormone.

Alcohol was Stanley's drug of choice. We celebrated New Year's Eve at the Stanley Club one year. We had a big spread of food, and people were having a marvelous time.

Then, Gerald Nicholson and Jack Niece got into it. They were both big men, mad and intoxicated. Like in some Western movies, their fight spilled out into the street. That wasn't the first time, nor the last time, those two fought.

Crack cocaine came into the community when I was mayor. I got called when a young man, high on cocaine, pulled a door off its hinges and sat with his rifle and whiskey bottle after beating his girlfriend.

I told our deputy sheriff, "Arrest these people. Get them out of here."

Not everyone wanted to see Stanley change. Most everyone didn't want to lose what made Stanley, "Stanley." To protect the town, we took advantage of rewriting the Comp Plan.

We rewrote our town's plan to keep Stanley rustic, old western, and connected to our ranching and mining roots. We believed that protecting Stanley would boost tourism while also complying with the law creating the Sawtooth National Recreation Area:

> SEC. 6. The Secretary may cooperate with other Federal agencies with State and local public agencies, and with private individuals and agencies in the development and operation of facilities and services in the area in furtherance of the purposes of this Act, including but not limited to, the restoration and maintenance of the historic setting and background of the frontier ranch-type town of Stanley.
>
> The Sawtooth National Recreation Area Act,
> Public Law 92-400

Lower Stanley hated our Comp Plan and went to war with Stanley. For context, these two towns have been at odds from the start. The Post Office and the school moved back and forth until 1947 when Stanley became a bona fide "city." Lower Stanley folks would come to City Council meetings, and we'd wait for the verbal guns to come out. Eventually, Lower Stanley prevailed and opted out of our Comp Plan. Still, the plan served as a hedge against growing pressures from developers. Eventually, development pressures prevailed.

In 1993, the citizens of Stanley elected me to the City Council for two years; in 1995, I was elected for a four-year term before I was mayor from 1996 to 1999. I am proud of my community service.

But, when society's laws happen to collide with rural realities, stand back.

We had an exciting experience in the 1990s related to the national focus on Idaho salmon listed under the federal Endangered Species Act. Those famous fish once thrived near Stanley, numbering in the thousands, but now face extinction.

In Stanley, the Forest Service Law Enforcement Officer (LEO), Steve Lipus, was charged with enforcing laws and USFS regulations to protect salmon. Steve was also one of our star EMTs.

Locals knew that downstream dams were killing many salmon born upstream in Idaho. But rather than dam owners fixing the problem, Idaho's rivers, rural river towns, and local businesses took the brunt.

In 1996, with salmon facing the threat of extinction, the Forest Service adopted draconian rules to protect salmon and their spawning beds ("redds") from whitewater rafters. Those rules required rafters to limit raft numbers, portage around the redds, and keep out of the river during certain times.

Both Idaho Fish & Game and Forest Service personnel took heat for enforcing rules to protect salmon spawning beds.

Sparks started to fly immediately. People knew the dams were killing salmon, but rafters and local rafting companies were paying the price. The sense of injustice was strong. Locals focused their anger on local law enforcement: Steve Lipus with the Forest Service and Gary Gadwa with the Idaho Department of Fish and Game.

Steve and Gary were Stanley's fabled EMT "Goat Patrol," who climbed high into the Sawtooths to rescue people. During the salmon crisis, they might be saving lives one day and facing angry rafters or dodging bullets the next. There was a real risk of someone "shooting the messengers" — Gary and Steve — and we needed to lower the temperature. As a community, we needed to stop talking around each other and start talking to each other and listening face-to-face.

Stanley held collaborative group meetings weekly for about four months with outside help from a professional facilitator. At the Community Center, we sat at group tables with a whiteboard. We started by expressing varying views of the problem. Then, people would write down possible solutions, what laws and rules could be in the way, and what actions might help. Eventually, we found consensus. We all cared about the wild salmon in the Salmon River. The attacks on our local agency staff stopped, at least in Stanley.

In 2000, Sawtooth NRA officials began a new environmental assessment that led to new rules. Eventually, in 2004, the Forest Service relaxed restrictions while still requiring rafters to protect salmon redds and returning salmon, but in less draconian ways.

It is an outrage that those four dams on the Lower Snake River continue harming Stanley people, other rural river towns, tribes, and the entire ecosystem of the Salmon River country. They need to go. At long last, forces are aligning to get that done. Still, what stayed with me was the model that Stanley people provided: members of a small community sitting down together in civil discourse and working for solutions.

The City of Stanley and I turned fifty in 1997: we celebrated. As Stanley's mayor, I asked the town's organizations to assemble history boards listing volunteers that we displayed in the Community Center. Everyone in town had their name on one or multiple history boards. On our fiftieth birthday, we were a community of volunteers. Yet, in a tiny town like ours, change can come fast.

"Gentrification" is the genteel word for what happened in Stanley, Idaho.

People with wealth were coming. As assessed property values inflated, so did property taxes, forcing out locals. Custer County, seated in Challis, was happy to have Stanley's property taxes. As the county tax assessor told Marie, "Stanley will be the Sun Valley of Custer County."

What happens to a community when working people can't afford to live there? In Stanley, working people camped in the woods during the summer. The Forest Service's rule that campers must move every two weeks made that more challenging. Over a few years, Stanley became more like the Wood River Valley, where gentrification forced working-class people out of Ketchum south to Hailey, followed by Bellevue, and then even further south. Without worker housing, gentrification pushes out low-income people and hollows out the community.

The lifeblood of Stanley, of any small town, is its volunteers. Stanley's fiftieth anniversary celebrated an entire community of volunteers. What happens with gentrification?

When it comes down to government versus rich people, who usually prevails? In our litigious society, anyone can sue anyone if you have money. Towns like Stanley have limited budgets to defend their city codes. If city officials don't uniformly enforce laws to avoid litigation, you negate them or open your city to lawsuits. Making exceptions becomes the "camel's nose under the tent," eventually voiding the Comp Plan, gutting building codes, and undoing efforts to protect the town. Rustic Stanley? It's history. While the valley still has characters, it now also has McMansions. The Forest Service has a responsibility to manage the Sawtooth NRA. However, the agency's annual budget for managing the NRA is a tiny fraction of some newcomers' wealth.

The Forest Service can't pick and choose, punishing locals who do it right by not punishing those who do wrong. Otherwise, you create a double standard. The 1973 New York Times article, "*Will success spoil Stanley, Idaho? A frontier town sells its privacy for dollars*," predicted the future for Stanley and the Sawtooth NRA:

> "Today Stanley qualifies as a kind of real estate man's dream: a brand-new, barely discovered Western playground, rich in the requisites—mountains, lakes, fish, deer and forests—that have brought bundles of cash, if not tranquility, to places like Jackson, Wyoming; Sun Valley, Idaho; and Lake Tahoe, California."

Over the years, Stanley has had its angels willing to write checks, people like Dan Mahoney and Teresa Heinz Kerry, who supported the clinic and ambulance. Before you get your chest pain, can't talk from a stroke, or find yourself trapped in your wrecked vehicle leaking gasoline, reflect on who you'll call. Go ahead, dial 911. What EMT in Stanley is left to volunteer at three am to climb in the ambulance and come to help you?

The rural healthcare system that Marie crocheted together in this part of the world depended on volunteers. Unfortunately, gentrification threatens rural EMS in this part of Idaho. People with wealth who helped create this EMS problem need to be part of the solution: To whom much is given, much is expected.

Everyone knows your name in Stanley. After I left and moved to Boise, I've lived in my neighborhood for eighteen years and still don't know others on my block. The Mountain Mamas would gather clothes and kitchen goods if someone had a house fire. Once, we were all at the church for a wedding when the alarm went off: "Fire at Dirty Dora's!" The whole town got up and left. Dora was burning weeds at the edge of her log buildings, and fire spread to her cabins.

If you needed a special screw, you didn't drive three hours to the closest hardware store. Instead, you called a neighbor. "Do you have a ...?" "Can I borrow a ...?" If "yes," the next time you went to town, you might buy two: one for you and one to replace your neighbor's. The Smith family ran Stanley's hardware store, but shipping supplies was difficult and expensive, and they closed.

Although we had telephones (with long-distance charges), computers, the internet, and social media did not consume our waking hours. Instead, we talked to each other more. "How's the family?" "Where're you going hunting this fall?" "Did you hear about the dead moose they found in the river?"

For Stanley, I lived through a time when we built our homes, businesses, and community. I wouldn't change that for anything. Still, you don't know what you've got until it's gone.

That Marie and the community triumphed against such odds in opening the Stanley Clinic and Stanley Ambulance is a testament in no small part to our community's volunteers. I lived through a special time in Stanley when nearly everyone volunteered. Indeed, the lifeblood of a community is volunteerism. Unfortunately, you've lost a community's soul once you lose your volunteers.

Nothing is forever, not even the mountains. I was born into impermanence: my father wrapped it into my name and life with the Buddha and Khema story. As for each of us, there comes a day when we say goodbye. In 2005, I closed the office door at Danners Cabin for the last time and moved to Boise for chemo and to continue getting my primary healthcare from Marie.

"Bunny, do you ever think about the good old days?" a friend asked. Were the old days "good?" Yes. And they were hard. We didn't know how hard they were because that was all we knew. I am grateful. I became part of a community I helped to build and, later, lead. I'm thankful to Marie for all she did for our community and many others.

After I left, Stanley's mayor sent a certificate of thanks that I've kept close:

City of Stanley

Living in a small community such as Stanley, Idaho, has its pleasures and pains, good times and times of struggle, but the heart of a community is in its residents and its leaders.

The City of Stanley is proud to have called you both.

There is an adage that states "you never know what you have until it's gone" and the city of Stanley has lost part of itself with your move and your absence as a friend, advocate, and soldier fighting for Stanley's causes. You will be missed for years to come. We want to thank you for your years of dedication, patience, and perseverance as a valued member of our community. Please accept this certificate as a small token of our admiration, appreciation and utmost respect.

Thank you.
Mayor, Paul Frantellizzi

38

EMERGENCY CALL: KEN & BERNIE HARTZ

"Base station to Unit 1. Marie, you're needed at the clinic." I carried my EMS radio, Unit 1, wherever I went. Unfortunately, radio reception in the mountains was spotty with dead spaces. Even the radio's emergency band, accessing StateComm, was unreliable. So, we depended on radio reception at the clinic and the intersection of Highway 21 with Highway 75 by the Salmon River.

When the Stanley Ambulance transported patients to the Sun Valley Moritz Hospital ER, the crew entered a radio dead zone after crossing Galena Summit.

We could not communicate with the ER staff until the Stanley Ambulance passed the Sawtooth NRA headquarters several miles down the pass toward Ketchum. Unfortunately, holes in EMS radio reception carried consequences. One impacted a BSU freshman with a traumatic head injury.

We got the emergency call at Don and Sharon Cutler's home, where we had gathered for the first snowmobile club meeting of the year. We scrambled and headed west to near Banner Summit. There, lying in the middle of Highway 21, was the BSU student, thrown from his vehicle.

The young man had a massive head injury. He needed helicopter transport, and I repeatedly tried to reach StateComm: but nothing.

Unable to connect, we loaded him into the Stanley Ambulance and headed for the Sun Valley ER to avoid further delays. It wasn't until we reached the intersection of Highways 21 and 75 in Stanley that I was able to connect to StateComm.

They lined up air transport from Sun Valley's ER to Salt Lake City because no neurosurgeon was available in Boise. The BSU freshman made it to Salt Lake City but didn't survive.

The Sawtooth country has its Bermuda Triangles, haunted by repeated terrible accidents: the highway curve at Beaver Creek near Smiley Creek, the old metal bridge over the Salmon River near the Fish Hatchery, that highway curve near the Stanley Museum just upriver from Lower Stanley, and the old "T" at Redfish Lake near The Visitor Center. At the "T" driving toward the lake, you could turn right toward Redfish Lake Lodge or turn left toward the North Shore Picnic Area and boat launch. Straight ahead was a clump of trees and the beach.

Even in winter, the Redfish T contributed to trauma cases. A woman who had never snowmobiled rented a machine at Smiley Creek, and by the time she approached Redfish Lake, she may have felt experienced. She wasn't. The novice snowmobiler missed the turn at the T, plowed into a tree, and shattered her femur.

In the snow, we cut off her pants. The femur was not piercing the skin, so the fracture was closed. Still, I could feel moving bone fragments. Her blood pressure was low and dropping.

We placed a Hare traction splint with major arteries at risk, reducing her pain. I got the catheter into a vein and started fluids for the injured snowmobiler.

Our team loaded her onto a sled and snowmobiled her to the highway and the waiting Stanley Ambulance. Wintertime ambulance transports over Galena Summit are slower, but she remained stable. Her X-ray at the hospital ER revealed what looked like broken eggshells, confirming our field diagnosis. Instead of snowmobile thrills, her life's trail led to the OR, recovery, and months of rehab.

Rural ambulances need dependable drivers. One driver and EMT who volunteered for more than thirty-five years was Ken Hartz, with support from his wife, Bernice. Ken was available, willing to help, and a good driver.

Ken and Bernice came to the Valley in 1975 with their young daughter, Janice, searching for summer jobs with the Sawtooth NRA. The two Pennsylvania teachers found summertime work at the Redfish Lake Visitors' Center.

Ken and Bernice were staffing the center in 1981 when the T intersection converted to a curve, closing the road to the lodge. That Redfish Lake intersection forever changed the lives of these two schoolteachers.

KEN & BERNIE HARTZ, IN THEIR OWN WORDS

Ken: Bernice and I were at the Redfish Lake Visitors Center when you could hear — almost feel — the crash and then the screaming.

Roland Miller, a future volunteer EMT for the Stanley Ambulance, grabbed the first-aid kit and ran for the door. I followed.

Near the middle of the old T intersection, a motorcycle was on its side. Two young riders were lying on the ground. I'm the guy that gets squeamish gutting a deer. Within a few minutes, I was up to my elbows with blood and stool, helping a teenage boy who had ripped open his rectum.

The motorcycle had crashed through the barrier logs, and the two male teenaged riders wore muscle shirts and gym shorts: no helmets or shoes. At high speed on gravel and pavement, skin doesn't do well. Both motorcycle riders had terrible cases of road rash.

The quiet accident victims may be in the worst shape. Some trauma victims can scream at the scene, and we tend to focus on them first. That evening at the Redfish T intersection, one motorcycle rider was yelling for help. We stabilized him on a backboard, and he did end up having a broken back. But the other motorcycle rider, the quiet one, was in greater peril.

When the second teenager hit the pavement, the impact ripped open his anus toward his coccyx, exposing his rectum with protruding pelvis. Feces and blood covered him and then us. He wasn't screaming; instead, he was quietly moaning. Bernice called 911.

Marie and the Stanley Ambulance arrived. Marie started the IV, ran the Lactated Ringers wide open, and the patient's blood pressure began to climb out of shock range. Marie and the EMTs used sterile dressings and direct pressure to stop the bleeding.

After stabilizing both teenagers' spines, we transported them from Redfish Lake to Sun Valley ER. An air ambulance carried them to regional trauma teams standing by.

Bernice and I are schoolteachers, and we had basic first-aid training. Some people might have run in the other direction by looking at the awful scene. Instead, we stayed, took deep breaths, rolled up our sleeves, and helped those two kids. Later that evening, Bernice and I discussed what we'd been through and decided we wanted to do more to help. The Stanley Ambulance needed drivers. I had driven our campers and fifth wheel to and from Pennsylvania, so I volunteered to drive the ambulance. That was in 1981. I continued volunteering for the Stanley Ambulance as a driver and, later, as an EMT until 2013.

Roland Miller

Ken Hartz, first responder, training for mountain rescues

Bernice: For Ken and me, volunteering for emergencies became a family affair. Our daughter, Janice, directed traffic and carried supplies, and I helped with communications. In the early 1980s, EMS depended on Forest Service radios, although we relied on a repeater and line-of-sight communication.

Ken: "Ken, meet me at the clinic, and I'll go over the ambulance with you," Ted Hendricks directed me.

Ted was the Stanley Ranger District's warehouseman and a regular volunteer as an ambulance driver. He was enthusiastic about me joining the EMS team as a volunteer ambulance driver. Ted showed me how to turn it on and the switches for the lights and sirens. That was it. Later that night, I got my first emergency call. It was Marie.

"Ken, can you drive?" Marie asked. "We need you. There's no one else."

Using ambulance flashers was standard, but we used sirens only for extreme emergencies or moving traffic out of our way. Especially poor form is pulling into an ER's ambulance bay with sirens blaring. When we arrived at the Sun Valley ER on my first ambulance run, I carefully flipped off the switches. Unknown to me, the siren had another controller under the floor mat. Exiting the driver's seat, I stepped on the siren switch, making for my dramatic introduction to the Sun Valley ER staff. The ER nurses just looked at me, not saying a word.

While I never had formal training as a volunteer ambulance driver other than Ted's tutorial, I did train others. Drivers of rural ambulances need to know the vehicle is top-heavy and affected by the wind. Ted stressed that you had to round out the corners and not square them. You take as much of the road as you can safely utilize. And all those switches? You learn and memorize them. Learning to drive for a rural volunteer ambulance service was on-the-job training.

Ambulance drivers are required to know where the equipment was: backboards, splints, dressings, and oxygen tubing. When we arrived at an accident scene, I helped the EMTs retrieve equipment and other supplies from the ambulance.

We weren't on call for emergency runs in an all-volunteer rural ambulance service, yet we were always on call. When I started volunteering in 1981, Marie had given up trying to maintain a schedule for EMTs and drivers. We didn't have enough volunteers for an EMS schedule to work early on. Later, EMS volunteers with the Forest Service and Idaho Fish and Game carried radios with emergency frequencies, and most turned out for emergency calls anyway. EMTs and drivers preferred to respond rather than work from a set schedule. It worked because they did respond and showed up to help.

When medical emergencies happened, one of the College of Idaho premed interns at the clinic would pick up the telephone and start calling. The phone would ring, and I'd respond to the call, driving fast to the clinic while watching for deer and elk. I'd move the ambulance out of the garage, usually waiting for EMTs before heading out. Information about how many were injured, severity, and location usually came with that first emergency call. Marie joined us in the ambulance or drove straight to the scene, often arriving first.

One safety feature in the ambulance was the automatic transmission, rather than a stick-shift manual transmission, which freed up one hand to hold the EMS radio. Still, driving the Stanley Ambulance on the curvy highway along the Salmon River, bumpy backcountry dirt roads, or over Galena Summit could be unsafe, especially in bad mountain weather or on ice.

We had some near misses. We were returning from a downriver run on a curve of Highway 75 compressed between river and cliff. I saw a big lowboy truck and trailer speeding toward us, crossing into our lane. I hit the brakes and veered toward the roadside, nearly hitting the rock face. The lowboy and ambulance almost collided.

Ambulance drivers watch for deer or elk, objects on the roads, and tourists, the latter being the worst. Some would pass us as we drove over Galena Summit with lights flashing! We'd write down license plate numbers and give them to Idaho State Police who, sometimes, would issue tickets.

We got a call about a possible heart attack. Roland Miller was the EMT, and I was the driver. We headed toward Sun Valley with the patient when I came upon a women's bicycle race, 100-200 racers in a pack that covered the highway. Fortunately, the bicyclists were still down on the valley floor where Highway 75 is straight, not on the curves over Galena Summit. The race had monitors on little motorcycles who helped too. With their help, I drove the ambulance on the wrong side of the road between racers and won the race that mattered: getting the patient to the ER.

Ambulance response times can mean the difference between life and death. It might take an hour or more to get to someone and then even longer to get them over the hill to the ER. Stanley has one ambulance. We cover a vast area. Response times are longer if we are out on a run when another emergency call comes in. Marie would hunker down in the borrow pit with the patient until the ambulance could get there. Ambulance services in Blaine County might rendezvous with us partway, taking our patient and allowing us to return to the waiting emergency call.

We had hell days when we might get three, four, or even five ambulance runs back-to-back. One day I got the call and drove the first run. Then, we got an emergency call for a second run on the way back: a motorcycle accident near Smiley Creek. We transported this victim to the Sun Valley ER. (More on this motorcyclist, who turned out to be famous, later.)

On our return, we got a third emergency call. Jimbo Funderberg, whose dad owned Jerry's Country Store in Lower Stanley, volunteered to drive that run. Unfortunately, an airplane crashed at the Stanley airstrip while the ambulance was out. Although no one was killed or seriously injured, we ended up with a fourth ambulance run for one

Roland Miller

of the crash victims. Meanwhile, Marie also had a clinic full of patients. That was a long day.

On the trip back from Sun Valley, from Galena Summit, we'd radio Marie. She would telephone Don Sessions at Sessions Lodge, a gas station and motel with a restaurant that Don's wife, Nedra, managed. It might be three am when we pulled into Sessions: Don had gotten out of bed, turned on his pumps, waited for us, and then filled the ambulance's gas tank. Don and his wife, Nedra, were stalwart supporters of the Stanley Clinic and Stanley Ambulance — lovely folks and part of the greater Stanley community.

Bernice: Ken could volunteer for the ambulance because he worked under USFS Law Enforcement Officer Steve Lipus, rather than simply staffing the Redfish Lake Visitors Center. In addition to working in Forest Service law enforcement, Ken also served as a first responder. After thirty-one years of teaching, Ken and I took an "early out" and retired from public education. Rather than returning to Pennsylvania, we stayed in Stanley. Steve Lipus connected us with the owners of the Sawtooth Hotel, Steve and Kathy Cole, and they asked us to caretake their hotel. I worked at the school as a teacher's aide. Finally, Ken could take and complete Marie's 1997 EMT course just two years before she left the Stanley Clinic.

We shared a double-wide trailer behind the ranger station for several summers with a volunteer EMT, Roland Miller. Often, Roland and Ken would both be out on the Stanley Ambulance. I took comfort in monitoring the radio, knowing where the ambulance crew was and where they were going. Sometimes, I would go to the ranger station or the Redfish Lake Visitors Center for better radio reception. At the Visitors Center, I could communicate with a lookout on the Boise National Forest, who could also help monitor backcountry emergencies.

Ken: "Hey, Ken, where are we?" EMTs would ask. They're in the back of the ambulance, focused on caring for patients. Sometimes, the journey posed challenges. Elk standing in the road? "EMTs, hold on!" More often, letting anxious EMTs know arrival times for the ER, especially if the patient is unstable, is another way the ambulance driver can help the team.

As we drove down Galena Summit into the Wood River Valley, we lost radio communication until we approached Ketchum. It was always a relief to reconnect with the ER staff, especially if we were transporting an unstable patient. We'd turn that corner from Highway 75 onto Saddle Road before Ketchum, heading for the Sun Valley ER, and turning that corner was almost like being at a car wreck scene when you first hear the sounds of helicopter blades coming over the Sawtooth Mountains. "Oh, thank God," and you breathe a sigh of relief: almost there.

One tight sphincter moment was when the ambulance's electrical system went out and the crew had to drive home with flashlights held out the two side windows. We had several momentary blackouts before the power would kick back on. Once, the crew ran a cord from an ambulance outlet to an aircraft landing light to illuminate an accident scene. That overloaded the system and screwed up the electrical.

Marie remembers when Jimbo drove Stanley's first new ModVan ambulance into town in 1974; it was a big deal for the Stanley community. People had worked hard to raise the money. Later, after placing the order for another ModVan, Stanley had to wait a year for delivery. The delay was caused by the ambulance's unique suspension — and because *Baywatch*, the TV drama about lifeguards, got theirs while Stanley stood second in line.

Bernice: Ken and I joined the rest of the Stanley community in raising money for the Stanley Ambulance. The existence of the Stanley Ambulance depends on people willing to reach into their pockets and donate. Financing a rural ambulance, even staffed with volunteers, depends on people paying their ambulance bills.

Marie and the clinic board dealt with the shortfalls when people didn't pay their bills. Keeping a rural ambulance service running is a team effort, including the finances. Marie recalls a Custer County program where the county paid the ambulance bill, and the patient paid back the county over time. Essentially, people who couldn't pay borrowed from taxpayers. EMS is expensive. In a bad accident, we used a lot of equipment. If Life Flight is involved, the bills can be astronomically high.

Ken: The old Redfish Lake T intersection might have been the site of a significant explosion that killed us all. Alcohol was involved. This guy borrowed his friend's new red truck. He lost control as he accelerated around the corner near the Redfish Lake Visitor Center.

We were inside the Visitor Center, showing our weekly nature movie for campers. Roland was running the movie projector, and tourists were eating popcorn when we heard the truck skidding and crashing. We grabbed the first aid kit and ran outside.

It was one weird sight: the red truck had rolled and was now sideways atop a pine tree. Although the vehicle hammered the tree, it wasn't damaged badly. Nevertheless, little bits of glass were everywhere.

The patient smelled of alcohol. He didn't answer our triage questions ("What year is this? Do you know where you are?"). Instead, he was confused and flailing around, and just seemed to become more agitated.

Bernice got the job of trying to talk him down and help hold him while Roland did an initial physical exam. Pieces of glass were getting into our gloves and clothes. That is when Bernice was transfixed by what she saw: liquid leaking from the truck bed.

"Hey, Roland? We might have a problem," Bernice said. "Do you think that's gasoline?" Leading to that awful, unasked question: Are we about to explode?

Roland put his finger to the liquid, then his nose.

"Beer."

The Stanley Ambulance pulled up to the curve near the Visitor Center. Jimbo was driving. Despite Bernice's best efforts to talk and hold him down, the patient was flailing his arms and legs. Roland added his weight to help, but our patient just lifted Roland. At the time, Jimbo carried surplus weight and sat on our patient's legs. The fellow nearly bucked off both Jimbo and Roland. Eventually, Marie helped with sedation, and the patient became calm enough for ambulance transport over the hill.

Agency staff in places like the Sawtooth NRA are essential first responders. Before Marie, Forest Service staff were mainly on their own, responding to emergencies. Over the years, other agencies have helped. For example, we had a domestic incident at Sunny Gulch campground just down the highway from the Redfish Lake turnoff. Two brothers were fighting. We ended up with eight law enforcement officers responding, including the Forest Service, Idaho State Police, the deputy sheriff for Custer County, Idaho Fish and Game, and Tribal Fish and Game. We had to work together in the field.

Business and agency support for rural EMS has declined, and budget cuts in Forest Service law enforcement also gutted the ranks of first responders. For the Visitor Center at Redfish Lake, in the mid-1980s, we had a staff of four or five seasonal employees and one or two volunteers. Years later, the Forest Service closed the Visitor Center. In the 1970s, we had just under twenty wilderness/seasonal backcountry rangers in the backcountry. By 2014 only one to three wilderness rangers patrolled the backcountry, and nonagency funds paid some of their salaries.

The same story applies to Forest Service law enforcement: In the mid-1980s, we had eight seasonal staff. Over thirty years, that staffing dropped to a single seasonal staff person. Congressional budget-cutting eliminated law enforcement personnel who also served as first responders. Increasing numbers of tourists with decreasing law enforcement personnel means trouble.

Transferring the Sawtooth NRA from the Forest Service to the Park Service won't fix the staffing problems. Both agencies are in the same boat. Yet, simultaneously with COVID, America rediscovered the great outdoors and our nation's public lands. As a result, demands for services shot through the roof. Those demands fell on agencies emaciated from years of budget-cutting, which, in turn, gutted the ranks of volunteer EMTs.

"Custer County Dispatch to Stanley, we have an emergency. Please respond." What if no one responds?

Ken: We all felt relief when the ambulance pulled up at the scene, and there was Marie; when Marie jumped in the ambulance as we headed out from the Stanley Clinic. We felt better with the professional on board.

With Marie approaching seventy, she and we knew she couldn't continue. Snowmobiling from her home at ten to thirty degrees below zero for emergency calls or seeing clinic patients became harder, as did back-to-back ambulance runs while juggling clinic patients. Marie loved what she did, but nothing is forever. Still, through it all, she stayed in touch with what was happening. She kept the balls in the air.

Stanley's volunteer EMTs and drivers might have had concerns but never panicked, knowing we had a team. We all knew who the leader was, too. We all knew who held it together. Her name was Marie. What the volunteer EMTs and drivers were able to accomplish under her guidance was a miracle.

Stanley Ambulance Crew, with Ken Hartz (1943 – 2024) standing on the far left.

PART EIGHT

HANDING OFF

"Closed" sign on the door of the clinic. After Marie "retired," the community struggled to find another Advanced Practice Provider — until Amy Klingler, P.A.

39

EMERGENCY CALL: ROLAND MILLER

To close your eyes
will not ease another's pain.

Chinese Proverb

The husband and wife riding their motorcycle collided with a bull on the highway near Fisher Creek: dead. The husband-and-wife motorcyclists slammed into the back of a Winnebago near Grandjean: dead. The young girl passenger whose intoxicated biker drove into a tree at a Redfish Lake campground: dead. Motorcycle riders colliding with a pickup truck over the highway centerline near Robinson Bar Ranch: a mass casualty event.

Motorcycles are death machines. My oldest son wanted a motorcycle in the worst way and finally got one after he left home. So many motorcycle stories end badly, especially for riders who don't wear helmets and leathers, drive too fast, drink, and take chances.

In Stanley, motorcycles gave us traumatic brain injuries, spine and femur fractures, and "road rash"— skin abrasions embedded with sand and gravel. Without protection, skin sliding across pavement turns to hamburger. In busy trauma centers, nurses tire of picking out debris. I always used lidocaine for local anesthesia before using a scrub brush to remove sand and gravel. These were usually the younger riders; the older ones sometimes didn't survive.

Some differences stand out between urban and rural EMS. Urban EMS has a more extensive funding base and more resources while serving a larger, dense population. With hospitals nearby, ambulance crews can "load and go."

In contrast, many rural communities struggle financially to support EMS and depend much more upon volunteers. Ambulance transports can take hours. Rural or urban, EMS is about networking and marshaling resources. EMS works best with the skillful and strategic coordination of all available resources. EMS, done well, is able to bridge the urban-rural divide.

Marie and Stanley's EMTs responded to motorcycle crash morbidity and mortality. For Marie, motorcycles are death machines.

Roland Miller is an urban-rural EMT. He volunteered as a first responder in Stanley, Idaho, and Cape Canaveral, Florida, experiencing emergency calls in both settings.

During eighteen summers, he worked for the Forest Service, mostly in law enforcement, while volunteering for the Stanley Ambulance. During winters, Roland volunteered for Canaveral Fire Rescue, then in late spring, Roland would travel across America, climbing more than a mile elevation from Cape Canaveral to Stanley.

When the emergency call toned out over the EMS radio, you'd hear huffing, puffing, and then, "This...is...Roland." He is funny and a quick thinker.

In addition to being an EMT, Roland is also a photographer, naturalist, and author. Besides his photos of Stanley's EMTs and the Salmon River clinic gracing this book, Roland worked with Italian astronaut Paolo Nespoli to photograph the International Space Station's interior in the book *Interior Space: A Visual Exploration of the International Space Station.*

He taught photography at Eastern Florida State College and then Illinois' College of Lake County, where he became dean of its Communication Arts, Humanities, and Fine Arts division.

Roland is married to a nurse practitioner, Amy. In 1980, photography first brought Roland over Galena Summit into the Sawtooth country.

ROLAND MILLER, IN HIS OWN WORDS

My first time coming into the Sawtooth country was on June 15, 1980. I drove over Galena Summit in six inches of snow and thought, "This is another world." As you move through the pass, the Sawtooth Valley opens up before you, breathtakingly beautiful. It changed my life; I was never the same.

As a student at Utah State in Logan, I wanted what my friends wanted: summertime field work with natural resource agencies. But I wanted to work as a photographer. At one point in my senior year, I waited half an hour outside my major professor's office to ask him about a class assignment. Finally, he opened the door, and said, "Oh, I'm sorry, I was on the phone with somebody from the Forest Service. Speaking of that, how'd you like to work for the Forest Service as a photographer this summer?"

My new photography job was under a naturalist and decorated Navy veteran, Chuck Ebersole. Chuck oversaw the Visitors Center at Redfish Lake. Visitors could watch a slide show about the recently established Sawtooth National Recreation Area. While the program's audio worked fine, Chuck wanted new photographs. I was Chuck's photographer, "hired" as a volunteer with the Student Conservation Association at $35 per week with lodging.

I tagged along with mining engineers, recreation and wilderness staff, and naturalists to photograph the Sawtooth NRA. I fell in love with the Sawtooth Range and the White Cloud Mountains.

The summer of 1980 was my summer between undergraduate and graduate studies. When two college students working in law enforcement departed early for classes, Steve Lipus gave me a job and I moved to law enforcement. Chuck Ebersole wanted me back, but he required that I add three

Roland Miller and Big Red after transporting a body out of the north end of the Sawtooth Wilderness

natural resource classes to my graduate load. During my second summer, I got cross-wise with the ranger who banished me to Bowery Guard Station during my third summer. I loved it up there.

Trauma found me; I didn't go looking for it. In my second season in Stanley, I was the first to arrive at three bad accidents, often with Ken Hartz. Two people had spine fractures at one of those. Although the Forest Service provided first aid training, I was over my head and wanted more training. So, while in graduate school, I added an EMT course.

After patrolling in the White Clouds with Julie Meissner that third summer, we returned to Stanley for our weekend. We got flagged down along the Salmon River at Shotgun Rapids, class IV white water above Sunbeam Dam. Kids boating without whitewater experience hit the rapids and flipped. We could see one girl on the far shore. Others from the rafting party were standing along Highway 75, safe and happy to be alive.

We drove to the closest bridge and hiked along the river to get to the girl. She was okay. I pulled out my Forest Service radio, turned to the EMS channel, and provided an update: Roland Miller was a newly minted EMT.

"Hey Roland, can we put her on the back of a kayak and get her across?" Uh, really?

"No, we're not going to do that." The girl had nearly drowned once. I could see the news headline, "Girl drowns during rescue: freaked out, fell off kayak." Decisions confront first responders in the field, and that was my first.

Examining the girl, I saw multiple tiny cuts and abrasions. I pulled out my Band-Aid box. When I finished, little half-inch bandages covered her. We rafted her across the river and drove her to the clinic.

As I presented the case to Marie, she stared at the girl. "What the hell is this crap?" I said nothing, pretending it wasn't me, as Marie pulled off all my little Band-Aids. Thankfully, it wasn't life or death. Those would come soon enough.

My conflict with the ranger meant that after that third season, I was not hired back until personnel changed. So, instead, I worked as a naturalist and photographer at The Pinchot Institute for Conservation Studies, the ancestral home of Gifford Pinchot, the visionary life force of the early Forest Service. Eventually, I returned to Stanley as a naturalist.

Being an EMT on the Stanley Ambulance for three months a year wasn't enough to maintain my skills, so, during winter, I joined the Cape Canaveral fire department. As an EMT, I was good; as a firefighter, being generous, I was competent.

You cannot drink when you're on call as a first responder. I left my radio at home when I went to Stanley's three bars. Two fire department volunteers and I ordered beers at the Mountain Village Saloon one evening.

When the server placed the cold bottles on the table, my friends' pagers went off. Everyone in the fire department was always on call.

"Man in cardiac arrest at the junction of Highway 21 and Highway 75."

Our plans changed. "Why don't you two get the ambulance?" I asked. "I'm heading over there." Pedal to the metal, I drove a quarter mile to the highway intersection.

I pulled up to an all-black van that looked like a utility truck. As I parked, five guys in handcuffs hopped out. Two uniformed security guards stood outside the van, an older, heavy-set woman in charge and a young man trainee without a gun.

"I'm here about the cardiac arrest," I said, as I reached for my jump kit.

"Oh, there's no cardiac arrest," the woman security guard said. "He's just having chest pain."

All the handcuffed prisoners were out except for one handcuffed to the bench seat inside. As I checked his vitals, the woman reached past me and uncuffed him.

"Uh, you don't need to do that." Too late.

My prisoner-patient's vitals were perfect: blood pressure 120/80, pulse 65. The man stripped off his shirt so I could listen to his heart and lungs. A colossal scar ran across his chest. The man explained he lost a part of a lung in a prison knife fight.

A little alarm went off in my head. Why is a prison van driving through Stanley at night? The woman security guard explained that they were heading to Michigan after loading a prisoner in Challis. Really? Stanley is in the opposite direction from Michigan if you are in Challis.

The Stanley Ambulance arrived at the intersection. After handcuffing our patient to the gurney, we loaded and transported him to the clinic. Staffing the ambulance were EMTs Maryellen and Sparky Easom and a College of Idaho premed intern, Marilyn Moretti. Next to the gurney was a little shelf with supplies. I whispered, "Marilyn, remove everything. There should be nothing this guy can grab, even handcuffed."

Marilyn was sitting in the jump seat by his head. I leaned over, "If anything happens, you jump into the cab and shut the door. Don't open it for anybody."

We were impressed with the prisoner's use of medical terms: "I'm having substernal chest pressure radiating down my left arm." His vitals were okay. When Marie placed her stethoscope on his chest, he groaned, complaining of chest pain. Using a cardiologist-donated first-generation EKG machine with rubber suction cups, the EKG did not show ischemic changes.

Once Marie completed her evaluation, we reloaded our patient into the ambulance and headed for the ER in Sun Valley. The black van, with the weaponless trainee at the wheel and five prisoners in the back, trailed behind the Stanley Ambulance. I wanted the deputy, Joe Hess, to follow us, but he was miles out of town on a call. Eventually, Joe caught up with us at Galena Summit, and we had the deputy's flashers the rest of the way to the ER.

The woman security guard sat beside me on the bench, holding her clipboard with our patient's criminal record in front of us. He was serving time for attempted murder.

Written across the top margin of the document with two big asterisks on each side, it said, ** HIGH-SECURITY RISK FOR ESCAPE **.

I pointed to the alarming note and gave the guard a wide-eyed look. "Oh yes, he's escaped from every institution where he's been incarcerated," the uniformed woman said. "We have to watch him closely."

Marilyn could see the prisoner's face reflected in the windows at the ambulance's rear. "The whole way to Sun Valley, he kept looking around," she told me later. Our patient may have escaped from everywhere else, but not the Stanley Ambulance. I was more worried that he would grab Marilyn or Maryellen and try to hold them hostage or something crazy.

In the ER in Sun Valley, our prisoner-patient started reciting Edgar Allan Poe: "Once upon a midnight ... oh, my heart! The pain!" He clutched his chest while pushing away helping hands. Unfortunately, our patient's theatrics thwarted ER therapeutics. This young man knew just enough medical-ese to be dangerous and knew how to put on a heart attack show in police custody.

We handed off our chest pain prisoner to the ER staff without incident. Despite the convincing history, he did not have a cardiac event, and the black-painted van of prisoners continued to Michigan.

I used to joke about this bizarre ambulance run. It happened soon after Hollywood released *The Fugitive*. After all, in Stanley, that could have been Harrison Ford leaping out of the black prison van.

For those who paid their bill, the Stanley Ambulance was among Idaho's most expensive ambulance rides. The EMTs and drivers were free and Marie was paid practically nothing. The high cost resulted from the sheer distances and terrain, and maintaining and replacing EMS equipment. Ambulances are expensive, and gas mileage sucked. Stanley's four-wheel-drive ambulance got four miles per gallon. Marie made this clear despite the cost: the Stanley Ambulance is a vital public resource serving one of the nation's premier public recreation areas. We can't go back to the days of hauling injured tourists and locals over Galena Summit in Forest Service station wagons.

Our ambulance runs could make for long days and nights for the volunteer crew, usually lasting three to four hours; longer, if we had a patient in the wilderness. After transporting a patient to the ER in Sun Valley, there wasn't much to do on the hour-long trip back to the Stanley Clinic. We'd fill out paperwork, clean up what we could, watch the sunrise, and stop at Sessions Lodge to fill the gas tank. EMT boredom encourages creativity.

A guy had rolled his GMC Jimmy and trailer just south of Obsidian. I arrived as a Forest Protection Officer for the Forest Service, directing highway traffic while waiting for the wrecker.

The wrecker needed to make two trips to Ketchum. "Roland, would you mind staying with the trailer until I can get back?" the tow truck driver asked. Sure. I pulled out my lunch and started the paperwork with the highway reopened.

Fields of timothy hay along that stretch of highway were full of cows. Finally, I couldn't help myself, got out of my Forest Service rig, and walked over to the fence while eating my sandwich.

"Moo."

I tried a few more times. "Moo-ooo."

Amazingly, the cows walked toward me and then stopped. They fanned out in rows like I was the conductor of an orchestra. It was the funniest thing.

What if I mooed using the ambulance's PA system? I decided to try it on a return trip from the Sun Valley ER. I picked up the microphone as we approached Fisher Creek south of Obsidian. "Moo. Moo-ooo."

The cows looked stunned, then kicked up their hooves and ran alongside the ambulance.

We mooed the cows on several ambulance runs that summer. I didn't want to scare someone driving or upset a rancher, so I glanced first and mooed second. It was harmless fun, with a wider audience than we knew.

One day one of the ranchers, Marilyn Mueller, got bucked off her horse. We were transporting her over the hill, and I was tending to her as the ambulance headed toward Galena Summit, when suddenly, Marilyn said, "Roland, can I share something with you?"

"Of course, Marilyn. What is it?"

"I think I've heard this ambulance mooing."

"Really?" Pause. "You must have hit your head harder than we thought."

After that, I was a more careful cow communicator.

The following summer, I was in my Forest Service rig when the EMS radio started ... mooing! What? Then I realized it was Andy Gunderson, who had watched me mooing cows.

I grabbed my radio microphone, "Hey Andy, you've got the wrong mike." He used the EMS radio mike, not the ambulance's PA system microphone. The mooing stopped.

Idaho is an "open range" state. By law, drivers and not ranchers are liable when vehicles and livestock collide on highways crossing the open range. Unfortunately, one of my co-workers, Cindy, learned about open-range law the hard way.

I was dancing at the old Mountain Village Dance Hall and Saloon when lights flashed from Highway 75 below us. After looking out the window, I headed out the door. After all, lights and sirens get me out of the mood for dancing.

Cindy drove a bright yellow Volkswagen Thing, and I could see the wreckage of her car. Law enforcement had thrown a tarp over the accident's grotesque remains near the highway's centerline.

"Oh my God, Cindy!"

Wait, that mound was too big for Cindy. It turned out to be a dead bull from the ranch of Jay Neider. The animal exited the fence, wandered onto the highway, and met Cindy's car.

"Where's the driver? Where's Cindy?"

The officer replied she was at the clinic. I headed over.

Despite killing a bull and totaling her car, Cindy survived with only a tiny nose laceration. Marie was suturing when I walked in. While Marie sewed, I held Cindy's hand and talked to her.

Suddenly, I didn't feel right. I was becoming lightheaded, queasy, cold, and clammy. Until Marie sewed Cindy's nose, I never came close to fainting. I excused myself, left the room, sat down, and put my head between my legs. As an EMT, I could handle witnessing much worse carnage than the small tear in Cindy's nostril, but because she was someone I knew and cared about, it got to me.

Cindy's collision with that bull is part of a larger story. On the receiving end of human-versus-livestock trauma, Marie was a proponent of ending the open-range laws to prevent death and injury. At the legislature, when it came to the powerful lobby of Idaho's ranchers versus Marie and human health, the ranchers prevailed.

On I-84, a Suburban rolled at high speed, and other cars pulled over. I was driving from Stanley to Salt Lake City when I saw the wreck, turned on my emergency lights, stopped, and grabbed my jump kit.

An injured man was sitting on the open side of a car. Another man was shaving off hair from the wounded man's scalp. I couldn't believe what I was watching.

"Hi, I'm an EMT. Do you need any help?"

The man never looked up from his shaving job. "I'm a doctor. I'm just taking care of this guy's head wound. Do you have any butterfly bandages?" As the doctor shaved the man's head, he uncovered a tiny scalp laceration.

"I think I do," reaching into my jump kit. The butterfly dressings were government-issue and poor quality, but it's what I carried.

"These are terrible," the doctor said. "Don't you have anything better?"

I'm thinking, "You're in the middle of nowhere. Your patient rolled his car at high speed, got a head injury, may have an unstable neck, you're shaving his head for a tiny cut, and now you're mad about my butterfly bandages?" But, wearing my EMT game face, I said, "Sorry, that's all I have."

The injured driver was not paralyzed and was probably okay. The doctor was running this show. Before it got weirder or worse, I headed down the freeway.

Unstable patients can make for long and stressful rural ambulance runs. So, too, if you're hand-carrying patients in a litter out of the wilderness.

"Roland, can you help take a group from a medical meeting on a hike to Sawtooth Lake?" The request was from Dr. Mary Barinaga, helping with the annual meeting of the Wilderness Medical Society held that year in Sun Valley. Mary is from a sheep ranching family in Cambridge, Idaho. We became friends when she was a College of Idaho premed at the Stanley Clinic. Dr. Barinaga became the Assistant Dean for the Idaho WWAMI Education Program at the University of Washington School of Medicine.

A lovely day hike in the Sawtooth Wilderness seemed perfect for the Wilderness Medical Society. We hiked four miles with a 1,200-foot elevation gain to Alpine Lake and stopped for lunch on our way to Sawtooth Lake. After lunch, Mary took me aside.

"Roland, we might have a problem." The wife of one of the doctors was having lower back pain. The couple had been trying to get pregnant, and the wife had been receiving hormone injections. Mary was worried the pain was from a rupturing ovarian cyst. "By the way, she's anticoagulated on Coumadin."

"Mary, are you telling me she could bleed out up here?"

"No, but would you mind getting a set of vitals?"

The husband was a physician, and I handed off my BP cuff and stethoscope for him to check her out. I tended to

Roland Miller

Transporting a patient when helicopters are not an option

carry some basic medical supplies on hikes after running into medical emergencies regularly. After examining his wife, the doctor reassured Mary and me, "I think she can make it. She's in pain, but otherwise okay." But it was four miles back down the trail to a vehicle.

"We can land Life Flight here at the lake," I said. "We've done it before. But, once we head down the trail, we're committed. There's only one other meadow where we might land a helicopter."

"Oh no, she'll be fine."

My mind was screaming: ruptured ovarian cyst, anticoagulated on Coumadin, and hours of walking to the trailhead. What if she's bleeding? Her husband was a doctor, so I didn't want to tell him, "No, we're going to fly her out of here now." After all, I'm a first responder, not a doctor.

We started down the trail. The woman was hurting and started slowing down. I rechecked her vitals. Her blood pressure was holding. Still, I knew it was too late if her blood pressure started dropping.

"Let me call Marie and see what she says," I said. I wanted Marie to pick up on my coded language and back me up on helicopter transport. I got Marie on the EMS radio. After I described the situation, Marie responded that she deferred to those of us, including doctors, with the patient to make a better assessment. We kept on walking down the trail.

"I can't walk anymore. I'm hurting." We'd gotten a half mile down the trail past the meadow landing site. Except for the blood pressure holding, my worries were becoming a reality.

"We're going to call Stanley, get a litter team together, and carry you out," I said, trying to stay calm and reassuring. And that's what we did.

I radioed for help, and a rescue team carried the young woman out of the wilderness. In a nutshell, we ended up rescuing the Wilderness Medical Society.

Our patient's diagnosis was, indeed, a ruptured ovarian cyst. Her pain resolved before our patient arrived at the hospital. She and we were fortunate that there were no bleeding complications.

"Please help me, I can't get out" are scary words inside a wrecked vehicle. Hydraulic rescue tools — the jaws of life — come in handy. First responders might also try crawling inside. For crushed cars, I'm too big and won't fit. For car trauma, our female first responders often shimmied into a car wreck's tight spaces to rescue the trapped.

One wreck was on Galena Summit, and Marie crawled through the back window to get to the people trapped and injured inside. Another was a station wagon that rolled off Highway 21 and pancaked, trapping three women: Two with injuries, including a hip fracture. EMTs Maryellen Easom and Jan Skrukrud got those people out. We fondly referred to Maryellen and Jan as our "Munchkin EMTs:" They could get inside almost any wrecked vehicle.

For many vehicles, the structural system around the driver and passengers is a steel roll cage with pillars or posts. If you cut the pillars, you risk collapsing the car onto people trapped inside.

Another option, cutting through the bottom of the car, doesn't work. Even with skilled first responders and the right equipment, sometimes people die, trapped inside.

"I'm sorry to tell you this: Your husband didn't make it."

Delivering bad news is usually the responsibility of doctors. But what if you're a first responder in the field? How much do you disclose? I struggled with this during an ambulance run.

The Park Creek Overlook on Highway 21 is about eight miles west of Stanley. On that August day, a freak snowstorm dropped about an inch of snow. A husband and wife in their late forties drove toward Stanley in their pickup. On the long downhill slope past the overlook, the husband lost control. The pickup slid on the slush, rolling several times. The wrecked vehicle ejected the wife while trapping the husband behind the steering wheel.

An EMT from another community arrived first on the scene. We arrived in the Stanley Ambulance. I briefly saw the injured driver but left him with other EMTs to attend to the woman.

I determined that she was conscious, injured badly, though not critically, and needed transport. I went with her in the ambulance.

Inside the wrecked pickup, her husband was upside down. We knew he wouldn't live. By the time the first responders freed the man from behind the steering wheel, he was dead. The EMT who had arrived first kept talking with the dying man. Even if we could have extricated the trapped husband sooner, he wouldn't have survived transport.

During the hour-long ambulance ride, the injured woman kept asking me, "How's my husband? Is he okay?" What should I say?

"We don't have great radio connections in the mountains. We'll know more when we get to the hospital." I could have answered her question, but I didn't. She had multiple injuries, and I didn't want to tell her what I knew.

For first responders, trauma and death can be devastating. There was nothing he or anyone could do. The first responders couldn't extricate the husband alive.

Marie arranged for the EMT to talk with Sharlene Stahl, a psychologist who volunteered with the Stanley Clinic.

Injured or dead children were the worst for me, and I don't even have kids. First responders at the scene with infants and children will struggle with memories, possibly for the rest of their lives.

The emergency call was for a climbing accident along Highway 75, with one child seriously injured. Two boys who were best friends camped with one of the boy's parents. The two scrambled up a cliff and one fell, landed on rocks, and didn't respond. The other boy climbed down, alerted his parents, who called 911. The Custer County sheriff's office dispatched the Stanley Ambulance.

We brought the injured boy up the cliff using ropes, loaded him into the ambulance, and headed over the hill to Sun Valley.

I stayed behind and was struck by how devastated the little boy was after watching his friend fall. In the blink of an eye, his world fell apart.

"Your son needs to talk to a counselor. He's struggling with what he saw." Speaking to the parents, I was getting all choked up, one of the few times I almost lost it. For the parents, this was a nightmare come to life. On their watch, the boy had fallen and suffered a traumatic brain injury. And now, some first responder is warning them that their son might have mental health problems as a result.

The parents said little. For their son, the memory of his friend lying unconscious on the rocks probably changed his life forever.

In 1980, Marie showcased a motorcycle helmet at the clinic. The motorcyclist had attached his helmet to the bike's sissy bar, enjoying the freedom of the road without head protection, and lost control on Highway 75 near Fourth of July Creek. Ah, freedom.

At sixty miles per hour, when the motorcycle laid down, the pavement abraded the helmet, creating a tennis-ball-sized area that was paper-thin. The unprotected skull and brain do poorly in these circumstances, and the motorcyclist suffered a traumatic brain injury.

Recovering, the motorcyclist stopped by the clinic to retrieve his helmet. I was there delivering a message when he walked in. Marie didn't miss a beat. "Are you going to wear a helmet next time?" She gave the motorcyclist the third degree. For Marie, as a sole provider on the receiving end of preventable trauma, there's little gained by mincing words. We saw lots of motorcycle trauma.

"Motorcycle wreck, two people involved," came over the EMS radio. The location was just north of the Beaver Creek store. We arrived by ambulance. One rider was down, in the borrow pit and off the highway. I knelt at his side, introduced myself, and started my evaluation.

"Do you mind if I remove your sunglasses to check your eyes?"

"Yes, leave 'em alone."

"Okay." I quickly decided I wouldn't fight the patient to check his eyes. He was conscious, fully oriented, and capable of making decisions. His upper lip had a deep cut, but I didn't see other injuries.

We packaged him for c-spine precautions, dressed the lip wound, and loaded him into the ambulance. Inside, I asked again whether I could complete my evaluation by him removing his sunglasses. The second time was the charm, and he said, "Okay." After completing my exam, I pulled out the clipboard to complete the forms.

"What's your name?"

"Peter Cetera." Hmmm. I'm from Chicago, and I know a famous singer and celebrity with that same name. With barely a pause, I asked casually, "Oh, the musician?"

"Yeah."

Now I understood why he didn't want me to remove his sunglasses.

"Oh, cool. I'm from Chicago."

The two motorcyclists had been riding when one of them slowed down. They collided, sending Cetera flying into the borrow pit.

He was lucky only to suffer a lip laceration. Cetera was also adamant that we arrange for a plastic surgeon to meet him at the hospital. Although Cetera's request was unusual from an accident victim, that lip was not your average lip. Marie agreed and called the Sun Valley hospital to arrange for the requested surgeon.

Once our patient knew he was in good hands, he was a pleasant and regular guy. Peter Cetera was lucky.

Another "lucky" motorcyclist hit a deer and arrived at the clinic with an Idaho State Trooper. The injury was a quarter-sized chunk of skin gouged from a knee and a few minor abrasions. Still, the trooper seemed overwhelmed.

"You should be dead. You really should be dead," the officer repeated.

While the patient was very much alive, he *was* upset after killing a deer and wrecking his motorcycle. The trooper had come upon the rider, wrecked motorcycle, dead deer, and a lot of blood on the highway. "You should be dead."

About the third time, I gently led the trooper to the clinic waiting area. He was starting to freak me out, and I'm sure it wasn't comforting to the patient, either. The deer was dead. That motorcyclist lucked out. Others are not so fortunate.

Motorcyclists should be aware of objects ahead. A father, brother, and their three or four sons were riding that curvy river highway below Stanley near Sunbeam. Most in the group were new to motorcycles, and the family was training for a more extended family road trip.

A big rock was on the highway. One of the sons froze. He missed the rock but drove off the road. He landed near the river's edge, smashing into a boulder. He still had a pulse when Stanley's EMTs got to him. StateComm dispatched Life Flight for air ambulance transport.

We placed the young man into a stokes litter to move him up the steep riverbank to the highway. Standing in the borrow pit were his father, uncle, and brothers. In an instant, their world had changed.

As we loaded our patient into the helicopter, rescue breathing with a bag-valve-mask, one brother ran toward us, yelling. "I'm going with him. I'm going on this helicopter." He was ballistic.

"You can't. There's no room." I was trying my best to be empathetic.

"I'm going with him, God damn it. I'm not leaving my brother."

"I know how you feel." I stopped. "I'm sorry. I don't know how you feel. But, with weight restrictions, if you get into that helicopter, they'll never be able to take off, and your brother needs critical care as soon as possible."

One of the other first responders calmly suggested that they return to Stanley and get one of the fixed-wing pilots to agree to fly them to Boise. Thankfully, the brother's emotions finally yielded to his common sense, and he took the first responder's good advice.

That young motorcyclist lived for about two days. We hoped the family could gather in the neuro ICU and say goodbye before the doctors turned off the ventilator.

Marie hates motorcycles. For her, they are all machines of death.

For EMS, transport time to the hospital means interacting with your patient, which can be rewarding and emotional.

With our single ambulance, Marie, as part of triage, had to decide who needed ambulance transport. One ambulance can't be in multiple places at once.

Along with my Forest Service work in the summers, I worked a couple of nights a week entertaining guests with my guitar at the Idaho Rocky Mountain Ranch. A guest fell and broke his collarbone while mountain biking and returned to the ranch. The ranch manager, Sandra, asked me to put down my guitar and look at the injury. I did and agreed: a fractured clavicle.

"You don't need an ambulance," I said. "You'll be fine if someone can drive you over the hill to the ER. You have a broken collarbone. If you want, I'll put on a sling and swath to reduce pain and help stabilize your broken bone."

Usually, I keep my jump kit with me, but not that day. Instead, I turned to Sandra, "We'll need a sling. Do you happen to have any large napkins we can use?" Sandra returned from the lodge's dining room with green and red napkins. I knotted them together, unintentionally creating an alternating red and green sling and swath.

When I stepped back to examine my homemade medical aid, I told the patient, "Man, you look like some magic trick that went horribly wrong."

Back-to-back ambulance runs can take most of the day. For example, one day, Phil Enright and I did four ambulance runs, starting at nine in the morning and finishing at two-thirty in the morning the next day.

Our first call was an injured firefighter. Forest fires were burning downriver, and the man caught his leg between two logs, fell, and snapped his ankle. While some patients are stoic about pain, he wasn't one. We splinted the leg, loaded the firefighter in the ambulance, took him over the hill to the ER, and then returned to Stanley.

As we backed the ambulance into the clinic garage, we heard, "Dispatch to Stanley Ambulance. We have a middle-aged male having chest pain." Another firefighter; we retraced our path downriver to the fire camp. We transported him over the hill to the ER and returned to Stanley in the late afternoon.

"Challis Dispatch to Stanley Ambulance: We need you to respond to a motorcycle accident." That third emergency call came as we headed north out of Ketchum, past the Boulder Mountains, and started up the curves to Galena Summit. (Amazingly, we got that call; that's one place where the mountains block EMS radio reception.) A red-tailed hawk had flown into the face of a motorcyclist. The biker was wearing a helmet, protecting his head when he crashed. However, his slide along the roadway was so severe that the rough pavement removed the flesh off his leg like filleting a fish. The skin was gone, revealing real-life human anatomy: muscles, tendons, and bones. We placed the biker's mangled leg in an airvac splint for transport.

That biker never complained. Instead, he thanked us until Life Flight lifted off and flew him to Boise. Talk about fate: a hawk flying into your helmet riding a motorcycle at sixty miles per hour. That poor guy nearly lost his leg and struggled to walk again. The Ketchum community held fundraisers to help him pay his medical bills. That day, after watching the helicopter disappear over the Sawtooths, we headed home at twilight.

"Dispatch to Stanley Ambulance. Respond to a middle-aged female downriver with trouble breathing." Really? It was nine o'clock; I'd been in this ambulance for twelve hours, and now a fourth emergency call? We headed down the valley with lights flashing, gassed up at Sessions Lodge, and drove past Stanley and on past Sunbeam. Maryellen Easom arrived on the scene just as we got there. We opened the door to a small cabin.

Flailing in the bed was a female in her forties. On the couch was a man, her husband, intoxicated. We assumed alcohol, possibly drugs. I knelt at the woman's side to try and get a history, check her vitals, and then examine her. Suddenly, her arm headed up between my legs. I squeezed my knees together: The last thing I wanted was her grabbing me in the groin. Then, her arms and legs went flaccid, and she stopped breathing.

I checked her carotids; she had a pulse. "Grab the Ambu bag." We started rescue breathing using the bag valve mask.

"We need helicopter transport." We had a woman in respiratory arrest with no history from her drunk husband and no diagnosis. Especially at night, you can't land a helicopter in the river canyon, so we prepared to ambulance-transport her and meet Life Flight at Stanley's airport.

We parked along the runway, waiting for the helicopter. We waited. And waited. "Life Flight to Stanley Ambulance. Our apologies, but we'll have to cancel. Forest fires are burning between Boise and Stanley, and we'll have to abort."

During the transport to the airport, the woman started breathing on her own and woke up. The deputy sheriff brought her husband, who was more sober and coherent, to the ambulance. The couple talked, and then he left.

"She's not breathing," Maryellen yelled out. Crap. She'd watched her oxygen saturation start to plummet. The patient had a pulse.

Again, we started bagging her. Just in case, we put a CPR board under her. After twenty minutes, she woke up.

"She stopped breathing again."

The woman's respiratory arrest became routine: Sometimes she breathed, sometimes she didn't. Sometimes we bagged her, sometimes we didn't.

With heavy smoke blocking Life Flight, we left the airport in the ambulance and headed for Galena Summit and the Sun Valley ER.

She lived. Blood and urine tests didn't yield a diagnosis other than alcohol intoxication, fatal for her had it not been for the Stanley Ambulance. Her husband ended up in DTs several days later, but he survived, too.

Twice that day, we'd eaten takeout from Louie's in Ketchum, using the "ambulance pizza fund" created by the clinic board. However, by that fourth run, Ketchum had rolled up its sidewalks.

We drove over Galena Summit for the eighth time after our four back-to-back calls, the night sky filled with stars. At 2:30 in the morning, after seventeen and a half hours of riding the Stanley Ambulance, we finally parked at the Stanley Clinic.

Saving somebody's life is the most important thing we can do in law enforcement. Forest Service leadership supported us.

When the Forest Service got nervous about liabilities, it was decided that while we were in the ambulance, we were on paid administrative leave. A win-win: The agency avoided liability while we didn't lose our pay. Most importantly, we kept the Stanley Ambulance on the road, responding to emergency calls. Government agencies can support employees volunteering as first responders. In contrast, local shops, motels, restaurants, and river-rafting businesses struggle when employees answer emergency calls.

A small business owner in Stanley who responds to emergency calls as an EMT volunteer might have to shut down her business for half a day or more. That's lost income. Maintaining EMS can be a hardship for rural communities, especially when agencies mostly walk away from supporting EMS, as they have in Stanley.

Sadly, the Forest Service axed most of its seasonal forest protection officer crew. If you had a national park the size and visitation of the Sawtooth NRA, Congress would fund dozens of law enforcement staff. The National Park Service even staffs EMS ranger positions.

I'm surprised things haven't deteriorated more in the Sawtooth NRA. The lack of federal leadership and funding has left the Stanley community holding the bag to maintain the EMS.

Healthcare in rural communities is not a spectator sport — survival can depend on everyone pitching in. But the billionaires and millionaires buying up property around Stanley are not training as EMTs and volunteering for the ambulance. Unless we change this trajectory, too few volunteers can't sustain EMS. During the COVID pandemic summer of 2020, when people escaped to safer, unpopulated places like the Sawtooth NRA, the Stanley Ambulance was down to five volunteer EMTs, serving thousands of people. Congress needs to direct and fund federal agencies to support rural EMS as part of homeland security.

Having worked at The Pinchot Institute, I know that one strength of the Forest Service in its early years was its decentralization and connection to its local communities. The agency must return to its roots, reconnect with local communities like Stanley, and support rural EMS

September 11, 2001, was my last day working for the Forest Service. After Amy and I married, I couldn't find a job teaching photography in Salt Lake City, where she was working. Instead, I took a position teaching at a college in Illinois. Living in the Midwest ended my crazy summers in Stanley.

In Stanley, we did things by the book, although the training manual never covered 90 percent of the emergencies. Because of scarce resources, rivers and mountains, climate, and people and politics, creating a healthcare system in the early 1970s in the Sawtooth country must have seemed an impossible dream.

It's hard to imagine what it was like for Marie, at forty, to begin fighting this battle, let alone continue over the decades. All those walls she had to punch through to make the Stanley Clinic and Stanley Ambulance a reality. Remember, the first one through the wall gets bloody.

Today, we know what a nurse practitioner is. When Marie started, no one knew, not even her. She made it up as she went along, driven by the rural realities of Idaho's Sawtooth country. In doing so, Marie helped create and define a new healthcare profession.

Marie can be a tough old bird. When I brought my first patient to the clinic from the river rafting accident, I realized I didn't want to see the look Marie gave me again — from anybody. As long as I live, I'll never forget Marie ripping off all those little Band-Aids.

Storm ovr the Sawtooth Range from Shaw Mesa

40

SHOULDERS, NOT SHOES

Change is constant. As I approached seventy, time and aging increasingly tugged at my stethoscope. Handing off the Stanley Clinic and Stanley Ambulance to a community-appropriate, competent clinician took years of planning and preparation, yet still proved perplexing.

When thinking about rural healthcare, beach sandcastles and incoming tides come to mind. We spend years creating institutions that can provide rural patient care. Yet nothing lasts, not in the big scheme. No matter how great the need or virtuous our mission of caring for rural communities, the true test and our greatest challenges rest with handing off our rural clinics and ambulance services to the next generation.

Transitioning from founders to followers can take years, if ever. In this transition, the clinic board and I faced a fundamental question: Would our clinic and ambulance endure? And what does that say about the fragile health of rural clinics and rural ambulance services? The answer has life-and-death consequences.

I formally "retired" at the end of the hunting season 1999. Even after leaving, I returned to fill the gaps. The road to my replacement, Amy Klingler, was rocky. For a while, a closed sign hung in the window of the Stanley Clinic. Meanwhile, the volunteer EMTs kept the ambulance service alive. It's helpful to remember what the community went through to find Amy.

I assume you've never hired your replacement. Managers with HR support will hire and fire if you work in a hospital or larger clinic. Our Stanley Clinic story is different and probably closer to what other rural clinics experience.

We are a rural clinic-hospital taxing district, and the district's property owners elect our clinic's board of directors. Starting in the mid-1990s, I worked with my board to create and implement the process of hiring my replacement.

NPs and PAs applied, thinking Stanley would be a great place to practice. Most knew Stanley as a vacation place, a gateway to wilderness and rivers. Unfortunately, in seasonal recreational economies such as ours, vacation time for tourists is not vacation time for locals, including me. Hanging the sign "Gone Fishing" on the door doesn't work. I never felt easy leaving the valley, especially during the summer.

I drove to the Sunny Gulch campground four times near the Redfish Lake turnoff, parked, and scrambled down the hillside to try fishing the Salmon River. Emergency calls interrupted each time I started to fish. Finally, after four tries, I gave up on fishing.

At my home on Shaw Mesa, I paused patient care to ride our horses, Sucia, Matia, or Tamaz, carrying the portable radio. I loved those horseback rides looking out at my mountains, and when the emergency calls came, we galloped back to the house. I pulled off the saddle and bridle, ran for my car, and raced down the hill and highway to the clinic.

Stanley can look great in July or August. How about January or February, when Stanley has the lowest temperatures in the lower forty-eight states? Even on those arctic mornings, I had clinic patients or emergency calls and had to go to town.

During the heavy snow winters of the 1980s, record snowfall complicated my every move to get to and from my patients. So yes, while Sawtooth winters are glorious, they can be daunting.

If your life objective is to make a lot of money and buy lots of boy toys or expensive clothes and jewelry, don't go into patient care — especially avoid patient care in rural communities. Even by the mid-1970s, John made more money cleaning outhouses in three months at $2.25 an hour than I did on fee-for-service, seeing patients all year.

We gradually increased the salary so that, by the time I retired in 1999, we could offer the practitioner a decent salary and housing. I never got that salary, but incoming practitioners did.

Housing in Stanley is essential yet limited within the Sawtooth National Recreation Area. We could not offer Boise salaries and knew an incoming practitioner would need a place to live. The clinic apartment was the perfect lodging for the students and me, but not a substitute for housing Stanley's next practitioner. With community help, we provided housing in town so the clinician could walk to work. We wanted a place near the clinic so the next clinician could walk or run to the clinic if their car didn't start.

Once the clinic board accepted my mortality, we focused on the search and hiring process. We started advertising in professional journals and did what we could to get the word out in professional circles.

Stanley has a special attraction for unique people. Unfortunately, we learned that the right NP or PA is hard to find, especially when a spouse and kids are involved. Many practitioners who applied were young, just out of school, and married. You and your clinic board may go through the hiring process and select the perfect candidate. Then, the whole thing falls apart when the spouse or significant other doesn't fit in or can't find a job. Also, you want a clinician experienced in rural medicine, trauma, and other emergency care for a clinic and ambulance service like Stanley's. When they go home after the clinic closes or an ambulance run, you want them to have a supportive family life. Your new hire will not stay if their spouse is unhappy and wants to get out. And rural towns may not have childcare. A new-hire practitioner with kids would face the same painful choices that Debbie and I did.

When hiring my replacement, we looked for an advanced practice provider, NP or PA. The state licenses NPs to practice independently in Idaho, making them our preferred choice. Still, you may be unable to compete with Boise's salaries, so you must be flexible. In the end, hiring is more about finding the right person (and spouse) and less about the letters behind their name.

You'll also need to be careful and do your due diligence on background checks. "Well, he's a great guy and a solid clinician — when he's sober," doesn't work, especially in a rural community. If you show up at the scene impaired or even smelling of alcohol, you're putting a lot at risk. In a small town where everyone knows everybody, a practitioner with drug or alcohol problems won't conceal them for long. And once the word is out, you can't "unring the bell." If you are in the Valley, you are on call and have to function. You're it. There's no one else.

And finally, there's the isolation. For me, after my second divorce and my rape, it was enough to have my mountains and my dog. When it's below zero outside, you can be a mile from the Salmon River and hear it flowing as if it were a hundred feet away. Just out your door is skiing and snowmobiling, hiking and climbing, hunting and fishing, boating, and swimming in one of the most beautiful places on earth. Isolation? Boredom? As a practitioner in a small town, my life was rich, and I had one of the best and most exciting jobs in one of the most beautiful places on earth.

We had one applicant who seemed to hit all the marks. She was well-qualified, and we hired her. That hire went badly. You must bring a practitioner who can play in the same sandbox with others. We hired another NP who loved Stanley, the clinic, and housing and was an avid hunter and angler. He was the perfect match, except he had an alcohol problem. Perfect matches are in heaven. When hiring for a high-profile, high-stakes clinical position in a rural community, it's hard to find heaven on earth, let alone in Stanley.

We did hire a young man with children. His children initially went to school in Stanley during their first year. In the second year, the new NP's son started high school, which meant boarding out in Challis or riding a school bus on the river road for two to three hours daily. Finally, he moved to Salmon, Idaho, where he could make more money with better housing options. In addition, Salmon provided his young family with access to elementary, junior high, and high schools. Stanley could not compete.

If successful, you'll hire a solid practitioner devoted to your community, whose spouse finds employment and wants to stay, and who can figure out the educational puzzle. You may go through twenty practitioners before you get that one person who fits. Getting it right is a tall order for rural clinics. Making that match and finding the right person can mean everything. For Stanley, that right match turned out to be Amy Klingler.

Jim Stark

Marie and Amy Klingler, PA. Small communities may struggle for years to find the right clinician. Advance Practice Providers — NPs and PAs — help make healthcare a reality in rural Amercia.

AMY KLINGLER, PA, IN HER OWN WORDS

It was intimidating to take over after Marie, even though seven years had passed since her departure in 1999. I remember telling June Hansen, "I have these really big shoes to fill." Marie's spirit was and still is so alive in the clinic and the ambulance service.

June changed my perspective, saying, "Amy, don't fill Marie's shoes. Stand on her shoulders." That advice enabled me to redefine my relationship with Marie's legacy. Shoulders, not shoes, permitted me to do things as I needed to, moving forward with my dream job and life.

I grew up in Virginia, where I graduated from high school and college. Even as a child, I knew I wanted to live among mountains.

After college, I left home for Jackson, Wyoming. Near Pinedale, I worked on a guest ranch on a dirt road ten miles off the highway. The mountains were spectacular.

After working the summer, I planned on being a ski bum in Jackson. However, in 1997, I met and fell in love with Chris at the guest ranch where we worked. He was born and raised in Idaho Falls, so when we married, I also married into Idaho.

Eventually, I wanted to go into medicine. Chris and I moved to the university town of Moscow. There, I continued to struggle with basic life choices: whether to go back to school to become a physician, PA, or nurse practitioner. At that time, what I most wanted was to become a midwife.

Chris and I knew about Stanley and how special and spectacular it is. We also knew Stanley had a clinic. In 2000, we stopped by the clinic and met with the practitioner, a PA. At that moment, I knew what I wanted from life: to work in that clinic. That meant I did not need to attend medical school — indeed, I should not. The Stanley Clinic suits an NP or PA, not a physician. So, I chose that day: I would become a PA and someday return to Stanley, Idaho.

Being a practitioner in Stanley is my dream job, warts and all. I applied three times, the first right after graduating in August 2003. Unfortunately, Stanley is not a good place for a new graduate, something I've learned with time.I was offered a position at the clinic in 2004, but then the board decided to reorganize, closing the clinic except for an occasional visiting provider.

Eventually, the Stanley Clinic's medical director and supervising physician, Dr. Richard Paris, hired a PA who commuted from Challis. Dr. Paris also wanted a second practitioner to fill in part-time.

I was working as a PA in Twin Falls when I heard about the opening at Stanley's clinic and said, "Yes!"

After my second interview, I started covering the clinic on a few weekends. When a PA position opened up in Challis, like musical chairs, Stanley's PA moved to Challis. That opened the position in Stanley. I called to schedule my third interview.

After finishing my interview with the board at the Stanley Clinic, excited and relieved to have it over, I got in my car and headed south on Highway 75. Hungry, I started eating a sandwich. Going around the highway curve near the Redfish Lake turnoff, I looked down at my sandwich — and lost control of my car. I overcorrected, drove off the road, hit a tree, and totaled my car. Fortunately, my sole injury was a cut eyebrow.

Law enforcement, going the opposite direction, saw the whole thing. Concerned about more extensive injuries, Stanley's EMTs transported me by ambulance over the hill. That's how I concluded my third and final interview for my dream job, adding to the EMS lore.

Welcome to Stanley.

The issues of spouse and child were significant barriers for many of the practitioners staffing the clinic, especially Marie and me. Even conveniences people take for granted, like shopping in big-box stores, require you to leave the Valley and drive for hours.

Being the sole provider in a rural clinic can challenge a marriage. Chris has a degree in fish and wildlife and, for twenty years, has worked seasonally for the Forest Service. Like Marie and Cal, Chris and I've been out for dinner at the Kasino Club and had people pull up a chair to discuss their medical problems. The spouse/family issue was significant for all the men who came between Marie and me. I used to joke this is a job for a woman.

People in this town have been thinking about my child's high school education since I was pregnant. "Amy, what are you going to do? You know, the Stanley school only goes to the eighth grade." I know they cared about Grady's education, but they also cared about what would happen to the clinic when he went to high school.

I don't know if I would have had more than one child, but the demands of patient care, the community, and the high school issue encouraged Chris and me to limit ourselves to one child.

My son, Grady, is a freshman in high school right now. Being the sole practitioner in the Sawtooth country may be my dream job, but my son's education is essential. After agonizing, at one point, I concluded, "We'll move. We'll go to Ketchum or Challis or Boise. Someday, I'll return." Then I realized I'd never get this job back once I left.

Parents used to put their kids on a bus from Stanley to Challis High School, about ninety minutes each way. We haven't even had a bus driver for the past three years. Stanley has many young families right now who are either business owners in the community or committed to staying here. Our community is exploring new options, trying to expand the Stanley School to allow high school students to stay in the Valley and connect in person or online with high school classes.

What a struggle this has been. We had many conversations with my son in the seventh and eighth grades. We could move to Challis or Ketchum, and I would commute to the Stanley Clinic. Yes, we did explore online education, but that wasn't a good option for our family. We were concerned about the educational quality for our son and the additional workload for Chris and me. Then came COVID.

With the virus spreading in March 2020, the Stanley school went online. Forced to transition from learning in the classroom to online at home, Grady did well. Online learning was a good fit for him. Consequently, we added online learning to the list of options for high school. Ultimately, Grady made the decision: He would try online high school. He loves it, and we stayed in Stanley.

Unlike many rural towns, Stanley housing is unaffordable; it's outrageous. The clinic owns the house in which our family lives. We've paid rent for sixteen years. Providing a home to the healthcare provider is a huge benefit; we could not have moved to Stanley without it.

Marie's brilliant idea, backed by the clinic board, was for the clinic to provide affordable housing for staff.

"Amy, do you answer phone calls from patients at nine o'clock at night?" one of my College of Idaho premed interns asked.

"Of course, I answer phone calls," I replied. I added, "I also answer text messages at ten." Not answering when patients call or send texts worries me. But cell phones and texting add to the demands. Once, I answered a phone call on a chairlift while skiing in Colorado. "What are you doing?" Chris asked. "It's one of my patients," I replied. After all, we were only on a chairlift, not skiing. Still, it's hard to set boundaries.

When I sit down to dinner with my family and go to bed at night, I say a silent prayer that the tones don't go off. Although we have a well-trained volunteer ambulance crew, sometimes I need to respond. I'm the backup if there's no one else.

When the clinic board offered me the job in 2005, St. Luke's regional health care system was heavily involved in the clinic as our managing entity. St. Luke's was my employer when I started and contracted me to the Stanley Clinic, and provided me with health insurance, annual and sick leave, and other benefits. But rural health clinic regulations, written by Medicare, require that I be an employee of the Salmon River Clinic, not St. Luke's. To comply, I now work for the clinic board. So do the two other clinic staff members, our receptionist and nurse. While the Stanley Clinic's recent history intertwines with St. Luke's, we are also independent.

When I started, one of St. Luke's vice presidents, who was my supervisor and attended every clinic board meeting, was adamant that the ambulance and clinic were to be separate to prevent practitioner burnout. Consequently, in the beginning of my employment, I didn't have much to do with the Stanley Ambulance.

Remember, Stanley's EMTs are volunteers. How could I not support them? I cared about them as people and as first responders. Not helping the volunteer EMTs increasingly felt like abandonment. Eventually, the boundaries separating the clinic and ambulance changed.

For emergencies, I'm the backstop. If you call 911 in the Sawtooth country, the person answering the phone is the dispatch at the county sheriff's office in Challis. Dispatch tones out the emergency call to Stanley's volunteer EMTs. If there's not a crew, then dispatch calls me.

Those stories about Marie's dinners interrupted or going without sleep? That's reality. Everything blurs. Your professional life is part of your personal life. Technology has made that both easier and harder. I can turn on the EMS radio at the house and listen, feeling better for knowing what's happening. But that comes at a cost.

These days, the EMTs usually don't bring emergencies to the clinic; they head directly over the hill, especially in the middle of the night. The scariest times for me are those bad winter storms when you can't get helicopter transport and avalanches close the mountain passes. Those are times when I'm on high alert. I'll handle as much as possible at the clinic to protect our ambulance team.

Healthcare professionals walk through the Stanley Clinic door, talking about doing this job when they retire. "Oh, I want to live in the mountains and hunt and fish. I'll bring my family here, too." No. This job is incredibly demanding. You never know who will walk through that door with what problem. It could be a movie star from Sun Valley wanting medication before a river trip or a sheepherder who is dripping blood.

I work for a publicly elected clinic board. I answer to them and serve at their pleasure. Ours is a meaningful relationship. Board members usually run unopposed until they tire of the job. Community support and volunteers keep the clinic doors open and keep Stanley's ambulance service alive. In this part of Idaho, sustaining healthcare is a core volunteer group with a lifelong commitment to the Stanley Clinic and Stanley Ambulance. These people have up to five decades of volunteer community service. It's stunning. Bev Angel was at our EMT training today — you can count on Bev. Andy Gunderson still drives. LuAnn Kuhn, over sixty-five, is one of our core volunteers, and so is Phil Enright, over seventy, responding day and night. Sparky and Maryellen Easom were well into their sixties when they reluctantly stepped down from taking emergency calls. Maryellen continues volunteering, and the community elected her to serve on the clinic board.

Today, we have fewer EMTs responding to emergency calls. For one thing, people want schedules. Marie recalls scheduling EMTs for emergency calls during the 1970s and having all the EMTs show up anyway. So, she stopped scheduling. That's changed.

Winter weekends can be busy. Summers can be crushing. One solution is to pay EMTs to be on call for emergencies. We are working to raise money to sustain that program. Otherwise, we're left hoping that when people call 911, volunteer EMTs will respond. The mindset that you're compensated financially for everything you do is alien in this part of Idaho. Instead, people commit time to their initial EMT education and continue to train. But an entire generation of volunteers is aging. Stanley is changing.

Many second homeowners and people use the community's services, but they're not volunteering and giving back to sustain local community services. As more and wealthier people move in and don't step up, demands for services fall on fewer aging volunteers — some in their sixties and seventies.

What do we do? We've tried to balance community expectations about responding to emergency calls with the reality that we don't have enough volunteer EMTs. We've had to start partially compensating our EMTs to cover emergency calls. Where does the funding come from in a tiny town of fifty to sixty year-round residents, but more second homeowners and over a million visitors?

For a volunteer force, compensation is a one-way street. Once you head down that road, it's hard to go back. Someone must do the fundraising. So, what was once a volunteer position morphs into a second job with compensation. Remember, Stanley is a difficult place to live. It's expensive to live here and even more costly to own a home. Employers are less willing to let workers leave their jobs to respond to emergencies.

The clinic budget has also changed. When Marie started, she did it all: cleaning, stocking, patient care, billing and insurance forms, teaching EMT classes, and responding to emergency calls. That wasn't sustainable for Marie and isn't for us.

We now have a full-time RN and contract out our billing and cleaning. It still feels overwhelming at times.

Just as Marie had Dr. Bryan Stone and other physician preceptors, I've had incredible support from my physician preceptor of sixteen years, Dr. Paris, and his wife, Dr. Woods, who provides backup support. Our ambulance medical director is separate. First, there was Dr. Keith Sivertson, and now Dr. Terry O'Connor. The support of these physicians and their family medicine and emergency medicine colleagues is critical for the Salmon River Clinic and Stanley Ambulance.

Medicare requires physicians precepting PAs to be on-site two days a month. However, Stanley has an exemption because of distances, mountain passes, winter weather, and lower patient volumes. Dr. Paris is here one day a month, just as Dr. Stone was for Marie.

We schedule patients at the clinic who want to see Dr. Paris. Then, he and I spend several hours reviewing charts. I randomly select some, and I specifically pull others because I want his input.

"Dr. Paris, we talked about this patient on the phone. I want to provide some follow-up." Or, "This is my diagnosis and treatment plan — would you do something differently?" Working with an attending physician committed to medical education is such a good experience, in some ways resembling ongoing residency training.

As with NPs, PAs' roles are evolving and moving towards independent practice, if slowly. As with all healthcare providers, we must have good judgment and personal integrity to know our limits. Within those boundaries, we develop clinical skills and wisdom that come with caring for people year after year. Being the sole healthcare provider in mountain country means pushing boundaries.

Isolation is a blessing and a curse for the Stanley Clinic and rural healthcare. Sometimes, you want to call 911, then remember you are 911. Fortunately, the Wood River Emergency Department and the air ambulance services know how isolated we are and do everything they can to help us and our patients.

Rural practitioners work independently, and that is special while anxiety-provoking. "What do I do now?" you ask. I can't walk down the hall and run a case by a colleague: "What do you think about this x-ray finding?" or "How would you manage this patient?"

The ER docs and hospitalists in the Wood River Valley have been fantastic and understand the limits of the Stanley Clinic.

Sometimes, in contrast, when I call Boise or Idaho Falls to transfer a patient, they ask, "What's the CBC?" We didn't do one. "Well, did you do chemistries?" No. "What's the chest X-ray show?" Stanley doesn't have an X-ray. "How about the head CT scan?" Really? In Stanley?

When I call the ER at St. Luke's Wood River Valley, the ER docs know most diagnostics are not available to me, certainly not "stat." They also know me as a colleague and are gracious with their time to help me work through cases.

COVID unmasked the importance of integrating into more extensive healthcare systems. Working alone in a rural community, I can't imagine researching COVID policies and making decisions alone.

When I started, the patient numbers at the clinic were low, especially during the winter. I was concerned about maintaining my skills and my brain. So, I began working one day a month at St. Luke's urgent care clinic in the Wood River Valley. On a single winter day in Ketchum, I might see as many patients as a couple of weeks at the Stanley Clinic.

I also started staffing a family planning clinic one day a month in Challis for Eastern Idaho Public Health and became an editor of the National Journal for Physician Assistants in 2006. Journal articles' peer review and editing have been excellent learning methods. Given Stanley's isolation, reaching out, networking, and doing work that maintains my clinical skills are critical.

The internet brings medical knowledge to my computer at the Stanley Clinic. Before computers, Marie kept a library of medical texts and a long list of phone numbers. I still have a full bookshelf at the clinic, but I use online medical resources to provide answers to my clinical questions.

If you work in healthcare in a city, you miss something extraordinary about the rural practice of medicine. In rural medicine, what you do defines who you are in a small community where everyone knows your name. I have friends who are also my patients. In rural healthcare, that line between your professional and personal lives fades almost to nonexistence.

"Amy, it's so weird having you as my primary care provider," a friend recently disclosed. Some locals have elected to leave the valley for healthcare because we are friends. Still, I'm honored when people come to me for their healthcare and join me at a dinner party the following week. Getting to know a person as more than a patient enriches and deepens relationships while improving the quality of care.

I have to set boundaries. I work hard to protect patient privacy. If you and I meet at the grocery store or the post office, I won't ask about your health. You may ask me about medical issues, but I won't ask you. Instead, see me in the clinic. At least I am sure to remember to chart our conversation.

During Stanley's live music and street dances on Thursday nights during the summer, I joke about becoming Lucy in the Peanuts cartoon, setting up my little advice booth on the unpaved streets of Stanley. I'll look in your ears or check your toes, and you can leave money in the donation jar for the ambulance.

As if the demands of family medicine and responding to emergencies weren't enough, there are days when I've also been a veterinarian, a dentist, an electrician, and a plumber.

Daily realities of staffing an isolated, rural clinic encourage you to be flexible.

A perennial question is whether we should do X-rays. Marie struggled with this issue, even installing lead in the walls of one of the clinic rooms before abandoning the X-ray option. My job is challenging enough without being an X-ray tech and then being responsible for interpreting the films. Also, people don't need one more excuse not to go over the hill to the hospital. And the liability: You take the X-ray, review it, miss the fracture, and tell your patient, "Looks normal. I don't see a fracture. Enjoy your rafting trip on the raft the Middle Fork." Then, two days later, the radiologist's interpretation comes back, "Fracture." Or "Probable fracture, recommend further imaging." That's not a responsibility I'm willing to take on.

As much as this is my dream job, I know it's not forever. It wasn't for Marie, either. That day came when she walked out the clinic door for the last time, a day of goodbyes, sadness, tears, and memories. Is there anything in life that matches this experience for Marie and me?

What do you need to know if you're interested in rural medicine? First, be open to being on a steep learning curve while becoming part of your community. As with Marie, knowing and trusting a rural community's healthcare provider takes time. I joke it took me ten years before the Stanley Clinic got busy. "Amy's still here after ten years. Looks like she'll stick around after all. Maybe I'll go see her."

So, you're interested in rural medicine: How will you pay for your education? State and federal loan repayment programs for care providers are critical to rural healthcare, which faces shortages across America. Generally, the payback commitment is two years. The loan repayment program helped finance my own PA training. I worked in Jerome to repay my student loans through the National Health Service Corps. The loan repayment program has a track record of success for rural communities.

Geography is destiny in making life choices. These mountains brought me here and have held me for the last eighteen years. Everything else came from that, including my commitment to rural practice. I know Stanley's clinic is a coveted job, despite the years it took for the clinic board to hire someone who was a good fit. The outcome can be excellent for the community and the clinician when there is a good match.

More than anything, I'm grateful for what Marie created and her contributions to medicine and rural healthcare. In my own way, standing on her shoulders, I'm trying to continue what she started.

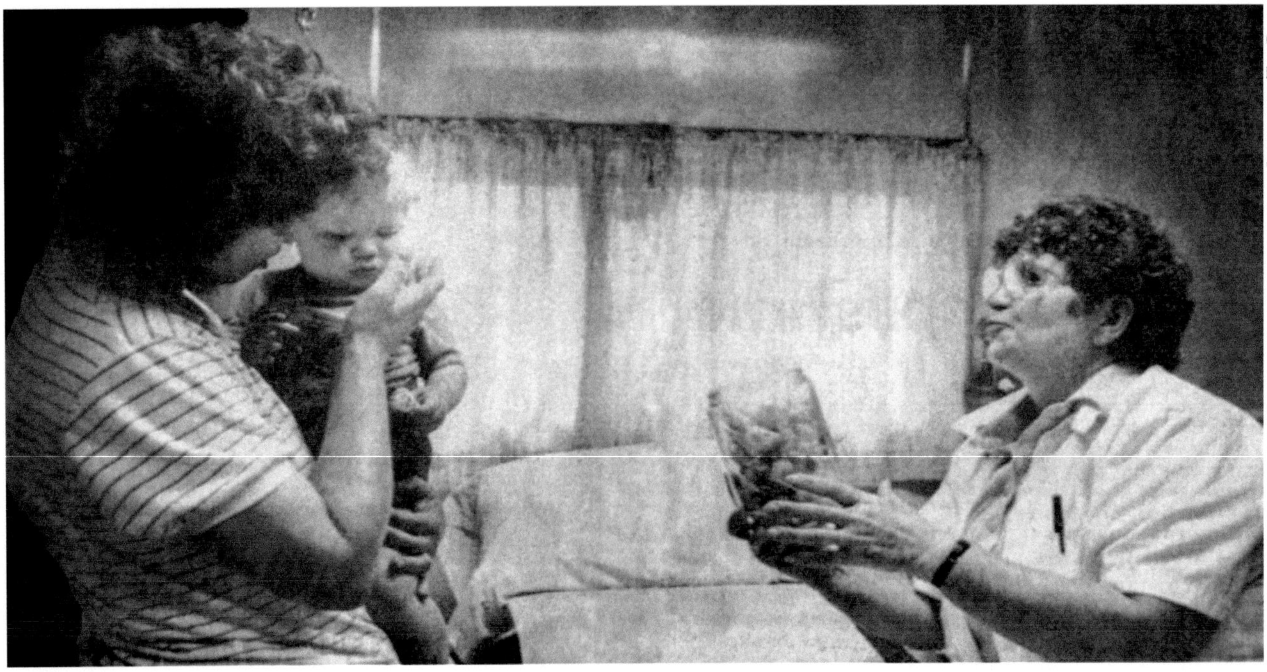

Image source Terri Davis

Marie Osborn charms 13-month-old Alison Stephens of Idaho Falls after an ear examination. Her mom, Ann Stephens, who was camping with the family, brought her to Osborn's office. From "Mountain Nurse: she's a camper's best friend and lifeline" by Larry Gardner, The Idaho Statesman, Boise, Idaho, August 7, 1987

41

EMS: CROSSING THE RURAL-URBAN DIVIDE

It's not easy to get out to folks in nearly 6,000 square miles of rural Custer County, and it's a lot more difficult in winter. I don't think it ever occurred to Marie, who was small of stature and big of heart, that she couldn't do something because she wasn't a man. Marie just did it.

Carole King, songwriter and singer

When you walk into the Stanley Clinic needing medical care, you are a patient no matter your station in life. During the busy summer tourist season, the College of Idaho premed interns reach for clipboards:

- You are asked for your name ("Spell it, please"), your contact information, medical insurance (if any), chief complaint, allergies, and medications.
- We will want your blood pressure, your pulse, and your temperature.
- We'll ask you to sit in the reception room until a treatment room is available, then walk you back.

Whether you are worth billions or homeless, the process is the same. We are all born with belly buttons.

"Here is a gown. Take off your clothes, please. There's a sheet on the bed." We ask our patients, some total strangers, to undress, and they do. History and physical exam are the first steps to diagnosis, and diagnosis is the first step to treatment.

Sun Valley, Idaho, just sixty miles away, sent movie stars and other celebrities for an occasional visit to the Sawtooths or whitewater rafting on the Middle Fork of the Salmon River. Bill Harrah was one of our first famous residents. He founded Harrah's Hotel and Casinos, which is now part of Caesars Entertainment. In the 1970s, Bill bought the west end of Stanley's Ace of Diamonds Street and about half of the town before he died.

He treated celebrity performers to Stanley and his Middle Fork Lodge, which were part of his Stanharrah operations.

"You can talk to Mr. Harrah for an hour, and when you get done, you don't know any more than when you started," said Maxine Baptiste to a New York Times reporter. Maxine managed the Armada Café for Stanharrah operations. Maxine looked like Aunt Bee in Mayberry RFD and could laugh even with her café packed with hungry customers.

Bill owned 1,100 vintage cars, the world's most extensive collection then. He displayed his antique cars, one at a time, in a glassed-in building across from Maxine's cafe. He especially loved showing his Stanley Steamer.

Bill and his wife, Verna, were regular good-weather residents of Stanley, not so much in the winter. Once Bill brought his two adopted sons, John and Tony, into the Stanley Clinic. I gave them 20 cc syringes. As boys discover, syringes make great squirt guns. Bill also brought celebrities to Stanley. Walking to the post office, I might see Burt Reynolds or Jim Nabors.

We were stunned when reporters announced Bill's death in his mid-sixties at the Mayo Clinic (St. Mary's Hospital in Rochester), during surgery to repair an aortic aneurysm. My son John had just studied surgical pathology at the Mayo Clinic months earlier. The Mayo Clinic was the destination for many in trouble, including some of the world's elite.

One morning at the Stanley Clinic, I was alone cleaning a treatment room when I heard the door open.

"Hello? Anyone here?"

I knew that voice. It was … of course, it was David Hartman, the first host of ABC's *Good Morning, America*. "Come on in," I yelled from the back of the clinic. "I'll be right there."

I also provided care for two singers from New York. The first was passing through Stanley on her way to an audition the next day. She had a terrible sore throat and was just miserable.

"I don't have any money," she said with a raspy voice.

"Pay your bill when you can," I replied. We were still in the old clinic back then. I cultured her throat and started her on antibiotics.

After achieving success, the singer again passed through Stanley about ten years later. She stopped by the new clinic, shared how she had made it in the world, and paid her bill.

The second singer from New York settled down to live locally: Carole King. Carole lived in two worlds: the concrete canyons of New York City and the river canyons of Custer County, Idaho. In Washington D.C., Carole met my son, John, testifying in a congressional hearing to protect wilderness. Straddling two worlds gives Carole a first-person understanding of the rural-urban divide that few other American leaders have.

I remember the first time I met Carole as a patient. I'm doubly disadvantaged being female and short. Height helps men and women in leadership roles. When first impressions count, being tall commands attention and begets respect. "I thought you'd be taller," was one deflating comment by people looking down at me in my white coat and stethoscope.

When Carole King first walked into the clinic, and I looked up at her by only a few inches, I smiled: Even short women can do great things.

CAROLE KING, IN HER OWN WORDS

I admire and respect dedicated medical professionals. I am so grateful for those called to care for others, especially Marie and EMTs who volunteer in rural communities.

In 1981, I came to Robinson Bar Ranch. The ranch is near where Warm Springs Creek flows into the Salmon River. We're about twenty miles downriver from Stanley. Fortunately, I didn't have to use the Stanley Clinic often and never had a life-threatening injury. I lived at the ranch most of the time, but sometimes, I had to go away for work. The ranch caretakers might get hurt, cutting themselves on a sharp tool. When you're injured, that's all you think about. They knew to head for the clinic — and Marie.

Marie looked after people in this vast area, with few roads and long spaces between towns and gas stations. Her impact on our rural county was immense and lasting.

The ranch house at Robinson Bar Ranch is set back from the Salmon River. Beyond the pasture, trees block views of the river. This part of the river is called "the Narrows." The river flows through a steep canyon with a series of white-water rapids. I know that stretch of river and have rafted it several times. Above the river, the highway twists through the canyon. Drivers entering the canyon are caught unaware. I'm not in the first category and I'm hoping not to be in the second, but in these parts you'll hear many times, "There are two kinds of people in Custer County: Them that's drove into the river, and them that's gonna drive into the river." Thankfully, there was Marie Osborn.

There are two kinds of people in Custer County: them that's drove into the river, and them that's gonna drive into the river.

When you'd see Marie at the clinic, she was no-nonsense, professional, and capable. You sensed her being calm, competent, and in control.

Don't take good healthcare for granted anywhere, especially in rural areas. The closest hospital was eighty miles from the ranch, over Galena Summit to Sun Valley or downriver to Salmon. City people don't have to consider whether emergency care is available, although money is a worry. Too often, however, it's a big challenge for rural people to get the healthcare they need.

Coming from the city, I was struck by rural people's self-sufficiency. You learn quickly to handle minor emergencies. For more serious medical problems, that's when you called Marie. Marie's reputation was storied. If it was severe and Marie couldn't handle it, she'd get you where you needed to be.

Stanley and Challis were my communities. Challis was the county seat for Custer County. Over the years, I got to know people in both communities. There is something special in these places. If you are in trouble and pull over to the side of the road, someone will stop and offer to help.

There is an attitude of helping each other even if you have different political beliefs. None of that matters when people are hurt and need help during a crisis. You have neighbors and a neighborhood in a big city, but it's different.

Marie will leave a legacy that will endure. She had the commitment, administrative skills, and ability to persuade people to support rural healthcare and EMS. Creating a healthcare system in that part of rural Idaho is every bit as big as her medical capability.

42

BREAKING TRAIL THAT OTHERS MAY FOLLOW

"And each one there has one thing shared:
They have sweated beneath the same sun,
Looked up in wonder at the same moon,
And wept when it was all done,
For being done too soon.
For being done too soon."

Neil Diamond

Emergency lights flash from the ambulance and the deputy's SUV. Our EMS radios are chattering. Near the wrecked, upside-down car, the EMTs and I anxiously monitor our patient's vitals: The blood pressure is marginal, and pulse is thready despite the IV fluids. How much longer before the air ambulance?

Then, a whisper, we hear it: *chuff, chuff, chuff.* Sounds grow louder. We see the helicopter moving against the peaks of the Sawtooth Range, flying over the trees, and coming down the valley.

Oh. Thank. God.

Until I die, I will remember the relief washing over me when I hear that helicopter while kneeling next to a critical patient. That sound means my patient has a chance.

Later, we watch the helicopter lift off, bracing ourselves against the rotors' downdraft. Then, finally, the aircraft grows smaller and disappears. Quiet returns. At that moment, the silence is almost sacred. EMTs and law enforcement start cleaning up while talking about when they got the emergency call, especially if it was bad.

When it's over at a trauma scene, especially if it's a bad outcome, you look at each other and then away. If someone is about to lose it, a hug is in order. The team gathers and debriefs, checking in and talking through. Beyond the first responders are the survivors. Where are they? How are they? With major trauma, human life changes abruptly. For some, life ends and leaves survivors beginning a journey of loss and "what ifs." As a first responder, you can help comfort and connect survivors with resources. When the helicopter takes off or the ambulance door closes, there is still more to do.

Small communities have the added dimension that emergency calls involve first responders' family and friends. Those can be especially hard when outcomes are bad. But the worst emergency calls? The kids. Those are the emergency calls you never forget.

Sunday mornings at the Stanley Clinic are usually quiet. I drove from my home on Shaw Mesa to the clinic. Waiting for the first walk-in patients, I enjoyed the calm while cleaning, stocking, talking with the premeds, sharing stories with Deputy Jim Parkhouse, and catching up on my paperwork.

"Camp Bradley to the Stanley Clinic: We need help." Getting a call from Camp Bradley wasn't unusual. The Valley's scouting and church camps sent us a lot of business.

For Camp Bradley, each Boy Scout was to have a physical exam before arriving at camp. Most did, but not all. Some parents sent their sons without physicals. Scout leaders then asked me to do them.

During the clinic's early years, weekly, I drove out to Camp Bradley, did physicals, and joined the Scouts for dinner before returning to town. When the boys came into the room for their physicals, many were wide-eyed and silent. The older Scouts had warned them, "She's going to do a rectal exam." I didn't.

Firecracker injuries were another problem. The Scouts would smash firecrackers between two rocks, and shrapnel could go anywhere. One scout had an eye injury requiring a referral to an ophthalmologist in Twin Falls.

Scoutmasters would arrive clean, spic and span, with all their badges displayed. One leader was dressed in a crisp and creased scouting uniform when he walked into the clinic complaining of noise in his ear.

He recalled leaving Twin Falls for the drive to Stanley, brushing away a fly from his head. I placed the speculum in his auditory canal and looked.

"That noise you're hearing? I hate to tell you this, but it's coming from maggots inside your ear," I said calmly, my stomach churning. That pregnant fly had deposited her eggs in a warm, dark ear canal, and they hatched.

Not knowing how to treat ear maggots, I called my physician preceptor, Dr. Gwinner, in Hailey. "Just put oil in the ear," he advised. "The oil will kill the maggots and relieve the discomfort." I used a dropper to release oil into the ear canal. It worked.

Camp Bradley had no telephone during those years. Camp leaders would barrel down the dirt road and Highway 21 for serious injuries. We settled on providing the camp with a portable radio with EMS channels to access the clinic. That way, scouting leaders could radio me with what to expect.

The camp leader's voice over the EMS radio that Sunday morning was frantic. "Marie, we need help. We've had a head-on collision. Kids are hurt, some badly."

We called for EMTs, pulled the ambulance out of the clinic garage, and headed west on Highway 21 with lights flashing. We turned onto the dirt road and drove until we saw wrecked vehicles.

It was bedlam. Kids were crying. Kids were screaming. Kids were bleeding, making grunting noises, and lying still, not breathing.

The drivers in the collision survived and didn't know what to do. How could they, with so many kids hurt? Where do you begin with a mass-casualty event involving children?

One volunteer EMT, Julie Meissner, had a day off from her job as a river guide when the emergency call went out. Before becoming an EMT, Julie had ski patrol and backcountry experience.

Once, Julie took a week off from guiding on the Middle Fork to work on building her house, only to get called for eight emergencies in seven days.

Here is Julie's story as a first responder for the multiple casualty event at Camp Bradley:

When we arrived, we saw multiple cars stopped along the dirt road, pointed in both directions. Exiting the ambulance, we watched a tall young boy ran down the road, screaming. Although he didn't look injured, he was later diagnosed with a traumatic brain injury.

"Check each car," Marie directed the EMTs.

We went from vehicle to vehicle, assessing the people inside. I ran up to a pickup with an older couple inside. Between them was their grandson, a boy maybe seven years old. The truck's cab had just one seat, and a stick shift was up from the floor.

"It hurts!" The boy bent over, sobbing and in pain. His hands clutched his abdomen. Not wearing a seatbelt when his grandfather hit the brake, the boy had hurtled forward onto the stick shift.

"Can you help him?" the grandfather pleaded. Then, the grandmother exited the truck to make room for me.

I got into the cab to try and comfort the boy. Time can be weird during emergencies. How much time passed, maybe five minutes? Fifteen? Meanwhile, Marie went vehicle to vehicle to check on each of us, doing her triage and figuring out who was going on that first helicopter. She arrived at the truck where I was and looked at the boy.

"He's going first," Marie said to me. I looked at Marie and was surprised. Really, this boy? She saw something I didn't. Marie could look at this boy — and the mass casualty scene — and determine priorities.

The helicopter landed to the east of the road. With so many injured, we organized to transport patients by air and ground ambulances. The crew loaded the boy and other patients, lifted off, and headed over the Sawtooth peaks for Boise, returning for the next load. As it turns out, the boy ruptured his spleen when he hit the stick shift. He would have bled to death had Marie not sent him on that first flight to Boise and into the operating room.

Marie talks about the relief she feels when she first hears that helicopter. That day, the relief I felt came from Marie. I knew something was wrong with the boy. I had no experience putting it together that he might die from internal injuries. Marie did. You learn and pay it forward.

The Camp Bradley incident involved two trucks colliding on a narrow, one-lane road just below the crest of a hill. Riding in those vehicles were boys ages ten to fourteen, unrestrained by seatbelts.

When we called for help, almost every EMT in the Valley came, as well as those from Challis and Ketchum. For the injured boys, we needed every EMT, every ambulance, and every helicopter.

We had recently practiced a mass-casualty response at the Forest Service parking lot. We had not, however, trained for anything this intense, with so many children injured.

Mass casualties demand a tightly coordinated effort. Communication is key. But as usual, mountains blocked our radio communications with central dispatch in Boise. So, instead, we got through to the sheriff's office in Challis. Challis dispatch called StateComm for helicopters and sent the call for Challis and Ketchum to send their ambulances.

Our first responders were terrific. As a team, we triaged, got backboards and C-collars on, started oxygen and IVs, and controlled bleeding. We feared head traumas and internal injuries, especially if the vitals were bad. You can't know the extent of traumatic injuries in a mass casualty event in the field.

After the last helicopter lifted off for Boise and the Stanley, Challis, and Ketchum ambulances headed for Sun Valley, bedlam gave way to quiet.

Remaining behind were EMTs, law enforcement, and people from the scout camp. Trash, IV bags, tubing, wrappings for dressings, and equipment littered the crash scene.

"Let's get this cleaned up," I said. We needed to get ready for the next call. As the mother of five, I could only think: Those could have been my boys.

I had a similar gut-wrenching feeling back in 1971 when those four kids were severely injured in a car wreck, and it took over two and a half hours for the ambulance to arrive from Hailey. Almost no emergency medical services were in place to help those kids.

Two decades later, confronted with multiple injured Boy Scouts on the road to Camp Bradley, it was apparent that an Emergency Medical Services revolution had swept over rural America. Responding to the Camp Bradley disaster were trained EMTs, paramedics, ambulance drivers, law enforcement, dedicated air ambulance pilots, and healthcare staff, all working together as a team and coordinated through Idaho EMS.

"We serve to bring control out of the uncontrollable," summarized Sparky Easom, who volunteered as an EMT for the Stanley Ambulance for decades.

By responding to emergencies and healthcare challenges in Idaho's Sawtooth country, the community of Stanley, Idaho, helped to drive that EMS revolution.

Any man's death diminishes me,
because I am involved in mankind,
and therefore never send to know for whom the bell tolls;
It tolls for thee.

John Donne, "No Man Is an Island"

In the early years, just about all of Stanley's business owners cooperated in letting their staff take time away to respond to emergency calls as volunteer EMTs. In Stanley, people make their money during the summer. Unfortunately, that's also when people get hurt.

Although EMS needs are year-round, emergency calls spike during summer with climbing, boating, and motor vehicle accidents. Since we relied on volunteer EMTs, the business owners were helping the community by subsidizing the Stanley ambulance with their employees.

Amy Klingler and the hospital district's elected board are now paying EMTs to be on call for emergencies, and a stipend for ambulance runs. What was once a pizza fund to reward and feed a hungry ambulance crew with takeout from Louie's Pizza in Ketchum is now a program of financial incentives. So far, the system is working.

Traffic ticket fines are another possible revenue source for funding rural EMS. In the 1990s, I tried and failed at the Idaho Legislature to have a portion of traffic tickets earmarked for rural EMS. Traffic ticket fines help pay judges' salaries and their retirement.

As one legislator and supporter of EMS explained, "Marie, traffic ticket money is a sacred cow. Using some of that money for rural EMS won't happen."

With so many lives at stake in our rural communities, we should not give up.

What about the agencies? For decades, two law enforcement officers — one federal and one state — volunteered as EMTs and anchored our first-responder teams.

What would it take for the Forest Service and Idaho Fish and Game to build on the legacy of previous employees who served as EMTs?

In exploring solutions for rural EMS, few people have lived and breathed EMS the way Idaho's EMS founder, Paul Anderson, has. Paul created and led Idaho's statewide EMS network from 1973 – 1992. I've asked Paul to share his recommendations for sustaining volunteer EMTs at the heart of rural EMS:

PAUL ANDERSON, IN HIS OWN WORDS

When Idaho EMS began in 1973, we focused on recruiting volunteers to take EMS training who would respond to emergency calls, essential for a viable statewide emergency response system.

Looking at the finances, most rural areas of Idaho do not generate enough emergency revenue to make EMS a viable business proposition. There are too few emergencies for rural EMS to pencil out without volunteers.

Starting in the 1950s, before 911, I remember going out on emergency vehicles to rural communities that had no emergency services — no EMTs, no ambulances, and no Quick Response Units (QRUs).

People needing help in those communities waited one or more hours for an ambulance. People died waiting.

By the early 1970s, EMS was a new field with new EMT, paramedic, and QRU training programs. People were excited about being part of a vital, cutting-edge program that held the promise of saving lives across America.

When we had training, several dozen people might turn out in rural towns across Idaho to train and then to become volunteers as part of their community's new EMS and rescue units.

Thousands of new EMS volunteers strengthened local fire departments and created new first responder teams. We can never fully calculate nor appreciate the service these unsung heroes provide — not just to their local communities but to society.

For rural EMS units, a week might go by without an emergency call, and then two or three calls occur during a single night.

Rural first responders must be ready, trained, and equipped to respond day or night to emergencies whenever they occur.

Here is the elephant in the room: As it has been stated several times in *Moving Mountains*, the volunteerism that makes rural EMS possible is in decline.

Ron Dunagan

Paul and Marie at Idaho StateComm, July, 2023. EMS crosses the urban-rural divide, requiring teamwork and tight communication.

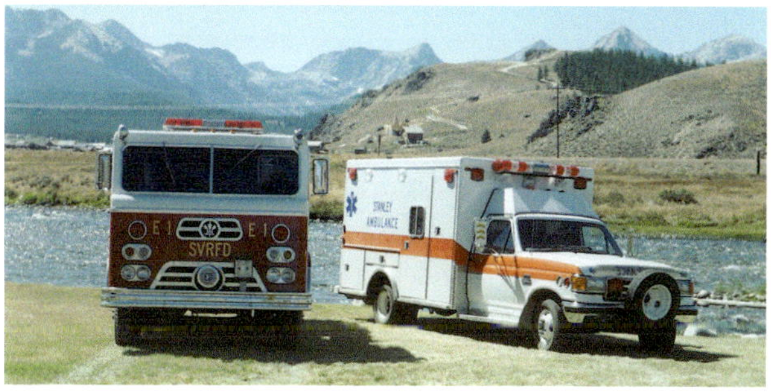

"When I first came to Stanley, I worked as a backcountry ranger," Stanley EMT Julie Meissner recalls:

> We had wilderness rangers in nearly every drainage. We had law enforcement here. The Agency staff volunteered as EMTs. Now? There's just one law enforcement officer for the whole region. Failing to fund and fill staff positions for the Sawtooth NRA impacts the Stanley Ambulance. Fewer EMTs are left to cover emergency calls.

Unfortunately, the EMS experience in Stanley is not unique. For rural EMS to endure, we must recruit, train, and retain new volunteer first responders. Rural communities across America struggle to respond with enough trained and certified EMS volunteers. The inequities for rural healthcare — the driving force for Marie to open the Stanley Clinic and Stanley Ambulance service — are still with us. The population of Idaho's Treasure Valley (Boise, Meridian, Nampa, Caldwell, Eagle, Star, and more) is rapidly approaching one million Call volume is sufficient to support paid EMS staff. Unfortunately, that model generally does not work for rural communities, resulting in vulnerabilities and inequities.

How do we ensure adequate EMS for rural communities? When Senator Frank Church stood on the floor of the US Senate and spoke about Stanley's 1958 Pontiac ambulance with exhaust fumes coming up through holes in the floorboards, he succeeded in getting his colleagues to better support rural ambulance services. For Idaho, state leaders could declare EMS and rescue services as "essential services" for the people of Idaho and visitors to the state. If volunteers are the backbone of rural EMS, and we're losing the ability to recruit and retain volunteers, declaring EMS an essential service will expand the options for finding solutions.

The smaller the town, the more difficult it can be to recruit and retain volunteer EMTs. A rural community with a population of 500–1000 might field an adequate team of volunteers. But that's a reach for a town like Stanley, with fewer than 100 year-round residents.

Other factors are the time and distance needed to transport a patient to the nearest hospital. For volunteer EMTs, being up all night transporting a patient will make it harder to show up for work in the morning.

Frequent emergency calls can lead to problems between employers and volunteers. Especially for small rural businesses, even the most supportive employer may balk at the costs of allowing volunteer EMTs to leave work repeatedly for emergency calls. The smaller the pool of volunteer EMTs, the more the burden falls on one or two EMTs and their employers.

Given the looming crisis in rural EMS, here are three options that could help.

1. Agencies need to help: county, state, and federal

Each year, over a million people visit the Sawtooth NRA. Local property owners voted overwhelmingly to tax themselves to fund healthcare. Meanwhile, the Forest Service is the largest property owner yet pays virtually nothing to support the ambulance and clinic. Before 1972, local Forest Service staff were the first responders, borrowing employee station wagons as makeshift ambulances to haul the injured over Galena Summit to Sun Valley. Forest Service seasonal and permanent employees became the backbone of Stanley's volunteer EMT program. No longer, in part, because positions go unfilled in the federal agency.

Federal, state, and county agencies often have offices and personnel in rural communities. These agencies need to do more to support rural EMS. While recognizing that for communities, "one size fits one," we also point to the Stanley model: Agency staff filling critical roles in sustaining the ambulance and rescue teams. Other agencies in a position to help include county roads departments and the Idaho Transportation Department (with personnel throughout the state).

Agencies could work with HR specialists to rewrite job descriptions and encourage staff to volunteer as first responders. Rewards and other incentives within agency systems could include community service in EMS. Furthermore, agency staff are vested in maintaining viable EMS in the rural communities where they and their families live. Failure to support EMS can mean the difference between life and death. EMS is a shared responsibility.

2. Partially compensate volunteer EMTs

With fewer volunteers, those responsible for EMS units are starting to offer partial compensation to recruit and retain EMTs.

EMS units with a higher volume of emergency calls (500-1000 calls in a year) are more likely to partially compensate EMS volunteers than those with lower volumes (100-200). Lower-volume EMS units are likely to spend more on operational expenses to keep their vehicles operating and equipped, making them less able to compensate their volunteers.

Uniformly compensating volunteer EMTs in rural communities will require new funding sources and systems. While recognizing a spectrum of needs, rural EMS units in greatest need are often those unable to generate adequate funds and, therefore, least able to compensate their volunteers partially.

3. Partial retirement or supplemental retirement fund

Another incentive might be to provide a state EMS retirement fund to help those who have volunteered for

EMS and rescue work in rural Idaho communities. The fund would supplement retirement income with a payment related to the number of years of volunteer EMS/rescue service provided to the state EMS system. If someone has provided ten or twenty years of volunteer EMS service, their retirement benefit should be more than that of someone who has volunteered for five years, for instance.

Who would pay? Rural EMS units would be unable to do so, leaving that to the state. The state still gets a bargain by saving millions on donated volunteer time and expertise of rural EMTs. Compared to state funding for state police and highway maintenance, the state's cost for EMS is a bargain.

A fourth and unacceptable option is to do nothing. Hollowing out EMS will return Idaho to where we started in the 1960s. People will call 911 for help ... and wait. People will die waiting.

Building and sustaining EMS is not a rural versus urban issue. People living in urban areas visit rural areas and get hurt. When a medical emergency occurs, the person needs help immediately, not later. Failing to find solutions to the declining number of volunteer EMTs risks Idaho's progress over the past fifty years. We all depend on those heroes who take the call at three in the morning, get out of bed, and head out to help their neighbor or a total stranger.

On September 20, 1997, Forest Service Law Enforcement Officer Steve Lipus and Forest Protection Officer Ken Hartz were patrolling near Alturas Lake when they got the call for a car wreck thirteen miles away, near Obsidian. Steve recalls:

> When we got the emergency call, Ken and I were in the Alturas Lake area in separate Forest Service vehicles. My law enforcement vehicle was equipped to run code (lights and siren), and I arrived first on the scene. A van had lost control and rolled. Multiple injured people were along the edge of the highway and in the ditch.
>
> Ken drove to town for the ambulance and additional EMTs. I stayed with six adult patients, women and men, many with severe traumatic injuries.
>
> Inside the van, the steering wheel pinned the driver. He had sustained blunt-force chest injuries, open head wounds, and an obstructed airway. In my triage assessment, while also attempting to establish an airway, I concluded he would not survive. I moved on to help save others while radioing StateComm for air ambulance support.
>
> I was relieved to see the Stanley Ambulance arrive. When Ken Hartz got out, I learned there were no EMTs aboard, but they were responding. That ambulance meant Ken and I had equipment and oxygen to stabilize the injured. One formidable challenge was communication, as our patients were all from India. I called again for more EMTs.
>
> Meanwhile, Gary Gadwa, Senior Conservation Officer with the Idaho Department of Fish and Game, heard my desperate radio call for EMTs. Gary was on patrol west of Stanley. Gary reported that he was about forty miles out but would bring the EMS Director for St. Luke's, Keith Seviertson, and make a "code run" to my location. Dr. Seviertson brought considerable medical experience to the scene and later reported, "That was the fastest code run I have ever made in my entire career."
>
> Soon, EMTs and members of the volunteer fire department arrived. As with other multi-casualty incidents, folks in the Stanley community — volunteer EMTs, clinic staff, Sawtooth Valley Rural Fire Department, and law enforcement — dropped whatever they were doing to respond to the call and help someone in need. As EMTs arrived, I assigned them to patients based on my initial triage.
>
> The driver was declared deceased. Life Flight airlifted one critical patient to Boise. The Stanley Ambulance transported multiple patients over the hill to Sun Valley.
>
> Afterward, all Stanley EMTs, clinic staff, and fire department volunteers who were involved attended a critical incident debriefing with Marie and psychologist Sharlene Stahl. These meetings are confidential. Still, I can disclose the comfort and support others provided. In all my years as a volunteer EMT, that was the only time I had to make a life-and-death triage

decision. I will always wonder if I did the right thing. In this, I am not alone.

Later, we received a letter from Burley, Idaho, physician Dr. Wendell L. Wells and his wife, Mary, who were on the scene and provided this reflection:

The single-car accident involved six people, two of whom were critically injured. Passing cars were asked to call for help. I am a family physician and had a few first aid supplies in my truck.

Time passes slowly when you're caring for such injured people, but very soon a member of the [Forest Service law enforcement] was on the scene. He listened to the condition of those injured and understood that air evacuation was necessary and had Life Flight in the air quickly. He also had extrication equipment en route and EMTs to assist in rescue efforts.

My wife and I were impressed with the professionalism and compassion shown by the firefighters, EMTs, ambulance crew, law officers, [Idaho Fish and Game] personnel (one of whom had the great idea to collect the Life Flight physician he knew was hunting in the area to come and help at the accident scene), and other local residents who gave assistance at the roadside tragedy.

Your community and county should be proud of your efforts. I doubt that many who travel through this beautiful area are aware of the many dedicated people who stand ready to help.

The following year, in 1998, my family and I left Stanley for Boise for a new position with the Forest Service.

Long before Stanley's EMTs, people in need depended on what the Bible named "Good Samaritans." My Kentucky grandmother, Mother Tatum, was one. She traveled throughout her community, delivering babies and nursing neighbors in need.

Service to others comes with a cost. In the fall of 1918, Mother Tatum was attending to her fellow Kentuckians and may have carried influenza home. Influenza killed her husband and plunged the Tatum family into poverty. Still, Mother Tatum never stopped providing her nursing service to others throughout her life.

From the time I was four or five years old, I wanted to be a nurse. Kentucky Nurses on Horseback, who rode into Appalachia to help rural people who had no healthcare, was what captured my dreams as a girl growing up in Kentucky and Indiana during the Great Depression. Eventually, I did house calls by horseback in Idaho's Sawtooth country. Still, I was less a Kentucky Nurse on Horseback and more an Idaho Nurse Practitioner on snowmobile.

Looking back, it's incredible how little things can start a movement. Something else adds to it, and something else adds more. You don't have a big strategic plan or even a checklist. Instead, you finish one task and go on to the next. In those first years, there was no grand plan or vision for the nurse practitioner as a profession or rural EMS. There was just the reality of responding to people needing help.

In 1971, I set out to provide emergency care services in Idaho's Sawtooth and Salmon River country. I did not set out to change the world. Once I started, though, I had to see it through. Partly, it was the utter lack of healthcare in Stanley and the Sawtooth Valley. Also, in the man's world of the early 1970s, I was driven to prove that a woman could do this work.

For me personally, there were consequences. This life cost me my marriage, fractured my family, left me on the edge of poverty, and landed me in frequent hearings before legislative committees, the Board of Medicine, and the Board of Pharmacy.

But in the end, the Stanley Clinic and Stanley Ambulance stood. So did the nurse practitioner as a profession in Idaho and far beyond, and so did rural EMS.

Now in my nineties and blind, above the couch where I sit during my days and sleep at night are Mother Teresa's words, "Not all of us can do great things. But we can do small things with great love." While I can't see her words any longer, I know they are there and take comfort in them.

"They told me you can do miracles," the distraught mother insisted. Her seven-year-old son swung the hatchet at their campsite, the blade landing on the hand of his four-year-old brother, cleaving off four fingers. The fingers arrived with the parents, along with their owner. The mother insisted I could reattach the fingers and make the hand whole.

"I am not God." I do not create, and I do not control destiny.

I wrapped those four little pale and bloody fingers in gauze, poured on betadine, dialed a hand surgeon, and sent the family to Boise and an operating room.

Sometimes, despite everything you can do, people die. The car wrecks, drownings, gunshot wounds, chest pains, overdoses, suicides, mountain climbing accidents, and more: Your best won't always change the outcome. You kneel over the body and pronounce your patient dead. Then you stand to hug the survivors, sobbing with grief. "I'm so sorry." You step back and realize it was their time, that sometimes you cannot change the inevitable. You hold it together. Then you go home and fall apart.

How many times am I reminded that medics don't perform miracles? One case remains with me: A young woman dancer dreaming of becoming a ballerina. She and her young hunter boyfriend were traveling in a Ford Mustang with a loaded rifle between them. He spotted a deer, grabbed his rifle, and it went off. The bullet destroyed the young dancer's ankle.

She wouldn't let anyone touch her or leave the car until I arrived. I don't know how she knew my name. When I examined the gunshot wound, I found her foot was attached only by the Achilles tendon. The bone was gone. I put her in an air splint and put her on a board, and the EMTs transported her back to Boise and the operating room. The orthopedic surgeons reattached her foot as best they could.

Some people wanted more than I could give. One example began when Bud James, operating our radio base station out of the Mountain Village motel during the early 1970s, called me for help. I drove to the motel parking lot. A woman wearing a slip had a mass protruding between her legs. It was her uterus. Her husband, worried and not knowing what it was, had brought his wife from their campsite to town. After many pregnancies, her pelvic floor collapsed, and her uterus dropped out of her body. I ended up sending her over the hill to Sun Valley. Later, she died.

The surviving husband and father of their many children came to the clinic. He told me about his wife dying. He wanted me to marry him because I could care for his kids. I didn't want to hurt his feelings, but I said no, and he left.

Later that fall, I was alone in the clinic when I heard someone in the reception room. When I stepped into the room, I saw him.

"I want to talk with you," he said. I tried to make small talk, saying that I hoped he and his kids were doing better after his wife's passing.

"My sister is helping with the kids," he said. "Marie, things have to change. I want you to marry me. I've thought a lot about it. I know you can take care of the kids just fine."

For some men, women are property. I said "No" a second time. Fortunately, he never returned.

Almost from the start, I sensed the importance of what we were doing in Stanley, Idaho.

I planned to write this book in those first years to finance my retirement. Now, fifty years later, I write this book to honor the many people who made the Stanley Clinic and Stanley Ambulance possible and supported me in becoming Idaho's first nurse practitioner.

In 1971, I could not have done what I did if I had been a twenty-two-year-old RN with my BSN fresh out of nurses training. Instead, my curriculum vitae included raising three sons and two daughters, losing twins, and nearly dying from mastitis. My husband was squeamish at the sight of blood, so I attended to my family's medical problems of lacerations, fractures, bad burns, hernias, allergic reactions, chokings, earaches, skin disorders, and more. It was as though the first half of my life helped prepare me to provide healthcare in Idaho's Sawtooth country.

You don't know how experiences may impact the rest of your life. How could you? Only by looking back can we hope to understand our life's journey.

For your rural patients, it helps if you share some of the same life experiences that they're experiencing. Unlike a new graduate, you may not be on top of the latest developments. But you bring different knowledge, a wisdom that only comes from living life and caring for others over the years.

Idaho is a relatively small community covering a formidable geography. In the 1960s and early 1970s, Cal and I were part of that community through IBM, our advocacy work in public education, and our kids' ski racing. People we knew — Gov. Andrus, John Hutchinson, Don Ness, and so many others — joined with locals in Stanley, the Wood River Valley, and beyond to open doors and access resources to create the Stanley Clinic and Stanley Ambulance.

Given what I went through, I'm at peace saying I was the right person, in the right place, at the right time.

What we were doing was a new idea. No one had ever done it. Within a few years of starting, I was making more and more trips to Boise as the politics became increasingly more unpleasant.

There were doctors in positions of power, all men, who could not concede that a woman nurse practitioner could provide patient care in underserved communities where a physician would not practice.

Who defended me in those hearings? The people of Stanley, my physician preceptors, especially Dr. Stone, the Board of Nursing, the College of Idaho premed interns, and my family. A middle-aged woman could never have walked this path alone, especially in Idaho in the 1970s.

At the time, I did not fully realize that I was blazing a trail for others to follow, narrow at first but widening with time into a fully integrated part of healthcare systems. In 1971, six years after Loretta Ford EdD, PNP, FAAN, and Henry Silver, MD, started the first nurse practitioner program to improve pediatric care access, Idaho was the first state to license NPs. I was the first nurse practitioner licensed in Idaho. My training and practice focused on emergency medicine and, soon after that, family medicine.

During my training in southern Idaho, Seattle, Salt Lake City, and Chicago, I was almost always the first nurse practitioner people had met. Those of us who went first created the profession as we went along. Today, the number of licensed NPs in the United States exceeds 300,000, and our profession has expanded internationally.

Jack See, owner of Redfish Lake Lodge, presents Marie with a dozen yellow roses at the community's farewell celebration.

There is nothing else like it. Over the years, I had multiple job offers at multiples of my salary. But I loved my mountains, being able to help others, and not knowing what was going to come through the door. I loved the adrenaline rush of emergency calls.

More than just providing healthcare, I was also part of my community: organizing Thanksgiving dinner, ensuring the Christmas tree was up in the community building, and helping plan the Christmas party.

Chateau Drug in Ketchum gave me a discount, and the Chamber of Commerce allocated the money so that I could buy presents Santa Claus would give to each child in Stanley at the Christmas dinner. They all got to sit on Santa's lap. Naughty or nice, each child got a gift. And each gift was wrapped by the Mountain Mamas.

Walking from the clinic to the post office to pick up the mail, I'd hear, "Hi Marie! Hi Marie!" from the kids. Everyone knows your name and who you are. The kids never cried, except when they knew they had to get shots.

The lead photo in a 1973 National Geographic Magazine article about Idaho was dancing at the Stanley Stomp in the heart of Idaho. The Braun Brothers, a beloved bluegrass band, started and grew up in Stanley before leaving for Challis. Our Arts and Crafts Fair, hosted by the Mountain Mamas, featured all handmade items. We started small, and then it grew so big the Mountain Mamas had to hire someone to run it. Eventually, it outgrew the Mountain Mamas, and someone else took it over.

I did not start this journey as a young woman. By the late 1990s, I was pushing seventy, living alone on Shaw Mesa, still on 24/7 emergency call, seeing clinic patients, and running women's clinics in Challis and Salmon. Life is not forever. And oh, how I wish I could continue doing this work.

"Getting old is not for sissies," Cal repeatedly warned as he got older. Mind you, I loved chopping my firewood; it's such a frustration reliever. But winters got harder. Climbing up the snowbank, starting the snowmobile, and heading out to the highway to see patients became an increasing problem by my late sixties. Those twelve highway miles to town in the winter could be scary. My body, and especially my eyesight, were beginning to weaken.

There comes a time when you know this doesn't go on forever. I had to find my replacement and say goodbye, painful as that would be. You have to set a date. You have to give your board and community a deadline. People focus when facing a deadline. After working with the board to ensure housing and a more competitive salary for my replacement, in 1998, I gave the board a year.

I had agreed to continue working until we could hire my replacement. Once the new healthcare provider was on board, I would split time in the fall between the clinics in Stanley and Idaho City while helping with the transition. The community planned my farewell celebration at Redfish Lake Lodge for May 30, 1999.

That day turned out to be the most interesting farewell you could imagine. Friends, family, and current and former EMTs arrived at Redfish Lake Lodge. It seemed like the entire Stanley community was there. I had dressed up with my new cowboy boots and a nice pantsuit. Just before the party started, we got an emergency call. A car had lost control, left Highway 21 west of town, and rolled. The driver was severely injured. Despite everything we could do, he later died.

The car had rolled into a swampy, mucky area. After we stabilized the patient and loaded him into the Stanley Ambulance for transport to Sun Valley, the remaining EMTs and I headed to my farewell party at Redfish. My new cowboy boots were ruined, and blood and muck were all over my clothes and white coat. I tried to clean up the best I could.

It seemed appropriate that my last day would be like the rest of the days. The EMTs and I arrived at Redfish Lake Lodge with blood, muck, and all. The EMTs, too, were dressed for my farewell party when the call came. "Well, here we are, take it or leave it," I thought as we walked into the welcoming crowd. And, of course, the people of Stanley didn't miss a beat. It seemed like nothing had changed, and nothing was going to change.

What a champagne and horseshit experience. Incredible joy followed by heartbreak. When you encounter an accident, do you stop and offer to help? When someone is in trouble, do you run toward them to help, do nothing, or run away? With that adrenaline rush, I run toward people who need help. That's who I am.

After I left Stanley, I continued to see patients in rural Horseshoe Bend, Emmett, Idaho City, and finally, low-income patients in Boise. I loved my work, but it wasn't the same without emergency calls. A month after I turned eighty, losing my vision from macular degeneration, I took off my stethoscope and hung up my white coat for the final time. I could no longer see to care for my patients safely.

For the Stanley Clinic, I could have gone on until I dropped. On my last day, I wasn't filled with regret as much as deep sadness. Sure, I was relieved that the Stanley Clinic and Stanley Ambulance would continue, but I wanted it to be with me, and that wasn't physically possible. Still, I didn't want it to end.

If it's appropriate to cry with your patient, you do that, but don't cry for yourself. On that final day, I had to go. I closed the door, walked down the clinic steps, got in my car, and left Stanley. When I walked into my home on Shaw Mesa, I sat down, looked at the Sawtooth peaks, and sobbed.

"Take care of the moments; the years take care of themselves — Carpe Diem." Cal included that wisdom on the back of his "retirement card" that he handed out by the thousands. The years did take care of themselves. However, the passage of years in the high country brought change.

Our family aluminum canoe, the CalMar, rests among the thistles near the woodpile. Named after our Bellingham Bay sailboat, our family canoe once floated the Boise River and then Redfish, Stanley, and Alturas Lakes during IBM and family campouts. Heavy snow crushed, dented, and punctured the boat. My sons have offered to haul it away, but I can't bring myself to let it go. Instead, what remains of the CalMar stays near my Sawtooth home, overlooking the mountains and Salmon River. There are too many memories of Cal and the kids in that canoe. After I'm gone, it can go.

Nearby is the tack house. Open the tack house door, and it's as though time stood still. Saddles and bridles are dust-covered and unused for years. Our horses, Sucia and Macia, are long gone. Still, if you give quiet space to your imagination, you can see Cal in his scruffy white cowboy hat riding Sucia in the Boise foothills, drinking a beer, and singing.

Past the woodpile is our doghouse, a sawed-off top of an outhouse. The Osborn family has so many memories of dogs: Frankie, Socks, Mort, and my beloved Mousse. After losing Mousse, I could never again experience the pain of losing my dog.

The aspen tree we planted has become a small grove turning glorious golden against October's deep blue skies. These and the lodgepole pine trees help screen new houses on Shaw Mesa. Unfortunately, the "rustic western style" of architecture mandated to protect the Sawtooth National Recreation Area from blight is mostly a memory, a casualty of time — and Forest Service neglect.

In the garage, the IBM Selectric typewriter gathers dust. In November 1953, Cal walked up to the IBM recruiter's desk at the University of Washington. IBM hired Cal to sell typewriters — and sell he did. IBM moved the Osborn family to Boise in 1963. IBM brought the Osborn family to Redfish Lake for its annual campout and later supported Cal and me in opening the Stanley Clinic. That relic of a dust-covered typewriter? It's a memory gold mine.

Upstairs is the Singer sewing machine, not the old treadle but the new electric one I insisted Cal buy in the 1960s. Colored spools of thread are eye-catchers, even in the corner shadows.

The memories that sewing machine created: Debbie's nurse uniform, Melinda's tap-dancing costumes, Halloween costumes, two leather drum-major uniforms for the Boise High School marching band, matching pajamas for my three sons and Cal, costumes for the Sound of Music and other off-Broadway productions in Boise, and my dresses for IBM's 100 Percent Club and Golden Circle events. Whether clothes or lacerations, I loved to sew. Today, my sewing machine sits in a corner, unused.

Old picture frames from Silver City remain upstairs, reminders of our early days exploring Idaho. The seven Osborns piled into our International Travelall, heading out to ghost towns, old cemeteries, rivers, and campgrounds. Those cemeteries seem closer now. Cal's ashes mostly reside at the Idaho State Veterans Cemetery, although some are buried with Cory. My ashes will come home to the Sawtooth country, the place we came to love the most.

I used to take comfort in the fact that while so much in life is transitory, the Sawtooth Mountains would remain unchanged. Now, I know better. The 1983 Borah Peak earthquake shook my home on Shaw Mesa, sounding like a freight train speeding toward me, cracking the foundation of my log cabin. Other earthquakes have followed, forever changing mountain landmarks. The Arrowhead, so named because it looked like a massive rock arrowhead perched on the Sawtooth Crest above Hell Roaring Lake, collapsed during a 6.4 earthquake in early 2020. That earthquake also toppled the summit boulder atop the Finger of Fate where my sons, Calvin and Jerry, once stood before a descent that nearly ended Jerry's life. The Stanley Lake Inlet Campground and beach, where our family camped so many summers during the 1960s, collapsed into the lake during that earthquake.

In my years in the Sawtooth country, while much remains, much has changed.

Stanley still has three liquor licenses and three bars. Across from the Kasino Club is the old three-room red log cabin, our first clinic. The 1958 Pontiac hearse ambulance is long gone—Sawtooth country now has a modern ambulance.

Looking east from the old clinic is the former home of Bill Harrah, the Reno gambling magnate, and his wife Verna, both clinic supporters. Across the street from the old Harrah home are the ruins of the Stanley schoolhouse, a Quonset hut. A new schoolhouse sits up the hill overlooking the mountains.

Walking westward, the Sawtooth Hotel still stands as rustic and stately as ever. Larry McCoy's store has a new name, within earshot of the old Rod and Gun Club. Gone to memory are the Smith family's hardware store, the old Stanley Club with its beautiful woodwork, and the New York City knock-off "Waldorf Hysteria."

Walking toward Highway 21, you come to the Salmon River Clinic with the Stanley Ambulance. Inside that building are enough memories to fill a book. The Jesse Leonard memorial garden on the north end of the clinic has grown: May it long be a comfort to Joe and Sheila.

Stanley is changing. The year-round population in 1963 was thirty-seven and is now sixty-three. That's deceptive, though; more than a million tourists visit the Sawtooth National Recreation Area during the summer, and that number is increasing. Meanwhile, gentrification is driving up property values.

Recruiting, training, and retaining volunteers to staff the Stanley Ambulance is ever more challenging. Whatever your station in life, when it's your turn, you'll want to ensure someone answers your 911 call. You need to make certain that the Stanley Ambulance and the Salmon River Clinic are there for you and people you love through training, volunteerism, and donations.

Do not go where the path may lead,
go instead where there is no path
and leave a trail.

Ralph Waldo Emerson

When we opened the Stanley Clinic in 1972, there were no nurse practitioners in Idaho. Someone had to go first. That RN was me. Now, with broad public support and Board of Nursing advocacy, the nurse practitioner as a healthcare professional is established and positioned to care for people in underserved communities, rural and urban, in the United States and beyond.

When I started, NPs did not have prescriptive authority. But, after conflicts with the Boards of Pharmacy and Board of Medicine that landed me in investigative hearings and left my physician preceptor on probation for twenty-five years, nurse practitioners can now write prescriptions, including opioids.

When I started, Idaho law required me to have a physician preceptor. Of my $1,000 annual income, fifteen percent went to pay my preceptor. Now, in Idaho, physician preceptors are no longer required, thanks to the hard work of Sen. Sheila Sorensen, also an NP. NPs are licensed independent practitioners or "LIPs." I was lucky: I had great physician preceptors, and Dr. Stone declined the fifteen percent fee.

When I started in 1971, three professional boards — Pharmacy, Medicine, and Nursing — provided my oversight. By the late 1970s, conflicts emerged between the three professional boards, placing my high-profile work at the Stanley Clinic in the crosshairs. The outcome? The Board of Pharmacy bowed out, followed by the Board of Medicine.

Now, the nurse practitioner profession in Idaho is governed solely by the Board of Nursing.

I want to thank Bud James and the entire Stanley community for traveling to Boise and defending me in those tumultuous, historic legislative hearings. Two nursing leaders, Leola Daniels and Eileen Merrell, defended my work and opened doors. Nurse practitioners everywhere owe Leola, Eileen, Bud, and the Stanley community a debt of gratitude.

When I started, there was no Idaho State EMS. There was also no clinic or ambulance, just Forest Service Ranger Tom Kovalicky's personal station wagon.

The work of Dr. Mike Copass and others in starting Medic 1 in Seattle and, later, Airlift Northwest became a model for the nation.

Idaho took a leading role under Paul Anderson in networking EMS across the state using the novel mountaintop radio system, then backfilling holes in the network. With its 1958 ambulance and volunteer EMTs, Stanley enabled Paul to build the statewide system far more quickly. Today, we take StateComm and the Idaho EMS system for granted. We shouldn't.

When I started, we had no radio communications and mostly didn't have telephones. Emergency calls went to the clinic board president, Marvin Larson, who lived in the valley below Shaw Mesa and would look for my orange VW bug and then drive up to get me. People, learning of our need, donated CB radios.

Then, with the help of Idaho EMS and the Robert Wood Johnson Foundation, we integrated into the statewide emergency communication system, StateComm. Radio dispatch moved from the motel to the sheriff's office in Challis. Despite best efforts and technology, the mountains still exert their power, and radio communications can be spotty.

When I started, there was no 911. Stanley was among the first in the state to establish a 911 service because those with telephones had the same 774 prefixes.

When I started, we depended on Forest Service helicopters and a new DOD program to respond to civilian emergencies: MAST helicopters flying out of Mountain Home Air Force Base. Thanks to Dr. Copass and others, we now have dedicated air ambulance services throughout the region.

When I started, there were no EMTs in Stanley and only a few in Idaho. With help from a McCall nurse, Sandy Cottrell, who began teaching the EMT class I finished after my training in Seattle, Stanley graduated one of the first EMT classes in Idaho. Volunteer EMTs in Stanley and throughout rural America are unsung heroes who are the backbone of the emergency response system. We fail to support them at our own risk.

When I started, ambulances still looked like hearses with almost no equipment. Senator Church highlighted our ambulance to urge his Senate colleagues to support rural EMS better. Back home in Stanley, with donation jars, lots of request letters to patients and supporters, Mountain Mamas' quilt raffles, and help from Idaho EMS, in 1975, we finally bought our first "mod-van ambulance," stocked with life-saving equipment and communication equipment. Today, the cost of an ambulance (without staffing) is north of $100,000, a formidable sum for rural communities.

When I started, our clinic was a three-room log cabin rental donated and shared with a school teacher. Then, like a prairie barn-raising, the Stanley community teamed with businesses and individuals throughout Idaho to build a modern, well-stocked clinic. That same clinic and ambulance still anchor a rural healthcare system serving locals and visitors in those thousands of square miles of central Idaho.

Soon after I started, premeds slept in sleeping bags on the clinic's floor and cooked on a hot plate in the garage. Then the clinic board added living quarters, prompted by a premed, Kelly Mutch, answering a nighttime knock on the clinic door in his shorts; and by my nearly dying when I snowmobiled off a cliff in a ground blizzard coming home from clinic. In 2025, the College of Idaho premed internship program will mark its fiftieth year, providing invaluable experience in rural healthcare to future physicians.

When I started, some and perhaps many women in the Salmon River Country did not have regular women's healthcare. Some had none. That changed with the pink postal reminder cards landing in mailboxes from Stanley to Salmon and even Idaho Falls and Boise. Women scheduled their vacation in the mountains to coincide with their annual gynecological exams, preferring affordable care from a woman clinician.

When I started, I was the wife of an IBM executive. With IBM's support, Cal helped me open the Stanley Clinic, start the Stanley Ambulance, and become Idaho's first nurse practitioner.

When I started, I had five kids in the Boise schools: elementary, junior high, and high school. My kids have grown up, married, with children of their own.

One daughter, Debbie, who stayed with me after the divorce, later graduated from Stanley's one-room schoolhouse, a Quonset hut. Eventually, Debbie left Stanley to become an ICU and then ER nurse working on the front lines of the COVID pandemic in New York City, Los Angeles, and Idaho.

When I started ....

I am amazed at how much the world has changed, and I have been part of that change. Many close friends and family are gone. Meanwhile, some ideas endure, grow, and transcend human frailties and mortality. EMS has flourished. The nurse practitioner idea caught fire, spreading across America and the world.

I didn't set out to do great things. I didn't even set out to be a nurse practitioner. As I told the head of the Idaho Hospital Association while sunbathing by the pool in Sun Valley, I just wanted someone to do something about the inequities of rural healthcare in America. Fate, or perhaps some higher power, intervened. The rest is history. Once I started, I could not and would not turn back.

When there is no path, you must make one. If your cause is just and you are true, others will follow.

EPILOGUE: CHRISTMAS EVE, 2022

"50th Anniversary of NP Practice"

Etched onto champagne flutes celebrating the 50th anniversary of the Nurse Practitioner in Idaho, the first state to license NPs

Jim Stark

The current and former EMTs of the Stanley Ambulance, with Marie and Amy Klingler at the 50th anniversary of the Salmon River Clinic and the Stanley Ambulance

First and most importantly, I wish you the best this holiday season. I love Christmas, and this is my 92nd. May you always hold Christmas in your heart.

After a career as a nurse practitioner doing emergency and family care, my life at an independent living facility is sedate. Other than neighbors setting off fire alarms with burnt toast and the occasional fire truck and ambulance, there's not much to write about. I am grateful when my newspaper arrives and my son, Cal, walks in with a café latte or Cobb salad.

2022 was the 50th anniversary of significant events in my life. A half-century ago, in 1972, I became an emergency-care nurse practitioner, opened the Salmon River Emergency Clinic and ambulance service, and helped graduate Stanley's first class of volunteer EMTs. At age 41, all this was possible because of my husband, Cal, and our five kids. We don't do much, if anything, alone.

On May 21, 2022, three days after my 91st birthday and a glorious spring day, the College of Idaho awarded me an honorary doctorate degree for my work in advancing rural

The College of Idaho recognized Marie's contribution to rural healthcare and commitment to teaching with an honorary doctorate

healthcare. Starting in 1975, premeds from the College interned at the Stanley Clinic, most of whom went on to become physicians. Among them was my youngest son, John, who helped start the program.

Standing at the graduation podium, looking out at hundreds of young people heading out into the world, I encouraged them to follow their hearts and blaze their own trail that others might follow.

That was a special day. In the audience were people important to me: my physician preceptor, Dr. Bryan Stone; former premed students Dr. Katie Reynolds (now my doctor), Dr. Mary Barinaga, Craig Pierce, and others; John Hutchinson of the Idaho Hospital Association who got me started; Paul Anderson, Idaho EMS's creator; sister Susie and husband, Bob; EMTs from Stanley including Steve and Teresa Lipus; and all five of my children and many from their families. Wow.

The College's former ski coach, Ron Bonneau, and his wife, Michele, also came. Graduation day was also their wedding anniversary. At the reception afterward, the couple tearfully recounted how a bee had stung Ron, who started to swell and suddenly struggled to breathe. Just before completely losing his airway, he arrived at the clinic. I injected epinephrine and stopped the anaphylactic reaction. The husband and wife came to say thank you for saving Ron's life and giving them a lifetime of anniversaries.

Not all of my former premed students could be in Caldwell on that beautiful spring day. Instead, one who went on to medical school, Jacob Clendenon, sent a letter for the event.

Mayo Clinic
Transplant Center | Jacksonville, Florida

I first met Marie Osborn in the summer of 1996, between my Sophomore and Junior years in college. I still remember my excitement when I found out I had been selected for the premedical internship at the Salmon River Emergency Clinic. I had heard the experience was fun, and it would, after all, look great on my resumé. In retrospect, I could never have imagined the profound impact of working with Marie on my life and career.

My first impression of Marie was that she was intimidating and, quite frankly, a bit terrifying. When she gave me "the look," it felt like she was taking the true measure of my soul. I was, and remain to this day, impressed by her breath of knowledge and clinical acumen. She commanded every situation with calm competence, clinical skill, and unwavering resolve.

Over two short summers, Marie taught me many valuable clinical and technical skills. More importantly, she taught me the incredible value of compassion for my patients. Marie selflessly dedicated herself to providing the best care possible for her many patients. She balanced the responsibilities of delivering exceptional patient care and teaching us often clueless students with effortless grace, all with often limited resources and at all hours of the day and night.

The experience I gained at the Salmon River Emergency Clinic instilled self-confidence and self-reliance. I also learned that it is okay to ask for help. Despite her impressive medical knowledge, Marie sometimes encountered a clinical situation where the correct diagnosis or best treatment was unclear. She was never too proud to call a colleague for advice. Humility, curiosity, and the willingness to continually learn in the pursuit of helping patients are all hallmarks of a great clinician, and Marie is a great clinician.

I am humbled by the responsibility that Marie entrusted to me as an intern. I now understand that teaching and trusting students with the care of patients is incredibly hard and can only come from self-confidence and a great depth of personal experience.

I have had a handful of genuinely great teachers throughout my medical training and career. Marie, however, was my first and most profoundly influential mentor. I am proud to know Marie. I am humbled by her willingness to teach and her role in pioneering a new field of medicine that has and will continue to better the lives of so many patients.

Marie, words can never adequately convey my gratitude to you. Your compassion, selflessness, and resolve embody the ideal I strive for in the care of my patients. It is an honor knowing you. Thank you.

Sincerely,

Jacob Clendenon, MD
Transplant Surgeon
Mayo Clinic

In Stanley, we had a patient with terrible dental trauma, his teeth shoved into the jaw after a bar fight in the early morning. Dr. Clendenon's dad was a dentist in Nampa. I remember Jacob calling his father at 2 or 3 in the morning, and we were so grateful for his help.

The second 50th-anniversary event in 2022 was a gala celebration in Boise, marking 50 years of the nurse practitioner profession in Idaho. Escorting me were Randall Hudspeth, a nurse practitioner and executive director for the Idaho Center for Nursing, and his wife, Ingrid, an RN who volunteers with Ronald McDonald House Charities of Idaho.

What a great evening, unexpected yet unforgettable. The vast ballroom was packed with nurse practitioners — women and men — from all over Idaho, including people I hadn't seen for years. It's hard to imagine, but when I started nursing school, doctors were men, nurses were women, and gender defined both professions. How the world has changed in the past half-century.

I laughed so hard that my jaw still hurt the next day. Idaho was the first state to license nurse practitioners, and everyone wanted their picture taken with Idaho's first nurse practitioner.

As a gift, the NPs sent me home with eight champagne flutes. Looking around that room at so many nurse practitioners, I felt pride and amazement at how our profession has grown.

The third event was a party in Stanley. On October 15, the community celebrated the 50th anniversary of the Salmon River Clinic and Stanley Ambulance and launched a fundraising drive to support Stanley's EMTs. So many friends and former colleagues turned out: Stanley's volunteer EMTs and ambulance drivers; premed interns, past and present, including Dr. Ken Harris with wife Sarah and Dr. Kelly Mutch; Amy Klingler PA, who now runs the clinic; past and current physician preceptors Dr. Stone and Dr. Paris; Dr. Rob Pierce, a veterinarian who saved my dog Mousse from drowning; and friends and family. It was a Stanley homecoming filled with stories, hugs, and laughter.

Jim Stark

Dave Kimpton, Marie, and Tom Kovalicky. Forest Service staff Tom and Dave supported Marie in opening the Salom River Clinic in 1972. Dave trained as an EMT and continued serving on the clinic's board a half-century later.

Finally, as this year of celebrations ends, I save my most special Christmas wishes for my five kids and their families.

2022 has been a champagne year. Thank you for being part of my life. Onward.

— *Marie Osborn, ARNP*

AFTERWORD

Roland Miller

If you drive into Stanley, you might not notice a little brown-sided building on the corner of Niece Avenue and Highway 21. If you have a safe and healthy visit, you might never observe the Salmon River Clinic; set against the backdrop of the Sawtooths, the clinic wouldn't be the first thing to catch your eye. If your kids don't need stitches, a tetanus shot, or a fishhook removed from their cheek, you might never know there are two examining rooms separated by a lab the size of a modest walk-in closet. If you never find yourself lying on the table in the "stirrup" room, you might never gaze up at the ceiling to see the poster of the turkey with a fanned-out tail proclaiming, "I'm so happy here I could just shit."

You might not realize that there is an apartment for housing the interns who come to submerge themselves in the summer craziness of myriad medical emergencies. You might never know that inside the garage is a state-of-the-art ambulance, the fourth replacement in a succession of ambulances that have provided thousands and thousands of miles of service.

If you do discover the ambulance, you might wonder why countless volunteer Emergency Medical Technicians (EMTs) spend months driving themselves to grueling night classes and later biennial recertification classes so they can drop what they are doing at a moment's notice to respond to the latest call for help.

Why do they willingly climb out of their warm beds, sometimes for the second time that night, and endure sub-zero temperatures to extricate an accident victim from a mangled automobile and drive them the 60+ miles to the nearest hospital? And how do they muster the fortitude to respond to the next call for assistance when all their best efforts fail?

Why does a sparsely populated community like Stanley have such valuable medical services? Why don't residents have to take their children to Challis or Ketchum for immunizations, throat cultures, or blood tests? Why do visitors to the area have such immediate access to these vital Emergency Medical Services?

If you ask around, you would hear of a diminutive nurse practitioner named Marie, and the next word you'd hear would be "dedication." Mother of five, crocheter of afghans, gourmet cook, and NFL fan, she came to the Sawtooth country in the late 1960s and recognized the need.

She saw a rural, isolated community completely without medical services. She begged, controlled, intimidated, explained, demonstrated, lobbied, and inspired a community with her tireless determination and optimism. Fundraisers, donations, volunteers, and, eventually, the establishment of a taxing district built the clinic on the corner.

Always leading by example, she willingly hopped on her snow machine at any hour to ride the two miles to the highway or drive the 15 miles to town to respond to a call for help. When the weather threatened, she spent many nights in the clinic apartment "just in case." Before the State Veterinary Board officially frowned some years ago, she could remove the most embedded porcupine quills from your dog's nose or inoculate your horse.

When she retired in 1999, hundreds of people, many of them former residents of Stanley's earlier years, came from all over the state and beyond to wish her well, express their gratitude, and demonstrate their love for the woman who came to Stanley and moved mountains.

— Teresa Lipus
Volunteer EMT, Stanley Ambulance

THE OFFICE OF THE GOVERNOR
PROCLAMATION

WHEREAS, prior to 1972, Custer and Blaine Counties had no rural health care access north of Galena Summit, west of Lowman, and east of Challis, Idaho; and

WHEREAS, Emergency Medical Services were only available by public service officials including the U.S. Forest Service and Department of Fish and Game; and

WHEREAS, in 1971, Marie Osborn RN, identified a critical need and lack of services following a horrific accident in the Stanley area and was compelled to action for better response and care; and

WHEREAS, the Idaho Hospital Association became aware of the request for need to support rural healthcare in the Sawtooth country and supported Marie to become a nurse practitioner, Idaho's first, at a time when Idaho was the first in the nation to license nurse practitioners; and

WHEREAS, in 1971, Stanley, Idaho, was among the first communities to start an Emergency Medical Technician (EMT) system under the development and training of Marie Osborn; and

WHEREAS, the EMT program has been an all-volunteer team of dedicated community citizens up until now; and

WHEREAS, Idaho Search and Rescue partnered to coordinate efforts for local emergency medical needs; and

WHEREAS, in 1972, the Salmon River Emergency Clinic opened in a rustic cabin with support from the local community, physician preceptors, Marie's family, and many others; and

WHEREAS, the first ambulance, a 1958 Pontiac purchased from military surplus, was acquired for the newly formed emergency clinic, and helicopter assist was provided by Mountain Home Air Force Base, Forest Service helicopters and, later, LifeFlight and other air ambulance services; and

WHEREAS, a new clinic building opened at 1975 and was constructed by residents of Stanley with cooperative support and materials from Boise Cascade and many other donations to build the clinic out of the ground; and

WHEREAS, Marie Osborn developed a women's health practice of care in rural central Idaho; and

WHEREAS, Stanley, Idaho was the first community in the state to implement a 9-1-1 system; and

WHEREAS, first responder and local law enforcement response has grown to a coordinated effort including the coroner and other physical and mental health systems; and

WHEREAS, the College of Idaho in 1975 began training pre-med students and is now in its 47th year for an internship program, and many students are now physicians shaped by their experience and contributing back to Idahoans; and

WHEREAS, since 2006, Amy Klingler, PA, has staffed the clinic for the needs of the community and tourists who continue to visit this country; and

WHEREAS, today, the Sawtooth Country medical access system is robust, but the challenge is to keep momentum alive and a new frontier on volunteers and systems becomes a threat to continued existence of this legacy;

NOW, THEREFORE, I, BRAD LITTLE, Governor of the State of Idaho, do hereby proclaim October 15, 2022, to be

**The 50th Anniversary of the
Salmon River Clinic and Stanley Ambulance**

in Idaho, and I encourage all Idahoans to join me in this special observance.

BRAD LITTLE, GOVERNOR
LAWRENCE DENNEY, SECRETARY OF STATE

STANLEY EMTS AND AMBULANCE DRIVERS

1972 – 2024

Kitty Anderson
Bev Angel
Kirk Bachman
Hannah Baybutt
Jeff Bitton
Jason Brunson
Jesse Buhler
Phil Coonts
Fred Dauber
Marilyn Dauber
Allie Dixon
Bob Downing
Johnson Duncan
Alan "Sparky" Easom
Maryellen Easom
Vicki Ebert
Phil Enright
Doug Everett
E. Beverly Everett
Jimbo Funderburg
Barb James
Fred Judd
Gary Gadwa
Lois Glenn
Bob Griswold
Andy Gunderson
Launna Gunderson
Ken Hartz
Tanner Haskins
John Haugh
Quincy Heithecker
Verlon Herndon
Ted Hendricks
Skylar Herbert
Steve Herrett
Mike Horn
Bill James
Luke Johnson
Bruce Kaufman
Linda Kaufman
Dave Kimpton
Danny King
Linda King
Amy Klingler
Allen Knight
Gretchen Koberness
Tom Kops
Tom Kovalicky
LuAnn Kuhn
Bill Leavell
Joe Leonard
Sophie Librett
Steve Lipus
Teresa Lipus
Rich Loeske
Ramsey Marquis
Amanda Mathews
Larry McCoy
Makena McDonald
Dennis McGonigal
Michelle Medsker
Julie Meissner
Joe Miczulski
Roland Miller
Dennis Moore
George Nedelea
Gerald Nicholson
Brent Nyborg
Kelsey O'Kelly
Debbie Osborn (Wilder)
Marie Osborn
John Pape
Robert Pearce
Megan Phelps
Bryce Reese
Jody Robb
Steve Rogers
Kathy Rogerson
Jan Skrukrud
Elin Smith
Marcus Smith
Ron Smith
Troy Spurgeon
Burton Stanley
Cassie Stanley
Chris Stephens
Dick Stoney
Bill Stutz
Jackson Sweet
Timmer Verhagh
Jeri West
Lauren Wright
Matthew Yost
Zoe Young

***This list may be incomplete. For EMTs and drivers not listed, our apologies**

Roland Miller

RURAL HEALTHCARE CLINICAL TRAINING

Salmon River Clinic
College of Idaho PreMed Interns*
1975 – 2024

Pete Angleton
Katie Ball
Mary Barinaga
Mari Bjorneberg
Mary Brown
Jake Bruner
Jesse Buhler
Hailey Chambers
Jake Clendenon
Kendra Coonse
Emily Dickerson
Laura Fink
KT Fisher
Brian Gable
Patrice Gibson
Matt Goodwin
Kencee Amyx Graves
Jessica Hansen
Dausen Harker
Ken Harris
Fawn Hoffman
Dawna Jacobsen (Kramer)
Katie James (Reynolds)
Peter John
Isabel Lete
Donna Kinney
Mary Anne Klepich
Blake Mitchell
Abucar Mohamed
Marilyn Moretti
Kevin Mott
Kelly Mutch
Marisa Hegbloom Nagle
Shane Newton
Mike Nowling
John Osborn
Rich Patten
Angela Pellant
Megan Phelps
Craig Pierce
Karly Pippitt
Carrie Jean Queen
Brad Ratcliff
Nancy Reincke
Robert Rigley
Kaitlyn Roberts
Cyndi Robison
Kent Rohweder
Lindsay Barclay Sales
Karen Sept
Jocele Skinner
Elynn Smith
Tim Soran
Sharon Stanley
Mary James Stredder
John Sype
Matt Tagaki
Alex Tanabe
Michelle Thompson
Caly Thurston
Chris Tietsort
Erick Valenzuela
Timmer Verhaegh
Dylan Walker
Hailey Woods
Dannen Wright
Zoe Young
Brian Zeranski

***Some interns also became EMTs, volunteering on the Stanley Ambulance.**

TRAINING NURSE PRACTITIONERS AND MEDICAL STUDENTS

Preceptors for NP and medical students, including:

- University of Washington, School of Medicine, Department of Family Medicine, 1981–1999
- University of Wyoming, School of Nursing, Family Nurse Practitioner Program
- Idaho State University, School of Nursing, Family Nurse Practitioner Program
- Gonzaga University, School of Nursing, Family Nurse Practitioner Program
- Intercollegiate Center for Nursing Education (Spokane), Family Nurse Practitioner Program
- Emory University, Nell Hodgson Woodruff School of Nursing (Atlanta), Family Nurse Practitioner Program

BOARD OF DIRECTORS, SALMON RIVER CLINIC

1972 – 2024*

Bev Angel
Judy Archbald
Phil Coonts
Dan Crabtree
Charlene Cvecich
Bob Downing
Maryellen Easom
Sid Edwards
Bill James
Rita James
Jerry Funderburg
Gary Gadwa
Dorothy Giffin
Cliff Hansen
Donna Hoitsma
Linda Kaufman
Dave Kimpton
Fern Larson
Marvin Larson
Annie Legg
Dave Lesser
Steve Lipus
Helen Lumpkin
Sandy Lumpkin
Freda Nicholson
Ruth Niece
Dave Pinney
Jocelyn Plass
Betty Rember
Jack See
Noel Sitton
Brent Snider
Jack Stands
Margaret Watkins
Michelle Wetzel
Ted Williams
Phyllis Williams
Sandra Willingham

*** Since 1979, the Directors have served the Salmon River Clinic Hospital District**

ABOUT THE AUTHORS

Marie Osborn, ARNP, is Idaho's first Nurse Practitioner. She obtained her BSN from Ball State University in 1953, completed emergency medicine training at Harborview Medical Center/University of Washington in 1972, and was in the first class of the Family Nurse Practitioner Program at the University of Utah in 1975. Marie staffed the Salmon River Emergency Clinic and Stanley Ambulance from 1972 – 1999. After retiring from the Stanley Clinic, Marie continued to see patients in rural Idaho communities, then low-income clinics in Boise until 2012. She returns to her Sawtooth home and the mountains she loves as her health allows.

John Osborn, MD, specializes in Internal Medicine and has provided care for military veterans since 1985, including as physician advisor to Camp Chaparral for Native American veterans with PTSD. John graduated from the College of Idaho in 1979, the University of Washington School of Medicine (1983) through the WWAMI program, and Internal Medicine Spokane (1986). Along with Derrick Jensen and George Draffan, he is an author of Railroads and Clearcuts: Legacy of Congress's 1864 Northern Pacific Railroad Land Grant. From 1988 – 2000, John chronicled the closing of frontiers and historic change in America's Northwest as editor of the journal Transitions: www.lib.uidaho.edu/digital/transitions/ His work in ethics includes POLST (Washington State) and the One River, Ethics Matter project for the Columbia River. He is married to Rachael — they live on Vashon Island, where they garden and press apple cider.

INDEX

Please note that italicized page numbers in this index indicate illustrations.